THE LIFE OF
SAMUEL JOHNSON, LL.D.

SAMUEL JOHNSON
by Sir Joshua Reynolds
in the collection of Courage Barclay & Simonds, Ltd.

THE LIFE OF

SAMUEL JOHNSON

LL.D.

BY JAMES BOSWELL, ESQ.

———————

With marginal comments and markings
from two copies annotated by

HESTER LYNCH THRALE PIOZZI

Prepared for publication
with an Introduction by

EDWARD G. FLETCHER

IN THREE VOLUMES
I

———————

THE HERITAGE PRESS
New York

INTRODUCTION

I

JAMES BOSWELL first met Samuel Johnson the evening of May 16, 1763. Johnson was fifty-four; less than a year before, he had been relieved from a lifetime of drudgery and poverty by the grant of a pension (the generosity of a Whig king to an inveterate Tory subject). In the twenty-six years since he had come to London he had made for himself a position of literary and critical pre-eminence. Boswell was only twenty-two, an ambitious young Scot of good family who thought very well of himself and who possessed literary tastes, although he knew he was expected to follow his father and grandfather in the law—in fact, he had come to London nine months before on his way to Holland to pursue his legal studies.

Here is the way the meeting is described by Arthur Murphy, actor, dramatist, and member of the Johnson circle, who says (probably inaccurately) that he was present to observe it:

'This writer went with him into the shop of Davies, the bookseller. . . . Davies came running to him, almost out of breath with joy: "The Scots gentleman is come, Sir; his principal wish is to see you; he is now in the back parlour." "Well, well, I'll see the gentleman," said Johnson. He walked towards the room. Mr. Boswell was the person. This writer followed, with no small curiosity. "I find," said Mr. Boswell, "that I am come to London, at a bad time, when great popular prejudice has gone forth against us North Britons; but, when I am talking to you, I am talking to a large and liberal mind, and you know that I cannot help coming from Scotland." "Sir," said Johnson, "no more can the rest of your countrymen." '

Here is Boswell's record in his *Journal*:

'I drank tea at Davies's in Russell Street, and about seven came in the great Mr. Samuel Johnson, whom I have so long wished to see. Mr. Davies introduced me to him. As I knew his mortal antipathy at the Scotch, I cried to Davies, "Don't tell him where I come from." However, he said, "From Scotland."

"Mr. Johnson," said I, "indeed I come from Scotland, but I cannot help it." "Sir," replied he, "that, I find, is what a very great many of your countrymen cannot help."

'Mr. Johnson is a man of a most dreadful appearance. He is a very big man, is troubled with sore eyes, the palsy & the King's evil. He is slovenly in his dress & speaks with a most uncouth voice. Yet his knowledge, and strength of expression, command vast respect and render him excellent company. He has great humour and is a worthy man. But his dogmatic roughness and manner is disagreeable.'

Here is Boswell's account in the *Life*:

'At last, on Monday the 16th of May, when I was sitting in Mr. Davies's back-parlour, after having drunk tea with him and Mrs. Davies, Johnson unexpectedly came into the shop; and Mr. Davies having perceived him through the glass-door in the room in which we were sitting, advancing towards us,— he announced his awful approach to me, somewhat in the manner of an actor in the part of Horatio, when he addresses Hamlet on the appearance of his father's ghost, "Look, my Lord, it comes." I found that I had a very perfect idea of Johnson's figure, from the portrait painted by Sir Joshua Reynolds . . . the first picture his friend did for him, which Sir Joshua very kindly presented to me. . . . Mr. Davies mentioned my name, and respectfully introduced me to him. I was much agitated; and recollecting his prejudice against the Scotch, of which I had heard much, I said to Davies, "Don't tell where I come from."—"From Scotland," cried Davies, roguishly. "Mr. Johnson, (said I) I do indeed come from Scotland, but I cannot help it." . . . This speech was somewhat unlucky; for with that quickness of wit for which he was so remarkable, he seized the expression "come from Scotland," which I used in the sense of being of that country; and, as if I had said that I had come away from it, or left it, retorted, "That, Sir, I find, is what a very great many of your countrymen cannot help." This stroke stunned me a good deal; and when we had sat down, I felt myself not a little embarrassed, and apprehensive of what might come next.'

The facts in these three accounts of the famous meeting are substantially the same; the difference lies in the artistic skill with which Boswell has presented them in the *Life*.

Boswell had to leave Davies' back parlor and Johnson to go on to another engagement. Davies' assurance to him—

'Don't be uneasy. I can see he likes you very well'—encouraged Boswell to foster the acquaintance. When he visited Johnson for the second time, on June 13th, he was asked to come frequently. He wrote himself notes to see Johnson often, even two or three times a week. On July 14th he wrote a friend, 'I had the honour of supping *tête-à-tête* with Mr. Johnson last night. . . . We sat till between two and three. He took me by the hand cordially and said, "My dear Boswell! I love you very much." Now, Temple, can I help indulging vanity?'

The friendship developed. When Boswell left England for Holland, Johnson, whom he had first met less than three months before, made a two-day stage coach trip to see him off from Harwich. They were friends, true and real friends, for the remaining twenty years of Johnson's life. During these years Boswell visited England fifteen times and was with Johnson for some part, at least, of about two hundred and seventy-five days; besides this they were together for a little over three months when Johnson visited Scotland and the Hebrides in 1773.

When they were apart, they exchanged letters, irregularly (there are some one hundred and twenty of Boswell's to some one hundred and five of Johnson's). 'You are not to think yourself forgotten,' Johnson wrote Boswell, in Utrecht, December 8, 1763, 'that you have had no letter from me. I love to see my friends, to hear from them, to talk to them, and to talk of them; but it is not without a considerable effort of resolution that I prevail upon myself to write. . . .' 'My regard for you is so radicated and fixed that it is become part of my mind, and cannot be effaced but by some cause uncommonly violent,' Johnson wrote him in 1775, and, early in January, three years later, 'In the first month of the present year I very highly esteem and very cordially love you. I hope to tell you this at the beginning of every year as long as we live.'

Just when Boswell decided to write Johnson's life it is impossible to say. As early as 1764, however, the year after Boswell had first met him, he remarked in a letter to Johnson: 'If you die before me, I shall endeavour to do honour to your memory,' and his procedure was already, ideally, 'to make a memorandum every night of what I have seen during the day. By this means I have my materials always secured.' Thus did the *Journal* come into being, and it was from this *Journal* (supplemented, of course, in various ways) that the *Life* was made. Geoffrey Scott's fascinating sixth volume of *The Boswell Papers—The Making of the Life of Johnson* (1929)—shows us precisely how Boswell worked up his material.

Boswell diligently collected information about Johnson from anyone who could furnish him with anecdotes or letters, and with the help of his own shorthand preserved a good deal of Johnson's actual conversation. It is a foolish and uninformed notion, however, that imagines Boswell always crowding Johnson's steps, ever ready to pull out of a pocket the little notebook in which (in some eighteenth-century variety of Pitman) to scrawl with all speed lest he miss a few syllables of the great man's remarks. His 'short-hand' was not a stenography, but simply his own system of abbreviating words to facilitate the quick jotting down of something to help him recollect it when he came to bring his journal up to date, or when he could find the time to enter and expand his notes in his *Journal*.

It is another false Boswell legend that even in a social group he was ever ready to pull out a notebook or a scrap of paper and record then and there what was being said. Mrs. Hester Thrale (of whom much more presently) once begged Johnson's permission to write something down directly, 'before anything could intervene that might make me forget the force of the expressions: a trick, which I have however seen played steadily [a printer's misreading of *stealthily*?] on common occasions, of sitting down at the other end of the room to write at the moment what should be said in company, either *by* Dr. Johnson or *to* him—a trick I never practiced myself, nor approved of in another. There is something so ill-bred, and so inclining to treachery in this conduct, that were it commonly adopted, all confidence would soon be exiled from society. . . .' This may or may not be a criticism of Boswell, and if it is, it may be deliberately misleading, to put him in a bad light, based only upon the most occasional examples of such behavior.

Boswell trusted his long memory of what was said, as Mrs. Thrale herself declares elsewhere. He was not likely to withdraw from a conversation and so miss something Johnson might say. Fanny Burney has described, with exaggeration, Boswell's attentive listening: 'He leant his ear almost to the shoulders of the Doctor; and his mouth dropped open to catch every syllable that might be uttered; nay, he seemed not only to dread losing a word, but to be anxious not to miss a breathing. . . .'

Johnson's conversations as printed in the *Life* are not to be taken as verbatim records of what he actually said, such as an accurate, unedited transcript of a taped recording would be. They are Boswell's reconstitution of the conversation from his notes and his memory of the occasion—a reconstitution in which his aim was to recapture the reality of the talk, which from his intimate knowledge of Johnson's personality, his mind, and his conversational style, he was supremely competent to do. The success of his achievement is another evidence of the foolishness of the opinion that the fascinating record of Johnson's conversation is some sort of happy accident and that this record is artless, little more than some sort of naïve, naturalistic reporting.

Johnson died in December 1784. In September 1785, Boswell published his *Journal of a Tour to the Hebrides with Samuel Johnson, LL.D.*, a first trial of the biographical method he was to employ in the *Life*; its frankness met with a great deal of criticism and dispraise. At the end of this book, under the heading 'Preparing for the Press,' Boswell announced that he was writing a life of Johnson.

Mrs. Thrale published her *Anecdotes of the Late Samuel Johnson* in March 1786. In 1787 appeared an eleven-volume edition of Johnson's works, the first volume of which was a six-hundred-page biography by Sir John Hawkins, a London attorney who had long known Johnson. Mrs. Thrale published her *Letters to and from the Late Samuel Johnson* in 1788. Boswell's great *Life* was published on April 16, 1791.

Dr. Frederick A. Pottle, Sterling professor of English at Yale University, who knows more about Boswell than any other living man, has spoken of Boswell's 'passion for knowing the varieties of human nature.' In 1934, at the end of his work on the Malahide Castle material which was published in *The Boswell Papers*, he wrote of the *Journal*:

'Boswell's *Journal* is painful to read because, while we are laughing with him and at him, while we are being shocked at him and disgusted with him, the scales fall from our eyes and we come suddenly to see that he is ourselves. He is the articulate and honest expression of that state of being which nearly all of us experience: of piety that seldom issues in righteousness; of primordial indecencies mocking our boast of civilization; of ambitions misdirected and beyond our strength; of warring motives which can never be reconciled; of childish dreams carried over into mature life.'

Whatever Boswell's contemporaries may have thought of him, and whatever others may have thought of him since (and there is no lack of those who have found him neither likable nor admirable), no judgment of him can overlook the triumph of his literary accomplishment. That the *Life* was and is a masterpiece is a critical commonplace, but it already seems apparent that his *Journal* (which, with interruptions and gaps, is a running account of his life from 1758 on) is likely to take its place as an equally great masterpiece.

II

JOHNSON first met Mrs. Thrale in 1765, two years after his first meeting with Boswell. It was presumably on a Wednesday afternoon in March, about four o'clock, the customary dining hour of the Thrales. He was introduced by Arthur Murphy, whom we have already met. Twelve years later, in 1777, Mrs. Thrale wrote in her diary: 'We liked each other so well that the next Thursday was appointed for the same Company to meet . . . and since then Johnson has remained, till this Day, our constant Acquaintance, Visitor, Companion and Friend.'

Henry Thrale, Johnson's host, was probably thirty-six years old, a good-looking, even handsome businessman who in 1758 had inherited from his father a profitable brewery in Southwark and a country house and extensive estate at Streatham, about six miles out of London. Thrale had attended Oxford, toured Europe, and then returned to a pleasant bachelor's life in London. Whatever his reasons for courting Hester Lynch Salusbury, they were married in October 1763—an entirely rational, arranged union, for there was no love on either side. He brought his bride (and her mother, to whom he had been very attentive during the courtship) home to the country estate his father had built—Streatham Place or Streatham Park.

Thrale was unimaginative and rather coldly unemotional. He was in all ways conventionally correct and dignified, but with a fondness for a pretty woman (his infidelities were gossiped about). He was given to a rather reckless spending of his profits, when he had them, rather than to building a suitable reserve for emergencies. He had some interest in literature and in literary and artistic people.

Mrs. Thrale was twenty-one in the year of her marriage. She had been born in Wales, and brought up in London since she was six. Always precocious, she was rather well if somewhat irregularly educated. She was a plumpish woman less than five feet tall, not pretty in any ordinary sense, but animated, with chestnut brown hair, light grey eyes, a loud, somewhat harsh voice and a flaunting rather than a reticent manner, 'warm-hearted, generous, sweet-tempered . . . replete with wit and pleasantry' and evincing unusual 'powers of entertainment.'

Between September 1764 and June 1778 Mrs. Thrale bore her husband twelve children. Only four of these lived beyond the age of ten: their daughters Hester Maria (Queeney), Susanna, Sophia, and Frances; the Thrales' first son died suddenly at the age of nine in 1776; their only other son had died in infancy the year before.

The Thrale town house was in an unfashionable section of London, the old bankside area of Shakespeare's days, next to the Thrale brewery in Deadman's End. The Thrales had few visitors there at first, chiefly her husband's three sisters with their businessman husbands and Thrale's former bachelor friends.

Johnson dined regularly with the Thrales at the house in the borough each week during the first months of 1765. That fall Thrale became a candidate for the House of Commons. He was elected, and remained a member of Parliament until he was defeated in 1780 during the illness which ended with his death the following spring. When her childbearing permitted it, his wife was a vigorous campaigner for Thrale. Johnson likewise helped him in his political activities, and in addition interested himself in his business, particularly from 1772 on, when Thrale's reckless experimentation with a new method of brewing almost ruined him.

When business picked up again, Thrale began to remodel and improve Streatham. One of the additions was a new library, for which he commissioned from Sir Joshua Reynolds a series of thirteen portraits which hung on its walls. These included likenesses of Johnson, Burke, Goldsmith, Garrick, and Reynolds himself.

Sometime towards the middle of 1766 Johnson joined the Thrales at Streatham for a stay of several months. From that time on, for the next sixteen years, he passed much of his time with the family at Streatham or at Deadman's End. To him the two houses were 'home'; the Thrales were 'my Master' and 'my Mistress.' When the Thrales went to Brighton (where Thrale had bought a house in 1767), as they regularly did in the late summer or early autumn, Johnson often visited them there, where he sometimes rode with Thrale's hunting companions and was once highly pleased when one of these remarked, 'Why, Johnson rides as well, for aught I see, as the most illiterate fellow in England.' Johnson went with the Thrales to Wales in 1774, to France in 1775, and would have accompanied them on the projected Italian trip of 1776 if it had not been cancelled because of the death of Thrale's only heir.

Gradually, and largely because of Johnson, the Thrale dining room and drawing room became distinguished for their company: Sir Joshua Reynolds, Oliver Goldsmith, Edmund Burke, David Garrick, James Beattie, Dr. Charles Burney, and many others. Boswell first met Mrs. Thrale in 1768; he first visited Streatham in 1769.

On June 8, 1778, Henry Thrale suffered his first stroke. It left him in a state of 'sometimes . . . Torpor, sometimes . . . Violence . . . restless & fanciful to an extream Degree. . . .' He gave himself up to immoderate eating and whatever pleasure he could find in a constant flow of company and in restless visits and trips. In January 1781 the Thrales, for the London season, moved into a rented, furnished house in fashionable Grosvenor Square, where, as in the other Thrale houses, there was always a room for Johnson's use. On April 2 and 3 Thrale devoured enormous dinners; the result was an apoplexy of which he died April 4.

The will, which left Johnson a small legacy of £200, named him one of the four executors of the estate. Mrs. Thrale was left the contents of the houses at Streatham and in Southwark, the use of the Streatham estate for life, and £30,000 if the brewery were sold, as it was within two months.

Shortly, for the first time in her life, she felt herself to be in love. She was forty. The man was the same age, an Italian musician named Gabriele Piozzi who had come to England in 1776, whom she had first met (and ridiculed by her mimicry behind his back) in February 1778. He had given Queeney music lessons in Brighton during the summer of 1780 and after that in London, and had been a frequent guest at her parties at Streatham and in Grosvenor Square.

Johnson was now, in the spring of 1781, seventy-one years old, unwell, and increasingly irritable. With Thrale dead and Mrs. Thrale a wealthy and eligible widow, their relationship could never again be what it had been. 'Do not let Mr. Piozzi nor any body else put me quite out of your head,' he wrote her in April 1782, 'and do not think that any body will love you like, Yours, &c.' 'Shall we ever exchange confidence by the fireside again?' he wrote her on March 10, 1784. Should she become Johnson's companion and nurse for the remaining years of his life (his father had lived to be seventy-five and his mother nearly ninety) or should she take what life now offered her—marriage with Piozzi, who loved her and whom she loved?

In her indecision, she thought of taking her three older daughters abroad; she let Streatham, which she did not have the means to keep up properly. One Sunday, October 6, 1782, Johnson dined for the last time in this 'home' where he had been treated so well and made so comfortable. For the last time he stood in the library, looking at Reynolds' portraits on the walls. Three of the subjects—Goldsmith, Garrick, Thrale—were already dead; in two years and two months he would be, too. The next day Johnson and the

Thrales went to Brighton, where he was so savage that he
received almost no invitations—'people ... almost ran
from him.'

Mrs. Thrale decided to remain in London for the winter,
and—in the face of her daughters' antagonism and the advice of her friends (for he was a foreigner, a Catholic, and,
as a musician, not quite a gentleman)—to encourage Piozzi's proposal. After he had banished himself and been re-
called, in June 1784 Mrs. Thrale formally notified the
executors of the Thrale estate that she intended to remarry,
and at the same time wrote Johnson apologizing for not
having been more open with him about her plans. Johnson
violently disapproved of the match and did everything that
he could to dissuade her. In the next to the last letter he
wrote her, July 2, 1784, he said: 'If the last act is yet to do,
I who long thought you the first of human kind, entreat
that before your fate is irrevocable, I may once more see
you.' Her reply two days later said: 'You have always
commanded my Esteem, and long enjoy'd the Fruits of a
Friendship never infringed by one harsh Expression on my
Part, during twenty Years of familiar Talk. Never did I
oppose your Will, or controal your Wish: nor can your un-
merited Severity itself lessen my Regard.' In his final letter
to her, July 8, he wrote: 'Whatever I can contribute to
your happiness, I am ready to repay for that kindness
which soothed twenty years of a life radically wretched. ...
The tears stand in my eyes. ... I am with great affection
Your most humble servant. ...'

Hester Thrale and Gabriele Piozzi were married in London on July 3, 1784. They left England for France and
Italy in early September. News of Johnson's death in
London on December 13 reached her in Milan. By early
1785 she was being asked by Sir John Hawkins, who was to
write the official biography, for anecdotes.

For seventeen years she had herself been collecting material about Johnson for use in some sort of memoir or life.
She now urged a correspondent in London to get for her
anecdotes about the early and the last years of his life. 'I
used to tell him in Jest,' she wrote in *Thraliana*, 'that his
Biographers would be at a Loss concerning some Orange-
Peel he used to keep in his pocket, and many a joke we had

about the Lives that would be published: "Rescue me out of all their hands My dear, & do it *yourself*," said he: "Taylor, Adams, & Hector will furnish you with juvenile Anecdotes, & Baretti will give you all the rest that you have not already. . . ." '

With her in Italy, Mrs. Piozzi had only her *Thraliana*, however; the rest of her Johnsonian material, including their letters, was in a bank vault in London, and she did not care to return so soon to England. So instead of writing the work she had originally projected—an intermingling of letters, anecdotes, and other miscellaneous material, in several volumes—she determined to make one little book out of the material she had with her in *Thraliana* and her recollections.

Anecdotes of the Late Samuel Johnson, LL.D., During the Last Twenty Years of His Life appeared on March 25, 1786. The first edition of a thousand copies had been sold by evening; three other printings soon followed. The Piozzis returned to England in March 1787. With the help of a young friend, drawing on Johnson's letters to her, a few poems by him, her own letters to him, and some letters of Johnson to Hill Boothby, she made a two-volume work, *Letters to and from the Late Samuel Johnson*, which was published March 8, 1788.

Mrs. Thrale's *Anecdotes* remains an interesting little book. Her letters to Johnson, especially in their original, unrevised form, now at last available in R. W. Chapman's great edition of Johnson's letters, illuminate Johnson's life. Her *British Synonymy*, a two-volume work published in 1794, had the commendable purpose of indicating shades of meaning and connotation between synonyms and near-synonyms. Mrs. Piozzi's no longer readable two-volume *Observations and Reflections made in the Course of a Journey through France, Italy, and Germany* (1789) was criticized, as her *Anecdotes* had been, for its colloquial style, but it may have helped to hasten the disintegration, toward the end of the century, of the stilted stiffness of the pseudo-Johnsonese of literary mediocrities.

Dr. Johnson's lively companion will always hold the esteem and admiration of Johnsonians for all she did for him in the long years of their friendship. She is indubitably one of the most interesting literary ladies in the whole range of English literature—more interesting, if less significant, than many of the women who have been the authors of books far more important than any of hers. As long as Boswell's *Life* is read, Johnsonians will respect, admire, and, in a Johnsonian sense, love her.

<h1 style="text-align:center">III</h1>

WHEN Johnson first met Boswell and Mrs. Thrale, he was in his middle fifties. He was the author, by then, of a considerable amount of journalistic writing, of two series of periodical essays, of a play, of a short novel, of a small body of poetry, and of a dictionary. During the years that he knew them he published an edition of Shakespeare, his journal of a trip to Scotland and the Hebrides with Boswell, and the biographical and critical prefaces to an edition of the English poets.

Johnson's only play, *Irene*, he carried with him when he first went to London from Lichfield in 1737. To persuade some theatrical impresario to produce it was one of the reasons for his trip. He was not successful. Ten years later, when Garrick had established himself on the London stage, he produced it for his friend and former teacher for nine performances. The play does not make Johnson a dramatist of any consequence.

The total bulk of Johnson's poetry is small. *The Vanity of Human Wishes* (1749), his first published work to have his name on the title page, is a great verse satire, one of the greatest in any language.

There are two hundred and eight of the biweekly *Rambler* essays (they appeared from March 20, 1750, to March 14, 1752). They belong to a typical eighteenth-century literary genre—the periodical essay—today remembered chiefly for Addison and Steele and their *Tatler* and *Spectator*. Johnson's rather involved style in these essays is chiefly responsible for the popular notion of how he always wrote and spoke. Johnson is reported to have said that his other works were wine and water, but his *Rambler* papers were pure wine. He wrote another, shorter series of one hundred and four periodical essays, *The Idler*, which appeared in *The Universal Chronicle* from April 1758 to April 1760.

In June 1746 Johnson had agreed with Dodsley and other

booksellers to write a new dictionary of the English language, the need for which had for some time been apparent; earlier eighteenth-century compilations contained such definitions as 'an animal well known' for *mouse* and 'a round utensil for various uses' for *wheel*. If Johnson, on the other hand, sometimes wrote such definitions as that of *cough*, 'a convulsion of the lungs, vellicated by some sharp serosity. It is pronounced *coff*,' he was at any rate not shirking the dictionary maker's primary job of definition.

Because he wished to have plenty of working room for the undertaking (he made use of six amanuenses, five of them Scots) and to be near his publishers' printers, he took at this time a house in Gough (pronounced *Goff*) Square, off Fleet Street.

Johnson had hoped to finish his work on it in three years, but it took him nine; the *Dictionary* was published April 15, 1775, in two large folio volumes weighing some twenty-seven pounds.

Johnson did two things that have been done in every good dictionary ever since: he discriminated between different senses of a word, and he provided examples in quotations of the actual uses of words in contexts. It was a dictionary that could be read with profit, interest, and amusement. Its large store of quotations provided an educational force that cannot be calculated. Of like importance was its effect on the stabilization of English spelling and pronunciation, although this effect was probably much less than it has sometimes been said to be. Most readers of Johnson's letters will be somewhat surprised at Johnson's own use of capitals and punctuation marks, and the variety of his spellings.

If Johnson had done nothing other than compile his *Dictionary*, he would have a very honorable position among men of letters. Carlyle wrote that in the *Dictionary*, considered alone of Johnson's writings, one could trace 'a great intellect, a genuine man.' It has been described in the mid-twentieth century as a landmark in the development of language and of human thought. Probably nearly fifty thousand copies were sold in Johnson's lifetime; for a century after his death it continued to be sold in revised and supplemented versions. Some years ago the work of restoration on Lichfield Cathedral provided the figure, on a buttress, of Johnson holding a copy of his *Dictionary*.

Johnson's short novel, *Rasselas*, appeared anonymously April 19, 1759. Johnson told a friend that he wrote it 'in the evenings of one week,' which was probably the week following the death of his mother in Lichfield. It is likely that the popular story that he wrote *Rasselas* to pay for his mother's funeral has at least some truth in it, yet Johnson's well-known remark, 'No man but a blockhead ever wrote, except for money,' should not be taken as literally as some have taken it. It is perhaps unintentionally ambiguous. The notion of writing something simply for the pleasure of writing it or because of some undeniable compulsion to write it was foreign to him, but he had no assurance that he would make money from *Irene* when he wrote the play, and he was under no necessity to make the money that he received for his *Lives of the Poets*.

As early as 1745, when he published some *Miscellaneous Observations on the Tragedy of Macbeth*, Johnson had in mind a new edition of Shakespeare. In 1756 he published *Proposals* for such an edition, to be issued by subscription at the end of the following year. For various reasons, he was very dilatory in completing the edition, which did not appear until the fall of 1765. It is the long 'Preface' of nearly seventy pages that remains of most interest; this is one of the best pieces of eighteenth-century Shakespeare criticism which no Shakespearian can afford to be unfamiliar with or to underrate.

In 1777 about forty London booksellers invited Johnson to write short lives as prefaces to an edition of English poets. Johnson did not choose the poets; he was not editorially responsible for the texts or the form that the work took. He must have had in mind the sort of thing he spoke of to Boswell at Ulinish, in September 1773, when they were on their Scottish expedition: 'Talking of biography, he said he did not know any literary man's life in English well-written. It should tell us his studies, his manner of life, the means by which he attained to excellence, his opinion of his own works, and such particulars.'

Four volumes of the *English Poets* appeared in 1779, with twenty-two lives; six more volumes in 1781 with thirty lives; the *Lives* alone were published in 1781, and in a new edition in 1783. A considerable part of the work of writing and of correcting proofs Johnson did during visits to Streatham and Southwark.

Many modern readers find in the *Lives of the Poets* some of Johnson's most interesting pages. Biographers since Johnson have written many lives with many more facts, and a greater attention to the most carefully verified accuracy of the facts, than Johnson assembled. 'To adjust the minute events of literary history, is tedious and troublesome,' Johnson wrote; 'it requires, indeed, no great force of understanding, but often depends upon inquiries which there is no opportunity of making, or is to be fetched from books and pamphlets not always at hand.' The *Lives* still make good reading; even in disagreement with Johnson's opinions, a reader can see that they are the criticism of a highly penetrating intelligence.

IV

ANY READER of Boswell's *Life* naturally becomes curious as to what Johnson looked like, and the chances are that (especially, perhaps, because of Macaulay) what he imagines is more or less a caricature of the Johnson that Boswell and Mrs. Thrale knew. To offset this legendary, improperly imagined Johnson, there are, for one thing, a number of representations of him. Only those who will look long and carefully at reproductions of the portraits by Barry, Opie, and Reynolds, of the Wedgwood profile on the title page of the McAdam-Hyde edition of the *Diaries* (1958), of the Turner engraving from Humphrey's drawing in Bates' *Johnson*, and of the engraving of Barry's sketch in Krutch's *Johnson* can properly imagine the Johnson his contemporaries knew.

It is not to be forgotten that there are different Johnsons —the huge, lumbering young man of his impoverished and difficult early London years; the Johnson whose life was made so much easier by his pension and whose behavior and outward appearance were both modified and civilized by the Thrales (he told Mr. Thrale that he had never 'sought to please till past thirty years old, considering the matter as hopeless'); the old man, ill, and no longer having

Mrs. Thrale to soften his life and make it more agreeable for him.

Johnson's stepdaughter, Lucy Porter, remembered him as being, in his early thirties, lean, lank, bony, noticeably scarred, wearing his own straight, stiff hair (which we know was medium brown, later touched with grey), likely to make odd gesticulations and convulsive starts, which came unexpectedly and were likely to seem somewhat ridiculous.

Mrs. Thrale remembered him, when she first knew him, as remarkably tall, an unusually strong man with exceedingly large limbs, with prominent, noticeable features and a 'rugged' complexion, 'though the original complexion had certainly been fair,' nearsighted and with imperfect sight in one eye, 'his eyes . . . of a light-grey colour . . . wild . . . piercing . . . and at times . . . fierce. . . .'

That he should have been likened to a bear (he even made the comparison himself) was probably inevitable, but it is well to recall that his friend Goldsmith once said of him that the only thing bearish about him was his skin. Until Boswell denied it, the story circulated that it was Boswell's father who had made the following observation: 'James, you told me this man was not a star of the first magnitude in the literary world only, but a very constellation of stars: You are perfectly right, James, and his name is the Ursa Major.'

'The great delight of his life was conversation and mental intercourse,' Sir John Hawkins wrote of him. 'I have heard him assert that a tavern chair was the throne of human felicity. . . . "Wine there exhilarates my spirits, and prompts me to free conversation and an interchange of discourses with those whom I most love [but it is well to remember that for years Johnson drank no wine, and limited himself to water, tea, and lemonade]: I dogmatise and am contradicted, and in this conflict of opinions and sentiments I find delight."' When Johnson talked, he talked to win.

It is a misconception of many who have read about Johnson but have not read Johnson that he normally wrote (and spoke) only in excessively long, elaborately constructed, rhetorical sentences, composed mostly of polysyllabic words. Mrs. Thrale wrote that he used big words 'only when little ones would not express his meaning as clearly, or when the elevation of the thought would have been disgraced by a dress less superb,' and Boswell agreed with her: 'Mr. Johnson's language is suitable to his sentiments. He uses large words because he has large ideas.'

The truth is that Johnson had several styles. The prose style of the *Lives of the Poets* is considerably simpler than that of the *Rambler* essays; any reader of his letters can find in them a remarkable range of deliberately different effects. This is true also of his conversation, as the publication of *Thraliana* and *The Boswell Papers* has made very plain.

In his conversational interchanges, he seems to have enunciated words deliberately and in a rather loud voice. He was not, as some have incorrectly imagined, the sort of talker who is always over-ready to get in the first word and to allow others little chance of expressing themselves: 'Tom Tyers described me the best. He once said to me, "Sir, you are like a ghost: you never speak till you are spoken to." '

Professor Pottle, in the understanding passage about Boswell already quoted, speaks of how, in reading Boswell's *Journal*, we are likely to find ourselves in something that Boswell tells us about himself with a frankness that rather astonishes, and perhaps somewhat frightens us. Something of the same sort is true of Johnson, but in a rather different way. Who can read Johnson's conversations, his letters, or his works without treasuring them for their skillful wording, their enormous common sense, their satirical penetration, their wit, their intelligence, and without relishing many of them as amazingly pertinent to one's own behavior, personality, and experience? As for example:

'A man may write at any time, if he will set himself doggedly to it.'

'This was a good dinner enough, to be sure; but it was not a dinner to *ask* a man to.'

'A man should keep his friendship in constant repair.'

'I hope I will never be deterred from detecting what I think a cheat, by the menaces of a ruffian.'

'It matters not how a man dies, but how he lives.'

'That fellow seems to me to possess but one idea, and that is a wrong one.'

'Every man has a lurking wish to appear considerable in his native place.'

'A man will turn over half a library to make one book.'
'Patriotism is the last refuge of a scoundrel.'
'Knowledge is of two kinds. We know a subject ourselves, or we know where we can find information upon it.'

Another popular misconception about Johnson is that he was somehow the invention of Boswell—that from what Boswell managed to find out about a man who would otherwise have been an obscure and mediocre background-figure in the literary and subliterary life of the period, Boswell created a colossus, and persuaded the world to accept his creation as the man himself. That this is not true is readily shown by even a slight acquaintance with the enormous body of material about Boswell and Johnson. If it were true, however, it would only demonstrate a further aspect of Boswell's versatility; for any writer of fiction or drama who could create a character like Johnson, or who could successfully write a fictionalized biography built around a more or less fictionalized character like Johnson, placed against a historically authentic background, would surely be a remarkable writer and deserve a high place in literature.

Johnson's melancholy is a subject that seems to be of more interest today than it ever was before. Melancholy, in some of its various senses (especially as mere boredom or some variety of mild depression) was a fashionable eighteenth-century complaint. Mrs. Thrale complained of it to Johnson, as did Boswell. The evidence is clear that neither of them ever knew the terrifying, severe depression that Johnson experienced from time to time.

According to Hawkins, Johnson thought he had inherited this from his father. Its first crisis seems to have come in 1729 when he was twenty years old. He left Oxford and consulted a Birmingham doctor who informed him, after reading a full description of his symptoms (in Latin), that they clearly pointed toward madness. There was another crisis toward the middle of 1766, which the Thrales comprehended well enough to invite him to come to live with them at Streatham.

Johnson's depression never became psychotic. It was the sort of severe depression that leaves one bewildered and desperate and terrified in some suburb of hell, but that does not push one into hell itself. It was in such a mood that Johnson bought and one day gave to Mrs. Thrale to keep for him such a padlock as was used to fasten the manacles which confined the insane in eighteenth-century asylums.

Johnson was never insane, but we shall never know how close he may have come to insanity. We do know that he desperately feared insanity. This, or declarations by Johnson in severe depression that he was indeed insane, was the secret that Mrs. Thrale only confided to her *Thraliana* in 1785, after his death: 'Poor Johnson! I see they will leave *nothing untold* that I laboured so long to keep secret; & I was so very delicate in trying to conceal his fancied Insanity, that I retained no Proofs of it—or hardly any—nor even mentioned it in these Books, lest by my dying first *they* might be printed and the Secret (for such I thought it) discovered.' Johnson had confided his fear to others. Tyers in 1784 in his periodical sketch spoke of Johnson's convulsive seizures, and revealed that 'he was afraid of his disorder's seizing his head, and took all possible care that his understanding should not be deranged'; and Hawkins, in his *Life* of 1787, spoke of Johnson's dread of such a calamity.

Nothing is more admirable about Johnson than that he managed somehow to last out these periods of severe depression. However he contrived it, his mind never went under long enough to incapacitate or to kill him.

Macaulay remarked of Johnson in the last paragraph of his *Encyclopaedia Britannica* article that 'Boswell's book has done for him more than the best of his own books could do. The memory of other authors is kept alive by their works. But the memory of Johnson keeps many of his works alive.' We value Johnson, he is saying—and primarily because of Boswell—as a man, rather than for what he wrote. This is a typical nineteenth-century judgment, and until recently it has precluded all others. In 1907 Walter Raleigh, professor of English at Oxford, began the last paragraph of his Leslie Stephen lecture on Johnson with this statement: 'This is the greatness of Johnson, that he is greater than his works. He thought of himself as a man, not as an author; and of literature as a means, not as an end in itself.'

On the other hand we find such conclusions as these by Professor James L. Clifford of Columbia University in 1958:

'What our age needs is a better understanding of the deep wisdom and sanity contained in Johnson's writings. . . . It is in his works that Johnson's significance lies. . . . He was a major writer, one of the great figures of English literature. . . . It is in his writings, rather than in the witty, explosive remarks so marvellously set down by Boswell, that Johnson has most to say to our generation.'

If today we had as slight a knowledge of Johnson the man as we have of many a writer, we would not be likely to find him, as a man, particularly memorable. If we knew him today only through his works, we would value him more highly than he was customarily valued for at least a century (say 1825–1925).

We are already within a quarter-century of the two-hundredth anniversary of his death. For us he is not, on the one hand, Johnson the author, and on the other, Johnson the subject of Boswell's great *Life*. For us he is admirable, and great, because he was a remarkable and great man—a greatness which shows itself in Boswell's record of his life and on page after page of his writings, including his letters.

Macaulay's assertion that the *Life* would be read as long as the English language is known, we feel to be as true a prophecy today as when Macaulay made it. Boswell's *Life* has assuredly made both Johnson and his biographer immortal figures. It is impossible to imagine a time when Boswell's *Life* will not be read, for it is a greatly told life of a great man.

EDWARD G. FLETCHER

A NOTE ON THE TEXT

THE TWO SETS of Piozzi marginalia which are the special feature of this edition of James Boswell's *Life of Samuel Johnson, LL.D.* are from an 1816 edition of the *Life* (the eighth) now at the Houghton Library at Harvard University, and from an 1807 edition (the fifth) now the property of Donald and Mary Hyde of North Branch, New Jersey.

The history of the former has been recorded by Percival Merritt in *Harvard Library Notes* for April 1926. Mrs. Piozzi bought it in November 1816 from Upham, a Bath bookseller. In September 1823 it was sold 'at the Emporium in Manchester' by a Mr. Broster, of Chester, who probably obtained it from Mrs. Piozzi's adopted son, Sir John Salusbury Piozzi Salusbury. It was at this time probably bought by one J. Webster, who pencilled a few comments and a few crosses into it, and jotted down some page references. Webster's books were sold 'at Mr. Evans's' in April 1826. The *Life* apparently came into the possession of the Reverend Henry Wellesley, of New Inn Hall, Oxford, who lent it to Hayward when he was working on his life of Mrs. Piozzi. Wellesley's library was sold in November 1866; the *Life* seems to have been purchased by Sir William Augustus Fraser, whose bookplate is now in each of the four volumes. When Fraser's library was sold at Sotheby's in April 1901, Quaritch bought the *Life*. Miss Amy Lowell probably secured it from Quaritch. She bequeathed it to Harvard in 1925, where it is now part of The Amy Lowell Collection of Books and Manuscripts.

Miss Lowell used to read from the marginalia to her friends, 'in a manner suggestive of the charm of Madame Piozzi herself.' A. Edward Newton heard her do so, and misunderstanding the edition annotated, wrote in *The Amenities of Book-Collecting* (1918), 'Who does not envy her the possession of the first edition of Boswell's "Life of Johnson," filled with the marginalia of the one person in the world whose knowledge of the old man rivaled that of the great biographer himself?' It is clear from a passage in

Thraliana that Mrs. Piozzi read a copy of the first edition, but whether she annotated it, and where the copy now is, are unknown.

The Harvard copy has nearly 575 marginalia. In addition to these, it contains about a thousand marks of one sort or another. Hayward printed in the first edition of his work on Mrs. Piozzi (1861) about twenty-five of these marginalia, and in the second edition (1861) about fifty more. G. B. Hill knew Hayward's book, and used a few of the marginalia in his edition of the *Life* (1887). In *Doctor Johnson's Mrs. Thrale*, J. H. Lobban in 1910 reprinted about fifty-five of them. A. E. Newton printed part of one, which he presumably remembered Amy Lowell reading, in the June 1918 *Atlantic Monthly* and in *The Amenities of Book-Collecting*. Merritt, in the April 1926 *Harvard Library Notes*, quoted about twenty, only a few of which had not previously appeared in Hayward. L. F. Powell had a typescript of them which he used in his revision of Hill (1934), but he quotes or refers to only about seventy-five.

The Hyde set of the *Life* is probably the annotated copy which was in the possession of Bohn the publisher about 1860. It was 'for long in the library of one of the most famous collectors of the nineteenth century.' It was owned for a time by Minna Steele Smith. In 1925 it was in the hands of the English bookseller, Charles Sawyer, who sold it to Colonel Ralph Isham. The Hydes acquired it at the auction of Isham's library after his death. This 1807 edition of the *Life* has about 450 marginalia, and contains about 100 marginal marks, underscorings, etc.

The 1807 and 1816 sets contain about sixty identical or almost identical marginalia, perhaps copied one from the other, and about eighty-five passages which have more or less similar marginalia in the two editions. All the marginalia are written in ink, but not, as the varying character of the handwriting shows, at the same time. The occasional dates, in fact, prove this. The marginal marks, etc., are also in ink, except that in the Harvard set many were made with a red or violet crayon.

Miss Smith printed about fifty of the Isham marginalia in *The London Mercury* for January 1922. A short article about the Isham copy in the London *Times* for December

30, 1925 (quoted almost entire in the New York *Evening Post Literary Review*, January 23, 1926) quoted six of them.

The text used in this edition is that of the eighth edition, 1816, printed by C. Baldwin for Cadell and Davies, the text of the Harvard annotated set. It has been exactly followed, except for a few changes in punctuation and capitalization, and the correction of a few printer's slips.

The devices used in printing the marginalia are, I trust, clear. Every comment and every indication of a mark is followed by an 'H' or an 'I' (sometimes both) to indicate which of the two annotated sets it is from (H for *Harvard* and H for *Hyde* obviously would not do, so it is necessary to revert to I for *Isham*). To indicate the position in the 1807 or 1816 texts of each marginal line, we have quoted the two first and two last words beginning and ending the line or lines against which it is placed. It is not always perfectly clear just what word or phrase Mrs. Piozzi intended a question mark or an exclamation mark to refer to; we have sometimes had to choose between two possibilities. A small reference letter in the text indicates a marginal note. The exact reference of some of the marginalia is, also, not wholly clear. The spelling, punctuation, and capitalization of the marginalia are Mrs. Piozzi's, though occasionally we may have printed a small letter where Mrs. Piozzi intended a capital, a dash where she intended dots (or vice versa), sometimes a period where she used a colon. All her dashes have been reduced to a common length and all her strings of dots to three. Dots in the marginalia never indicate omission.

All footnotes not credited in the text are by James Boswell, the author of the *Life*. Notes signed J. BOSWELL are by his second son, James Boswell, Jr. Chief among the other identified annotators are Edmond MALONE, Dr. Charles BURNEY, Alexander CHALMERS, Reverend Dr. KEARNEY, James DODSLEY, John COURTENAY, Reverend J. B. BLAKEWAY, Thomas WARTON, John NICHOLS, and James BEATTIE.

The publisher and the editor are greatly indebted to the Librarian of the Harvard College Library for permission to print the marginalia from the Harvard copy of the *Life*, and to Donald and Mary Hyde for the use of their copy. I am under a special obligation in my Introduction to the preliminary materials in the various volumes of *The Boswell Papers* edited by Frederick A. Pottle and others.

The frontispiece portraits of Dr. Johnson and Mrs. Piozzi in Volumes I and III, respectively, are in the possession of Courage Barclay & Simonds, Ltd., London, and are reproduced with their kind permission. The portrait of James Boswell in Volume II is reproduced through the courtesy of the National Galleries of Scotland, Edinburgh.

E. G. F.

THE

L I F E

OF

SAMUEL JOHNSON, LL.D.

COMPREHENDING

AN ACCOUNT OF HIS STUDIES
AND NUMEROUS WORKS,

IN CHRONOLOGICAL ORDER;

A SERIES OF HIS EPISTOLARY CORRESPONDENCE
AND CONVERSATIONS WITH MANY EMINENT PERSONS;

AND

VARIOUS ORIGINAL PIECES OF HIS COMPOSITION,
NEVER BEFORE PUBLISHED.

THE WHOLE EXHIBITING A VIEW OF LITERATURE AND LITERARY MEN
IN GREAT-BRITAIN, FOR NEAR HALF A CENTURY,
DURING WHICH HE FLOURISHED.

IN TWO VOLUMES.

BY JAMES BOSWELL, ESQ.

————*Quò fit ut* OMNIS
Votiva pateat veluti descripta tabella
VITA SENIS.————   HORAT.

VOLUME THE FIRST.

LONDON:
PRINTED BY HENRY BALDWIN,
FOR CHARLES DILLY, IN THE POULTRY.
M DCC XCI.

DEDICATION

TO

SIR JOSHUA REYNOLDS

MY DEAR SIR,

EVERY liberal motive that can actuate an Authour in the dedication of his labours, concurs in directing me to you, as the person to whom the following Work should be inscribed.

IF there be a pleasure in celebrating the distinguished merit of a contemporary, mixed with a certain degree of vanity not altogether inexcusable, in appearing fully sensible of it, where can I find one, in complimenting whom I can with more general approbation gratify those feelings? Your excellence not only in the Art over which you have long presided with unrivalled fame, but also in Philosophy and elegant Literature, is well known to the present, and will continue to be the admiration of future ages. Your equal and placid temper, your variety of conversation, your true politeness, by which you are so amiable in private society, and that enlarged hospitality which has long made your house a common centre of union for the great, the accomplished, the learned, and the ingenious; all these qualities I can, in perfect confidence of not being accused of flattery, ascribe to you.

IF a man may indulge an honest pride, in having it known to the world, that he has been thought worthy of particular attention by a person of the first eminence in the age in which he lived, whose company has been universally courted, I am justified in availing myself of the usual privilege of a Dedication, when I mention that there has been a long and uninterrupted friendship between us.

I F gratitude should be acknowledged for favours received, I have this opportunity, my dear Sir, most sincerely to thank you for the many happy hours which I owe to your kindness,—for the cordiality with which you have at all times been pleased to welcome me,—for the number of valuable acquaintances to whom you have introduced me,—for the *noctes cænæque Deûm*, which I have enjoyed under your roof.

I F a work should be inscribed to one who is master of the subject of it, and whose approbation, therefore, must ensure it credit and success, the Life of Dr. Johnson is, with the greatest propriety, dedicated to Sir Joshua Reynolds, who was the intimate and beloved friend of that great man; the friend, whom he declared to be 'the most invulnerable man he knew; whom, if he should quarrel with him, he should find the most difficulty how to abuse.' You, my dear Sir, studied him, and knew him well: you venerated and admired him. Yet, luminous as he was upon the whole, you perceived all the shades which mingled in the grand composition; all the little peculiarities and slight blemishes which marked the literary Colossus. Your very warm commendation of the specimen which I gave in my 'Journal of a Tour to the Hebrides,' of my being able to preserve his conversation in an authentick and lively manner, which opinion the Public has confirmed, was the best encouragement for me to persevere in my purpose of producing the whole of my stores.

I N one respect this Work will, in some passages, be different from the former. In my 'Tour,' I was almost unboundedly open in my communications, and from my eagerness to display the wonderful fertility and readiness of Johnson's wit, freely shewed to the world its dexterity, even when I was myself the object of it. I trusted that I should be liberally understood, as knowing very well what

I was about, and by no means as simply unconscious of the pointed effects of the satire. I own, indeed, that I was arrogant enough to suppose that the tenour of the rest of the book would sufficiently guard me against such a strange imputation. But it seems I judged too well of the world; for, though I could scarcely believe it, I have been undoubtedly informed, that many persons, especially in distant quarters, not penetrating enough into Johnson's character, so as to understand his mode of treating his friends, have arraigned my judgement, instead of seeing that I was sensible of all that they could observe.

It is related of the great Dr. Clarke, that when in one of his leisure hours he was unbending himself with a few friends in the most playful and frolicksome manner, he observed Beau Nash approaching; upon which he suddenly stopped;—'My boys, (said he,) let us be grave: here comes a fool.' The world, my friend, I have found to be a great fool, as to that particular on which it has become necessary to speak very plainly. I have, therefore, in this Work been more reserved; and though I tell nothing but the truth, I have still kept in my mind that the whole truth is not always to be exposed. This, however, I have managed so as to occasion no diminution of the pleasure which my book should afford; though malignity may sometimes be disappointed of its gratifications.

I am,

My dear Sir,

Your much obliged friend,

And faithful humble servant,

London,

April 20, 1791.

JAMES BOSWELL

ADVERTISEMENT
TO THE FIRST EDITION

I AT last deliver to the world a Work which I have long promised, and of which, I am afraid, too high expectations have been raised. The delay of its publication must be imputed, in a considerable degree, to the extraordinary zeal which has been shewn by distinguished persons in all quarters to supply me with additional information concerning its illustrious subject; resembling in this the grateful tribes of ancient nations, of which every individual was eager to throw a stone upon the grave of a departed Hero, and thus to share in the pious office of erecting an honourable monument to his memory.

The labour and anxious attention with which I have collected and arranged the materials of which these volumes are composed, will hardly be conceived by those who read them with careless facility. The stretch of mind and prompt assiduity by which so many conversations were preserved,[a] I myself, at some distance of time, contemplate with wonder; and I must be allowed to suggest, that the nature of the work, in other respects, as it consists of innumerable detached particulars, all which, even the most minute, I have spared no pains to ascertain with a scrupulous authenticity, has occasioned a degree of trouble far beyond that of any other species of composition. Were I to detail the books which I have consulted and the inquiries which I have found it necessary to make by various channels, I should probably be thought ridiculously ostentatious. Let me only observe, as a specimen of my trouble, that I have sometimes been obliged to run half over London, in order to fix a date correctly; which, when I had accomplished, I well knew would obtain me no praise, though a failure would have been to my discredit. And after all, perhaps, hard as it may be, I shall not be surprised if omissions or mistakes be pointed out with invidious severity. I have also been extremely careful as to the exactness of my quotations; holding that there is a respect due to the publick, which

[a] *Excellent!* [1]

should oblige every Authour to attend to this, and never to presume to introduce them with,—'I think I have read;'—or—'If I remember right;'[a]*—when the originals may be examined.*

I beg leave to express my warmest thanks to those who have been pleased to favour me with communications and advice in the conduct of my Work. But I cannot sufficiently acknowledge my obligations to my friend Mr. MALONE, *who was so good as to allow me to read to him almost the whole of my manuscript, and make such remarks as were greatly for the advantage of the Work; though it is but fair to him to mention, that upon many occasions I differed from him, and followed my own judgement. I regret exceedingly that I was deprived of the benefit of his revision, when not more than one half of the book had passed through the press; but after having completed his very laborious and admirable edition of* SHAKSPEARE, *for which he generously would accept of no other reward but that fame which he has so deservedly obtained, he fulfilled his promise of a long-wished-for visit to his relations in Ireland; from whence his safe return* finibus Atticis *is desired by his friends here, with all the classical ardour of* Sic te Diva potens Cypri; *for there is no man in whom more elegant and worthy qualities are united; and whose society, therefore, is more valued by those who know him.*

It is painful to me to think, that while I was carrying on this Work, several of those to whom it would have been most interesting have died. Such melancholy disappointments we know to be incident to humanity; but we do not feel them the less. Let me particularly lament the Reverend THOMAS WARTON, *and the Reverend Dr.* ADAMS. *Mr.* WARTON, *amidst his variety of genius and learning, was an excellent Biographer. His contributions to my Collection are highly estimable; and as he had a true relish of my* 'Tour to the Hebrides,' *I trust I should now have been gratified with a larger share of his kind approbation. Dr.* ADAMS, *eminent as the Head of a College, as a writer, and as a most amiable man, had known* JOHNSON *from his early years, and was his friend through life. What reason I had to hope for the countenance of that venerable Gentleman to this Work, will appear from what he wrote to me upon a former occasion from Oxford, November* 17, 1785:— 'Dear Sir, I hazard this letter, not knowing where it will find you, to thank you for your very agreeable "Tour," which I found here on my return from the country, and in which you have depicted our friend so perfectly to my fancy, in every attitude, every scene and situation, that I have thought myself in the company, and of the party almost throughout. It has given very general satisfaction; and those who have found most fault with a passage here and there, have agreed that they could not help going through, and being entertained with the whole. I wish, indeed, some few gross expressions had been softened, and a few of our hero's foibles had been a little more shaded; but it is useful to see the weaknesses incident to great minds; and you have given us Dr. Johnson's authority that in history all ought to be told.'

underlined:

Such a sanction to my faculty[a] *of giving a just representation* faculty [1]
of Dr. JOHNSON *I could not conceal. Nor will I suppress my* [a] *faculty!!* [1]
satisfaction in the consciousness, that by recording so considerable a
portion of the wisdom and wit of 'the brightest ornament of the
eighteenth century,'* *I have largely provided for the instruction*
and entertainment of mankind.

London, April 20, 1791.

---

* See Mr. Malone's Preface to his edition of Shakspeare.

ADVERTISEMENT

TO THE SECOND EDITION

THAT I was anxious for the success of a Work which had employed much of my time and labour, I do not wish to conceal: but whatever doubts I at any time entertained, have been entirely removed by the very favourable reception with which it has been honoured. That reception has excited my best exertions to render my Book more perfect; and in this endeavour I have had the assistance not only of some of my particular friends, but of many other learned and ingenious men, by which I have been enabled to rectify some mistakes, and to enrich the Work with many valuable additions. These I have ordered to be printed separately in quarto, for the accommodation of the purchasers of the first edition. May I be permitted to say that the typography of both editions does honour to the press of Mr. HENRY BALDWIN, now Master of the Worshipful Company of Stationers, whom I have long known as a worthy man and an obliging friend.

In the strangely mixed scenes of human existence, our feelings are often at once pleasing and painful. Of this truth, the progress of the present Work furnishes a striking instance. It was highly gratifying to me that my friend, Sir JOSHUA REYNOLDS, to whom it is inscribed, lived to peruse it, and to give the strongest testimony to its fidelity; but before a second edition, which he contributed to improve, could be finished, the world has been deprived of that most valuable man; a loss of which the regret will be deep, and lasting, and extensive, proportionate to the felicity which he diffused through a wide circle of admirers and friends.

In reflecting that the illustrious subject of this Work, by being more extensively and intimately known, however elevated before, has risen in the veneration and love of mankind, I feel a satisfaction beyond what fame can afford. We cannot, indeed, too much or too often admire his wonderful powers of mind, when we consider that the principal store of wit and wisdom which this Work contains, was not a particular selection from his general conversation, but was merely his occasional talk at such times as I had the good fortune to be in his company; and, without doubt, if his discourse at other periods had been collected with the same attention, the whole tenor of what he uttered would have been found equally excellent.

His strong, clear, and animated enforcement of religion, morality, loyalty, and subordination, while it delights and improves the wise and the good, will, I trust, prove an effectual antidote to that detestable sophistry which has been lately imported from France, under the false name of Philosophy, *and with a malignant industry has been employed against the peace, good order, and happiness of society, in our free and prosperous country; but, thanks be to* GOD, *without producing the pernicious effects which were hoped for by its propagators.*

It seems to me, in my moments of self-complacency, that this extensive biographical work, however inferior in its nature, may in one respect be assimilated to the ODYSSEY. *Amidst a thousand entertaining and instructive episodes the* HERO *is never long out of sight; for they are all in some degree connected with him; and* HE, *in the whole course of the History, is exhibited by the Authour for the best advantage of his readers:*

> —Quid virtus et quid sapientia possit,
> Utile proposuit nobis exemplar Ulyssen.

Should there be any cold-blooded and morose mortals who really dislike this Book, I will give them a story to apply. When the great DUKE OF MARLBOROUGH, *accompanied by* LORD CADOGAN, *was one day reconnoitring the army in Flanders, a heavy rain came on, and they both called for their cloaks.* LORD CADOGAN'S *servant, a good humoured alert lad, brought his Lordship's in a minute. The Duke's servant, a lazy sulky dog, was so sluggish, that his Grace being wet to the skin, reproved him, and had for answer with a grunt, 'I came as fast as I could;' upon which the Duke calmly said,—'* CADOGAN, *I would not for a thousand pounds have that fellow's temper.'*

There are some men, I believe, who have, or think they have, a very small share of vanity. Such may speak of their literary fame

in a decorous style of diffidence. But I confess, that I am so formed
by nature and by habit, that to restrain the effusion of delight, on
having obtained such fame, to me would be truly painful. Why then
should I suppress it? Why 'out of the abundance of the heart'
should I not speak? Let me then mention with a warm, but no
insolent exultation, that I have been regaled with spontaneous
praise of my work by many and various persons eminent for their
rank, learning, talents, and accomplishments; much of which
praise I have under their hands to be reposited in my archives at
Auchinleck. *An honourable and reverend friend speaking of the*
favourable reception of my volumes, even in the circles of fashion
and elegance, said to me, 'you have made them all talk Johnson.' —
Yes, I may add, I have Johnsonised *the land; and I trust they*
will not only talk, *but* think, Johnson.

To enumerate those to whom I have been thus indebted, would be
tediously ostentatious. I cannot however but name one, whose praise
is truly valuable, not only on account of his knowledge and abilities,
but on account of the magnificent, yet dangerous embassy, in which
he is now employed, which makes every thing that relates to him
peculiarly interesting. LORD MACARTNEY *favoured me with*
his own copy of my book, with a number of notes, of which I have
availed myself. On the first leaf I found in his Lordship's hand-
writing, an inscription of such high commendation, that even I, vain
as I am, cannot prevail on myself to publish it.

[July 1, 1793.]

ADVERTISEMENT
TO THE THIRD EDITION

———

SEVERAL valuable letters, and other curious matter, having been communicated to the Authour too late to be arranged in that chronological order which he had endeavoured uniformly to observe in his work, he was obliged to introduce them in his Second Edition, by way of ADDENDA, *as commodiously as he could. In the present edition they have been distributed in their proper places. In revising his volumes for a new edition, he had pointed out where some of these materials should be inserted; but unfortunately, in the midst of his labours, he was seized with a fever, of which, to the great regret of all his friends, he died on the 19th of May, 1795. All the Notes that he had written in the margin of the copy which he had in part revised, are here faithfully preserved; and a few new Notes have been added, principally by some of those friends to whom the Authour in the former editions acknowledged his obligations. Those subscribed with the letter* B. *were communicated by Dr.* BURNEY; *those to which the letters* J. B. *are annexed, by the Rev.* J. B. BLAKEWAY, *of Shrewsbury, to whom Mr.* BOSWELL *acknowledged himself indebted for some judicious remarks on the first edition of his work: and the letters* J. B—. O. *are annexed to some remarks furnished by the Authour's second son, a Student of Brazen-Nose College in Oxford. Some valuable observations were communicated by* JAMES BINDLEY, *Esq. First Commissioner in the Stamp-Office, which have been acknowledged in their proper places. For all those without any signature, Mr.* MALONE *is answerable.—Every new remark, not written by the Authour, for the sake of distinction has been enclosed within crotchets; in one instance, however, the printer, by mistake, has affixed this mark to a note relative to the Rev.* THOMAS FYSCHE PALMER, (*see* vol. iii. p. 223,) *which was written by Mr.* BOSWELL, *and therefore ought not to have been thus distinguished.*

I have only to add, that the proof-sheets of the present edition not having passed through my hands, I am not answerable for any typographical errours that may be found in it. Having, however, been printed at the very accurate press of Mr. Baldwin, I make no doubt it will be found not less perfect than the former edition; the greatest care having been taken, by correctness and elegance, to do justice to one of the most instructive and entertaining works in the English language.

EDM. MALONE

April 8, 1799.

ADVERTISEMENT

TO THE FOURTH EDITION

In this edition are inserted some new letters of which the greater part has been obligingly communicated by the Reverend Doctor VYSE, Rector of Lambeth. Those written by Dr. JOHNSON concerning his mother in her last illness, furnish a new proof of his great piety and tenderness of heart, and therefore cannot but be acceptable to the readers of this very popular work. Some new notes also have been added, which, as well as the observations inserted in the third edition, and the letters now introduced, are carefully included within crotchets, that the authour may not be answerable for any thing which had not the sanction of his approbation. The remarks of his friends are distinguished as formerly, except those of Mr. MALONE, to which the letter M. is now subjoined. Those to which the letter K. is affixed, were communicated by my learned friend, the Reverend Doctor KEARNEY, formerly Senior Fellow of Trinity College, Dublin, and now beneficed in the diocese of Raphoe in Ireland, of which he is Archdeacon.

Of a work which has been before the publick for thirteen years with increasing approbation, and of which near four thousand copies have been dispersed, it is not necessary to say more; yet I cannot refrain from adding, that, highly as it is now estimated, it will, I am confident, be still more valued by posterity a century hence, when all the actors in the scene shall be numbered with the dead; when the excellent and extraordinary man, whose wit and wisdom are here recorded, shall be viewed at a still greater distance; and the instruction and entertainment they afford, will at once produce reverential gratitude, admiration, and delight.

E. M.

June 20, 1804.

A CHRONOLOGICAL CATALOGUE

OF THE PROSE WORKS*

OF SAMUEL JOHNSON, LL.D.

[N.B. To those which he himself acknowledged is added *acknowl.* To those which may be fully believed to be his from internal evidence, is added *intern. evid.*]

1735. ABRIDGEMENT and translation of Lobo's Voyage to Abyssinia. *acknowl.*

1738. Part of a translation of Father Paul Sarpi's History of the Council of Trent. *acknowl.*

[N.B. As this work, after some sheets were printed, suddenly stopped, I know not whether any part of it is now to be found.]

FOR THE GENTLEMAN'S MAGAZINE

Preface. *intern. evid.*

Life of Father Paul. *acknowl.*

1739. A complete vindication of the Licenser of the Stage from the malicious and scandalous aspersions of Mr. Brooke, authour of Gustavus Vasa. *acknowl.*

Marmor Norfolciense: or, an Essay on an ancient prophetical inscription in monkish rhyme, lately discovered near Lynne in Norfolk: by PROBUS BRITANNICUS. *acknowl.*

FOR THE GENTLEMAN'S MAGAZINE

Life of Boerhaave. *acknowl.*

Address to the Reader. *intern. evid.*

* I do not here include his Poetical Works; for, excepting his Latin Translation of Pope's Messiah, his London, and his Vanity of Human Wishes imitated from Juvenal; his Prologue on the opening of Drury Lane Theatre by Mr. Garrick, and his Irene, a Tragedy, they are very numerous, and in general short; and I have promised a complete edition of them, in which I shall with the utmost care ascertain their authenticity, and illustrate them with notes and various readings.

Appeal to the Publick in behalf of the Editor. *intern. evid.*

Considerations on the case of Dr. Trapp's Sermons; a plausible attempt to prove that an authour's work may be abridged without injuring his property. *acknowl.*

1740.   FOR THE GENTLEMAN'S MAGAZINE

Preface. *intern. evid.*

Life of Admiral Drake. *acknowl.*

Life of Admiral Blake. *acknowl.*

Life of Philip Barretier. *acknowl.*

Essay on Epitaphs. *acknowl.*

1741.   FOR THE GENTLEMAN'S MAGAZINE

Preface. *intern. evid.*

A free translation of the Jests of Hierocles, with an introduction. *intern. evid.*

Debate on the *Humble Petition and Advice* of the Rump Parliament to Cromwell in 1657, to assume the Title of King; abridged, methodized and digested. *intern. evid.*

Translation of Abbé Guyon's Dissertation on the Amazons. *intern. evid.*

Translation of Fontenelle's Panegyrick on Dr. Morin. *intern. evid.*

1742.   FOR THE GENTLEMAN'S MAGAZINE

Preface. *intern. evid.*

Essay on the Account of the Conduct of the Duchess of Marlborough. *acknowl.*

An Account of the Life of Peter Burman. *acknowl.*

The Life of Sydenham, afterwards prefixed to Dr. Swan's Edition of his Works. *acknowl.*

Proposals for printing Bibliotheca Harleiana, or a Catalogue of the Library of the Earl of Oxford, afterwards prefixed to the first Volume of that Catalogue, in which the Latin Accounts of the Books were written by him. *acknowl.*

Abridgement, entitled Foreign History. *intern. evid.*

Essay on the Description of China, from the French of Du Halde. *intern. evid.*

1743. Dedication to Dr. Mead of Dr. James's Medicinal Dictionary. *intern. evid.*[a]

[a] *Acknowledged to H. L. P.* [H]

FOR THE GENTLEMAN'S MAGAZINE

Preface. *intern. evid.*

Parliamentary Debates under the name of Debates in the Senate of Lilliput, from Nov. 19, 1740, to Feb. 23, 1742–3, inclusive. *acknowl.*

Considerations on the Dispute between Crousaz and Warburton on Pope's Essay on Man. *intern. evid.*

A Letter, announcing that the Life of Mr. Savage was speedily to be published by a person who was favoured with his Confidence. *intern. evid.*

Advertisement for Osborne concerning the Harleian Catalogue. *intern. evid.*

1744. Life of Richard Savage. *acknowl.*

Preface to the Harleian Miscellany. *acknowl.*

FOR THE GENTLEMAN'S MAGAZINE

Preface. *intern. evid.*

1745. Miscellaneous Observations on the Tragedy of Macbeth, with remarks on Sir T. H.'s (Sir Thomas Hanmer's) Edition of Shakspeare, and Proposals for a new Edition of that Poet. *acknowl.*

1747. Plan for a Dictionary of the ENGLISH LANGUAGE, addressed to Philip Dormer, Earl of Chesterfield. *acknowl.*

FOR THE GENTLEMAN'S MAGAZINE

1748. Life of Roscommon. *acknowl.*

Foreign History, November. *intern. evid.*

FOR MR. DODSLEY'S PRECEPTOR

Preface. *acknowl.*

Vision of Theodore the Hermit. *acknowl.*

1750. The RAMBLER, the first Paper of which was published 20th of March this year, and the last 17th of March, 1752, the day on which Mrs. Johnson died.* *acknowl.*

* [This is a mistake. The last number of the Rambler appeared on the *fourteenth* of March, three days before Mrs. Johnson died. See vol. i. p. 157. MALONE.]

Letter in the General Advertiser to excite the attention of the Publick to the Performance of Comus, which was next day to be acted at Drury-Lane Playhouse for the Benefit of Milton's Grand-daughter. *acknowl.*

Preface and Postscript to Lauder's Pamphlet, entitled, 'An Essay on Milton's Use and Imitation of the Moderns in his Paradise Lost.' *acknowl.*

1751. Life of Cheynel, in the Miscellany called 'The Student.' *acknowl.*

Letter for Lauder, addressed to the Reverend Dr. John Douglas, acknowledging his Fraud concerning Milton in terms of suitable Contrition. *acknowl.*

Dedication to the Earl of Middlesex of Mrs. Charlotte Lennox's 'Female Quixote.' *intern. evid.*

1753. Dedication to John Earl of Orrery, of Shakspeare Illustrated, by Mrs. Charlotte Lennox. *acknowl.*

During this and the following year he wrote and gave to his much loved friend Dr. Bathurst the Papers in the Adventurer, signed T. *acknowl.*

1754. Life of Edw. Cave, in the Gentleman's Magazine. *acknowl.*

1755. A DICTIONARY, with a Grammar and History, of the ENGLISH LANGUAGE. *acknowl.*

An Account of an Attempt to ascertain the Longitude at Sea, by an exact Theory of the Variations of the Magnetical Needle, with a Table of the Variations at the most remarkable Cities in Europe, from the year 1660 to 1860. *acknowl.* This he wrote for Mr. Zachariah Williams, an ingenious ancient Welch Gentleman, father of Mrs. Anna Williams, whom he for many years kindly lodged in his House. It was published with a Translation into Italian by Signor Baretti. In a Copy of it which he presented to the Bodleian Library at Oxford, is pasted a Character of the late Mr. Zachariah Williams, plainly written by Johnson. *intern. evid.*

1756. An Abridgement of his Dictionary. *acknowl.*

Several Essays in the Universal Visiter, which there is some difficulty in ascertaining. All that are marked with two Asterisks have been ascribed to him, although I am confident from internal Evidence, that we should except from these 'The Life of Chaucer,' 'Reflections on the State of Portugal,' and 'An Essay on Architecture:' And from the same Evidence I am confident that he wrote 'Further Thoughts on Agriculture,' and 'A Dissertation on the State of Literature and Authours.' The Dissertation on the Epitaphs written by Pope he afterwards acknowledged, and added to his 'Idler.'

Life of Sir Thomas Browne prefixed to a new Edition of his Christian Morals. *acknowl.*

In the LITERARY MAGAZINE: or, UNIVERSAL REVIEW, which began in January 1756

His ORIGINAL ESSAYS are

The Preliminary Address. *intern. evid.*

An Introduction to the Political State of Great Britain. *intern. evid.*

Remarks on the Militia Bill. *intern. evid.*

Observations on his Britannick Majesty's Treaties with the Empress of Russia and the Landgrave of Hesse Cassel. *intern. evid.*

Observations on the Present State of Affairs. *intern. evid.*

Memoirs of Frederick III. King of Prussia. *intern. evid.*

In the same MAGAZINE his REVIEWS are of the following Books: 'Birch's History of the Royal Society.'—'Browne's Christian Morals.'—'Warton's Essay on the Writings and Genius of Pope, Vol. I.'—'Hampton's Translation of Polybius.'—'Sir Isaac Newton's Arguments in Proof of a Deity.'—'Borlase's History of the Isles of Scilly.'—'Home's Experiments on Bleaching.'—'Browne's History of Jamaica.'—'Hales on Distilling Sea Waters, Ventilators in Ships, and curing an ill Taste in Milk.'—'Lucas's Essay on Waters.'—'Keith's Catalogue of the Scottish Bishops.' —'Philosophical Transactions, Vol. XLIX.'—'Miscellanies by Elizabeth Harrison.'—'Evans's Map and Account of the Middle Colonies in America.'—'The Cadet, a Military Treatise.'—'The Conduct of the Ministry relating to the present War impartially examined.' *intern. evid.*

'Mrs. Lennox's Translation of Sully's Memoirs.'—
'Letter on the Case of Admiral Byng.'—'Appeal to the
People concerning Admiral Byng.'—'Hanway's Eight
Days' Journey, and Essay on Tea.'—'Some further
Particulars in Relation to the Case of Amiral Byng, by
a Gentleman of Oxford.' *acknowl.*

Mr. Jonas Hanway having written an angry Answer to
the Review of his Essay on Tea, Johnson in the same
Collection made a reply to it. *acknowl.* This is the only
Instance, it is believed, when he condescended to take
Notice of any Thing that had been written against
him; and here his chief Intention seems to have been
to make Sport.

Dedication to the Earl of Rochford of, and Preface to,
Mr. Payne's Introduction to the Game of Draughts.
acknowl.

Introduction to the London Chronicle, an Evening Paper
which still subsists with deserved credit. *acknowl.*

1757. Speech on the Subject of an Address to the Throne after
the Expedition to Rochefort: delivered by one of his
Friends in some public Meeting: it is printed in the
Gentleman's Magazine for October 1785. *intern. evid.*

The first two paragraphs of the Preface to Sir William
Chambers's Designs of Chinese Buildings, &c. *acknowl.*

1758. THE IDLER, which began April 5, in this year, and was
continued till April 5, 1760. *acknowl.*

An Essay on the Bravery of the English Common
Soldiers was added to it, when published in Volumes.
acknowl.

1759. Rasselas Prince of Abyssinia, a Tale. *acknowl.*

Advertisement for the Proprietors of the Idler against
certain Persons who pirated those Papers as they came
out singly in a News-paper called the Universal
Chronicle, or Weekly Gazette. *intern. evid.*

For Mrs. Charlotte Lennox's English Version of
Brumoy,—'A Dissertation on the Greek Comedy,' and
the General Conclusion of the Book. *intern. evid.*

Introduction to the World Displayed, a Collection of
Voyages and Travels. *acknowl.*

Three Letters in the Gazetteer, concerning the best plan
for Blackfriars Bridge. *acknowl.*

1760. Address of the Painters to George III. on his Accession
to the Throne. *intern. evid.*

Dedication of Baretti's Italian[a] and English Dictionary
to the Marquis of Abreu, then Envoy-Extraordinary
from Spain at the Court of Great Britain. *intern. evid.*

Review in the Gentleman's Magazine, of M. Tytler's
acute and able Vindication of Mary Queen of Scots.
acknowl.

Introduction to the Proceedings of the Committee for
Cloathing the French Prisoners. *acknowl.*

underlined:
Italian [1]

[a] *Qu*—Spanish; *what
had D'Abreu to do
with Italian?* [1]

1761. Preface to Rolt's Dictionary of Trade and Commerce.
acknowl.

Corrections and Improvements for Mr. Gwyn the
Architect's Pamphlet, entitled 'Thoughts on the
Coronation of George III.' *acknowl.*

1762. Dedication to the King, of the Reverend Dr. Kennedy's
Complete System of Astronomical Chronology unfolding the Scriptures, Quarto Edition. *acknowl.*[b]

Preface to the Catalogue of the Artist's Exhibition.
intern. evid.

[b] *& a Dedication to
the King of Somebody's
Treatise on the Globes
—I forget whose—an
Optician he was, I
think. Qu: if not
Adams.* [1]

1763. Character of Collins in the Poetical Calendar, published
by Fawkes and Woty. *acknowl.*

Dedication to the Earl of Shaftsbury of the edition of
Roger Ascham's English Works, published by the
Reverend Mr. Bennett. *acknowl.*

The Life of Ascham, also prefixed to that edition.
acknowl.

Review of Telemachus, a Masque, by the Rev. George
Graham, of Eton College, in the Critical Review.
acknowl.

Dedication to the Queen of Mr. Hoole's Translation
of Tasso. *acknowl.*

Account of the Detection of the Imposture of the Cock-
Lane Ghost, published in the Newspapers and
Gentleman's Magazine. *acknowl.*

1764. Part of a Review of Grainger's 'Sugar Cane, a Poem,'
in the London Chronicle. *acknowl.*

Review of Goldsmith's Traveller, a Poem, in the Critical
Review. *acknowl.*

1765. The Plays of William Shakspeare, in eight volumes, 8vo. with Notes. *acknowl.*

1766. The Fountains, a Fairy Tale, in Mrs. Williams's Miscellanies. *acknowl.*

1767. Dedication to the King of Mr. Adams's Treatise on the Globes. *acknowl.*

1769. Character of the Reverend Mr. Zachariah Mudge, in the London Chronicle. *acknowl.*

1770. The False Alarm. *acknowl.*

1771. Thoughts on the late Transactions respecting Falkland's Islands. *acknowl.*

1772. Defence of a Schoolmaster; dictated to me for the House of Lords. *acknowl.*

Argument in Support of the Law of *Vicious Intromission;* dictated to me for the Court of Session in Scotland. *acknowl.*

1773. Preface to Macbean's 'Dictionary of Ancient Geography.' *acknowl.*

Argument in Favour of the Rights of Lay Patrons; dictated to me for the General Assembly of the Church of Scotland. *acknowl.*

1774. The Patriot. *acknowl.*

1775. A Journey to the Western Islands of Scotland. *acknowl.*

Proposals for publishing the Works of Mrs. Charlotte Lennox, in Three Volumes Quarto. *acknowl.*

Preface to Baretti's Easy Lessons in Italian and English. *intern. evid.*

Taxation no Tyranny; an Answer to the Resolutions and Address of the American Congress. *acknowl.*

Argument on the Case of Dr. Memis; dictated to me for the Court of Session in Scotland. *acknowl.*

Argument to prove that the Corporation of Stirling was corrupt; dictated to me for the House of Lords. *acknowl.*

1776. Argument in Support of the Right of immediate, and personal reprehension from the Pulpit; dictated to me. *acknowl.*

Proposals for publishing an Analysis of the Scotch Celtick Language, by the Reverend William Shaw. *acknowl.*

1777. Dedication to the King of the Posthumous Works of Dr. Pearce, Bishop of Rochester. *acknowl.*

Additions to the Life and Character of that Prelate; prefixed to those Works. *acknowl.*

Various Papers and Letters in Favour of the Reverend Dr. Dodd. *acknowl.*

1780. Advertisement for his Friend Mr. Thrale to the Worthy Electors of the Borough of Southwark. *acknowl.*

The first Paragraph of Mr. Thomas Davies's Life of Garrick. *acknowl.*

1781. Prefaces, Biographical and Critical, to the Works of the most eminent English Poets: afterwards published with the Title of Lives of the English Poets. *acknowl.*

Argument on the Importance of the Registration of Deeds; dictated to me for an Election Committee of the House of Commons. *acknowl.*

On the Distinction between TORY and WHIG; dictated to me. *acknowl.*

On Vicarious Punishments, and the great Propitiation for the Sins of the World, by JESUS CHRIST; dictated to me. *acknowl.*

Argument in favour of Joseph Knight, an African Negro, who claimed his Liberty in the Court of Session in Scotland, and obtained it; dictated to me. *acknowl.*

Defence of Mr. Robertson, Printer of the Caledonian Mercury, against the Society of Procurators in Edinburgh, for having inserted in his Paper a ludicrous Paragraph against them; demonstrating that it was not an injurious Libel; dictated to me. *acknowl.*

1782. The greatest part, if not the whole, of a Reply, by the Reverend Mr. Shaw, to a Person at Edinburgh, of the Name of Clarke, refuting his arguments for the authenticity of the Poems published by Mr. James Macpherson as Translations from Ossian. *intern. evid.*

1784. List of the Authours of the Universal History, deposited in the British Museum, and printed in the Gentleman's Magazine for December, this year. *acknowl.*

VARIOUS YEARS

Letters to Mrs. Thrale. *acknowl.*

Prayers and Meditations, which he delivered to the Rev. Mr. Strahan, enjoining him to publish them. *acknowl.*

Sermons, *left for Publication* by John Taylor, LL.D. Prebendary of Westminster, and given to the World by the Rev. Samuel Hayes, A. M. *intern evid.**

Such was the number and variety of the Prose Works of this extraordinary man, which I have been able to discover, and am at liberty to mention; but we ought to keep in mind, that there must undoubtedly have been many more which are yet concealed; and we may add to the account, the numerous Letters which he wrote, of which a considerable part are yet unpublished. It is hoped that those persons in whose possession they are, will favour the world with them.

JAMES BOSWELL

[* To this List of the Writings of Dr. Johnson, Mr. Alexander Chalmers, with considerable probability, suggests to me that we may add the following:

IN THE GENTLEMAN'S MAGAZINE

1747. Lauder's Proposals for printing the *Adamus Exul* of Grotius. Vol. 20. p. 404.

1750. Address to the Publick, concerning Miss Williams's Miscellanies. Vol. 20. p. 428.

1753. Preface.
Notice of Mr. Edward Cave's death, inserted in the last page of the Index.

IN THE LITERARY MAGAZINE

1756. 'Observations on the foregoing letter;' i.e. A letter on the American Colonies. Vol. 1. p. 66. MALONE.]

THE LIFE OF
SAMUEL JOHNSON, LL.D.

'After my death I wish no other herald,
No other speaker of my living actions,
To keep mine honour from corruption,
But such an honest chronicler as Griffith.'*

SHAKSPEARE, *Henry VIII*

---

* See Dr. Johnson's letter to Mrs. Thrale, dated Ostick in Skie, September 30, 1773: 'Boswell writes a regular journal of our travels, which I think contains as much of what I say and do, as of all other occurrences together; "*for such a faithful chronicler* is *Griffith.*" '

THE LIFE OF
SAMUEL JOHNSON
LL.D.

To write the Life of him who excelled all mankind in writing the lives of others, and who, whether we consider his extraordinary endowments, or his various works, has been equalled by few in any age, is an arduous, and may be reckoned in me a presumptuous task.

Had Dr. Johnson written his own Life, in conformity with the opinion which he has given,[1] that every man's life may be best written by himself; had he employed in the preservation of his own history, that clearness of narration and elegance of language in which he has embalmed so many eminent persons, the world would probably have had the most perfect example of biography that was ever exhibited. But although he at different times, in a desultory manner, committed to writing many particulars of the progress of his mind and fortunes, he never had persevering diligence enough to form them into a regular composition. Of these memorials a few have been preserved; but the greater part was consigned by him to the flames, a few days before his death.

As I had the honour and happiness of enjoying his friendship for upwards of twenty years; as I had the scheme of writing his life constantly in view; as he was well apprised of this circumstance, and from time to time obligingly satisfied my enquiries, by communicating to me the incidents of his early years; as I acquired a facility in recollecting, and was very assiduous in recording, his conversation, of which the extraordinary vigour and vivacity constituted one of the first features of his character; and as I have spared no pains in obtaining materials concerning him, from every quarter where I could discover

[1] Idler, No. 84.

that they were to be found, and have been favoured with the most liberal communications by his friends; I flatter myself that few biographers have entered upon such a work as this, with more advantages; independent of literary abilities, in which I am not vain enough to compare myself with some great names who have gone before me in this kind of writing.

Since my work was announced, several Lives and Memoirs of Dr. Johnson have been published, the most voluminous of which is one compiled for the booksellers of London, by Sir John Hawkins, Knight,[1] a man, whom, during my long intimacy with Dr. Johnson, I never saw in his company, I think, but once, and I am sure not above twice. Johnson might have esteemed him for his decent, religious demeanour, and his knowledge of books and literary history; but from the rigid formality of his manners, it is evident that they never could have lived together with companionable ease and familiarity; nor had Sir John Hawkins that nice perception which was necessary to mark the finer and less obvious parts of Johnson's character. His being appointed one of his executors, gave him an opportunity of taking possession of such fragments of a diary and other papers as were left; of which, before delivering them up to the residuary legatee, whose property they were, he endeavoured to extract the substance. In this he has not been very successful, as I have found upon a perusal of those papers, which have been since transferred to me. Sir John Hawkins's ponderous labours, I must acknowledge, exhibit a *farrago*, of which a considerable portion is not devoid of entertainment to the lovers of literary gossiping; but besides its being swelled out with

[1] The greatest part of this book was written while Sir John Hawkins was alive: and I avow, that one object of my strictures was to make him feel some compunction for his illiberal treatment of Dr. Johnson. Since his decease, I have suppressed several of my remarks upon his work. But though I would not 'war with the dead' *offensively*, I think it necessary to be strenuous in *defence* of my illustrious friend, which I cannot be, without strong animadversions upon a writer who has greatly injured him. Let me add, that though I doubt I should not have been very prompt to gratify Sir John Hawkins with any compliment in his life-time, I do now frankly acknowledge, that, in my opinion, his volume, however inadequate and improper as a life of Dr. Johnson, and however discredited by unpardonable inaccuracies in other respects, contains a collection of curious anecdotes and observations, which few men but its authour could have brought together.

long unnecessary extracts from various works, (even one of several leaves from Osborne's Harleian Catalogue, and those not compiled by Johnson, but by Oldys,) a very small part of it relates to the person who is the subject of the book; and, in that, there is such an inaccuracy in the statement of facts, as in so solemn an authour is hardly excusable, and certainly makes his narrative very unsatisfactory. But what is still worse, there is throughout the whole of it a dark uncharitable cast, by which the most unfavourable construction is put upon almost every circumstance in the character and conduct of my illustrious friend; who, I trust, will, by a true and fair delineation, be vindicated both from the injurious misrepresentations of this authour, and from the slighter aspersions of a lady who once lived in great intimacy with him.

There is, in the British Museum, a letter from Bishop Warburton to Dr. Birch, on the subject of biography; which, though I am aware it may expose me to a charge of artfully raising the value of my own work, by contrasting it with that of which I have spoken, is so well conceived and expressed, that I cannot refrain from here inserting it:

'I SHALL endeavour, (says Dr. Warburton,) to give you what satisfaction I can in any thing you want to be satisfied in any subject of Milton, and am extremely glad you intend to write his life. Almost all the life-writers we have had before Toland and Desmaiseaux, are indeed strange insipid creatures; and yet I had rather read the worst of them, than be obliged to go through with this of Milton's, or the other's life of Boileau, where there is such a dull, heavy succession of long quotations of disinteresting passages, that it makes their method quite nauseous. But the verbose, tasteless Frenchman seems to lay it down as a principle, that every life must be a book, and what's worse, it proves a book without a life; for what do we know of Boileau, after all his tedious stuff? You are the only one, (and I speak it without a compliment,) that by the vigour of your stile and sentiments, and the real importance of your materials, have the art, (which one would imagine no one could have missed,) of adding agreements[a] to the

underlined:
agreements [1]
[a] *Agrèmens* [1]

most agreeable subject in the world, which is literary
history.'[1]   'Nov. 24, 1737.'

Instead of melting down my materials into one mass,
and constantly speaking in my own person, by which I
might have appeared to have more merit in the execution
of the work, I have resolved to adopt and enlarge upon
the excellent plan of Mr. Mason, in his Memoirs of Gray.
Wherever narrative is necessary to explain, connect, and
supply, I furnish it to the best of my abilities; but in the
chronological series of Johnson's life, which I trace as
distinctly as I can, year by year, I produce, wherever it is
in my power, his own minutes, letters, or conversation,
being convinced that this mode is more lively, and will
make my readers better acquainted with him, than even
most of those were who actually knew him, but could
know him only partially; whereas there is here an accumulation of intelligence from various points, by which his
character is more fully understood and illustrated.

Indeed I cannot conceive a more perfect mode of
writing any man's life, than not only relating all the most
important events of it in their order, but interweaving
what he privately wrote, and said, and thought; by which
mankind are enabled as it were to see him live, and to
'live o'er each scene' with him, as he actually advanced
through the several stages of his life. Had his other friends
been as diligent and ardent as I was, he might have been
almost entirely preserved. As it is, I will venture to say
that he will be seen in this work more completely than
any man who has ever yet lived.

underlined:
panegyrick, praise [1]

[a] Panegyrick must be
Praise. What a Nov-
elty! [1]

And he will be seen as he really was; for I profess to write,
not his panegyrick, which must be all. praise,[a] but his Life;
which, great and good as he was, must not be supposed
to be entirely perfect. To be as he was, is indeed subject
of panegyrick enough to any man in this state of being;
but in every picture there should be shade as well as light,
and when I delineate him without reserve, I do what he
himself recommended, both by his precept and his example.

'If the biographer writes from personal knowledge, and
makes haste to gratify the publick curiosity, there is danger

[1] Brit. Mus. 4320, Ayscough's Catal. Sloane MSS.

lest his interest, his fear, his gratitude, or his tenderness, overpower his fidelity, and tempt him to conceal, if not to invent. There are many who think it an act of piety to hide the faults or failings of their friends, even when they can no longer suffer by their detection; we therefore see whole ranks of characters adorned with uniform pane-gyrick, and not to be known from one another but by extrinsick and casual circumstances. "Let me remember, (says Hale,) when I find myself inclined to pity a criminal, that there is likewise a pity due to the country." If we owe regard to the memory of the dead, there is yet more respect to be paid to knowledge, to virtue, and to truth.'[1]

What I consider as the peculiar value of the following work, is, the quantity it contains of Johnson's conversation; which is universally acknowledged to have been eminently instructive and entertaining; and of which the specimens that I have given upon a former occasion, have been received with so much approbation, that I have good grounds for supposing that the world will not be indifferent to more ample communications of a similar nature.

That the conversation of a celebrated man, if his talents have been exerted in conversation, will best display his character, is, I trust, too well established in the judgement of mankind, to be at all shaken by a sneering observation of Mr. Mason, in his Memoirs of Mr. William Whitehead, in which there is literally no *Life*, but a mere dry narrative of facts. I do not think it was quite necessary to attempt a depreciation of what is universally esteemed, because it was not to be found in the immediate object of the in-genious writer's pen; for in truth, from a man so still and so tame, as to be contented to pass many years as the domestick companion of a superannuated lord and lady, conversation could no more be expected, than from a Chinese mandarin on a chimney-piece, or the fantastick figures on a gilt leather skreen.

If authority be required, let us appeal to Plutarch, the prince of ancient biographers. Οὔτε ταῖς ἐπιφανεστάταις πράξεσι πάντως ἔνεστι δήλωσις ἀρετῆς ἢ κακίας, ἀλλὰ πρᾶγμα βραχὺ πολλάκις, καὶ ῥῆμα, καὶ παιδιά τις ἔμφασιν ἤθους ἐποίησεν μᾶλλον ἢ μάχαι μυριόνεκροι, παρατάξεις αἱ μέγισται, καὶ πολιορκία πόλεων. 'Nor is

---

[1] Rambler, No. 60.

it always in the most distinguished atchievements that men's virtues or vices may be best discerned; but very often an action of small note, a short saying, or a jest, shall distinguish a person's real character more than the greatest sieges, or the most important battles.'[1]

To this may be added the sentiments of the very man whose life I am about to exhibit. 'The business of the biographer is often to pass slightly over those performances and incidents which produce vulgar greatness, to lead the thoughts into domestick privacies, and display the minute details of daily life, where exteriour appendages are cast aside, and men excel each other only by prudence and by virtue. The account of Thuanus is with great propriety said by its authour to have been written, that it might lay open to posterity the private and familiar character of that man, *cujus ingenium et candorem ex ipsius scriptis sunt olim semper miraturi*, whose candour and genius will to the end of time be by his writings preserved in admiration.

'There are many invisible circumstances, which whether we read as enquirers after natural or moral knowledge, whether we intend to inlarge our science or increase our virtue, are more important than publick occurrences. Thus Sallust, the great master of nature, has not forgot in his account of Catiline to remark, that his walk was now quick, and again slow, as an indication of a mind revolving with violent commotion. Thus the story of Melancthon affords a striking lecture on the value of time, by informing us, that when he had made an appointment, he expected not only the hour, but the minute to be fixed, that the day might not run out in the idleness of suspense; and all the plans and enterprises of De Wit are now of less importance to the world than that part of his personal character, which represents him as careful of his health, and negligent of his life.

'But biography has often been allotted to writers, who seem very little acquainted with the nature of their task, or very negligent about the performance. They rarely afford any other account than might be collected from publick papers, but imagine themselves writing a life, when they exhibit a chronological series of actions or preferments; and have so little regard to the manners or

[1] Plutarch's Life of Alexander.—Langhorne's Translation.

behaviour of their heroes, that more knowledge may be gained of a man's real character, by a short conversation with one of his servants, than from a formal and studied narrative, begun with his pedigree, and ended with his funeral.

'There are indeed, some natural reasóns why these narratives are often written by such as were not likely to give much instruction or delight, and why most accounts of particular persons are barren and useless. If a life be delayed till interest and envy are at an end, we may hope for impartiality, but must expect little intelligence; for the incidents which give excellence to biography are of a volatile and evanescent kind, such as soon escape the memory, and are rarely transmitted by tradition. We know how few can pourtray a living acquaintance, except by his most prominent and observable particularities, and the grosser features of his mind; and it ʼmay be easily imagined how much of this little knowledge may be lost in imparting it, and how soon a succession of copies will lose all resemblance of the original.'[1]

I am fully aware of the objections which may be made to the minuteness on some occasions of my detail of Johnson's conversation, and how happily it is adapted for the petty exercise of ridicule, by men of superficial understanding, and ludicrous fancy; but I remain firm and confident in my opinion, that minute particulars are frequently characteristick, and always amusing, when they relate to a distinguished man. I am therefore exceedingly unwilling that any thing, however slight, which my illustrious friend thought it worth his while to express, with any degree of point, should perish. For this almost superstitious reverence, I have found very old and venerable authority, quoted by our great modern prelate, Secker, in whose tenth sermon there is the following passage:

'*Rabbi David Kimchi*, a noted Jewish Commentator, who lived about five hundred years ago, explains that passage in the first Psalm, *His leaf also shall not wither*, from Rabbins yet older than himself, thus: That *even the idle talk*, so he expresses it, *of a good man ought to be regarded;* the most superfluous things he saith are always of some value. And

[1] Rambler, No. 60.

other ancient authours have the same phrase, nearly in the same sense.'

Of one thing I am certain, that considering how highly the small portion which we have of the table-talk and other anecdotes of our celebrated writers is valued, and how earnestly it is regretted that we have not more, I am justified in preserving rather too many of Johnson's sayings, than too few; especially as from the diversity of dispositions it cannot be known with certainty beforehand, whether what may seem trifling to some, and perhaps to the collector himself, may not be most agreeable to many; and the greater number that an authour can please in any degree, the more pleasure does there arise to a benevolent mind.

To those who are weak enough to think this a degrading task, and the time and labour which have been devoted to it misemployed, I shall content myself with opposing the authority of the greatest man of any age, JULIUS CÆSAR, of whom Bacon observes, that 'in his book of Apophthegms which he collected, we see that he esteemed it more honour to make himself but a pair of tables, to take the wise and pithy words of others, than to have every word of his own to be made an apophthegm or an oracle.'[1]

Having said thus much by way of introduction, I commit the following pages to the candour of the Publick.

SAMUEL JOHNSON was born at Lichfield, in Stafford-shire, on the 18th of September, N.S. 1709; and his initiation into the Christian church was not delayed; for his baptism is recorded, in the register of St. Mary's parish in that city, to have been performed on the day of his birth: His father is there stiled *Gentleman*, a circumstance of which an ignorant panegyrist has praised him for not being proud; when the truth is, that the appellation of Gentleman, though now lost in the indiscriminate assumption of *Esquire*, was commonly taken by those who could not boast of gentility. His father was Michael Johnson, a native of Derbyshire, of obscure extraction, who settled in Lichfield as a bookseller and stationer. His mother was Sarah Ford, descended of an ancient race of substantial

[1] Bacon's Advancement of Learning, Book I.

yeomanry in Warwickshire. They were well advanced in
years when they married, and never had more than two
children, both sons; Samuel, their first-born, who lived to
be the illustrious character whose various excellence I am
to endeavour to record, and Nathanael, who died in his
twenty-fifth year.[1]

Mr. Michael Johnson was a man of a large and robust
body, and of a strong and active mind; yet, as in the most
solid rocks veins of unsound substance are often discovered,
there was in him a mixture of that disease, the nature of
which eludes the most minute enquiry,[a] though the effects
are well known to be a weariness of life, an unconcern
about those things which agitate the greater part of mankind, and a general sensation of gloomy wretchedness.
From him then his son inherited, with some other qualities,
'a vile melancholy,' which in his too strong expression of
any disturbance of the mind, 'made him mad all his life,
at least not sober.'[2] Michael was, however, forced by the
narrowness of his circumstances to be very diligent in
business, not only in his shop, but by occasionally resorting
to several towns in the neighbourhood,[3] some of which
were at a considerable distance from Lichfield. At that
time booksellers' shops in the provincial towns of England
were very rare, so that there was not one even in Birmingham, in which town old Mr. Johnson used to open a shop
every market-day. He was a pretty good Latin scholar,
and a citizen so creditable as to be made one of the

[a] *it was a scrophulous Complaint* King's Evil *wch. is Parent of many Diseases.* [1]

[1] [Nathanael was born in 1712, and died in 1737. Their father, Michael
Johnson, was born at Cubley in Derbyshire, in 1656, and died at Lichfield
in 1731, at the age of seventy-six. Sarah Ford, his wife, was born at King's
Norton, in the county of Worcester, in 1669, and died at Lichfield, in January
1759, in her ninetieth year.—King's-Norton Dr. Johnson supposed to be in
Warwickshire, (see his inscription for his mother's tomb,) but it is in
Worcestershire, probably on the confines of the county of Warwick.—
MALONE.]

[2] Journal of a Tour to the Hebrides, 3d edit. p. 213.

[3] Extract of a Letter, dated 'Trentham, St. Peter's day, 1716,' written by
the Rev. George Plaxton, Chaplain at that time to Lord Gower, which may
serve to show the high estimation in which the Father of our great Moralist
was held:— 'Johnson, the Lichfield Librarian, is now here; he propagates
learning all over this diocese, and advanceth knowledge to its just height;
all the Clergy here are his Pupils, and suck all they have from him; Allen
cannot make a warrant without his precedent, nor our quondam John Evans
draw a recognizance *sine directione Michaelis.*'

Gentleman's Magazine, October, 1791.

magistrates of Lichfield; and, being a man of good sense, and skill in his trade, he acquired a reasonable share of wealth, of which however he afterwards lost the greatest part, by engaging unsuccessfully in a manufacture of parchment. He was a zealous high-church man and royalist, and retained his attachment to the unfortunate house of Stuart, though he reconciled himself, by casuistical arguments of expediency and necessity, to take the oaths imposed by the prevailing power.

There is a circumstance in his life somewhat romantick, but so well authenticated, that I shall not omit it. A young woman of Leek, in Staffordshire, while he served his apprenticeship there, conceived a violent passion for him; and though it met with no favourable return, followed him to Lichfield, where she took lodgings opposite to the house in which he lived, and indulged her hopeless flame. When he was informed that it so preyed upon her mind that her life was in danger, he with a generous humanity went to her and offered to marry her, but it was then too late: Her vital power was exhausted; and she actually exhibited one of the very rare instances of dying for love. She was buried in the cathedral of Lichfield; and he, with a tender regard, placed a stone over her grave with this inscription:

Here lies the body of

Mrs. ELIZABETH BLANEY, a stranger:

She departed this life

20 of September, 1694.

Johnson's mother was a woman of distinguished under-standing.[1] I asked his old school-fellow, Mr. Hector, surgeon,

[1] [It was not, however, much cultivated, as we may collect from Dr. Johnson's own account of his early years, published by R. Phillips, 8vo. 1805, a work undoubtedly authentick, and which, though short, is curious, and well worthy of perusal. 'My father and mother (says Johnson) had not much happiness from each other. They seldom conversed; for my father could not bear to talk of his affairs; and my mother, *being unacquainted with books,* cared not to talk of any thing else. Had my mother been more literate, they had been better companions. She might have sometimes introduced her unwelcome topick with more success, if she could have diversified her conversation. Of business she had no distinct conception; and therefore her discourse was composed only of complaint, fear, and suspicion. Neither of them ever tried to calculate the profits of trade, or the expences of living. My mother concluded that we were poor, because we lost by some of our

of Birmingham, if she was not vain of her son. He said, 'she had too much good sense to be vain, but she knew her son's value.' Her piety was not inferiour to her understanding; and to her must be ascribed those early impressions of religion upon the mind of her son, from which the world afterwards derived so much benefit. He told me, that he remembered distinctly having had the first notice of Heaven, 'a place to which good people went,' and hell, 'a place to which bad people went,' communicated to him by her, when a little child in bed with her; and that it might be the better fixed in his memory, she sent him to repeat it to Thomas Jackson, their man-servant; he not being in the way, this was not done; but there was no occasion for any artificial aid for its preservation.

In following so very eminent a man from his cradle to his grave, every minute particular, which can throw light on the progress of his mind, is interesting. That he was remarkable, even in his earliest years, may easily be supposed; for to use his own words in his Life of Sydenham, 'That the strength of his understanding, the accuracy of his discernment, and the ardour of his curiosity, might have been remarked from his infancy, by a diligent observer, there is no reason to doubt. For, there is no instance of any man, whose history has been minutely related, that did not in every part of life discover the same proportion of intellectual vigour.'

In all such investigations it is certainly unwise to pay too much attention to incidents which the credulous relate with eager satisfaction, and the more scrupulous or witty enquirer considers only as topicks of ridicule: Yet there is a traditional story of the infant Hercules of toryism, so curiously characteristick, that I shall not withhold it. It was communicated to me in a letter from Miss Mary Adye, of Lichfield.

'When Dr. Sacheverel was at Lichfield, Johnson was not quite three years old. My grandfather Hammond observed

trades; but the truth was, that my father, having in the early part of his life contracted debts, never had trade sufficient to enable him to pay them, and to maintain his family: he got something, but not enough. It was not till about 1768, that I thought to calculate the returns of my father's trade, and by that estimate his probable profits. This, I believe, my parents never did.' —MALONE.]

him at the cathedral perched upon his father's shoulders, listening and gaping at the much celebrated preacher. Mr. Hammond asked Mr. Johnson how he could possibly think of bringing such an infant to church, and in the midst of so great a croud. He answered, because it was impossible to keep him at home; for, young as he was, he believed he had caught the publick spirit and zeal for Sacheverel, and would have staid for ever in the church, satisfied with beholding him.'

Nor can I omit a little instance of that jealous independence of spirit, and impetuosity of temper, which never forsook him. The fact was acknowledged to me by himself, upon the authority of his mother. One day, when the servant who used to be sent to school to conduct him home, had not come in time, he set out by himself, though he was then so near-sighted, that he was obliged to stoop down on his hands and knees to take a view of the kennel before he ventured to step over it. His school-mistress, afraid that he might miss his way, or fall into the kennel, or be run over by a cart, followed him at some distance. He happened to turn about and perceive her. Feeling her careful attention as an insult to his manliness, he run back to her in a rage, and beat her, as well as his strength would permit.

Of the power of his memory, for which he was all his life eminent to a degree almost incredible, the following early instance was told me in his presence at Lichfield, in 1776, by his step-daughter, Mrs. Lucy Porter, as related to her by his mother. When he was a child in petticoats, and had learnt to read, Mrs. Johnson one morning put the common prayer-book into his hands, pointed to the collect for the day, and said, 'Sam, you must get this by heart.' She went up stairs, leaving him to study it: but by the time she had reached the second floor, she heard him following her. 'What's the matter?' said she. 'I can say it,' he replied; and repeated it distinctly, though he could not have read it more than twice.

But there has been another story of his infant precocity generally circulated, and generally believed, the truth of which I am to refute upon his own authority. It is told,[1]

a & now all is over!! I do protest he told them to me himself as I printed them; & I believe he made them. [1]

[1] Anecdotes of Dr. Johnson, by Hester Lynch Piozzi, p. 11.[a] Life of Dr. Johnson by Sir John Hawkins, p. 6.

that, when a child of three years old, he chanced to tread upon a duckling, the eleventh of a brood, and killed it; upon which, it is said, he dictated to his mother the following epitaph:

'Here lies good master duck,
    Whom Samuel Johnson trod on;
    If it had liv'd, it had been *good luck*,
    For then we'd had an *odd one*.'

There is surely internal evidence that this little composition combines in it, what no child of three years old could produce, without an extension of its faculties by immediate inspiration; yet Mrs. Lucy Porter, Dr. Johnson's step-daughter, positively maintained to me, in his presence, that there could be no doubt of the truth of this anecdote, for she had heard it from his mother. So difficult is it to obtain an authentick relation of facts, and such authority may there be for errour; for he assured me, that his father made the verses, and wished to pass them for his child's. He added, 'my father was a foolish old man; that is to say, foolish in talking of his children.'[1]

Young Johnson had the misfortune to be much afflicted with the scrophula, or king's-evil, which disfigured a countenance naturally well formed, and hurt his visual

[1] This anecdote of the duck, though disproved by internal and external evidence, has nevertheless, upon supposition of its truth,[a] been made the foundation of the following ingenious and fanciful reflections of Miss Seward, amongst the communications concerning Dr. Johnson with which she has been pleased to favour me:—'These infant numbers contain the seeds of those propensities which through his life so strongly marked his character, of that poetick talent which afterwards bore such rich and plentiful fruits; for, excepting his orthographick works, every thing which Dr. Johnson wrote was Poetry, whose essence consists not in numbers, or in jingle, but in the strength and glow of a fancy, to which all the stores of nature and of art stand in prompt administration; and in an eloquence which conveys their blended illustrations in a language "more tuneable than needs or rhyme or verse to add more harmony."

'The above little verses also shew that superstitious bias which "grew with his growth, and strengthened with his strength," and, of late years particularly, injured his happiness, by presenting to him the gloomy side of religion, rather than that bright and cheering one which gilds the period of closing life with the light of pious hope.'

This is so beautifully imagined, that I would not suppress it. But, like many other theories, it is deduced from a supposed fact, which is, indeed, a fiction.[b]

[a] *& true it was.* [1]

underlined:
fiction [1]
[b] *no* Indeed. [1]

nerves so much, that he did not see at all with one of his
eyes, though its appearance was little different from that
of the other. There is amongst his prayers, one inscribed
'*When my* EYE *was restored to its use*,'[1] which ascertains a
defect that many of his friends knew he had, though I
never perceived it.[2] I supposed him to be only near-
sighted; and indeed I must observe, that in no other[a]
respect could I discern any defect in his vision; on the
contrary, the force of his attention and perceptive quickness made him see and distinguish all manner of objects,
whether of nature or of art, with a nicety that is rarely to
be found. When he and I were travelling in the Highlands
of Scotland, and I pointed out to him a mountain which I
observed resembled a cone, he corrected my inaccuracy,
by shewing me, that it was indeed pointed at the top, but
that one side of it was larger than the other. And the
ladies with whom he was acquainted agree, that no man
was more nicely and minutely critical in the elegance of
female dress. When I found that he saw the romantick
beauties of Islam, in Derbyshire, much better than I did,
I told him that he resembled an able performer upon a
bad instrument. How false and contemptible then are all
the remarks which have been made to the prejudice either
of his candour or of his philosophy, founded upon a
supposition that he was almost blind. It has been said, that
he contracted this grievous malady from his nurse.[3] His
mother, yielding to the superstitious notion, which, it is
wonderful to think, prevailed so long in this country, as
to the virtue of the regal touch; a notion, which our kings
encouraged, and to which a man of such enquiry and such
judgement as Carte could give credit; carried him to
London, where he was actually touched by Queen Anne.[4]

[a] *yes yes; his Eye*
trembled in a very odd
way—not the Lid, but
the Eye. [1]

[1] Prayers and Meditations, p. 27.

[2] [Speaking himself of the imperfection of one of his eyes, he said to Dr.
Burney, 'the dog was never good for much.' BURNEY.]

[3] [Such was the opinion of Dr. Swinfen. Johnson's eyes were very soon
discovered to be bad, and to relieve them, an issue was cut in his left arm.
At the end of ten weeks from his birth, he was taken home from his nurse, 'a
poor diseased infant, almost blind.' See a work, already quoted, entitled
'An Account of the life of Dr. Samuel Johnson, from his birth to his eleventh
year; written by himself.' 8vo. 1805. MALONE.]

[4] [He was only thirty months old, when he was taken to London to be
touched for the evil. During this visit, he tells us, his mother purchased for

Mrs. Johnson indeed, as Mr. Hector informed me, acted by the advice of the celebrated Sir John Floyer, then a physician in Lichfield. Johnson used to talk of this very frankly; and Mrs. Piozzi has preserved his very picturesque description of the scene, as it remained upon his fancy. Being asked if he could remember Queen Anne,—'He had (he said) a confused, but somehow a sort of solemn recollection of a lady in diamonds, and a long black hood.'[1] This touch, however, was without any effect. I ventured to say to him, in allusion to the political principles in which he was educated, and of which he ever retained some odour, that 'his mother had not carried him far enough; she should have taken him to ROME.'

He was first taught to read English by Dame Oliver, a widow, who kept a school for young children in Lichfield. He told me she could read the black letter, and asked him to borrow for her, from his father, a bible in that character. When he was going to Oxford, she came to take leave of him, brought him, in the simplicity of her kindness, a present of gingerbread, and said he was the best scholar she ever had. He delighted in mentioning this early compliment; adding, with a smile, that 'this was as high a proof of his merit as he could conceive.' His next instructor in English was a master, whom, when he spoke of him to me, he familiarly called Tom Brown, who, said he, 'published a spelling-book, and dedicated it to the UNIVERSE; but, I fear, no copy of it can now be had.'

He began to learn Latin with Mr. Hawkins, usher, or under-master of Lichfield school, 'a man (said he) very skilful in his little way.' With him he continued two years, and then rose to be under the care of Mr. Hunter, the head-master, who, according to his account, 'was very severe, and wrong-headedly severe. He used (said he) to beat us unmercifully; and he did not distinguish between ignorance and negligence; for he would beat a boy equally for not knowing a thing, as for neglecting to know it. He would ask a boy a question, and if he did not answer it, he

him a small silver cup and spoon. 'The cup,' he affectingly adds, 'was one of the last pieces of plate which dear Tetty sold, in our distress. I have now the spoon. She bought at the same time two tea-spoons, and till my manhood, she had no more.' Ibid. MALONE.]

[1] Anecdotes, p. 10.

would beat him, without considering whether he had an
opportunity of knowing how to answer it. For instance, he
would call up a boy and ask him Latin for a candlestick,
which the boy could not expect to be asked. Now, Sir, if a
boy could answer every question, there would be no need
of a master to teach him.'

It is, however, but justice to the memory of Mr. Hunter
to mention, that though he might err in being too severe,
the school of Lichfield was very respectable in his time.
The late Dr. Taylor, Prebendary of Westminster, who was
educated under him, told me that 'he was an excellent
master, and that his ushers were most of them men of
eminence; that Holbrook, one of the most ingenious men,
best scholars, and best preachers of his age, was usher
during the greatest part of the time that Johnson was at
school. Then came Hague, of whom as much might be
said, with the addition that he was an elegant poet. Hague
was succeeded by Green, afterwards Bishop of Lincoln,
whose character in the learned world is well known. In
the same form with Johnson was Congreve, who afterwards
became chaplain to Archbishop Boulter, and by that
connection obtained good preferment in Ireland. He was
a younger son of the ancient family of Congreve, in Staffordshire, of which the poet was a branch. His brother sold the
estate. There was also Lowe, afterwards Canon of Windsor.'

Indeed Johnson was very sensible how much he owed
to Mr. Hunter. Mr. Langton one day asked him how he
had acquired so accurate a knowledge of Latin, in which,
I believe, he was exceeded by no man of his time; he said,
'My master whipt me very well. Without that, Sir, I
should have done nothing.' He told Mr. Langton, that
while Hunter was flogging his boys unmercifully, he used
to say, 'And this I do to save you from the gallows.'
Johnson, upon all occasions, expressed his approbation
of enforcing instruction by means of the rod.[1] 'I would
rather (said he) have the rod to be the general terrour to
all, to make them learn, than tell a child, if you do thus,
or thus, you will be more esteemed than your brothers or

[1] [Johnson's observations to Dr. Rose, on this subject, may be found in a
subsequent part of this work. See vol. ii. near the end of the year 1775.
BURNEY.]

sisters. The rod produces an effect which terminates in itself. A child is afraid of being whipped, and gets his task, and there's an end on't; whereas, by exciting emulation and comparisons of superiority, you lay the foundation of lasting mischief; you make brothers and sisters hate each other.'

When Johnson saw some young ladies in Lincolnshire who were remarkably well behaved, owing to their mother's strict discipline and severe correction, he exclaimed, in one of Shakspeare's lines a little varied,[1]

'*Rod*, I will honour thee for this thy duty.'

That superiority over his fellows, which he maintained with so much dignity in his march through life, was not assumed from vanity and ostentation, but was the natural and constant effect of those extraordinary powers of mind, of which he could not but be conscious by comparison; the intellectual difference, which in other cases of comparison of characters, is often a matter of undecided contest, being as clear in his case as the superiority of stature in some men above others. Johnson did not strut or stand on tip-toe; he only did not stoop. From his earliest years, his superiority was perceived and acknowledged. He was from the beginning Ἄναξ ἀνδρῶν, a king of men. His school-fellow, Mr. Hector, has obligingly furnished me with many particulars of his boyish days; and assured me that he never knew him corrected at school, but for talking and diverting other boys from their business. He seemed to learn by intuition; for though indolence and procrastination were inherent in his constitution, whenever he made an exertion he did more than any one else. In short, he is a memorable instance of what has been often observed, that the boy is the man in miniature; and that the distinguishing characteristicks of each individual are the same, through the whole course of life. His favourites used to receive very liberal assistance from him; and such was the submission and deference with which he was treated, such the desire to obtain his regard, that three of the boys, of whom Mr. Hector was sometimes one, used to come in

two marginal lines:
That superiority . . .
particulars of [H]

queried:
the distinguishing
characteristicks etc. [H]

---

[1] [More than a little. The line is in KING HENRY VI. Part ii. act iv. sc. last: 'Sword, I will hallow thee for this thy deed.' MALONE.]

the morning as his humble attendants, and carry him to school. One in the middle stooped, while he sat upon his back, and one on each side supported him; and thus he was borne triumphant. Such a proof of the early predominance of intellectual vigour is very remarkable, and does honour to human nature.—Talking to me once himself of his being much distinguished at school, he told me, 'they never thought to raise me by comparing me to any one; they never said, Johnson is as good a scholar as such a one; but such a one is as good a scholar as Johnson; and this was said but of one, but of Lowe; and I do not think he was as good a scholar.'

He discovered a great ambition to excel, which roused him to counteract his indolence. He was uncommonly inquisitive; and his memory was so tenacious, that he never forgot any thing that he either heard or read. Mr. Hector remembers having recited to him eighteen verses, which, after a little pause, he repeated *verbatim*, varying only one epithet, by which he improved the line.

He never joined with the other boys in their ordinary diversions: his only amusement was in winter, when he took a pleasure in being drawn upon the ice by a boy barefooted, who pulled him along by a garter fixed round him; no very easy operation, as his size was remarkably large. His defective sight, indeed, prevented him from enjoying the common sports; and he once pleasantly remarked to me, 'how wonderfully well he had contrived to be idle without them.' Lord Chesterfield, however, has justly observed in one of his letters, when earnestly cautioning a friend against the pernicious effects of idleness, that active sports are not to be reckoned idleness in young people; and that the listless torpor of doing nothing alone deserves that name. Of this dismal inertness of disposition, Johnson had all his life too great a share.[a] Mr. Hector relates, that 'he could not oblige him more than by sauntering away the hours of vacation in the fields, during which he was more engaged in talking to himself than to his companion.'

Dr. Percy, the Bishop of Dromore, who was long intimately acquainted with him, and has preserved a few anecdotes concerning him, regretting that he was not a

marginal notes:

marginal line:
how wonderfully . . .
however, has [H]

underlined:
listless torpor [I]

[a] *So had Lord Chatham . . . at Recreation hours he would lie on his Back upon a bench staring at the Sky, while the other Boys were at Play, Lord Westcote said; & his Companions hated him for it.* [H]

So had the great Ld Chatham when a Boy.

more diligent collector, informs me, that 'when a boy he was immoderately fond of reading romances of chivalry, and he retained his fondness for them through life; so that (adds his Lordship) spending part of a summer at my parsonage-house in the country, he chose for his regular reading the old Spanish romance of FELIXMARTE OF HIRCANIA, in folio, which he read quite through. Yet I have heard him attribute to these extravagant fictions that unsettled turn of mind which prevented his ever fixing in any profession.'

Billy Lyttelton said he wd. lye on a bench on his Back staring at the Sun with his fine Eyes, whilst other Boys were at Study or at Play: he loved neither. [1]

After having resided for some time at the house of his uncle,[1] Cornelius Ford, Johnson was, at the age of fifteen, removed to the school of Stourbridge, in Worcestershire, of which Mr. Wentworth was then master. This step was taken by the advice of his cousin, the Rev. Mr. Ford, a man in whom both talents and good dispositions were disgraced by licentiousness,[2] but who was a very able judge of what was right. At this school he did not receive so much benefit as was expected. It has been said, that he acted in the capacity of an assistant to Mr. Wentworth in teaching the younger boys. 'Mr. Wentworth (he told me) was a very able man, but an idle man, and to me very severe; but I cannot blame him much. I was then a big boy; he saw I did not reverence him; and that he should get no honour by me. I had brought enough with me, to carry me through; and all I should get at his school would be ascribed to my own labour, or to my former master. Yet he taught me a great deal.'

He thus discriminated, to Dr. Percy, Bishop of Dromore, his progress at his two grammar-schools. 'At one, I learned much in the school, but little from the master; in the other, I learnt much from the master, but little in the school.'

The Bishop also informs me, that 'Dr. Johnson's father, before he was received at Stourbridge, applied to have him admitted as a scholar and assistant to the Rev. Samuel Lea, M.A., head master of Newport school, in Shropshire; (a very diligent good teacher, at that time in high

---

[1] [Cornelius Ford, according to Sir John Hawkins, was his cousin-german, being the son of Dr. Joseph [Q. Nathanael,] Ford, an eminent physician, who was brother to Johnson's mother. MALONE.]

[2] He is said to be the original of the parson in Hogarth's Modern Midnight Conversation.[a]

[a] *Johnson told me that he was so. [1]*

reputation, under whom Mr. Hollis is said, in the Memoirs
of his Life, to have been also educated.)[1] This application
to Mr. Lea was not successful; but Johnson had afterwards
the gratification to hear that the old gentleman, who lived
to a very advanced age, mentioned it as one of the most
memorable events of his life, that 'he was *very near* having
that great man for his scholar.'

He remained at Stourbridge little more than a year,
and then he returned home, where he may be said to have
loitered, for two years, in a state very unworthy his
uncommon abilities. He had already given several proofs
of his poetical genius, both in his school-exercises and in
other occasional compositions. Of these I have obtained a
considerable collection, by the favour of Mr. Wentworth,
son of one of his masters, and of Mr. Hector, his school-
fellow and friend; from which I select the following
specimens:

Translation of VIRGIL. Pastoral I

MELIBŒUS

Now, Tityrus, you, supine and careless laid,
Play on your pipe beneath this beechen shade;
While wretched we about the world must roam,
And leave our pleasing fields and native home,
Here at your ease you sing your amorous flame,
And the wood rings with Amarillis' name.

TITYRUS

Those blessings, friend, a deity bestow'd,
For I shall never think him less than God;
Oft on his altar shall my firstlings lie,
Their blood the consecrated stones shall dye:
He gave my flocks to graze the flowery meads,
And me to tune at ease th' unequal reeds.

MELIBŒUS

My admiration only I exprest,
(No spark of envy harbours in my breast)
That, when confusion o'er the country reigns,
To you alone this happy state remains.

[1] As was likewise the Bishop of Dromore many years afterwards.

Here I, though faint myself, must drive my goats,
Far from their antient fields and humble cots.
This scarce I lead, who left on yonder rock
Two tender kids, the hopes of all the flock.
Had we not been perverse and careless grown,
This dire event by omens was foreshown;
Our trees were blasted by the thunder stroke,
And left-hand crows, from an old hollow oak,
Foretold the coming evil by their dismal croak.[a]

[a] *it was a Single Crow:—ever ominous in all Countries.* [H]

Translation of HORACE. Book I. Ode xxii

THE man, my friend, whose conscious heart
   With virtue's sacred ardour glows,
Nor taints with death the envenom'd dart,
   Nor needs the guard of Moorish bows;

Though Scythia's icy cliffs he treads,
   Or horrid Africk's faithless sands;
Or where the fam'd Hydaspes spreads
   His liquid wealth o'er barbarous lands.

For while by Chloe's image charm'd,
   Too far in Sabine woods I stray'd;
Me singing, careless and unarm'd,
   A grizly wolf surprised, and fled.

No savage more portentous stain'd
   Apulia's spacious wilds with gore;
No fiercer Juba's thirsty land,
   Dire nurse of raging lions, bore.

Place me where no soft summer gale
   Among the quivering branches sighs;
Where clouds condens'd for ever veil
   With horrid gloom the frowning skies:

Place me beneath the burning line,
   A clime deny'd to human race:
I'll sing of Chloe's charms divine,
   Her heav'nly voice, and beauteous face.

Translation of HORACE. Book II. Ode ix

CLOUDS do not always veil the skies,
    Nor showers immerse the verdant plain;
Nor do the billows always rise,
    Or storms afflict the ruffled main.

Nor, Valgius, on th' Armenian shores
    Do the chain'd waters always freeze;
Not always furious Boreas roars,
    Or bends with violent force the trees.

But you are ever drown'd in tears,
    For Mystes dead you ever mourn;
No setting Sol can ease your care,
    But finds you sad at his return.

The wise experienc'd Grecian sage
    Mourn'd not Antilochus so long;
Nor did King Priam's hoary age
    So much lament his slaughter'd son.

Leave off, at length, these woman's sighs,
    Augustus' numerous trophies sing;
Repeat that prince's victories,
    To whom all nations tribute bring.

Niphates rolls an humbler wave,
    At length the undaunted Scythian yields,
Content to live the Roman's slave,
    And scarce forsakes his native fields.

Translation of part of the Dialogue between HECTOR *and*
ANDROMACHE; *from the Sixth Book of* HOMER'S
ILIAD

SHE ceas'd; then godlike Hector answer'd kind,
(His various plumage sporting in the wind)
That post, and all the rest, shall be my care;
But shall I, then, forsake the unfinished war?
How would the Trojans brand great Hector's name!
And one base action sully all my fame,

Acquired by wounds and battles bravely fought!
Oh! how my soul abhors so mean a thought.
Long since I learn'd to slight this fleeting breath,
And view with cheerful eyes approaching death.
The inexorable sisters have decreed
That Priam's house, and Priam's self shall bleed:
The day will come, in which proud Troy shall yield,
And spread its smoking ruins o'er the field.
Yet Hecuba's, nor Priam's hoary age,
Whose blood shall quench some Grecian's thirsty rage,
Nor my brave brothers, that have bit the ground,
Their souls dismiss'd through many a ghastly wound,
Can in my bosom half that grief create,
As the sad thought of your impending fate:
When some proud Grecian dame shall tasks impose,
Mimick your tears, and ridicule your woes;
Beneath Hyperia's waters shall you sweat,
And, fainting, scarce support the liquid weight:
Then shall some Argive loud insulting cry,
Behold the wife of Hector, guard of Troy!
Tears, at my name, shall drown those beauteous eyes,
And that fair bosom heave with rising sighs!
Before that day, by some brave hero's hand
May I lie slain, and spurn the bloody sand.

To a YOUNG LADY *on her* BIRTH-DAY[1]

THIS tributary verse receive, my fair,
Warm with an ardent lover's fondest pray'r.
May this returning day for ever find
Thy form more lovely, more adorn'd thy mind;
All pains, all cares, may favouring heav'n remove,
All but the sweet solicitudes of love![a]
May powerful nature join with grateful art
To point each glance, and force it to the heart!
O then, when conquered crowds confess thy sway,
When ev'n proud wealth and prouder wit obey,
My fair, be mindful of the mighty trust,
Alas! 'tis hard for beauty to be just.

[a] *That is a Line in some other Poem I forget what.* [1]

[1] Mr. Hector informs me, that this was made almost *impromptu*, in his presence.

Those sovereign charms with strictest care employ;
Nor give the generous pain, the worthless joy:
With his own form acquaint the forward fool,
Shewn in the faithful glass of ridicule;
Teach mimick censure her own faults to find, ⎫
No more let coquettes to themselves be blind, ⎬
So shall Belinda's charms improve mankind. ⎭

THE YOUNG AUTHOUR[1]

WHEN first the peasant, long inclined to roam,
Forsakes his rural sports and peaceful home,
Pleas'd with the scene the smiling ocean yields,
He scorns the verdant meads and flow'ry fields;
Then dances jocund o'er the watery way,
While the breeze whispers, and the streamers play:
Unbounded prospects in his bosom roll,
And future millions lift his rising soul;
In blissful dreams he digs the golden mine,
And raptur'd sees the new-found ruby shine.
Joys insincere! thick clouds invade the skies,
Loud roar the billows, high the waves arise;
Sick'ning with fear, he longs to view the shore,
And vows to trust the faithless deep no more.
So the young Authour, panting after fame,
And the long honours of a lasting name,
Entrusts his happiness to human kind,
More false, more cruel, than the seas or wind.
'Toil on, dull croud, in extacies he cries,
For wealth or title, perishable prize;
While I those transitory blessings scorn,
Secure of praise from ages yet unborn.'
This thought once form'd, all council comes too late,
He flies to press, and hurried on his fate;
Swiftly he sees the imagin'd laurels spread,
And feels the unfading wreath surround his head.
Warn'd by another's fate, vain youth be wise,
Those dreams were Settle's once, and Ogilby's:

[1] This he inserted, with many alterations, in the Gentleman's Magazine, 1743.

[He, however, did not add his name. See Gent. Mag. vol. xiii. p. 378. MALONE.]

The pamphlet spreads, incessant hisses rise,
To some retreat the baffled writer flies;
Where no sour criticks snarl, no sneers molest,
Safe from the tart lampoon, and stinging jest;
There begs of heaven a less distinguish'd lot,
Glad to be hid, and proud to be forgot.[a]

[a] This *is worth them all*, This *we see is done con Amore.* [1]

EPILOGUE, *intended to have been spoken by a* LADY *who was to personate the Ghost of* HERMIONE[1]

YE blooming train, who give despair or joy,
Bless with a smile, or with a frown destroy;
In whose fair cheeks destructive Cupids wait,
And with unerring shafts distribute fate;
Whose snowy breasts, whose animated eyes,
Each youth admires, though each admirer dies;
Whilst you deride their pangs in barb'rous play, ⎫
Unpitying see them weep, and hear them pray, ⎬
And unrelenting sport ten thousand lives away; ⎭
For you, ye fair, I quit the gloomy plains;
Where sable night in all her horrour reigns;
No fragrant bowers, no delightful glades,
Receive the unhappy ghosts of scornful maids.
For kind, for tender nymphs the myrtle blooms,
And weaves her bending boughs in pleasing glooms:
Perennial roses deck each purple vale,
And scents ambrosial breathe in every gale:
Far hence are banish'd vapours, spleen, and tears,
Tea, scandal, ivory teeth, and languid airs:
No pug, nor favourite Cupid there enjoys
The balmy kiss, for which poor Thyrsis dies;
Form'd to delight, they use no foreign arms,
Nor torturing whalebones pinch them into charms;
No conscious blushes there their cheeks inflame,
For those who feel no guilt can know no shame;
Unfaded still their former charms they shew,
Around them pleasures wait, and joys for ever new.
But cruel virgins meet severer fates;
Expell'd and exil'd from the blissful seats,

[1] Some young ladies at Lichfield having proposed to act 'The Distressed Mother,' Johnson wrote this, and gave it to Mr. Hector to convey it privately to them.

To dismal realms, and regions void of peace,
Where furies ever howl, and serpents hiss.
O'er the sad plains perpetual tempests sigh,
And pois'nous vapours, black'ning all the sky,
With livid hue the fairest face o'ercast,
And every beauty withers at the blast:
Where'er they fly their lovers' ghosts pursue,
Inflicting all those ills which once they knew;
Vexation, Fury, Jealousy, Despair,
Vex ev'ry eye, and every bosom tear;
Their foul deformities by all descry'd,
No maid to flatter, and no paint to hide.
Then melt, ye fair, while crowds around you sigh,
Nor let disdain sit lowring in your eye;
With pity soften every awful grace,
And beauty smile auspicious in each face;
To ease their pains exert your milder power,
So shall you guiltless reign, and all mankind adore.

The two years which he spent at home, after his return
from Stourbridge, he passed in what he thought idleness,
and was scolded by his father for his want of steady application. He had no settled plan of life, nor looked forward
at all, but merely lived from day to day. Yet he read a
great deal in a desultory manner, without any scheme of
study, as chance threw books in his way, and inclination
directed him through them. He used to mention one
curious instance of his casual reading, when but a boy.
Having imagined that his brother had hid some apples
behind a large folio upon an upper shelf in his father's
shop, he climbed up to search for them. There were no
apples; but the large folio proved to be Petrarch, whom
he had seen mentioned, in some preface, as one of the
restorers of learning. His curiosity having been thus excited,
he sat down with avidity, and read a great part of the book.
What he read during these two years, he told me, was not
works of mere amusement, 'not voyages and travels, but
all literature, Sir, all ancient writers, all manly: though
but little Greek, only some of Anacreon and Hesiod: but
marginal line: *which were . . . that when* [H] in this irregular manner (added he) I had looked into a
great many books, which were not commonly known at

the Universities, where they seldom read any books but
what are put into their hands by their tutors; so that when
I came to Oxford, Dr. Adams, now master of Pembroke
College, told me, I was the best qualified for the University
that he had ever known come there.'

In estimating the progress of his mind during these two
years, as well as in future periods of his life, we must not
regard his own hasty confession of idleness; for we see,
when he explains himself, that he was acquiring various
stores; and, indeed he himself concluded the account, with
saying, 'I would not have you think I was doing nothing
then.' He might, perhaps, have studied more assiduously;
but it may be doubted, whether such a mind as his was
not more enriched by roaming at large in the fields of
literature, than if it had been confined to any single spot.
The analogy between body and mind is very general, and
the parallel will hold as to their food, as well as any other
particular. The flesh of animals who feed excursively, is
allowed to have a higher flavour than that of those who
are cooped up. May there not be the same difference
between men who read as their taste prompts, and men
who are confined in cells and colleges to stated tasks?

marginal line:
animals who . . .
cooped up [H]

That a man in Mr. Michael Johnson's circumstances
should think of sending his son to the expensive University
of Oxford, at his own charge, seems very improbable. The
subject was too delicate to question Johnson upon; but I
have been assured by Dr. Taylor, that the scheme never
would have taken place, had not a gentleman of Shropshire, one of his schoolfellows, spontaneously undertaken
to support him at Oxford, in the character of his companion: though, in fact, he never received any asisstance
whatever from that gentleman.

He, however, went to Oxford, and was entered a
Commoner of Pembroke College, on the 31st of October,
1728, being then in his nineteenth year.

The Reverend Dr. Adams, who afterwards presided
over Pembroke College with universal esteem, told me he
was present, and gave me some account of what passed
on the night of Johnson's arrival at Oxford. On that
evening, his father, who had anxiously accompanied him,
found means to have him introduced to Mr. Jorden, who

was to be his tutor. His being put under any tutor, reminds
us of what Wood says of Robert Burton, authour of the
'Anatomy of Melancholy,' when elected student of Christ
Church; 'for form's sake, *though he wanted not a tutor*, he was
put under the tuition of Dr. John Bancroft, afterwards
Bishop of Oxon.'[1]

His father seemed very full of the merits of his son, and
told the company he was a good scholar, and a poet, and
wrote Latin verses. His figure and manner appeared
strange to them; but he behaved modestly, and sat silent,
till upon something which occurred in the course of
conversation, he suddenly struck in and quoted Macrobius;
and thus he gave the first impression of that more extensive
reading in which he had indulged himself.

His tutor, Mr. Jorden, fellow of Pembroke, was not, it
seems, a man of such abilities as we should conceive
requisite for the instructor of Samuel Johnson, who gave
me the following account of him. 'He was a very worthy
man, but a heavy man, and I did not profit much by his
instructions. Indeed, I did not attend him much. The first
day after I came to college, I waited upon him, and then
staid away four. On the sixth, Mr. Jorden asked me why
I had not attended. I answered I had been sliding in
Christ Church meadow. And this I said with as much
nonchalance as I am now[2] talking to you. I had no notion
that I was wrong or irreverent to my tutor.' BOSWELL.
'That, Sir, was great fortitude of mind.' JOHNSON. 'No,
Sir; stark insensibility.'[3]

The fifth of November was at that time kept with great
solemnity at Pembroke College, and exercises upon the
subject of the day were required. Johnson neglected to
perform his, which is much to be regretted; for his vivacity
of imagination, and force of language, would probably
have produced something sublime upon the gunpowder
plot. To apologise for his neglect, he gave in a short copy
of verses, intitled *Somnium*, containing a common thought;
'that the Muse had come to him in his sleep, and whispered,

---

[1] Athen. Oxon. edit. 1721, i. 627.   [2] Oxford, 20th March, 1776.

[3] It ought to be remembered, that Dr. Johnson was apt, in his literary as
well as moral exercises, to overcharge his defects. Dr. Adams informed me,
that he attended his tutor's lectures, and also the lectures in the College
Hall, very regularly.

that it did not become him to write on such subjects as politicks; he should confine himself to humbler themes:' but the versification was truly Virgilian.

He had a love and respect for Jorden, not for his literature, but for his worth. 'Whenever (said he) a young man becomes Jorden's pupil, he becomes his son.'

Having given such a specimen of his poetical powers, he was asked by Mr. Jorden, to translate Pope's Messiah into Latin verse, as a Christmas exercise. He performed it with uncommon rapidity, and in so masterly a manner, that he obtained great applause from it, which ever after kept him high in the estimation of his College, and, indeed, of all the University.

marginal line: *Pope's Messiah . . . a Christmas* [H]

It is said, that Mr. Pope expressed himself concerning it in terms of strong approbation. Dr. Taylor told me, that it was first printed for old Mr. Johnson, without the knowledge of his son, who was very angry when he heard of it. A Miscellany of Poems collected by a person of the name of Husbands, was published at Oxford in 1731. In that Miscellany Johnson's Translation of the Messiah appeared, with this modest motto from Scaliger's Poeticks, '*Ex alieno ingenio Poeta, ex suo tantum versificator.*'

marginal line: *Husbands, was . . . the Messiah* [H]

I am not ignorant that critical objections have been made to this and other specimens of Johnson's Latin Poetry. I acknowledge myself not competent to decide on a question of such extreme nicety. But I am satisfied with the just and discriminative eulogy pronounced upon it by my friend Mr. Courtenay.

'And with like ease his vivid lines assume
The garb and dignity of ancient Rome.—
Let college *verse-men* trite conceits express,
Trick'd out in splendid shreds of Virgil's dress:
From playful Ovid cull the tinsel phrase,
And vapid notions hitch in pilfer'd lays;
Then with mosaic art the piece combine,
And boast the glitter of each dulcet line:
Johnson adventur'd boldly to transfuse
His vigorous sense into the Latin muse;
Aspir'd to shine by unreflected light,
And with a Roman's ardour *think* and write.

He felt the tuneful Nine his breast inspire,
And, like a master, wak'd the soothing lyre:
Horatian strains a grateful heart proclaim,
While Sky's wild rocks resound his Thralia's name. —
Hesperia's plant, in some less skilful hands,
To bloom a while, factitious heat demands:
Though glowing Maro a faint warmth supplies,
The sickly blossom in the hot-house dies:
By Johnson's genial culture, art, and toil,
Its root strikes deep, and owns the fost'ring soil;
Imbibes our sun through all its swelling veins,
And grows a native of Britannia's plains.' [1]

The 'morbid melancholy,' which was lurking in his
constitution, and to which we may ascribe those particularities, and that aversion to regular life, which, at a very
early period marked his character, gathered such strength
in his twentieth year, as to afflict him in a dreadful manner.
While he was at Lichfield, in the college vacation of the
year 1729, he felt himself overwhelmed with an horrible
hypochondria, with perpetual irritation, fretfulness, and
impatience; and with a dejection, gloom, and despair,
which made existence misery. From this dismal malady
he never afterwards was perfectly relieved: and all his
labours, and all his enjoyments, were but temporary
interruptions of its baleful influence. How wonderful, how
unsearchable are the ways of GOD! Johnson, who was
blest with all the powers of genius and understanding in a
degree far above the ordinary state of human nature, was
at the same time visited with a disorder so afflictive, that
they who know it by dire experience, will not envy his
exalted endowments. That it was, in some degree, occasioned by a defect in his nervous system, that inexplicable
part of our frame, appears highly probable. He told
Mr. Paradise that he was sometimes so languid and
inefficient, that he could not distinguish the hour upon the
town-clock.[a]

Johnson, upon the first violent attack of this disorder,
strove to overcome it by forcible exertions. He frequently

[a] *Did he mean Lich-
field? & did he make a
wonder of that? he
never at his best could
see at such a Distance.*
[1]

[1] Poetical Review of the Literary and Moral Character of Dr. Johnson,
by John Courtnay, Esq. M.P.

walked to Birmingham and back again, and tried many
other expedients, but all in vain. His expression concerning
it to me was 'I did not then know how to manage it.' His
distress became so intolerable, that he applied to Dr.
Swinfen, physician in Lichfield, his god-father, and put
into his hands a state of his case, written in Latin. Dr.
Swinfen was so much struck with the extraordinary
acuteness, research, and eloquence of this paper, that in
his zeal for his god-son he shewed it to several people. His
daughter, Mrs. Desmoulins, who was many years humanely
supported in Dr. Johnson's house in London, told me, that
upon his discovering that Dr. Swinfen had communicated
his case, he was so much offended, that he was never
afterwards fully reconciled to him. He indeed had good
reason to be offended; for though Dr. Swinfen's motive
was good, he inconsiderately betrayed a matter deeply
interesting and of great delicacy, which had been entrusted
to him in confidence: and exposed a complaint of his young
friend and patient, which, in the superficial opinion of the
generality of mankind, is attended with contempt and
disgrace.

But let not little men triumph upon knowing that
Johnson was an HYPOCHONDRIACK, was subject to
what the learned, philosophical, and pious Dr. Cheyne
has so well treated under the title of 'The English Malady.'
Though he suffered severely from it, he was not therefore
degraded. The powers of his great mind might be troubled,
and their full exercise suspended at times; but the mind
itself was ever entire. As a proof of this, it is only necessary
to consider, that, when he was at the very worst, he composed that state of his own case, which shewed an uncommon vigour, not only of fancy and taste, but of
judgement. I am aware that he himself was too ready to
call such a complaint by the name of *madness;* in conformity
with which notion, he has traced its gradations, with
exquisite nicety, in one of the chapters of his RASSELAS.
But there is surely a clear distinction between a disorder
which affects only the imagination and spirits, while the
judgement is sound, and a disorder by which the judgement itself is impaired. This distinction was made to me
by the late Professor Gaubius of Leyden, physician to the

Prince of Orange, in a conversation which I had with him several years ago, and he expanded it thus: 'If (said he) a man tells me that he is grievously disturbed, for that he *imagines* he sees a ruffian coming against him with a drawn sword, though at the same time he is *conscious* it is a delusion, I pronounce him to have a disordered imagination; but if a man tells me that he *sees* this, and in consternation calls to me to look at it, I pronounce him to be *mad*.'

It is a common effect of low spirits or melancholy, to make those who are afflicted with it imagine that they are actually suffering those evils which happen to be most strongly presented to their minds. Some have fancied themselves to be deprived of the use of their limbs, some to labour under acute diseases, others to be in extreme poverty; when, in truth, there was not the least reality in any of the suppositions; so that when the vapours were dispelled, they were convinced of the delusion. To Johnson, whose supreme enjoyment was the exercise of his reason, the disturbance or obscuration of that faculty was the evil most to be dreaded. Insanity, therefore, was the object of his most dismal apprehension; and he fancied himself seized by it, or approaching to it, at the very time when he was giving proofs of a more than ordinary soundness and vigour of judgement. That his own diseased imagination should have so far deceived him, is strange; but it is stranger still that some of his friends should have given credit to his groundless opinion, when they had such undoubted proofs that it was totally fallacious; though it is by no means surprising that those who wish to depreciate him, should, since his death, have laid hold of this circumstance, and insisted upon it with very unfair aggravation.

Amidst the oppression and distraction of a disease which very few have felt in its full extent, but many have experienced in a slighter degree, Johnson, in his writings, and in his conversation, never failed to display all the varieties of intellectual excellence. In his march through this world to a better, his mind still appeared grand and brilliant, and impressed all around him with the truth of Virgil's noble sentiment—

'*Igneus est ollis vigor et cœlestis origo.*'

The history of his mind as to religion is an important article. I have mentioned the early impressions made upon his tender imagination by his mother, who continued her pious cares with assiduity, but, in his opinion, not with judgement. 'Sunday (said he) was a heavy day to me when I was a boy. My mother confined me on that day, and made me read "The Whole Duty of Man," from a great part of which I could derive no instruction. When, for instance, I had read the chapter on theft, which from my infancy I had been taught was wrong, I was no more convinced that theft was wrong than before; so there was no accession of knowledge. A boy should be introduced to such books, by having his attention directed to the arrangement, to the style, and other excellencies of composition; that the mind being thus engaged by an amusing variety of objects may not grow weary.'

He communicated to me the following particulars upon the subject of his religious progress. 'I fell into an inattention to religion, or an indifference about it, in my ninth year. The church at Lichfield, in which we had a seat, wanted reparation, so I was to go and find a seat in other churches; and having bad eyes, and being awkward about this, I used to go and read in the fields on Sunday. This habit continued till my fourteenth year; and still I find a great reluctance to go to church. I then became a sort of lax *talker* against religion, for I did not much *think* against it; and this lasted till I went to Oxford, where it would not be *suffered*. When at Oxford, I took up "Law's Serious Call to a Holy Life," expecting to find it a dull book, (as such books generally are,) and perhaps to laugh at it. But I found Law quite an overmatch for me; and this was the first occasion of my thinking in earnest of religion, after I became capable of rational enquiry.'[1] From this

[1] Mrs. Piozzi has given a strange fantastical account of the original of Dr. Johnson's belief in our most holy religion. 'At the age of *ten* years his mind was disturbed by scruples of infidelity, which preyed upon his spirits, and made him very uneasy,[a] the more so, as he revealed his uneasiness to none, being naturally (as he said) of a sullen temper, and reserved disposition. He searched, however, diligently, but fruitlessly, for evidences of the truth of revelation; and, at length, *recollecting* a book he had *once* seen [*I suppose at five years old*] in his father's shop, intitled *De veritate Religionis, &c.* he began to think himself *highly culpable* for neglecting such a means of information, and took himself severely to task for this *sin*, adding many acts

[a] *he told me this* himself; *I did not dream it, & could not have invented it, or heard it from others. I will* Swear *he told me as I told the* Public, *& swear it* (*if they will*) *when in my last Moments. In 1808* They *cannot be far distant.* [1]

time forward religion was the predominant object of his thoughts; though, with the just sentiments of a conscientious christian, he lamented that his practice of its duties fell far short of what it ought to be.

This instance of a mind such as that of Johnson being first disposed, by an unexpected incident, to think with anxiety of the momentous concerns of eternity, and of 'what he should do to be saved,' may for ever be produced in opposition to the superficial and sometimes profane contempt that has been thrown upon those occasional impressions which it is certain many christians have experienced; though it must be acknowledged that weak minds, from an erroneous supposition that no man is in a state of grace who has not felt a particular conversion, have, in some cases, brought a degree of ridicule upon them; a ridicule, of which it is inconsiderate or unfair to make a general application.

How seriously Johnson was impressed with a sense of religion, even in the vigour of his youth, appears from the following passage in his minutes kept by way of diary: 'Sept. 7, 1736. I have this day entered upon my 28th year. Mayest thou, O God, enable me, for JESUS CHRIST's sake, to spend this in such a manner, that I may receive comfort from it at the hour of death, and in the day of judgement! Amen.'

The particular course of his reading while at Oxford, and during the time of vacation which he passed at home,

of voluntary, and, to others, unknown *penance*. The first opportunity which offered, of course, he seized the book with avidity; but, on examination, *not finding himself scholar enough to peruse its contents*, set his heart at rest; and not thinking to enquire whether there were any English books written on the subject, followed his usual amusements and *considered his conscience as lightened of a crime*. He redoubled his diligence to learn the language that contained the information he most wished; but from the pain which *guilt* [*namely having omitted to read what he did not understand*] had given him, he now began to deduce the soul's immortality; [*a sensation of pain in this world being an unquestionable proof of existence in another*] which was the point that belief first stopped at; *and from that moment resolving to be a Christian*, became one of the most zealous and pious ones our nation ever produced.' Anecdotes, p. 17.

This is one of the numerous misrepresentations of this lively lady, which it is worth while to correct; for if credit should be given to such a childish, irrational, and ridiculous statement of the foundation of Dr. Johnson's faith in Christianity, how little credit would be due to it. Mrs. Piozzi[a] seems to wish, that the world should think Dr. Johnson also under the influence of that easy logick, *Stet pro ratione voluntas*.

[a] *Mrs. Piozzi thought & knew that she was telling Truth* [1]

cannot be traced. Enough has been said of his irregular
mode of study. He told me, that from his earliest years he
loved to read poetry, but hardly ever read any poem to an
end; that he read Shakspeare at a period so early, that the
speech of the Ghost in Hamlet terrified him when he was
alone; that Horace's Odes were the compositions in which
he took most delight, and it was long before he liked his
Epistles and Satires. He told me what he read *solidly* at
Oxford was Greek; not the Grecian historians, but Homer
and Euripides, and now and then a little Epigram; that
the study of which he was the most fond was Metaphysicks,
but he had not read much, even in that way. I always
thought that he did himself injustice in his account of what
he had read, and that he must have been speaking with
reference to the vast portion of study which is possible,
and to which a few scholars in the whole history of literature have attained; for when I once asked him whether
a person whose name I have now forgotten, studied hard,
he answered 'No, Sir. I do not believe he studied hard.
I never knew a man who studied hard. I conclude, indeed,
from the effects, that some men have studied hard, as
Bentley and Clarke.' Trying him by that criterion upon
which he formed his judgement of others, we may be
absolutely certain, both from his writings and his conversation, that his reading was very extensive. Dr. Adam
Smith, than whom few were better judges on this subject,
once observed to me, that 'Johnson knew more books than
any man alive.' He had a peculiar facility in seizing at
once what was valuable in any book, without submitting
to the labour of perusing it from beginning to end. He had,
from the irritability of his constitution, at all times, an
impatience and hurry when he either read or wrote. A
certain apprehension arising from novelty, made him
write his first exercise at College twice over; but he never
took that trouble with any other composition: and we
shall see that his most excellent works were struck off at a
heat, with rapid exertion.[1]

[1] [He told Dr. Burney, that he never wrote any of his works that were
printed, twice over. Dr. Burney's wonder at seeing several pages of his
'Lives of the Poets,' in Manuscript, with scarce a blot or erasure, drew this
observation from him. MALONE.]

marginal line:
when he . .. and it [H]

Yet he appears, from his early notes or memorandums in my possession, to have at various times attempted, or at least planned, a methodical course of study, according to computation, of which he was all his life fond, as it fixed his attention steadily upon something without, and prevented his mind from preying upon itself. Thus I find in his handwriting the number of lines in each of two of Euripides's Tragedies, of the Georgicks of Virgil, of the first six books of the Æneid, of Horace's Art of Poetry, of three of the books of Ovid's Metamorphosis, of some parts of Theocritus, and of the tenth Satire of Juvenal; and a table, showing at the rate of various numbers a day, (I suppose verses to be read,) what would be, in each case, the total amount in a week, month, and year.

marginal line:
in Pembroke . . . learn-
ing will [H]

No man had a more ardent love of literature, or a higher respect for it, than Johnson. His apartment in Pembroke College was that upon the second floor over the gateway. The enthusiast of learning will ever contemplate it with veneration. One day, while he was sitting in it quite alone, Dr. Panting, then master of the College, whom he called 'a fine Jacobite fellow,' overheard him uttering this soliloquy in his strong emphatic voice: 'Well, I have a mind to see what is done in other places of learning. I'll go and visit the Universities abroad. I'll go to France and Italy. I'll go to Padua.—And I'll mind my business. For an *Athenian* blockhead is the worst of all blockheads.'[1]

Dr. Adams told me that Johnson, while he was at Pembroke College, 'was caressed and loved by all about him, was a gay and frolicksome fellow, and passed there the happiest part of his life.' But this is a striking proof of the fallacy of appearances, and how little any of us know of the real internal state even of those whom we see most frequently; for the truth is, that he was then depressed by poverty, and irritated by disease. When I mentioned to him this account as given me by Dr. Adams, he said, 'Ah,

[1] I had this anecdote from Dr. Adams, and Dr. Johnson confirmed it. Bramston, in his 'Man of Taste,' has the same thought:

'Sure, of all blockheads, scholars are the worst.'

[Johnson's meaning however, is, that a scholar who is a blockhead, must be the worst of all blockheads, because he is without excuse. But Bramston, in the assumed character of an ignorant coxcomb, maintains, that *all* scholars are blockheads, on account of their scholarship. J. BOSWELL.]

Sir, I was mad and violent. It was bitterness which they mistook for frolick. I was miserably poor, and I thought to fight my way by my literature and my wit; so I disregarded all power and all authority.'

The Bishop of Dromore observes in a letter to me, 'The pleasure he took in vexing the tutors and fellows has been often mentioned. But I have heard him say, what ought to be recorded to the honour of the present venerable master of that College, the Reverend William Adams, D.D. who was then very young, and one of the junior fellows; that the mild but judicious expostulations of this worthy man, whose virtue awed him, and whose learning he revered, made him really ashamed of himself, 'though I fear (said he) I was too proud to own it.'

'I have heard from some of his contemporaries that he was generally seen lounging at the College gate, with a circle of young students round him, whom he was entertaining with wit, and keeping from their studies, if not spiriting them up to rebellion against the College discipline, which in his maturer years he so much extolled.'

He very early began to attempt keeping notes or memorandums, by way of a diary of his life. I find, in a parcel of loose leaves, the following spirited resolution, to contend against his natural indolence: '*Oct.* 1729. *Desidiæ valedixi; syrenis istius cantibus surdam posthac aurem obversurus.* — I bid farewell to Sloth, being resolved henceforth not to listen to her syren strains.' I have also in my possession a few leaves of another *Libellus*, or little book, entitled ANNALES, in which some of the early particulars of his history are registered in Latin.

I do not find that he formed any close intimacies with his fellow-collegians. But Dr. Adams told me that he contracted a love and regard for Pembroke College, which he retained to the last. A short time before his death he sent to that College, a present of all his works, to be deposited in their library; and he had thoughts of leaving to it his house at Lichfield; but his friends[a] who were about him very properly dissuaded him from it, and he bequeathed it to some poor relations. He took a pleasure in boasting of the many eminent men who had been educated at Pembroke. In this list are found the names

underlined:
friends [1]

[a] *A Man's* Friends *as they are called, are always* Friends *to his Relations;—not to* him: These *People, prefer'd you see Beggars with whom they were not acquainted, to the Fame of their* Friend [1]

of Mr. Hawkins the Poetry Professor, Mr. Shenstone, Sir William Blackstone, and others;[1] not forgetting the celebrated popular preacher, Mr. George Whitefield, of whom, though Dr. Johnson did not think very highly, it must be acknowledged that his eloquence was powerful, his views pious and charitable, his assiduity almost incredible; and, that since his death, the integrity of his character has been fully vindicated. Being himself a poet, Johnson was peculiarly happy in mentioning how many of the sons of Pembroke were poets; adding, with a smile of sportive triumph, 'Sir, we are a nest of singing birds.'

He was not, however, blind to what he thought the defects of his own college: and I have, from the information of Dr. Taylor, a very strong instance of that rigid honesty which he ever inflexibly preserved. Taylor had obtained his father's consent to be entered of Pembroke, that he might be with his school-fellow Johnson, with whom, though some years older than himself, he was very intimate. This would have been a great comfort to Johnson. But he fairly told Taylor that he could not, in conscience, suffer him to enter where he knew he could not have an able tutor. He then made enquiry all round the University, and having found that Mr. Bateman, of Christ-Church, was the tutor of highest reputation, Taylor was entered of that College. Mr. Bateman's lectures were so excellent, that Johnson used to come and get them at second-hand from Taylor, till his poverty being so extreme, that his shoes were worn out, and his feet appeared through them, he saw that this humiliating circumstance was perceived by the Christ-church men, and he came no more. He was too proud to accept of money, and somebody having set a pair of new shoes at his door, he threw them away with indignation. How must we feel when we read such an anecdote of Samuel Johnson!

His spirited refusal of an eleemosynary supply of shoes, arose, no doubt, from a proper pride. But, considering his ascetic disposition at times, as acknowledged by himself in his Meditations, and the exaggeration with which some have treated the peculiarities of his character, I should not wonder to hear it ascribed to a principle of superstitious

[1] See Nash's History of Worcestershire, Vol. I. p. 529.

mortification; as we are told by Tursellinus, in his Life of
St. Ignatius Loyola, that this intrepid founder of the order
of Jesuits, when he arrived at Goa, after having made a
severe pilgrimage through the eastern desarts, persisted
in wearing his miserable shattered shoes, and when new
ones were offered him, rejected them as an unsuitable
indulgence.

The *res angusta domi* prevented him from having the
advantage of a complete academical education. The friend
to whom he had trusted for support had deceived him.
His debts in College, though not great, were increasing;
and his scanty remittances from Lichfield, which had all
along been made with great difficulty, could be supplied
no longer, his father having fallen into a state of insolvency.
Compelled, therefore, by irresistible necessity, he left the
College in autumn, 1731, without a degree, having been
a member of it little more than three years.

Dr. Adams, the worthy and respectable master of
Pembroke College, has generally had the reputation of
being Johnson's tutor. The fact, however, is, that in 1731,
Mr. Jorden quitted the College, and his pupils were
transferred to Dr. Adams; so that had Johnson returned,
Dr. Adams *would have been his tutor*. It is to be wished, that
this connection had taken place. His equal temper, mild
disposition, and politeness of manners, might have insensibly softened the harshness of Johnson, and infused
into him those more delicate charities, those *petites morales*,
in which, it must be confessed, our great moralist was more
deficient than his best friends could fully justify. Dr. Adams
paid Johnson this high compliment. He said to me at
Oxford, in 1776, 'I was his nominal tutor; but he was
above my mark.' When I repeated it to Johnson, his eyes
flashed with grateful satisfaction, and he exclaimed, 'That
was liberal and noble.'

And now (I had almost said *poor*) Samuel Johnson
returned to his native city, destitute, and not knowing
how he should gain even a decent livelihood. His father's
misfortunes in trade rendered him unable to support his
son; and for some time there appeared no means by which
he could maintain himself. In the December of this year
his father died.

The state of poverty in which he died, appears from a note in one of Johnson's little diaries of the following year, which strongly displays his spirit and virtuous dignity of mind. '1732, *Julii* 15. *Undecim aureos deposui, quo die quicquid ante matris funus (quod serum sit precor) de paternis bonis sperari licet, viginti scilicet libras, accepi. Usque adeo mihi fortuna fingenda est. Interea, ne paupertate vires animi languescant, nec in flagitia egestas abigat, cavendum.* —I layed by eleven guineas on this day, when I received twenty pounds, being all that I have reason to hope for out of my father's effects, previous to the death of my mother; an event which, I pray GOD may be very remote. I now therefore see that I must make my own fortune. Meanwhile, let me take care that the powers of my mind be not debilitated by poverty, and that indigence do not force me into any criminal act.'

Johnson was so far fortunate, that the respectable character of his parents, and his own merit, had, from his earliest years, secured him a kind reception in the best families at Lichfield. Among these I can mention Mr. Howard, Dr. Swinfen, Mr. Simpson, Mr. Levett, Capt. Garrick, father of the great ornament of the British stage; but above all, Mr. Gilbert Walmsley,[1] Registrar of the Ecclesiastical Court of Lichfield, whose character, long after his decease, Dr. Johnson has, in his life of Edmund Smith, thus drawn in the glowing colours of gratitude:

'Of Gilbert Walmsley, thus presented to my mind, let me indulge myself in the remembrance. I knew him very early; he was one of the first friends that literature procured me, and I hope, that at least, my gratitude made me worthy of his notice.

[1] Mr. Warton informs me, 'that this early friend of Johnson was entered a Commoner of Trinity College, Oxford, aged 17, in 1698; and is the author of many Latin verse translations in the Gentleman's Magazine. One of them is a translation of

'My time, O ye Muses, was happily spent,' &c.

He died August 3, 1751, and a monument to his memory has been erected in the cathedral of Lichfield, with an inscription written by Mr. Seward, one of the Prebendaries.

[His translation of 'My time, O ye Muses,' &c. may be found in the Gentleman's Magazine for 1745, vol. xv. p. 102. It is there subscribed with his name. MALONE.]

'He was of an advanced age, and I was only not a boy, yet he never received my notions with contempt. He was a whig, with all the virulence and malevolence of his party; yet difference of opinion did not keep us apart. I honoured him and he endured me.

'He had mingled with the gay world without exemption from its vices or its follies; but had never neglected the cultivation of his mind. His belief of revelation was unshaken; his learning preserved his principles; he grew first regular, and then pious.

'His studies had been so various, that I am not able to name a man of equal knowledge. His acquaintance with books was great, and what he did not immediately know, he could, at least, tell where to find. Such was his amplitude of learning, and such his copiousness of communication, that it may be doubted whether a day now passes, in which I have not some advantage from his friendship.

'At this man's table I enjoyed many cheerful and instructive hours, with companions, such as are not often found—with one who has lengthened, and one who has gladdened life; with Dr. James, whose skill in physick will be long remembered; and with David Garrick, whom I hoped to have gratified with this character of our common friend. But what are the hopes of man! I am disappointed by that stroke of death, which has eclipsed the gaiety of nations, and impoverished the public stock of harmless pleasure.'

marginal line: *of death . . . harmless pleasure* [H]

In these families he passed much time in his early years. In most of them, he was in the company of ladies, particularly at Mr. Walmsley's, whose wife and sisters-in-law, of the name of Aston, and daughters of a Baronet, were remarkable for good breeding; so that the notion which has been industriously circulated and believed, that he never was in good company till late in life, and, consequently had been confirmed in coarse and ferocious manners by long habits, is wholly without foundation. Some of the ladies have assured me, they recollected him well when a young man, as distinguished for his complaisance.

And that his politeness was not merely occasional and temporary, or confined to the circles of Lichfield, is ascertained by the testimony of a lady, who, in a paper with which I have been favoured by a daughter of his intimate friend and physician, Dr. Lawrence, thus describes Dr. Johnson some years afterwards:

'As the particulars of the former part of Dr. Johnson's life do not seem to be very accurately known, a lady hopes that the following information may not be unacceptable.

'She remembers Dr. Johnson on a visit to Dr. Taylor, at Ashbourn, some time between the end of the year 37, and the middle of the year 40; she rather thinks it to have been after he and his wife were removed to London. During his stay at Ashbourn, he made frequent visits to Mr. Meynell, at Bradley, where his company was much desired by the ladies of the family, who were, perhaps, in point of elegance and accomplishments, inferiour to few of those with whom he was afterwards acquainted. Mr. Meynell's eldest daughter was afterwards married to Mr. Fitzherbert,[a] father to Mr. Alleyne Fitzherbert, lately minister to the court of Russia. Of her, Dr. Johnson said, in Dr. Lawrence's study, that she had the best understanding he ever met with in any human being. At Mr. Meynell's he also commenced that friendship with Mrs. Hill Boothby, sister to the present Sir Brook Boothby, which continued till her death. The *young woman whom he used to call Molly Aston*,[1] was sister to Sir Thomas Aston, and daughter to a Baronet; she was also sister to the wife of his friend, Mr. Gilbert Walmsley.[2] Besides his intimacy with the above-mentioned persons, who were surely people of rank and education, while he was yet at Lichfield he used to be frequently at the house of Dr. Swinfen, a gentleman of very ancient family in Staffordshire, from which, after the death of his elder brother, he inherited a good estate. He was, besides, a physician of very extensive practice; but for want of due attention to the management

underlined:
Fitzherbert [1]
[a] *who hang'd himself.*
[1]

[1] The words of Sir John Hawkins, p. 316.

[2] [Sir Thomas Aston, Bart. who died in January, 1724-5, left one son, named Thomas also, and eight daughters. Of the daughters, Catherine married Johnson's friend, the Hon. Henry Hervey; Margaret, Gilbert Walmsley. Another of these ladies married the Rev. Mr. Gastrell. Mary, or *Molly* Aston, as she was usually called, became the wife of Captain Brodie of the Navy. Another sister, who was unmarried, was living at Lichfield in 1776. MALONE.]

of his domestic concerns, left a very large family in indigence. One of his daughters, Mrs. Desmoulins, afterwards found an asylum in the house of her old friend, whose doors were always open to the unfortunate, and who well observed the precept of the Gospel, for he "was kind to the unthankful and to the evil."'

In the forlorn state of his circumstances, he accepted of an offer to be employed as usher in the school of Market-Bosworth, in Leicestershire, to which it appears, from one of his little fragments of a diary, that he went on foot, on the 16th of July.—'*Julii* 16. *Bosvortiam pedes petii*.' But it is not true, as has been erroneously related, that he was assistant to the famous Anthony Blackwall, whose merit has been honoured by the testimony of Bishop Hurd,[1] who was his scholar; for Mr. Blackwall died on the 8th of April, 1730,[2] more than a year before Johnson left the University.

This employment was very irksome to him in every respect, and he complained grievously of it in his letters to his friend, Mr. Hector, who was now settled as a surgeon at Birmingham. The letters are lost; but Mr. Hector recollects his writing 'that the poet had described the dull sameness of his existence in these words, "*Vitam continet una dies*" (one day contains the whole of my life); that it was unvaried as the note of the cuckow; and that he did not know whether it was more disagreeable for him to teach, or the boys to learn, the grammar rules.' His general aversion to this painful drudgery was greatly enhanced by a disagreement between him and Sir Wolstan Dixie,[a] the patron of the school, in whose house, I have been told, he officiated as a kind of domestic chaplain, so far, at least, as to say grace at table, but was treated with what he represented as intolerable harshness; and, after suffering

[a] *I remember my Mother relating ludicrous stories of this Sr. Wolston Dixie's Ignorance & Brutality—but knew not he had ever anything to do with Dr. Johnson till I read it here now in 1808.* [1]

[1] [There is here (as Mr. James Boswell observes to me) a slight inaccuracy. Bishop Hurd, in the Epistle Dedicatory prefixed to his Commentary on Horace's Art of Poetry, &c. does not praise Blackwall, but the Rev. Mr. Budworth, head-master of the grammar school at Brewood in Staffordshire, who had himself been bred under Blackwall. See vol iii. near the end, where, from the information of Mr. John Nichols, Johnson is said to have applied in 1736 to Mr. Budworth, to be received by him as an assistant in his school in Staffordshire. MALONE.]

[2] See Gent. Mag. Dec. 1784, p. 957.

for a few months such complicated misery,[1] he relinquished a situation which all his life afterwards he recollected with the strongest aversion, and even a degree of horrour. But it is probable that at this period, whatever uneasiness he may have endured, he laid the foundation of much future eminence by application to his studies.

Being now again totally unoccupied, he was invited by Mr. Hector to pass some time with him at Birmingham, as his guest, at the house of Mr. Warren, with whom Mr. Hector lodged and boarded. Mr. Warren was the first established bookseller in Birmingham, and was very attentive to Johnson, who he soon found could be of much service to him in his trade, by his knowledge of literature; and he even obtained the assistance of his pen in furnishing some numbers of a periodical Essay printed in the newspaper, of which Warren was proprietor. After very diligent enquiry, I have not been able to recover those early specimens of that particular mode of writing by which Johnson afterwards so greatly distinguished himself.

He continued to live as Mr. Hector's guest for about six months, and then hired lodgings in another part of the town,[2] finding himself as well situated at Birmingham as he supposed he could be any where, while he had no settled plan of life, and very scanty means of subsistence. He made some valuable acquaintances there, amongst whom were Mr. Porter, a mercer, whose widow he afterwards married, and Mr. Taylor, who by his ingenuity in mechanical inventions, and his success in trade, acquired an immense fortune. But the comfort of being near Mr. Hector, his old school fellow and intimate friend, was Johnson's chief inducement to continue here.

In what manner he employed his pen at this period, or whether he derived from it any pecuniary advantage, I have not been able to ascertain. He probably got a little money from Mr. Warren; and we are certain, that he

---

[1] [It appears from a letter of Johnson's to a friend, which I have read, dated Lichfield, July 27, 1732, that he had left Sir Wolstan Dixie's house, recently before that letter was written. He then had hopes of succeeding either as master or usher, in the school of Ashburne. MALONE.]

[2] [In June 1733, Sir John Hawkins states, from one of Johnson's diaries, that he lodged in Birmingham at the house of a person named Jarvis, probably a relation of Mrs. Porter, whom he afterwards married. MALONE.]

executed here one piece of literary labour, of which Mr. Hector has favoured me with a minute account. Having mentioned that he had read at Pembroke College a Voyage to Abyssinia, by Lobo, a Portuguese Jesuit, and that he thought an abridgement and translation of it from the French into English might be an useful and profitable publication, Mr. Warren and Mr. Hector joined in urging him to undertake it. He accordingly agreed; and the book not being to be found in Birmingham, he borrowed it of Pembroke College. A part of the work being very soon done, one Osborn, who was Mr. Warren's printer, was set to work with what was ready, and Johnson engaged to supply the press with copy as it should be wanted; but his constitutional indolence soon prevailed, and the work was at a stand. Mr. Hector, who knew that a motive of humanity would be the most prevailing argument with his friend, went to Johnson, and represented to him, that the printer could have no other employment till this undertaking was finished, and that the poor man and his family were suffering. Johnson upon this exerted the powers of his mind, though his body was relaxed. He lay in bed with the book, which was a quarto, before him, and dictated while Hector wrote. Mr. Hector carried the sheets to the press, and corrected almost all the proof sheets, very few of which were even seen by Johnson. In this manner, with the aid of Mr. Hector's active friendship, the book was completed, and was published in 1735, with London upon the title-page, though it was in reality printed at Birmingham, a device too common with provincial publishers. For this work he had from Mr. Warren only the sum of five guineas.

This being the first prose work of Johnson, it is a curious object of enquiry how much may be traced in it of that style which marks his subsequent writings with such peculiar excellence; with so happy an union of force, vivacity, and perspicuity. I have perused the book with this view, and have found that here, as I believe in every other translation, there is in the work itself no vestige of the translator's own style; for the language of translation being adapted to the thoughts of another person, insensibly follows their cast, and as it were runs into a mould that is ready prepared.

Thus, for instance, taking the first sentence that occurs at the opening of the book, p. 4, 'I lived here above a year, and completed my studies in divinity; in which time some letters were received from the fathers of Ethiopia, with an account that Sultan Segned, Emperour of Abyssinia, was converted to the church of Rome; that many of his subjects had followed his example, and that there was a great want of missionaries to improve these prosperous beginnings. Every body was very desirous of seconding the zeal of our fathers, and of sending them the assistance they requested; to which we were the more encouraged, because the Emperour's letter informed our Provincial, that we might easily enter his dominions by the way of Dancala; but, unhappily, the secretary wrote Geila for Dancala, which cost two of our fathers their lives.' Every one acquainted with Johnson's manner will be sensible that there is nothing of it here; but that this sentence might have been composed by any other man.

But, in the Preface, the Johnsonian style begins to appear; and though use had not yet taught his wing a permanent and equable flight, there are parts of it which exhibit his best manner in full vigour. I had once the pleasure of examining it with Mr. Edmund Burke, who confirmed me in this opinion, by his superiour critical sagacity, and was, I remember, much delighted with the following specimen:

'The Portuguese traveller, contrary to the general vein of his countrymen, has amused his reader with no roman-tick absurdity, or incredible fictions; whatever he relates, whether true or not, is at least probable; and he who tells nothing exceeding the bounds of probability, has a right to demand that they should believe him who cannot contradict him.

'He appears by his modest and unaffected narration, to have described things as he saw them, to have copied nature from the life, and to have consulted his senses, not his imagination. He meets with no basilisks that destroy with their eyes, his crocodiles devour their prey with-out tears, and his cataracts fall from the rocks without deafening the neighbouring inhabitants.

'The reader will here find no regions cursed with

irremediable barrenness, or blest with spontaneous fecundity;[a] no perpetual gloom, or unceasing sunshine; nor are the nations here described, either devoid of all sense of humanity, or consummate in all private or social virtues. Here are no Hottentots without religious policy or articulate language; no Chinese perfectly polite, and completely skilled in all sciences; he will discover, what will always be discovered by a diligent and impartial enquirer, that wherever human nature is to be found, there is a mixture of vice and virtue, a contest of passion and reason; and that the Creator doth not appear partial in his distributions, but has balanced, in most countries, their particular inconveniences by particular favours.'

Here we have an early example of that brilliant and energetick expression, which upon innumerable occasions in his subsequent life, justly impressed the world with the highest admiration.

Nor can any one, conversant with the writings of Johnson, fail to discern his hand in this passage of the Dedication to John Warren, Esq. of Pembrokeshire, though it is ascribed to Warren the bookseller. 'A generous and elevated mind is distinguished by nothing more certainly than an eminent degree of curiosity;[1] nor is that curiosity ever more agreeably or usefully employed, than in examining the laws and customs of foreign nations. I hope, therefore, the present I now presume to make, will not be thought improper; which, however, it is not my business as a dedicator to commend, nor as a bookseller to depreciate.'

It is reasonable to suppose, that his having been thus accidentally led to a particular study of the history and manners of Abyssinia, was the remote occasion of his writing, many years afterwards, his admirable philosophical tale, the principal scene of which is laid in that country.

Johnson returned to Lichfield early in 1734, and in August that year he made an attempt to procure some little subsistence by his pen; for he published proposals for printing by subscription the Latin Poems of Politian:[2]

a There recurs an Idea of the same Kind in the Prologue to Irene 'and spare him Ladies, tho' his Lovers live.' [1]

---

[1] See RAMBLER, No. 103.

[2] May we not trace a fanciful similarity between Politian, and Johnson? Huetius, speaking of Paulus Pelissonius Fontanerius, says '—in quo Natura, ut olim in Angelo Politiano, deformitatem oris excellentis ingenii præstantia compensavit.' Comment. de reb. ad eum pertin. Edit. Amstel. 1718. p. 200.

'*Angeli Politiani Poemata Latina, quibus, Notas cum historiâ
Latinæ poeseos à Petrarchæ ævo ad Politiani tempora deductâ,
et vitâ Politiani fusius quam antehac enarratâ, addidit* SAM.
JOHNSON.'[1]

It appears that his brother Nathanael had taken up his
father's trade; for it is mentioned that 'subscriptions are
taken in by the Editor, or N. Johnson, bookseller, of
Lichfield.' Notwithstanding the merit of Johnson, and the
cheap price at which this book was offered, there were not
subscribers enough to insure a sufficient sale; so the work
never appeared, and probably, never was executed.

We find him again this year at Birmingham, and there
is preserved the following letter from him to Mr. Edmund
Cave,[2] the original compiler and editor of the Gentleman's
Magazine:

'TO MR. CAVE

'SIR,   '*Nov.* 25, 1734

'As you appear no less sensible than your readers of
the defects of your poetical article, you will not be displeased, if, in order to the improvement of it, I communicate to you the sentiments of a person, who will undertake,
on reasonable terms, sometimes to fill a column.

'His opinion is, that the publick would not give you a
bad reception, if, beside the current wit of the month,
which a critical examination would generally reduce to a
narrow compass, you admitted not only poems, inscrip-
tions, &c. never printed before, which he will sometimes
supply you with; but likewise short literary dissertations
in Latin or English, critical remarks on authours ancient
or modern, forgotten poems that deserve revival, or loose
pieces, like Floyer's,[3] worth preserving. By this method,
your literary article, for so it might be called, will, he

---

[1] The book was to contain more than thirty sheets, the price to be two
shillings and sixpence at the time of subscribing, and two shillings and
sixpence at the delivery of a perfect book in quires.

[2] Miss Cave, the grand-niece of Mr. Edw. Cave, has obligingly shewn me
the originals of this and the other letters of Dr. Johnson, to him, which were
first published in the Gentleman's Magazine, with notes by Mr. John
Nichols, the worthy and indefatigable editor of that valuable miscellany,
signed N.; some of which I shall occasionally transcribe in the course of this
work.

[3] Sir John Floyer's Treatise on Cold Baths. Gent. Mag. 1734. p. 197.

thinks, be better recommended to the publick than by low jests, awkward buffoonery, or the dull scurrilities of either party.

'If such a correspondence will be agreeable to you, be pleased to inform me in two posts, what the conditions are on which you shall expect it. Your late offer[1] gives me no reason to distrust your generosity. If you engage in any literary projects besides this paper, I have other designs to impart, if I could be secure from having others reap the advantage of what I should hint.

'Your letter by being directed to *S. Smith*, to be left at the Castle in Birmingham, Warwickshire, will reach

'Your humble Servant'

Mr. Cave has put a note on this letter, 'Answered Dec. 2.' But whether any thing was done in consequence of it we are not informed.

Johnson had, from his early youth, been sensible to the influence of female charms. When at Stourbridge school, he was much enamoured of Olivia Lloyd, a young quaker, to whom he wrote a copy of verses, which I have not been able to recover;[2] but with what facility and elegance he

[1] A prize of fifty pounds for the best poem 'on Life, Death, Judgement, Heaven, and Hell.' See Gentleman's Magazine, vol iv. p. 560. NICHOLS.

[2] [He also wrote some amatory verses, before he left Staffordshire, which our author appears not to have seen. They were addressed 'to Miss Hickman, playing on the spinet.' At the back of this early poetical effusion, of which the original copy, in Johnson's hand-writing, was obligingly communicated to me by Mr. John Taylor, is the following attestation:

'Written by the late Dr. Samuel Johnson, on my mother, then Miss Hickman, playing on the Spinet. J. Turton.'

Dr. Turton, the physician, the writer of this certificate, who died in April, 1806, in his 71st year, was born in 1735. The verses in question therefore, which have been printed in some late editions of Johnson's poems, must have been written before that year.—Miss Hickman, it is believed, was a lady of Staffordshire.

The concluding lines of this early copy of verses have much of the vigour of Johnson's poetry in his maturer years:

'When old Timotheus struck the vocal string,
Ambitious fury fir'd the Grecian king:
Unbounded projects lab'ring in his mind,
He pants for room, in one poor world confin'd.
Thus wak'd to rage by musick's dreadful power,
He bids the sword destroy, the flame devour.

could warble the amorous lay, will appear from the following lines which he wrote for his friend Mr. Edmund Hector.

VERSES *to a* LADY, *on receiving from her a* SPRIG *of* MYRTLE

'What hopes, what terrours does thy gift create,
Ambiguous emblem of uncertain fate!
The myrtle, ensign of supreme command,
Consign'd by Venus to Melissa's hand;
Not less capricious than a reigning fair,
Now grants, and now rejects a lover's prayer.
In myrtle shades oft sings the happy swain,
In myrtle shades despairing ghosts complain:
The myrtle crowns the happy lovers' heads,
The unhappy lover's grave the myrtle spreads;
O then the meaning of thy gift impart,
And ease the throbbings of an anxious heart!
Soon must this bough, as you shall fix his doom,
Adorn Philander's head, or grace his tomb.'[1]

His juvenile attachments to the fair sex were, however, very transient: and it is certain, that he formed no criminal connection whatsoever. Mr. Hector, who lived with him

Had Stella's gentle touches mov'd the lyre,
Soon had the monarch felt a nobler fire;
No more delighted with disastrous war,
Ambitious only now to please the fair,
Resign'd his thirst of empire to her charms,
And found a thousand world's in Stella's arms.'
                                            MALONE.]

[1] Mrs. Piozzi gives the following account of this little composition from Dr. Johnson's own relation to her, on her inquiring whether it was rightly attributed to him.—'I think it is now just forty years ago, that a young fellow had a sprig of myrtle given him by a girl he courted, and asked me to write him some verses that he might present her in return. I promised, but forgot; and when he called for his lines at the time agreed on—Sit still a moment, (says I) dear Mund, and I'll fetch them thee—So stepped aside for five minutes, and wrote the nonsense you now keep such a stir about.' *Anecdotes*, p. 34.
    In my first edition I was induced to doubt the authenticity of this account, by the following circumstantial statement in a letter to me from Miss Seward, of Lichfield:—'I *know* those verses were addressed to Lucy Porter, when he was enamoured of her in his boyish days, two or three years before he had seen her mother, his future wife. He wrote them at my grandfather's,

in his younger days in the utmost intimacy and social freedom, has assured me, that even at that ardent season his conduct was strictly virtuous in that respect; and that though he loved to exhilarate himself with wine, he never knew him intoxicated but once.

In a man whom religious education has secured from licentious indulgences, the passion of love, when once it has seized him, is exceedingly strong; being unimpaired by dissipation, and totally concentrated in one object.

and gave them to Lucy in the presence of my mother, to whom he shewed them on the instant. She used to repeat them to me, when I asked her for *the Verses Dr. Johnson gave her on a Sprig of Myrtle, which he had stolen or begged from her bosom*. We all know honest Lucy Porter to have been incapable of the mean vanity of applying to herself a compliment not *intended* for her.' Such was this lady's statement, which I make no doubt she supposed to be correct; but it shews how dangerous it is to trust too implicitly to traditional testimony and ingenious inference; for Mr. Hector has lately assured me that Mrs. Piozzi's account is in this instance accurate, and that he was the person for whom Johnson wrote those verses, which have been erroneously ascribed to Mr. Hammond.

I am obliged in so many instances to notice Mrs. Piozzi's incorrectness of relation, that I gladly seize this opportunity of acknowledging, that however often, she is not always inaccurate.

The authour having been drawn into a controversy with Miss Anna Seward, in consequence of the preceding statement (which may be found in the Gentleman's Magazine, Vol. lxiii and lxiv,) received the following letter from Mr. Edmund Hector, on the subject:

'DEAR SIR,

'I am sorry to see you are engaged in altercation with a Lady, who seems unwilling to be convinced of her errors. Surely it would be more ingenuous to acknowledge than to persevere.

'Lately, in looking over some papers I meant to burn, I found the original manuscript of the myrtle, with the date on it, 1731, which I have inclosed.

'The true history (which I could swear to) is as follows: Mr. Morgan Graves, the elder brother of a worthy Clergyman near Bath, with whom I was acquainted, waited upon a Lady in this neighbourhood, who at parting presented him the branch. He shewed it me, and wished much to return the compliment in verse. I applied to Johnson, who was with me, and in about half an hour dictated the verses which I sent to my friend.

'I most solemnly declare, at that time, Johnson was an entire stranger to the Porter family; and it was almost two years after that I introduced him to the acquaintance of Porter, whom I bought my cloaths of.

'If you intend to convince this obstinate woman, and to exhibit to the publick the truth of your narrative, you are at liberty to make what use you please of this statement.

'I hope you will pardon me for taking up so much of your time. Wishing you *multos et felices annos*, I shall subscribe myself

'Your obliged humble servant,

'E. HECTOR'

'*Birmingham*,
Jan. 9th, 1794.'

This was experienced by Johnson, when he became the fervent admirer of Mrs. Porter, after her first husband's death.[1] Miss Porter told me, that when he was first introduced to her mother, his appearance was very forbidding: he was then lean and lank, so that his immense structure of bones was hideously striking to the eye, and the scars of the scrophula were deeply visible. He also wore his hair, which was straight and stiff, and separated behind: and he often had, seemingly, convulsive starts and odd gesticulations, which tended to excite at once surprise and ridicule. Mrs. Porter was so much engaged by his conversation that she overlooked all these external disadvantages, and said to her daughter, 'this is the most sensible man that I ever saw in my life.'

Though Mrs. Porter was double the age of Johnson,[2] and her person and manner, as described to me by the late Mr. Garrick, were by no means pleasing to others,[3] she must have had a superiority of understanding and talents,[4] as she certainly inspired him with a more than

[1] [It appears from Mr. Hector's letter, that Johnson became acquainted with her three years before he married her. MALONE.]

[2] [Mrs. Johnson's maiden name was Jervis.—Though there was a great disparity of years between her and Dr. Johnson, she was not quite so old as she is here represented, having only completed her forty-eighth year in the month of February preceding her marriage, as appears by the following extract from the parish-register of Great Peatling, in Leicestershire, which was obligingly made at my request, by the Hon. and Rev. Mr. Ryder, Rector of Lutterworth, in that county:

'Anno Dom. 1688-[-9] Elizabeth, the daughter of William Jervis, Esq. and Mrs. Anne his wife, born the fourth day of February and mané, baptized 16th day of the same month by Mr. Smith, Curate of Little Peatling.

'John Allen, Vicar'

The family of Jervis, Mr. Ryder informs me, once possessed nearly the whole lordship of Great Peatling (about 2000 acres,) and there are many monuments of them in the Church; but the estate is now much reduced. The present representative of this ancient family is Mr. Charles Jervis, of Hinckley, Attorney at Law. MALONE.]

[3] [That in Johnson's eyes she was handsome, appears from the epitaph which he caused to be inscribed on her tomb-stone not long before his own death, and which may be found in a subsequent page, under the year 1752. MALONE.]

[4] [The following account of Mrs. Johnson, and her family, is copied from a paper (chiefly relating to Mrs. Anna Williams) written by Lady Knight at Rome, and transmitted by her to the late John Hoole, Esq. the translator of Metastasio, &c. by whom it was inserted in the European Magazine for October 1799:

ordinary passion; and she having signified her willingness
to accept of his hand, he went to Lichfield to ask his
mother's consent to the marriage; which he could not but
be conscious was a very imprudent scheme, both on
account of their disparity of years, and her want of
fortune. But Mrs. Johnson knew too well the ardour of her
son's temper, and was too tender a parent to oppose his
inclinations.

I know not for what reason the marriage ceremony was
not performed at Birmingham; but a resolution was taken
that it should be at Derby, for which place the bride and
bridegroom set out on horseback, I suppose in very good
humour. But though Mr. Topham Beauclerk used archly

'Mrs. Williams's account of Mrs. Johnson was, that she had a good understanding, and great sensibility, but inclined to be satirical. Her first husband
died insolvent; her sons were much disgusted with her for her second
marriage, perhaps because they being struggling to get advanced in life,
were mortified to think she had allied herself to a man who had not any
visible means of being useful to them; however, she always retained her
affection for them. While they [Dr. and Mrs. Johnson] resided in Gough
Square, her son, the officer, knocked at the door, and asked the maid, if her
mistress was at home. She answered, "Yes, Sir; but she *is* sick in bed."
"O," says he, "if it's so, tell her that her son Jervis called to know how she
did;" and was going away. The maid begged she might run up to tell her
mistress, and without attending his answer, left him. Mrs. Johnson, enraptured
to hear her son was below, desired the maid to tell him she longed to
embrace him. When the maid descended, the gentleman was gone, and poor
Mrs. Johnson was much agitated by the adventure: it was the only time he
ever made an effort to see her. Dr. Johnson did all he could to console his
wife, but told Mrs. Williams, "Her son is uniformly undutiful; so I conclude,
like many other sober men, he might once in his life be drunk, and in that
fit nature got the better of his pride."'

The following anecdotes of Dr. Johnson are recorded by the same lady:

'One day that he came to my house to meet many others, we told him
that we had arranged our party to go to Westminster Abbey: would not he
go with us? "*No*," he replied, "*not while I can keep out.*"

'Upon our saying that the friends of a lady had been in great fear lest she
should make a certain match, he said, "We that are *his* friends have had
great fears for him."

'Dr. Johnson's political principles ran high, both in church and state:
he wished power to the King and to the Heads of the Church, as the laws
of England have established; but I know he disliked absolute power; and
I am very sure of his disapprobation of the doctrines of the church of Rome;
because about three weeks before we came abroad, he said to my Cornelia,
"you are going where the ostentatious pomp of church ceremonies attracts
the imagination; but if they want to persuade you to change, you must
remember, that by increasing your faith, you may be persuaded to become
Turk." If these were not the words, I have kept up to the express meaning.'
MALONE.]

to mention Johnson's having told him with much gravity, 'Sir, it was a love marriage on both sides,' I have had from my illustrious friend the following curious account of their journey to church upon the nuptial morn:—'Sir, she had read the old romances, and had got into her head the fantastical notion that a woman of spirit should use her lover like a dog. So, Sir, at first she told me that I rode too fast, and she could not keep up with me: and, when I rode a little slower, she passed me, and complained that I lagged behind. I was not to be made the slave of caprice; and I resolved to begin as I meant to end. I therefore pushed on briskly, till I was fairly out of her sight. The road lay between two hedges, so I was sure she could not miss it; and I contrived that she should soon come up with me. When she did, I observed her to be in tears.'

This, it must be allowed, was a singular beginning of connubial felicity; but there is no doubt that Johnson, though he thus shewed a manly firmness, proved a most affectionate and indulgent husband to the last moment of Mrs. Johnson's life: and in his 'Prayers and Meditations,' we find very remarkable evidence that his regard and fondness for her never ceased, even after her death.

He now set up a private academy, for which purpose he hired a large house, well situated near his native city. In the Gentleman's Magazine for 1736, there is the following advertisement: 'At Edial, near Lichfield, in Staffordshire, young gentlemen are boarded and taught the Latin and Greek languages, by SAMUEL JOHNSON.' But the only pupils that were put under his care were the celebrated David Garrick and his brother George, and a Mr. Offely, a young gentleman of good fortune who died early. As yet, his name had nothing of that celebrity which afterwards commanded the highest attention and respect of mankind. Had such an advertisement appeared after the publication of his LONDON, or his RAMBLER, or his DICTIONARY, how would it have burst upon the world! with what eagerness would the great and the wealthy have embraced an opportunity of putting their sons under the learned tuition of SAMUEL JOHNSON. The truth, however, is, that he was not so well qualified for being a teacher of elements, and a conductor in learning by

marginal line:
were put ... celebrated
David (H)

regular gradations, as men of inferiour powers of mind.
His own acquisitions had been made by fits and starts, by
violent irruptions into the regions of knowledge; and it
could not be expected that his impatience would be
subdued, and his impetuosity restrained, so as to fit him
for a quiet guide to novices. The art of communicating
instruction, of whatever kind, is much to be valued; and
I have ever thought that those who devote themselves to
this employment, and do their duty with diligence and
success, are entitled to very high respect from the com-
munity, as Johnson himself often maintained. Yet I am
of opinion, that the greatest abilities are not only not
required for this office, but render a man less fit for it.
    While we acknowledge the justness of Thomson's
beautiful remark,

marginal line:
violent irruptions . . .
and it (H)

queried:
While we acknowledge
etc. [H]

> 'Delightful task! to rear the tender thought,
> And teach the young idea how to shoot!'

we must consider that this delight is perceptible only by
'a mind at ease,' a mind at once calm and clear; but that
a mind gloomy and impetuous, like that of Johnson,
cannot be fixed for any length of time in minute attention,
and must be so frequently irritated by unavoidable slowness and errour in the advances of scholars, as to perform
the duty, with little pleasure to the teacher, and no great
advantage to the pupils. Good temper is a most essential
requisite in a preceptor. Horace paints the character
as *bland:*

> '—— *Ut pueris olim dant crustula* blandi
>   *Doctores, elementa velint ut discere prima.*'

    Johnson was not more satisfied with his situation as the
master of an academy, than with that of the usher of a
school; we need not wonder, therefore, that he did not
keep his academy above a year and a half. From Mr.
Garrick's account he did not appear to have been pro-
foundly reverenced by his pupils. His oddities of manner,
and uncouth gesticulations, could not but be the subject
or merriment to them; and in particular, the young rogues
used to listen at the door of his bed-chamber, and peep
through the key-hole, that they might turn into ridicule

his tumultuous and awkward fondness for Mrs. Johnson, whom he used to name by the familiar appellation of *Tetty* or *Tetsey*, which like *Betty* or *Betsey*, is provincially used as a contraction for *Elizabeth*, her christian name, but which to us seems ludicrous, when applied to a woman of her age and appearance. Mr. Garrick described her to me as very fat, with a bosom of more than ordinary protuberance, with swelled cheeks, of a florid red, produced by thick painting, and increased by the liberal use of cordials; flaring and fantastick in her dress, and affected both in her speech and her general behaviour. I have seen Garrick exhibit her, by his exquisite talent of mimickry, so as to excite the heartiest burst of laughter; but he, probably, as is the case in all such representations, considerably aggravated the picture.

That Johnson well knew the most proper course to be pursued in the instruction of youth, is authentically ascertained by the following paper in his own hand-writing, given about this period to a relation, and now in the possession of Mr. John Nichols:

'SCHEME *for the* CLASSES *of a* GRAMMAR SCHOOL

'When the introduction, or formation of nouns and verbs, is perfectly mastered, let them learn[a]

'Corderius by Mr. Clarke, beginning at the same time to translate out of the introduction, that by this means they may learn the syntax. Then let them proceed to

'Erasmus, with an English translation, by the same authour.

'Class II. Learns Eutropius and Cornelius Nepos, or Justin, with the translation.

'N.B. The first class gets for their part every morning the rules which they have learned before, and in the afternoon learns the Latin rules of the nouns and verbs.

'They are examined in the rules which they have learned, every Thursday and Saturday.

'The second class does the same whilst they are in Eutropius; afterwards their part is in the irregular nouns and verbs, and in the rules for making and scanning verses. They are examined as the first.

[a] *and this was the Method he took in teaching Lady Keith then Miss Thrale; & he offer'd, nay wish'd to teach Fanny Burney, now Madame D'Arblaye, at the same Time: but her Father did not approve.* [1]

'Class III. Ovid's Metamorphoses in the morning, and Cæsar's Commentaries in the afternoon.

'Practise in the Latin rules till they are perfect in them; afterwards in Mr. Leeds's Greek Grammar. Examined as before.

'Afterwards they proceed to Virgil, beginning at the same time to write themes and verses, and to learn Greek; from thence passing on to Horace, &c. as shall seem most proper.

'I know not well what books to direct you to, because you have not informed me what study you will apply yourself to. I believe it will be most for your advantage to apply yourself wholly to the languages, till you go to the university. The Greek authours I think it best for you to read are these:

'Cebes	
'Ælian	
'Lucian by Leeds	Attick
'Xenophon	
'Homer	Ionick
'Theocritus	Dorick
'Euripides	Attick and Dorick

'Thus you will be tolerably skilled in all the dialects, beginning with the Attick, to which the rest must be referred.

'In the study of Latin, it is proper not to read the latter authours, till you are well versed in those of the purest ages; as Terence, Tully, Cæsar, Sallust, Nepos, Velleius Paterculus, Virgil, Horace, Phædrus.

'The greatest and most necessary task still remains, to attain a habit of expression, without which knowledge is of little use. This is necessary in Latin, and more necessary in English; and can only be acquired by a daily imitation of the best and correctest authours.

'SAM. JOHNSON'

While Johnson kept his academy, there can be no doubt that he was insensibly furnishing his mind with various knowledge; but I have not discovered that he wrote any thing except a great part of his tragedy of IRENE.

Mr. Peter Garrick, the elder brother of David, told me that he remembered Johnson's borrowing the Turkish History of him, in order to form his play from it. When he had finished some part of it, he read what he had done to Mr. Walmsley, who objected to his having already brought his heroine into great distress, and asked him, 'how can you possibly contrive to plunge her into deeper calamity!'[a] Johnson, in sly allusion to the supposed oppressive proceedings of the court of which Mr. Walmsley was registrar, replied, 'Sir, I can put her into the Spiritual Court!'

Mr. Walmsley, however, was well pleased with this proof of Johnson's abilities as a dramatick writer, and advised him to finish the tragedy, and produce it on the stage.

Johnson now thought of trying his fortune in London, the great field of genius and exertion, where talents of every kind have the fullest scope, and the highest encouragement. It is a memorable circumstance that his pupil David Garrick went thither at the same time,[1] with intent to complete his education, and follow the profession of the law, from which he was soon diverted by his decided preference for the stage.

This joint expedition of those two eminent men to the metropolis, was many years afterwards noticed in an allegorical poem on Shakspeare's Mulberry-tree, by Mr. Lovibond, the ingenious authour of 'The Tears of Old-May-day.'

They were recommended to Mr. Colson,[2] an eminent

[a] no very wise Enquiry for so wise a Man— Irene suffers no Calamity till just at last, & suffers that by an Accidental Delay of some Messenger: as Johnson has managed it. Every Tragic heroine on our Stage suffers more than Irene & commonly deserves it less. [1]

[1] Both of them used to talk pleasantly of this their first journey to London. Garrick, evidently meaning to embellish a little, said one day in my hearing, 'we rode and tied.' And the Bishop of Killaloe, [Dr. Barnard,] informed me, that at another time, when Johnson and Garrick were dining together in a pretty large company, Johnson humorously ascertaining the chronology of something, expressed himself thus: 'that was the year when I came to London with two-pence half-penny in my pocket.' Garrick overhearing him, exclaimed, 'eh? what do you say? with two-pence half-penny in your pocket?'—JOHNSON, 'Why, yes; when I came with two-pence half-penny in *my* pocket, and thou, Davy, with three half-pence in thine.'

[2] [The Reverend John Colson was bred at Emmanuel College in Cambridge, and in 1728, when George the Second visited that University, was created Master of Arts. About that time he became First Master of the Free School at Rochester, founded by Sir Joseph Williamson. In 1739, he was appointed Lucasian Professor of Mathematics in the University of Cambridge, on the death of Professor Sanderson, and held that office till 1759, when he died. He published Lectures on Experimental Philosophy, translated from the French of l'Abbé Nodet, 8vo. 1732, and some other tracts.

mathematician and master of an academy, by the following letter from Mr. Walmsley:

'*To the Reverend Mr.* COLSON

'DEAR SIR,   'Lichfield, March 2, 1737

'I had the favour of yours, and am extremely obliged to you; but I cannot say I had a greater affection for you upon it than I had before, being long since so much endeared to you, as well by an early friendship, as by your many excellent and valuable qualifications; and, had I a son of my own, it would be my ambition, instead of sending him to the University, to dispose of him as this young gentleman is.

'He, and another neighbour of mine, one Mr. Samuel Johnson, set out this morning for London together. David Garrick is to be with you early the next week, and Mr. Johnson to try his fate with a tragedy, and to see to get himself employed in some translation, either from the Latin or the French. Johnson is a very good scholar and poet, and I have great hopes will turn out a fine tragedy-writer. If it should any way lie in your way, doubt not but you would be ready to recommend and assist your countryman.

'G. WALMSLEY'

How he employed himself upon his first coming to London is not particularly known.[1] I never heard that he found any protection or encouragement by the means of Mr. Colson, to whose academy David Garrick went. Mrs. Lucy Porter told me, that Mr. Walmsley gave him a letter of introduction to Lintot his bookseller, and that Johnson wrote some things for him; but I imagine this to

Our author, it is believed, was mistaken in stating him to have been Master of an Academy. Garrick, probably, during his short residence at Rochester, lived in his house as a private pupil.

The character of GELIDUS, the philosopher, in the Rambler, (No. 24) was meant to represent this gentleman. See Mrs. Piozzi's ANECDOTES, &c. p. 49. MALONE.]

[1] One curious anecdote was communicated by himself to Mr. John Nichols. Mr. Wilcox, the bookseller, on being informed by him that his intention was to get his livelihood as an authour, eyed his robust frame attentively, and with a significant look, said, 'You had better buy a porter's knot.' He however added, 'Wilcox was one of my best friends.'

marginal line:
you had . . . however
added [H]

be a mistake, for I have discovered no trace of it, and I am pretty sure he told me, that Mr. Cave was the first publisher by whom his pen was engaged in London.

He had a little money when he came to town, and he knew how he could live in the cheapest manner. His first lodgings were at the house of Mr. Norris, a staymaker, in Exeter-street, adjoining Catherine-street, in the Strand. 'I dined (said he) very well for eight-pence, with very good company, at the Pine-Apple in New-street, just by. Several of them had travelled. They expected to meet every day; but did not know one another's names. It used to cost the rest a shilling, for they drank wine; but I had a cut of meat for six-pence, and bread for a penny, and gave the waiter a penny; so that I was quite well served, nay, better than the rest, for they gave the waiter nothing.'

He at this time, I believe, abstained entirely from fermented liquors: a practice to which he rigidly conformed for many years together, at different periods of his life.

His OFELLUS in the *Art of Living in London*, I have heard him relate, was an Irish painter, whom he knew at Birmingham, and who had practised his own precepts of economy for several years in the British capital. He assured Johnson, who, I suppose, was then meditating to try his fortune in London, but was apprehensive of the expence, 'that thirty pounds a year was enough to enable a man to live there without being contemptible. He allowed ten pounds for cloaths and linen. He said a man might live in a garret at eighteen-pence a week; few people would inquire where he lodged: and if they did, it was easy to say, "Sir, I am to be found at such a place." By spending three-pence in a coffee-house, he might be for some hours every day in very good company; he might dine for six-pence, breakfast on bread and milk for a penny, and do without supper. On *clean-shirt-day* he went abroad, and paid visits.' I have heard him more than once talk of his frugal friend, whom he recollected with esteem and kindness, and did not like to have one smile at the recital. 'This man (said he, gravely) was a very sensible man, who perfectly understood common affairs: a man of a great deal of knowledge of the world, fresh from life, not strained through books. He borrowed a horse and ten pounds at Birmingham. Finding himself master of so much money, he set off for West Chester, in order to get to Ireland. He returned the horse, and probably the ten pounds too, after he got home.'

Considering Johnson's narrow circumstances in the early part of his life, and particularly at the interesting æra of his launching into the ocean of London, it is not to be wondered at, that an actual instance, proved by experience, of the possibility of enjoying the intellectual luxury of social life upon a very small income, should deeply engage his attention, and be ever recollected by him as a circumstance of much importance. He amused himself, I remember, by computing how much more expence was absolutely necessary to live upon the same scale with that which his friend described, when the value of money was diminished by the progress of commerce.[a] It may be estimated that double the money might now with difficulty be sufficient.

[a] *I never heard him mention the Friend, but he often amused his Mind with that sort of Talk.* [1]

Amidst this cold obscurity, there was one brilliant circumstance to cheer him; he was well acquainted with Mr. Henry Hervey,[1] one of the branches of the noble family of that name, who had been quartered at Lichfield as an officer of the army, and had at this time a house in London, where Johnson was frequently entertained, and had an opportunity of meeting genteel company. Not very long before his death, he mentioned this, among other particulars of his life, which he was kindly communicating to me; and he described this early friend 'Harry Hervey,' thus: 'He was a vicious man, but very kind to me. If you call a dog HERVEY, I shall love him.'

He told me he had now written only three acts of his IRENE, and that he retired for some time to lodgings at

---

[1] The Honourable Henry Hervey, third son of the first Earl of Bristol, quitted the army and took orders. He married a sister of Sir Thomas Aston, by whom he got the Aston Estate, and assumed the name and arms of that family. Vide Collins's Peerage.

[The Honourable Henry Hervey was nearly of the same age with Johnson, having been born about nine months before him, in the year 1709. He married Catharine, the sister of Sir Thomas Aston, in 1739; and as that lady had seven sisters, she probably succeeded to the Aston Estate on the death of her brother under his will.[b] Mr. Hervey took the degree of Master of Arts at Cambridge, at the late age of thirty-five, in 1744; about which time, it is believed, he entered into holy orders. MALONE.]

underlined:
her brother . . . his will
[1]

[b] *perhaps not, & I believe not. Eldest Daughters are made eldest Sons yet in Wales & were so in Cheshire ½ a Century ago.* [1]

Greenwich, where he proceeded in it somewhat further, and used to compose, walking in the Park; but did not stay long enough at that place to finish it.

At this period we find the following letter from him to Mr. Edward Cave, which, as a link in the chain of his literary history, it is proper to insert:

'TO MR. CAVE

'Greenwich, next door to the Golden Heart,
Church-street, July 12, 1737

'SIR,

'HAVING observed in your papers very uncommon offers of encouragement to men of letters, I have chosen, being a stranger in London, to communicate to you the following design, which, I hope, if you join in it, will be of advantage to both of us.

'The History of the Council of Trent having been lately translated into French, and published with large Notes by Dr. Le Courayer, the reputation of that book is so much revived in England, that, it is presumed, a new translation of it from the Italian, together with Le Courayer's Notes from the French, could not fail of a favourable reception.

'If it be answered, that the History is already in English, it must be remembered, that there was the same objection against Le Courayer's undertaking, with this disadvantage, that the French had a version by one of their best translators, whereas you cannot read three pages of the English History without discovering that the style is capable of great improvements; but whether those improvements are to be expected from this attempt, you must judge from the specimen, which, if you approve the proposal, I shall submit to your examination.

'Suppose the merit of the versions equal, we may hope that the addition of the Notes will turn the balance in our favour, considering the reputation of the Annotator.

'Be pleased to favour me with a speedy answer, if you are not willing to engage in this scheme; and appoint me a day to wait upon you, if you are.

'I am, Sir,
'Your humble servant,
'SAM. JOHNSON'

It should seem from this letter, though subscribed with his own name, that he had not yet been introduced to Mr. Cave. We shall presently see what was done in consequence of the proposal which it contains.

In the course of the summer he returned to Lichfield, where he had left Mrs. Johnson, and there he at last finished his tragedy, which was not executed with his rapidity of composition upon other occasions, but was slowly and painfully elaborated. A few days before his death, while burning a great mass of papers, he picked out from among them the original unformed sketch of this tragedy, in his own hand-writing, and gave it to Mr. Langton, by whose favour a copy of it is now in my possession. It contains fragments of the intended plot, and speeches for the different persons of the drama, partly in the raw materials of prose, partly worked up into verse; as also a variety of hints for illustration, borrowed from the Greek, Roman, and modern writers. The hand-writing is very difficult to be read, even by those who were best acquainted with Johnson's mode of penmanship, which at all times was very particular. The King having graciously accepted of this manuscript as a literary curiosity, Mr. Langton made a fair and distinct copy of it, which he ordered to be bound up with the original and the printed tragedy; and the volume is deposited in the King's library. His Majesty was pleased to permit Mr. Langton to take a copy of it for himself.

The whole of it is rich in thought and imagery, and happy expressions; and of the *disjecta membra* scattered throughout, and as yet unarranged, a good dramatic poet might avail himself with considerable advantage. I shall give my readers some specimens of different kinds, distinguishing them by the Italick character.

> '*Nor think to say here will I stop,*
> *Here will I fix the limits of transgression,*
> *Nor farther tempt the avenging rage of heaven.*
> *When guilt like this once harbours in the breast,*
> *Those holy beings, whose unseen direction*
> *Guides through the maze of life the steps of man,*
> *Fly the detested mansions of impiety,*
> *And quit their charge to horrour and to ruin.*'

A small part only of this interesting admonition is preserved in the play, and is varied, I think, not to advantage:

'The soul once tainted with so foul a crime,
No more shall glow with friendship's hallow'd ardour,
Those holy beings whose superior care
Guides erring mortals to the paths of virtue,
Affrighted at impiety like thine,
Resign their charge to baseness and to ruin.'

'I feel the soft infection
Flush in my cheek, and wander in my veins.
Teach me the Grecian arts of soft persuasion.'

'Sure this is love, which heretofore I conceived the dream of idle
maids, and wanton poets.'

'Though no comets or prodigies foretold the ruin of Greece,
signs which heaven must by another miracle enable us to understand,
yet might it be foreshewn, by tokens no less certain, by the vices
which always bring it on.'

This last passage is worked up in the tragedy itself, as
follows:

LEONTIUS

'——————That power that kindly spreads
The clouds, a signal of impending showers,
To warn the wand'ring linnet to the shade,
Beheld, without concern, expiring Greece,
And not one prodigy foretold our fate.

DEMETRIUS

'A thousand horrid prodigies foretold it;
A feeble government, eluded laws,
A factious populace, luxurious nobles,
And all the maladies of sinking States.
When public villainy, too strong for justice,
Shews his bold front, the harbinger of ruin,
Can brave Leontius call for airy wonders,
Which cheats interpret, and which fools regard?
When some neglected fabrick nods beneath
The weight of years, and totters to the tempest,
Must heaven despatch the messengers of light,
Or wake the dead, to warn us of its fall?'

MAHOMET (to IRENE). '*I have tried thee, and joy to find that thou deservest to be loved by Mahomet,—with a mind great as his own. Sure, thou art an errour of nature, and an exception to the rest of thy sex, and art immortal; for sentiments like thine were never to sink into nothing. I thought all the thoughts of the fair had been to select the graces of the day, dispose the colours of the flaunting (flowing) robe, tune the voice and roll the eye, place the gem, choose the dress, and add new roses to the fading cheek, but—sparkling.*'

Thus in the tragedy:

'Illustrious maid, new wonders fix me thine;
   Thy soul completes the triumphs of thy face;
   I thought, forgive my fair, the noblest aim,
   The strongest effort of a female soul
   Was but to choose the graces of the day,
   To tune the tongue, to teach the eyes to roll,
   Dispose the colours of the flowing robe,
   And add new roses to the faded cheek.'

I shall select one other passage, on account of the doctrine which it illustrates. IRENE observes, '*that the Supreme Being will accept of virtue, whatever outward circumstances it may be accompanied with, and may be delighted with varieties of worship:* but is answered; *That variety cannot affect that Being, who, infinitely happy in his own perfections, wants no external gratifications; nor can infinite truth be delighted with falsehood; that though he may guide or pity those he leaves in darkness, he abandons those who shut their eyes against the beams of day.*'

Johnson's residence at Lichfield, on his return to it at this time, was only for three months; and as he had as yet seen but a small part of the wonders of the Metropolis, he had little to tell his townsmen. He related to me the following minute anecdote of this period: 'In the last age, when my mother lived in London, there were two sets of people, those who gave the wall, and those who took it: the peaceable and the quarrelsome. When I returned to Lichfield, after having been in London, my mother asked me, whether I was one of those who gave the wall, or those who took it. *Now* it is fixed that every man keeps to the right; or, if one is taking the wall, another yields it; and it is never a dispute.'[1]

He now removed to London with Mrs. Johnson; but her daughter, who had lived with them at Edial, was left with her relations in the country. His lodgings were for some time in Woodstock-street, near Hanover-square, and afterwards in Castle-street, near Cavendish-square. As there is something pleasingly interesting, to many, in tracing so great a man through all his different habitations, I shall, before this work is concluded, present my readers with an exact list of his lodgings and houses, in order of time, which, in placid condescension to my respectful curiosity, he one evening dictated to me, but without specifying how long he lived at each. In the progress of his life I shall have occasion to mention some of them as connected with particular incidents, or with the writing of particular parts of his works. To some, this minute attention may appear trifling; but when we consider the punctilious exactness with which the different houses in which Milton resided have been traced by the writers of his life, a similar enthusiasm may be pardoned in the biographer of Johnson.

His tragedy being by this time, as he thought, completely finished and fit for the stage, he was very desirous that it should be brought forward. Mr. Peter Garrick told me, that Johnson and he went together to the Fountain tavern, and read it over, and that he afterwards solicited Mr. Fleetwood, the patentee of Drury-lane theatre, to have it acted at his house; but Mr. Fleetwood would not accept it, probably because it was not patronized by some man of high rank; and it was not acted till 1749, when his friend David Garrick was manager of that theatre.

THE GENTLEMAN'S MAGAZINE, begun and carried on by Mr. Edward Cave, under the name of SYLVANUS URBAN, had attracted the notice and esteem of Johnson, in an eminent degree, before he came to London as an adventurer in literature. He told me, that when he first saw St. John's Gate, the place where that deservedly popular miscellany was originally printed, he 'beheld it with reverence.' I suppose, indeed, that every young

marginal line:
lodgings were . . .
Castle-street [H]

[1] Journal of a Tour to the Hebrides, 3d edit. p. 232.

authour has had the same kind of feeling for the magazine
or periodical publication which has first entertained him,
and in which he has first had an opportunity to see himself
in print, without the risk of exposing his name. I myself
recollect such impressions from 'THE SCOTS MAGA-
ZINE,' which was begun at Edinburgh in the year 1739,
and has been ever conducted with judgement, accuracy,
and propriety. I yet cannot help thinking of it with an
affectionate regard. Johnson has dignified the Gentleman's
Magazine, by the importance with which he invests the
life of Cave; but he has given it still greater lustre by the
various admirable Essays which he wrote for it.

Though Johnson was often solicited by his friends to
make a complete list of his writings, and talked of doing
it, I believe with a serious intention that they should all
be collected on his own account, he put it off from year to
year, and at last died without having done it perfectly. I
have one in his own hand-writing, which contains a certain
number; I indeed doubt if he could have remembered
every one of them, as they were so numerous, so various,
and scattered in such a multiplicity of unconnected publications; nay, several of them published under the names
of other persons, to whom he liberally contributed from
the abundance of his mind. We must, therefore, be content
to discover them, partly from occasional information given
by him to his friends, and partly from internal evidence.[1]

His first performance in the Gentleman's Magazine,
which for many years was his principal source for employment and support, was a copy of Latin verses, in March
1738, addressed to the editor in so happy a style of compliment, that Cave must have been destitute both of taste
and sensibility, had he not felt himself highly gratified.

marginal line:
*His first . . . Gentle-
man's Magazine* [H]

Ad URBANUM*

URBANE, *nullis fesse laboribus,*
URBANE, *nullis victe calumniis,*
Cui fronte sertum in eruditâ
Perpetuò viret et virebit;

[1] While in the course of my narrative I enumerate his writings, I shall take
care that my readers shall not be left to waver in doubt, between certainty
and conjecture, with regard to their authenticity; and, for that purpose, shall

Quid moliatur gens imitantium,
Quid et minetur, solicitus parùm,
Vacare solis perge Musis,
Juxta animo studiisque felix.

Linguæ procacis plumbea spicula,
Fidens, superbo frange silentio;
Victrix per obstantes catervas
Sedulitas animosa tendet.

Intende nervos, fortis, inanibus
Risurus olim nisibus æmuli
Intende jam nervos, habebis
Participes operæ Camœnas.

Non ulla Musis pagina gratior,
Quam quæ severis ludicra jungere
Novit, fatigatamque nugis
Utilibus recreare mentem.

Texente Nymphis serta Lycoride,
Rosæ ruborem sic viola adjuvat
Immista, sic Iris refulget
Æthereis variata fucis.[1]   S. J.

It appears that he was now enlisted by Mr. Cave as a regular coadjutor in his magazine, by which he probably obtained a tolerable livelihood. At what time, or by what

mark with an *asterisk* (*) those which he acknowledged to his friends, and with a *dagger* (†) those which are ascertained to be his by internal evidence. When any other pieces are ascribed to him, I shall give my reasons.

[1] A translation of this Ode, by an unknown correspondent, appeared in the Magazine for the month of May following:

'Hail URBAN! indefatigable man,
Unwearied yet by all thy useful toil!
Whom num'rous slanderers assault in vain;
Whom no base calumny can put to foil.
But still the laurel on thy learned brow
Flourishes fair, and shall for ever grow.

'What mean the servile imitating crew,
What their vain blust'ring, and their empty noise,
Ne'er seek: but still thy noble ends pursue,
Unconquer'd by the rabble's venal voice,
Still to the Muse thy studious mind apply,
Happy in temper, as in industry.

means, he had acquired a competent knowledge both of French and Italian, I do not know; but he was so well skilled in them, as to be sufficiently qualified for a translator. That part of his labour which consisted in emendation and improvement of the productions of other contributors, like that employed in levelling ground, can be perceived only by those who had an opportunity of comparing the original with the altered copy. What we certainly know to have been done by him in this way, was the Debates in both houses of Parliament, under the name of 'The Senate of Lilliput,' sometimes with feigned denominations of the several speakers, sometimes with denominations formed of the letters of their real names, in the manner of what is called anagram, so that they might easily be decyphered. Parliament then kept the press in a kind of mysterious awe, which made it necessary to have recourse to such devices. In our time it has acquired an unrestrained freedom, so that the people in all parts of the kingdom have a fair, open, and exact report of the actual proceedings

'The senseless sneerings of an haughty tongue,
Unworthy thy attention to engage,
    Unheeded pass: and tho' they mean thee wrong,
By manly silence disappoint their rage.
    Assiduous diligence confounds its foes,
    Resistless, tho' malicious crowds oppose.

'Exert thy powers, nor slacken in the course,
Thy spotless fame shall quash all false reports:
    Exert thy powers, nor fear a rival's force,
But thou shalt smile at all his vain efforts;
    Thy labours shall be crown'd with large success;
    The Muse's aid thy Magazine shall bless.

'No page more grateful to th' harmonious nine
Than that wherein thy labours we survey;
    Where solemn themes in fuller splendour shine,
(Delightful mixture,) blended with the gay,
    Where in improving, various joys we find,
    A welcome respite to the wearied mind.

'Thus when the nymphs in some fair verdant mead,
Of various flow'rs a beauteous wreath compose,
    The lovely violet's azure-painted head
Adds lustre to the crimson-blushing rose.
    Thus splendid Iris, with her varied dye,
    Shines in the æther, and adorns the sky.'

                                    'BRITON'

of their representatives and legislators, which in our constitution is highly to be valued; though, unquestionably,
there has of late been too much reason to complain of the
petulance with which obscure scribblers have presumed
to treat men of the most respectable character and
situation.

This important article of the Gentleman's Magazine
was, for several years, executed by Mr. William Guthrie,
a man who deserves to be respectably recorded in the
literary annals of this country. He was descended of an
ancient family in Scotland; but having a small patrimony,
and being an adherent of the unfortunate house of Stuart,
he could not accept of any office in the state; he therefore
came to London, and employed his talents and learning
as an 'Authour by profession.' His writings in history,
criticism, and politicks, had considerable merit.[1] He was
the first English historian who had recourse to that
authentick source of information, the Parliamentary
Journals; and such was the power of his political pen, that,
at an early period, Government thought it worth their
while to keep it quiet by a pension, which he enjoyed till
his death. Johnson esteemed him enough to wish that his
life should be written. The debates in Parliament, which
were brought home and digested by Guthrie, whose
memory, though surpassed by others who have since
followed him in the same department, was yet very quick
and tenacious, were sent by Cave to Johnson for his
revision; and, after some time, when Guthrie had attained
to greater variety of employment, and the speeches were
more and more enriched by the accession of Johnson's
genius, it was resolved that he should do the whole himself,
from the scanty notes furnished by persons employed to
attend in both houses of Parliament. Sometimes, however,
as he himself told me, he had nothing more communicated
to him than the names of the several speakers, and the
part which they had taken in the debate.

Thus was Johnson employed during some of the best

[1] How much poetry he wrote, I know not; but he informed me that he
was the authour of the beautiful little piece, 'The Eagle and Robin Red-
breast,' in the collection of poems entitled. 'THE UNION,' though it is
there said to be written by Archibald Scott, before the year 1600.

years of his life, as a mere literary labourer 'for gain, not glory,' solely to obtain an honest support. He however indulged himself in occasional little sallies, which the French so happily express by the term *jeux d'esprit*, and which will be noticed in their order, in the progress of this work.

But what first displayed his transcendent powers, and 'gave the world assurance of the MAN,' was his 'LONDON, a Poem, in Imitation of the Third Satire of Juvenal,' which came out in May this year, and burst forth with a splendour, the rays of which will for ever encircle his name. Boileau had imitated the same satire with great success, applying it to Paris: but an attentive comparison will satisfy every reader, that he is much excelled by the English Juvenal. Oldham had also imitated it, and applied it to London: all which performances concur to prove, that great cities, in every age, and in every country, will furnish similar topicks of satire. Whether Johnson had previously read Oldham's imitation, I do not know; but it is not a little remarkable, that there is scarcely any coincidence found between the two performances, though upon the very same subject. The only instances are, in describing London as the *sink* of foreign worthlessness:

'———— the *common shore*,
  Where France does all her filth and ordure pour.'
                                        OLDHAM

  'The *common shore* of Paris and of Rome.'
                                        JOHNSON

and,

  'No calling or profession comes amiss,
  A *needy monsieur* can be what he please.'
                                        OLDHAM

  'All sciences a *fasting monsieur* knows.'
                                        JOHNSON

The particulars which Oldham has collected, both as exhibiting the horrours of London, and of the times,

contrasted with better days, are different from those óf
Johnson, and in general well chosen, and well exprest.[1]

There are, in Oldham's imitation, many prosaick verses
and bad rhymes, and his poem sets out with a strange
inadvertent blunder:

> 'Tho' much concern'd to *leave* my dear old friend,
> I must, however, *his* design commend
> Of fixing in the country——.'

It is plain he was not going to leave his *friend;* his friend
was going to leave *him.* A young lady at once corrected
this with good critical sagacity, to

> 'Tho' much concern'd to *lose* my dear old friend.'

There is one passage in the original, better transfused by
Oldham than by Johnson:

ᵃ *Oh so true!* [H]

> '*Nil habet infelix paupertas durius in se,*
> *Quàm quod ridiculos homines facit.*'ᵃ

which is an exquisite remark on the galling meanness and
contempt annexed to poverty: JOHNSON's imitation is,

> 'Of all the griefs that harass the distrest,
> Sure the most bitter is a scornful jest.'

OLDHAM's, though less elegant, is more just:

> 'Nothing in poverty so ill is borne,
> As its exposing men to grinning scorn.'

Where, or in what manner this poem was composed, I
am sorry that I neglected to ascertain with precision, from
Johnson's own authority. He has marked upon his corrected
copy of the first edition of it, 'Written in 1738;' and, as it

marginal line:
of it . . . evident that
[H]

[1] I own it pleased me to find amongst them one trait of the manners of
the age in London, in the last century, to shield from the sneer of English
ridicule, what was some time ago too common a practice in my native city
of Edinburgh!

> 'If what I've said can't from the town affright,
> Consider other *dangers of the night;*
> When brickbats are from upper stories thrown,
> And *emptied chamber pots come pouring down*
> *From garret windows.*'

was published in the month of May in that year, it is evident that much time was not employed in preparing it for the press. The history of its publication I am enabled to give in a very satisfactory manner; and judging from myself, and many of my friends, I trust that it will not be uninteresting to my readers.

We may be certain, though it is not expressly named in the following letters to Mr. Cave, in 1738, that they all relate to it:

'TO MR. CAVE

'Castle-street, Wednesday Morning.
'SIR,   [No date. 1738]

'WHEN I took the liberty of writing to you a few days ago, I did not expect a repetition of the same pleasure so soon; for a pleasure I shall always think it, to converse in any manner with an ingenious and candid man; but having the inclosed poem in my hands to dispose of for the benefit of the authour, (of whose abilities I shall say nothing, since I send you his performance,) I believed I could not procure more advantageous terms from any person than from you, who have so much distinguished yourself by your generous encouragement of poetry; and whose judgement of that art nothing but your commen- dation of my trifle[1] can give me any occasion to call in question. I do not doubt but you will look over this poem with another eye, and reward it in a different manner from a mercenary bookseller, who counts the lines he is to purchase, and considers nothing but the bulk. I cannot help taking notice, that besides what the authour may hope for on account of his abilities, he has likewise another claim to your regard, as he lies at present under very disadvantageous circumstances of fortune. I beg, therefore, that you will favour me with a letter to-morrow, that I may know what you can afford to allow him, that he may either part with it to you, or find out, (which I do not expect,) some other way more to his satisfaction.

'I have only to add, that as I am sensible I have tran- scribed it very coarsely, which, after having altered it, I was obliged to do, I will, if you please to transmit the

---

[1] [His Ode 'Ad Urbanum,' probably. NICHOLS.]

sheets from the press, correct it for you; and take the trouble
of altering any stroke of satire which you may dislike.

'By exerting on this occasion your usual generosity,
you will not only encourage learning, and relieve distress,
but (though it be in comparison of the other motives of
very small account) oblige in a very sensible manner, Sir,

'Your very humble Servant,

'SAM. JOHNSON'

'TO MR. CAVE

'SIR,   'Monday, No. 6, Castle-street

'I AM to return you thanks for the present you were
so kind as to send by me, and to intreat that you will be
pleased to inform me by the penny-post whether you
resolve to print the poem. If you please to send it me by
the post, with a note to Dodsley, I will go and read the
lines to him, that we may have his consent to put his name
in the title-page. As to the printing, if it can be set immediately about, I will be so much the authour's friend,
as not to content myself with mere solicitations in his
favour. I propose, if my calculation be near the truth, to
engage for the reimbursement of all that you shall lose
by an impression of 500; provided, as you very generously
propose, that the profit, if any, be set aside for the authour's
use, excepting the present you made, which, if he be a
gainer, it is fit he should repay. I beg that you will let one
of your servants write an exact account of the expence of
such an impression, and send it with the poem, that I may
know what I engage for. I am very sensible, from your
generosity on this occasion, of your regard to learning,
even in its unhappiest state; and cannot but think such a
temper deserving of the gratitude of those who suffer so
often from a contrary disposition. I am, Sir,

'Your most humble Servant,

'SAM. JOHNSON'

'TO MR. CAVE

'SIR,   [No date]

'I WAITED on you to take the copy to Dodsley's: as
I remember the number of lines which it contains, it will

be no longer than EUGENIO,[1] with the quotations, which must be subjoined at the bottom of the page; part of the beauty of the performance (if any beauty be allowed it) consisting in adapting Juvenal's sentiments to modern facts and persons. It will, with those additions, very conveniently make five sheets. And since the expence will be no more, I shall contentedly insure it, as I mentioned in my last. If it be not therefore gone to Dodsley's, I beg it may be sent me by the penny-post, that I may have it in the evening. I have composed a Greek Epigram to Eliza,[2] and think she ought to be celebrated in as many different languages as Lewis le Grand. Pray send me word when you will begin upon the poem, for it is a long way to walk. I would leave my Epigram, but have not daylight to transcribe it. I am, Sir,

'Your's, &c.

'SAM. JOHNSON'

'TO MR. CAVE

'SIR,   [*No date*]

'I am extremely obliged by your kind letter, and will not fail to attend you to-morrow with IRENE, who looks upon you as one of her best friends.

'I was to-day with Mr. Dodsley, who declares very warmly in favour of the paper you sent him, which he desires to have a share in, it being, as he says, *a creditable thing to be concerned in.* I knew not what answer to make till I had consulted you, nor what to demand on the authour's part, but am very willing that, if you please, he should have a part in it, as he will undoubtedly be more diligent to disperse and promote it. If you can send me word to-morrow what I shall say to him, I will settle matters, and bring the poem with me for the press, which, as the town empties, we cannot be too quick with. I am, Sir,

'Your's, &c.

'SAM. JOHNSON'

[1] A poem, published in 1737, of which see an account in vol. ii. under April 30, 1773.

[2] [The learned Mrs. Elizabeth Carter. This lady, of whom frequent mention will be found in these Memoirs, was daughter of Nicholas Carter, D.D. She died in Clarges-street, Feb. 19, 1806, in her eighty-ninth year. MALONE.]

To us who have long known the manly force, bold spirit, and masterly versification of this poem, it is a matter of curiosity to observe the diffidence with which its authour brought it forward into publick notice, while he is so cautious as not to avow it to be his own production; and with what humility he offers to allow the printer to 'alter any stroke of satire which he might dislike.' That any such alteration was made, we do not know. If we did, we could not but feel an indignant regret; but how painful is it to see that a writer of such vigorous powers of mind was actually in such distress, that the small profit which so short a poem, however excellent, could yield, was courted as a 'relief.'

It has been generally said, I know not with what truth, that Johnson offered his 'London' to several booksellers, none of whom would purchase it. To this circumstance Mr. Derrick alludes in the following lines of his 'FORTUNE, A RHAPSODY:'

> 'Will no kind patron JOHNSON own?
> Shall JOHNSON friendless range the town?
> And every publisher refuse
> The offspring of his happy Muse?'

But we have seen that the worthy, modest, and ingenious Mr. Robert Dodsley, had taste enough to perceive its uncommon merit, and thought it creditable to have a share in it. The fact is, that, at a future conference, he bargained for the whole property of it, for which he gave Johnson ten guineas; who told me, 'I might perhaps have accepted of less; but that Paul Whitehead had a little before got ten guineas for a poem; and I would not take less than Paul Whitehead.'

marginal line: property of . . . ten guineas [H]

I may here observe, that Johnson appeared to me to undervalue Paul Whitehead upon every occasion when he was mentioned, and, in my opinion, did not do him justice; but when it is considered that Paul Whitehead was a member of a riotous and profane club, we may account for Johnson's having a prejudice against him. Paul Whitehead was, indeed, unfortunate in being not only slighted

by Johnson, but violently attacked by Churchill, who
utters the following imprecation:

> 'May I (can worse disgrace on manhood fall?)
> Be born a Whitehead, and baptized a Paul!'

yet I shall never be persuaded to think meanly of the
authour of so brilliant and pointed a satire as 'MANNERS.'

Johnson's 'London' was published in May, 1738;[1] and
it is remarkable, that it came out on the same morning
with Pope's satire, entitled '1738;' so that England had
at once its Juvenal and Horace as poetical monitors. The
Reverend Dr. Douglas, now Bishop of Salisbury, to whom
I am indebted for some obliging communications, was
then a student at Oxford, and remembers well the effect
which 'London' produced. Every body was delighted
with it; and there being no name to it, the first buz of the
literary circles was, 'here is an unknown poet, greater
even than Pope.' And it is recorded in the Gentleman's
Magazine of that year,[2] that it 'got to the second edition
in the course of a week.'

One of the warmest patrons of this poem on its first
appearance was General OGLETHORPE, whose 'strong
benevolence of soul' was unabated during the course of a
very long life; though it is painful to think, that he had
but too much reason to become cold and callous, and
discontented with the world, from the neglect which he
experienced of his publick and private worth, by those in
whose power it was to gratify so gallant a veteran with

---

[1] Sir John Hawkins, p. 86, tells us, 'The event is *antedated*, in the poem of
"London;" but in every particular, except the difference of a year, what is
there said of the departure of Thales, must be understood of Savage, and
looked upon as *true history*.' This conjecture is, I believe, entirely groundless.
I have been assured that Johnson said he was not so much as acquainted
with Savage, when he wrote his 'London.' If the departure mentioned in
it was the departure of Savage, the event was not *antedated* but *foreseen;* for
'London' was published in May, 1738, and Savage did not set out for
Wales till July, 1739. However well Johnson could defend the credibility
of *second sight*, he did not pretend that he himself was possessed of that
faculty.

[The assertion that Johnson was not even acquainted with Savage, when
he published his 'LONDON,' may be doubtful. Johnson took leave of Savage
when he went to Wales in 1739, and must have been acquainted with him
before that period.[a] See his Life of Savage. A. CHALMERS.]

[2] Page 269.

[a] *I thought we were all
convinced that Thales
was Savage* [1]

marks of distinction. This extraordinary person was as remarkable for his learning and taste, as for his other eminent qualities; and no man was more prompt, active, and generous, in encouraging merit. I have heard Johnson gratefully acknowledge, in his presence, the kind and effectual support which he gave to his 'London,' though unacquainted with its authour.

POPE, who then filled the poetical throne without a rival, it may reasonably be presumed, must have been particularly struck by the sudden appearance of such a poet; and, to his credit, let it be remembered, that his feelings and conduct on the occasion were candid and liberal. He requested Mr. Richardson, son of the painter, to endeavour to find out who this new authour was. Mr. Richardson, after some inquiry, having informed him that he had discovered only that his name was Johnson, and that he was some obscure man, Pope said, 'He will soon be *deterré*.'[1] We shall presently see, from a note written by Pope,[2] that he was himself afterwards more successful in his inquiries than his friend.

That in this justly celebrated poem may be found a few rhymes which the critical precision of English prosody at this day would disallow, cannot be denied; but with this small imperfection, which in the general blaze of its excellence is not perceived, till the mind has subsided into cool attention, it is, undoubtedly, one of the noblest productions in our language both for sentiment and expression. The nation was then in that ferment against the Court and the Ministry, which some years after ended in the downfall of Sir Robert Walpole; and as it has been said, that Tories are Whigs when out of place; and Whigs Tories when in place; so, as a Whig Administration ruled with what force it could, a Tory Opposition had all the animation and all the eloquence of resistance to power, aided by the common topicks of patriotism, liberty, and independence! Accordingly, we find in Johnson's 'London' the most spirited invectives against tyranny and oppression, the warmest predilection for his own country, and the purest love of virtue; interspersed with traits of his

[1] Sir Joshua Reynolds, from the information of the younger Richardson.
[2] [See p. 90. MALONE.]

own particular character and situation, not omitting his
prejudices as a 'true-born Englishman,'[1] not only against
foreign countries, but against Ireland and Scotland. On
some of these topicks I shall quote a few passages:

> 'The cheated nation's happy fav'rites see;
> Mark whom the great caress, who frown on me.'

> 'Has heaven reserv'd, in pity to the poor,
> No pathless waste, or undiscover'd shore?
> No secret island in the boundless main?
> No peaceful desart yet unclaim'd by Spain?
> Quick let us rise, the happy seats explore,
> And bear Oppression's insolence no more.'

> 'How, when competitors like these contend,
> Can *surly Virtue* hope to find a friend?'

> 'This mournful truth is every where confess'd,
> SLOW RISES WORTH, BY POVERTY DEPRESS'D!'

We may easily conceive with what feeling a great mind
like his, cramped and galled by narrow circumstances,
uttered this last line, which he marked by capitals. The
whole of the poem is eminently excellent, and there are
in it such proofs of a knowledge of the world, and of a
mature acquaintance with life, as cannot be contemplated
without wonder, when we consider that he was then only
in his twenty-ninth year, and had yet been so little in the
'busy haunts of men.'

marginal line:
when we . . . twenty-ninth [H]

Yet, while we admire the poetical excellence of this
poem, candour obliges us to allow, that the flame of
patriotism and zeal for popular resistance with which it
is fraught, had no just cause. There was, in truth, *no*
'oppression;' the 'nation' was *not* 'cheated.' Sir Robert
Walpole was a wise and a benevolent minister, who
thought that the happiness and prosperity of a commercial
country like ours, would be best promoted by peace,
which he accordingly maintained with credit, during a

underlined:
ought [H]

[1] It is, however, remarkable, that he uses the epithet, which undoubtedly,
since the union between England and Scotland, ought to denominate the
natives of both parts of our island.

> 'Was early taught a BRITON's rights to prize.'

marginal line:
ought to . . . our
island [H]

very long period. Johnson himself afterwards honestly acknowledged the merit of Walpole, whom he called 'a fixed star;' while he characterised his opponent, Pitt, as a 'meteor.' But Johnson's juvenile poem was naturally impregnated with the fire of opposition, and upon every account was universally admired.

Though thus elevated into fame, and conscious of uncommon powers, he had not that bustling confidence, or I may rather say, that animated ambition, which one might have supposed would have urged him to endeavour at rising in life. But such was his inflexible dignity of character, that he could not stoop to court the great; without which, hardly any man has made his way to a high station. He could not expect to produce many such works as his 'LONDON,' and he felt the hardships of writing for bread; he was, therefore, willing to resume the office of a schoolmaster, so as to have a sure, though moderate income for his life; and an offer being made to him of the mastership of a school,[1] provided he could

---

[1] In a billet written by Mr. Pope in the following year, this school is said to have been in *Shropshire;* but as it appears from a letter from Earl Gower, that the trustees of it were 'some worthy gentlemen in Johnson's neighbour-hood,' I in my first edition suggested that Pope must have, by mistake, written Shropshire, instead of Staffordshire. But I have since been obliged to Mr. Spearing, attorney-at-law, for the following information:—'William Adams, formerly citizen and haberdasher of London, founded a school at Newport, in the county of Salop, by deed dated 27th November, 1656, by which he granted the "yearly sum of *sixty pounds* to such able and learned schoolmaster, from time to time, being of godly life and conversation, who should have been educated at one of the Universities of Oxford or Cambridge, and had taken the degree of *Master of Arts*, and was well read in the Greek and Latin tongues, as should be nominated from time to time by the said William Adams, during his life, and after the decease of the said William Adams by the governours (namely, the Master and Wardens of the Haber-dashers' Company of the City of London) and their successors." The manour and lands out of which the revenues for the maintenance of the school were to issue are situate *at Knighton and Adbaston, in the county of Stafford.*' From the foregoing account of this foundation, particularly the circumstances of the salary being sixty pounds, and the degree of Master of Arts being a requisite qualification in the teacher, it seemed probable that this was the school in contemplation; and that Lord Gower erroneously supposed that the gentlemen who possessed the lands, out of which the revenues issued, were trustees of the charity.

Such was probable conjecture. But in the Gentleman's Magazine for May, 1793, there is a letter from Mr. Henn, one of the masters of the school of Appleby, in Leicestershire, in which he writes as follows:

'I compared time and circumstance together, in order to discover whether

obtain the degree of Master of Arts, Dr. Adams was applied to, by a common friend, to know whether that could be granted him as a favour from the University of Oxford. But though he had made such a figure in the literary world, it was then thought too great a favour to be asked.

Pope, without any knowledge of him but from his 'London,' recommended him to Earl Gower, who endeavoured to procure for him a degree from Dublin, by the following letter to a friend of Dean Swift:

'SIR,

'MR. SAMUEL JOHNSON (authour of LONDON, a satire, and some other poetical pieces) is a native of this country,ª and much respected by some worthy gentlemen in his neighbourhood, who are trustees of a charity-school now vacant; the certain salary is sixty pounds a year, of which they are desirous to make him master; but, unfortunately, he is not capable of receiving their bounty, which *would make him happy for life*, by not being *a Master of Arts;* which, by the statutes of this school, the master of it must be.

marginal line:
native of . . . by some
[H]
ª *country* corrected to
county [H]

'Now these gentlemen do me the honour to think that I have interest enough in you, to prevail upon you to write to Dean Swift, to persuade the University of Dublin to send a diploma to me, constituting this poor man Master of Arts in their University. They highly extol the man's learning and probity; and will not be persuaded, that the University will make any difficulty of conferring such a

the school in question might not be this of Appleby. Some of the trustees at that period were "worthy gentlemen of the neighbourhood of Lichfield." Appleby itself is not far from the neighbourhood of Lichfield: the salary, the degree requisite, together with the *time of election*, all agreeing with the statutes of Appleby. The election, as said in the letter, "could not be delayed longer than the 11th of next month," which was the 11th of September, just three months after the annual audit-day of Appleby school, which is always on the 11th of June; and the statutes enjoin, *ne ullius præceptorum electio diutius tribus mensibus moraretur*, &c.

'These I thought to be convincing proofs that my conjecture was not ill-founded, and that, in a future edition of that book, the circumstance might be recorded as fact.

'But what banishes every shadow of doubt is the *Minute-book* of the school, which declares the head-mastership to be *at that time* VACANT.'

I cannot omit returning thanks to this learned gentleman for the very handsome manner in which he has in that letter been so good as to speak of this work.

favour upon a stranger, if he is recommended by the Dean. They say, he is not afraid of the strictest examination, though he is of so long a journey; and will venture it, if the Dean thinks it necessary; choosing rather to die upon the road, *than be starved to death in translating for booksellers;* which has been his only subsistence for some time past.

'I fear there is more difficulty in this affair, than those good-natured gentlemen apprehend; especially as their election cannot be delayed longer than the 11th of next month. If you see this matter in the same light that it appears to me, I hope you will burn this, and pardon me for giving you so much trouble about an impracticable thing; but, if you think there is a probability of obtaining the favour asked, I am sure your humanity, and propensity to relieve merit in distress, will incline you to serve the poor man, without my adding any more to the trouble I have already given you, than assuring you that I am, with great truth, Sir,

'Your faithful servant,

'GOWER'

'Trentham, Aug. 1, 1739.'

It was, perhaps, no small disappointment to Johnson that this respectable application had not the desired effect; yet how much reason has there been, both for himself and his country, to rejoice that it did not succeed, as he might probably have wasted in obscurity those hours in which he afterwards produced his incomparable works.

About this time he made one other effort to emancipate himself from the drudgery of authorship. He applied to Dr. Adams, to consult Dr. Smalbroke of the Commons, whether a person might be permitted to practise as an advocate there, without a doctor's degree in Civil Law. 'I am (said he) a total stranger to these studies; but whatever is a profession, and maintains numbers, must be within the reach of common abilities, and some degree of industry.' Dr. Adams was much pleased with Johnson's design to employ his talents in that manner, being confident he would have attained to great eminence. And, indeed, I cannot conceive a man better qualified to make a distinguished figure as a lawyer; for, he would have brought

marginal line:
and maintains . . . the reach [H]

to his profession a rich store of various knowledge, an uncommon acuteness, and a command of language, in which few could have equalled, and none have surpassed him. He who could display eloquence and wit in defence of the decision of the House of Commons upon Mr. Wilkes's election for Middlesex, and of the unconstitutional taxation of our fellow-subjects in America, must have been a powerful advocate in any cause. But here, also, the want of a degree was an insurmountable bar.

He was, therefore, under the necessity of persevering in that course, into which he had been forced; and we find that his proposal from Greenwich to Mr. Cave, for a translation of Father Paul Sarpi's History, was accepted.[1]

Some sheets of this translation were printed off, but the design was dropt; for it happened, oddly enough, that another person of the name of Samuel Johnson, Librarian of St. Martin's in the Fields, and Curate of that parish, engaged in the same undertaking, and was patronised by the Clergy, particularly by Dr. Pearce, afterwards Bishop of Rochester. Several light skirmishes passed between the rival translators, in the news-papers of the day; and the consequence was that they destroyed each other, for neither of them went on with the work. It is much to be regretted, that the able performance of that celebrated genius FRA PAOLO, lost the advantage of being incorporated into British literature by the masterly hand of Johnson.

[1] In the Weekly Miscellany, October 21, 1738, there appeared the following advertisement: 'Just published, proposals for printing the History of the Council of Trent, translated from the Italian of Father Paul Sarpi; with the Authour's Life, and Notes theological, historical, and critical, from the French edition of Dr. Le Courayer. To which are added, Observations on the History, and Notes and Illustrations from various Authours, both printed and manuscript. By S. Johnson. 1. The work will consist of two hundred sheets, and be two volumes in quarto, printed on good paper and letter. 2. The price will be 18s. each volume, to be paid, half a guinea at the delivery of the first volume, and the rest at the delivery of the second volume in sheets. 3. Twopence to be abated for every sheet less than two hundred. It may be had on a large paper, in three volumes, at the price of three guineas; one to be paid at the time of subscribing, another at the delivery of the first, and the rest at the delivery of the other volumes. The work is now in the press, and will be diligently prosecuted. Subscriptions are taken in by Mr. Dodsley in Pall-Mall, Mr. Rivington in St. Paul's Church-yard, by E. Cave at St. John's Gate, and the Translator, at No. 6, in Castle-street, by Cavendish-square.'

I have in my possession, by the favour of Mr. John
Nichols, a paper in Johnson's hand-writing, entitled
'Account between Mr. Edward Cave and Sam. Johnson,
in relation to a version of Father Paul, &c. begun August
the 2d, 1738;' by which it appears, that from that day to
the 21st of April, 1739, Johnson received for this work
49l. 7s. in sums of one, two, three, and sometimes four
guineas at a time, most frequently two. And it is curious
to observe the minute and scrupulous accuracy with which
Johnson had pasted upon it a slip of paper, which he has
entitled 'Small account,' and which contains one article,
'Sept. 9th, Mr. Cave laid down 2s. 6d.' There is subjoined
to this account, a list of some subscribers to the work,
partly in Johnson's hand-writing, partly in that of another
person; and there follows a leaf or two on which are
written a number of characters which have the appearance of a short hand, which, perhaps, Johnson was then
trying to learn.

'TO MR. CAVE

'SIR,   'Wednesday

'I DID not care to detain your servant while I wrote
an answer to your letter, in which you seem to insinuate
that I had promised more than I am ready to perform.
If I have raised your expectations by any thing that may
have escaped my memory, I am sorry; and if you remind
me of it, shall thank you for the favour. If I made fewer
alterations than usual in the Debates, it was only because
there appeared, and still appears to be, less need of alteration. The verses to Lady Firebrace[1] may be had when
you please, for you know that such a subject neither
deserves much thought, nor requires it.

'The Chinese Stories[2] may be had folded down when
you please to send, in which I do not recollect that you
desired any alterations to be made.

'An answer to another query I am very willing to write,
and had consulted with you about it last night, if there had

[1] They afterwards appeared in the Gentleman's Magazine with this
title—'Verses to Lady Firebrace, at Bury Assizes.'

[2] [Du Halde's Description of China was then publishing by Mr. Cave in
weekly numbers, whence Johnson was to select pieces for the embellishment
of the Magazine. NICHOLS.]

been time; for I think it the most proper way of inviting such a correspondence as may be an advantage to the paper, not a load upon it.

'As to the Prize Verses, a backwardness to determine their degrees of merit is not peculiar to me. You may, if you please, still have what I can say; but I shall engage with little spirit in an affair, which I shall *hardly* end to my own satisfaction, and *certainly* not to the satisfaction of the parties concerned.[1]

'As to Father Paul, I have not yet been just to my proposal, but have met with impediments, which, I hope, are now at an end; and if you find the progress hereafter not such as you have a right to expect, you can easily stimulate a negligent translator.

'If any or all of these have contributed to your discontent, I will endeavour to remove it; and desire you to propose the question to which you wish for an answer.

'I am, Sir,
'Your humble servant,
'SAM. JOHNSON'

'TO MR. CAVE

'SIR,   [*No date*]

'I AM pretty much of your opinion, that the Commentary cannot be prosecuted with any appearance of success; for as the names of the authours concerned are of more weight in the performance than its own intrinsick merit, the publick will be soon satisfied with it. And I think the Examen should be pushed forward with the utmost expedition. Thus, "This day, &c. An Examen of Mr. Pope's Essay, &c. containing a succinct Account of the Philosophy of Mr. Leibnitz on the System of the Fatalists, with a Confutation of their Opinions, and an Illustration of the Doctrine of Free-will;" [with what else you think proper.]

'It will, above all, be necessary to take notice, that it is a thing distinct from the Commentary.

'I was so far from imagining they stood still,[2] that I

---

[1] [The premium of forty pounds proposed for the best poem on the Divine Attributes is here alluded to. NICHOLS.]

[2] [The Compositors in Mr. Cave's printing-office, who appear by this letter to have then waited for copy. NICHOLS.]

conceived them to have a good deal before-hand, and therefore was less anxious in providing them more. But if ever they stand still on my account, it must doubtless be charged to me; and whatever else shall be reasonable, I shall not oppose; but beg a suspense of judgement till morning, when I must entreat you to send me a dozen proposals, and you shall then have copy to spare.

'I am, Sir,

'Your's, *impransus,*

'SAM. JOHNSON'

'Pray muster up the Proposals if you can, or let the boy recall them from the booksellers.'

But although he corresponded with Mr. Cave concerning a translation of Crousaz's Examen of Pope's Essay on Man, and gave advice as one anxious for its success, I was long ago convinced by a perusal of the Preface, that this translation was erroneously ascribed to him; and I have found this point ascertained beyond all doubt, by the following article in Dr. Birch's Manuscripts in the British Museum:

'ELISÆ CARTERÆ, S. P. D. THOMAS BIRCH

'*Versionem tuam Examinis Crousaziani jam perlegi. Summam styli et elegantiam, et in re difficillimâ proprietatem, admiratus.*
'*Dabam Novemb.* 27° 1738.'[1]

Indeed Mrs. Carter has lately acknowledged to Mr. Seward, that she was the translator of the 'Examen.'

It is remarkable, that Johnson's last quoted letter to Mr. Cave concludes with a fair confession that he had not a dinner; and it is no less remarkable, that though in this state of want himself, his benevolent heart was not insensible to the necessities of an humble labourer in literature, as appears from the very next letter:

'TO MR. CAVE

'DEAR SIR,   [*No date*]

'You may remember I have formerly talked with you about a Military Dictionary. The eldest Mr. Macbean,

[1] Birch MSS. Brit. Mus. 4323.

who was with Mr. Chambers, has very good materials for
such a work, which I have seen, and will do it at a very
low rate.[1] I think the terms of War and Navigation might
be comprised, with good explanations, in one 8vo. Pica,
which he is willing to do for twelve shillings a sheet, to be
made up a guinea at the second impression. If you think
on it, I will wait on you with him.

marginal line:
terms of . . . be comprised [H]

'I am, Sir,
'Your humble servant,
'SAM. JOHNSON'
'Pray lend me Topsel on Animals.'

I must not omit to mention, that this Mr. Macbean[a]
was a native of Scotland.

In the Gentleman's Magazine of this year, Johnson
gave a Life of Father Paul;* and he wrote the Preface to
the Volume,† which, though prefixed to it when bound,
is always published with the Appendix, and is therefore
the last composition belonging to it. The ability and nice
adaptation with which he could draw up a prefatory
address, was one of his peculiar excellencies.

underlined:
Mr. Macbean [I]
[a] & lived to be very old   he was a hanger on upon Johnson in my Time; & he spoke of him as a good Hebraist. [I]

It appears too, that he paid a friendly attention to
Mrs. Elizabeth Carter; for in a letter from Mr. Cave to
Dr. Birch, November 28, this year, I find 'Mr. Johnson
advises Miss C. to undertake a translation of *Boethius de
Cons.*[b] because there is prose and verse, and to put her
name to it when published.' This advice was not followed;
probably from an apprehension that the work was not
sufficiently popular for an extensive sale. How well
Johnson himself could have executed a translation of this
philosophic poet, we may judge from the following
specimen which he has given in the Rambler: (*Motto to
No.* 7.)

[b] he advised Me to do it many years after—& I did do two or three odes. [I]

> '*O qui perpetuâ mundum ratione gubernas,*
> *Terrarum cœlique sator!——*
> *Disjice terrenæ nebulas et pondera molis,*
> *Atque tuo splendore mica! Tu namque serenum,*
> *Tu requies tranquilla piis. Te cernere finis,*
> *Principium, vector, dux, semita, terminus, idem.*'

[1] This book was published.

'O THOU whose power o'er moving worlds presides,
Whose voice created, and whose wisdom guides,
On darkling man in pure effulgence shine,
And cheer the clouded mind with light divine.
'Tis thine alone to calm the pious breast,
With silent confidence and holy rest;
From thee, great God! we spring, to thee we tend,
Path, motive, guide, original, and end!'

In 1739, beside the assistance which he gave to the
Parliamentary Debates, his writings in the Gentleman's
Magazine were, 'The Life of Boerhaave,'* in which it is
to be observed, that he discovers that love of chymistry
which never forsook him; 'An Appeal to the Publick in
behalf of the Editor;'† 'An Address to the Reader;'†
'An Epigram both in Greek and Latin to Eliza,'* and also
English verses to her;* and 'A Greek Epigram to Dr.
Birch.'* It has been erroneously supposed, that an Essay
published in that Magazine this year, entitled 'The
Apotheosis of Milton,' was written by Johnson; and on
that supposition it has been improperly inserted in the
edition of his works by the Booksellers, after his decease.
Were there no positive testimony as to this point, the style
of the performance, and the name of Shakspeare not being
mentioned in an Essay professedly reviewing the principal
English poets, would ascertain it not to be the production
of Johnson. But there is here no occasion to resort to internal evidence; for my Lord Bishop of Salisbury (Dr.
Douglas) has assured me that it was written by Guthrie.
His separate publications were, 'A Complete Vindication
of the Licensers of the Stage, from the malicious and scandalous Aspersions of Mr. Brooke, Authour of Gustavus
Vasa,'* being an ironical Attack upon them for their
Suppression of that Tragedy; and, 'Marmor Norfolciense;
or an Essay on an ancient prophetical Inscription, in
monkish Rhyme, lately discovered near Lynne, in Norfolk,
by PROBUS BRITANNICUS.'* In this performance, he,
in a feigned inscription, supposed to have been found in
Norfolk, the county of Sir Robert Walpole, then the obnoxious prime minister of this country, inveighs against
the Brunswick succession, and the measures of government

consequent upon it.[1] To this supposed prophecy he added a Commentary, making each expression apply to the times, with warm Anti-Hanoverian zeal.

This anonymous pamphlet, I believe, did not make so much noise as was expected, and, therefore, had not a very extensive circulation. Sir John Hawkins relates, that 'warrants were issued, and messengers employed to apprehend the author; who, though he had forborne to subscribe his name to the pamphlet, the vigilance of those in pursuit of him had discovered;' and we are informed, that he lay concealed in Lambeth-marsh till the scent after him grew cold. This, however, is altogether without foundation, for Mr. Steele, one of the Secretaries of the Treasury, who amidst a variety of important business, politely obliged me with his attention to my inquiry, informed me, that 'he directed every possible search to be made in the records of the Treasury and Secretary of State's Office, but could find no trace whatever of any warrant having been issued to apprehend the authour of this pamphlet.'

'Marmor Norfolciense' became exceedingly scarce, so that I for many years endeavoured in vain to procure a copy of it. At last I was indebted to the malice of one of Johnson's numerous petty adversaries, who, in 1775, published a new edition of it, 'with Notes and a Dedication to SAMUEL JOHNSON, LL.D. by TRIBUNUS;' in which some puny scribbler invidiously attempted to found upon it a charge of inconsistency against its authour, because he had accepted of a pension from his present Majesty, and had written in support of the measures of government. As a mortification to such impotent malice, of which there are so many instances towards men of eminence, I am happy to relate, that this *telum imbelle* did not reach its exalted object, till about a year after it thus appeared, when I mentioned it to him, supposing that he knew of the re-publication. To my surprise, he had not yet heard of it. He requested me to go directly and get it for him, which I did. He looked at it and laughed, and seemed to be much diverted with the feeble efforts of his unknown adversary, who, I hope, is alive to read this

[1] The Inscription and the Translation of it are preserved in the London Magazine for the year 1739, p. 244.

account. 'Now (said he) here is somebody who thinks he
has vexed me sadly: yet if it had not been for you, you
rogue, I should probably never have seen it.'

As Mr. Pope's note concerning Johnson, alluded to in
a former page, refers both to his 'London,' and his 'Marmor Norfolciense,' I have deferred inserting it till now.
I am indebted for it to Dr. Percy, the Bishop of Dromore,
who permitted me to copy it from the original in his
possession. It was presented to his Lordship by Sir Joshua
Reynolds, to whom it was given by the son of Mr. Richardson the painter, the person to whom it is addressed. I
have transcribed it with minute exactness, that the
peculiar mode of writing, and imperfect spelling of that
celebrated poet, may be exhibited to the curious in
literature. It justifies Swift's epithet of 'paper-sparing
Pope,' for it is written on a slip no larger than a common
message-card, and was sent to Mr. Richardson, along
with the imitation of Juvenal.

'This is imitated by one Johnson who put in for a
Publick-school in Shropshire,[1] but was disappointed. He
has an infirmity of the convulsive kind, that attacks him
sometimes, so as to make Him a sad Spectacle.[a] Mr. P.
from the Merit of This Work which was all the knowledge
he had of Him endeavoured to serve Him without his own
application; & wrote to my L^d. gore, but he did not
succeed. Mr Johnson published afterw^{ds}. another Poem in
Latin with Notes the whole very Humerous call'd the
Norfolk Prophecy.'   'P.'

a Pope's care for a Man's Personal Appearance is comical enough; his own being so miserable. [1]

Johnson had been told of this note; and Sir Joshua
Reynolds informed him of the compliment which it
contained, but, from delicacy, avoided shewing him the
paper itself. When Sir Joshua observed to Johnson that he
seemed very desirous to see Pope's note, he answered,
'Who would not be proud to have such a man as Pope so
solicitous in inquiring about him?'

The infirmity to which Mr. Pope alludes, appeared to
me also, as I have elsewhere[2] observed, to be of the
convulsive kind, and of the nature of that distemper called
St. Vitus's dance; and in this opinion I am confirmed by

[1] See note, p. 80.   [2] Journal of a Tour to the Hebrides, 3d edit. p. 8.

the description which Sydenham gives of that disease. 'This disorder is a kind of convulsion. It manifests itself by halting or unsteadiness of one of the legs, which the patient draws after him like an ideot. If the hand of the same side be applied to the breast, or any other part of the body, he cannot keep it a moment in the same posture, but it will be drawn into a different one by a convulsion, notwithstanding all his efforts to the contrary.' Sir Joshua Reynolds, however, was of a different opinion, and favoured me with the following paper.

'Those motions or tricks of Dr. Johnson are improperly called convulsions. He could sit motionless when he was told so to do, as well as any other man. My opinion is, that it proceeded from a habit[1] which he had indulged himself in,[a] of accompanying his thoughts with certain untoward actions, and those actions always appeared to me as if they were meant to reprobate some part of his past conduct. Whenever he was not engaged in conversation, such thoughts were sure to rush into his mind; and, for this reason, any company, any employment whatever, he preferred to being alone.[b] The great business of his life (he said) was to escape from himself; this disposition he considered as the disease of his mind, which nothing cured but company.

[a] *Reynolds was right so far I think* [1]

[b] *I dare say the King saw none of these odd Gesticulations,—nor did he much use them at Church* [1]
marginal line: *this disposition . . . but company* [H]

'One instance of his absence of mind and particularity, as it is characteristick of the man, may be worth relating. When he and I took a journey together into the West, we visited the late Mr. Banks, of Dorsetshire; the conversation turning upon pictures, which Johnson could not well see, he retired to a corner of the room, stretching out his right leg as far as he could reach before him, then bringing up his left leg, and stretching his right still further on. The old gentleman observing him, went up to him, and in a very courteous manner assured him, though it was not a new house, the flooring was perfectly safe. The Doctor started from his reverie, like a person waked out of his sleep, but spoke not a word.'

[1] [Sir Joshua Reynolds's notion on this subject is confirmed by what Johnson himself said to a young lady, the niece of his friend Christopher Smart. See a note by Mr. Boswell on some particulars communicated by Reynolds, in vol. iii. under March 30, 1783. MALONE.]

While we are on this subject, my readers may not be displeased with another anecdote, communicated to me by the same friend, from the relation of Mr. Hogarth.

Johnson used to be a pretty frequent visitor at the house of Mr. Richardson, authour of Clarissa, and other novels of extensive reputation. Mr. Hogarth came one day to see Richardson,ᵃ soon after the execution of Dr. Cameron, for having taken arms for the house of Stuart in 1745-6; and being a warm partisan of George the Second, he observed to Richardson, that certainly there must have been some very unfavourable circumstances lately discovered in this particular case, which had induced the King to approve of an execution for rebellion so long after the time when it was committed, as this had the appearance of putting a man to death in cold blood,¹ and was very unlike his Majesty's usual clemency. While he was talking, he perceived a person standing at a window in the room, shaking his head, and rolling himself about in a strange ridiculous manner. He concluded that he was an ideot, whom his relations had put under the care of Mr. Richardson, as a very good man. To his great surprize, however, this figure stalked forwards to where he and Mr. Richardson were sitting, and all at once took up the argument, and burst out into an invective against George the Second, as one, who, upon all occasions, was unrelenting and barbarous; mentioning many instances, particularly, that when an officer of high rank had been acquitted by a Court Martial, George the Second had with his own hand struck his name off the list. In short, he displayed such a power of eloquence, that Hogarth looked at him with

ᵃ *I have heard Hogarth speak of Johnson when I was a child; & I recollect his saying ' That Man not only believes in the Bible but I think he believes nothing that is not in the Bible. I told Doctor Johnson that he said so, and Johnson laugh'd* [1]

marginal line: *the Second . . . his name* [H]

¹ Impartial posterity may, perhaps, be as little inclined as Dr. Johnson was, to justify the uncommon rigour exercised in the case of Dr. Archibald Cameron. He was an amiable and truly honest man; and his offence was owing to a generous, though mistaken principle of duty. Being obliged, after 1746, to give up his profession as a physician, and to go into foreign parts, he was honoured with the rank of Colonel, both in the French and Spanish service. He was a son of the ancient and respectable family of Cameron, of Lochiel; and his brother who was the Chief of that brave clan, distinguished himself by moderation and humanity, while the Highland army marched victorious through Scotland. It is remarkable of this Chief, that though he had earnestly remonstrated against the attempt as hopeless, he was of too heroick a spirit not to venture his life and fortune in the cause, when personally asked by him whom he thought his Prince.

astonishment, and actually imagined that this ideot had been at the moment inspired. Neither Hogarth nor Johnson were made known to each other at this interview.

In 1740 he wrote for the Gentleman's Magazine the 'Preface,'† the 'Life of Admiral Blake,'* and the first parts of those of 'Sir Francis Drake,'* and 'Philip Barretier,'*[1] both which he finished the following year. He also wrote an 'Essay on Epitaphs,'* and an 'Epitaph on Philips, a Musician,'* which was afterwards published with some other pieces of his, in Mrs. Williams's Miscellanies. This Epitaph is so exquisitely beautiful, that I remember even Lord Kames, strangely prejudiced as he was against Dr. Johnson, was compelled to allow it very high praise. It has been ascribed to Mr. Garrick, from its appearing at first with the signature G; but I have heard Mr. Garrick declare, that it was written by Dr. Johnson, and give the following account of the manner in which it was composed. Johnson and he were sitting together; when, amongst other things, Garrick repeated an Epitaph upon this Philips by a Dr. Wilkes, in these words:

'Exalted soul! whose harmony could please
The love-sick virgin, and the gouty ease;
Could jarring discord, like Amphion, move
To beauteous order and harmonious love;
Rest here in peace, till angels bid thee rise,
And meet thy blessed Saviour in the skies.'

Johnson shook his head at these common-place funeral lines, and said to Garrick, 'I think, Davy, I can make a better.' Then stirring about his tea for a little while, in a state of meditation, he almost extempore produced the following verses:

'Philips, whose touch harmonious could remove
The pangs of guilty power or hapless love;
Rest here, distress'd by poverty no more,
Here find that calm thou gav'st so oft before;

[1] [To which in 1742 he made very large additions, which have never yet been incorporated in any edition of Barretier's Life. A. CHALMERS.]

a and Saints embrace thee with a Love like mine   is a Line in Pope's Eloisa [H]

Sleep, undisturb'd, within this peaceful shrine,
Till angels wake thee with a note like thine!'[1][a]

At the same time that Mr. Garrick favoured me with this anecdote, he repeated a very pointed Epigram by Johnson, on George the Second and Colley Cibber, which has never yet appeared, and of which I know not the exact date. Dr. Johnson afterwards gave it to me himself:

'Augustus still survives in Maro's strain,
And Spenser's verse prolongs Eliza's reign;
Great George's acts let tuneful Cibber sing;
For Nature form'd the Poet for the King.'

In 1741 he wrote for the Gentleman's Magazine the 'Preface,'† 'Conclusion of his Lives of Drake and Barretier,'* 'A free translation of the Jests of Hierocles, with an Introduction;'† and, I think, the following pieces: 'Debate on the Proposal of Parliament to Cromwell, to assume the Title of King, abridged, modified, and digested;'†

---

[1] [The epitaph of Phillips is in the porch of Wolverhampton church. The prose part of it is curious:

'Near this place lies
CHARLES CLAUDIUS PHILLIPS,
Whose absolute contempt of riches
and inimitable performances upon the violin,
made him the admiration of all that knew him.
He was born in Wales,
made the tour of Europe,
and, after the experience of both kinds of fortune,
Died in 1732.'

Mr. Garrick appears not to have recited the verses correctly, the original being as follows. One of the various readings is remarkable, as it is the germ of Johnson's concluding line:

'Exalted soul, *thy various sounds* could please
The love sick virgin, and the gouty ease;
Could jarring *crowds*, like *old* Amphion, move
To beauteous order and harmonious love;
Rest here in peace, till Angels bid thee rise,
And meet thy Saviour's *consort* in the skies.'

Dr. Wilkes, the authour of these lines, was a Fellow of Trinity College, in Oxford, and rector of Pitchford, in Shropshire: he collected materials for a history of that county, and is spoken of by Brown Willis, in his History of Mitred Abbies, vol. ii. p. 189. But he was a native of Staffordshire; and to the antiquities of that county was his attention chiefly confined. Mr. Shaw has had the use of his papers. BLAKEWAY.]

'Translation of Abbé Guyon's Dissertation on the Amazons;'✝ 'Translation of Fontenelle's Panegyrick on Dr. Morin.'✝ Two notes upon this appear to me undoubtedly his. He this year, and the two following, wrote the Parliamentary Debates. He told me himself, that he was the sole composer of them for those three years only. He was not, however, precisely exact in his statement, which he mentioned from hasty recollection; for it is sufficiently evident, that his composition of them began November 19, 1740, and ended February 23, 1742–3.

It appears from some of Cave's letters to Dr. Birch, that Cave had better assistance for that branch of his Magazine than has been generally supposed; and that he was indefatigable in getting it made as perfect as he could.

Thus 21st July, 1735, 'I trouble you with the inclosed, because you said you could easily correct what is here given for Lord C———ld's speech. I beg you will do so as soon as you can for me, because the month is far advanced.'

And 15th July, 1737, 'As you remember the debates so far as to perceive the speeches already printed are not exact, I beg the favour that you will peruse the inclosed, and, in the best manner your memory will serve, correct the mistaken passages, or add any thing that is omitted. I should be very glad to have something of the Duke of N———le's speech, which would be particularly of service.

'A gentleman has Lord Bathurst's speech to add something to.'

And July 3, 1744, 'You will see what stupid, low, abominable stuff is put[1] upon your noble and learned friend's[2] character, such as I should quite reject, and endeavour to do something better towards doing justice to the character. But as I cannot expect to attain my desire in that respect, it would be a great satisfaction, as well as an honour to our work, to have the favour of the genuine speech. It is a method that several have been pleased to take, as I could shew, but I think myself under a restraint. I shall say so far, that I have had some by a third hand, which I understood well enough to come from

---

[1] I suppose in another compilation of the same kind.
[2] Doubtless, Lord Hardwick.

the first; others by penny-post, and others by the speakers themselves, who have been pleased to visit St. John's gate, and show particular marks of their being pleased.'[1]

There is no reason, I believe, to doubt the veracity of Cave. It is, however, remarkable, that none of these letters are in the years during which Johnson alone furnished the Debates, and one of them is in the very year after he ceased from that labour. Johnson told me, that as soon as he found that the speeches were thought genuine, he determined that he would write no more of them; 'for he would not be accessary to the propagation of falsehood.' And such was the tenderness of his conscience, that a short time before his death he expressed his regret for his having been the authour of fictions, which had passed for realities.

He nevertheless agreed with me in thinking, that the debates which he had framed were to be valued as orations upon questions of publick importance. They have accordingly been collected in volumes, properly arranged, and recommended to the notice of parliamentary speakers by a preface, written by no inferior hand.[2] I must, however, observe, that although there is in those debates a wonderful store of political information, and very powerful eloquence, I cannot agree that they exhibit the manner of each particular speaker, as Sir John Hawkins seems to think. But, indeed, what opinion can we have of his judgement, and taste in public speaking, who presumes to give, as the characteristicks of two celebrated orators, 'the deep-mouthed rancour of Pulteney, and the yelping pertinacity of Pitt.'[3]

marginal line:
celebrated orators . . .
of Pitt [H]

This year I find that his tragedy of I R E N E had been for some time ready for the stage, and that his necessities made him desirous of getting as much as he could for it without delay; for there is the following letter from Mr. Cave to Dr. Birch, in the same volume of manuscripts in the British Museum, from which I copied those above quoted. They were most obligingly pointed out to me by

[1] Birch's MSS. in the British Museum, 4302.

[2] I am assured that the editor is Mr. George Chalmers, whose commercial works are well known and esteemed.

[3] Hawkins's Life of Johnson, p. 100.

Sir William Musgrave, one of the Curators of that noble repository.

'Sept. 9, 1741

'I HAVE put Mr. Johnson's play into Mr. Gray's[1] hands, in order to sell it to him, if he is inclined to buy it; but I doubt whether he will or not. He would dispose of the copy, and whatever advantage may be made by acting it. Would your society,[2] or any gentleman, or body of men that you know, take such a bargain? He and I are very unfit to deal with theatrical persons. Fleetwood was to have acted it last season, but Johnson's diffidence or   [3]   prevented it.'

I have already mentioned that 'Irene' was not brought into publick notice till Garrick was manager of Drury-lane theatre.

In 1742[4] he wrote for the Gentleman's Magazine the 'Preface,'† the 'Parliamentary Debates,'* 'Essay on the Account of the Conduct of the Duchess of Marlborough,'* then the popular topick of conversation. This Essay is a short but masterly performance. We find him in No. 13 of his Rambler, censuring a profligate sentiment in that 'Account;' and again insisting upon it strenuously in conversation.[5] 'An Account of the Life of Peter Burman,'* I believe chiefly taken from a foreign publication; as, indeed, he could not himself know much about Burman; 'Additions to his Life of Barretier;'* 'The Life of Sydenham,'* afterwards prefixed to Dr. Swan's edition of his works; 'Proposals for printing Bibliotheca Harleiana, or a Catalogue of the Library of the Earl of Oxford.'* His

[1] A bookseller of London.

[2] Not the Royal Society: but the Society for the encouragement of learning, of which Dr. Birch was a leading member. Their object was, to assist authours in printing expensive works. It existed from about 1735 to 1746, when, having incurred a considerable debt, it was dissolved.

[3] There is no erasure here, but a mere blank: to fill up which may be an exercise for ingenious conjecture.

[4] [From one of his letters to a friend, written in June 1742, it should seem that he then purposed to write a play on the subject of Charles the Twelfth, of Sweden, and to have it ready for the ensuing winter. The passage alluded to, however, is somewhat ambiguous; and the work which he then had in contemplation may have been a history of that monarch. MALONE.]

[5] Journal of a Tour to the Hebrides, 3d edit. p. 167.

account of that celebrated collection of books, in which
he displays the importance to literature, of what the
French call a *catalogue raisonné*, when the subjects of it are
extensive and various, and it is executed with ability,
cannot fail to impress all his readers with admiration of
his philological attainments. It was afterwards prefixed to
the first volume of the Catalogue, in which the Latin
accounts of books were written by him. He was employed
in this business by Mr. Thomas Osborne, the bookseller,
who purchased the library for 13,000*l.* a sum which
Mr. Oldys says, in one of his manuscripts, was not more
than the binding of the books had cost; yet, as Dr. Johnson
assured me, the slowness of the sale was such, that there
was not much gained by it. It has been confidently related,
with many embellishments, that Johnson one day knocked
Osborne down in his shop, with a folio, and put his foot
upon his neck. The simple truth I had from Johnson
himself. 'Sir, he was impertinent to me, and I beat him.
But it was not in his shop: it was in my own chamber.'

A very diligent observer may trace him where we should
not easily suppose him to be found. I have no doubt that
he wrote the little abridgement entitled 'Foreign History,'
in the Magazine for December. To prove it, I shall quote
the Introduction. 'As this is that season of the year in
which Nature may be said to command a suspension of
hostilities, and which seems intended, by putting a short
stop to violence and slaughter, to afford time for malice
to relent, and animosity to subside; we can scarce expect
any other account than of plans, negociations and treaties,
of proposals for peace, and preparations for war.' As also
this passage: 'Let those who despise the capacity of the
Swiss, tell us by what wonderful policy, or by what happy
conciliation of interests, it is brought to pass, that in a
body made up of different communities and different
religions, there should be no civil commotions, though
the people are so warlike, that to nominate and raise an
army is the same.'

I am obliged to Mr. Astle for his ready permission to
copy the two following letters, of which the originals are
in his possession. Their contents shew that they were
written about this time, and that Johnson was now

marginal line:
manuscripts, was . . .
the slowness [H]

engaged in preparing an historical account of the British
Parliament.

'TO MR. CAVE

'SIR,   [*No date*]

'I BELIEVE I am going to write a long letter, and
have therefore taken a whole sheet of paper. The first
thing to be written about is our historical design.

'You mentioned the proposal of printing in numbers,
as an alteration in the scheme, but I believe you mistook,
some way or other, my meaning; I had no other view
than that you might rather print too many of five sheets
than of five and thirty.

'With regard to what I shall say on the manner of
proceeding, I would have it understood as wholly indifferent to me, and my opinion only, not my resolution.
Emptoris sit eligere.

'I think the insertion of the exact dates of the most
important events in the margin, or of so many events as
may enable the reader to regulate the order of facts with
sufficient exactness, the proper medium between a journal,
which has regard only to time, and a history which ranges
facts according to their dependence on each other, and
postpones or anticipates according to the convenience of
narration. I think the work ought to partake of the spirit
of history, which is contrary to minute exactness, and of
the regularity of a journal, which is inconsistent with
spirit. For this reason, I neither admit numbers or dates,
nor reject them.

marginal line:
*numbers or . . . reject
them* [H]

'I am of your opinion with regard to placing most of
the resolutions, &c. in the margin, and think we shall
give the most complete account of Parliamentary proceedings that can be contrived. The naked papers, without
an historical treatise interwoven, require some other book
to make them understood. I will date the succeeding
facts with some exactness, but I think in the margin. You
told me on Saturday that I had received money on this
work, and found set down 13*l.* 2*s.* 6*d.* reckoning the half
guinea of last Saturday. As you hinted to me that you
had many calls for money, I would not press you too hard,
and therefore shall desire only, as I send it in, two guineas

for a sheet of copy; the rest you may pay me when it may be more convenient; and even by this sheet payment I shall, for some time, be very expensive.

'The Life of Savage I am ready to go upon; and in Great Primer, and Pica notes, I reckon on sending in half a sheet a day; but the money for that shall likewise lye by in your hands till it is done. With the debates, shall not I have business enough? if I had but good pens.

'Towards Mr. Savage's Life what more have you got? I would willingly have his trial, &c. and know whether his defence be at Bristol, and would have his collection of Poems, on account of the Preface; — "The Plain Dealer."[1] — all the magazines that have any thing of his or relating to him.

'I thought my letter would be long, but it is now ended; and I am, Sir,

'Your's, &c.

'SAM. JOHNSON'

'The boy found me writing this almost in the dark, when I could not quite easily read yours.

'I have read the Italian: — nothing in it is well.

'I had no notion of having any thing for the inscription.[2] I hope you don't think I kept it to extort a price. I could think of nothing, till to-day. If you could spare me another guinea for the history, I should take it very kindly, to-night; but if you do not, I shall not think it an injury.——I am almost well again.'

'TO MR. CAVE
'SIR,

'You did not tell me your determination about the *Soldier's Letter*,[3] which I am confident was never printed. I think it will not do by itself, or in any other place, so well as the Mag. Extraordinary. If you will have it at all, I believe you do not think I set it high, and I will be glad if what you give, you will give quickly.

---

[1] 'The Plain Dealer' was published in 1724, and contained some account of Savage.

[2] [Perhaps the Runick Inscription, Gent. Mag. vol. xii. p. 132. MALONE.]

[3] I have not discovered what this was.

'You need not be in care about something to print, for I have got the State Trials, and shall extract Layer, Atterbury, and Macclesfield from them, and shall bring them to you in a fortnight; after which I will try to get the South Sea Report.'

[*No date nor signature.*]

I would also ascribe to him an 'Essay on the Description of China, from the French of Du Halde.'✝

His writings in the Gentleman's Magazine in 1743, are, the Preface,✝ the Parliamentary Debates,✝ 'Considerations on the Dispute between Crousaz and Warburton, on Pope's Essay on Man;'✝ in which while he defends Crousaz, he shews an admirable metaphysical acuteness and temperance in controversy; 'Ad Lauram parituram Epigramma[1];'* and, 'A Latin Translation of Pope's Verses on his Grotto;'* and as he could employ his pen

---

[1] *Angliacas inter pulcherrima Laura puellas,*
    Mox uteri pondus depositura grave,
    Adsit, Laura, tibi facilis Lucina dolenti,
    Neve tibi noceat prænituisse Deæ.

Mr. Hector was present when this Epigram was made *impromptu.* The first line was proposed by Dr. James, and Johnson was called upon by the company to finish it, which he instantly did.

[The following elegant Latin Ode, which appeared in the Gentleman's Magazine for 1743, (vol. xiii. p. 548,) was many years ago pointed out to James Bindley, Esq. as written by Johnson, and may safely be attributed to him.

AD ORNATISSIMAM PUELLAM

VANÆ sit arti, sit studio modus,
    Formosa virgo: sit speculo quies,
Curamque quærendi decoris
    Mitte, supervacuosque cultus,
Ut fortuitis verna coloribus
Depicta vulgo rura magis placent,
    Nec invident horto nitenti
        Divitias operosiores:

Lenique fons cum murmure pulchrior
Obliquat ultro præcipitem fugam
    Inter reluctantes lapillos, et
        Ducit aquas temerè sequentes:

Utque inter undas, inter et arbores,
Jam vere primo dulce strepunt aves,
    Et arte nulla gratiores
        Ingeminant sine lege cantus:

with equal success upon a small matter as a great, I suppose him to be the authour of an advertisement for Osborne, concerning the great Harleian Catalogue.

But I should think myself much wanting, both to my illustrious friend and my readers, did I not introduce here, with more than ordinary respect, an exquisitely beautiful Ode, which has not been inserted in any of the collections of Johnson's poetry, written by him at a very early period, as Mr. Hector informs me, and inserted in the Gentleman's Magazine of this year.

FRIENDSHIP, *an* ODE*

FRIENDSHIP, peculiar boon of heav'n,
    The noble mind's delight and pride,
To men and angels only giv'n,
    To all the lower world deny'd.

While love unknown among the blest,
    Parent of thousand wild desires,
The savage and the human breast
    Torments alike with raging fires;

> Nativa sic te gratia, te nitor
> Simplex decebit, te veneres tuæ;
>   Nudus Cupido suspicatur
>   Artifices nimis apparatûs.
>
> Ergo fluentem tu; malè sedula,
> Ne sæva inuras semper acu comam;
>   Nec sparsa odorato nitentes
>   Pulvere dedecores capillos;
>
> Quales nec olim vel Ptolemæia
> Jactabat uxor, sidereo in choro
>   Utcunque devotæ refulgent
>   Verticis exuviæ decori;
>
> Nec diva mater, cum similem tuæ
> Mentita formam, et pulchrior aspici,
>   Permisit incomptas protervis
>   Fusa comas agitare ventis.

In vol. xiv. p. 46, of the same work, an elegant Epigram was inserted, in answer to the foregoing Ode, which was written by Dr. Inyon of Pulham, in Norfolk, a physician, and an excellent classical scholar:

Ad Authorem Carminis AD ORNATISSIMAM PUELLAM

O cui non potuit, quia culta, placere puella,
    Quî speras Musam posse placere tuam? MALONE.]

With bright, but oft destructive, gleam,
  Alike o'er all his lightnings fly;
Thy lambent glories only beam
  Around the fav'rites of the sky.

Thy gentle flows of guiltless joys
  On fools and villains ne'er descend;
In vain for thee the tyrant sighs,
  And hugs a flatterer for a friend.

Directress of the brave and just,
  O guide us through life's darksome way!
And let the tortures of mistrust
  On selfish bosoms only prey.

Nor shall thine ardour cease to glow,
  When souls to blissful climes remove:
What rais'd our virtue here below,
  Shall aid our happiness above.

Johnson had now an opportunity of obliging his school-fellow Dr. James, of whom he once observed, 'no man brings more mind to his profession.' James published this year his 'Medicinal Dictionary,' in three volumes folio. Johnson, as I understood from him, had written, or assisted in writing, the proposals for this work; and being very fond of the study of physick, in which James was his master, he furnished some of the articles. He, however, certainly wrote for it the Dedication to Dr. Mead,✝ which is conceived with great address, to conciliate the patronage of that very eminent man.[1]

[1]'TO DR. MEAD

'SIR,

'THAT the *Medicinal Dictionary* is dedicated to you, is to be imputed only to your reputation for superior skill in those sciences which I have endeavoured to explain and facilitate: and you are, therefore, to consider this address, if it be agreeable to you, as one of the rewards of merit; and if otherwise, as one of the inconveniencies of eminence.

'However you shall receive it, my design cannot be disappointed; because this publick appeal to your judgement will shew that I do not found my hopes of approbation upon the ignorance of my readers, and that I fear his censure least, whose knowledge is most extensive.[a] I am, Sir,

[a]*Very neat indeed.* [t]

'Your most obedient humble servant,

'R. JAMES'

It has been circulated, I know not with what authenticity, that Johnson considered Dr. Birch as a dull writer,
and said of him, 'Tom Birch is as brisk as a bee in conversation; but no sooner does he take a pen in his hand, than
it becomes a torpedo to him, and benumbs all his faculties.'
That the literature of this country is much indebted to
Birch's activity and diligence must certainly be acknowledged. We have seen that Johnson honoured him with a
Greek Epigram; and his correspondence with him, during
many years, proves that he had no mean opinion of him.

'TO DR. BIRCH

'SIR,   'Thursday, Sept. 29, 1743
   'I HOPE you will excuse me for troubling you on an
occasion on which I know not whom else I can apply to;
I am at a loss for the Lives and Characters of Earl Stanhope,
the two Craggs, and the minister Sunderland; and beg
that you will inform [me] where I may find them, and
send any pamphlets, &c. relating to them to Mr. Cave to
be perused for a few days by, Sir,

'Your most humble servant,
'SAM. JOHNSON'

His circumstances were at this time embarrassed; yet
his affection for his mother was so warm, and so liberal,
that he took upon himself a debt of her's, which, though
small in itself, was then considerable to him. This appears
from the following letter which he wrote to Mr. Levett,
of Lichfield, the original of which lies now before me.

'TO MR. LEVETT; IN LICHFIELD

'SIR,   'December 1, 1743
   'I AM extremely sorry that we have encroached so
much upon your forbearance with respect to the interest,
which a great perplexity of affairs hindered me from
thinking of with that attention that I ought, and which
I am not immediately able to remit to you, but will pay it
(I think twelve pounds,) in two months. I look upon this,
and on the future interest of that mortgage, as my own

debt; and beg that you will be pleased to give me directions how to pay it, and not mention it to my dear mother. If it be necessary to pay this in less time, I believe I can do it; but I take two months for certainty, and beg an answer whether you can allow me so much time. I think myself very much obliged to your forbearance, and shall esteem it a great happiness to be able to serve you. I have great opportunities of dispersing any thing that you may think it proper to make publick. I will give a note for the money, payable at the time mentioned, to any one here that you shall appoint. I am, Sir,

> 'Your most obedient
> > 'And most humble servant,
> > > 'SAM. JOHNSON'
> > > 'At Mr. Osborne's, bookseller, in Gray's Inn.'

I T does not appear that he wrote any thing in 1774 for the Gentleman's Magazine, but the Preface.✝ His life of Barretier was now re-published in a pamphlet by itself. But he produced one work this year, fully sufficient to maintain the high reputation which he had acquired. This was 'THE LIFE OF RICHARD SAVAGE;'* a man, of whom it is difficult to speak impartially, without wondering that he was for some time the intimate companion of Johnson; for his character[1] was marked by profligacy, insolence, and ingratitude: yet, as he undoubtedly had a warm and vigorous, though unregulated mind, had seen life in all its varieties, and been much in the company of the statesmen and wits of his time, he could communicate to Johnson an abundant supply of such materials as

---

[1] As a specimen of his temper, I insert the following letter from him to a noble Lord, to whom he was under great obligations, but who, on account of his bad conduct, was obliged to discard him. The original was in the hands of the late Francis Cockayne Cust, Esq. one of his Majesty's Counsel learned in the law:

'*Right Honourable* BRUTE *and* BOOBY,

'I FIND you want (as Mr. ———[a] is pleased to hint,) to swear away my life, that is, the life of your creditor, because he asks you for a debt.— The publick shall soon be acquainted with this, to judge whether you are not fitter to be an Irish Evidence, than to be an Irish Peer.—I defy and despise you.   'I am,

> 'Your determined adversary,
> > 'R. S.'

[a] *I suppose Ld. Tyrconnel* [1]

his philosophical curiosity most eagerly desired; and as
Savage's misfortunes and misconduct had reduced him
to the lowest state of wretchedness as a writer for bread,
his visits to St. John's Gate naturally brought Johnson
and him together.[1]

It is melancholy to reflect, that Johnson and Savage
were sometimes in such extreme indigence,[2] that they
could not pay for a lodging; so that they have wandered
together whole nights in the streets.[3] Yet in these almost
incredible scenes of distress, we may suppose that Savage
mentioned many of the anecdotes with which Johnson

[1] Sir John Hawkins gives the world to understand, that Johnson, 'being
an admirer of genteel manners, was captivated by the address and demeanour of Savage, who, as to his exterior, was to a remarkable degree accomplished.'—Hawkins's Life, p. 52. But Sir John's notions of gentility must
appear somewhat ludicrous, from his stating the following circumstance as
presumptive evidence that Savage was a good swordsman: 'That he understood the exercise of a gentleman's weapon, may be inferred from the use
made of it in that rash encounter which is related in his Life.' The dexterity
here alluded to was, that Savage, in a nocturnal fit of drunkenness, stabbed
a man at a coffee-house, and killed him: for which he was tried at the Old
Bailey, and found guilty of murder.

Johnson, indeed, describes him as having 'a grave and manly deportment,
a solemn dignity of mien; but which, upon a nearer acquaintance, softened
into an engaging easiness of manners.' How highly Johnson admired him
for that knowledge which he himself so much cultivated, and what kindness
he entertained for him, appears from the following lines in the Gentleman's
Magazine for April, 1738, which I am assured were written by Johnson:

'*Ad* RICARDUM SAVAGE.

'*Humani studium generis cui pectore fervet*
O colat humanum te foveatque genus.'

[2] [The following striking proof of Johnson's extreme indigence, when
he published the Life of Savage, was communicated to Mr. Boswell, by
Mr. Richard Stowe, of Apsley, in Bedfordshire, from the information of
Mr. Walter Harte, authour of the Life of Gustavus Adolphus:

'Soon after Savage's Life was published, Mr. Harte dined with Edward
Cave, and occasionally praised it. Soon after, meeting him, Cave said,
"You made a man very happy t'other day."—"How could that be," says
Harte; "nobody was there but ourselves." Cave answered, by reminding
him that a plate of victuals was sent behind a screen, which was to Johnson,
dressed so shabbily, that he did not choose to appear: but on hearing the
conversation, he was highly delighted with the encomiums on his book.'
MALONE.]

[3] [As Johnson was married before he settled in London, and must have
always had a habitation for his wife, some readers have wondered, how he
ever could have been driven to stroll about with Savage, all night, for want
of a lodging. But it should be remembered, that Johnson, at different
periods, had lodgings in the vicinity of London; and his finances certainly
would not admit of a double establishment. When, therefore, he spent a

afterwards enriched the life of his unhappy companion, and those of other Poets.

He told Sir Joshua Reynolds, that one night in particular, when Savage and he walked round St. James's-square for want of a lodging, they were not at all depressed by their situation; but in high spirits and brimful of patriotism, traversed the square for several hours, inveighed against the minister, and 'resolved they would *stand by their country.*'

I am afraid, however, that by associating with Savage, who was habituated to the dissipation and licentiousness of the town, Johnson, though his good principles remained steady, did not entirely preserve that conduct, for which, in days of greater simplicity, he was remarked by his friend Mr. Hector; but was imperceptibly led into some indulgencies which occasioned much distress to his virtuous mind.

That Johnson was anxious that an authentick and favourable account of his extraordinary friend should first get possession of the publick attention, is evident from a letter which he wrote in the Gentleman's Magazine for August of the year preceding its publication.

'MR. URBAN,

'As your collections show how often you have owed the ornaments of your poetical pages to the correspondence of the unfortunate and ingenious Mr. Savage, I doubt not but you have so much regard to his memory as to en-courage any design that may have a tendency to the preservation of it from insults or calumnies; and therefore, with some degree of assurance, intreat you to inform the publick, that his life will speedily be published by a person who was favoured with his confidence, and received from himself an account of most of the transactions which he proposes to mention, to the time of his retirement to Swansea in Wales.

convivial day in London, and found it too late to return to any country residence he may occasionally have had, having no lodging in town, he was obliged to pass the night in the manner described above; for, though at that period, it was not uncommon for two men to sleep together, Savage, it appears, could accommodate him with nothing but his company in the open air.—The Epigram given above, which doubtless was written by Johnson, shews that their acquaintance commenced before April, 1738. See p. 77, n. MALONE.]

'From that period, to his death in the prison of Bristol, the account will be continued from materials still less liable to objection; his own letters, and those of his friends, some of which will be inserted in the work, and abstracts of others subjoined in the margin.

'It may be reasonably imagined, that others may have the same design; but as it is not credible that they can obtain the same materials, it must be expected they will supply from invention the want of intelligence; and that under the title of "The Life of Savage," they will publish only a novel, filled with romantick adventures, and imaginary amours. You may therefore, perhaps, gratify the lovers of truth and wit, by giving me leave to inform them in your Magazine, that my account will be published in 8vo. by Mr. Roberts, in Warwick-lane.'

[*No Signature.*]

In February, 1744, it accordingly came forth from the shop of Roberts, between whom and Johnson I have not traced any connection, except the casual one of this publication. In Johnson's 'Life of Savage,' although it must be allowed that its moral is the reverse of— '*Respicere exemplar vitæ morumque jubebo*,' a very useful lesson is inculcated, to guard men of warm passions from a too free indulgence of them; and the various incidents are related in so clear and animated a manner, and illumi-nated throughout with so much philosophy, that it is one of the most interesting narratives in the English language. Sir Joshua Reynolds told me, that upon his return from Italy he met with it in Devonshire, knowing nothing of its authour, and began to read it while he was standing with his arm leaning against a chimney-piece. It seized his attention so strongly, that, not being able to lay down the book till he had finished it, when he attempted to move, he found his arm totally benumbed. The rapidity with which this work was composed, is a wonderful circum-stance. Johnson has been heard to say, 'I wrote forty-eight of the printed octavo pages of the Life of Savage at a sitting; but then I sat up all night.'[1]

[1] Journal of a Tour to the Hebrides, 3d edit. p. 35.

He exhibits the genius of Savage to the best advantage, in the specimens of his poetry which he has selected, some of which are of uncommon merit. We, indeed, occasionally find such vigour and such point, as might make us suppose that the generous aid of Johnson had been imparted to his friend. Mr. Thomas Warton made this remark to me; and, in support of it, quoted from the poem entitled 'The Bastard,' a line in which the fancied superiority of one 'stamped in Nature's mint with extasy,' is contrasted with a regular lawful descendant of some great and ancient family:

'No tenth transmitter of a foolish face.'

But the fact is, that this poem was published some years before Johnson and Savage were acquainted.

It is remarkable, that in this biographical disquisition there appears a very strong symptom of Johnson's prejudice against players; a prejudice which may be attributed to the following causes: first, the imperfection of his organs, which were so defective that he was not susceptible of the fine impressions which theatrical excellence produces upon the generality of mankind; secondly, the cold rejection of his tragedy; and, lastly, the brilliant success of Garrick, who had been his pupil, who had come to London at the same time with him, not in a much more prosperous state than himself, and whose talents he undoubtedly rated low, compared with his own. His being outstripped by his pupil in the race of immediate fame, as well as of fortune, probably made him feel some indignation, as thinking that whatever might be Garrick's merits in his art, the reward was too great when compared with what the most successful efforts of literary labour could attain. At all periods of his life Johnson used to talk contemptuously of players; but in this work he speaks of them with peculiar acrimony; for which, perhaps, there was formerly too much reason from the licentious and dissolute manners of those engaged in that profession. It is but justice to add, that in our own time such a change has taken place, that there is no longer room for such an unfavourable distinction.

His schoolfellow and friend, Dr. Taylor, told me a pleasant anecdote of Johnson's triumphing over his pupil,

David Garrick. When that great actor had played some
little time at Goodman's-fields, Johnson and Taylor went
to see him perform, and afterwards passed the evening
at a tavern with him and old Giffard. Johnson, who was
ever depreciating stage-players, after censuring some
mistakes in emphasis, which Garrick had committed in
the course of that night's acting, said, 'the players, Sir,
have got a kind of rant, with which they run on, without
any regard either to accent or emphasis.' Both Garrick
and Giffard were offended at this sarcasm, and endeavoured to refute it; upon which Johnson rejoined, 'Well
now, I'll give you something to speak, with which you are
little acquainted, and then we shall see how just my
observation is. That shall be the criterion. Let me hear
you repeat the ninth Commandment, "Thou shalt not bear
false witness against thy neighbour."' Both tried at it, said
Dr. Taylor, and both mistook the emphasis, which should
be upon *not* and *false witness*.[1] Johnson put them right, and
enjoyed his victory with great glee.

His 'Life of Savage' was no sooner published, than the
following liberal praise was given to it, in 'The Champion,'
a periodical paper: 'This pamphlet is, without flattery to
its authour, as just and well written a piece as of its kind
I ever saw; so that at the same time that it highly deserves,
it certainly stands very little in need of this recommendation. As to the history of the unfortunate person, whose
memoirs compose this work, it is certainly penned with
equal accuracy and spirit, of which I am so much the
better judge, as I know many of the facts mentioned to be
strictly true, and very fairly related. Besides, it is not only
the story of Mr. Savage, but innumerable incidents relating
to other persons, and other affairs, which renders this a
very amusing, and, withal, a very instructive and valuable
performance. The author's observations are short, significant, and just, as his narrative is remarkably smooth,
and well disposed. His reflections open to all the recesses

---

[1] I suspect Dr. Taylor was inaccurate in this statement. The emphasis
should be equally upon *shalt* and *not*, as both concur to form the negative
injunction; and *false witness*, like the other acts prohibited in the Decalogue,
should not be marked by any peculiar emphasis, but only be distinctly
enunciated.
[A moderate emphasis should be placed on *false*. KEARNEY.]

of the human heart; and, in a word, a more just or pleasant, a more engaging or a more improving treatise, on all the excellencies and defects of human nature, is scarce to be found in our own, or perhaps, any other language.'[1]

Johnson's partiality for Savage made him entertain no doubt of his story, however extraordinary and improbable. It never occurred to him to question his being the son of the Countess of Macclesfield, of whose unrelenting barbarity he so loudly complained, and the particulars of which are related in so strong and affecting a manner in Johnson's Life of him. Johnson was certainly well warranted in publishing his narrative, however offensive it might be to the lady and her relations, because her alledged unnatural and cruel conduct to her son, and shameful avowal of guilt, were stated in a Life of Savage now lying before me, which came out so early as 1727, and no attempt had been made to confute it, or to punish the authour or printer as a libeller: but for the honour of human nature, we should be glad to find the shocking tale not true; and from a respectable gentleman[2] connected with the lady's family, I have received such information and remarks, as joined to my own inquiries, will, I think, render it at least somewhat doubtful, especially when we consider that it must have originated from the person himself who went by the name of Richard Savage.

If the maxim, *falsum in uno, falsum in omnibus*, were to be received without qualification, the credit of Savage's narrative, as conveyed to us, would be annihilated; for it contains some assertions which, beyond a question, are not true.

1. In order to induce a belief that the Earl Rivers, on account of a criminal connection with whom, Lady Macclesfield is said to have been divorced from her husband, by Act of Parliament,[3] had a peculiar anxiety about the child which she bore to him, it is alledged, that

[1] This character of the Life of Savage was not written by Fielding, as has been supposed, but most probably by Ralph, who, as appears from the minutes of the Partners of 'The Champion,' in the possession of Mr. Reed of Staple Inn, succeeded Fielding in his share of the paper, before the date of that eulogium.[a]

[2] The late Francis Cockayne Cust, Esq., one of his Majesty's Counsel.

[3] 1697.

[a] *Seward always said that Colonel Brett upon his Deathbed express'd his Belief that Savage was not the Son of Lady Macclesfield.* [1]

his Lordship gave him his own name, and had it duly recorded in the register of St. Andrew's, Holborn. I have carefully inspected that register, but no such entry is to be found.[1]

2. It is stated, that 'Lady Macclesfield having lived for some time upon very uneasy terms with her husband, thought a publick confession of adultery the most obvious and expeditious method of obtaining her liberty;' and Johnson, assuming this to be true, stigmatises her with indignation, as 'the wretch who had, without scruple, proclaimed herself an adultress.'[2] But I have perused the Journals of both houses of Parliament at the period of her divorce, and there find it authentically ascertained, that so far from voluntarily submitting to the ignominious

---

[1] [Mr. Cust's reasoning, with respect to the filiation of Richard Savage, always appeared to me extremely unsatisfactory; and is entirely overturned by the following decisive observations, for which the reader is indebted to the unwearied researches of Mr. Bindley.—The story on which Mr. Cust so much relies, that Savage was a supposititious child, not the son of Lord Rivers and Lady Macclesfield, but the offspring of a shoemaker, introduced in consequence of her real son's death, was, without doubt, grounded on the circumstance of Lady Macclesfield's having, in 1696, previously to the birth of Savage, had a daughter by the Earl Rivers, who died in her infancy: a fact, which, as the same gentleman observes to me, was proved in the course of the proceedings on Lord Macclesfield's Bill of Divorce. Most fictions of this kind have some admixture of truth in them. MALONE.]

[From 'the Earl of Macclesfield's Case,' which, in 1697-8, was presented to the Lords, in order to procure an act of divorce, it appears, that 'Anne, Countess of Macclesfield, under the name of Madam SMITH, was delivered of a male child in Fox Court, near Brook-street, Holborn, by Mrs. Wright, a midwife, on Saturday the 16th of January, 1696-7, at six o'clock in the morning, who was baptized on the Monday following, and registered by the name of RICHARD, the son of John Smith, by Mr. Burbridge, assistant to Dr. Manningham's Curate for St. Andrew's, Holborn: that the child was christened on Monday the 18th of January, in Fox Court; and, from the privacy, was supposed by Mr. Burbridge to be 'a by-blow, or bastard.' It also appears, that during her delivery, the lady wore a mask; and that Mary Pegler on the next day after the baptism (Tuesday) took a male-child, whose mother was called Madam Smith, from the house of Mrs. Pheasant, in Fox Court, [running from Brook Street into Gray's-Inn Lane,] who went by the name of Mrs. Lee.

Conformable to this statement is the entry in the Register of St. Andrew's, Holborn, which is as follows, and which unquestionably records the baptism of Richard Savage, to whom Lord Rivers gave his own Christian name, prefixed to the assumed surname of his mother: Jan. 1696-7. 'RICHARD, son of John Smith and Mary, in Fox Court, in Gray's-Inn Lane, baptised the 18th.' BINDLEY.]

[2] No divorce can be obtained in the Courts, on confession of the party. There must be proofs. KEARNEY.]

charge of adultery, she made a strenuous defence by her Counsel; the bill having been first moved the 15th of January, 1697–8, in the house of Lords, and proceeded on, (with various applications for time to bring up witnesses at a distance, &c.) at intervals, till the 3d of March, when it passed. It was brought to the Commons, by a message from the Lords, the 5th of March, proceeded on the 7th, 10th, 11th, 14th, and 15th, on which day, after a full examination of witnesses on both sides, and hearing of Counsel, it was reported without amendments, passed, and carried to the Lords. That Lady Macclesfield was convicted of the crime of which she was accused, cannot be denied; but the question now is, whether the person calling himself Richard Savage was her son.

It has been said,[1] that when Earl Rivers was dying, and anxious to provide for all his natural children, he was informed by Lady Macclesfield that her son by him was dead. Whether, then, shall we believe that this was a malignant lie, invented by a mother to prevent her own child from receiving the bounty of his father, which was accordingly the consequence, if the person whose life Johnson wrote, was her son; or shall we not rather believe that the person who then assumed the name of Richard Savage was an impostor, being in reality the son of the shoe-maker, under whose wife's care[2] Lady Macclesfield's child was placed; that after the death of the real Richard Savage, he attempted to personate him; and that the fraud being known to Lady Macclesfield, he was therefore repulsed by her with just resentment.

There is a strong circumstance in support of the last supposition; though it has been mentioned as an aggravation of Lady Macclesfield's unnatural conduct, and that is, her having prevented him from obtaining the benefit of a legacy left to him by Mrs. Lloyd, his godmother. For if there was such a legacy left, his not being able to obtain payment of it, must be imputed to his consciousness that he was not the real person. The just

[1] [By Johnson, in his Life of Savage. MALONE.]

[2] [This, as an accurate friend remarks to me, is not correctly stated.[a] The shoemaker under whose care Savage was placed, with a view to his becoming his apprentice, was not the husband of his nurse.—See Johnson's Life of Savage. Lives of the Poets, vol. iii. p. 131. edit. 1732. J. BOSWELL.]

[a] *Mr. Seward assur'd me that Colonel Brett declared upon his Death-bed, that Savage was not Son to the Countess of Macclesfield* H. L. P. [H]

inference should be, that by the death of Lady Macclesfield's child before its god-mother, the legacy became
lapsed, and therefore that Johnson's Richard Savage was
an impostor.

If he had a title to the legacy, he could not have found
any difficulty in recovering it; for had the executors
resisted his claim, the whole costs, as well as the legacy,
must have been paid by them, if he had been the child
to whom it was given.

The talents of Savage, and the mingled fire, rudeness,
pride, meanness, and ferocity of his character,[1] concur in
making it credible that he was fit to plan and carry on an
ambitious and daring scheme of imposture, similar
instances of which have not been wanting in higher
spheres, in the history of different countries, and have
had a considerable degree of success.

Yet, on the other hand, to the companion of Johnson,
(who, through whatever medium he was conveyed into
this world,—be it ever so doubtful 'To whom related, or
by whom begot,' was, unquestionably, a man of no
common endowments,) we must allow the weight of
general repute as to his *Status* or parentage, though illicit;
and supposing him to be an impostor, it seems strange
that Lord Tyrconnel, the nephew of Lady Macclesfield,
should patronise him, and even admit him as a guest in
his family.[2] Lastly, it must ever appear very suspicious,

[1] Johnson's companion appears to have persuaded that lofty-minded man,
that he resembled him in having a noble pride; for Johnson, after painting
in strong colours the quarrel between Lord Tyrconnel and Savage, asserts
that 'the spirit of Mr. Savage, indeed, never suffered him to solicit a reconciliation: he returned reproach for reproach, and insult for insult.' But the
respectable gentleman to whom I have alluded, has in his possession a letter
from Savage, after Lord Tyrconnel had discarded him, addressed to the
Reverend Mr. Gilbert, his Lordship's Chaplain, in which he requests him,
in the humblest manner, to represent his case to the Viscount.

[2] Trusting to Savage's information, Johnson represents this unhappy
man's being received as a companion by Lord Tyrconnel, and pensioned
by his Lordship, as posterior to Savage's conviction and pardon. But I am
assured, that Savage had received the voluntary bounty of Lord Tyrconnel,
and had been dismissed by him long before the murder was committed, and
that his Lordship was very instrumental in procuring Savage's pardon, by
his intercession with the Queen, through Lady Hertford. If, therefore, he
had been desirous of preventing the publication by Savage, he would have
left him to his fate. Indeed I must observe, that although Johnson mentions
that Lord Tyrconnel's patronage of Savage was 'upon his promise to lay

that three different accounts of the Life of Richard Savage, one published in 'The Plain Dealer,' in 1724, another in 1727, and another by the powerful pen of Johnson, in 1744, and all of them while Lady Macclesfield was alive, should, notwithstanding the severe attacks upon her, have been suffered to pass without any publick and effectual contradiction.

I have thus endeavoured to sum up the evidence upon the case, as fairly as I can; and the result seems to be, that the world must vibrate in a state of uncertainty as to what was the truth.

This digression, I trust, will not be censured, as it relates to a matter exceedingly curious, and very intimately connected with Johnson, both as a man and an authour.[1]

He this year wrote the 'Preface to the Harleian Miscellany.'* The selection of the pamphlets of which it was composed was made by Mr. Oldys, a man of eager curiosity, and indefatigable diligence, who first exerted that spirit of inquiry into the literature of the old English writers, by which the works of our great dramatic poet have of late been so signally illustrated.

In 1745 he published a pamphlet entitled, 'Miscellaneous Observations on the Tragedy of Macbeth, with Remarks on Sir T. H.'s (Sir Thomas Hanmer's) Edition

marginal line:
Miscellaneous Observations . . . of Macbeth [H]

aside his design of exposing the cruelty of his mother,' the great biographer has forgotten that he himself has mentioned, that Savage's story had been told several years before in 'The Plain Dealer;' from which he quotes this strong saying of the generous Sir Richard Steele, that the 'inhumanity of his mother had given him a right to find every good man his father.' At the same time it must be acknowledged, that Lady Macclesfield and her relations might still wish that her story should not be brought into more conspicuous notice by the satirical pen of Savage.

[1] Miss Mason, after having forfeited the title of Lady Macclesfield by divorce, was married to Colonel Brett, and, it is said, was well known in all the polite circles. Colley Cibber, I am informed, had so high an opinion of her taste and judgement as to genteel life and manners, that he submitted every scene of his 'Careless Husband' to Mrs. Brett's revisal and correction. Colonel Brett was reported to be free in his gallantry with his Lady's Maid. Mrs. Brett came into a room one day in her own house, and found the Colonel and her maid both fast asleep in two chairs. She tied a white handkerchief round her husband's neck, which was a sufficient proof that she had discovered his intrigue; but she never at any time took notice of it to him. This incident as I am told, gave occasion to the well-wrought scene of Sir Charles and Lady Easy and Edging.

cross:
was married etc. [H]

of Shakspeare.'* To which he affixed, proposals for a new edition of that poet.

As we do not trace any thing else published by him during the course of this year, we may conjecture that he was occupied entirely with that work. But the little encouragement which was given by the publick to his anonymous proposals for the execution of a task which Warburton was known to have undertaken, probably damped his ardour. His pamphlet, however, was highly esteemed, and was fortunate enough to obtain the appro-bation even of the supercilious Warburton himself, who, in the Preface to his Shakspeare published two years afterwards, thus mentioned it: 'As to all those things which have been published under the titles of *Essays, Remarks, Observations*, &c. on Shakspeare, if you except some Critical Notes on Macbeth, given as a specimen of a projected edition, and written, as appears, by a man of parts and genius, the rest are absolutely below a serious notice.'

Of this flattering distinction shewn to him by Warburton,

marginal line:
entertained by . . . to me [H]

a very grateful remembrance was ever entertained by Johnson, who said, 'He praised me at a time when praise was of value to me.'

In 1746 it is probable that he was still employed upon his Shakspeare, which perhaps he laid aside for a time, upon account of the high expectations which were formed of Warburton's edition of that great poet. It is somewhat curious, that his literary career appears to have been almost totally suspended in the years 1745 and 1746, those years which were marked by a civil war in Great-Britain, when a rash attempt was made to restore the House of Stuart to the throne. That he had a tenderness for that unfortunate House, is well known; and some may fanci-fully imagine, that a sympathetick anxiety impeded the exertion of his intellectual powers: but I am inclined to think, that he was, during this time, sketching the outlines of his great philological work.

None of his letters during those years are extant, so far as I can discover. This is much to be regretted. It might afford some entertainment to see how he then expressed himself to his private friends concerning State affairs. Dr. Adams informs me, that 'at this time a favourite object which he had in contemplation was "The Life of Alfred;" in which, from the warmth with which he spoke about it, he would, I believe, had he been master of his own will, have engaged himself, rather than on any other subject.'

index sign:
The Life of Alfred etc.
[1]

In 1747 it is supposed that the Gentleman's Magazine for May was enriched by him with five short poetical pieces, distinguished by three asterisks. The first is a translation, or rather a paraphrase, of a Latin Epitaph on Sir Thomas Hanmer. Whether the Latin was his, or not, I have never heard, though I should think it probably was, if it be certain that he wrote the English; as to which my only cause of doubt is, that his slighting character of Hanmer as an editor, in his 'Observations on Macbeth,' is very different from that in the Epitaph. It may be said, that there is the same contrariety between the character in the Observations, and that in his own Preface to Shakspeare; but a considerable time elapsed between the one publication and the other, whereas the Observations and the Epitaph came close together. The others are, 'To Miss ——, on her giving the Authour a gold and silk net-work Purse of her own weaving;' 'Stella in Mourning;' 'The Winter's Walk;' 'An Ode;' and, 'To Lyce, an elderly Lady.' I am not positive that all these were his productions;[1] but as 'The Winter's Walk' has never been controverted to be his, and all of them have the same mark, it is reasonable to conclude that they are all written by the same hand. Yet to the Ode, in which we find a passage very characteristick of him, being a learned description of the gout,

> 'Unhappy, whom to beds of pain
> *Arthritick* tyranny consigns;'

there is the following note, 'The authour being ill of the gout:' but Johnson was not attacked with that distemper

---

[1] [In the UNIVERSAL VISITER, to which Johnson contributed, the mark which is affixed to some pieces unquestionably his, is also found subjoined to others, of which he certainly was not the authour. The mark therefore will not ascertain the poems in question to have been written by him. Some of them were probably the productions of Hawkesworth, who, it is believed, was afflicted with the gout. The verses on a purse were inserted afterwards in Mrs. Williams's Miscellanies, and are, unquestionably, Johnson's. MALONE.]

till a very late period of his life. May not this, however, be a poetical fiction? Why may not a poet suppose himself to have the gout, as well as suppose himself to be in love, of which we have innumerable instances, and which has been admirably ridiculed by Johnson in his 'Life of Cowley'? I have also some difficulty to believe that he could produce such a group of *conceits* as appear in the verses to Lyce, in which he claims for this ancient person-age as good a right to be assimilated to *heaven,* as nymphs whom other poets have flattered; he therefore ironically ascribes to her the attributes of the *sky,* in such stanzas as this:

> 'Her teeth the *night* with *darkness* dies,
>   She's *starr'd* with pimples o'er;
> Her tongue like nimble *lightning* plies,
>   And can with *thunder* roar.'

But as at a very advanced age he could condescend to trifle in *namby-pamby* rhymes, to please Mrs. Thrale and her daughter, he may have, in his earlier years, composed such a piece as this.

It is remarkable, that in this first edition of 'The Winter's Walk,' the concluding line is much more Johnsonian than it was afterwards printed; for in subsequent editions, after praying Stella to 'snatch him to her arms,' he says,

> 'And *shield* me from the *ills* of life.'

Whereas in the first edition it is

> 'And *hide* me from the *sight* of life.'

A horrour at life in general is more consonant with Johnson's habitual gloomy cast of thought.[a]

I have heard him repeat with great energy the following verses, which appeared in the Gentleman's Magazine for April this year; but I have no authority to say they were his own. Indeed one of the best criticks of our age suggests to me, that 'the word *indifferently* being used in the sense of *without concern,* and being also very unpoetical, renders it improbable that they should have been his composition.'

'*On Lord* LOVAT'S *Execution*

> 'Pity'd by *gentle minds* KILMARNOCK died;
>   The *brave,* BALMERINO, were on thy side;

RADCLIFFE, unhappy in his crimes of youth,
Steady in what he still mistook for truth,
Beheld his death so decently unmov'd,
The *soft* lamented, and the *brave* approv'd.
But LOVAT's fate indifferently we view,
True to no *King*, to no *religion* true:
No *fair* forgets the *ruin* he has done;
No *child* laments the *tyrant* of his *son;*
No *tory* pities, thinking what he was;
No *whig* compassions, *for he left the cause;*
The *brave* regret not, for he was not brave;
The *honest* mourn not, knowing him a knave!'[1]

This year his old pupil and friend, David Garrick, having become joint patentee and manager of Drury-lane theatre, Johnson honoured his opening of it with a Prologue,* which for just and manly dramatick criticism on the whole range of the English stage, as well as for poetical excellence,[2] is unrivalled. Like the celebrated Epilogue to the 'Distressed Mother,' it was, during the season, often called for by the audience. The most striking and brilliant passages of it have been so often repeated, and are so well recollected by all the lovers of the drama, and of poetry, that it would be superfluous to point them out.—In the Gentleman's Magazine for December this

two marginal lines:
as well . . . is unrivalled
[H]
marginal line:
Mother,' it . . . and
brilliant [H]

[1] These verses are somewhat too severe on the extraordinary person who is the chief figure in them; for he was undoubtedly brave. His pleasantry during his solemn trial (in which, by the way, I have heard Mr. David Hume observe, that we have one of the very few speeches of Mr. Murray, now Earl of Mansfield, authentically given) was very remarkable. When asked if he had any questions to put to Sir Everard Fawkener, who was one of the strongest witnesses against him, he answered 'I only wish him joy of his young wife.' And after sentence of death, in the horrible terms in such cases of treason, was pronounced upon him, and he was retiring from the bar, he said, 'Fare you well, my Lords, we shall not all meet again in one place.' He behaved with perfect composure at his execution, and called out 'Dulce et decorum est pro patriâ mori.'

two marginal lines:
brave. His . . . by the
[H]

[2] My friend Mr. Courtenay, whose eulogy on Johnson's Latin Poetry has been inserted in this Work, is no less happy in praising his English Poetry.

But hark, he sings! the strain even Pope admires;
Indignant virtue her own bard inspires,
Sublime as Juvenal he pours his lays,
And with the Roman shares congenial praise;—
In glowing numbers now he fires the age,
And Shakspeare's sun relumes the clouded stage.

year, he inserted an 'Ode on Winter,' which is, I think, an admirable specimen of his genius for lyrick poetry.

But the year 1747 is distinguished as the epoch, when Johnson's arduous and important work, his DICTIONARY OF THE ENGLISH LANGUAGE, was announced to the world, by the publication of its Plan or PROSPECTUS.

How long this immense undertaking had been the object of his contemplation, I do not know. I once asked him by what means he had attained to that astonishing knowledge of our language, by which he was enabled to realize a design of such extent and accumulated difficulty. He told me, that 'it was not the effect of particular study; but that it had grown up in his mind insensibly.' I have been informed by Mr. James Dodsley, that several years before this period, when Johnson was one day sitting in his brother Robert's shop, he heard his brother suggest to him that a Dictionary of the English Language would be a work that would be well received by the publick; that Johnson seemed at first to catch at the proposition; but, after a pause, said, in his abrupt decisive manner, 'I believe I shall not undertake it.' That he, however, had bestowed much thought upon the subject, before he published his 'Plan,' is evident from the enlarged, clear, and accurate views which it exhibits; and we find him mentioning in that tract, that many of the writers whose testimonies were to be produced as authorities, were selected by Pope; which proves that he had been furnished, probably by Mr. Robert Dodsley, with whatever hints that eminent poet had contributed towards a great literary project, that had been the subject of important consideration in a former reign.

The booksellers who contracted with Johnson, single and unaided, for the execution of a work, which in other countries has not been effected but by the co-operating exertions of many, were Mr. Robert Dodsley, Mr. Charles Hitch, Mr. Andrew Millar, the two Messieurs Longman, and the two Messieurs Knapton. The price stipulated was fifteen hundred and seventy-five pounds.

The 'Plan' was addressed to Philip Dormer, Earl of Chesterfield, then one of his Majesty's Principal Secretaries of State; a nobleman who was very ambitious of literary distinction, and who, upon being informed of the design, had expressed himself in terms very favourable to its success. There is, perhaps, in every thing of any consequence, a secret history which it would be amusing to know, could we have it authentically communicated. Johnson told me,[1] 'Sir, the way in which the plan of my Dictionary came to be inscribed to Lord Chesterfield, was this: I had neglected to write it by the time appointed. Dodsley suggested a desire to have it addressed to Lord Chesterfield. I laid hold of this as a pretext for delay, that it might be better done, and let Dodsley have his desire. I said to my friend, Dr. Bathurst, "Now if any good comes of my addressing to Lord Chesterfield, it will be ascribed to deep policy, when, in fact, it was only a casual excuse for laziness."'

It is worthy of observation, that the 'Plan' has not only the substantial merit of comprehension, perspicuity, and precision, but that the language of it is unexceptionably excellent; it being altogether free from that inflation of style, and those uncommon but apt and energetick words, which in some of his writings have been censured, with more petulance than justice; and never was there a more dignified strain of compliment than that in which he courts the attention of one, who, he had been persuaded to believe, would be a respectable patron.

'With regard to questions of purity or propriety, (says he) I was once in doubt whether I should not attribute to myself too much in attempting to decide them, and whether my province was to extend beyond the proposition of the question, and the display of the suffrages on each side; but I have been since determined by your Lordship's opinion, to interpose my own judgement, and shall therefore endeavour to support what appears to me most consonant to grammar and reason. Ausonius thought that modesty forbade him to plead inability for a task to which Cæsar had judged him equal:

Cur me posse negem, posse quod ille putat?

And I may hope, my Lord, that since you, whose authority in our language is so generally acknowledged, have

[1] September 22, 1777, going from Ashbourne in Derbyshire, to see Islam.

commissioned me to declare my own opinion, I shall be considered as exercising a kind of vicarious jurisdiction: and that the power which might have been denied to my own claim, will be readily allowed me as the delegate of your Lordship.'

This passage proves, that Johnson's addressing his 'Plan' to Lord Chesterfield was not merely in consequence of the result of a report by means of Dodsley, that the Earl favoured the design; but that there had been a particular communication with his Lordship concerning it. Dr. Taylor told me, that Johnson sent his 'Plan' to him in manuscript, for his perusal; and that when it was lying upon his table, Mr. William Whitehead happened to pay him a visit, and being shewn it, was highly pleased with such parts of it as he had time to read, and begged to take it home with him, which he was allowed to do; that from him it got into the hands of a noble Lord, who carried it to Lord Chesterfield. When Taylor observed this might be an advantage, Johnson replied, 'No, Sir, it would have come out with more bloom, if it had not been seen before by any body.'

marginal line: replied, 'No . . . any body [H]

The opinion conceived of it by another noble authour, appears from the following extract of a letter from the Earl of Orrery to Dr. Birch:

'Caledon, Dec. 30, 1747

'I have just now seen the specimen of Mr. Johnson's Dictionary, addressed to Lord Chesterfield. I am much pleased with the plan, and I think the specimen is one of the best that I have ever read. Most specimens disgust, rather than prejudice us in favour of the work to follow; but the language of Mr. Johnson's is good, and the arguments are properly and modestly expressed. However, some expressions may be cavilled at, but they are trifles. I'll mention one: the *barren* laurel. The laurel is not barren, in any sense whatever; it bears fruits and flowers. *Sed hæ sunt nugæ,* and I have great expectations from the performance.'[1]

That he was fully aware of the arduous nature of the undertaking, he acknowledges; and shews himself perfectly sensible of it in the conclusion of his 'Plan;' but he had a

[1] Birch MSS. Brit. Mus. 4303.

noble consciousness of his own abilities, which enabled him to go on with undaunted spirit.

Dr. Adams found him one day busy at his Dictionary, when the following dialogue ensued.—'ADAMS. This is a great work, Sir. How are you to get all the etymologies? JOHNSON. Why, Sir, here is a shelf with Junius, and Skinner, and others; and there is a Welch gentleman who has published a collection of Welch proverbs, who will help me with the Welch. ADAMS. But, Sir, how can you do this in three years? JOHNSON. Sir, I have no doubt that I can do it in three years. ADAMS. But the French Academy, which consists of forty members, took forty years to compile their Dictionary. JOHNSON. Sir, thus it is. This is the proportion. Let me see; forty times forty is sixteen hundred. As three to sixteen hundred, so is the proportion of an Englishman to a Frenchman.' With so much ease and pleasantry could he talk of that prodigious labour which he had undertaken to execute.

The publick has had, from another pen,[1] a long detail of what had been done in this country by prior Lexicographers; and no doubt Johnson was wise, to avail himself of them, so far as they went: but the learned, yet judicious research of etymology, the various, yet accurate display of definition, and the rich collection of authorities, were reserved for the superiour mind of our great philologist. For the mechanical part he employed, as he told me, six amanuenses; and let it be remembered by the natives of North-Britain, to whom he is supposed to have been so hostile, that five of them were of that country. There were two Messieurs Macbean; Mr. Shiels, who, we shall hereafter see, partly wrote the Lives of the Poets to which the name of Cibber is affixed:[2] Mr. Stewart, son of Mr. George Stewart, bookseller at Edinburgh; and a Mr. Maitland. The sixth of these humble assistants was Mr. Peyton,[a] who, I believe, taught French, and published some elementary tracts.

underlined:
Mr. Peyton [1]
[a] *Poor Soul.* [1]

To all these painful labourers Johnson shewed a

[1] See Sir John Hawkins's Life of Johnson.

[Sir John Hawkins's list of former English Dictionaries is, however, by no means complete. MALONE.]

[2] See vol. ii. under April 10, 1776.

never-ceasing kindness, so far as they stood in need of it. The elder Mr. Macbean had afterwards the honour of being Librarian to Archibald, Duke of Argyle, for many years, but was left without a shilling. Johnson wrote for him a Preface to 'A System of Ancient Geography;' and, by the favour of Lord Thurlow, got him admitted a poor brother of the Charterhouse. For Shiels, who died of a consumption, he had much tenderness; and it has been thought that some choice sentences in the Lives of the Poets were supplied by him. Peyton, when reduced to penury, had frequent aid from the bounty of Johnson, who at last was at the expence of burying him and his wife.

While the Dictionary was going forward, Johnson lived part of the time in Holborn, part in Gough-square, Fleet-street; and he had an upper room fitted up like a counting-house for the purpose, in which he gave to the copyists their several tasks. The words partly taken from other dictionaries, and partly supplied by himself, having been first written down with spaces left between them, he delivered in writing their etymologies, definitions, and various significations. The authorities were copied from the books themselves, in which he had marked the passages with a black-lead pencil, the traces of which could easily be effaced. I have seen several of them, in which that trouble had not been taken; so that they were just as when used by the copyists. It is remarkable that he was so attentive in the choice of the passages in which words were authorised, that one may read page after page of his Dictionary with improvement and pleasure; and it should not pass unobserved, that he has quoted no authour whose writings had a tendency to hurt sound religion and

^a *It has been observed 20 Times* [1] morality.^a

The necessary expence of preparing a work of such magnitude for the press, must have been a considerable deduction from the price stipulated to be paid for the copyright. I understand that nothing was allowed by the booksellers on that account; and I remember his telling me, that a large portion of it having, by mistake, been

marginal line: *the paper . . . it tran-scribed* [H]

written upon both sides of the paper, so as to be inconvenient for the compositor, it cost him twenty pounds to have it transcribed upon one side only.

He is now to be considered as 'tugging at his oar,' as engaged in a steady continued course of occupation, sufficient to employ all his time for some years; and which was the best preventive of that constitutional melancholy which was ever lurking about him, ready to trouble his quiet. But his enlarged and lively mind could not be satisfied without more diversity of employment, and the pleasure of animated relaxation.[1] He therefore not only exerted his talents in occasional composition, very different from Lexicography, but formed a club in Ivy-lane, Paternoster-row, with a view to enjoy literary discussion, and amuse his evening hours. The members associated with him in this little society were, his beloved friend Dr. Richard Bathurst, Mr. Hawkesworth, afterwards well known by his writings, Mr. John Hawkins, an attorney,[2] and a few others of different professions.

In the Gentleman's Magazine for May of this year he wrote a 'Life of Roscommon,'* with Notes; which he afterwards much improved, (indenting the notes into text,) and inserted amongst his Lives of the English Poets.

Mr. Dodsley this year brought out his PRECEPTOR, one of the most valuable books for the improvement of young minds that has appeared in any language; and to this meritorious work Johnson furnished 'The Preface,'* containing a general sketch of the book, with a short and perspicuous recommendation of each article; as also, 'The Vision of Theodore, the Hermit, found in his Cell,'* a most beautiful allegory of human life, under the figure

marginal line:
recommendation of . . .
a most [H]

[1] [For the sake of relaxation from his literary labours, and probably also for Mrs. Johnson's health, he this Summer visited Tunbridge Wells, then a place of much greater resort than it is at present. Here he met Mr. Cibber, Mr. Garrick, Mr. Samuel Richardson, Mr. Whiston, Mr. Onslow, (the Speaker,) Mr. Pitt, Mr. Lyttelton, and several other distinguished persons. In a print, representing some of 'the remarkable characters' who were at Tunbridge Wells in 1748, and copied from a drawing of the same size, (See RICHARDSON'S CORRESPONDENCE,) Dr. Johnson stands the first figure.[a] MALONE.]

[a] *So he does.* [J]

[2] He was afterwards for several years Chairman of the Middlesex Justices, and upon occasion of presenting an address to the King, accepted the usual offer of Knighthood. He is authour of 'A History of Musick,' in five volumes in quarto. By assiduous attendance upon Johnson in his last illness, he obtained the office of one of his executors; in consequence of which, the booksellers of London employed him to publish an edition of Dr. Johnson's works, and to write his Life.

of ascending the mountain of Existence. The Bishop of Dromore heard Dr. Johnson say, that he thought this was the best thing he ever wrote.ᵃ

In January, 1749, he published 'THE VANITY OF HUMAN WISHES, being the Tenth Satire of Juvenal imitated.'* He, I believe, composed it the preceding year.[1] Mrs. Johnson, for the sake of country air, had lodgings at Hampstead, to which he resorted occasionally, and there the greatest part, if not the whole, of this imitation was written. The fervid rapidity with which it was produced, is scarcely credible. I have heard him say, that he composed seventy lines of it in one day, without putting one of them upon paper till they were finished. I remember when I once regretted to him that he had not given us more of Juvenal's Satires, he said, he probably should give more, for he had them all in his head; by which I understood, that he had the originals and correspondent allusions floating in his mind, which he could, when he pleased, embody and render permanent without much labour. Some of them, however, he observed were too gross for imitation.

The profits of a single poem, however excellent, appear to have been very small in the last reign, compared with

what a publication of the same size has since been known to yield. I have mentioned upon Johnson's own authority, that for his LONDON he had only ten guineas; and now,

after his fame was established, he got for his 'Vanity of Human Wishes' but five guineas more, as is proved by an authentick document in my possession.[2]

It will be observed, that he reserves to himself the right of printing one edition of this satire, which was his practice upon occasion of the sale of all his writings; it being his

---

[1] Sir John Hawkins, with solemn inaccuracy, represents this poem as a consequence of the indifferent reception of his tragedy. But the fact is, that the poem was published on the 9th of January, and the tragedy was not acted till the 6th of the February following.

[2] 'Nov. 25, 1748, I received of Mr. Dodsley fifteen guineas, for which I assign to him the right of copy of an Imitation of the Tenth Satire of Juvenal, written by me; reserving to myself the right of printing one edition.

SAM. JOHNSON'

'London, 29 June, 1786. A true copy, from the original in Dr. Johnson's hand-writing. JAˢ. DODSLEY'

fixed intention to publish at some period, for his own profit, a complete collection of his works.

His 'Vanity of Human Wishes' has less of common life, but more of a philosophick dignity than his 'London.' More readers, therefore, will be delighted with the pointed spirit of 'London,' than with the profound reflection of 'The Vanity of Human Wishes.' Garrick, for instance, observed in his sprightly manner, with more vivacity than regard to just discrimination, as is usual with wits, 'When Johnson lived much with the Herveys, and saw a good deal of what was passing in life, he wrote his "London," which is lively and easy: when he became more retired, he gave us his "Vanity of Human Wishes," which is as hard as Greek. Had he gone on to imitate another satire, it would have been as hard as Hebrew.'[1a]

But 'The Vanity of Human Wishes' is, in the opinion of the best judges, as high an effort of ethick poetry as any language can shew. The instances of variety of disappointment are chosen so judiciously, and painted so strongly, that, the moment they are read, they bring conviction to every thinking mind.

That of the scholar must have depressed the too sanguine expectations of many an ambitious student.[2] That

marginal line:
some period . . . his works [H]

underlined:
Hebrew [H]
[a] *which is not as hard as either of the others* [H]
marginal line:
But ' The . . . instances of [H]

[1] From Mr. Langton.

[2] In this poem one of the instances mentioned of unfortunate learned men is *Lydiat:*

'Hear Lydiat's Life, and Galileo's end.'

The History of Lydiat being little known, the following account of him may be acceptable to many of my readers. It appeared as a note in the Supplement to the Gentleman's Magazine for 1748, in which some passages extracted from Johnson's poem were inserted, and it should have been added in the subsequent editions.—'A very learned divine and mathematician, fellow of New College, Oxon, and Rector of Okerton, near Banbury. He wrote, among many others, a Latin treatise " *De natura cæli, &c.*" in which he attacked the sentiments of Scaliger and Aristotle, not bearing to hear it urged, *that some things are true in philosophy, and false in divinity.* He made above 600 Sermons on the harmony of the Evangelists. Being unsuccessful in publishing his works, he lay in the prison of Bocardo at Oxford, and in the King's Bench, till Bishop Usher, Dr. Laud, Sir William Boswell, and Dr. Pink, released him by paying his debts. He petitioned King Charles I. to be sent into Ethiopia, &c. to procure MSS. Having spoken in favour of Monarchy and bishops, he was plundered by the parliament forces, and twice carried away prisoner from his rectory; and afterwards had not a shirt to shift him in three months, without he borrowed it, and died very poor in 1646.'

of the warrior, Charles of Sweden, is, I think, as highly
finished a picture as can possibly be conceived.

Were all the other excellencies of this poem annihilated,
it must ever have our grateful reverence from its noble
conclusion; in which we are consoled with the assurance
that happiness may be attained, if we 'apply our hearts'
to piety:

> 'Where then shall hope and fear their objects find?
> Shall dull suspense corrupt the stagnant mind?
> Must helpless man, in ignorance sedate,
> Roll darkling down the torrent of his fate?
> Shall no dislike alarm, no wishes rise,
> No cries attempt the mercy of the skies?
> Inquirer, cease; petitions yet remain,
> Which Heav'n may hear, nor deem Religion vain.
> Still raise for good the supplicating voice,
> But leave to Heaven the measure and the choice.
> Safe in His hand, whose eye discerns afar
> The secret ambush of a specious pray'r;
> Implore his aid, in his decisions rest,
> Secure, whate'er he gives, he gives the best:
> Yet when the sense of sacred presence fires,
> And strong devotion to the skies aspires,
> Pour forth thy fervours for a healthful mind,
> Obedient passions, and a will resign'd;
> For love, which scarce collective man can fill;
> For patience, sovereign o'er transmuted ill;
> For faith, which panting for a happier seat,
> Counts death kind Nature's signal for retreat,
> These goods for man the laws of Heaven ordain,
> These goods He grants, who grants the power to gain;
> With these celestial wisdom calms the mind,
> And makes the happiness she does not find.'[1]

[1] [In this poem, a line in which the danger attending on female beauty
is mentioned, has very generally, I believe, been misunderstood:
> 'Yet VANE could tell what ills from beauty spring,
> And Sedley curs'd the form that pleas'd a king.'

The lady mentioned in the first of these verses, was not the celebrated
Lady Vane, whose memoirs were given to the publick by Dr. Smollett, but
Anne Vane, who was mistress to Frederick, Prince of Wales, and died in
1736, not long before Johnson settled in London. Some account of this lady
was published, under the title of The Secret History of Vanella, 8vo. 1732.

Garrick being now vested with theatrical power by being manager of Drury-lane theatre, he kindly and generously made use of it to bring out Johnson's tragedy, which had been long kept back for want of encouragement. But in this benevolent purpose he met with no small difficulty from the temper of Johnson, which could not brook that a drama which he had formed with much study, and had been obliged to keep more than the nine years of Horace, should be revised and altered at the pleasure of an actor. Yet Garrick knew well, that without some alterations it would not be fit for the stage. A violent dispute having ensued between them, Garrick applied to the Reverend Dr. Taylor to interpose. Johnson was at first very obstinate. 'Sir, (said he) the fellow wants me to make Mahomet run mad, that he may have an opportunity of tossing his hands and kicking his heels.'[1] He was, however, at last, with difficulty, prevailed on to comply with Garrick's wishes, so as to allow of some changes; but still there were not enough.

Dr. Adams was present the first night of the representation of IRENE, and gave me the following account: 'Before the curtain drew up, there were catcalls whistling, which alarmed Johnson's friends. The Prologue, which was written by himself in a manly strain, soothed the

See also Vanella in the Straw, 4to, 1732. In Mr. Boswell's TOUR TO THE HEBRIDES, (p. 37, 4th edit.) we find some observations respecting the lines in question:

'In Dr. Johnson's VANITY OF HUMAN WISHES there is the following passage:

> 'The teeming mother anxious for her race,
> Begs for each birth the fortune of a face;
> Yet Vane,' &c.

'Lord Hailes told him, [Johnson] he was mistaken in the instances he had given of unfortunate fair ones, for neither Vane nor Sedley had a title to that description.'—His lordship therefore thought, that the lines should rather have run thus:

> Yet *Shore* could tell——
> And *Valiere*[a] curs'd——

'Our friend (he added in a subsequent note, addressed to Mr. Boswell on this subject) chose Vane, who was far from being well-look'd, and Sedley, who was so ugly that Charles II. said—his brother had her by way of penance.'— MALONE.]

[1] Mahomet was in fact played by Mr. Barry, and Demetrius by Mr. Garrick: but probably at this time the parts were not yet cast.

underlined with grave accent added to first 'e': Valiere [1]

[a] *The Accent would not have fallen right upon the last Lady, besides that She was Mademoiselle* de la Valiere: *Valiere is* a Place. [1]

audience,[1] and the play went off tolerably, till it came to the conclusion, when Mrs. Pritchard, the heroine of the piece, was to be strangled upon the stage, and was to speak two lines with the bow-string round her neck. The audience cried out *"Murder! Murder!"*[2] She several times attempted to speak; but in vain. At last she was obliged to go off the stage alive.' This passage was afterwards struck out, and she was carried off to be put to death behind the scenes, as the play now has it. The Epilogue, as Johnson informed me, was written by Sir William Yonge.[a] I know not how his play came to be thus graced by the pen of a person then so eminent in the political world.

Notwithstanding all the support of such performers as Garrick, Barry, Mrs. Cibber, Mrs. Pritchard, and every advantage of dress and decoration, the tragedy of Irene did not please the publick.[3] Mr. Garrick's zeal carried it

[a] *& is very sprightly.*
[1]

---

[1] The expression used by Dr. Adams was 'soothed.' I should rather think the audience was *awed* by the extraordinary spirit and dignity of the following lines:

> 'Be this at least his praise, be this his pride,
> To force applause no modern arts are tried:
> Should partial catcalls all his hopes confound,
> He bids no trumpet quell the fatal sound;
> Should welcome sleep relieve the weary wit,
> He rolls no thunders o'er the drowsy pit;
> No snares to captivate the judgement spreads,
> Nor bribes your eyes, to prejudice your heads.
> Unmov'd, though witlings sneer and rivals rail,
> Studious to please, yet not asham'd to fail,
> He scorns the meek address, the suppliant strain,
> With merit needless, and without it vain;
> In Reason, Nature, Truth, he dares to trust;
> Ye fops be silent, and ye wits be just!'

[2] [This shews, how ready modern audiences are to condemn in a new play what they have frequently endured very quietly in an old one. Rowe has made Moneses in TAMERLANE die by the bow-string, without offence. MALONE.]

[3] [I know not what Sir John Hawkins means by the *cold reception* of IRENE. [See note, p. 126.] I was at the first representation, and most of the subsequent. It was much applauded the first night, particularly the speech on *to-morrow*. It ran nine nights at least. It did not indeed become a stock-play, but there was not the least opposition during the representation, except the first night in the last act, where Irene was to be strangled on the stage, which *John* could not bear, though a dramatick poet may stab or slay by hundreds. The bow-string was not a Christian nor an ancient Greek or Roman death. But this offence was removed after the first night, and Irene went off the stage to be strangled.—Many stories were circulated at the time, of the authour's being observed at the representation to be dissatisfied with

through for nine nights, so that the authour had his three nights' profits; and from a receipt signed by him, now in the hands of Mr. James Dodsley, it appears that his friend, Mr. Robert Dodsley, gave him one hundred pounds for the copy, with his usual reservation of the right of one edition.

IRENE, considered as a poem, is entitled to the praise of superiour excellence. Analysed into parts, it will furnish a rich store of noble sentiments, fine imagery, and beautiful language; but it is deficient in pathos, in that delicate power of touching the human feelings, which is the principal end of the drama.[1] Indeed Garrick has complained to me, that Johnson not only had not the faculty of producing the impressions of tragedy, but that he had not the sensibility to perceive them. His great friend Mr. Walmsley's

some of the speeches and conduct of the play, himself; and, like la Fontaine, expressing his disapprobation aloud. BURNEY.]

[Mr. Murphy, in his Life of Johnson, p. 53, says, 'the amount of the three benefit nights for the tragedy of IRENE, it is to be feared, were not very considerable, as the profit, that stimulating motive, never invited the authour to another dramatick attempt.'

On the word 'profit,' the late Mr. Isaac Reed, in his copy of that Life, which I purchased at the sale of his library, has added a manuscript note, containing the following receipts on Johnson's three benefit nights:

	£		
'3d night's receipt - - - -	177	1	6
6th - - - - - - - - - -	106	4	0
9th - - - - - - - - - -	101	11	6
	384	17	0
Charges of the House - - - -	189	0	0
Profit - - - - - - - - - -	195	17	0
He also received for the Copy -	100	0	0
In all - - - - - - - - - -	295	17	0 '

In a preceding page (52) Mr. Murphy says, 'IRENE was acted at Drury-lane on Monday, Feb. 6, and from that time, without interruption, to Monday, February the 20th, being in all thirteen nights.'

On this Mr. Reed somewhat indignantly has written—'This is false. It was acted only nine nights, and never repeated afterwards. Mr. Murphy, in making the above calculation, includes both the Sundays and Lent-days.'

The blunder, however, is that of the Monthly Reviewer, from whom Murphy took, without acknowledgment, the greater part of his Essay. M. R. vol. lxxvii. p. 135. A. CHALMERS.]

[1] Aaron Hill (vol. ii. p. 355), in a letter to Mr. Mallet, gives the following account of Irene after having seen it: 'I was at the anomalous Mr. Johnson's benefit, and found the play his proper representative; strong sense ungraced by sweetness or decorum.'[a]

underlined: *anomalous* [1]

[a] *Bravo! A: Hill.* [1]

marginal line:
had not . . . in that [H]

prediction, that he would 'turn out a fine tragedy writer,' was, therefore, ill-founded. Johnson was wise enough to be convinced that he had not the talents necessary to write successfully for the stage, and never made another attempt in that species of composition.

When asked how he felt upon the ill success of his tragedy, he replied, 'Like the Monument;' meaning that he continued firm and unmoved as that column. And let it be remembered, as an admonition to the *genus irritabile* of dramatick writers, that this great man, instead of peevishly complaining of the bad taste of the town, submitted to its decision without a murmur. He had, indeed, upon all occasions a great deference for the general opinion: 'A man (said he) who writes a book, thinks himself wiser or wittier than the rest of mankind; he supposes that he can instruct or amuse them, and the publick to whom he appeals, must, after all, be the judges of his pretensions.'

On occasion of this play being brought upon the stage, Johnson had a fancy that as a dramatick authour his dress should be more gay than what he ordinarily wore; he therefore appeared behind the scenes, and even in one of the side boxes, in a scarlet waistcoat, with rich gold lace, and a gold-laced hat. He humourously observed to Mr. Langton, 'that when in that dress he could not treat people with the same ease as when in his usual plain clothes.' Dress indeed, we must allow, has more effect even upon strong minds than one should suppose, without having had the experience of it. His necessary attendance while his play was in rehearsal, and during its performance, brought him acquainted with many of the performers of both sexes, which produced a more favourable opinion of their profession than he had harshly expressed in his Life of Savage. With some of them he kept up an acquaintance as long as he and they lived, and was ever ready to shew them acts of kindness. He for a considerable time used to frequent the *Green-Room*, and seemed to take delight in dissipating his gloom, by mixing in the sprightly chit-chat of the motley circle then to be found there. Mr. David Hume related to me from Mr. Garrick, that Johnson at last denied himself this amusement, from considerations of rigid virtue; saying, 'I'll come no more behind your scenes, David; for the silk stockings and white bosoms of your actresses excite my amorous propensities.'[a]

In 1750 he came forth in the character for which he was eminently qualified, a majestick teacher of moral and religious wisdom. The vehicle which he chose was that of a periodical paper, which he knew had been, upon former occasions, employed with great success. The Tatler, Spectator, and Guardian, were the last of the kind published in England, which had stood the test of a long trial; and such an interval had now elapsed since their publication, as made him justly think that, to many of his readers, this form of instruction would, in some degree, have the advantage of novelty. A few days before the first of his Essays came out, there started another competitor for fame in the same form, under the title of 'The Tatler Revived,' which I believe was 'born but to die.' Johnson was, I think, not very happy in the choice of his title,— 'The Rambler;' which certainly is not suited to a series of grave and moral discourses; which the Italians have literally, but ludicrously, translated by *Il Vagabondo*,[b] and which has been lately assumed as the denomination of a vehicle of licentious tales, 'The Rambler's Magazine.' He gave Sir Joshua Reynolds the following account of its getting this name; 'What *must* be done, Sir, *will* be done. When I was to begin publishing that paper, I was at a loss how to name it. I sat down at night upon my bedside, and resolved that I would not go to sleep till I had fixed its title. The Rambler seemed the best that occurred, and I took it.'[1]

With what devout and conscientious sentiments this paper was undertaken, is evidenced by the following prayer, which he composed and offered up on the

[a] *apparently said in Jest by Johnson, and certainly related in Jest by Garrick.* [I]

[b] *L'Errante is the right Way to translate it.* [H]
L'Errante not Il Vagabondo [I]

---

[1] I have heard Dr. Warton mention, that he was at Mr. Robert Dodsley's with the late Mr. Moore, and several of his friends, considering what should be the name of the periodical paper which Moore had undertaken. Garrick proposed the *Sallad*, which, by a curious coincidence, was afterwards applied to himself by Goldsmith:

'Our Garrick's a sallad, for in him we see
Oil, vinegar, sugar, and saltness agree!'

At last, the company having separated, without any thing of which they approved having been offered, Dodsley himself thought of *The World*.

occasion: 'Almighty GOD, the giver of all good things, without whose help all labour is ineffectual, and without whose grace all wisdom is folly: grant, I beseech Thee, that in this undertaking thy Holy Spirit may not be withheld from me, but that I may promote thy glory, and the salvation of myself and others: grant this, O Lord, for the sake of thy son, JESUS CHRIST. Amen.'[1]

The first paper of the Rambler was published on Tuesday the 20th of March, 1749–50: and its authour was enabled to continue it, without interruption, every Tuesday and Saturday, till Saturday the 17th of March,[2] 1752, on which day it closed. This is a strong confirmation of the truth of a remark of his, which I have had occasion to quote elsewhere,[3] that 'a man may write at any time, if he will set himself doggedly to it;' for, notwithstanding his constitutional indolence, his depression of spirits, and his labour in carrying on his Dictionary, he answered the stated calls of the press twice a week from the stores of his mind, during all that time; having received no assistance, except four billets in No. 10, by Miss Mulso, now Mrs. Chapone; No. 30, by Mrs. Catharine Talbot; No. 97, by Mr. Samuel Richardson, whom he describes in an introductory note as 'An authour who has enlarged the knowledge of human nature, and taught the passions to move at the command of virtue;' and Numbers 44 and 100, by Mrs. Elizabeth Carter.

Posterity will be astonished when they are told, upon the authority of Johnson himself, that many of these discourses, which we should suppose had been laboured with all the slow attention of literary leisure, were written in haste as the moment pressed, without even being read over by him before they were printed. It can be accounted for only in this way; that by reading and meditation, and a very close inspection of life, he had accumulated a great

marginal line:
received no . . . Mr. Samuel [H]

marginal line:
the command . . . Elizabeth Carter [H]

[1] Prayers and Meditations, p. 9.

[2] [This is a mistake, into which the authour was very pardonably led by the inaccuracy of the original folio edition of the Rambler, in which the concluding paper of that work is dated on 'Saturday, March 17.' But Saturday was in fact the *fourteenth* of March. This circumstance, though it may at first appear of very little importance, is yet worth notice; for Mrs. Johnson died on the *seventeenth* of March. MALONE.]

[3] Journal of a Tour to the Hebrides, 3d edit. p. 28.

fund of miscellaneous knowledge, which, by a peculiar promptitude of mind, was ever ready at his call, and which he had constantly accustomed himself to clothe in the most apt and energetick expression. Sir Joshua Reynolds once asked him by what means he had attained his extraordinary accuracy and flow of language. He told him, that he had early laid it down as a fixed rule to do his best on every occasion, and in every company: to impart whatever he knew in the most forcible language he could put it in; and that by constant practice, and never suffering any careless expressions to escape him, or attempting to deliver his thoughts without arranging them in the clearest manner, it became habitual to him.[1]

marginal lines:
fund of . . . expression.
Sir [H]

marginal line:
deliver his . . . to him
[H]

Yet he was not altogether unprepared as a periodical writer; for I have in my possession a small duodecimo volume, in which he has written, in the form of Mr. Locke's Common-Place Book, a variety of hints for essays on different subjects. He has marked upon the first blank leaf of it, 'To the 128th page, collections for the RAMBLER;' and in another place, 'In fifty-two there were seventeen provided; in 97—21; in 190—25.' At a subsequent period (probably after the work was finished) he added, 'In all, taken of provided materials, 30.'

Sir John Hawkins, who is unlucky upon all occasions, tells us, that 'this method of accumulating intelligence had been practised by Mr. Addison, and is humourously described in one of the Spectators, wherein he feigns to have dropped his paper of *notanda*, consisting of a diverting medley of broken sentences and loose hints, which he tells us he had collected, and meant to make use of. Much of the same kind is Johnson's Adversaria.'[2] But the truth is, that there is no resemblance at all between them. Addison's note was a fiction, in which unconnected fragments of his lucubrations were purposely jumbled together, in as odd a manner as he could, in order to produce a laughable effect. Whereas Johnson's abbreviations are all

[1] [The rule which Dr. Johnson observed, is sanctioned by the authority of two great writers of antiquity: 'Ne id quidem tacendum est, quod eidem Ciceroni placet, nullum nostrum usquam negligentem esse sermonem: *quicquid loquemur, ubicunque, sit pro sua scilicet portione perfectum.*' Quinctil. x. 7. MALONE.]

[2] Hawkins's Life of Johnson, p. 268.

distinct, and applicable to each subject of which the head
is mentioned.

For instance, there is the following specimen:

Youth's Entry, &c.

'Baxter's account of things in which he had changed his
mind as he grew up. Voluminous.—No wonder.—If every
man was to tell, or mark, on how many subjects he has
changed, it would make vols. but the changes not always
observed by man's self.—From pleasure to bus. [*business*]
to quiet; from thoughtfulness to reflect. to piety; from
dissipation to domestic. by imperfect gradat. but the
change is certain. Dial *non progredi, progress. esse conspicimus.*
Look back, consider what was thought at some dist. period.

'*Hope predom. in youth. Mind not willingly indulges unpleasing
thoughts.* The world lies all enamelled before him, as a
distant prospect sun-gilt;[1]—inequalities only found by
coming to it. *Love is to be all joy—children excellent—*Fame to
be constant—caresses of the great—applauses of the
learned—smiles of Beauty.

'*Fear of disgrace—Bashfulness—*Finds things of less
importance. Miscarriages forgot like excellencies;—if
remembered, of no import. Danger of sinking into negligence of reputation;—lest the fear of disgrace destroy
activity.

'*Confidence in himself.* Long tract of life before him.—No
thought of sickness.—Embarrassment of affairs.—Distraction of family. Publick calamities.—No sense of the
prevalence of bad habits. Negligent of time—ready to
undertake—careless to pursue—all changed by time.

'*Confident of others—*unsuspecting as unexperienced—
imagining himself secure against neglect, never imagines
they will venture to treat him ill. Ready to trust; expecting
to be trusted. Convinced by time of the selfishness, the
meanness, the cowardice, the treachery of men.

'Youth ambitious, as thinking honours easy to be had.

'Different kinds of praise pursued at different periods.
Of the gay in youth,—dang. hurt, &c. despised.

---

[1] This most beautiful image of the enchanting delusion of youthful
prospect has not been used in any of Johnson's essays.

'Of the fancy in manhood. Ambit.—stocks—bargains.—
Of the wise and sober in old age—seriousness—formality—
maxims, but general—only of the rich, otherwise age is
happy—but at last every thing referred to riches—no having
fame, honour, influence, without subjection to caprice.

'Horace.

'Hard it would be if men entered life with the same
views with which they leave it, or left as they enter it.—
No hope—no undertaking—no regard to benevolence—
no fear of disgrace, &c.

'Youth to be taught the piety of age—age to retain the
honour of youth.'

This, it will be observed, is the sketch of Number 196
of the Rambler. I shall gratify my readers with another
specimen:

marginal line:
196 of . . . *another*
specimen [H]

Confederacies difficult; why.

'Seldom in war a match for single persons—nor in
peace; therefore kings make themselves absolute. Confederacies in learning—every great work the work of one.
Bruy. Scholars' friendship like ladies. Scribebamus, &c.
Mart.[1] The apple of discord—the laurel of discord—the
poverty of criticism. Swift's opinion of the power of six
geniuses united. That union scarce possible. His remarks
just;—man a social, not steady nature. Drawn to man by
words, repelled by passions. Orb drawn by attraction, rep.
[*repelled*] by centrifugal.

'Common danger unites by crushing other passions—
but they return. Equality hinders compliance. Superiority
produces insolence and envy. Too much regard in each to
private interest;—too little.

'The mischiefs of private and exclusive societies.—The
fitness of social attraction diffused through the whole. The
mischiefs of too partial love of our country. Contraction
of moral duties.—δι φιλοι ου φιλος.

'Every man moves upon his own center, and therefore
repels others from too near a contact, though he may
comply with some general laws.

---

[1] [Lib. xii. 96. 'In Tuccam æmulum omnium suorum studiorum.'
MALONE.]

'Of confederacy with superiors every one knows the inconvenience. With equals, no authority;—every man his own opinion—his own interest.

'Man and wife hardly united;—scarce ever without children. Computation, if two to one against two, how many against five? If confederacies were easy—useless;—many oppresses many.—If possible only to some, dangerous. *Principum amicitias*.'

Here we see the embryo of Number 45 of the Adventurer; and it is a confirmation of what I shall presently have occasion to mention, that the papers in that collection marked T. were written by Johnson.

This scanty preparation of materials will not, however, much diminish our wonder at the extraordinary fertility of his mind; for the proportion which they bear to the number of essays which he wrote, is very small; and it is remarkable, that those for which he had made no preparation, are as rich and as highly finished, as those for which the hints were lying by him. It is also to be observed, that the papers formed from his hints are worked up with such strength and elegance, that we almost lose sight of the hints, which become like 'drops in the bucket.' Indeed, in several instances, he has made a very slender use of them, so that many of them remain still unapplied.[1]

As the Rambler was entirely the work of one man, there was, of course, such a uniformity in its texture, as very much to exclude the charm of variety; and the grave and often solemn cast of thinking, which distinguished it from other periodical papers, made it, for some time, not generally liked. So slowly did this excellent work, of which

[1] Sir John Hawkins has selected from this little collection of materials, what he calls the 'Rudiments of two of the papers of the Rambler.' But he has not been able to read the manuscript distinctly. Thus he writes, p. 266, 'Sailor's fate any mansion;' whereas the original is 'Sailor's life my aversion.' He has also transcribed the unappropriated hints on *Writers for bread*, in which he decyphers these notable passages, one in Latin, *fatui non famæ*, instead of *fami non famæ*; Johnson having in his mind what Thuanus says of the learned German antiquary and linguist, Xylander, who, he tells us, lived in such poverty, that he was supposed *fami non famæ scribere*; and another in French, *Degenté de fate et affamé d'argent*, instead of *Degouté de fame* (an old word for *renommé*) *et affamé d'argent*. The manuscript being written in an exceedingly small hand, is indeed very hard to read; but it would have been better to have left blanks than to write nonsense.

marginal line:
have been . . . write
nonsense [H]

twelve editions have now issued from the press, gain upon
the world at large, that even in the closing number the
authour says, 'I have never been much a favourite of the
publick.'[1]

Yet, very soon after its commencement, there were who
felt and acknowledged its uncommon excellence. Verses in
its praise appeared in the newspapers; and the editor of the
Gentleman's Magazine mentions, in October, his having
received several letters to the same purpose from the learned.
'The Student, or Oxford and Cambridge Miscellany,' in
which Mr. Bonnel Thornton and Mr. Colman were the
principal writers, describes it as 'a work that exceeds any
thing of the kind ever published in this kingdom, some of
the Spectators excepted,—if indeed they may be excepted.'
And afterwards, 'May the publick favours crown his merits,
and may not the English, under the auspicious reign of
GEORGE the Second, neglect a man, who, had he lived
in the first century, would have been one of the greatest

---

[1] [The Ramblers certainly were little noticed at first. Smart, the poet, first
mentioned them to me as excellent papers, before I had heard any one else
speak of them. When I went into Norfolk, in the autumn of 1751, I found but
one person, (the Rev. Mr. Squires, a man of learning, and a general purchaser of new books,) who knew any thing of them. But he had been misinformed concerning the true authour, for he had been told they were written
by a Mr. Johnson of Canterbury, the son of a clergyman who had had a
controversy with Bentley: and who had changed the readings of the old
ballad entitled *Norton Falgate*, in Bentley's bold style, (*meo periculo*) till not a
single word of the original song was left. Before I left Norfolk in the year
1760, the Ramblers were in high favour among persons of learning and
good taste. Others there were, devoid of both, who said that the *hard words*
in the Rambler were used by the authour to render his Dictionary indispensably necessary. BURNEY.]

[It may not be improper to correct a slight errour in the preceding note,
though it does not at all affect the principal object of Dr. Burney's remark.
The clergyman above alluded to, was Mr. Richard Johnson, Schoolmaster
at Nottingham, who in 1717 published an octavo volume in Latin, against
Bentley's edition of Horace, entitled ARISTARCHUS ANTI-BENTLEIANUS.
In the middle of this Latin work (as Mr. Bindley observes to me,) he has
introduced four pages of English criticism, in which he ludicrously corrects,
in Bentley's manner, one stanza, not of the ballad the hero of which lived in
Norton Falgate, but of a ballad celebrating the achievements of TOM
BOSTOCK; who in a sea-fight performed prodigies of valour. The stanza,
on which this ingenious writer has exercised his wit, is as follows:

'Then old Tom Bostock he fell to the work,
He pray'd like a Christian, but fought like a Turk,
And cut 'em off all in a jerk,
Which nobody can deny,' &c. MALONE.]

favourites of Augustus.' This flattery of the monarch had no effect. It is too well known, that the second George never was an Augustus to learning or genius.

Johnson told me, with an amiable fondness, a little pleasing circumstance relative to this work.[a] Mrs. Johnson, in whose judgement and taste he had great confidence, said to him, after a few numbers of the Rambler had come out, 'I thought very well of you before; but I did not imagine you could have written any thing equal to this.' Distant praise, from whatever quarter, is not so delightful as that of a wife whom a man loves and esteems. Her approbation may be said to 'come home to his *bosom;*' and being so near, its effect is most sensible and permanent.

Mr. James Elphinston, who has since published[b] various works, and who was ever esteemed by Johnson as a worthy man,[c] happened to be in Scotland while the Rambler was coming out in single papers at London. With a laudable zeal at once for the improvement of his countrymen, and the reputation of his friend, he suggested and took the charge of an edition of those Essays at Edinburgh, which followed progressively the London publication.[1]

The following letter written at this time, though not dated, will show how much pleased Johnson was with this publication, and what kindness and regard he had for Mr. Elphinston.

'TO MR. JAMES ELPHINSTON

'DEAR SIR,   [*No date*]

'I CANNOT but confess the failures of my corre-spondence, but hope the same regard which you express

[a] *he told me the same Thing in the same Words.* [H]

underlined:
has since published [I]

[b] *Yes—Martial!!* [I]

underlined:
worthy man [H]

[c] *which he was* not, *but he was a* Scotch-man. [H]

---

[1] It was executed in the printing-office of Sands, Murray, and Cochran, with uncommon elegance, upon writing paper, of a duodecimo size, and with the greatest correctness: and Mr. Elphinston enriched it with trans-lations of the mottos. When completed, it made eight handsome volumes. It is, unquestionably, the most accurate and beautiful edition of this work; and there being but a small impression, it is now become scarce, and sells at a very high price.

[With respect to the correctness of this edition, the authour probably derived his information from some other person, and appears to have been misinformed; for it was *not* accurately printed, as we learn from Mr. A. Chalmers. J. BOSWELL.]

for me on every other occasion, will incline you to forgive me. I am often, very often, ill; and, when I am well, am obliged to work: and, indeed, have never much used myself to punctuality. You are, however, not to make unkind inferences, when I forbear to reply to your kindness; for be assured, I never receive a letter from you without great pleasure, and a very warm sense of your generosity and friendship, which I heartily blame myself for not cultivating with more care. In this, as in many other cases, I go wrong, in opposition to conviction; for I think scarce any temporal good equally to be desired with the regard and familiarity of worthy men. I hope we shall be some time nearer to each other, and have a more ready way of pouring out our hearts.

'I am glad that you still find encouragement to proceed in your publication, and shall beg the favour of six more volumes to add to my former six, when you can, with any convenience, send them me. Please to present a set in my name, to Mr. Ruddiman,[1] of whom, I hear, that his learning is not his highest excellence. I have transcribed the mottos, and returned them, I hope not too late, of which I think many very happily performed. Mr. Cave has put the last in the magazine,[2] in which I think he did well. I beg of you to write soon, and to write often, and to write long letters, which I hope in time to repay you; but you must be a patient creditor. I have, however, this of gratitude, that I think of you with regard, when I do not, perhaps, give the proofs which I ought, of being, Sir,

'Your most obliged and
'Most humble servant,

'SAM. JOHNSON'

[1] Mr. Thomas Ruddiman, the learned grammarian of Scotland, well known for his various excellent works, and for his accurate editions of several authours. He was also a man of a most worthy private character. His zeal for the Royal House of Stuart did not render him less estimable in Dr. Johnson's eye.

[2] [If the Magazine here referred to be that for October, 1752, (See GENT. MAG. vol. 22, p. 468,) then this letter belongs to a later period. If it relates to the Magazine for Sept. 1750, (See GENT. MAG. vol. 20, p. 406,) then it may be ascribed to the month of October in that year, and should have followed the subsequent letter. MALONE.]

This year he wrote to the same gentleman another letter upon a mournful occasion.

'TO MR. JAMES ELPHINSTON

'DEAR SIR,   'September 25, 1750

'You have, as I find by every kind of evidence, lost an excellent mother; and I hope you will not think me incapable of partaking of your grief. I have a mother, now eighty-two years of age, whom, therefore, I must soon lose, unless it please GOD that she should rather mourn for me. I read the letters in which you relate your mother's death to Mrs. Strahan, and think I do myself honour, when I tell you that I read them with tears; but tears are neither to *you* nor to *me* of any farther use, when once the tribute of nature has been paid. The business of life summons us away from useless grief, and calls us to the exercise of those virtues of which we are lamenting our deprivation. The greatest benefit which one friend can confer upon another, is to guard, and excite, and elevate, his virtues. This your mother will still perform, if you diligently preserve the memory of her life, and of her death: a life, so far as I can learn, useful, wise, and innocent; and a death resigned, peaceful, and holy. I cannot forbear to mention, that neither reason nor revelation denies you to hope, that you may increase her happiness by obeying her precepts; and that she may, in her present state, look with pleasure upon every act of virtue to which her instructions or example have contributed. Whether this be more than a pleasing dream, or a just opinion of separate spirits, is, indeed, of no great importance to us, when we consider ourselves as acting under the eye of GOD; yet, surely, there is something pleasing in the belief, that our separation from those whom we love is merely corporeal; and it may be a great incitement to virtuous friendship, if it can be made probable, that that union that has received the divine approbation shall continue to eternity.

'There is one expedient by which you may, in some degree, continue her presence. If you write down minutely what you remember of her from your earliest years, you will read it with great pleasure, and receive from it many

index sign:
you may increase etc.
[I]

index sign:
a great incitement etc.
[H]

hints of soothing recollection, when time shall remove her yet farther from you, and your grief shall be matured to veneration. To this, however painful for the present, I cannot but advise you, as to a source of comfort and satisfaction in the time to come; for all comfort and all satisfaction is sincerely wished you by, dear Sir,

> 'Your most obliged, most obedient,
>> 'And most humble servant,
>>> 'SAM. JOHNSON'

The Rambler has increased in fame as in age. Soon after its first folio edition was concluded, it was published in six duodecimo volumes;[1] and its authour lived to see ten numerous editions of it in London, beside those of Ireland and Scotland.

I profess myself to have ever entertained a profound veneration for the astonishing force and vivacity of mind, which the Rambler exhibits. That Johnson had penetration enough to see, and seeing would not disguise the general misery of man in this state of being, may have given rise to the superficial notion of his being too stern a philosopher. But men of reflection will be sensible that he has given a true representation of human existence, and that he has, at the same time, with a generous benevolence displayed every consolation which our state affords us; not only those arising from the hopes of futurity, but such as may be attained in the immediate progress through life. He has not depressed the soul to despondency and indifference. He has every where inculcated study, labour, and exertion. Nay, he has shewn, in a very odious light, a man, whose practice is to go about darkening the views of others, by

---

[1] [This is not quite accurate. In the GENT. MAG. for Nov. 1751, while the work was yet proceeding, is an advertisement, announcing that *four* volumes of the Rambler would speedily be published; and it is believed that they were published in the next month. The fifth and sixth volumes, with tables of contents and translations of the mottos, were published in July 1752, by Payne, (the original publisher,) three months after the close of the work.

When the Rambler was collected into volumes, Johnson revised and corrected it throughout. Mr. Boswell was not aware of this circumstance, which has lately been discovered and accurately stated by Mr. Alexander Chalmers in a new edition of these and various other periodical Essays, under the title of 'the British Essayists.' MALONE.]

perpetual complaints of evil, and awakening those considerations of danger and distress, which are, for the most
part, lulled into a quiet oblivion. This he has done
very strongly in his character of Suspirius,[1] from which
Goldsmith took that of Croaker, in his comedy of 'The
Good-natured Man,' as Johnson told me he acknowledged
to him, and which is, indeed, very obvious.

To point out the numerous subjects which the Rambler
treats, with a dignity and perspicuity which are there
united in a manner which we shall in vain look for any
where else, would take up too large a portion of my book,
and would, I trust, be superfluous, considering how
universally those volumes are now disseminated. Even the
most condensed and brilliant sentences which they contain,
and which have very properly been selected under the
name of 'BEAUTIES,'[2] are of considerable bulk. But I
may shortly observe, that the Rambler furnishes such an
assemblage of discourses on practical religion and moral
duty, of critical investigations, and allegorical and oriental
tales, that no mind can be thought very deficient that has,
by constant study and meditation, assimilated to itself all
that may be found there. No. 7, written in Passion-week
on abstraction and self-examination, and No. 110, on
penitence and the placability of the Divine Nature, cannot
be too often read. No. 54, on the effect which the death
of a friend should have upon us, though rather too dis-
piriting, may be occasionally very medicinal to the mind.
Every one must suppose the writer to have been deeply
impressed by a real scene; but he told me that was not the
case; which shews how well his fancy could conduct him
to the 'house of mourning.' Some of these more solemn
papers, I doubt not, particularly attracted the notice of
Dr. Young, the authour of 'The Night Thoughts,' of whom
my estimation is such, as to reckon his applause an honour
even to Johnson. I have seen volumes of Dr. Young's copy

---

[1] No. 55.

[2] Dr. Johnson was gratified by seeing this selection, and wrote to Mr.
Kearsley, bookseller, in Fleet-street, the following note:

'Mr. Johnson sends compliments to Mr. Kearsley, and begs the favour
of seeing him as soon as he can. Mr. Kearsley is desired to bring with him
the last edition of what he has honoured with the name of BEAUTIES.'

'May 20, 1782.'

of the Rambler, in which he has marked the passages
which he thought particularly excellent, by folding down
a corner of the page; and such as he rated in a super-
eminent degree are marked by double folds. I am sorry
that some of the volumes are lost. Johnson was pleased
when told of the minute attention with which Young had
signified his approbation of his Essays.

I will venture to say, that in no writings whatever can
be found more *bark and steel for the mind,* if I may use the
expression; more that can brace and invigorate every
manly and noble sentiment. No. 32 on patience, even
under extreme misery, is wonderfully lofty, and as much
above the rant of stoicism, as the Sun of Revelation is
brighter than the twilight of Pagan philosophy. I never
read the following sentence without feeling my frame
thrill: ' I think there is some reason for questioning whether
the body and mind are not so proportioned, that the one
can bear all which can be inflicted on the other; whether
virtue cannot stand its ground as long as life, and whether
a soul well principled will not be sooner separated than
subdued.' [a]

To this Truth, bear Witness all the Martyrs. [H]

Though instruction be the predominant purpose of the
Rambler, yet it is enlivened with a considerable portion
of amusement. Nothing can be more erroneous than the
notion which some persons have entertained, that Johnson
was then a retired authour, ignorant of the world; and,
of consequence, that he wrote only from his imagination,
when he described characters and manners. He said to
me, that before he wrote that work, he had been 'running
about the world,' as he expressed it, more than almost any
body; and I have heard him relate, with much satisfaction,
that several of the characters in the Rambler were drawn
so naturally, that when it first circulated in numbers, a
club in one of the towns in Essex imagined themselves to
be severally exhibited in it, and were much incensed
against a person who, they suspected, had thus made them
objects of publick notice; nor were they quieted till authentick assurance was given them, that the Rambler was
written by a person who had never heard of any one of
them. Some of the characters are believed to have been
actually drawn from the life, particularly that of Prospero

from Garrick,[1] who never entirely forgave its pointed satire. For instances of fertility of fancy, and accurate description of real life, I appeal to No. 19, a man who wanders from one profession to another, with most plausible reasons for every change: No. 34, female fastidiousness and timorous refinement: No. 82, a Virtuoso who has collected curiosities: No. 88, petty modes of entertaining a company, and conciliating kindness: No. 182, fortune-hunting: No. 194—195, a tutor's account of the follies of his pupil: No. 197—198, legacy-hunting: He has given a specimen of his nice observation of the mere external appearances of life, in the following passage in No. 179, against affectation, that frequent and most disgusting quality: 'He that stands to contemplate the crowds that fill the streets of a populous city, will see many passengers, whose air and motions it will be difficult to behold without contempt and laughter: but if he examine what are the appearances that thus powerfully excite his risibility, he will find among them neither poverty nor disease, nor any involuntary or painful defect. The disposition to derision and insult, is awakened by the softness of foppery, the swell of insolence, the liveliness of levity, or the solemnity of grandeur; by the sprightly trip, the stately walk, the formal strut, and the lofty mien; by gestures intended to catch the eye, and by looks elaborately formed as evidences of importance.'

Every page of the Rambler shews a mind teeming with classical allusion and poetical imagery: illustrations from other writers are, upon all occasions, so ready, and mingle so easily in his periods, that the whole appears of one uniform vivid texture.

The style of this work has been censured by some shallow criticks as involved and turgid, and abounding with antiquated and hard words. So ill-founded is the first part of

---

[1] [That of GELIDUS in No. 24, from Professor Coulson, (see p. 58 of this vol.) and that of EUPHUES in the same paper, which, with many others, was doubtless drawn from the life. EUPHUES, I once thought, might have been intended to represent either Lord Chesterfield or Soame Jenyns: but Mr. Bindley, with more probability, thinks, that George Bubb Dodington, who was remarkable for the homeliness of his person, and the finery of his dress, was the person meant under that character. MALONE.]

this objection, that I will challenge all who may honour this book with a perusal, to point out any English writer whose language conveys his meaning with equal force and perspicuity. It must, indeed, be allowed, that the structure of his sentences is expanded, and often has somewhat of the inversion of Latin; and that he delighted to express familiar thoughts in philosophical language; being in this the reverse of Socrates, who, it is said, reduced philosophy to the simplicity of common life. But let us attend to what he himself says in his concluding paper: 'When common words were less pleasing to the ear, or less distinct in their signification, I have familiarised the terms of philosophy, by applying them to popular ideas.'[1] And, as to the second part of this objection, upon a late careful revision of the work, I can with confidence say, that it is amazing how few of those words, for which it has been unjustly characterised, are actually to be found in it; I am sure, not the proportion of one to each paper. This idle charge has been echoed from one babbler to another, who have confounded Johnson's Essays with Johnson's Dictionary; and because he thought it right in a Lexicon of our language to collect many words which had fallen into disuse, but were supported by great authorities, it has been imagined that all of these have been interwoven into his own compositions. That some of them have been adopted by him unnecessarily, may, perhaps, be allowed; but, in general they are evidently an advantage, for without them his stately ideas would be confined and cramped. 'He that thinks with more extent than another, will want words of larger meaning.'[2] He once told me, that he had formed his style upon that of Sir William Temple, and upon Chambers's Proposal for his Dictionary.[3] He certainly was mistaken; or if he imagined at first that he was imitating

---

[1] Yet his style did not escape the harmless shafts of pleasant humour; for the ingenious Bonnell Thornton published a mock Rambler in the Drury-lane Journal.[a]

[2] Idler, No. 70.

[3] [The Paper here alluded to, was, I believe, Chambers's Proposal for a second and improved edition of his Dictionary, which, I think, appeared in 1738. This proposal was probably in circulation in 1737, when Johnson first came to London. MALONE.]

[a] *I never saw it . . . but what a Man Boswell is! to whom Friend & Foe are alike Entertaining: . . . and who delights in the Ridicule as in the Applause of those he pretends to admire.* [H]

ª *as Rowe fancied him-*
self imitating Shake-
speare in Jane Shore
[1]

Temple,ª he was very unsuccessful;[1] for nothing can be more unlike than the simplicity of Temple, and the richness of Johnson. Their styles differ as plain cloth and brocade. Temple, indeed, seems equally erroneous in supposing that he himself had formed his style upon Sandys's View of the State of Religion in the Western parts of the World.

The style of Johnson was, undoubtedly, much formed upon that of the great writers in the last century, Hooker, Bacon, Sanderson, Hakewell, and others; those 'GIANTS,' as they were well characterised by A GREAT PERSONAGE, whose authority, were I to name him, would stamp a reverence on the opinion.

We may, with the utmost propriety, apply to his learned style that passage of Horace, a part of which he has taken as the motto to his Dictionary:

'*Cum tabulis animum censoris sumet honesti;*
Audebit quæcumque parùm splendoris habebunt
Et sine pondere erunt, et honore indigna ferentur,
Verba movere loco, quamvis invita recedant,
Et versentur adhuc intra penetralia Vestæ.
Obscurata diu populo bonus eruet, atque
Proferet in lucem speciosa vocabula rerum,
Quæ priscis memorata Catonibus atque Cethegis,
Nunc situs informis premit et deserta vetustas:
Adsciscet nova, quæ genitor produxerit usus:
Vehemens, et liquidus, puroque simillimus amni,
Fundet opes Latiumque beabit divite linguâ.'[2]

To so great a master of thinking, to one of such vast and various knowledge as Johnson, might have been

---

[1] [The authour appears to me to have misunderstood Johnson in this instance. He did not, I conceive, mean to say, that, when he first began to write, he made Sir William Temple his model, with a view to form a style that should resemble his in all its parts; but that he formed his style on that of Temple and others; by taking from each those characteristic excellencies which were most worthy of imitation.—See this matter further explained in vol. ii. under April 9, 1778; where, in a conversation at Sir Joshua Reynolds's, Johnson himself mentions the particular improvements which Temple made in the English style. These, doubtless, were the objects of his imitation, so far as that writer was his model. MALONE.]

[2] Horat. Epist. Lib. ii. Epist. ii.

allowed a liberal indulgence of that licence which Horace
claims in another place:

'————— *Si forté necesse est*
Indiciis monstrare recentibus abdita rerum,
Fingere cinctutis non exaudita Cethegis
Continget, dabiturque licentia sumpta pudenter:
Et nova fictaque nuper habebunt verba fidem, si
Græco fonte cadant, parcè detorta. Quid autem
Cæcilio Plautoque dabit Romanus, ademptum
Virgilio Varioque? Ego cur, acquirere pauca
Si possum, invideor; cum lingua Catonis et Enni
Sermonem patrium ditaverit, et nova rerum
Nomina protulerit? Licuit, semperque licebit
Signatum præsente notâ producere nomen.'[1]

Yet Johnson assured me, that he had not taken upon
him to add more than four or five words to the English
language, of his own formation; and he was very much
offended at the general licence by no means 'modestly
taken' in his time, not only to coin new words, but to use
many words in senses quite different from their established
meaning, and those frequently very fantastical.

Sir Thomas Brown, whose Life Johnson wrote, was
remarkably fond of Anglo-Latin diction; and to his
example we are to ascribe Johnson's sometimes indulging
himself in this kind of phraseology.[2] Johnson's comprehension of mind was the mould for his language. Had his
conceptions been narrower, his expression would have been
easier. His sentences have a dignified march; and, it is
certain, that his example has given a general elevation to
the language of his country, for many of our best writers
have approached very near to him; and, from the influence
which he has had upon our composition, scarcely any thing
is written now that is not better expressed than was usual
before he appeared to lead the national taste.

[1] Horat. De Arte Poetica.

[2] The observation of his having imitated Sir Thomas Brown has been
made by many people; and lately it has been insisted on, and illustrated by
a variety of quotations from Brown, in one of the popular Essays written by
the Reverend Mr. Knox, master of Tunbridge-school, whom I have set down
in my list of those who have sometimes not unsuccessfully imitated Dr.
Johnson's style.[a]

[a] *Mrs. Barbauld did
it best.* [1]

This circumstance, the truth of which must strike every critical reader, has been so happily enforced by Mr. Courtenay, in his 'Moral and Literary Character of Dr. Johnson,' that I cannot prevail on myself to withhold it, notwithstanding his, perhaps, too great partiality for one of his friends:

'By nature's gifts ordain'd mankind to rule,
He, like a Titian, form'd his brilliant school;
And taught congenial spirits to excel,
While from his lips impressive wisdom fell.
Our boasted GOLDSMITH felt the sovereign sway;
From him deriv'd the sweet, yet nervous lay.
To Fame's proud cliff he bade our Raffaelle rise:
Hence REYNOLDS' pen with REYNOLDS' pencil vies.
With Johnson's flame melodious BURNEY glows,
While the grand strain in smoother cadence flows.
And you, MALONE, to critick learning dear,
Correct and elegant, refin'd though clear,
By studying him, acquir'd that classick taste,
Which high in Shakspeare's fane thy statue plac'd.
Near Johnson STEEVENS stands, on scenick ground,
Acute, laborious, fertile, and profound.
Ingenious HAWKESWORTH to this school we owe,
And scarce the pupil from the tutor know.
Here early parts accomplish'd JONES sublimes,
And science blends with Asia's lofty rhymes:
Harmonious JONES! who in his splendid strains
Sings Camdeo's sports, on Agra's flowery plains,
In Hindu fictions while we fondly trace
Love and the Muses, deck'd with Attick grace.
Amid these names can BOSWELL be forgot,
Scarce by North Britons now esteem'd a Scot?[1]

[1] [The following observation in Mr. Boswell's *Journal of a Tour to the Hebrides* may sufficiently account for that Gentleman's being 'now scarcely esteemed a Scot' by many of his countrymen: 'If he [Dr. Johnson] was particularly prejudiced against the Scots, it was because they were more in his way; because he thought their success in England rather exceeded the due proportion of their real merit; and because he could not but see in them that nationality which, I believe, no liberal-minded Scotchman will deny.' Mr. Boswell, indeed, is so free from national prejudices, that he might with equal propriety have been described as—

'Scarce by *South* Britons now esteem'd a Scot.'

COURTENAY.]

Who to the sage devoted from his youth,
Imbib'd from him the sacred love of truth;
The keen research, the exercise of mind,
And that best art, the art to know mankind. —
Nor was his energy confin'd alone
To friends around his philosophick throne;
Its influence wide improv'd our letter'd isle,
And lucid vigour mark'd the general style:
As Nile's proud waves, swoln from their oozy bed,
First o'er the neighbouring meads majestick spread;
Till gathering force, they more and more expand,
And with new virtue fertilise the land.'

Johnson's language, however, must be allowed to be too masculine for the delicate gentleness of female writing. His ladies, therefore, seem strangely formal, even to ridicule; and are well denominated by the names which he has given them, as Misella, Zozima, Properantia, Rhodoclia.

It has of late been the fashion to compare the style of Addison and Johnson, and to depreciate, I think, very unjustly, the style of Addison as nerveless and feeble, because it has not the strength and energy of that of Johnson. Their prose may be balanced like the poetry of Dryden and Pope. Both are excellent, though in different ways. Addison writes with the ease of a gentleman. His readers fancy that a wise and accomplished companion is talking to them; so that he insinuates his sentiments and taste into their minds by an imperceptible influence. Johnson writes like a teacher. He dictates to his readers as if from an academical chair. They attend with awe and admiration; and his precepts are impressed upon them by his commanding eloquence. Addison's style, like a light wine, pleases every body from the first. Johnson's like a liquor of more body, seems too strong at first, but, by degrees, is highly relished; and such is the melody of his periods, so much do they captivate the ear, and seize upon the attention, that there is scarcely any writer, however inconsiderable, who does not aim, in some degree, at the same species of excellence. But let us not ungratefully undervalue that beautiful style, which has pleasingly conveyed to us much instruction and entertainment. Though comparatively weak, opposed to Johnson's Herculean vigour, let us not call it positively feeble. Let us remember the character of his style, as given by Johnson himself: 'What he attempted, he performed; he is *never feeble*, and he did not wish to be energetick; he is never rapid, and he never stagnates. His sentences have neither studied amplitude, nor affected brevity: his periods, though not diligently rounded, are voluble and easy.[1] Whoever wishes to attain an English style, familiar but not coarse, and elegant but not ostentatious, must give his days and nights to the volumes of Addison.'[2]

Though the Rambler was not concluded till the year 1752, I shall under this year, say all that I have to observe upon it. Some of the translations of the mottos by himself, are admirably done. He acknowledges to have received 'elegant translations' of many of them from Mr. James Elphinston; and some are very happily translated by a Mr. *F. Lewis*, of whom I never heard more, except that Johnson thus described him to Mr. Malone: 'Sir, he lived in London, and hung loose upon society.'[3] The concluding

[1] [When Johnson shewed me a proof-sheet of the character of Addison, in which he so highly extols his style, I could not help observing, that it had not been his own model, as no two styles could differ more from each other.[a] —'Sir, Addison had his style, and I have mine.'—When I ventured to ask him, whether the difference did not consist in this, that Addison's style was full of idioms, colloquial phrases, and proverbs; and his own more strictly grammatical, and free from such phraseology and modes of speech as can never be literally translated or understood by foreigners; he allowed the discrimination to be just.—Let any one who doubts it, try to translate one of Addison's Spectators into Latin, French, or Italian; and though so easy, familiar, and elegant, to an Englishman, as to give the intellect no trouble; yet he would find the transfusion into another language extremely difficult, if not impossible. But a Rambler, Adventurer, or Idler, of Johnson, would fall into any classical or European language, as easily as if it had been originally conceived in it.[b] BURNEY.]

[a] *I remember Dr. Johnson telling Doctor Burney that he made him his Model of Style in the Journey to the Hebrides; but we only laughed, Thinking no Styles could resemble each other less than Johnson's and Burney's.* [J]

[b] *beautifully imagined, & perfectly true. Bravo Burney! 1820.* [H]

[2] I shall probably, in another work, maintain the merit of Addison's poetry, which has been very unjustly depreciated.

[3] [In the Gentleman's Magazine, for October 1752, p. 468, he is styled 'the Rev. Francis Lewis, of Chiswick.' The late Lord Macartney, while he resided at Chiswick, at my request, made some inquiry concerning him at that place, but no intelligence was obtained.

The translations of the mottos supplied by Mr. Elphinston, appeared first in the Edinburgh edition of the Rambler, and in some instances were revised and improved, probably by Johnson, before they were inserted in the London octavo edition. The translations of the mottos affixed to the

paper of his Rambler is at once dignified and pathetick. I cannot, however, but wish that he had not ended it with an unnecessary Greek verse, translated[1] also into an English couplet. It is too much like the conceit of those dramatick poets, who used to conclude each act with a rhyme; and the expression in the first line of his couplet, 'Celestial powers,' though proper in Pagan poetry, is ill suited to Christianity, with 'a conformity' to which he consoles himself. How much better would it have been, to have ended with the prose sentence 'I shall never envy the honours which wit and learning obtain in any other cause, if I can be numbered among the writers who have given ardour to virtue, and confidence to truth.'

His friend Dr. Birch, being now engaged in preparing an edition of Ralegh's smaller pieces, Dr. Johnson wrote the following letter to that gentleman:

'TO DR. BIRCH

'SIR,   'Gough-square, May 12, 1750

'KNOWING that you are now preparing to favour the publick with a new edition of Ralegh's miscellaneous pieces, I have taken the liberty to send you a Manuscript, which fell by chance within my notice. I perceive no proofs of forgery in my examination of it; and the owner tells me, that as *he* has heard, the hand-writing is Sir Walter's. If you should find reason to conclude it genuine, it will be a kindness to the owner, a blind person,[2] to recommend it to the booksellers. I am, Sir,

'Your most humble servant,
'SAM. JOHNSON'

His just abhorrence of Milton's political notions was ever strong. But this did not prevent his warm admiration of Milton's great poetical merit, to which he has done illustrious justice, beyond all who have written upon the subject. And this year he not only wrote a Prologue, which was spoken by Mr. Garrick before the acting of Comus at

first thirty numbers of the Rambler, were published, from the Edinburgh edition, in the Gentleman's Magazine for September 1750, before the work was collected into volumes. MALONE.]

[1] [Not in the original edition, in folio. MALONE.]

[2] Mrs. Williams is probably the person meant.

Drury-lane theatre, for the benefit of Milton's grand-daughter, but took a very zealous interest in the success of the charity. On the day preceding the performance, he published the following letter in the 'General Advertiser,' addressed to the printer of that paper:

'SIR,

'THAT a certain degree of reputation is acquired merely by approving the works of genius, and testifying a regard to the memory of authours, is a truth too evident to be denied; and therefore to ensure a participation of fame with a celebrated poet, many, who would, perhaps, have contributed to starve him when alive, have heaped expensive pageants upon his grave.[1]

'It must, indeed, be confessed, that this method of becoming known to posterity with honour, is peculiar to the great, or at least to the wealthy; but an opportunity now offers for almost every individual to secure the praise of paying a just regard to the illustrious dead, united with the pleasure of doing good to the living. To assist industrious indigence, struggling with distress and debilitated by age, is a display of virtue, and an acquisition of happiness and honour.

'Whoever, then, would be thought capable of pleasure in reading the works of our incomparable Milton, and not so destitute of gratitude as to refuse to lay out a trifle in rational and elegant entertainment, for the benefit of his living remains, for the exercise of their own virtue, the increase of their reputation, and the pleasing consciousness of doing good, should appear at Drury-lane theatre to-morrow, April 5, when Comus will be performed for the benefit of Mrs. Elizabeth Foster, grand-daughter to the authour,[2] and the only surviving branch of his family.

'N.B. There will be a new prologue on the occasion, written by the authour of Irene, and spoken by Mr. Garrick; and, by particular desire, there will be added to the Masque a dramatick satire, called Lethe, in which Mr. Garrick will perform.'

[1] [Alluding probably to Mr. Auditor Benson. See the Dunciad, b. iv. MALONE.]

[2] [Mrs. Elizabeth Foster died May 9, 1754. A. CHALMERS.]

In 1751 we are to consider him as carrying on both his Dictionary and Rambler. But he also wrote 'The Life of Cheynel,'* in the miscellany called 'The Student;' and the Reverend Dr. Douglas having with uncommon acuteness clearly detected a gross forgery and imposition upon the public by William Lauder, a Scotch schoolmaster, who had with equal impudence and ingenuity, represented Milton as a plagiary from certain modern Latin poets, Johnson, who had been so far imposed upon as to furnish a Preface and Postscript to his work, now dictated a letter for Lauder, addressed to Dr. Douglas, acknowledging his fraud in terms of suitable contrition.[1]

This extraordinary attempt of Lauder was no sudden effort. He had brooded over it for many years: and to this hour it is uncertain what his principal motive was, unless it were a vain notion of his superiority, in being able, by whatever means, to deceive mankind. To effect this, he produced certain passages from Grotius, Masenius, and others, which had a faint resemblance to some parts of the 'Paradise Lost.' In these he interpolated some fragments of Hog's Latin translation of that poem, alleging that the mass thus fabricated was the archetype from which Milton copied. These fabrications he published from time to time in the Gentleman's Magazine; and, exulting in his

[1] Lest there should be any person, at any future period, absurd enough to suspect that Johnson was a partaker in Lauder's fraud, or had any knowledge of it, when he assisted him with his masterly pen, it is proper here to quote the words of Dr. Douglas, now Bishop of Salisbury, at the time when he detected the imposition. 'It is to be hoped, nay it is *expected*, that the elegant and nervous writer, whose judicious sentiments and inimitable style point out the authour of Lauder's Preface and postscript, will no longer allow one to *plume himself with his feathers*, who appeareth so little to deserve assistance: and assistance which I am persuaded would never have been communicated, had there been the least suspicion of those facts which I have been the instrument of conveying to the world in these sheets.' *Milton no Plagiary*, 2d edit. p. 78. And his Lordship has been pleased now to authorise me to say, in the strongest manner, that there is no ground whatever for any unfavourable reflection against Dr. Johnson, who expressed the strongest indignation against Lauder.

[Lauder renewed his attempts on Milton's character in 1754, in a pamphlet entitled, 'The Grand Impostor detected, or Milton convicted of forgery against King Charles I.;'—which was reviewed, probably by Johnson, in the Gent. Mag. 1754, p. 97. A. CHALMERS.]

['Lauder afterwards went to Barbadoes, where he died very miserably about the year 1771. MALONE.]

fancied success, he in 1750 ventured to collect them into a
pamphlet, entitled 'An Essay on Milton's Use and Imitation of the Moderns in his Paradise Lost.' To this
pamphlet Johnson wrote a Preface, in full persuasion of
Lauder's honesty, and a Postscript recommending, in the
most persuasive terms, a subscription for the relief of a
grand-daughter of Milton, of whom he thus speaks: 'It is
yet in the power of a great people to reward the poet whose
name they boast, and from their alliance to whose genius
they claim some kind of superiority to every other nation
of the earth; that poet, whose works may possibly be read
when every other monument of British greatness shall be
obliterated; to reward him, not with pictures or with
medals, which, if he sees, he sees with contempt, but with
tokens of gratitude, which he, perhaps, may even now
consider as not unworthy the regard of an immortal spirit.'
Surely this is inconsistent with 'enmity towards Milton,'
which Sir John Hawkins imputes to Johnson upon this
occasion, adding, 'I could all along observe that Johnson
seemed to approve not only of the design, but of the argument; and seemed to exult in a persuasion, that the reputation of Milton was likely to suffer by this discovery. That
he was not privy to the imposture, I am well persuaded;
that he wished well to the argument, may be inferred
from the Preface, which indubitably was written by
Johnson.' Is it possible for any man of clear judgement to
suppose that Johnson, who so nobly praised the poetical
excellence of Milton in a Postscript to this very 'discovery,'
as he then supposed it, could, at the same time, exult in a
persuasion that the great poet's reputation was likely to
suffer by it? This is an inconsistency of which Johnson was
incapable; nor can any thing more be fairly inferred from
the Preface, than that Johnson, who was alike distinguished
for ardent curiosity and love of truth, was pleased with an
investigation by which both were gratified. That he was
actuated by these motives, and certainly by no unworthy
desire to depreciate our great epick poet, is evident from
his own words; for, after mentioning the general zeal of
men of genius and literature, 'to advance the honour, and
distinguish the beauties of Paradise Lost,' he says, 'Among
the inquiries to which this ardour of criticism has naturally

given occasion, none is more obscure in itself, or more worthy of rational curiosity, than a retrospect of the progress of this mighty genius in the construction of his work; a view of the fabrick gradually rising, perhaps, from small beginnings, till its foundation rests in the centre, and its turrets sparkle in the skies; to trace back the structure through all its varieties, to the simplicity of its first plan; to find what was first projected, whence the scheme was taken, how it was improved, by what assistance it was executed, and from what stores the materials were collected; whether its founder dug them from the quarries of Nature, or demolished other buildings to embellish his own.'[1]—Is this the language of one who wishes to blast the laurels of Milton?

Though Johnson's circumstances were at this time far from being easy, his humane and charitable disposition was constantly exerting itself. Mrs. Anna Williams, daughter of a very ingenious Welsh physician, and a woman of more than ordinary talents and literature, having come to London in hopes of being cured of a cataract in both her eyes, which afterwards ended in total blindness, was kindly received as a constant visitor at his house while Mrs. Johnson lived; and, after her death, having come under his roof in order to have an operation upon her eyes performed with more comfort to her than in lodgings, she had an apartment from him during the rest of her life, at all times when he had a house.

In 1752 he was almost entirely occupied with his Dictionary. The last paper of his Rambler was published March 2,[2] this year; after which, there was a cessation for

[1] ['Proposals [written evidently by Johnson] for printing the ADAMUS EXUL of Grotius, with a Translation and Notes by Wm. Lauder, A.M.' Gent. Mag. 1747. vol. 17. p. 404. MALONE.]

[2] [Here the author's memory failed him, for, according to the account given in a former page, (see p. 134,) we should here read March 17; but in truth, as has been already observed, the Rambler closed on Saturday the *fourteenth* of March; at which time Mrs. Johnson was near her end, for she died on the following Tuesday, March 17. Had the concluding paper of that work been written on the day of her death, it would have been still more extraordinary than it is, considering the extreme grief into which the author was plunged by that event.—The melancholy cast of that concluding essay is sufficiently accounted for by the situation of Mrs. Johnson at the time it was written; and her death three days afterwards put an end to the Paper. MALONE.]

some time of any exertion of his talents as an essayist. But, in the same year, Dr. Hawkesworth, who was his warm admirer, and a studious imitator of his style, and then lived in great intimacy with him, began a periodical paper, entitled, 'THE ADVENTURER,' in connection with other gentlemen, one of whom was Johnson's much-loved friend, Dr. Bathurst; and, without doubt, they received many valuable hints from his conversation, most of his friends having been so assisted in the course of their works.

That there should be a suspension of his literary labours during a part of the year 1752, will not seem strange, when it is considered that soon after closing his Rambler, he suffered a loss which, there can be no doubt, affected him with the deepest distress. For on the 17th of March, O.S. his wife died. Why Sir John Hawkins should unwarrantably take upon him even to *suppose* that Johnson's fondness for her was *dissembled* (meaning simulated or assumed,) and to assert, that if it was not the case, 'it was a lesson he had learned by rote,' I cannot conceive; unless it proceeded from a want of similar feelings in his own breast. To argue from her being much older than Johnson, or any other circumstances, that he could not really love her, is absurd; for love is not a subject of reasoning, but of feeling, and therefore there are no common principles upon which one can persuade another concerning it. Every man feels for himself, and knows how he is affected by particular qualities in the person he admires, the impressions of which are too minute and delicate to be substantiated in language.

The following very solemn and affecting prayer was found after Dr. Johnson's decease, by his servant, Mr. Francis Barber, who delivered it to my worthy friend the Reverend Mr. Strahan, Vicar of Islington, who at my earnest request has obligingly favoured me with a copy of it, which he and I compared with the original. I present it to the world as an undoubted proof of a circumstance in the character of my illustrious friend, which, though some whose hard minds I never shall envy, may attack as superstitious, will I am sure endear him more to numbers of good men. I have an additional, and that a personal

motive for presenting it, because it sanctions what I myself
have always maintained and am fond to indulge:

'April 26, 1752, being after 12 at Night of the 25th

'O Lord! Governour of heaven and earth, in whose
hands are embodied and departed Spirits, if thou hast
ordained the Souls of the Dead to minister to the Living,
and appointed my departed Wife to have care of me, grant
that I may enjoy the good effects of her attention and
ministration, whether exercised by appearance, impulses,
dreams, or in any other manner agreeable to thy Government. Forgive my presumption, enlighten my ignorance,
and however meaner agents are employed, grant me the
blessed influences of thy holy Spirit, through Jesus Christ
our Lord. Amen.'

What actually followed upon this most interesting piece
of devotion by Johnson, we are not informed; but I, whom
it has pleased GOD to afflict in a similar manner to that
which occasioned it, have certain experience of benignant
communication by dreams.[a]

That his love for his wife was of the most ardent kind,
and, during the long period of fifty years, was unimpaired
by the lapse of time, is evident from various passages in the
series of his Prayers and Meditations, published by the
Reverend Mr. Strahan, as well as from other memorials,
two of which I select, as strongly marking the tenderness
and sensibility of his mind.

'March 28, 1753. I kept this day as the anniversary of
my Tetty's death, with prayer and tears in the morning.
In the evening I prayed for her conditionally, if it
were lawful.'

'April 23, 1753. I know not whether I do not too much
indulge the vain longings of affection; but I hope they
intenerate my heart, and that when I die like my Tetty,
this affection will be acknowledged in a happy interview,
and that in the mean time I am incited by it to piety. I
will, however, not deviate too much from common and
received methods of devotion.'

Her wedding-ring, when she became his wife, was, after
her death, preserved by him, as long as he lived, with an

underlined:
*I, certain, experience,
fifty years* [H]
[a] *Oh Dear! oh dear!* [H]

exclamation point,
index sign, under-
lined:
certain, dreams [I]

affectionate care, in a little round wooden box, in the inside of which he pasted a slip of paper, thus inscribed by him in fair characters, as follows:

'*Eheu!*

Eliz. Johnson,

Nupta Jul. 9° 1736

Mortua, eheu!

Mart. 17° 1752.'[a]

After his death, Mr. Francis Barber, his faithful servant, and residuary legatee, offered this memorial of tenderness to Mrs. Lucy Porter, Mrs. Johnson's daughter; but she having declined to accept of it, he had it enamelled as a mourning ring for his old master, and presented it to his wife, Mrs. Barber, who now has it.

The state of mind in which a man must be upon the death of a woman whom he sincerely loves, had been in his contemplation many years before. In his I RENE, we find the following fervent and tender speech of Demetrius, addressed to his Aspasia:

'From those bright regions of eternal day,
    Where now thou shin'st amongst thy fellow saints,
    Array'd in purer light, look down on me!
    In pleasing visions and assuasive dreams,
    O! sooth my soul, and teach me how to lose thee.'

I have, indeed, been told by Mrs. Desmoulins, who, before her marriage, lived for some time with Mrs. Johnson at Hampstead, that she indulged herself in country air and nice living, at an unsuitable expence, while her husband was drudging in the smoke of London, and that she by no means treated him with that complacency which is the most engaging quality in a wife. But all this is perfectly compatible with his fondness for her, especially when it is remembered that he had a high opinion of her understanding, and that the impressions which her beauty, real or imaginary, had originally made upon his fancy, being continued by habit, had not been effaced, though she herself was doubtless much altered for the worse. The dreadful shock of separation took place in the night; and he immediately dispatched a letter to his friend, the Reverend Dr. Taylor, which, as Taylor told me, expressed grief in the strongest manner he had ever read; so that it is much to be regretted it has not been preserved.[1] The letter was brought to Dr. Taylor, at his house in the Cloysters, Westminster, about three in the morning; and as it signified an earnest desire to see him, he got up, and went to Johnson as soon as he was dressed, and found him in tears and in extreme agitation. After being a little while together, Johnson requested him to join with him in prayer. He then prayed extempore, as did Dr. Taylor; and thus by means of that piety which was ever his primary object, his troubled mind was, in some degree, soothed and composed.

The next day he wrote as follows:

'TO THE REVEREND DR. TAYLOR

'DEAR SIR,

'Let me have your company and instruction. Do not live away from me. My distress is great.

'Pray desire Mrs. Taylor to inform me what mourning I should buy for my mother and Miss Porter, and bring a note in writing with you.

'Remember me in your prayers, for vain is the help of man.

'I am, dear Sir, &c.

'March 18, 1752.'   'SAM. JOHNSON'

That his sufferings upon the death of his wife were severe, beyond what are commonly endured, I have no doubt, from the information of many who were then about him, to none of whom I give more credit than to Mr. Francis Barber, his faithful negro servant,[2] who came

---

[1] [In the Gentleman's Magazine for February, 1794, (p. 100,) was printed a letter pretending to be that written by Johnson on the death of his wife. But it is merely a transcript of the 41st number of 'The Idler,' on the death of a friend. A fictitious date, March 17, 1751, O. S. was added by some person, previously to this paper's being sent to the publisher of that miscellany, to give a colour to this deception. MALONE.]

[2] Francis Barber was born in Jamaica, and was brought to England in 1750 by Colonel Bathurst, father of Johnson's very intimate friend, Dr. Bathurst. He was sent, for some time, to the Reverend Mr. Jackson's school, at Barton, in Yorkshire. The Colonel by his will left him his freedom, and

into his family about a fortnight after the dismal event. These sufferings were aggravated by the melancholy

a *I never recover'd the Loss of my Wife, said he to me in the year 1780,—nor ever shall.* [1]

inherent in his constitution;[a] and although he probably was not oftener in the wrong than she was, in the little disagreements which sometimes troubled his married state, during which, he owned to me, that the gloomy irritability of his existence was more painful to him than ever, he might very naturally, after her death, be tenderly disposed to charge himself with slight omissions and offences, the sense of which would give him much uneasiness.[1] Accordingly we find, about a year after her decease, that he thus addressed the Supreme Being: 'O LORD, who givest the grace of repentance, and hearest the prayers of the penitent, grant that by true contrition I may obtain forgiveness of all the sins committed, and of all duties neglected, in my union with the wife whom thou hast taken from me; for the neglect of joint devotion, patient exhortation, and mild instruction.'[2] The kindness of his heart, notwithstanding the impetuosity of his temper, is well known to his friends; and I cannot trace the smallest foundation for the following dark and uncharitable assertion by Sir John Hawkins: 'The apparition of his

b *I never heard he saw any Apparition of her: when could it have been?* [1]

departed wife[b] was altogether of the terrifick kind, and hardly afforded him a hope that she was in a state of happiness.'[3] That he, in conformity with the opinion of many of the most able, learned, and pious Christians in all ages, supposed that there was a middle state after death, previous to the time at which departed souls are finally received to eternal felicity, appears, I think, unquestionably from his devotions:[4] 'And, O LORD, so far as it may

Dr. Bathurst was willing that he should enter into Johnson's service, in which he continued from 1752 till Johnson's death, with the exception of two intervals; in one of which, upon some difference with his master, he went and served an apothecary in Cheapside, but still visited Dr. Johnson occasionally; in another, he took a fancy to go to sea. Part of the time, indeed, he was, by the kindness of his master, at a school in Northamptonshire, that he might have the advantage of some learning.[c] So early, and so lasting a connection was there between Dr. Johnson and this humble friend.

c *he was at School since I knew Dr. Johnson—I used to joke him for schooling Frank so—when he would let me.* [1]

[1] [See his beautiful and affecting Rambler, No. 54. MALONE.]

[2] Prayers and Meditations, p. 19. [3] Hawkins's Life of Johnson, p. 316.

[4] [It does not appear that Johnson was fully persuaded that there was a middle state: his prayers being only *conditional*, i.e. if such a state existed. MALONE.]

be lawful in me, I commend to thy fatherly goodness *the soul of my departed wife;*[a] beseeching thee to *grant* her whatever is best in her *present state*, and *finally to receive her to eternal happiness.*'[1] But this state has not been looked upon with horrour, but only as less gracious.

He deposited the remains of Mrs. Johnson in the church of Bromley in Kent,[2] to which he was probably led by the residence of his friend Hawkesworth at that place. The funeral sermon which he composed for her, which was never preached, but having been given to Dr. Taylor, has been published since his death, is a performance of uncommon excellence, and full of rational and pious comfort to such as are depressed by that severe affliction which Johnson felt when he wrote it. When it is considered that it was written in such an agitation of mind, and in the short interval between her death and burial, it cannot be read without wonder.

From Mr. Francis Barber I have had the following authentick and artless account of the situation in which he found him recently after his wife's death: 'He was in great affliction. Mrs. Williams was then living in his house, which was in Gough-square. He was busy with the Dictionary. Mr. Shiels, and some others of the gentlemen who had formerly written for him, used to come about him. He had then little for himself, but frequently sent money to Mr. Shiels when in distress. The friends who visited him at that time, were chiefly Dr. Bathurst,[3] and Mr. Diamond, an

[a] *Yes, & the Soul of Henry Thrale too* [H & I]

---

[1] Prayers and Meditations, p. 20.

[2] [A few months before his death, Johnson honoured her memory by the following epitaph, which was inscribed on her tombstone, in the church of Bromley:

Hic conduntur reliquiæ
ELIZABETHÆ
Antiqua Jarvisiorum gente,
Peatlingæ, apud Leicestrienses, ortæ;
Formosæ, cultæ, ingeniosæ, piæ;
Uxoris, primis nuptiis, HENRICI PORTER,
Secundis, SAMUELIS JOHNSON:
Qui multum amatam, diuque defletam
Hoc lapide contexit.
Obiit Londini, Mense Mart.
A. D. MDCCLII.   MALONE.]

[3] Dr. Bathurst, though a physician of no inconsiderable merit, had not the good fortune to get much practice in London. He was, therefore, willing

apothecary in Cork-street, Burlington-gardens, with whom
he and Mrs. Williams generally dined every Sunday. There
was a talk of his going to Iceland with him, which would
probably have happened, had he lived. There were also
Mr. Cave, Dr. Hawkesworth, Mr. Ryland, merchant on
Tower-hill, Mrs. Masters, the poetess, who lived with Mr.
Cave, Mrs. Carter, and sometimes Mrs. Macaulay; also,
Mrs. Gardiner, wife of a tallow-chandler on Snow-hill, not
in the learned way, but a worthy good woman; Mr. (now
Sir Joshua) Reynolds; Mr. Miller, Mr. Dodsley, Mr.
Bouquet, Mr. Payne, of Paternoster-row, booksellers; Mr.
Strahan, the printer; the Earl of Orrery, Lord Southwell,
Mr. Garrick.'

Many are, no doubt, omitted in this catalogue of his
friends, and in particular, his humble friend Mr. Robert
Levet, an obscure practiser in physick amongst the lower
people, his fees being sometimes very small sums, sometimes
whatever provisions his patients could afford him; but
of such extensive practice in that way, that Mrs. Williams
has told me his walk was from Houndsditch to Marybone.
It appears from Johnson's diary, that their acquaintance
commenced about the year 1746; and such was Johnson's
predilection for him, and fanciful estimation of his moderate
abilities, that I have heard him say he should not be satisfied, though attended by all the College of Physicians,
unless he had Mr. Levet with him. Ever since I was
acquainted with Dr. Johnson, and many years before, as
I have been assured by those who knew him earlier, Mr.
Levet had an apartment in his house, or his chambers,
and waited upon him every morning, through the whole
course of his late and tedious breakfast. He was of a strange
grotesque appearance, stiff and formal in his manner, and
seldom said a word while any company was present.[1]

to accept of employment abroad, and, to the regret of all who knew him,
fell a sacrifice to the destructive climate, in the expedition against the
Havannah. Mr. Langton recollects the following passage in a letter from
Dr. Johnson to Mr. Beauclerk: 'The Havannah is taken;—a conquest too
dearly obtained; for, Bathurst died before it.
        "Vix Priamus tanti totaque Troja fuit." '

[1] [A more particular account of this person may be found in the Gentle-
man's Magazine for February 1785. It originally appeared in the St.
James's Chronicle, and, I believe, was written by the late George Steevens,
Esq. MALONE.]

The circle of his friends, indeed, at this time was extensive and various, far beyond what has been generally imagined. To trace his acquaintance with each particular person, if it could be done, would be a task, of which the labour would not be repaid by the advantage. But exceptions are to be made; one of which must be a friend so eminent as Sir Joshua Reynolds, who was truly his *dulce decus*, and with whom he maintained an uninterrupted intimacy to the last hour of his life. When Johnson lived in Castle-street, Cavendish-square, he used frequently to visit two ladies who lived opposite to him, Miss Cottereils,[a] daughters of Admiral Cotterell. Reynolds used also to visit there, and thus they met. Mr. Reynolds, as I have observed above, had, from the first reading of his Life of Savage, conceived a very high admiration of Johnson's powers of writing. His conversation no less delighted him; and he cultivated his acquaintance with the laudable zeal of one who was ambitious of general improvement. Sir Joshua, indeed, was lucky enough at their very first meeting to make a remark, which was so much above the common-place style of conversation, that Johnson at once perceived that Reynolds had the habit of thinking for himself. The ladies were regretting the death of a friend, to whom they owed great obligations; upon which Reynolds observed, 'You have, however, the comfort of being relieved from a burthen of gratitude.' They were shocked a little at this alleviating suggestion, as too selfish; but Johnson defended it in his clear and forcible manner, and was much pleased with the *mind*, the fair view of human nature,[1] which it exhibited, like some of the reflections of Rochefaucault. The consequence was, that he went home with Reynolds, and supped with him.

Sir Joshua told me a pleasant characteristical anecdote of Johnson about the time of their first acquaintance. When they were one evening together at the Miss Cotterells', the then Duchess of Argyle and another lady of high rank came in. Johnson thinking that the Miss

underlined:
Cotterells [H]

underlined:
Miss Cotterells [I]

[a] *one of whom married the Dean of Ossory— his Son by a former Wife. Yet lives: Hon. Mr. Villiers Lewis, or rather Hon. Villiers— suppressing his Father's Name. 1816* [H]

one married the Dean of Ossory—the other I know not if yet dead. Mrs. Lewis died seven years ago or more. [I]

two marginal lines:
at once . . . regretting the [H]

---

[1] [Johnson himself has a sentiment somewhat similar in his 87th Rambler: 'There are minds so impatient of inferiority, that their gratitude is a species of revenge, and they return benefits, not because recompence is a pleasure, but because obligation is a pain.' J. BOSWELL.]

Cotterells were too much engrossed by them, and that he and his friend were neglected, as low company of whom they were somewhat ashamed, grew angry: and resolving to shock their supposed pride, by making their great visiters imagine that his friend and he were low indeed, he addressed himself in a loud tone to Mr. Reynolds, saying, 'How much do you think you and I could get in a week, if we were to *work as hard* as we could?'—as if they had been common mechanicks.

His acquaintance with Bennet Langton, Esq. of Langton, in Lincolnshire, another much valued friend, commenced soon after the conclusion of his Rambler; which that gentleman, then a youth, had read with so much admiration, that he came to London chiefly with a view of endeavouring to be introduced to its authour. By a fortunate chance he happened to take lodgings in a house where Mr. Levet frequently visited; and having mentioned his wish to his landlady, she introduced him to Mr. Levet, who readily obtained Johnson's permission to bring Mr. Langton to him; as, indeed, Johnson, during the whole course of his life, had no shyness, real or affected, but was easy of access to all who were properly recommended, and even wished to see numbers at his *levee*, as his morning circle of company might, with strict propriety, be called. Mr. Langton was exceedingly surprised when the sage first appeared. He had not received the smallest intimation of his figure, dress, or manner. From perusing his writings, he fancied he should see a decent, well-drest, in short, a remarkably decorous philosopher. Instead of which, down from his bed-chamber, about noon, came, as newly risen, a huge uncouth figure, with a little dark wig which scarcely covered his head, and his clothes hanging loose about him. But his conversation was so rich, so animated, and so forcible, and his religious and political notions so congenial with those in which Langton had been educated, that he conceived for him that veneration and attachment which he ever preserved. Johnson was not the less ready to love Mr. Langton, for his being of a very ancient family; for I have heard him say, with pleasure, 'Langton, Sir, has a grant of free warren from Henry the Second; and Cardinal Stephen Langton, in King John's reign, was of this family.'

Mr. Langton afterwards went to pursue his studies at Trinity College, Oxford, where he formed an acquaintance with his fellow-student, Mr. Topham Beauclerk; who, though their opinions and modes of life were so different, that it seemed utterly improbable that they should at all agree, had so ardent a love of literature, so acute an understanding, such elegance of manners, and so well discerned the excellent qualities of Mr. Langton, a gentleman eminent not only for worth and learning, but for an inexhaustible fund of entertaining conversation, that they became intimate friends.

Johnson, soon after this acquaintance began, passed a considerable time at Oxford. He at first thought it strange that Langton should associate so much with one who had the character of being loose, both in his principles and practice: but, by degrees, he himself was fascinated. Mr. Beauclerk's being of the St. Alban's family, and having, in some particulars, a resemblance to Charles the Second, contributed, in Johnson's imagination, to throw a lustre upon his other qualities; and in a short time, the moral, pious Johnson, and the gay, dissipated Beauclerk, were companions. 'What a coalition! (said Garrick, when he heard of this:) I shall have my old friend to bail out of the Round-house.' But I can bear testimony that it was a very agreeable association. Beauclerk was too polite, and valued learning and wit too much, to offend Johnson by sallies of infidelity or licentiousness; and Johnson delighted in the good qualities of Beauclerk, and hoped to correct the evil. Innumerable were the scenes in which Johnson was amused by these young men. Beauclerk could take more liberty with him, than any body with whom I ever saw him; but, on the other hand, Beauclerk was not spared by his respectable companion, when reproof was proper. Beauclerk had such a propensity to satire, that at one time Johnson said to him, 'You never open your mouth but with intention to give pain; and you have often given me pain, not from the power of what you said, but from seeing your intention.' At another time applying to him, with a slight alteration, a line of Pope, he said,

marginal line:
from the . . . to him [H]

'Thy love of folly, and thy scorn of fools—

Every thing thou dost shews the one, and every thing thou say'st the other.' At another time he said to him, 'Thy body is all vice, and thy mind all virtue.' Beauclerk not seeming to relish the compliment, Johnson said, 'Nay, Sir, Alexander the Great, marching in triumph into Babylon, could not have desired to have had more said to him.'

Johnson was some time with Beauclerk at his house at Windsor, where he was entertained with experiments in natural philosophy. One Sunday, when the weather was very fine, Beauclerk enticed him, insensibly, to saunter about all the morning. They went into a church-yard, in the time of divine service, and Johnson laid himself down at his ease upon one of the tomb-stones. 'Now, Sir, (said Beauclerk) you are like Hogarth's Idle Apprentice.' When Johnson got his pension, Beauclerk said to him, in the humourous phrase of Falstaff, 'I hope you'll now purge and live cleanly, like a gentleman.'

One night, when Beauclerk and Langton had supped at a tavern in London, and sat till about three in the morning, it came into their heads to go and knock up Johnson, and see if they could prevail on him to join them in a ramble. They rapped violently at the door of his chambers in the Temple, till at last he appeared in his shirt, with his little black wig on the top of his head, instead of a nightcap, and a poker in his hand, imagining, probably, that some ruffians were coming to attack him. When he discovered who they were, and was told their errand, he smiled, and with great good humour agreed to their proposal: 'What, is it you, you dogs! I'll have a frisk with you.'[1] He was soon dressed, and they sallied forth together into Covent-Garden, where the green-grocers and fruiterers were beginning to arrange their hampers, just come in from the country. Johnson made some attempts to help them; but the honest gardeners stared so at his figure and manner, and odd interference, that he soon saw his services were not relished. They then repaired to one of the neighbouring taverns, and made a bowl of that liquor called *Bishop*,

---

[1] [Johnson, as Mr. Kemble observes to me, might here have had in his thoughts the words of Sir John Brute, (a character which doubtless he had
^a *Yes, & by Quin too.* seen represented by Garrick,)[a] who uses nearly the same expression in 'the
[H]   Provoked Wife,' Act III. Sc. i. MALONE.]

which Johnson had always liked: while in joyous contempt
of sleep, from which he had been roused, he repeated the
festive lines,

> 'Short, O short then be thy reign,
> And give us to the world again!'[1]

They did not stay long, but walked down to the
Thames, took a boat, and rowed to Billingsgate. Beauclerk
and Johnson were so well pleased with their amusement,
that they resolved to persevere in dissipation for the rest
of the day: but Langton deserted them, being engaged to
breakfast with some young Ladies. Johnson scolded him
for 'leaving his social friends, to go and sit with a set of
wretched *un-idea'd* girls.' Garrick being told of this ramble,
said to him smartly, 'I heard of your frolick t'other night.
You'll be in the Chronicle.'[a] Upon which Johnson afterwards observed, '*He* durst not do such a thing. His *wife*
would not *let* him!'[b]

He entered upon this year 1753 with his usual piety, as
appears from the following prayer, which I transcribed
from that part of his diary which he burnt a few days before
his death:

'Jan. 1, 1753, N. S. which I shall use for the future.

'Almighty GOD, who hast continued my life to this day,
grant that, by the assistance of thy Holy Spirit, I may
improve the time which thou shalt grant me, to my eternal
salvation. Make me to remember, to thy glory, thy judge-
ments and thy mercies. Make me so to consider the loss
of my wife, whom thou hast taken from me, that it may
dispose me, by thy grace, to lead the residue of my life in
thy fear. Grant this, O LORD, for JESUS CHRIST'S
sake. Amen.'

He now relieved the drudgery of his Dictionary, and
the melancholy of his grief, by taking an active part in the
composition of 'The Adventurer,' in which he began to
write, April 10, marking his essays with the signature T,
by which most of his papers in that collection are

marginal line:
un-idea'd *girls* . . .
this ramble [H]

[a] *it was in 1752 his
own Wife died—this
could not have been
more than 3 Months
after* March. [H & I]

[b] *True* [H]

---

[1] Mr. Langton recollected, or Dr. Johnson repeated, the passage wrong.
The lines are in Lord Lansdowne's Drinking Song to Sleep, and run thus:

> 'Short, very short, be then thy reign,
> For I'm in haste to laugh and drink[c] again.'

[c] *laugh and drink
crossed out; live writ-
ten in* [I]
*was the way Johnson
repeated it to me* [I]

distinguished: those, however, which have that signature
and also that of *Mysargyrus*, were not written by him, but,
as I suppose, by Dr. Bathurst. Indeed Johnson's energy of
thought and richness of language, are still more decisive
marks than any signature. As a proof of this, my readers,
I imagine, will not doubt that number 39, on sleep, is his;
for it not only has the general texture and colour of his
style, but the authours with whom he was peculiarly
conversant are readily introduced in it in cursory allusion.
The translation of a passage in Statius[1] quoted in that
paper, and marked C. B. has been erroneously ascribed
to Dr. Bathurst, whose Christian name was Richard.
How much this amiable man actually contributed to 'The
Adventurer,' cannot be known. Let me add, that Hawkesworth's imitations of Johnson are sometimes so happy, that
it is extremely difficult to distinguish them, with certainty,
from the composition of his great archetype. Hawkesworth
was his closest imitator, a circumstance of which that writer
would once have been proud to be told; though, when he
had become elated by having risen into some degree of
consequence, he, in a conversation with me, had the
provoking effrontery to say he was not sensible of it.

Johnson was truly zealous for the success of 'The Adventurer;' and very soon after his engaging in it, he wrote
the following letter:

'TO THE REVEREND DR. JOSEPH WARTON

'DEAR SIR,

'I OUGHT to have written to you before now, but I
ought to do many things which I do not; nor can I, indeed,
claim any merit from this letter; for being desired by the
authours and proprietor of the Adventurer to look out for
another hand, my thoughts necessarily fixed upon you,
whose fund of literature will enable you to assist them with
very little interruption of your studies.

'They desire you to engage to furnish one paper a
month, at two guineas a paper, which you may very readily
perform. We have considered that a paper should consist

[1] [This is a slight inaccuracy. The Latin Sapphicks translated by C. B.
in that paper were written by Cowley, and are in his fourth book on Plants.
MALONE.]

of pieces of imagination, pictures of life, and disquisitions of literature. The part which depends on the imagination is very well supplied, as you will find when you read the paper; for descriptions of life, there is now a treaty almost made with an authour and an authoress;[1a] and the province of criticism and literature they are very desirous to assign to the commentator on Virgil.

'I hope this proposal will not be rejected, and that the next post will bring us your compliance. I speak as one of the fraternity, though I have no part in the paper, beyond now and then a motto; but two of the writers are my particular friends, and I hope the pleasure of seeing a third united to them, will not be denied to, dear Sir,

'Your most obedient,
'And most humble servant,
'March 8, 1753.'   'SAM. JOHNSON'

underlined:
authoress [1]
[a] *Qu: who?* [1]

The consequence of this letter was, Dr. Warton's enriching the collection with several admirable essays.

Johnson's saying 'I have no part in the paper, beyond now and then a motto,' may seem inconsistent with his being the authour of the papers marked T. But he had, at this time, written only one number;[2] and besides, even at

[1] [It is not improbable, that the 'authour and authouress, with whom a treaty was almost made,—for descriptions of life,' and who are mentioned in a manner that seems to indicate some connexion between them, were Henry, and his sister Sally, Fielding, as she was then popularly called. Fielding had previously been a periodical essayist, and certainly was well acquainted with life in all its varieties, more especially within the precincts of London; and his sister was a lively and ingenious writer. To this notion perhaps it may be objected, that no papers in THE ADVENTURER are known to be their productions. But it should be remembered, that of several of the Essays in that work the authours are unknown; and some of these may have been written by the persons here supposed to be alluded to. Nor would the objection be decisive, even if it were ascertained that neither of them contributed any thing to THE ADVENTURER; for the treaty above-mentioned might afterwards have been broken off. The negotiator, doubtless, was Hawkesworth, and not Johnson.—Fielding was at this time in the highest reputation; having, in 1751, produced his AMELIA, of which the whole impression was sold off on the day of its publication. MALONE.]

[2] [The authour, I conceive, is here in an errour. He had before stated, that Johnson began to write in 'the Adventurer' on April 10th (when No. 45 was published,) above a month after the date of his letter to Dr. Warton. The two papers published previously with the signature T, and subscribed MYSARGYRUS, (No. 34 and 41,) were written, I believe, by Bonnel

any after period, he might have used the same expression,
considering it as a point of honour not to own them; for
Mrs. Williams told me that, 'as he had *given* those Essays
to Dr. Bathurst, who sold them at two guineas each, he
never would own them; nay, he used to say, he did not
write them: but the fact was, that he *dictated* them, while
Bathurst wrote.' I read to him Mrs. Williams's account;
he smiled, and said nothing.

I am not quite satisfied with the casuistry by which
the productions of one person are thus passed upon the
world for the productions of another. I allow that not only
knowledge, but powers and qualities of mind may be
communicated; but the actual effect of individual exertion
never can be transferred, with truth, to any other than its
own original cause. One person's child may be made the
child of another person by adoption, as among the
Romans, or by the ancient Jewish mode of a wife having
children borne to her upon her knees, by her handmaid.
But these were children in a different sense from that of

Thornton, who contributed also all the papers signed A. This information
I received several years ago; but do not precisely remember from whom I
derived it. I believe, however, my informer was Dr. Warton.

With respect to No. 39, on Sleep, which our authour has ascribed to
Johnson, (see p. 170,) even if it were written by him, it would not be inconsistent with his statement to Dr. Warton; for it appeared on March 20th,
near a fortnight after the date of Johnson's letter to that gentleman.—But
on considering it attentively, though the style bears a strong resemblance
to that of Johnson, I believe it was written by his friend, Dr. Bathurst, and
perhaps touched in a few places by Johnson. Mr. Boswell has observed, that
'this paper not only has the general texture and colour of his style, but the
authours with whom he was peculiarly conversant are readily introduced
in it, in cursory allusion.' Now the authours mentioned in that paper are,
Fontenelle, Milton, Ramazzini, Madlle. de Scuderi, Swift, Homer, Baretier,
Statius, Cowley, and Sir Thomas Browne. With many of these, doubtless,
Johnson was particularly conversant; but I doubt whether he would have
characterised the expression quoted from Swift, as *elegant;* and with the
works of RAMAZZINI it is very improbable that he should have been
acquainted. Ramazzini was a celebrated physician, who died at Padua, in
1714, at the age of 81; with whose writings Dr. Bathurst may be supposed
to have been conversant. So also with respect to Cowley: Johnson, without
doubt, had read his Latin poem on plants; but Bathurst's profession
probably led him to read it with more attention than his friend had given
to it; and Cowley's eulogy on the POPPY would more readily occur to the
Naturalist and the Physician, than to a more general reader. I believe,
however, that the last paragraph of the paper on Sleep, in which Sir Thomas
Browne is quoted, to shew the propriety of prayer, before we lie down to
rest, was added by Johnson. MALONE.]

nature. It was clearly understood that they were not of the blood of their nominal parents. So in literary children, an authour may give the profits and fame of his composition to another man, but cannot make that other the real authour. A Highland gentleman, a younger branch of a family, once consulted me if he could not validly purchase the Chieftainship of his family from the Chief, who was willing to sell it. I told him it was impossible for him to acquire, by purchase, a right to be a different person from what he really was; for that the right of Chieftainship attached to the blood of primogeniture, and, therefore, was incapable of being transferred. I added, that though Esau sold his birth-right, or the advantages belonging to it, he still remained the first-born of his parents; and that whatever agreement a Chief might make with any of the clan, the Heralds-Office could not admit of the metamorphosis, or with any decency attest that the younger was the elder; but I did not convince the worthy gentleman.

Johnson's papers in the Adventurer are very similar to those of the Rambler; but being rather more varied in their subjects,[1] and being mixed with essays by other writers, upon topicks more generally attractive than even the most elegant ethical discourses, the sale of the work, at first, was more extensive. Without meaning, however, to depreciate the Adventurer, I must observe, that as the value of the Rambler came, in the progress of time, to be better known, it grew upon the publick estimation, and that its sale has far exceeded that of any other periodical papers since the reign of Queen Anne.

marginal line: *that its . . . Queen Anne* [H]

In one of the books of his diary I find the following entry:

'Apr. 3, 1753. I began the second vol. of my Dictionary, room being left in the first for Preface, Grammar, and History, none of them yet begun.

'O GOD, who hast hitherto supported me, enable me to proceed in this labour, and in the whole task of my present state; that when I shall render up, at the last day,

---

[1] [Dr. Johnson lowered and somewhat disguised his style, in writing the Adventurers, in order that his Papers might pass for those of Dr. Bathurst, to whom he consigned the profits. This was Hawkesworth's opinion.[a] [a] *& mine.* [I] BURNEY.]

an account of the talent committed to me, I may receive pardon, for the sake of JESUS CHRIST. Amen.'

He this year favoured Mrs. Lenox with a Dedication* to the Earl of Orrery, of her 'Shakspeare Illustrated.'[1]

In 1754 I can trace nothing published by him, except his numbers of the Adventurer, and 'The Life of Edward Cave,'* in the Gentleman's Magazine for February. In biography there can be no question that he excelled, beyond all who have attempted that species of composition; upon which, indeed, he set the highest value. To the minute selection of characteristical circumstances, for which the ancients were remarkable, he added a philosophical research, and the most perspicuous and energetick language. Cave was certainly a man of estimable qualities, and was eminently diligent and successful in his own business, which, doubtless, entitled him to respect. But he was peculiarly fortunate in being recorded by Johnson; who, of the narrow life of a printer and publisher, without any digressions or adventitious circumstances, has made an interesting and agreeable narrative.

The Dictionary, we may believe, afforded Johnson full occupation this year. As it approached to its conclusion, he probably worked with redoubled vigour, as seamen increase their exertion and alacrity when they have a near prospect of their haven.

Lord Chesterfield, to whom Johnson had paid the high compliment of addressing to his Lordship the Plan of his Dictionary, had behaved to him in such a manner as to excite his contempt and indignation. The world has been

a *Johnson told me that Richardson would not till very late make an Index for Grandison, because it would have destroy'd the Suspense of his Readers by shewing them which Lady obtained his Hero . . . without reading the Book to the End.* [H & I; I omits *them*]

b *Very curious—and an odd Friendship somehow between Men so completely dissimilar; The Elephant & Zebra drawing together.* 1820. [H] *curious!* [I]

[1] [Two of Johnson's Letters, addressed to Samuel Richardson, authour of CLARISSA, &c. the former dated March 9, 1750–1, the other September 26, 1753, are preserved in Richardson's CORRESPONDENCE, 8vo. 1804, vol. v. pp. 281–284. In the latter of these letters Johnson suggested to Richardson, the propriety of making an Index to his three works:[a] 'but while I am writing, (he adds) an objection arises; such an index to the three would look like the preclusion of a fourth, to which I will never contribute; for if I cannot benefit mankind, I hope never to injure them.' Richardson, however, adopted the hint; for in 1755 he published in octavo, 'A Collection of the Moral and Instructive Sentiments, Maxims, Cautions, and Reflections, contained in the Histories of Pamela, Clarissa, and Sir Charles Grandison, digested under proper heads.'

It is remarkable, that both to this book, and to the first two volumes of Clarissa, is prefixed a Preface, *by a friend.* The 'friend,' in this latter instance, was the celebrated Dr. Warburton.[b] MALONE.]

for many years amused with a story confidently told, and
as confidently repeated with additional circumstances,
that a sudden disgust was taken by Johnson upon occasion
of his having been one day kept long in waiting in his
Lordship's antechamber, for which the reason assigned
was, that he had company with him; and that at last,
when the door opened, out walked Colley Cibber; and
that Johnson was so violently provoked when he found
for whom he had been so long excluded, that he went
away in a passion, and never would return. I remember
having mentioned this story to George Lord Lyttleton,
who told me, he was very intimate with Lord Chesterfield;
and holding it as a well-known truth, defended Lord
Chesterfield by saying, that 'Cibber, who had been introduced familiarly by the back-stairs, had probably not been
there above ten minutes.' It may seem strange even to
entertain a doubt concerning a story so long and so
widely current, and thus implicitly adopted, if not sanctioned by the authority which I have mentioned; but
Johnson himself assured me, that there was not the least
foundation for it. He told me, that there never was any
particular incident which produced a quarrel between
Lord Chesterfield and him; but that his Lordship's continued neglect was the reason why he resolved to have no
connexion with him. When the Dictionary was upon the
eve of publication, Lord Chesterfield, who, it is said, had
flattered himself with expectations that Johnson would
dedicate the work to him, attempted, in a courtly manner,
to soothe and insinuate himself with the Sage, conscious,
as it should seem, of the cold indifference with which he
had treated its learned authour; and further attempted to
conciliate him, by writing two papers in 'The World,' in
recommendation of the work; and it must be confessed,
that they contain some studied compliments, so finely
turned, that if there had been no previous offence, it is
probable that Johnson would have been highly delighted.
Praise, in general, was pleasing to him; but by praise
from a man of rank and elegant accomplishments, he was
peculiarly gratified.

marginal line:
but Johnson . . . that
there [H]

His Lordship says, 'I think the publick in general, and
the republick of letters in particular, are greatly obliged

to Mr. Johnson, for having undertaken, and executed so
great and desirable a work. Perfection is not to be expected
from man: but if we are to judge by the various works of
Johnson already published, we have good reason to believe,
that he will bring this as near to perfection as any man
could do. The plan of it, which he published some years
ago, seems to me to be a proof of it. Nothing can be more
rationally imagined, or more accurately and elegantly
expressed. I therefore recommend the previous perusal
of it to all those who intend to buy the Dictionary, and
who, I suppose, are all those who can afford it.'

*   *   *   *   *   *   *   *

'It must be owned, that our language is, at present, in a
state of anarchy, and hitherto, perhaps, it may not have
been the worse for it. During our free and open trade,
many words and expressions have been imported, adopted,
and naturalized from other languages, which have greatly
enriched our own. Let it still preserve what real strength
and beauty it may have borrowed from others; but let it
not, like the Tarpeian maid, be overwhelmed and crushed
by unnecessary ornaments. The time for discrimination
seems to be now come. Toleration, adoption, and natural-
ization have run their lengths. Good order and authority
are now necessary. But where shall we find them, and at
the same time, the obedience due to them? We must have
recourse to the old Roman expedient in times of confusion,
and chuse a dictator. Upon this principle, I give my vote
for Mr. Johnson, to fill that great and arduous post; and
I hereby declare that I make a total surrender of all my
rights and privileges in the English language, as a free-born
British subject, to the said Mr. Johnson, during the term
of his dictatorship. Nay more, I will not only obey him
like an old Roman, as my dictator, but, like a modern
Roman, I will implicitly believe in him as my Pope, and
hold him to be infallible while in the chair, but no longer.
More than this he cannot well require; for, I presume,
that obedience can never be expected, when there is
neither terrour to enforce, nor interest to invite it.'[a]

[a] *a true saying ... &
exemptified* [sic] *in 1816
... when there is* no
*Obedience for that very
Reason. Parents, Hus-
bands, Schoolmasters &
Government in general
want both Interest to
induce Submission,—&
Power to enforce it ...
So everybody takes his
Course And bad at first,
we all grow worse.* [H]

*   *   *   *   *   *   *   *

'But a Grammar, a Dictionary, and a History of our

Language, through its several stages, were still wanting at home, and importunately called for from abroad. Mr. Johnson's labours will now, I dare say, very fully supply that want, and greatly contribute to the farther spreading of our language in other countries. Learners were discouraged, by finding no standard to resort to; and, consequently, thought it incapable of any. They will now be undeceived and encouraged.'

This courtly device failed of its effect. Johnson, who thought that 'all was false and hollow,' despised the honeyed words, and was even indignant that Lord Chesterfield should, for a moment, imagine, that he could be the dupe of such an artifice. His expression to me concerning Lord Chesterfield, upon this occasion, was, 'Sir, after making great professions, he had, for many years, taken no notice of me; but when my Dictionary was coming out, he fell a scribbling in "The World" about it. Upon which, I wrote him a letter expressed in civil terms, but such as might shew him that I did not mind what he said or wrote, and that I had done with him.'

This is that celebrated letter of which so much has been said, and about which curiosity has been so long excited, without being gratified. I for many years solicited Johnson to favour me with a copy of it, that so excellent a composition might not be lost to posterity. He delayed from time to time to give it me;[1] till at last in 1781, when we were on a visit at Mr. Dilly's, at Southill in Bedfordshire, he was pleased to dictate it to me from memory. He afterwards found among his papers a copy of it, which he had dictated to Mr. Baretti, with its title and corrections, in his own hand-writing. This he gave to Mr. Langton; adding that if it were to come into print, he wished it to be from that copy. By Mr. Langton's kindness, I am enabled to enrich

---

[1] Dr. Johnson appeared to have had a remarkable delicacy with respect to the circulation of this letter; for Dr. Douglas, Bishop of Salisbury, informs me, that having many years ago pressed him to be allowed to read it to the second Lord Hardwicke, who was very desirous to hear it, (promising at the same time, that no copy of it should be taken,) Johnson seemed much pleased that it had attracted the attention of a nobleman of such respectable character; but after pausing some time, declined to comply with the request, saying, with a smile, 'No, Sir; I have hurt the dog too much already;' or words to that purpose.

my work with a perfect transcript of what the world has so eagerly desired to see.

'TO THE RIGHT HONOURABLE THE EARL OF CHESTERFIELD

'MY LORD,   'February 7, 1755

'I HAVE been lately informed, by the proprietor of the World, that two papers, in which my Dictionary is recommended to the publick, were written by your Lordship. To be so distinguished, is an honour, which, being very little accustomed to favours from the great, I know not well how to receive, or in what terms to acknowledge.

'When, upon some slight encouragement, I first visited your Lordship, I was overpowered, like the rest of mankind, by the enchantment of your address, and could not forbear to wish that I might boast myself *Le vainqueur du vainqueur de la terre;*—that I might obtain that regard for which I saw the world contending; but I found my attendance so little encouraged, that neither pride nor modesty would suffer me to continue it. When I had once addressed your Lordship in publick, I had exhausted all the art of pleasing which a retired and uncourtly scholar can possess. I had done all that I could; and no man is well pleased to have his all neglected, be it ever so little.

'Seven years, my Lord, have now past, since I waited in your outward rooms, or was repulsed from your door; during which time I have been pushing on my work through difficulties, of which it is useless to complain, and have brought it, at last, to the verge of publication, without one act of assistance,[1] one word of encouragement, or one smile of favour. Such treatment I did not expect, for I never had a Patron before.

'The shepherd in Virgil grew at last acquainted with Love, and found him a native of the rocks.

'Is not a Patron, my Lord, one who looks with unconcern on a man struggling for life in the water, and, when

[1] The following note is subjoined by Mr. Langton. 'Dr. Johnson, when he gave me this copy of his letter, desired that I would annex to it his information to me, that whereas it is said in the letter that "no assistance has been received," he did once receive from Lord Chesterfield the sum of ten pounds; but as that was so inconsiderable a sum, he thought the mention of it could not properly find a place in a letter of the kind that this was.'

he has reached ground, encumbers him with help? The notice which you have been pleased to take of my labours, had it been early, had been kind; but it has been delayed till I am indifferent, and cannot enjoy it; till I am solitary, and cannot impart it;[1] till I am known, and do not want it. I hope it is no very cynical asperity, not to confess obligations where no benefit has been received, or to be unwilling that the Publick should consider me as owing that to a Patron, which Providence has enabled me to do for myself.

'Having carried on my work thus far with so little obligation to any favourer of learning, I shall not be disappointed though I should conclude it, if less be possible, with less; for I have been long wakened from that dream of hope, in which I once boasted myself with so much exultation,

'My Lord,

'Your Lordship's most humble

'Most obedient servant,

'SAM. JOHNSON'[2]

'While this was the talk of the town, (says Dr. Adams, in a letter to me) I happened to visit Dr. Warburton, who finding that I was acquainted with Johnson, desired me earnestly to carry his compliments to him, and to tell him, that he honoured him for his manly behaviour in rejecting these condescensions of Lord Chesterfield, and for resenting the treatment he had received from him with a proper spirit. Johnson was visibly pleased with this compliment,

[1] In this passage Dr. Johnson evidently alludes to the loss of his wife. We find the same tender recollection recurring to his mind upon innumerable occasions: and, perhaps no man ever more forcibly felt the truth of the sentiment so elegantly expressed by my friend Mr. Malone, in his Prologue to Mr. Jephson's tragedy of JULIA:

> 'Vain—wealth, and fame, and fortune's fostering care,
> If no fond breast the splendid blessings share;
> And, each day's bustling pageantry once past,
> There, only there, our bliss is found at last.'

exclamation point:
There, only there etc.
[H]

[2] Upon comparing this copy with that which Dr. Johnson dictated to me from recollection, the variations are found to be so slight, that this must be added to the many other proofs which he gave of the wonderful extent and accuracy of his memory. To gratify the curious in composition, I have deposited both the copies in the British Museum.

for he had always a high opinion of Warburton.'[1] Indeed, the force of mind which appeared in this letter, was congenial with that which Warburton himself amply possessed.

There is a curious minute circumstance which struck me, in comparing the various editions of Johnson's Imitations of Juvenal. In the tenth Satire one of the couplets upon the vanity of wishes even for literary distinction stood thus:

> 'Yet think what ills the scholar's life assail,
>   Toil, envy, want, the *garret*, and the jail.'

But after experiencing the uneasiness which Lord Chesterfield's fallacious patronage made him feel, he dismissed the word *garret* from the sad group, and in all the subsequent editions the line stands,

> 'Toil, envy, want, the *Patron*, and the jail.'

That Lord Chesterfield must have been mortified by the lofty contempt, and polite, yet keen, satire with which Johnson exhibited him to himself in this letter, it is impossible to doubt. He, however, with that glossy duplicity which was his constant study, affected to be quite unconcerned. Dr. Adams mentioned to Mr. Robert Dodsley that he was sorry Johnson had written his letter to Lord Chesterfield. Dodsley, with the true feelings of trade, said, 'he was very sorry too; for that he had a property in the Dictionary, to which his Lordship's patronage might have been of consequence.' He then told Dr. Adams, that Lord Chesterfield had shewn him the letter. 'I should have imagined (replied Dr. Adams) that Lord Chesterfield would have concealed it.' 'Poh! (said Dodsley) do you think a letter from Johnson could hurt Lord Chesterfield? Not at all, Sir. It lay upon his table, where any body might see it.

---

[1] Soon after Edwards's 'Canons of Criticism' came out, Johnson was dining at Tonson the Bookseller's, with Hayman the Painter and some more company. Hayman related to Sir Joshua Reynolds, that the conversation having turned upon Edwards's book, the gentlemen praised it much, and Johnson allowed its merit. But when they went farther, and appeared to put that authour upon a level with Warburton, 'Nay, (said Johnson,) he has given him some smart hits to be sure; but there is no proportion between the two men; they must not be named together. A fly, Sir, may sting a stately horse, and make him wince; but one is but an insect, and the other is a horse still.'

He read it to me; said, "this man has great powers," pointed out the severest passages, and observed how well they were expressed.' The air of indifference, which imposed upon the worthy Dodsley, was certainly nothing but a specimen of that dissimulation which Lord Chesterfield inculcated as one of the most essential lessons for the conduct of life. His Lordship endeavoured to justify himself to Dodsley from the charges brought against him by Johnson; but we may judge of the flimsiness of his defence, from his having excused his neglect of Johnson, by saying, that 'he had heard he had changed his lodgings, and did not know where he lived;' as if there could have been the smallest difficulty to inform himself of that circumstance, by enquiring in the literary circle with which his Lordship was well acquainted, and was, indeed, himself, one of its ornaments.

Dr. Adams expostulated with Johnson, and suggested, that his not being admitted when he called on him, was probably not to be imputed to Lord Chesterfield; for his Lordship had declared to Dodsley, that 'he would have turned off the best servant he ever had, if he had known that he denied him to a man who would have been always more than welcome;' and in confirmation of this, he insisted on Lord Chesterfield's general affability and easiness of access, especially to literary men. 'Sir, (said Johnson) that is not Lord Chesterfield; he is the proudest man this day existing.' 'No, (said Dr. Adams) there is one person, at least, as proud; I think, by your own account you are the prouder man of the two.' 'But mine (replied Johnson instantly) was *defensive* pride.' This, as Dr. Adams well observed, was one of those happy turns for which he was so remarkably ready.

marginal line: *was* defensive . . . *well observed* [H]

Johnson having now explicitly avowed his opinion of Lord Chesterfield, did not refrain from expressing himself concerning that nobleman with pointed freedom: 'This man (said he) I thought had been a Lord among wits; but, I find, he is only a wit among Lords!'[1] And when his

---

[1] [Johnson's character of Chesterfield seems to be imitated from—*inter doctos nobilissimus, inter nobiles doctissimus, inter utrosque optimus;* (ex Apuleio. v. Erasm.—Dedication of Adages to Lord Mountjoy;) and from ἰδιώτης ἐν φιλοσόφοις, φιλόσοφος ἐν ἰδιώταις. Proclus de Critia. KEARNEY.]

Letters to his natural son were published, he observed, that 'they teach the morals of a whore, and the manners of a dancing-master.'[1]

The character of a 'respectable Hottentot,' in Lord Chesterfield's Letters, has been generally understood to be meant for Johnson, and I have no doubt that it was. But I remember when the *Literary Property* of those letters was contested in the Court of Session in Scotland, and Mr. Henry Dundas,[2] one of the counsel for the proprietors, read this character as an exhibition of Johnson, Sir David Dalrymple, Lord Hailes, one of the Judges maintained, with some warmth, that it was not intended as a portrait of Johnson, but of a late noble Lord, distinguished for abstruse science. I have heard Johnson himself talk of the character, and say that it was meant for George Lord Lyttleton, in which I could by no means agree; for his Lordship had nothing of that violence which is a conspicuous feature in the composition. Finding that my illustrious friend could bear to have it supposed that it might be meant for him, I said, laughingly, that there was one trait which unquestionably did not belong to him; 'he throws his meat any where but down his throat.' 'Sir, (said he,) Lord Chesterfield never saw me eat in his life.'[a]

a which must have been strictly true [I]

[1] That collection of letters cannot be vindicated from the serious charge, of encouraging, in some passages, one of the vices most destructive to the good order and comfort of society, which his Lordship represents as mere fashionable gallantry; and, in others, of inculcating the base practice of dissimulation, and recommending, with disproportionate anxiety, a perpetual attention to external elegance of manners. But it must, at the same time, be allowed, that they contain many good precepts of conduct, and much genuine information upon life and manners, very happily expressed; and that there was considerable merit in paying so much attention to the improvement of one who was dependent upon his Lordship's protection; it has, probably, been exceeded in no instance by the most exemplary parent; and though I can by no means approve of confounding the distinction between lawful and illicit offspring, which is, in effect, insulting the civil establishment of our country, to look no higher; I cannot help thinking it laudable to be kindly attentive to those, of whose existence we have, in any way, been the cause. Mr. Stanhope's character has been unjustly represented as diametrically opposite to what Lord Chesterfield wished him to be. He has been called dull, gross, and aukward: but I knew him at Dresden, when he was Envoy to that court; and though he could not boast of the *graces*, he was, in truth, a sensible, civil, well-behaved man.

marginal line: he could . . . well-behaved man [H]

[2] Now [1792] one of his Majesty's principal Secretaries of State.

On the 6th of March came out Lord Bolingbroke's works, published by Mr. David Mallet. The wild and pernicious ravings, under the name of 'Philosophy,' which were thus ushered into the world, gave great offence to all well-principled men. Johnson, hearing of their tendency, which nobody disputed, was roused with a just indignation, and pronounced this memorable sentence upon the noble authour and his editor. 'Sir, he was a scoundrel, and a coward: a scoundrel for charging a blunderbuss against religion and morality; a coward, because he had not resolution to fire it off himself, but left half a crown to a beggarly Scotchman, to draw the trigger after his death!' Garrick, who I can attest from my own knowledge, had his mind seasoned with pious reverence, and sincerely disapproved of the infidel writings of several, whom in the course of his almost universal gay intercourse with men of eminence, he treated with external civility, distinguished himself upon this occasion. Mr. Pelham having died on the very day on which Lord Bolingbroke's works came out, he wrote an elegant Ode on his death, beginning

> 'Let others hail the rising sun,
> I bow to that whose course is run.'

in which is the following stanza:

> 'The same sad morn, to Church and State
> (So for our sins, 'twas fix'd by fate,)
>   A double stroke was given;
> Black as the whirlwinds of the North,
> St. John's fell genius issued forth,
>   And Pelham fled to heaven.'

Johnson this year found an interval of leisure to make an excursion to Oxford, for the purpose of consulting the libraries there. Of this, and of many interesting circumstances concerning him, during a part of his life when he conversed but little with the world, I am enabled to give a particular account, by the liberal communications of the Reverend Mr. Thomas Warton, who obligingly furnished me with several of our common friend's letters, which he illustrated with notes. These I shall insert in their proper places.

'TO THE REVEREND MR. THOMAS WARTON

'SIR,

'IT is but an ill return for the book with which you were pleased to favour me,[1] to have delayed my thanks for it till now. I am too apt to be negligent; but I can never deliberately shew my disrespect to a man of your character: and I now pay you a very honest acknowledgement, for the advancement of the literature of our native country. You have shewn to all, who shall hereafter attempt the study of our ancient authours, the way to success; by directing them to the perusal of the books which those authours had read. Of this method, Hughes,[2] and men much greater than Hughes, seem never to have thought. The reason why the authours, which are yet read, of the sixteenth century, are so little understood, is, that they are read alone; and no help is borrowed from those who lived with them, or before them. Some part of this ignorance I hope to remove by my book,[3] which now draws towards its end; but which I cannot finish to my mind, without visiting the libraries of Oxford, which I therefore hope to see in a fortnight.[4] I know not how long I shall stay, or where I shall lodge; but shall be sure to look for you at my arrival, and we shall easily settle the rest. I am, dear Sir,

'Your most obedient, &c.

'[London] July 16, 1754.'   'SAM JOHNSON'

Of his conversation while at Oxford at this time, Mr. Warton preserved and communicated to me the following memorial, which, though not written with all the care and attention which that learned and elegant writer bestowed on those compositions which he intended for the public eye, is so happily expressed in an easy style, that I should injure it by any alteration:

'When Johnson came to Oxford in 1754, the long

[1] Observations on Spenser's Fairy Queen, the first edition of which was now published.
[2] 'Hughes published an edition of Spenser.'
[3] 'His Dictionary.'
[4] 'He came to Oxford within a fortnight, and stayed about five weeks. He lodged at a house called Kettel-hall, near Trinity College. But during his visit at Oxford, he collected nothing in the libraries for his Dictionary.'

vacation was beginning, and most people were leaving the place. This was the first time of his being there, after quitting the University. The next morning after his arrival, he wished to see his old College, *Pembroke*. I went with him. He was highly pleased to find all the College-servants which he had left there still remaining, particularly a very old butler; and expressed great satisfaction at being recognised by them, and conversed with them familiarly. He waited on the master, Dr. Radcliffe, who received him very coldly. Johnson at least expected, that the master would order a copy of his Dictionary, now near publication; but the master did not choose to talk on the subject, never asked Johnson to dine, nor even to visit him, while he stayed at Oxford. After we had left the lodgings, Johnson said to me, " *There* lives a man, who lives by the revenues of literature, and will not move a finger to support it. If I come to live at Oxford, I shall take up my abode at Trinity." We then called on the Reverend Mr. Meeke, one of the fellows, and of Johnson's standing. Here was a most cordial greeting on both sides. On leaving him, Johnson said, "I used to think Meeke had excellent parts, when we were boys together at the college: but, alas!

'Lost in a convent's solitary gloom!' —

I remember, at the classical lecture in the Hall, I could not bear Meeke's superiority, and I tried to sit as far from him as I could, that I might not hear him construe."[a]

'As we were leaving the College, he said, "Here I translated Pope's Messiah. Which do you think is the best line in it?—My own favourite is,

' *Vallis aromaticas fundit Saronica nubes.*' "

I told him, I thought it a very sonorous hexameter. I did not tell him, it was not in the Virgilian style.[b] He much regretted that his *first* tutor was dead; for whom he seemed to retain the greatest regard. He said, "I once had been a whole morning sliding in Christ-Church meadows, and missed his lecture in logick. After dinner he sent for me to his room. I expected a sharp rebuke for my idleness, and went with a beating heart. When we were seated, he told me he had sent for me to drink a glass of wine with him,

[a] *very curious!* [1]

[b] *Better not: why should a Man be forced on Imitation?* [1]

and to tell me, he was *not* angry with me for missing his lecture. This was, in fact, a most severe reprimand. Some more of the boys were then sent for, and we spent a very pleasant afternoon." Besides Mr. Meeke, there was only one other Fellow of Pembroke now resident: from both of whom Johnson received the greatest civilities during this visit, and they pressed him very much to have a room in the College.

'In the course of this visit (1754,) Johnson and I walked three or four times to Ellsfield, a village beautifully situated about three miles from Oxford, to see Mr. Wise, Radclivian librarian, with whom Johnson was much pleased. At this place, Mr. Wise had fitted up a house and gardens, in a singular manner, but with great taste. Here was an excellent library, particularly a valuable collection of books in Northern literature, with which Johnson was often very busy. One day Mr. Wise read to us a dissertation which he was preparing for the press, intitled, "A History and Chronology of the fabulous Ages." Some old divinities of Thrace, related to the Titans, and called the CABIRI, made a very important part of the theory of this piece; and in conversation afterwards, Mr. Wise talked much of his CABIRI.[a] As we returned to Oxford in the evening, I outwalked Johnson, and he cried out *Sufflamina*, a Latin word, which came from his mouth with peculiar grace, and was as much as to say, *Put on your drag chain.* Before we got home, I again walked too fast for him; and he now cried out, "Why, you walk as if you were pursued by all the CABIRI in a body."[b] In an evening we frequently took long walks from Oxford into the country, returning to supper. Once, in our way home, we viewed the ruins of the abbies of Oseney and Rewley, near Oxford. After at least half an hour's silence, Johnson said, "I viewed them with indignation!" We had then a long conversation on Gothic buildings; and in talking of the form of old halls, he said, "In these halls, the fire-place was antiently always in the middle of the room, till the Whigs removed it on one side." —About this time there had been an execution of two or three criminals at Oxford on a Monday. Soon afterwards, one day at dinner, I was saying that Mr. Swinton, the chaplain of the gaol, and also a frequent preacher before

[a] *we now find out they were Shem, Ham, and Japhet.* [1]

[b] *how droll!* [1]

the University, a learned man, but often thoughtless and
absent, preached the condemnation-sermon on repentance,
before the convicts, on the preceding day, Sunday; and
that in the close he told his audience, that he should give
them the remainder of what he had to say on the subject,
the next Lord's Day. Upon which, one of our company,
a Doctor of Divinity, and a plain matter-of-fact man, by
way of offering an apology for Mr. Swinton, gravely
remarked, that he had probably preached the same sermon
before the University: "Yes, Sir, (says Johnson) but the
University were not to be hanged the next morning."[a]

underlined:
remainder, Lord's Day
[H]

'I forgot to observe before, that when he left Mr. Meeke,
(as I have told above) he added, "About the same time
of life, Meeke was left behind at Oxford to feed on a
Fellowship, and I went to London to get my living: now,
Sir, see the difference of our literary characters!"'

[a] *Like the Hangman
who when some Gener-
ous Fellow gave him a
Guinea, cried out Long
Life to your Honour,
while he was tying the
Knot.* [H]

The following letter was written by Dr. Johnson to
Mr. Chambers, of Lincoln College, afterwards Sir Robert
Chambers, one of the judges in India:[1]

'TO MR. CHAMBERS, OF LINCOLN COLLEGE

'DEAR SIR,

'THE commission which I delayed to trouble you
with at your departure, I am now obliged to send you; and
beg that you will be so kind as to carry it to Mr. Warton,
of Trinity, to whom I should have written immediately,
but that I know not if he be yet come back to Oxford.

'In the Catalogue of MSS. of Gr. Brit. see vol. I. pag. 18.
MSS. Bodl. MARTYRIUM XV. *martyrum sub Juliano,
auctore Theophylacto.*

'It is desired that Mr. Warton will enquire, and send
word, what will be the cost of transcribing this manuscript.

'Vol. II. p. 32. Num. 1022. 58. COLL. NOV.—
*Commentaria in Acta Apostol.—Comment. in Septem Epistolas
Catholicas.*

'He is desired to tell what is the age of each of these
manuscripts: and what it will cost to have a transcript
of the two first pages of each.

---

[1] Communicated by the Reverend Mr. Thomas Warton, who had the
original.

'If Mr. Warton be not in Oxford, you may try if you can get it done by any body else; or stay till he comes according to your own convenience. It is for an Italian *literato*.

'The answer is to be directed to his Excellency Mr. Zon, Venetian Resident, Soho-Square.

'I hope, dear Sir, that you do not regret the change of London for Oxford. Mr. Baretti is well, and Miss Williams;[1] and we shall all be glad to hear from you, whenever you shall be so kind as to write to, Sir,

'Your most humble servant,

'Nov. 21, 1754.'   'SAM. JOHNSON'

The degree of Master of Arts, which, it has been observed, could not be obtained for him at an early period of his life, was now considered as an honour of considerable importance, in order to grace the title-page of his Dictionary; and his character in the literary world being by this time deservedly high, his friends thought that, if proper exertions were made, the University of Oxford would pay

^a *I cannot comprehend why they delay'd it so.* [1]

him the compliment.[a]

'TO THE REVEREND MR. THOMAS WARTON

'DEAR SIR,

'I AM extremely obliged to you and to Mr. Wise, for the uncommon care which you have taken of my interest;[2] if you can accomplish your kind design, I shall certainly take me a little habitation among you.

> [1] 'I presume she was a relation of Mr. Zachariah Williams, who died in his eighty-third year, July 12, 1755. When Dr. Johnson was with me at Oxford, in 1755, he gave to the Bodleian Library a thin quarto of twenty-one pages, a work in Italian, with an English translation on the opposite page. The English title-page is this: 'An Account of an Attempt to ascertain the Longitude at Sea, by an exact Variation of the Magnetical Needle, &c. By Zachariah Williams. London, printed for Dodsley, 1755.' The English translation, from the strongest internal marks, is unquestionably the work of Johnson. In a blank leaf, Johnson has written the age, and time of death, of the author Z. Williams, as I have said above. On another blank leaf is pasted a paragraph from a newspaper, of the death and character of Williams, which is plainly written by Johnson. He was very anxious about placing this book in the Bodleian: and, for fear of any omission or mistake, he entered, in the great Catalogue, the title-page of it with his own hand.'
>
> [In this statement there is a slight mistake. The English account, which was written by Johnson, was the *original;* the Italian was a *translation*, done

^b *just so.* [1]

> by Baretti.[b] See p. 209. MALONE.]
>
> [2] 'In procuring him the degree of Master of Arts by diploma at Oxford.'

'The books which I promised to Mr. Wise,[1] I have not been able to procure: but I shall send him a Finnick Dictionary, the only copy, perhaps, in England, which was presented to me by a learned Swede: but I keep it back, that it may make a set of my own books of the new edition, with which I shall accompany it, more welcome. You will assure him of my gratitude.

'Poor dear Collins![2]—Would a letter give him any pleasure? I have a mind to write.

'I am glad of your hindrance in your Spenserian design,[3] yet I would not have it delayed. Three hours a day stolen from sleep and amusement will produce it. Let a Servitour[4]

[1] 'Lately fellow of Trinity College, and at this time Radclivian librarian, at Oxford. He was a man of very considerable learning, and eminently skilled in Roman and Anglo-Saxon antiquities. He died in 1767.'

[2] 'Collins (the poet) was at this time at Oxford, on a visit to Mr. Warton; but labouring under the most deplorable languor of body and dejection of mind.

[In a letter to Dr. Joseph Warton, written some months before, (March 8, 1754,) Dr. Johnson thus speaks of Collins:

'But how little can we venture to exult in any intellectual powers or literary attainments, when we consider the condition of poor Collins. I knew him a few years ago full of hopes, and full of projects, versed in many languages, high in fancy, and strong in retention. This busy and forcible mind is now under the government of those, who lately could not have been able to comprehend the least and most narrow of his designs. What do you hear of him? are there hopes of his recovery? or is he to pass the remainder of his life in misery and degradation? perhaps, with a complete consciousness of his calamity.'

In a subsequent letter to the same gentleman, (Dec. 24, 1754) he thus feelingly alludes to their unfortunate friend:

'Poor dear Collins! Let me know whether you think it would give him pleasure if I should write to him. I have often been *near* his state, and therefore have it in great commiseration.'

Again,—April 9, 1756:

'What becomes of poor dear Collins? I wrote him a letter which he never answered. I suppose writing is very troublesome to him. That man is no common loss. The moralists all talk of the uncertainty of fortune, and the transitoriness of beauty: but it is yet more dreadful to consider that the powers of the mind are equally liable to change, that understanding may make its appearance and depart, that it may blaze and expire.'[a]

See Biographical Memoirs of the late Reverend Dr. Joseph Warton, by the Rev. John Wool, A. M. 4to. 1806.

Mr. Collins, who was the son of a hatter at Chichester, was born December 25, 1720, and was released from the dismal state here so pathetically described, in 1756. MALONE.]

[a] *ay, ay, so it is; &* much *more. 1820* [H]
Oh Charming! [I]
marginal line:
Mr. Collins . . . 1756.
Malone [H]

[3] 'Of publishing a volume of observations on the best of Spenser's works. It was hindered by my taking pupils in this College.'

[4] 'Young students of the lowest rank at Oxford are so called.'

transcribe the quotations, and interleave them with references, to save time. This will shorten the work, and lessen the fatigue.

'Can I do any thing to promote the diploma? I would not be wanting to co-operate with your kindness; of which, whatever be the effect, I shall be, dear Sir,

'Your most obliged, &c.

'[London,] Nov. 28, 1754.'   'SAM. JOHNSON'

TO THE SAME

'DEAR SIR,

'I AM extremely sensible of the favour done me, both by Mr. Wise and yourself. The book[1] cannot, I think, be printed in less than six weeks, nor probably so soon; and I will keep back the title-page, for such an insertion as you seem to promise me. Be pleased to let me know what money I shall send you for bearing the expence of the affair; and I will take care that you may have it ready at your hand.

'I had lately the favour of a letter from your brother, with some account of poor Collins, for whom I am much concerned. I have a notion, that by very great temperance, or more properly abstinence, he may yet recover.

'There is an old English and Latin book of poems by Barclay, called "The Ship of Fools:" at the end of which are a number of *Eglogues*,—so he writes it, from *Egloga*,—which are probably the first in our language. If you cannot find the book, I will get Mr. Dodsley to send it you.

'I shall be extremely glad to hear from you again, to know, if the affair proceeds.[2] I have mentioned it to none of my friends, for fear of being laughed at for my disappointment.

'You know poor Mr. Dodsley has lost his wife; I believe he is much affected. I hope he will not suffer so much as I yet suffer for the loss of mine.

Οἴμι· τι δ' οἴμι; θνῆτα γὰρ πεπόνθαμεν.[3]

---

[1] 'His Dictionary.'   [2] 'Of the degree at Oxford.'

[3] [This verse is taken from the long lost BELLEROPHON, a tragedy by Euripides. It is preserved by Suidas in his Lexicon, Voc. Οἴμοι. II. p. 666, where the reading is, θνητά τοι πεπόνθαμεν. Rev. C. BURNEY.]

I have ever since seemed to myself broken off from mankind; a kind of solitary wanderer in the wild of life, without
any direction, or fixed point of view; a gloomy gazer on
the world to which I have little relation. Yet I would
endeavour, by the help of you and your brother, to supply
the want of closer union, by friendship: and hope to have
long the pleasure of being, dear Sir,

                              'Most affectionately your's,
'[London] Dec. 21, 1754.'   'SAM. JOHNSON'

In 1755 we behold him to great advantage; his degree
of Master of Arts conferred upon him, his Dictionary
published, his correspondence animated, his benevolence
exercised.

'TO THE REVEREND MR. THOMAS WARTON

'DEAR SIR,
    'I WROTE to you some weeks ago, but believe did not
direct accurately, and therefore know not whether you
had my letter. I would, likewise, write to your brother,
but know not where to find him. I now begin to see land,
after having wandered, according to Mr. Warburton's
phrase, in this vast sea of words. What reception I shall
meet with on the shore, I know not; whether the sound
of bells, and acclamations of the people, which Ariosto
talks of in his last Canto, or a general murmur of dislike,
I know not: whether I shall find upon the coast a Calypso
that will court, or a Polypheme that will resist. But if
Polypheme comes, have at his eye. I hope, however, the
criticks will let me be at peace; for though I do not much
fear their skill and strength, I am a little afraid of myself,[a]
and would not willingly feel so much ill-will in my bosom
as literary quarrels are apt to excite.
    'Mr. Baretti is about a work for which he is in great
want of Crescimbeni, which you may have again when
you please.
    'There is nothing considerable done or doing among
us here. We are not, perhaps, as innocent as villagers, but

underlined:
myself [H]

[a] *That is just what I
feel when Insulted; not
about literary tho',—
but social Quarrels:
The others are not
worth a Thought.* [H]

most of us seem to be as idle. I hope, however, you are busy; and should be glad to know what you are doing.

'I am, dearest, Sir,
'Your humble servant,

'[London] Feb. 4, 1755.'   'SAM. JOHNSON'

TO THE SAME

'DEAR SIR,

'I RECEIVED your letter this day, with great sense of the favour that has been done me;[1] for which I return my most sincere thanks; and entreat you to pay to Mr. Wise such returns as I ought to make for so much kindness so little deserved.

'I sent Mr. Wise the Lexicon, and afterwards wrote to him; but know not whether he had either the book or letter. Be so good as to contrive to enquire.

'But why does my dear Mr. Warton tell me nothing of himself? Where hangs the new volume?[2] Can I help? Let not the past labour be lost, for want of a little more: but snatch what time you can from the Hall, and the pupils, and the coffee-house, and the parks, and complete your design. I am, dear Sir, &c.   'SAM. JOHNSON'

'[London] Feb. 4, 1755.'

TO THE SAME

'DEAR SIR,

'I HAD a letter last week from Mr. Wise, but have yet heard nothing from you, nor know in what state my affair[3] stands; of which I beg you to inform me, if you can, to-morrow, by the return of the post.

'Mr. Wise sends me word, that he has not had the Finnick Lexicon yet, which I sent some time ago; and if he has it not, you must enquire after it. However, do not let your letter stay for that.

'Your brother, who is a better correspondent than you, and not much better, sends me word, that your pupils

---

[1] 'His degree had now past, according to the usual form, the suffrages of the heads of Colleges; but was not yet finally granted by the University. It was carried without a single dissentient voice.'

[2] 'On Spenser.'   [3] 'Of the degree.'

keep you in College: but do they keep you from writing too? Let them, at least, give you time to write to, dear Sir,

'Your most affectionate, &c.

'[London] Feb. 13, 1755.'   'SAM. JOHNSON'

TO THE SAME

'DEAR SIR,

'DR. KING[1] was with me a few minutes before your letter; this, however, is the first instance in which your kind intentions to me have ever been frustrated.[2] I have now the full effect of your care and benevolence; and am far from thinking it a slight honour, or a small advantage; since it will put the enjoyment of your conversation more frequently in the power of, dear Sir,

'Your most obliged and affectionate,

'SAM. JOHNSON'

'P.S. I have enclosed a letter to the Vice-Chancellor,[3] which you will read; and, if you like it, seal and give him.

'[London] Feb. 1755.'

As the Publick will doubtless be pleased to see the whole progress of this well-earned academical honour, I shall insert the Chancellor of Oxford's letter to the University,[4] the diploma, and Johnson's letter of thanks to the Vice-Chancellor.

'*To the Reverend Dr.* HUDDESFORD, *Vice-Chancellor of the* University *of* Oxford; *to be communicated to the Heads of Houses, and proposed in Convocation.*

'MR. VICE-CHANCELLOR, AND GENTLEMEN,

'MR. SAMUEL JOHNSON, who was formerly of Pembroke College, having very eminently distinguished himself by the publication of a series of Essays, excellently

[1] 'Principal of Saint Mary Hall at Oxford. He brought with him the diploma from Oxford.'

[2] 'I suppose Johnson means that my *kind intention* of being the *first* to give him the good news of the degree being granted was *frustrated*, because Dr. King brought it before my intelligence arrived.'

[3] 'Dr. Huddesford, President of Trinity College.'

[4] Extracted from the Convocation-Register, Oxford.

calculated to form the manners of the people, and in which the cause of religion and morality is every where maintained by the strongest powers of argument and language; and who shortly intends to publish a Dictionary of the English Tongue, formed on a new plan, and executed with the greatest labour and judgement; I persuade myself that I shall act agreeable to the sentiments of the whole University, in desiring that it may be proposed in convocation to confer on him the degree of Master of Arts by diploma, to which I readily give my consent; and am,

'Mr. Vice-Chancellor, and Gentlemen,

'Your affectionate friend and servant,

'Grosvenor-street, Feb. 4, 1755.'   'ARRAN'

Term. S^{cti.}
Hilarii.   'DIPLOMA MAGISTRI JOHNSON
1755.

'*CANCELLARIUS, Magistri et Scholares Universitatis Oxoniensis omnibus ad quos hoc presens scriptum prevenerit, salutem in Domino sempiternam.*

'*Cùm eum in finem gradus academici à majoribus nostris instituti fuerint, ut viri ingenio et doctrinâ præstantes titulis quoque præter cæteros insignirentur; cùmque vir doctissimus* Samuel Johnson *è Collegio Pembrochiensi, scriptis suis popularium mores informantibus dudum literato orbi innotuerit; quin et linguæ patriæ tum ornandæ tum stabiliendæ (Lexicon scilicet Anglicanum summo studio, summo à se judicio congestum propediem editurus) etiam nunc utilissimam impendat operam; Nos igitur Cancellarius, Magistri, et Scholares antedicti, nè virum de literis humanioribus optimè meritum diutius inhonoratum prætereamus, in solenni Convocatione Doctorum, Magistrorum, Regentium, et non Regentium, decimo die Mensis Februarii Anno Domini Millesimo Septingentesimo Quinquagesimo quinto habitâ, præfatum virum* Samuelem Johnson *(conspirantibus omnium suffragiis) Magistrum in Artibus renunciavimus et constituimus; eumque, virtute præsentis diplomatis, singulis juribus privilegiis et honoribus ad istum gradum quàquà pertinentibus frui et gaudere jussimus.*

'*In cujus rei testimonium sigillum Universitatis Oxoniensis præsentibus apponi fecimus.*

'*Datum in Domo nostræ Convocationis die 20° Mensis Feb. Anno Dom. prædicto.*

'*Diploma supra scriptum per Registrarium lectum erat, et ex decreto venerabilis Domûs communi Universitatis sigillo munitum.*'[1]

'*Londini. 4to Cal. Mart.* 1755.

'VIRO REVERENDO - - - - HUDDESFORD, S. T. P. UNIVERSITATIS OXONIENSIS VICE-CANCELLARIO DIGNISSIMO, S. P. D.

'SAM. JOHNSON.[2]

'*INGRATUS plane et tibi et mihi videar, nisi quanto me gaudio affecerint, quos nuper mihi honores (te, credo, auctore,) decrevit Senatus Academicus, literarum, quo tamen nihil levius, officio, significem; ingratus etiam, nisi comitatem, quâ vir eximius[3] mihi vestri testimonium amoris in manus tradidit, agnoscam et laudem. Si quid est, undè rei tam gratæ accedat gratia, hoc ipso magis mihi placet, quod eo tempore in ordines Academicos denuò cooptatus sim, quo tuam imminuere auctoritatem, famamque Oxonii lædere, omnibus modis conantur homines vafri, nec tamen acuti: quibus ego, prout viro umbratico licuit, semper restiti, semper restiturus. Qui enim, inter has rerum procellas, vel tibi vel Academiæ defuerit, illum virtuti et literis, sibique et posteris, defuturum existimo. Vale.*'

'TO THE REVEREND MR. THOMAS WARTON

'DEAR SIR,

'AFTER I received my diploma, I wrote you a letter of thanks, with a letter to the Vice-Chancellor, and sent another to Mr. Wise; but have heard from nobody since, and begin to think myself forgotten. It is true, I sent you a double letter, and you may fear an expensive correspondent; but I would have taken it kindly, if you had returned it treble: and what is a double letter to a *petty king*, that having *fellowship and fines*, can sleep without a *Modus in his head?*[4]

---

[1] The original is in my possession.

[2] [The superscription of this letter was not quite correct in the early editions of this work. It is here given from Dr. Johnson's original letter, now before me. MALONE.]

[3] We may conceive what a high gratification it must have been to Johnson to receive his diploma from the hands of the great Dr. KING, whose principles were so congenial with his own.

[4] 'The words in Italicks are allusions to passages in Mr. Warton's poem, called "THE PROGRESS OF DISCONTENT,' now lately published.'[a]

[a] & wch. Johnson always admired to the last [1]

'Dear Mr. Warton, let me hear from you, and tell me something, I care not what, so I hear it but from you. Something I will tell you:—I hope to see my Dictionary bound and lettered, next week;—*vastâ mole superbus*. And I have a great mind to come to Oxford at Easter; but you will not invite me. Shall I come uninvited, or stay here where nobody perhaps would miss me if I went? A hard choice! But such is the world to, dear Sir,

'Yours, &c.

'[London] March 20, 1755.'   'SAM. JOHNSON'

                    TO THE SAME
'DEAR SIR,

'THOUGH not to write, when a man can write so well, is an offence sufficiently heinous, yet I shall pass it by. I am very glad that the Vice-Chancellor was pleased with my note. I shall impatiently expect you at London, that we may consider what to do next. I intend in the winter to open a *Bibliothèque*, and remember, that you are to subscribe a sheet a year: let us try, likewise, if we cannot persuade your brother to subscribe another. My book is now coming *in luminis oras*. What will be its fate I know not, nor think much, because thinking is to no purpose. It must stand the censure of the *great vulgar and the small;* of those that understand it, and that understand it not. But in all this, I suffer not alone; every writer has the same difficulties, and, perhaps, every writer talks of them more than he thinks.

'You will be pleased to make my compliments to all my friends; and be so kind, at every idle hour, as to remember, dear Sir,

'Yours, &c.

'[London] March 25, 1755.'   'SAM. JOHNSON'

Dr. Adams told me, that this scheme of a *Bibliothèque* was a serious one: for upon his visiting him one day, he found his parlour floor covered with parcels of foreign and English literary journals, and he told Dr. Adams he meant to undertake a Review. 'How, Sir, (said Dr. Adams,) can you think of doing it alone? All branches of knowledge must be considered in it. Do you know Mathematicks?

Do you know Natural History?' Johnson answered, 'Why, Sir, I must do as well as I can. My chief purpose is to give my countrymen a view of what is doing in literature upon the continent; and I shall have, in a good measure, the choice of my subject, for I shall select such books as I best understand.' Dr. Adams suggested, that as Dr. Maty had just then finished his *Bibliothèque Britannique*, which was a well-executed work, giving foreigners an account of British publications, he might, with great advantage, assume him as an assistant. '*He* (said Johnson) the little black dog! I'd throw him into the Thames.' The scheme, however, was dropped.

In one of his little memorandum books I find the following hints for his intended Review or Literary Journal: '*The Annals of Literature, foreign as well as domestick*. Imitate Le Clerc—Bayle—Barbeyrac. Infelicity of Journals in England. Works of the learned. We cannot take in all. Sometimes copy from foreign Journalists. Always tell.'

'TO DR. BIRCH

'SIR,   'March 29th, 1755
   'I HAVE sent some parts of my Dictionary, such as were at hand, for your inspection. The favour which I beg is, that if you do not like them, you will say nothing. I am, Sir,   'Your most affectionate humble servant,
                                    'SAM. JOHNSON'

'TO MR. SAMUEL JOHNSON

'SIR,   'Norfolk-street, April 23, 1755
   'THE part of your Dictionary which you have favoured me with the sight of has given me such an idea of the whole, that I most sincerely congratulate the publick upon the acquisition of a work long wanted, and now executed with an industry, accuracy, and judgement, equal to the importance of the subject. You might, perhaps, have chosen one in which your genius would have appeared to more advantage, but you could not have fixed upon any other in which your labours would have done such substantial service to the present age and to posterity. I am

glad that your health has supported the application necessary to the performance of so vast a task; and can undertake to promise you as one (though perhaps the only) reward of it, the approbation and thanks of every well-wisher to the honour of the English language. I am, with the greatest regard,

'Sir,
'Your most faithful and
'Most affectionate humble servant,
'THO. BIRCH'

Mr. Charles Burney, who has since distinguished himself so much in the science of Musick, and obtained a Doctor's degree from the University of Oxford, had been driven from the capital by bad health, and was now residing at Lynne Regis in Norfolk. He had been so much delighted with Johnson's Rambler, and the plan of his Dictionary, that when the great work was announced in the newspapers as nearly finished, he wrote to Dr. Johnson, begging to be informed when and in what manner his Dictionary would be published; entreating, if it should be by subscription, or he should have any books at his own disposal, to be favoured with six copies for himself and friends.

In answer to this application, Dr. Johnson wrote the following letter, of which (to use Dr. Burney's own words) 'if it be remembered that it was written to an obscure young man, who at this time had not much distinguished himself even in his own profession, but whose name could never have reached the authour of THE RAMBLER, the politeness and urbanity may be opposed to some of the stories which have been lately circulated of Dr. Johnson's natural rudeness and ferocity.'

'TO MR. BURNEY, IN LYNNE REGIS, NORFOLK

'SIR,

'IF you imagine that by delaying my answer I intended to shew any neglect of the notice with which you have favoured me, you will neither think justly of yourself nor of me. Your civilities were offered with too much elegance not to engage attention; and I have too much pleasure in pleasing men like you, not to feel very sensibly the distinction which you have bestowed upon me.

'Few consequences of my endeavours to please or to benefit mankind have delighted me more than your friendship thus voluntarily offered, which now I have it I hope to keep, because I hope to continue to deserve it.

'I have no Dictionaries to dispose of for myself, but shall be glad to have you direct your friends to Mr. Dodsley, because it was by his recommendation that I was employed in the work.

'When you have leisure to think again upon me, let me be favoured with another letter; and another yet, when you have looked into my Dictionary. If you find faults, I shall endeavour to mend them; if you find none, I shall think you blinded by kind partiality: but to have made you partial in his favour, will very much gratify the ambition of, Sir,

'Your most obliged
'And most humble servant,

'Gough-square, Fleet-street,   'SAM. JOHNSON'
       April 8, 1755.'

Mr. Andrew Millar, bookseller in the Strand, took the principal charge of conducting the publication of Johnson's Dictionary; and as the patience of the proprietors was repeatedly tried and almost exhausted, by their expecting that the work would be compleated, within the time which Johnson had sanguinely supposed, the learned author was often goaded to dispatch, more especially as he had received all the copy money, by different drafts, a considerable time before he had finished his task. When the messenger who carried the last sheet to Millar returned, Johnson asked him, 'Well, what did he say?'—'Sir, (answered the messenger) he said, thank GOD I have done with him.' 'I am glad (replied Johnson, with a smile,) that he thanks GOD for any thing.'[1] It is remarkable, that those with whom Johnson chiefly contracted for his

---

[1] Sir John Hawkins, p. 341, inserts two notes as having passed formerly between Andrew Millar and Johnson, to the above effect. I am assured this was not the case. In the way of incidental remark it was a pleasant play of raillery. To have deliberately written notes in such terms would have been morose.

literary labours were Scotchmen, Mr. Millar and Mr. Strahan. Millar, though himself no great judge of literature, had good sense enough to have for his friends very able men, to give him their opinion and advice in the purchase of copyright; the consequence of which was his acquiring a very large fortune, with great liberality. Johnson said of him, 'I respect Millar, Sir; he has raised the price of literature.' The same praise may be justly given to Panckoucke, the eminent bookseller of Paris. Mr. Strahan's liberality, judgement, and success are well known.

'TO BENNET LANGTON, ESQ. AT LANGTON, NEAR
SPILSBY, LINCOLNSHIRE
'SIR,

'IT has been long observed, that men do not suspect faults which they do not commit; your own elegance of manners, and punctuality of complaisance, did not suffer you to impute to me that negligence of which I was guilty, and which I have not since atoned. I received both your letters, and received them with pleasure proportioned to the esteem which so short an acquaintance strongly impressed, and which I hope to confirm by nearer knowledge, though I am afraid that gratification will be for a time withheld.

'I have, indeed, published my Book,[1] of which I beg to know your father's judgement, and yours; and I have now staid long enough to watch its progress in the world. It has, you see, no patrons, and I think, has yet had no opponents, except the criticks of the coffee-house, whose outcries are soon dispersed into the air, and are thought on no more; from this, therefore, I am at liberty, and think of taking the opportunity of this interval to make an excursion, and why not then into Lincolnshire? or, to mention a stronger attraction, why not to dear Mr. Langton? I will give the true reason, which I know you will approve:—I have a mother more than eighty years old, who has counted the days to the publication of my book, in hopes of seeing me; and to her, if I can disengage myself here, I resolve to go.

'As I know, dear Sir, that to delay my visit for a reason

[1] His Dictionary.

like this, will not deprive me of your esteem, I beg it may not lessen your kindness. I have very seldom received an offer of friendship which I so earnestly desire to cultivate and mature. I shall rejoice to hear from you, till I can see you, and will see you as soon as I can; for when the duty that calls me to Lichfield is discharged, my inclination will carry me to Langton. I shall delight to hear the ocean roar, or see the stars twinkle, in the company of men to whom Nature does not spread her volume or utter her voice in vain.

'Do not, dear Sir, make the slowness of this letter a precedent for delay, or imagine that I approved the incivility that I have committed; for I have known you enough to love you, and sincerely to wish a further knowledge; and I assure you once more, that to live in a house that contains such a father and such a son, will be accounted a very uncommon degree of pleasure, by, dear Sir,

'Your most obliged,
'And most humble servant,

'May 6, 1755.'   'SAM. JOHNSON'

'TO THE REVEREND MR. THOMAS WARTON

'DEAR SIR,

'I AM grieved that you should think me capable of neglecting your letters; and beg you will never admit any such suspicion again. I purpose to come down next week, if you shall be there; or any other week, that shall be more agreeable to you. Therefore let me know. I can stay this visit but a week; but intend to make preparations for longer stay next time; being resolved not to lose sight of the University. How goes Apollonius?[1] Don't let him be forgotten. Some things of this kind must be done, to keep us up. Pay my compliments to Mr. Wise, and all my other friends. I think to come to Kettel-Hall.[2] I am, Sir,

'Your most affectionate, &c.

'[London] May 13, 1755.'   'SAM. JOHNSON'

[1] 'A translation of Apollonius Rhodius was now intended by Mr. Warton.'

[2] [Kettel-Hall is an ancient tenement, adjoining to Trinity College, built about the year 1615, by Dr. Ralph Kettel, then President, for the accommodation of Commoners of that Society. In this ancient *hostel*, then in a very

TO THE SAME
'DEAR SIR,

'IT is strange how many things will happen to inter-
cept every pleasure, though it [be] only that of two friends
meeting together. I have promised myself every day to
inform you when you might expect me at Oxford, and
have not been able to fix a time. This time, however, is,
I think, at last come; and I promise myself to repose in
Kettel-Hall, one of the first nights of the next week. I am
afraid my stay with you cannot be long; but what is the
inference? We must endeavour to make it chearful. I wish
your brother could meet us, that we might go and drink
tea with Mrs. Wise in a body. I hope he will be at Oxford,
or at his nest of British and Saxon antiquities.[1] I shall
expect to see Spenser finished, and many other things
begun. Dodsley is gone to visit the Dutch. The Dictionary
sells well. The rest of the world goes on as it did. Dear Sir,
'Your most affectionate, &c.

'[London] June 10, 1755.'   'SAM. JOHNSON'

TO THE SAME
'DEAR SIR,

'To talk of coming to you, and not yet to come, has
an air of trifling which I would not willingly have among
you; and which, I believe, you will not willingly impute to
me, when I have told you, that since my promise, two of
our partners[2] are dead, and that I was solicited to suspend
my excursion till we could recover from our confusion.

'I have not laid aside my purpose; for every day makes
me more impatient of staying from you. But death, you
know, hears not supplications, nor pays any regard to the
convenience of mortals. I hope now to see you next week;
but next week is but another name for to-morrow, which
has been noted for promising and deceiving.
'I am, &c.

'[London] June 24, 1755.'   'SAM. JOHNSON'

ruinous state, about forty years after Johnson had lodged there, Mr. Windham and the present writer were accommodated with two chambers, of
primitive simplicity, during the installation of the Duke of Portland as
Chancellor of the University of Oxford, in 1793. It has since been converted
into a commodious private house. MALONE.]
    [1] 'At Ellsfield, a village three miles from Oxford.'
    [2] 'Booksellers concerned in his Dictionary.'

TO THE SAME
'DEAR SIR,

'I TOLD you that among the manuscripts are some things of Sir Thomas More. I beg you to pass an hour in looking on them, and procure a transcript of the ten or twenty first lines of each, to be compared with what I have; that I may know whether they are yet published. The manuscripts are these:

'Catalogue of Bodl. MS. pag. 122. F. 3. Sir Thomas More.

1. Fall of angels. 2. Creation and fall of mankind. 3. Determination of the Trinity for the rescue of mankind.[a] 4. Five lectures of our Saviour's passion. 5. Of the institution of the Sacrament, three lectures. 6. How to receive the blessed body of our Lord sacramentally. 7. Neomenia, the new moon. 8. *De tristitia, tædio, pavore, et oratione Christi ante captionem ejus.*

'Catalogue, pag. 154. Life of Sir Thomas More. *Qu.* Whether Roper's? Page 363. *De resignatione Magni Sigilli in manus Regis per D. Thomam Morum.* Pag. 364. *Mori Defensio Moriæ.*

'If you procure the young gentleman in the library to write out what you think fit to be written, I will send to Mr. Prince the bookseller to pay him what you shall think proper.

'Be pleased to make my compliments to Mr. Wise, and all my friends. I am, Sir,

'Your affectionate, &c.

'[London] Aug. 7, 1755.' 'SAM. JOHNSON'

[a] *before hand with Parkhurst!* [1]

The Dictionary, with a Grammar and History of the English Language, being now at length published, in two volumes folio, the world contemplated with wonder so stupendous a work atchieved by one man, while other countries had thought such undertakings fit only for whole academies. Vast as his powers were, I cannot but think that his imagination deceived him, when he supposed that by constant application he might have performed the task in three years. Let the Preface be attentively perused, in which is given, in a clear, strong, and glowing style, a comprehensive, yet particular view of what he had done;

and it will be evident, that the time he employed upon it
was comparatively short. I am unwilling to swell my book
with long quotations from what is in every body's hands,
and I believe there are few prose compositions in the English
language that are read with more delight, or are more
impressed upon the memory, than that preliminary discourse. One of its excellencies has always struck me with
peculiar admiration; I mean the perspicuity with which
he has expressed abstract scientifick notions. As an instance
of this, I shall quote the following sentence: 'When the
radical idea branches out into parallel ramifications, how
can a consecutive series be formed of senses in their own
nature collateral?' We have here an example of what has
been often said, and I believe with justice, that there is for
every thought a certain nice adaptation of words which
none other could equal, and which, when a man has been
so fortunate as to hit, he has attained, in that particular
case, the perfection of language.

The extensive reading which was absolutely necessary
for the accumulation of authorities, and which alone may
account for Johnson's retentive mind being enriched with
a very large and various store of knowledge and imagery,
must have occupied several years. The Preface furnishes
an eminent instance of a double talent, of which Johnson
was fully conscious. Sir Joshua Reynolds heard him say,
'There are two things which I am confident I can do very
well: one is an introduction to any literary work, stating
what it is to contain, and how it should be executed in
the most perfect manner: the other is a conclusion, shewing
from various causes why the execution has not been equal
to what the authour promised to himself and to the publick.'

How should puny scribblers be abashed and disappointed, when they find him displaying a perfect theory of
lexicographical excellence, yet at the same time candidly
and modestly allowing that he 'had not satisfied his own
expectations.' Here was a fair occasion for the exercise
of Johnson's modesty, when he was called upon to compare
his own arduous performance, not with those of other
individuals, (in which case his inflexible regard to truth
would have been violated had he affected diffidence,) but
with speculative perfection; as he, who can outstrip all his

competitors in the race, may yet be sensible of his deficiency when he runs against time. Well might he say, that
'the English Dictionary was written with little assistance
of the learned;' for he told me, that the only aid which he
received was a paper containing twenty etymologies, sent
to him by a person then unknown, who he was afterwards
informed was Dr. Pearce, Bishop of Rochester. The etymologies, though they exhibit learning and judgement,
are not, I think, entitled to the first praise amongst the
various parts of this immense work. The definitions have
always appeared to me such astonishing proofs of acuteness
of intellect and precision of language, as indicate a genius
of the highest rank. This it is which marks the superiour
excellence of Johnson's Dictionary over others equally
or even more voluminous, and must have made it a work
of much greater mental labour than mere Lexicons, or
Word-Books, as the Dutch call them. They, who will make
the experiment of trying how they can define a few
words of whatever nature, will soon be satisfied of the
unquestionable justice of this observation, which I can
assure my readers is founded upon much study, and upon
communication with more minds than my own.

A few of his definitions must be admitted to be erroneous.
Thus, *Windward* and *Leeward*, though directly of opposite
meaning, are defined identically the same way;[1] as to
which inconsiderable specks it is enough to observe, that
his Preface announces that he was aware there might be
many such in so immense a work; nor was he at all disconcerted when an instance was pointed out to him. A
lady once asked him how he came to define *Pastern* the
knee of a horse: instead of making an elaborate defence, as
she expected, he at once answered, 'Ignorance, Madam,
pure ignorance.' His definition of *Network*, has been often
quoted with sportive malignity, as obscuring a thing in
itself very plain. But to these frivolous censures no other
answer is necessary than that with which we are furnished
by his own Preface. 'To explain, requires the use of terms
less abstruse than that which is to be explained, and such

marginal line:
told me . . . him by [H]

marginal line:
*a horse . . . answered,
'Ignorance* [H]

[1] [He owns in his Preface the deficiency of the technical part of his work;
and he said, he should be much obliged to me for definitions of musical
terms for his next edition, which he did not live to superintend. BURNEY.]

terms cannot always be found. For as nothing can be proved but by supposing something intuitively known, and evident without proof, so nothing can be defined but by the use of words too plain to admit of definition.[a] Sometimes easier words are changed into harder; as, burial, into sepulture or interment; dry, into desiccative; dryness, into siccity or aridity; fit, into paroxism; for, the easiest word, whatever it be, can never be translated into one more easy.'

His introducing his own opinions, and even prejudices, under general definitions of words, while at the same time the original meaning of the words is not explained, as his Tory, Whig, Pension, Oats, Excise,[1] and a few more, cannot be fully defended, and must be placed to the account of capricious and humorous indulgence. Talking to me upon this subject when we were at Ashbourne in 1777, he mentioned a still stronger instance of the predominance of his private feelings in the composition of this work, than any now to be found in it. 'You know, Sir, Lord Gower forsook the old Jacobite interest. When I came to the word Renegado, after telling that it meant "one who deserts to the enemy, a revolter," I added, Sometimes we say a GOWER.[b] Thus it went to the press: but the printer had more wit than I, and struck it out.'

Let it, however, be remembered, that this indulgence does not display itself only in sarcasm towards others, but sometimes in playful allusion to the notions commonly

[a] besides that there is commonly a Roman & a Runic Word for Every thing—He tells Italians that the awkward Word Burial means Sepulture or Interment. The Saxon Word is Easiest only to Anglo Saxons. [i]

[b] & he was obliged to Ld. Gower, See Page 109 [in this edition, vol. i, p. 82] [i]

[1] He thus defines Excise: 'A hateful tax levied upon commodities, and adjudged not by the common judges of property, but wretches hired by those to whom Excise is paid.' The Commissioners of Excise being offended by this severe reflection, consulted Mr. Murray, then Attorney-General, to know whether redress could be legally obtained. I wished to have procured for my readers a copy of the opinion which he gave, and which may now be justly considered as history: but the mysterious secresy of office it seems would not permit it. I am, however, informed, by very good authority, that its import was, that the passage might be considered as actionable; but that it would be more prudent in the board not to prosecute. Johnson never made the smallest alteration in this passage. We find he still retained his early prejudice against Excise; for in 'The Idler, No. 65,' there is the following very extraordinary paragraph: 'The authenticity of Clarendon's history, though printed with the sanction of one of the first Universities of the world, had not an unexpected manuscript been happily discovered, would, with the help of factious credulity, have been brought into question, by the two lowest of all human beings, a Scribbler for a party, and a Commissioner of Excise.' The persons to whom he alludes were Mr. John Oldmixon, and George Ducket, Esq.

entertained of his own laborious task. Thus; 'Grub-street, the name of a street in London, much inhabited by writers of small histories, *dictionaries*, and temporary poems; whence any mean production is called *Grub-street.*' — '*Lexicographer*, a writer of dictionaries, *a harmless drudge.*'

At the time when he was concluding his very eloquent Preface, Johnson's mind appears to have been in such a state of depression, that we cannot contemplate without wonder the vigorous and splendid thoughts which so highly distinguish that performance. 'I (says he) may surely be contented without the praise of perfection, which if I could obtain in this gloom of solitude, what would it avail me? I have protracted my work till most of those whom I wished to please have sunk into the grave; and success and miscarriage are empty sounds. I therefore dismiss it with frigid tranquillity, having little to fear or hope from censure or from praise.' That this indifference was rather a temporary than an habitual feeling, appears, I think, from his letters to Mr. Warton; and however he may have been affected for the moment, certain it is that the honours which his great work procured him, both at home and abroad, were very grateful to him. His friend the Earl of Corke and Orrery, being at Florence, pre-sented it to the *Academia della Crusca.* That Academy sent Johnson their *Vocabolario*, and the French Academy sent him their *Dictionnaire*, which Mr. Langton had the pleasure to convey to him.

It must undoubtedly seem strange, that the conclusion of his Preface should be expressed in terms so desponding, when it is considered that the authour was then only in his forty-sixth year. But we must ascribe its gloom to that miserable dejection of spirits to which he was constitution-ally subject, and which was aggravated by the death of his wife two years before. I have heard it ingeniously observed by a lady of rank and elegance,[a] that 'his melancholy was then at its meridian.' It pleased GOD to grant him almost thirty years of life after this time; and once when he was in a placid frame of mind, he was obliged to own to me that he had enjoyed happier days, and had many more friends, since that gloomy hour, than before.

It is a sad saying, that 'most of those whom he wished

exclamation point:
I have protracted etc.
[H]

exclamation points:
That this indifference
etc. [H]

[a] *Qu   who was She?* [I]

to please had sunk into the grave;' and his case at forty-five was singularly unhappy, unless the circle of his friends was very narrow. I have often thought, that as longevity is generally desired, and I believe, generally expected, it would be wise to be continually adding to the number of our friends, that the loss of some may be supplied by others. Friendship, 'the wine of life,' should, like a well-stocked cellar, be thus continually renewed; and it is consolatory to think, that although we can seldom add what will equal the generous *first growths* of our youth, yet friendship becomes insensibly old in much less time than is commonly imagined, and not many years are required to make it very mellow and pleasant. *Warmth* will, no doubt, make a considerable difference. Men of affectionate temper and bright fancy will coalesce a great deal sooner than those who are cold and dull.

The proposition which I have now endeavoured to illustrate was, at a subsequent period of his life, the opinion of Johnson himself. He said to Sir Joshua Reynolds, 'If a man does not make new acquaintance as he advances through life, he will soon find himself left alone. A man, Sir, should keep his friendship *in constant repair.*'

The celebrated Mr. Wilkes, whose notions and habits of life were very opposite to his, but who was ever eminent for literature and vivacity, sallied forth with a little *Jeu d'Esprit* upon the following passage in his Grammar of the English Tongue, prefixed to the Dictionary: '*H* seldom, perhaps never, begins any but the first syllable.' In an essay printed in 'the Publick Advertiser,' this lively writer enumerated many instances in opposition to this remark; for example, 'The authour of this observation must be a man of a quick *appre-hension*, and of a most *compre-hensive* genius.' The position is undoubtedly expressed with too much latitude.

This light sally, we may suppose, made no great impression on our Lexicographer; for we find that he did not alter the passage till many years afterwards.[1]

---

[1] In the third edition, published in 1773, he left out the words *perhaps never*, and added the following paragraph:

'It sometimes begins middle or final syllables in words compounded, as *block-head*, or derived from the Latin, as *comprehended.*'

He had the pleasure of being treated in a very different manner by his old pupil Mr. Garrick, in the following complimentary Epigram:

'*On* JOHNSON'S DICTIONARY

'TALK of war with a Briton, he'll boldly advance,
That one English soldier will beat ten of France;
Would we alter the boast from the sword to the pen,
Our odds are still greater, still greater our men;
In the deep mines of science though Frenchmen may toil,
Can their strength be compar'd to Locke, Newton, and Boyle?
Let them rally their heroes, send forth all their pow'rs,
Their verse-men and prose-men, then match them with ours!
First Shakspeare and Milton, like Gods in the fight,
Have put their whole drama and epick to flight;
In satires, epistles, and odes, would they cope,
Their numbers retreat before Dryden and Pope;
And Johnson, well-arm'd like a hero of yore,
Has beat forty French,[1] and will beat forty more!'

Johnson this year gave at once a proof of his benevolence, quickness of apprehension, and admirable art of composition, in the assistance which he gave to Mr. Zachariah Williams, father of the blind lady whom he had humanely received under his roof. Mr. Williams had followed the profession of physick in Wales; but having a very strong propensity to the study of natural philosophy, had made many ingenious advances towards a discovery of the longitude, and repaired to London in hopes of obtaining the great parliamentary reward. He failed of success; but Johnson having made himself master of his principles and experiments, wrote for him a pamphlet, published in quarto, with the following title: 'An Account of an Attempt to ascertain the Longitude at Sea, by an exact Theory of the Variation of the Magnetical Needle; with a Table of the Variations at the most remarkable Cities in Europe, from the year 1660 to 1860.'† To diffuse it more extensively, it was accompanied with an Italian translation

---

[1] The number of the French Academy employed in settling their language.

on the opposite page, which it is supposed was the work of Signor Baretti,[1] an Italian of considerable literature, who having come to England a few years before, had been employed in the capacity both of a language master and an authour, and formed an intimacy with Dr. Johnson. This pamphlet Johnson presented to the Bodleian Library.[2] On a blank leaf of it is pasted a paragraph cut out of a newspaper, containing an account of the death and character of Williams, plainly written by Johnson.[3]

In July this year he had formed some scheme of mental improvement, the particular purpose of which does not appear. But we find in his 'Prayers and Meditations,' p. 25, a prayer entitled, 'On the Study of Philosophy, as an instrument of living;' and after it follows a note, 'This study was not pursued.'

On the 13th of the same month he wrote in his Journal the following scheme of life, for Sunday: 'Having lived' (as he with tenderness of conscience expresses himself) 'not without an habitual reverence for the Sabbath, yet without that attention to its religious duties which Christianity requires;

'1. To rise early, and in order to it, to go to sleep early on Saturday.

'2. To use some extraordinary devotion in the morning.

'3. To examine the tenour of my life, and particularly the last week; and to mark my advances in religion, or recession from it.

[1] [This ingenious foreigner, who was a native of Piedmont, came to England about the year 1753, and died in London, May 5, 1789. A very candid and judicious account of him and his works, beginning with the words, 'So much asperity,' and written, it is believed, by a distinguished dignitary in the church, may be found in the Gentleman's Magazine, for that year, p. 469.[a] MALONE.]

[2] See note by Mr. Warton, p. 188. [from which it appears that '12th' in the next note means the 12th of July, 1755. MALONE.]

[3] 'On Saturday the 12th, about twelve at night, died Mr. Zachariah Williams, in his eighty-third year, after an illness of eight months, in full possession of his mental faculties. He has been long known to philosophers and seamen for his skill in magnetism, and his proposal to ascertain the longitude by a peculiar system of the variation of the compass. He was a man of industry indefatigable, of conversation inoffensive, patient of adversity and disease, eminently sober, temperate, and pious; and worthy to have ended life with better fortune.'

[a] *There was also a Panegyric on him in a Paper called the World conducted by Mr. Este.* [1]

'4. To read the Scripture methodically with such helps as are at hand.

'5. To go to church twice.

'6. To read books of Divinity, either speculative or practical.

'7. To instruct my family.

'8. To wear off by meditation any worldly soil contracted in the week.'

In 1756 Johnson found that the great fame of his Dictionary had not set him above the necessity of 'making provision for the day that was passing over him.'[1] No royal or noble patron extended a munificent hand to give independence to the man who had conferred stability on the language of his country. We may feel indignant that there should have been such unworthy neglect; but we must, at the same time, congratulate ourselves, when we consider, that to this very neglect, operating to rouse the natural indolence of his constitution, we owe many valuable productions, which otherwise, perhaps, might never have appeared.

He had spent, during the progress of the work, the money for which he had contracted to write his Dictionary. We have seen that the reward of his labour was only fifteen hundred and seventy-five pounds; and when the expence of amanuenses and paper, and other articles, are deducted, his clear profit was very inconsiderable. I once said to him, 'I am sorry, Sir, you did not get more for your Dictionary.' His answer was, 'I am sorry too. But it was very well. The booksellers are generous liberal-minded men.' He, upon all occasions, did ample justice to their character in this respect. He considered them as the patrons of literature; and, indeed, although they have eventually been considerable gainers by his Dictionary, it is to them that we owe its having been undertaken and

[1] [He was so far from being 'set above the necessity of making provision for the day that was passing over him,' that he appears to have been in this year in great pecuniary distress, having been arrested for debt; on which occasion his friend, Samuel Richardson, became his surety. See a letter from Johnson to him, on that subject, dated Feb. 19, 1756. Richardson's Correspondence, vol. v. p. 283. Malone.]

carried through at the risk of great expence, for they were not absolutely sure of being indemnified.

On the first day of this year[1] we find from his private devotions, that he had then recovered from sickness,[2] and in February, that his eye was restored to its use.[3] The pious gratitude with which he acknowledges mercies upon every occasion is very edifying; as is the humble submission which he breathes, when it is the will of his heavenly Father to try him with afflictions. As such dispositions become the state of man here, and are the true effects of religious discipline, we cannot but venerate in Johnson one of the most exercised minds that our holy religion hath ever formed. If there be any thoughtless enough to suppose such exercise the weakness of a great understanding, let them look up to Johnson, and be convinced that what he so earnestly practised must have a rational foundation.

His works this year were, an abstract or epitome, in octavo, of his folio Dictionary, and a few essays in a monthly publication, entitled, 'THE UNIVERSAL VISITER.' Christopher Smart, with whose unhappy vacillation of mind he sincerely sympathised, was one of the stated undertakers of this miscellany; and it was to assist him that Johnson sometimes employed his pen. All the essays marked with two *asterisks* have been ascribed to him; but I am confident, from internal evidence, that of these, neither 'The Life of Chaucer,' 'Reflections on the State of Portugal,' nor an 'Essay on Architecture,' were written by him. I am equally confident, upon the same evidence, that he wrote, 'Further Thoughts on Agriculture;'✝ being the sequel of a very inferiour essay on the same subject, and which, though carried on as if by the same hand, is both in thinking and expression so far above it, and so strikingly peculiar, as to leave no doubt of its true parent; and that he also wrote 'A Dissertation on the State of Literature

[1] [In April in this year, Johnson wrote a letter to Dr. Joseph Warton, in consequence of having read a few pages of that gentleman's newly published 'Essay on the Genius and Writings of Pope.' The only paragraph in it that respects Johnson's personal history is this: 'For my part I have not lately done much. I have been ill in the winter, and my eye has been inflamed; but I please myself with the hopes of doing many things, with which I have long pleased and deceived myself!' Memoirs of Dr. J. Warton, &c. 4to. 1806. MALONE.]

[2] Prayers and Meditations.   [3] Ibid. 27.

and Authours,'✝ and 'A Dissertation on the Epitaphs written by Pope.'* The last of these, indeed, he afterwards added to his 'Idler.' Why the essays truly written by him are marked in the same manner with some which he did not write, I cannot explain; but with deference to those who have ascribed to him the three essays which I have rejected, they want all the characteristical marks of Johnsonian composition.

He engaged also to superintend and contribute largely to another monthly publication, entitled 'THE LITERARY MAGAZINE, OR UNIVERSAL REVIEW;'* the first number of which came out in May this year. What were his emoluments from this undertaking, and what other writers were employed in it, I have not discovered. He continued to write in it, with intermissions, till the fifteenth number; and I think that he never gave better proofs of the force, acuteness, and vivacity of his mind, than in this miscellany, whether we consider his original essays, or his reviews of the works of others. The 'Preliminary Address'✝ to the publick, is a proof how this great man could embellish, with the graces of superiour composition, even so trite a thing as the plan of a magazine.

His original essays are, 'An Introduction to the Political State of Great Britain;'✝ 'Remarks on the Militia Bill;'✝ 'Observations on his Britannick Majesty's Treaties with the Empress of Russia and the Landgrave of Hesse Cassel;'✝ 'Observations on the Present State of Affairs;'✝ and, 'Memoirs of Frederick III. King of Prussia.'✝ In all these he displays extensive political knowledge and sagacity, expressed with uncommon energy and perspicuity, without any of those words which he sometimes took a pleasure in adopting, in imitation of Sir Thomas Browne; of whose 'Christian Morals' he this year gave an edition, with his 'Life'* prefixed to it, which is one of Johnson's best biographical performances. In one instance only in these essays has he indulged his *Brownism*. Dr. Robertson, the historian, mentioned it to me, as having at once convinced him that Johnson was the authour of the 'Memoirs of the King of Prussia.' Speaking of the pride which the old King, the father of his hero, took in being master of the tallest regiment in Europe, he says, 'To review this *towering* regiment was his daily pleasure; and to perpetuate it was so much his care, that when he met a tall woman he immediately commanded one of his *Titanian* retinue to marry her, that they might *propagate procerity.*' For this Anglo-Latian word *procerity*, Johnson had, however, the authority of Addison.

His reviews are of the following books: 'Birch's History of the Royal Society;'✝ 'Murphy's Gray's-Inn Journal;'✝ 'Warton's Essay on the Writings and Genius of Pope, Vol. I.'✝ 'Hampton's Translation of Polybius;'✝ 'Blackwell's Memoirs of the Court of Augustus;'✝ 'Russel's Natural History of Aleppo;'✝ 'Sir Isaac Newton's Arguments in Proof of a Deity;'✝ 'Borlase's History of the Isles of Scilly;'✝ 'Holme's Experiments on Bleaching;'✝ 'Browne's Christian Morals;'✝ 'Hales on distilling Sea-Water, Ventilators in Ships, and curing an ill Taste in Milk;'✝ 'Lucas's Essay on Waters;'✝ 'Keith's Catalogue of the Scottish Bishops;'✝ 'Browne's History of Jamaica;'✝ 'Philosophical Transactions, Vol. XLIX.'✝ 'Mrs. Lennox's Translation of Sully's Memoirs;'* 'Miscellanies by Elizabeth Harrison;'✝ 'Evans's Map and Account of the Middle Colonies in America;'✝ 'Letter on the Case of Admiral Byng;'* 'Appeal to the People concerning Admiral Byng;'* 'Hanway's Eight Days Journey, and Essay on Tea;'* 'The Cadet, a Military Treatise;'✝ 'Some further Particulars in Relation to the Case of Admiral Byng, by a Gentleman of Oxford;'* 'The Conduct of the Ministry relating to the present War impartially examined;'✝ 'A Free Inquiry into the Nature and Origin of Evil.'* All these from internal evidence, were written by Johnson: some of them I know he avowed, and have marked them with an *asterisk* accordingly. Mr. Thomas Davies indeed, ascribed to him the Review of Mr. Burke's 'Inquiry into the Origin of our ideas of the Sublime and Beautiful;' and Sir John Hawkins, with equal discernment, has inserted it in his collection of Johnson's works: whereas it has no resemblance to Johnson's composition, and is well known to have been written by Mr. Murphy, who has acknowledged it to me and many others.

It is worthy of remark, in justice to Johnson's political character, which has been misrepresented as abjectly

submissive to power, that his 'Observations on the present
State of Affairs,' glow with as animated a spirit of constitutional liberty as can be found any where. Thus he begins:
'The time is now come, in which every Englishman expects
to be informed of the national affairs; and in which he has
a right to have that expectation gratified. For, whatever
may be urged by Ministers, or those whom vanity or
interest make the followers of ministers, concerning the
necessity of confidence in our governours, and the presumption of prying with profane eyes into the recesses of
policy, it is evident that this reverence can be claimed only
by counsels yet unexecuted, and projects suspended in
deliberation. But when a design has ended in miscarriage
or success, when every eye and every ear is witness to
general discontent, or general satisfaction, it is then a
proper time to disentangle confusion and illustrate obscurity; to shew by what causes every event was produced,
and in what effects it is likely to terminate; to lay down
with distinct particularity what rumour always huddles
in general exclamation, or perplexes by indigested
narratives; to shew whence happiness or calamity is
derived, and whence it may be expected; and honestly to
lay before the people what inquiry can gather of the past,
and conjecture can estimate of the future.'

marginal line: *animated a . . . can be* [H]

marginal lines: *always huddles . . . the future* [H]

Here we have it assumed as an incontrovertible principle,
that in this country the people are the superintendents of
the conduct and measures of those by whom government
is administered; of the beneficial effect of which the present
reign afforded an illustrious example, when addresses
from all parts of the kingdom controuled an audacious
attempt to introduce a new power subversive of the
crown.

queried and under-
lined: *people* [H]

A still stronger proof of his patriotick spirit appears in
his review of an 'Essay on Waters, by Dr. Lucas,' of whom,
after describing him as a man well known to the world
for his daring defiance to power, when he thought it
exerted on the side of wrong, he thus speaks: 'The Irish
Ministers drove him from his native country by a procla-
mation, in which they charge him with crimes of which
they never intended to be called to the proof, and oppressed
him by methods equally irresistible by guilt and innocence.

'Let the man thus driven into exile, for having been the friend of his country, be received in every other place as a confessor of liberty; and let the tools of power be taught in time, that they may rob, but cannot impoverish.'

Some of his reviews in this Magazine are very short accounts of the pieces noticed, and I mention them only that Dr. Johnson's opinion of the works may be known, but many of them are examples of elaborate criticism, in the most masterly style. In his review of the 'Memoirs of the Court of Augustus,' he has the resolution to think and speak from his own mind, regardless of the cant transmitted from age to age, in praise of the ancient Romans. Thus: 'I know not why any one but a school-boy in his declamation should whine over the Commonwealth of Rome, which grew great only by the misery of the rest of mankind. The Romans, like others, as soon as they grew rich, grew corrupt; and in their corruption sold the lives and freedoms of themselves, and of one another.' Again, 'A people, who, while they were poor robbed mankind; and as soon as they became rich, robbed one another.' In his review of the Miscellanies in prose and verse, published by Elizabeth Harrison, but written by many hands, he gives an eminent proof at once of his orthodoxy and candour. 'The authours of the essays in prose seem generally to have imitated, or tried to imitate, the copiousness and luxuriance of Mrs. *Rowe*. This, however, is not all their praise; they have laboured to add to her brightness of imagery, her purity of sentiments. The poets have had Dr. *Watts* before their eyes; a writer, who, if he stood not in the first class of genius, compensated that defect by a ready application of his powers to the promotion of piety. The attempt to employ the ornaments of romance in the decoration of religion, was, I think, first made by Mr. *Boyle's Martyrdom of Theodora;* but *Boyle's* philosophical studies did not allow him time for the cultivation of style: and the completion of the great design was reserved for Mrs. *Rowe*. Dr. *Watts* was one of the first who taught the dissenters to write and speak like other men, by shewing them that elegance might consist with piety. They would have both done honour to a better society, for they had that charity which might well make their failings be forgotten, and with which the whole Christian world wish for communion. They were pure from all the heresies of an age, to which every opinion is become a favourite that the universal church has hitherto detested!

'This praise the general interest of mankind requires to be given to writers who please and do not corrupt, who instruct and do not weary. But to them all human eulogies are vain, whom I believe applauded by angels, and numbered with the just.'

His defence of tea against Mr. Jonas Hanway's violent attack upon that elegant and popular beverage, shews how very well a man of genius can write upon the slightest subject, when he writes, as the Italians say, *con amore:* I suppose no person ever enjoyed with more relish the infusion of that fragrant leaf than Johnson. The quantities which he drank of it at all hours were so great, that his nerves must have been uncommonly strong, not to have been extremely relaxed by such an intemperate use of it. He assured me that he never felt the least inconvenience from it; which is a proof that the fault of his constitution was rather a too great tension of fibres, than the contrary. Mr. Hanway wrote an angry answer to Johnson's review of his Essay on Tea, and Johnson, after a full and deliberate pause, made a reply to it; the only instance, I believe, in the whole course of his life, when he condescended to oppose any thing that was written against him. I suppose when he thought of any of his little antagonists, he was ever justly aware of the high sentiment of Ajax in Ovid:

> '*Iste tulit pretium jam nunc certaminis hujus,*
> *Qui, cùm victus erit, mecum certasse feretur.*'

marginal line:
Iste tulit . . . certasse
feretur [H]

But, indeed, the good Mr. Hanway laid himself so open to ridicule, that Johnson's animadversions upon his attack were chiefly to make sport.

The generosity with which he pleads the cause of Admiral Byng is highly to the honour of his heart and spirit. Though *Voltaire* affects to be witty upon the fate of that unfortunate officer, observing that he was shot '*pour encourager les autres,*' the nation has long been satisfied that his life was sacrificed to the political fervour of the times. In the vault belonging to the Torrington family,

two marginal lines:
has long . . . vault
belonging [H]

in the church of Southill, in Bedfordshire, there is the
following Epitaph upon his monument, which I have

ᵃWho wrote it? not
Johnson sure! [I]

transcribed:ᵃ

'TO THE PERPETUAL DISGRACE
OF PUBLICK JUSTICE,
THE HONOURABLE JOHN BYNG, ESQ.
ADMIRAL OF THE BLUE,
FELL A MARTYR TO POLITICAL
PERSECUTION,
MARCH 14, IN THE YEAR 1757;
WHEN BRAVERY AND LOYALTY
WERE INSUFFICIENT SECURITIES
FOR THE LIFE AND HONOUR OF
A NAVAL OFFICER.'

Johnson's most exquisite critical essay in the Literary
Magazine, and indeed any where, is his review of Soame
Jenyns's 'Inquiry into the Origin of Evil.' Jenyns was
possessed of lively talents, and a style eminently pure and
easy, and could very happily play with a light subject,

marginal line:
when he . . . he 'ven-
tured [H]

either in prose or verse; but when he speculated. on that
most difficult and excruciating question, the Origin of
Evil, he 'ventured far beyond his depth,' and, accordingly,
was exposed by Johnson, both with acute argument and
brilliant wit. I remember when the late Mr. Bicknell's
humorous performance, entitled 'The Musical Travels of

underlined:
Musical Travels,
Johnson [I]

Joel Collyer,' in which a slight attempt is made to ridicule

ᵇ *no   not Johnson*
but Burney. [I]

Johnson,ᵇ was ascribed to Soame Jenyns, 'Ha! (said
Johnson) I thought I had given *him* enough of it.'
His triumph over Jenyns is thus described by my friend
Mr. Courtenay in his 'Poetical Review of the literary and
moral Character of Dr. Johnson;' a performance of such
merit, that had I not been honoured with a very kind and
partial notice in it, I should echo the sentiments of men
of the first taste loudly in its praise:

'When specious sophists with presumption scan
The source of evil hidden still from man;
Revive Arabian tales, and vainly hope
To rival St. John, and his scholar Pope:
Though metaphysicks spread the gloom of night,
By reason's star he guides our aching sight;

The bounds of knowledge marks, and points the way
To pathless wastes, where wilder'd sages stray;
Where, like a farthing link-boy, Jenyns stands,
And the dim torch drops from his feeble hands.'[1a]

[a] *The last is a good Couplet—& worth all the rest.* [I]

This year Mr. William Payne, brother of the respectable bookseller of that name, published 'An Introduction to the Game of Draughts,' to which Johnson contributed a Dedication to the Earl of Rochford,* and a Preface,* both of which are admirably adapted to the treatise to which they are prefixed. Johnson, I believe, did not play at draughts after leaving College, by which he suffered; for it would have afforded him an innocent soothing relief from the melancholy which distressed him so often. I have heard him regret that he had not learnt to play at cards; and the game of draughts we know is peculiarly calculated to fix the attention without straining it. There is a composure and gravity in draughts which insensibly

[1] Some time after Dr. Johnson's death, there appeared in the newspapers and magazines an illiberal and petulant attack upon him, in the form of an Epitaph, under the name of Mr. Soame Jenyns, very unworthy of that gentleman, who had quietly submitted to the critical lash while Johnson lived. It assumed, as characteristicks of him, all the vulgar circumstances of abuse which had circulated amongst the ignorant. It was an unbecoming indulgence of puny resentment, at a time when he himself was at a very advanced age, and had a near prospect of descending to the grave. I was truly sorry for it; for he was then become an avowed, and (as my Lord Bishop of London, who had a serious conversation with him on the subject, assures me) a sincere Christian. He could not expect that Johnson's numerous friends would patiently bear to have the memory of their master stigmatized by no mean pen, but that, at least, one would be found to retort. Accordingly, this unjust and sarcastick Epitaph was met in the same publick field by an answer, in terms by no means soft, and such as wanton provocation only could justify:

'EPITAPH,

'*Prepared for a creature* not quite dead *yet*

'Here lies a little ugly nauseous elf,
Who judging only from his wretched self,
Feebly attempted, petulant and vain,
The "Origin of Evil" to explain.
A mighty Genius at this elf displeas'd,
With a strong critick grasp the urchin squeez'd.
For thirty years its coward spleen it kept,
Till in the dust the mighty Genius slept:
Then stunk and fretted in expiring snuff,
And blink'd at JOHNSON with its last poor puff.'[b]

[b] *whose was this? was it Boswell's? he seems to wish we may think so.* [I]

tranquillises the mind; and, accordingly, the Dutch are
fond of it, as they are of smoaking, of the sedative influence
of which, though he himself never smoaked, he had a high
opinion.[1] Besides, there is in draughts some exercise of the
faculties; and, accordingly, Johnson wishing to dignify the
subject in his Dedication with what is most estimable in
it, observes, 'Triflers may find or make any thing a trifle:
but since it is the great characteristick of a wise man to
see events in their causes, to obviate consequences, and
ascertain contingencies, your Lordship will think nothing
a trifle by which the mind is inured to caution, foresight,
and circumspection.'

As one of the little occasional advantages which he did
not disdain to take by his pen, as a man whose profession
was literature, he this year accepted of a guinea from
Mr. Robert Dodsley, for writing the introduction to 'The
London Chronicle,' an evening news-paper; and even in
so slight a performance exhibited peculiar talents. This
Chronicle still subsists, and from what I observed, when
I was abroad, has a more extensive circulation upon the
Continent than any of the English news-papers. It was
constantly read by Johnson himself; and it is but just to
observe, that it has all along been distinguished for good
sense, accuracy, moderation, and delicacy.

Another instance of the same nature has been communicated to me by the Reverend Dr. Thomas Campbell,
who has done himself considerable credit by his own
writings. 'Sitting with Dr. Johnson one morning alone, he
asked me if I had known Dr. Madden, who was authour
of the premium-scheme[2] in Ireland. On my answering in
the affirmative, and also that I had for some years lived in
his neighbourhood, &c. he begged of me that when I

---

[1] Journal of a Tour to the Hebrides, 3d. edit. p. 48.

[2] [In the College of Dublin, four quarterly Examinations of the students
are held in each year, in various prescribed branches of literature and
science; and premiums, consisting of books impressed with the College
Arms, are adjudged by Examiners (composed generally of the Junior
Fellows,) to those who have most distinguished themselves in the several
classes, after a very rigid trial, which lasts two days. This regulation, which
has subsisted about seventy years, has been attended with the most beneficial
effects.

Dr. Samuel Madden was the first proposer of premiums in that University.
They were instituted about the year 1734. He was also one of the founders

returned to Ireland, I would endeavour to procure for him a poem of Dr. Madden's, called "Boulter's Monument."[1] The reason (said he) why I wish for it, is this: when Dr. Madden came to London, he submitted that work to my castigation; and I remember I blotted a great many lines, and might have blotted many more without making the poem worse.[2] However, the Doctor was very thankful, and very generous, for he gave me ten guineas, *which was to me at that time a great sum.*'

He this year resumed his scheme of giving an edition of Shakspeare with notes. He issued Proposals of considerable length,[3] in which he shewed that he perfectly well knew what a variety of research such an undertaking required; but his indolence prevented him from pursuing it with that diligence which alone can collect those scattered facts, that genius, however acute, penetrating, and luminous, cannot discover by its own force. It is remarkable, that at this time his fancied activity was for the moment so vigorous, that he promised his work should be published before Christmas, 1757. Yet nine years elapsed before it saw the light. His throes in bringing it forth had been severe and remittent; and at last we may almost conclude that the Cæsarian operation was performed by the knife of Churchill, whose upbraiding satire, I dare say, made Johnson's friends urge him to dispatch.

> 'He for subscribers baits his hook,
>   And takes your cash; but where's the book?
>   No matter where; wise fear, you know,
>   Forbids the robbing of a foe;
>   But what, to serve our private ends,
>   Forbids the cheating of our friends?'

of the DUBLIN SOCIETY for the encouragement of arts and agriculture. In addition to the premiums which were and are still annually given by that society for this purpose, Dr. Madden gave others from his own fund. Hence he was usually called 'Premium Madden.' MALONE.]

[1] [Dr. Hugh Boulter, Archbishop of Armagh, and Primate of Ireland. He died Sept. 27, 1742, at which time he was, for the thirteenth time, one of the Lords Justices of that kingdom. Johnson speaks of him in high terms of commendation, in his Life of Ambrose Philips. BOSWELL.]

[2] [Dr. Madden wrote very bad verses. V. those prefixed to Leland's Life of Philip of Macedon, 4to. 1758. KEARNEY.]

[3] They have been reprinted by Mr. Malone in the Preface to his edition of Shakspeare.

About this period he was offered a living of considerable value in Lincolnshire, if he were inclined to enter into holy orders. It was a rectory in the gift of Mr. Langton, the father of his much-valued friend. But he did not accept of it; partly I believe from a conscientious motive, being persuaded that his temper and habits rendered him unfit for that assiduous and familiar instruction of the vulgar and ignorant, which he held to be an essential duty in a clergyman; and partly because his love of a London life was so strong, that he would have thought himself an exile in any other place, particularly if residing in the country. Whoever would wish to see his thoughts upon that subject displayed in their full force, may peruse the Adventurer, Number 126.

marginal line:
and partly . . . an
exile (H)

In 1757 it does not appear that he published any thing, except some of those articles in the Literary Magazine, which have been mentioned. That magazine, after Johnson ceased to write in it, gradually declined, though the popular epithet of *Antigallican* was added to it; and in July 1758 it expired. He probably prepared a part of his Shakspeare this year, and he dictated a speech on the subject of an address to the Throne, after the expedition to Rochfort, which was delivered by one of his friends, I know not in what publick meeting. It is printed in the Gentleman's Magazine for October 1785 as his, and bears sufficient marks of authenticity.

By the favour of Mr. Joseph Cooper Walker, of the Treasury, Dublin, I have obtained a copy of the following letter from Johnson to the venerable authour of 'Dissertations on the History of Ireland.'

'TO CHARLES O'CONNOR, ESQ.[1]

'SIR,

'I HAVE lately, by the favour of Mr. Faulkner, seen your account of Ireland, and cannot forbear to solicit a prosecution of your design. Sir William Temple complains

[1] [Of this gentleman, who died at his seat at Ballinegare, in the county of Roscommon, in Ireland, July 1, 1791, in his 82d year, some account may be found in the Gentleman's Magazine of that date. Of the work here alluded to by Dr. Johnson—'Dissertations on the History of Ireland'—a second and much improved edition was published by the authour in 1766. MALONE.]

that Ireland is less known than any other country, as to its ancient state. The natives have had little leisure, and little encouragement for enquiry; and strangers, not knowing the language, have had no ability.

'I have long wished that the Irish literature were cultivated.[1] Ireland is known by tradition to have been once the seat of piety and learning; and surely it would be very acceptable to all those who are curious either in the original of nations, or the affinities of languages, to be further informed of the revolution of a people so ancient, and once so illustrious.

'What relation there is between the Welsh and Irish language, or between the language of Ireland and that of Biscay, deserves enquiry. Of these provincial and unextended tongues, it seldom happens that more than one are understood by any one man; and, therefore, it seldom happens that a fair comparison can be made. I hope you will continue to cultivate this kind of learning, which has too long lain neglected, and which, if it be suffered to remain in oblivion for another century, may, perhaps, never be retrieved. As I wish well to all useful undertakings, I would not forbear to let you know how much you deserve in my opinion, from all lovers of study, and how much pleasure your work has given to, Sir,

'Your most obliged,
'And most humble servant,

'London, April 9, 1757.'   'SAM. JOHNSON'

'TO THE REVEREND MR. THOMAS WARTON

'DEAR SIR,

'DR. MARSILI,[a] of Padua, a learned gentleman,   [a] *Marsigli* [1]
and good Latin poet, has a mind to see Oxford. I have

---

[1] The celebrated oratour, Mr. Flood, has shewn himself to be of Dr. Johnson's opinion; having by his will bequeathed his estate, after the death of his wife Lady Frances, to the University of Dublin; desiring that immediately after the said estate shall come into their possession, they shall appoint two professors, one for the study of the native Erse or Irish language, and the other for the study of Irish antiquities and Irish history, and for the study of any other European language illustrative of, or auxiliary to, the study of Irish antiquities or Irish history; and that they shall give yearly

given him a letter to Dr. Huddesford,[1] and shall be glad
if you will introduce him, and shew him any thing in
Oxford.

'I am printing my new edition of Shakspeare.

'I long to see you all, but cannot conveniently come
yet. You might write to me now and then, if you were
good for any thing. But *honores mutant mores*. Professors
forget their friends.[2] I shall certainly complain to Miss
Jones.[3] I am,

'Your, &c.

'[London,] June 21, 1757.'   'SAM. JOHNSON'

'Please to make my compliments to Mr. Wise.'

Mr. Burney having enclosed to him an extract from the
review of his Dictionary in the *Bibliothèque des Savans*,[4] and
a list of subscribers to his Shakspeare, which Mr. Burney
had procured in Norfolk, he wrote the following answer:

'TO MR. BURNEY, IN LYNNE, NORFOLK

'SIR,

'THAT I may shew myself sensible of your favours,
and not commit the same fault a second time, I make
haste to answer the letter which I received this morning.
The truth is, the other likewise was received, and I wrote
an answer; but being desirous to transmit you some proposals and receipts, I waited till I could find a convenient

two liberal premiums for two compositions, one in verse, and the other in
prose, in the Irish language.'

[Since the above was written, Mr. Flood's Will has been set aside, after
a trial at bar, in the Court of Exchequer in Ireland. MALONE.]

[1] 'Now, or late, Vice-Chancellor.'

[2] 'Mr. Warton was elected Professor of Poetry at Oxford in the preceding
year.'

[3] 'Miss Jones lived at Oxford, and was often of our parties. She was a
very ingenious poetess, and published a volume of poems; and, on the
whole, was a most sensible, agreeable, and amiable woman. She was sister
to the Reverend River Jones, Chanter of Christ-Church cathedral at
Oxford, and Johnson used to call her the *Chantress*. I have heard him often
address her in this passage from "IL PENSEROSO:"

"Thee, Chantress, oft the woods among
        I woo," &c.

She died unmarried.'

[4] Tom. III. p. 482.

conveyance, and day was passed after day, till other things drove it from my thoughts; yet not so, but that I remember with great pleasure your commendation of my Dictionary. Your praise was welcome, not only because I believe it was sincere, but because praise has been very scarce. A man of your candour will be surprised when I tell you, that among all my acquaintance there were only two, who, upon the publication of my book, did not endeavour to depress me with threats of censure from the publick, or with objections learned from those who had learned them from my own preface. Your's is the only letter of goodwill that I have received; though, indeed, I am promised something of that sort from Sweden.

'How my new edition[1] will be received I know not; the subscription has not been very successful. I shall publish about March.

'If you can direct me how to send proposals, I should wish that they were in such hands.

'I remember, Sir, in some of the first letters with which you favoured me, you mentioned your lady. May I enquire after her? In return for the favours which you have shewn me, it is not much to tell you, that I wish you and her all that can conduce to your happiness. I am, Sir,

'Your most obliged,
'And most humble servant,
'SAM. JOHNSON'

'Gough-square, Dec. 24, 1757.'

In 1758 we find him, it should seem, in as easy and pleasant a state of existence, as constitutional unhappiness ever permitted him to enjoy.

'TO BENNET LANGTON, ESQ. AT LANGTON,
LINCOLNSHIRE

'DEAREST SIR,
'I MUST have indeed slept very fast, not to have been awakened by your letter. None of your suspicions are true; I am not much richer than when you left me; and, what is worse, my omission of an answer to your first letter, will prove that I am not much wiser. But I go on as

[1] Of Shakspeare.

I formerly did, designing to be some time or other both rich and wise; and yet cultivate neither mind nor fortune. Do you take notice of my example, and learn the danger of delay. When I was as you are now, towering in confidence of twenty-one, little did I suspect that I should be at forty-nine, what I now am.

'But you do not seem to need my admonition. You are busy in acquiring and in communicating knowledge, and while you are studying, enjoy the end of study, by making others wiser and happier. I was much pleased with the tale that you told me of being tutour to your sisters. I, who have no sisters nor brothers, look with some degree of innocent envy on those who may be said to be born to friends; and cannot see, without wonder, how rarely that native union is afterwards regarded. It sometimes, indeed, happens, that some supervenient cause of discord may overpower this original amity; but it seems to me more frequently thrown away with levity, or lost by negligence, than destroyed by injury or violence. We tell the ladies that good wives make good husbands; I believe it is a more certain position that good brothers make good sisters.

'I am satisfied with your stay at home, as Juvenal with his friend's retirement to Cumæ: I know that your absence is best, though it be not best for me.

underlined:
the *i* of *sibyllæ* and
the *y* of *Sybil* [H]

"*Quamvis digressu veteris confusus amici,*
Laudo tamen vacuis quod sedem figere Cumis
Destinet, atque unum civem donare Sibyllæ."

'*Langton* is a good *Cumæ*, but who must be Sybilla? Mrs. Langton is as wise as Sybil, and as good; and will live, if my wishes can prolong life, till she shall in time be as old. But she differs in this, that she has not scattered her precepts in the wind, at least not those which she bestowed upon you.

'The two Wartons just looked into the town, and were taken to see *Cleone*, where, David[1] says, they were starved for want of company to keep them warm. David and Doddy[2] have had a new quarrel, and, I think, cannot conveniently quarrel any more. "Cleone" was well acted by all the characters, but Bellamy left nothing to be

underlined:
Bellamy [I]

[1] Mr. Garrick.   [2] Mr. Dodsley, the Authour of Cleone.

desired.[a] I went the first night, and supported it as well   [a] *True* [1]
as I might; for Doddy, you know, is my patron, and I
would not desert him. The play was very well received.
Doddy, after the danger was over, went every night to the
stage-side, and cryed at the distress of poor Cleone.

'I have left off housekeeping, and therefore made
presents of the game which you were pleased to send me.
The pheasant I gave to Mr. Richardson,[1] the bustard to
Dr. Lawrence, and the pot I placed with Miss Williams,
to be eaten by myself. She desires that her compliments
and good wishes may be accepted by the family; and I
make the same request for myself.

'Mr. Reynolds has within these few days raised his
price to twenty guineas a head,[b] and Miss is much em-   [b] *curious* [1]
ployed in miniatures. I know not any body [else] whose
prosperity has increased since you left them.

'Murphy is to have his "Orphan of China" acted next
month; and is therefore, I suppose, happy. I wish I could
tell you of any great good to which I was approaching, but
at present my prospects do not much delight me; however,
I am always pleased when I find that you, dear Sir,
remember,

'Your affectionate, humble servant,

'Jan. 9, 1758.'   'SAM JOHNSON'

'TO MR. BURNEY, AT LYNNE, NORFOLK

'SIR,

'YOUR kindness is so great, and my claim to any
particular regard from you so little, that I am at a loss
how to express my sense of your favours;[2] but I am, indeed,
much pleased to be thus distinguished by you.

'I am ashamed to tell you that my Shakspeare will not
be out so soon as I promised my subscribers; but I did
not promise them more than I promised myself. It will,
however, be published before summer.

'I have sent you a bundle of proposals, which, I think,
do not profess more than I have hitherto performed. I

---

[1] Mr. Samuel Richardson, Authour of Clarissa.

[2] This letter was an answer to one, in which was inclosed a draft for the
payment of some subscriptions to his Shakspeare.

have printed many of the plays, and have hitherto left very few passages unexplained; where I am quite at loss, I confess my ignorance, which is seldom done by commentators.

'I have, likewise, inclosed twelve receipts; not that I mean to impose upon you the trouble of pushing them with more importunity than may seem proper, but that you may rather have more than fewer than you shall want. The proposals you will disseminate as there shall be an opportunity. I once printed them at length in the Chronicle, and some of my friends (I believe Mr. Murphy, who formerly wrote the Gray's-Inn Journal) introduced them with a splendid encomium.

'Since the Life of Browne, I have been a little engaged, from time to time, in the Literary Magazine, but not very lately. I have not the collection by me, and therefore cannot draw out a catalogue of my own parts, but will do it, and send it. Do not buy them, for I will gather all those that have any thing of mine in them, and send them to Mrs. Burney, as a small token of gratitude for the regard which she is pleased to bestow upon me.

'I am, Sir,
'Your most obliged
'And most humble servant,

'London, March 8, 1758.'   'SAM. JOHNSON'

Dr. Burney has kindly favoured me with the following memorandum, which I take the liberty to insert in his own genuine easy style. I love to exhibit sketches of my illustrious friend by various eminent hands.

'Soon after this, Mr. Burney, during a visit to the capital, had an interview with him in Gough-square, where he dined and drank tea with him, and was introduced to the acquaintance of Mrs. Williams. After dinner, Mr. Johnson proposed to Mr. Burney to go up with him into his garret, which being accepted, he there found about five or six Greek folios, a deal writing-desk, and a chair and a half. Johnson giving to his guest the entire seat, tottered himself on one with only three legs and one arm. Here he gave Mr. Burney Mrs. Williams's history, and

shewed him some volumes of his Shakspeare already
printed, to prove that he was in earnest. Upon Mr.
Burney's opening the first volume, at the Merchant of
Venice, he observed to him, that he seemed to be more
severe on Warburton than Theobald. "O poor Tib.! (said
Johnson) he was ready knocked down to my hands;
Warburton stands between me and him." "But, Sir, (said
Mr. Burney,) you'll have Warburton upon your bones,
won't you?" "No, Sir; he'll not come out: he'll only growl
in his den." "But you think, Sir, that Warburton is a
superiour critick to Theobald?"—"O, Sir, he'd make
two-and-fifty Theobalds, cut into slices! The worst of
Warburton is, that he has a rage for saying something,
when there's nothing to be said."—Mr. Burney then asked
him whether he had seen the letter which Warburton had
written in answer to a pamphlet addressed "To the most
impudent Man alive." He answered in the negative. Mr.
Burney told him it was supposed to be written by Mallet.
The controversy now raged between the friends of Pope and
Bolingbroke; and Warburton and Mallet were the leaders
of the several parties. Mr. Burney asked him then if he had
seen Warburton's book against Bolingbroke's Philosophy?
"No, Sir; I have never read Bolingbroke's impiety, and
therefore am not interested about its confutation."'

marginal line: *a rage . . . there's nothing* [H]

On the fifteenth of April he began a new periodical
paper, entitled 'THE IDLER,'* which came out every
Saturday in a weekly news-paper, called 'The Universal
Chronicle, or Weekly Gazette,' published by Newbery.[1]
These essays were continued till April 5, 1760. Of one
hundred and three, their total number, twelve were
contributed by his friends; of which, Numbers 33, 93,
and 96, were written by Mr. Thomas Warton; No. 67, by
Mr. Langton; and Nos. 76, 79, and 82, by Sir Joshua
Reynolds; the concluding words of No. 82, 'and pollute
his canvas with deformity,' being added by Johnson; as
Sir Joshua informed me.

marginal line: *which, Numbers . . . pollute his* [H]

[1] [This is a slight mistake. The first number of 'The Idler' appeared on the
15th of April, 1758, in No. 2 of the Universal Chronicle, &c., which was
published by J. Payne, for whom also the Rambler had been printed. On
the 29th of April this newspaper assumed the title of PAYNE's Universal
Chronicle, &c. MALONE.]

The IDLER is evidently the work of the same mind which produced the RAMBLER, but has less body and more spirit. It has more variety of real life, and greater facility of language. He describes the miseries of idleness, with the lively sensations of one who has felt them; and in his private memorandums while engaged in it, we find 'This year I hope to learn diligence.'[1] Many of these excellent essays were written as hastily as an ordinary letter. Mr. Langton remembers Johnson, when on a visit at Oxford, asking him one evening how long it was till the post went out; and on being told about half an hour, he exclaimed, 'then we shall do very well.' He upon this instantly sat down and finished an Idler, which it was necessary should be in London the next day. Mr. Langton having signified a wish to read it, 'Sir, (said he) you shall not do more than I have done myself.' He then folded it up, and sent it off.

Yet there are in the Idler several papers which shew as much profundity of thought, and labour of language, as any of this great man's writings. No. 14, 'Robbery of time;' No. 24, 'Thinking;' No. 41, 'Death of a friend;' No. 43, 'Flight of time;' No. 51, 'Domestick greatness unattainable;' No. 52, 'Self-denial;' No. 58, 'Actual, how short of fancied, excellence;' No. 89, 'Physical evil moral good;' and his concluding paper on 'The horrour of the last,' will prove this assertion. I know not why a motto, the usual trapping of periodical papers, is prefixed to very few of the Idlers, as I have heard Johnson commend the custom; and he never could be at a loss for one, his memory being stored with innumerable passages of the classicks. In this series of essays he exhibits admirable instances of grave humour, of which he had an uncommon share. Nor on some occasions has he repressed that power of sophistry which he possessed in so eminent a degree. In No. 11, he treats with the utmost contempt the opinion that our mental faculties depend, in some degree, upon the weather; an opinion, which they who have never experienced its truth are not to be envied, and of which he himself could not but be sensible, as the effects of weather upon him were very visible. Yet thus he declaims: 'Surely nothing is

[1] Prayers and Meditations, p. 30.

more reproachful to a being endowed with reason, than to resign its powers to the influence of the air, and live in dependence on the weather and the wind for the only blessings which nature has put into our power, tranquillity and benevolence.—This distinction of seasons is produced only by imagination operating on luxury. To temperance, every day is bright; and every hour is propitious to diligence. He that shall resolutely excite his faculties, or exert his virtues, will soon make himself superiour to the seasons; and may set at defiance the morning mist and the evening damp, the blasts of the east, and the clouds of the south.'

queried three times:
To temperance etc. [H]

queried:
may set at defiance etc. [H]

Alas! it is too certain, that where the frame has delicate fibres, and there is a fine sensibility, such influences of the air are irresistible. He might as well have bid defiance to the ague, the palsy, and all other bodily disorders. Such boasting of the mind is false elevation.

marginal line:
Alas! it . . . false elevation [H]

a second marginal line:
Such boasting etc. [H]

'I think the Romans call it Stoicism.'

But in this number of his Idler his spirits seem to run riot; for in the wantonness of his disquisition he forgets, for a moment, even the reverence for that which he held in high respect; and describes 'the attendant on a *Court*,' as one 'whose business is to watch the looks of a being, weak and foolish as himself.'

His unqualified ridicule of rhetorical gesture or action is not, surely, a test of truth; yet we cannot help admiring how well it is adapted to produce the effect which he wished. 'Neither the judges of our laws, nor the representatives of our people, would be much affected by laboured gesticulations, or believe any man the more because he rolled his eyes, or puffed his cheeks, or spread abroad his arms, or stamped the ground, or thumped his breast; or turned his eyes sometimes to the ceiling, and sometimes to the floor.'

A casual coincidence with other writers, or an adoption of a sentiment or image which has been found in the writings of another, and afterwards appears in the mind as one's own, is not unfrequent. The richness of Johnson's fancy, which could supply his page abundantly on all occasions, and the strength of his memory, which at once detected the real owner of any thought, made him less

liable to the imputation of plagiarism than, perhaps, any
of our writers. In the Idler, however, there is a paper, in
which conversation is assimilated to a bowl of punch,
where there is the same train of comparison as in a poem
by Blacklock, in his collection published in 1756; in which
a parallel is ingeniously drawn between human life and
that liquor. It ends,

> 'Say, then, physicians of each kind,
> Who cure the body or the mind,
> What harm in drinking can there be,
> Since punch and life so well agree?'

To the Idler, when collected in volumes, he added,
beside the Essay on Epitaphs, and the Dissertation on
those of Pope, an Essay on the Bravery of the English
common Soldiers. He, however, omitted one of the original
papers, which in the folio copy, is No. 22.[1]

'TO THE REVEREND MR. THOMAS WARTON

'DEAR SIR,

'YOUR notes upon my poet were very acceptable.
I beg that you will be so kind as to continue your searches.
It will be reputable to my work, and suitable to your
professorship, to have something of yours in the notes. As
you have given no directions about your name, I shall
therefore put it. I wish your brother would take the same
trouble. A commentary must arise from the fortuitous
discoveries of many men in devious walks of literature.
Some of your remarks are on plays already printed: but I
purpose to add an Appendix of Notes, so that nothing
comes too late.

'You give yourself too much uneasiness, dear Sir, about
the loss of the papers.[2] The loss is nothing, if nobody has
found them; nor even then, perhaps, if the numbers be
known. You are not the only friend that has had the same
mischance. You may repair your want out of a stock, which
is deposited with Mr. Allen, of Magdalen-Hall; or out of

---

[1] This paper may be found in Stockdale's supplemental volume, of
Johnson's Miscellaneous Pieces.
[2] 'Receipts for Shakspeare.'

a parcel which I have just sent to Mr. Chambers[1] for the use of any body that will be so kind as to want them. Mr. Langtons are well; and Miss Roberts,[a] whom I have at last brought to speak, upon the information which you gave me, that she had something to say.

> [a] *Qu—who was She?* [1]

'I am, &c.

'[London] April 14, 1758.'   'SAM. JOHNSON'

TO THE SAME

'DEAR SIR,

  'YOU will receive this by Mr. Baretti, a gentleman particularly intitled to the notice and kindness of the Professor of poesy. He has time but for a short stay, and will be glad to have it filled up with as much as he can hear and see.

  'In recommending another to your favour, I ought not to omit thanks for the kindness which you have shown to myself. Have you any more notes on Shakspeare? I shall be glad of them.

  'I see your pupil sometimes;[2] his mind is as exalted as his stature. I am half afraid of him; but he is no less amiable than formidable. He will, if the forwardness of his spring be not blasted, be a credit to you, and to the University. He brings some of my plays[3] with him, which he has my permission to shew you, on condition you will hide them from every body else.

'I am, dear Sir, &c.

'[London] June 1, 1758.'   'SAM. JOHNSON'

'TO BENNET LANGTON, ESQ. OF TRINITY COLLEGE,
OXFORD

'DEAR SIR,

  'THOUGH I might have expected to hear from you, upon your entrance into a new state of life at a new place, yet recollecting, (not without some degree of shame,) that I owe you a letter upon an old account, I think it my part

---

[1] 'Then of Lincoln College. Now Sir Robert Chambers, one of the Judges in India.'

[2] 'Mr. Langton.'

[3] 'Part of the impression of the Shakspeare, which Dr. Johnson conducted alone, and published by subscription. This edition came out in 1765.'

> marginal line:
> *Johnson conducted . . .*
> *This edition* [H]

to write first. This, indeed, I do not only from complaisance but from interest; for living on in the old way, I am very glad of a correspondent so capable as yourself, to diversify the hours. You have, at present, too many novelties about you to need any help from me to drive along your time.

'I know not any thing more pleasant, or more instructive, than to compare experience with expectation, or to register from time to time the difference between idea and reality. It is by this kind of observation that we grow daily less liable to be disappointed. You, who are very capable of anticipating futurity, and raising phantoms before your own eyes, must often have imagined to yourself an academical life, and have conceived what would be the manners, the views, and the conversation, of men devoted to letters; how they would choose their companions, how they would direct their studies, and how they would regulate their lives. Let me know what you expected, and what you have found. At least record it to yourself before custom has reconciled you to the scenes before you, and the disparity of your discoveries to your hopes has vanished from your mind. It is a rule never to be forgotten, that whatever strikes strongly, should be described while the first impression remains fresh upon the mind.

queried:
It is a rule etc. [H]

'I love, dear Sir, to think on you, and therefore, should willingly write more to you, but that the post will not now give me leave to do more than send my compliments to Mr. Warton, and tell you that I am, dear Sir, most affectionately,   'Your very humble servant,

'June 28, 1758.'   'SAM. JOHNSON'

'TO BENNET LANGTON, ESQ. AT LANGTON, NEAR
SPILSBY, LINCOLNSHIRE

'DEAR SIR,

'I SHOULD be sorry to think that what engrosses the attention of my friend, should have no part of mine. Your mind is now full of the fate of Dury;[1] but his fate is past,

---

[1] Major General Alexander Dury, of the first regiment of footguards, who fell in the gallant discharge of his duty, near St. Cas, in the well-known unfortunate expedition against France, in 1758. His lady and Mr. Langton's mother were sisters. He left an only son, Lieutenant-Colonel Dury, who has a company in the same regiment.

and nothing remains but to try what reflection will suggest
to mitigate the terrours of a violent death, which is more
formidable at the first glance, than on a nearer and more
steady view. A violent death is never very painful: the only
danger is, lest it should be unprovided. But if a man can
be supposed to make no provision for death in war, what
can be the state that would have awakened him to the
care of futurity? When would that man have prepared
himself to die, who went to seek death without preparation?
What then can be the reason why we lament more him
that dies of a wound, than him that dies of a fever? A man
that languishes with disease, ends his life with more pain,
but with less virtue: he leaves no example to his friends,[a]
nor bequeaths any honour to his descendants. The only
reason why we lament a soldier's death, is, that we think
he might have lived longer; yet this cause of grief is common to many other kinds of death, which are not so
passionately bewailed. The truth is, that every death is
violent which is the effect of accident; every death, which
is not gradually brought on by the miseries of age, or when
life is extinguished for any other reason than that it is
burnt out.[b] He that dies before sixty, of a cold or consumption, dies, in reality, by a violent death; yet his death
is borne with patience, only because the cause of his
untimely end is silent and invisible. Let us endeavour to
see things as they are, and then enquire whether we ought
to complain. Whether to see life as it is, will give us much
consolation, I know not; but the consolation which is
drawn from truth, if any there be, is solid and durable:
that which may be derived from errour, must be, like its
original, fallacious and fugitive.

> 'I am, dear, dear Sir,
> 'Your most humble Servant,

'Sept. 21, 1758.'   'SAM. JOHNSON'

In 1759, in the month of January, his mother died at
the great age of ninety, an event which deeply affected
him; not that 'his mind had acquired no firmness by the
contemplation of mortality;[1] but that his reverential
affection for her was not abated by years, as indeed he

underlined:
no example [H]

[a] *yet in his Letters he
speaks as if despising
Example.* [H]

[b] *This is one of
Johnson's 1st Rate
Letters.* [I]

---

[1] Hawkins's Life of Johnson, p. 395.

retained all his tender feelings even to the latest period of his life. I have been told, that he regretted much his not having gone to visit his mother for several years previous to her death. But he was constantly engaged in literary labours which confined him to London; and though he had not the comfort of seeing his aged parent, he contributed liberally to her support.

['TO MRS. JOHNSON, IN LICHFIELD[1]

'HONOURED MADAM,

'THE account which Miss [Porter] gives me of your health, pierces my heart. GOD comfort and preserve you and save you, for the sake of Jesus Christ.

'I would have Miss read to you from time to time the Passion of our Saviour, and sometimes the sentences in the Communion Service, beginning—*Come unto me, all ye that travail and are heavy laden, and I will give you rest.*

'I have just now read a physical book, which inclines me to think that a strong infusion of the bark would do you good. Do, dear mother, try it.

'Pray, send me your blessing, and forgive all that I have done amiss to you. And whatever you would have done, and what debts you would have paid first, or any thing else that you would direct, let Miss put it down; I shall endeavour to obey you.

'I have got twelve guineas[2] to send you, but unhappily am at a loss how to send it to-night. If I cannot send it to-night, it will come by the next post.

'Pray, do not omit any thing mentioned in this letter. GOD bless you for ever and ever.

'I am
'Your dutiful Son,

'Jan. 13, 1758.'[3]   'SAM. JOHNSON'

[1] [Since the publication of the third edition of this work, the following letters of Dr. Johnson, occasioned by the last illness of his mother, were obligingly communicated to Mr. Malone by the Rev. Dr. Vyse. They are placed here agreeably to the chronological order almost uniformly observed by the authour; and so strongly evince Dr. Johnson's piety, and tenderness of heart, that every reader must be gratified by their insertion. MALONE.]

[2] [Six of these twelve guineas Johnson appears to have borrowed from Mr. Allen, the Printer. See Hawkins's Life of Johnson, p. 366. n. MALONE.]

[3] [Written by mistake for 1759, as the subsequent letters shew. In the next

'TO MISS PORTER, AT MRS. JOHNSON'S,
IN LICHFIELD

'MY DEAR MISS,

'I THINK myself obliged to you beyond all expression of gratitude for your care of my dear mother. GOD grant it may not be without success. Tell Kitty,[1] that I shall never forget her tenderness for her mistress. Whatever you can do, continue to do. My heart is very full.

'I hope you received twelve guineas on Monday. I found a way of sending them by means of the Postmaster, after I had written my letter, and hope they came safe. I will send you more in a few days. GOD bless you all.

'I am, my dear,
'Your most obliged
'and most humble Servant,

'Jan. 16, 1759.'   'SAM. JOHNSON'

'Over the leaf is a letter to my mother.'

'DEAR HONOURED MOTHER,

'YOUR weakness afflicts me beyond what I am willing to communicate to you. I do not think you unfit to face death, but I know not how to bear the thought of losing you. Endeavour to do all you [can] for yourself. Eat as much as you can.

'I pray often for you; do you pray for me.—I have nothing to add to my last letter.

'I am, dear, dear Mother,
'Your dutiful Son,

'Jan. 16, 1759.'   'SAM. JOHNSON'

letter, he had inadvertently fallen into the same errour, but corrected it. On the *outside* of the letter of the 13th was written by another hand—'Pray acknowledge the receipt of this by return of post, without fail.' MALONE.]

[1] [Catharine Chambers, Mrs. Johnson's maid-servant. She died in October, 1767. See Dr. Johnson's PRAYERS AND MEDITATIONS, p. 71: 'Sunday, Oct. 18, 1767. Yesterday, Oct. 17, I took my leave for ever of my dear old friend, Catharine Chambers, who came to live with my mother about 1724, and has been but little parted from us since. She buried my father, my brother, and my mother. She is now fifty-eight years old.' MALONE.]

'TO MRS. JOHNSON, IN LICHFIELD

'DEAR HONOURED MOTHER,

'I FEAR you are too ill for long letters; therefore I
will only tell you, you have from me all the regard that
can possibly subsist in the heart. I pray GOD to bless you
for evermore, for Jesus Christ's sake. Amen.

'Let Miss write to me every post, however short.

'I am, dear Mother,
'Your dutiful Son,
'Jan. 18, 1759.'   'SAM. JOHNSON'

'TO MISS PORTER, AT MRS. JOHNSON'S,
IN LICHFIELD

'DEAR MISS,

'I WILL, if it be possible, come down to you. GOD
grant I may yet [find] my dear mother breathing and
sensible. Do not tell her, lest I disappoint her. If I miss to
write next post, I am on the road.

'I am, my dearest Miss,
'Your most humble servant,
'Jan. 20, 1759.'   'SAM. JOHNSON'

'*On the other side.*'

'DEAR HONOURED MOTHER,[1]

'NEITHER your condition nor your character make
it fit for me to say much. You have been the best mother,
and I believe the best woman in the world. I thank you
for your indulgence to me, and beg forgiveness of all that
I have done ill, and all that I have omitted to do well.[2]
GOD grant you his Holy Spirit, and receive you to

---

[1] [This letter was written on the second leaf of the preceding, addressed
to Miss Porter. MALONE.]

[2] [So, in the Prayer which he composed on this occasion: 'Almighty
GOD, merciful Father, in whose hands are life and death, sanctify unto me
the sorrow which I now feel. *Forgive me whatever I have done unkindly to my
Mother, and whatever I have omitted to do kindly.* Make me to remember her good
precepts and good example, and to reform my life according to thy holy
word, &c.' PRAYERS AND MEDITATIONS, p. 31. MALONE.]

everlasting happiness, for Jesus Christ's sake. Amen. Lord Jesus receive your spirit. Amen.

> 'I am, dear, dear Mother,
> 'Your dutiful Son,

'Jan. 20, 1759.'   'SAM. JOHNSON'

'TO MISS PORTER, IN LICHFIELD

'You will conceive my sorrow for the loss of my mother, of the best mother. If she were to live again, surely I should behave better to her. But she is happy, and what is past is nothing to her; and for me, since I cannot repair my faults to her, I hope repentance will efface them. I return you and all those that have been good to her my sincerest thanks, and pray GOD to repay you all with infinite advantage. Write to me, and comfort me, dear child. I shall be glad likewise, if Kitty will write to me. I shall send a bill of twenty pounds in a few days, which I thought to have brought to my mother; but GOD suffered it not. I have not power or composure to say much more. GOD bless you, and bless us all.

> 'I am, dear Miss,
> 'Your affectionate humble Servant,

'Jan. 23, 1759.'[1]   'SAM. JOHNSON']

Soon after this event, he wrote his 'RASSELAS, PRINCE OF ABYSSINIA:'* concerning the publication of which Sir John Hawkins guesses vaguely and idly, instead of having taken the trouble to inform himself with authentick precision. Not to trouble my readers with a repetition of the Knight's reveries, I have to mention, that the late Mr. Strahan the printer told me, that Johnson wrote it, that with the profits he might defray the expence of his mother's funeral, and pay some little debts which she had left. He told Sir Joshua Reynolds, that he composed it in the evenings of one week,[2] sent it to the press in portions as it was written, and had never since read it

---

[1] [Mrs. Johnson probably died on the 20th or 21st of January, and was buried on the day this letter was written. MALONE.]

[2] [RASSELAS was published in March or April, 1759.]

a *he told Murphy so*
in my hearing, & told
us all. [H]

over.[1a] Mr. Strahan, Mr. Johnston, and Mr. Dodsley, purchased it for a hundred pounds, but afterwards paid him twenty-five pounds more, when it came to a second edition.

Considering the large sums which have been received for compilations, and works requiring not much more genius than compilations, we cannot but wonder at the very low price which he was content to receive for this admirable performance; which, though he had written nothing else, would have rendered his name immortal in the world of literature. None of his writings has been so extensively diffused over Europe; for it has been translated into most, if not all, of the modern languages. This Tale, with all the charms of oriental imagery, and all the force and beauty of which the English language is capable, leads us through the most important scenes of human life, and shews us that this stage of our being is full of 'vanity and vexation of spirit.' To those who look no further than the present life, or who maintain that human nature has not fallen from the state in which it was created, the instruction of this sublime story will be of no avail. But they who think justly, and feel with strong sensibility, will listen with eagerness and admiration to its truth and wisdom. Voltaire's CANDIDE, written to refute the system of Optimism, which it has accomplished with brilliant success, is wonderfully similar in its plan and conduct to Johnson's RASSELAS; insomuch, that I have heard Johnson say, that if they had not been published so closely one after the other that there was not time for imitation, it would have been in vain to deny that the scheme of that which came latest, was taken from the other. Though the proposition illustrated by both these works was the same, namely, that in our present state there is more evil than good, the intention of the writers was very different. Voltaire, I am afraid, meant only by wanton profaneness to obtain a sportive victory over religion, and to discredit the belief of a superintending Providence: Johnson meant, by shewing the unsatisfactory nature of things temporal,

1 [See vol. iii. under June 2, 1781. Finding it then accidentally in a chaise with Mr. Boswell, he read it eagerly.—This was doubtless long after his declaration to Sir Joshua Reynolds. MALONE.]

to direct the hopes of man to things eternal. Rasselas, as was observed to me by a very accomplished lady,[a] may be considered as a more enlarged and more deeply philosophical discourse in prose, upon the interesting truth, which in his 'Vanity of Human Wishes' he had so successfully enforced in verse.

[a] *True enough; but I wonder who was the Lady? Mrs. Boswell perhaps.* [1]

The fund of thinking which this work contains is such, that almost every sentence of it may furnish a subject of long meditation. I am not satisfied if a year passes without my having read it through; and at every perusal, my admiration of the mind which produced it is so highly raised, that I can scarcely believe that I had the honour of enjoying the intimacy of such a man.

queried: *at every perusal* etc. [H]

I restrain myself from quoting passages from this excellent work, or even referring to them, because I should not know what to select, or, rather, what to omit. I shall, however, transcribe one, as it shews how well he could state the arguments of those who believe in the appearance of departed spirits; a doctrine which it is a mistake to suppose that he himself ever positively held:

'If all your fear be of apparitions, (said the Prince,) I will promise you safety: there is no danger from the dead; he that is once buried will be seen no more.

'That the dead are seen no more, (said Imlac,) I will not undertake to maintain, against the concurrent and unvaried testimony of all ages, and of all nations. There is no people, rude or learned, among whom apparitions of the dead are not related and believed. This opinion, which prevails as far as human nature is diffused, could become universal only by its truth; those that never heard of one another, would not have agreed in a tale which nothing but experience can make credible. That it is doubted by single cavillers, can very little weaken the general evidence; and some who deny it with their tongues, confess it by their fears.'

queried: *those that* etc. [H]

Notwithstanding my high admiration of Rasselas, I will not maintain that the 'morbid melancholy' in Johnson's constitution may not, perhaps, have made life appear to him more insipid and unhappy than it generally is: for I am sure that he had less enjoyment from it than I have. Yet, whatever additional shade his own particular sensations may have thrown on his representation of life, attentive observation and close enquiry have convinced me, that there is too much reality in the gloomy picture. The truth, however, is, that we judge of the happiness and misery of life differently at different times, according to the state of our changeable frame. I always remember a remark made to me by a Turkish lady, educated in France: '*Ma foi, Monsieur, notre bonheur depend de la façon que notre sang circule.*' This have I learnt from a pretty hard course of experience, and would, from sincere benevolence, impress upon all who honour this book with a perusal, that until a steady conviction is obtained, that the present life is an imperfect state, and only a passage to a better, if we comply with the divine scheme of progressive improvement; and also that it is a part of the mysterious plan of Providence, that intellectual beings must 'be made perfect through suffering;' there will be a continual recurrence of disappointment and uneasiness. But if we walk with hope in 'the mid-day sun' of revelation, our temper and disposition will be such, that the comforts and enjoyments in our way will be relished, while we patiently support the inconveniences and pains. After much speculation and various reasonings, I acknowledge myself convinced of the truth of Voltaire's conclusion, '*Après tout c'est un monde passable.*' But we must not think too deeply:

'——where ignorance is bliss,
'Tis folly to be wise.'

is, in many respects, more than poetically just. Let us cultivate, under the command of good principles, '*la théorie des sensations agréables;*' and, as Mr. Burke once admirably counselled a grave and anxious gentleman, 'live pleasant.'

The effect of Rasselas, and of Johnson's other moral tales, is thus beautifully illustrated by Mr. Courtenay:

'Impressive truth, in splendid fiction drest,
    Checks the vain wish, and calms the troubled breast;
O'er the dark mind a light celestial throws,
    And sooths the angry passions to repose;
As oil effus'd illumes and smooths the deep,
When round the bark the foaming surges sweep.'[1]

[1] Literary and Moral Character of Johnson.

It will be recollected, that during all this year he carried
on his IDLER,[1] and, no doubt, was proceeding, though
slowly, in his edition of Shakspeare. He, however, from
that liberality which never failed, when called upon to
assist other labourers in literature, found time to translate for Mrs. Lennox's English version of Brumoy. 'A
Dissertation on the Greek Comedy,'† and 'The General
Conclusion of the Book.'†

An enquiry into the state of foreign countries was an
object that seems at all times to have interested Johnson.
Hence Mr. Newbery found no great difficulty in persuad-
ing him to write the Introduction* to a collection of
voyages and travels published by him under the title
of 'The World Displayed:' the first volume of which
appeared this year, and the remaining volumes in
subsequent years.

---

[1] This paper was in such high estimation before it was collected into
volumes, that it was seized on with avidity by various publishers of newspapers and magazines, to enrich their publications. Johnson, to put a stop
to this unfair proceeding, wrote for the Universal Chronicle the following
advertisement; in which there is, perhaps, more pomp of words than the
occasion demanded:

'London, Jan. 5, 1759. ADVERTISEMENT. The proprietors of the paper
intitled "The Idler," having found that those essays are inserted in the newspapers and magazines with so little regard to justice or decency, that the
Universal Chronicle, in which they first appear, is not always mentioned,
think it necessary to declare to the publishers of those collections, that
however patiently they have hitherto endured these injuries, made yet more
injurious by contempt, they have now determined to endure them no
longer. They have already seen essays, for which a very large price is paid,
transferred, with the most shameless rapacity, into the weekly or monthly
compilations, and their right, at least for the present, alienated from them,
before they could themselves be said to enjoy it. But they would not willingly
be thought to want tenderness, even for men by whom no tenderness hath
been shewn. The past is without remedy, and shall be without resentment.
But those who have been thus busy with their sickles in the fields of their
neighbours, are henceforward to take notice, that the time of impunity
is at an end. Whoever shall, without our leave, lay the hand of rapine upon
our papers, is to expect that we shall vindicate our due, by the means which
justice prescribes, and which are warranted by the immemorial prescriptions
of honourable trade. We shall lay hold, in our turn, on their copies, degrade
them from the pomp of wide margin and diffuse typography, contract them
into a narrow space, and sell them at an humble price; yet not with a view
of growing rich by confiscations, for we think not much better of money
got by punishment than by crimes. We shall therefore, when our losses are
repaid, give what profit shall remain to the Magdalens; for we know not who
can be more properly taxed for the support of penitent prostitutes, than
prostitutes in whom there yet appears neither penitence nor shame.'

I would ascribe to this year the following letter to a son of one of his early friends at Lichfield, Mr. Joseph Simpson, Barrister, and authour of a tract, entitled 'Reflections on the Study of the Law.'

'TO JOSEPH SIMPSON, ESQ.

'DEAR SIR,

'YOUR father's inexorability not only grieves but amazes me: he is your father; he was always accounted a wise man; nor do I remember any thing to the disadvantage of his good nature; but in his refusal to assist you there is neither good nature, fatherhood, nor wisdom. It is the practice of good nature to overlook faults which have already, by the consequences, punished the delinquent. It is natural for a father to think more favourably than others of his children; and it is always wise to give assistance, while a little help will prevent the necessity of greater.

'If you married imprudently, you miscarried at your own hazard, at an age when you had a right of choice. It would be hard if the man might not choose his own wife, who has a right to plead before the Judges of his country.

'If your imprudence has ended in difficulties and inconveniences, you are yourself to support them; and, with the help of a little better health, you would support them and conquer them. Surely, that want which accident and sickness produces, is to be supported in every region of humanity, though there were neither friends nor fathers in the world. You have certainly from your father the highest claim of charity, though none of right: and therefore I would counsel you to omit no decent nor manly degree of importunity. Your debts in the whole are not large, and of the whole but a small part is troublesome. Small debts are like small shot; they are rattling on every side, and can scarcely be escaped without a wound: great debts are like cannon; of loud noise, but little danger. You must, therefore, be enabled to discharge petty debts, that you may have leisure, with security, to struggle with the rest. Neither the great nor little debts disgrace you. I am

marginal line:
every side . . . *loud*
noise [H]

sure you have my esteem for the courage with which you contracted them, and the spirit with which you endure them. I wish my esteem could be of more use. I have been invited, or have invited myself to several parts of the kingdom; and will not incommode my dear Lucy by coming to Lichfield, while her present lodging is of any use to her. I hope, in a few days, to be at leisure, and to make visits. Whither I shall fly is a matter of no importance. A man unconnected is at home every where; unless he may be said to be at home no where. I am sorry, dear Sir, that where you have parents, a man of your merits, should not have a home. I wish I could give it you. I am, my dear Sir,

'Affectionately yours,

'SAM. JOHNSON'

He now refreshed himself by an excursion to Oxford, of which the following short characteristical notice, in his own words, is preserved:—' * * * is now making tea for me. I have been in my gown ever since I came here. It was, at my first coming, quite new and handsome. I have swum thrice, which I had disused for many years. I have proposed to Vansittart[1] climbing over the wall, but he has refused me. And I have clapped my hands till they are sore, at Dr. King's speech.'[2]

His negro servant, Francis Barber, having left him, and been some time at sea, not pressed as has been supposed, but with his own consent, it appears from a letter to John Wilkes, Esq. from Dr. Smollett, that his master kindly interested himself in procuring his release from a state of life of which Johnson always expressed the utmost abhorrence. He said, 'No man will be a sailor who has contrivance enough to get himself into a jail; for being in a ship is being in a jail, with the chance of being drowned.'[3] And at another time, 'A man in a jail has

marginal line: *get himself . . . drowned.' And* [H]

[a] *I wonder he declined any Frolic . . . he was a good Frolicker enough:—walked to Oxford, his Carriage accompanying him; & a Sumpter Horse oddly set out with Portables as he called his Writing-Desk, his Wardrobe &c.* [H]

[1] Dr. Robert Vansittart, of the ancient and respectable family of that name in Berkshire. He was eminent for learning and worth, and much esteemed by Dr. Johnson.[a]

[2] Gentleman's Magazine, April, 1785.

[3] Journal of a Tour to the Hebrides, 3d edit. p. 126.

more room, better food, and commonly better company.'[1]
The letter was as follows:

'DEAR SIR,   'Chelsea, March 16, 1759

'I AM again your petitioner, in behalf of that great
CHAM[2] of literature, Samuel Johnson. His black servant,
whose name is Francis Barber, has been pressed on board
the Stag frigate, Captain Angel, and our lexicographer is
in great distress. He says the boy is a sickly lad, of a delicate
frame, and particularly subject to a malady in his throat,
which renders him very unfit for his Majesty's service. You
know what matter of animosity the said Johnson has
against you: and I dare say you desire no other opportunity
of resenting it, than that of laying him under an obligation.
He was humble enough to desire my assistance on this
occasion, though he and I were never cater-cousins; and
I gave him to understand that I would make application
to my friend Mr. Wilkes, who, perhaps, by his interest
with Dr. Hay and Mr. Elliot, might be able to procure
the discharge of his lacquey. It would be superfluous to
say more on the subject, which I leave to your own
consideration; but I cannot let slip this opportunity of
declaring that I am, with the most inviolable esteem and
attachment, dear Sir,

'Your affectionate obliged humble servant,

'T. SMOLLETT'

[1] Journal of a Tour to the Hebrides, 3d edit. p. 251.

[2] In my first edition this word was printed *Chum*, as it appears in one
of Mr. Wilkes's Miscellanies, and I animadverted on Dr. Smollett's ignorance; for which let me propitiate the *manes* of that ingenious and benevolent
gentleman. CHUM was certainly a mistaken reading for CHAM, the title
of the Sovereign of Tartary, which is well applied to Johnson, the Monarch
of Literature: and was an epithet familiar to Smollett. See 'Roderick
Random,' chap. 56. For this correction I am indebted to Lord Palmerston,
whose talents and literary acquirements accord well with his respectable
pedigree of TEMPLE.

[After the publication of the second edition of this work, the authour was
furnished by Mr. Abercrombie, of Philadelphia, with the copy of a letter
written by Dr. John Armstrong, the poet, to Dr. Smollett, at Leghorn,
containing the following paragraph:

'As to the K. Bench patriot, it is hard to say from what motive he published
a letter of yours asking some trifling favour of him in behalf of somebody for
whom the great CHAM of literature, Mr. Johnson, had interested himself.'
MALONE.]

Mr. Wilkes, who upon all occasions has acted as a private gentleman, with most polite liberality, applied to his friend Sir George Hay, then one of the Lords Commissioners of the Admiralty; and Francis Barber was discharged, as he has told me, without any wish of his own. He found his old master in Chambers of the Inner Temple, and returned to his service.

What particular new scheme of life Johnson had in view this year, I have not discovered; but that he meditated one of some sort, is clear from his private devotions, in which we find,[1] 'the change of outward things which I am now to make;' and 'Grant me the grace of thy Holy Spirit, that the course which I am now beginning may proceed according to thy laws, and end in the enjoyment of thy favour.' But he did not, in fact, make any external or visible change.

At this time there being a competition among the architects of London to be employed in the building of Blackfriars-bridge, a question was very warmly agitated whether semicircular or elliptical arches were preferable. In the design offered by Mr. Mylne the elliptical form was adopted, and therefore it was the great object of his rivals to attack it. Johnson's regard for his friend Mr. Gwyn induced him to engage in this controversy against Mr. Mylne;[2] and after being at considerable pains to study the

[1] Prayers and Meditations, pp. 30 and 40.

[2] Sir John Hawkins has given a long detail of it, in that manner, vulgarly, but significantly, called rigmarole; in which, amidst an ostentatious exhibition of arts and artists, he talks of 'proportions of a column being taken from that of the human figure, and adjusted by Nature—masculine and feminine—in a man, sesquioctave of the head, and in a woman sesquinonal; nor has he failed to introduce a jargon of musical terms, which do not seem much to correspond with the subject, but serve to make up the heterogeneous mass. To follow the Knight through all this, would be an useless fatigue to myself, and not a little disgusting to my readers. I shall, therefore, only make a few remarks upon his statement.—He seems to exult in having detected Johnson in procuring 'from a person eminently skilled in mathematicks and the principles of architecture, answers to a string of questions drawn up by himself, touching the comparative strength of semicircular and elliptical arches.' Now I cannot conceive how Johnson could have acted more wisely. Sir John complains that the opinion of that excellent mathematician, Mr. Thomas Simpson, did not preponderate in favour of the semicircular arch. But he should have known, that however eminent Mr. Simpson was in the higher parts of abstract mathematical science, he was little versed in mixed and practical mechanicks. Mr. Muller, of Woolwich Academy, the

subject, he wrote three several letters in the Gazetteer, in opposition to his plan.

If it should be remarked that this was a controversy which lay quite out of Johnson's way, let it be remembered, that after all, his employing his powers of reasoning and eloquence upon a subject which he had studied on the moment, is not more strange than what we often observe in lawyers, who, as *Quicquid agunt homines* is the matter of law-suits, are sometimes obliged to pick up a temporary knowledge of an art or science, of which they understood nothing till their brief was delivered, and appear to be much masters of it. In like manner, members of the legislature frequently introduce and expatiate upon subjects of which they have informed themselves for the occasion.

In 1760 he wrote 'An Address of the Painters to George III. on his Accession to the Throne of these Kingdoms,'† which no monarch ever ascended with more sincere congratulations from his people. Two generations of foreign

marginal line:
an art . . . be much [H]

scholastick father of all the great engineers which this country has employed for forty years, decided the question by declaring clearly in favour of the elliptical arch.

It is ungraciously suggested, that Johnson's motive for opposing Mr. Mylne's scheme may have been his prejudice against him as a native of North Britain; when, in truth, as has been stated, he gave the aid of his able pen to a friend, who was one of the candidates; and so far was he from having any illiberal antipathy to Mr. Mylne, that he afterwards lived with that gentleman upon very agreeable terms of acquaintance, and dined with him at his house. Sir John Hawkins, indeed, gives full vent to his own prejudice in abusing Blackfriars-bridge, calling it 'an edifice, in which beauty and symmetry are in vain sought for; by which the citizens of London have perpetuated their own disgrace, and subjected a whole nation to the reproach of foreigners.' Whoever has contemplated *placido lumine*, this stately, elegant, and airy structure, which has so fine an effect, especially on approaching the capital on that quarter, must wonder at such unjust and ill-tempered censure; and I appeal to all foreigners of good taste, whether this bridge be not one of the most distinguished ornaments of London. As to the stability of the fabrick, it is certain that the city of London took every precaution to have the best Portland stone for it; but as this is to be found in the quarries belonging to the publick, under the direction of the Lords of the Treasury, it so happened that parliamentary interest, which is often the bane of fair pursuits, thwarted their endeavours. Notwithstanding this disadvantage, it is well known that not only has Blackfriars-bridge never sunk either in its foundation or in its arches, which were so much the subject of contest, but any injuries which it has suffered from the effects of severe frosts have been already, in some measure, repaired with sounder stone, and every necessary renewal can be completed at a moderate expence.

princes had prepared their minds to rejoice in having
again a King, who gloried in being 'born a Briton.' He also
wrote for Mr. Baretti the Dedication✝ of his Italian and
English Dictionary, to the Marquis of Abreu, then Envoy-
Extraordinary from Spain at the Court of Great-Britain.

Johnson was now either very idle or very busy with his
Shakspeare; for I can find no other publick composition
by him except an Introduction to the proceedings of the
Committee for cloathing the French Prisoners;* one of the
many proofs that he was ever awake to the calls of
humanity; and an account which he gave in the Gentleman's Magazine of Mr. Tytler's acute and able vindication
of Mary, Queen of Scots.* The generosity of Johnson's
feelings shines forth in the following sentence: 'It has now
been fashionable, for near half a century, to defame and
vilify the house of Stuart, and to exalt and magnify the
reign of Elizabeth. The Stuarts have found few apologists,
for the dead cannot pay for praise;[a] and who will, without
reward, oppose the tide of popularity? Yet there remains
still among us, not wholly extinguished, a zeal for truth,
a desire of establishing right in opposition to fashion.'

> [a] *Elizabeth was as dead as Stuart.* [1]

In this year I have not discovered a single private letter
written by him to any of his friends. It should seem, however, that he had at this period a floating intention of
writing a history of the recent and wonderful successes
of the British arms in all quarters of the globe; for among
his resolutions or memorandums, September 18, there is,
'Send for books for Hist. of War.'[1] How much is it to be
regretted that this intention was not fulfilled. His majestick
expression would have carried down to the latest posterity
the glorious achievements of his country, with the same
fervent glow which they produced on the mind at the
time. He would have been under no temptation to deviate
in any degree from truth, which he held very sacred, or
to take a licence, which a learned divine told me he once
seemed, in a conversation, jocularly to allow to historians,
'There are (said he) inexcusable lies, and consecrated lies.
For instance, we are told that on the arrival of the news
of the unfortunate battle of Fontenoy, every heart beat,
and every eye was in tears. Now we know that no man eat

---

[1] Prayers and Meditations, p. 42.

his dinner the worse,[a] but there *should* have been all this concern; and to say there *was*, (smiling) may be reckoned a consecrated lie.'

This year Mr. Murphy, having thought himself ill-treated by the Reverend Dr. Franklin, who was one of the writers of 'The Critical Review,' published an indignant vindication in 'A Poetical Epistle to Samuel Johnson, A.M.' in which he compliments Johnson in a just and elegant manner:

'Transcendant Genius! whose prolifick vein
Ne'er knew the frigid poet's toil and pain;
To whom APOLLO opens all his store,
And every Muse presents her sacred lore;
Say, pow'rful JOHNSON, whence thy verse is fraught
With so much grace, such energy of thought;
Whether thy JUVENAL instructs the age
In chaster numbers, and new points his rage;
Or fair IRENE sees, alas! too late
Her innocence exchang'd for guilty state;
Whate'er you write, in every golden line
Sublimity and elegance combine;
Thy nervous phrase impresses every soul,
While harmony gives rapture to the whole.'

Again, towards the conclusion:

'Thou then, my friend, who see'st the dang'rous strife
In which some demon bids me plunge my life,
To the Aonian fount direct my feet,
Say, where the Nine thy lonely musings meet?
Where warbles to thy ear the sacred throng,
Thy moral sense, thy dignity of song?
Tell, for you can, by what unerring art
You wake to finer feelings every heart;
In each bright page some truth important give,
And bid to future times thy RAMBLER live.'

I take this opportunity to relate the manner in which an acquaintance first commenced between Dr. Johnson and Mr. Murphy. During the publication of 'The Gray's-Inn Journal,' a periodical paper which was successfully carried on by Mr. Murphy alone, when a very young man, he happened to be in the country with Mr. Foote; and having mentioned that he was obliged to go to London in order to get ready for the press one of the numbers of that Journal, Foote said to him: 'You need not go on that account. Here is a French magazine, in which you will find a very pretty oriental tale; translate that, and send it to your printer.' Mr. Murphy having read the tale, was highly pleased with it, and followed Foote's advice. When he returned to Town, this tale was pointed out to him in 'The Rambler,' from whence it had been translated into the French magazine. Mr. Murphy then waited upon Johnson, to explain this curious incident. His talents, literature, and gentleman-like manners, were soon perceived by Johnson, and a friendship was formed which was never broken.[1]

'TO BENNET LANGTON, ESQ. AT LANGTON, NEAR SPILSBY, LINCOLNSHIRE

'DEAR SIR,

'You that travel about the world, have more materials for letters, than I who stay at home: and should, therefore, write with frequency equal to your opportunities. I should be glad to have all England surveyed by you, if you would impart your observations in narratives as agreeable as

[1] [When Mr. Murphy first became acquainted with Dr. Johnson, he was about thirty-one years old. He died at Knightsbridge, June 18, 1805, it is believed in his eighty-second year.[a]

In an account of this gentleman, published recently after his death, he is reported to have said, that 'he was but *twenty-one*, when he had the impudence to write a periodical paper, during the time that Johnson was publishing the Rambler.'—In a subsequent page, in which Mr. Boswell gives an account of his first introduction to Johnson, will be found a striking instance of the incorrectness of Mr. Murphy's memory; and the assertion above-mentioned, if indeed he made it, which is by no means improbable, furnishes an additional proof of his inaccuracy; for both the facts asserted are unfounded. He appears to have been eight years older than twenty-one, when he began the Gray's-Inn Journal; and that paper, instead of running a race with Johnson's production, did not appear till after the closing of the Rambler, which ended March 14, 1752. The first number of the Gray's-Inn Journal made its appearance about seven months afterwards, in a news-paper of the time, called the Craftsman, October 21, 1752; and in that form the first forty-nine numbers were given to the publick. On Saturday, Sept. 29, 1753, it assumed a new form, and was published as a distinct periodical paper; and in that shape it continued to be published till the 21st of Sept. 1754, when it finally closed; forming in the whole one hundred and one

[a] *Poor Fellow!* [H]
Eheu!! poor Murphy [I]

your last. Knowledge is always to be wished to those who can communicate it well. While you have been riding and running, and seeing the tombs of the learned, and the camps of the valiant, I have only staid at home, and intended to do great things, which I have not done. Beau[1] went away to Cheshire, and has not yet found his way back. Chambers passed the vacation at Oxford.

'I am very sincerely solicitous for the preservation or curing of Mr. Langton's sight, and am glad that the chirurgeon at Coventry gives him so much hope. Mr. Sharpe is of opinion that the tedious maturation of the cataract is a vulgar errour, and that it may be removed as soon as it is formed. This notion deserves to be considered; I doubt whether it be universally true; but if it be true in some cases, and those cases can be distinguished, it may save a long and uncomfortable delay.

'Of dear Mrs. Langton you give me no account; which is the less friendly, as you know how highly I think of her, and how much I interest myself in her health. I suppose you told her of my opinion, and likewise suppose it was not followed; however, I still believe it to be right.

'Let me hear from you again, wherever you are, or whatever you are doing; whether you wander or sit still,

Essays, in the folio copy. The extraordinary paper mentioned in the text, is No. 38 of the second series, published on June 15, 1754; which is a re-translation from the French version of Johnson's Rambler, No. 190. It was omitted in the re-publication of these Essays in two volumes 12mo. in which one hundred and four are found, and in which the papers are not always dated on the days when they really appeared; so that the motto prefixed to this Anglo-Gallick Eastern tale, *obscuris vera involvens*, might very properly have been prefixed to this work, when re-published. Mr. Murphy did not, I believe, wait on Johnson recently after the publication of this adumbration of one of his Ramblers, as seems to be stated in the text; for, in his concluding Essay, Sept. 21, 1754, we find the following paragraph:

'Besides, why may not a person rather choose an air of bold negligence, than the obscure diligence of pedants and writers of affected phraseology. For my part, I have always thought an easy style more eligible than a pompous diction, lifted up by metaphor, amplified by epithet, and dignified by too frequent insertions of the Latin idiom.' It is probable that the Rambler was here intended to be censured, and that the author, when he wrote it, was not acquainted with Johnson, whom, from his first introduction, he endeavoured to conciliate. Their acquaintance, therefore, it may be presumed, did not commence till towards the end of this year 1754. Murphy however had highly praised Johnson in the preceding year, No. 14 of the second series, Dec. 22, 1753. MALONE.]

[1] Topham Beauclerk, Esq.

plant trees or make *Rusticks*,[1] play with your sisters or muse alone; and in return I will tell you the success of Sheridan, who at this instant is playing Cato, and has already played Richard twice. He had more company the second than the first night, and will make I believe a good figure in the whole, though his faults seem to be very many; some of natural deficience, and some of laborious affectation. He has, I think, no power of assuming either that dignity or elegance which some men, who have little of either in common life, can exhibit on the stage. His voice when strained is unpleasing, and when low is not always heard. He seems to think too much on the audience, and turns his face too often to the galleries.[a]

'However, I wish him well; and among other reasons, because I like his wife.[2]

'Make haste to write to, dear Sir,
            'Your most affectionate servant,
'Oct. 18, 1760.'   'SAM. JOHNSON'

In 1761 Johnson appears to have done little. He was still, no doubt, proceeding in his edition of Shakspeare; but what advances he made in it cannot be ascertained. He certainly was at this time not active; for, in his scrupulous examination of himself on Easter eve, he laments, in his too rigorous mode of censuring his own conduct, that his life, since the communion of the preceding Easter, had been 'dissipated and useless.'[3] He, however, contributed this year the Preface* to 'Rolt's Dictionary of Trade and Commerce,' in which he displays such a clear and comprehensive knowledge of the subject, as might lead the reader to think that its authour had devoted all his life to it. I asked him, whether he knew much of Rolt, and of his work. 'Sir, (said he) I never saw the man, and never read the book. The booksellers wanted a Preface to a Dictionary of Trade and Commerce. I knew very well what such a Dictionary should be, and I wrote a Preface

[a] *how true all this is of old Sheridan!* [I]

marginal line:
Sir, (said . . . to a [H]

---

[1] Essays with that title, written about this time by Mr. Langton, but not published.

[2] Mrs. Sheridan was authour of 'Memoirs of Miss Sydney Biddulph,' a novel of great merit, and of some other pieces.—See her character, p. 275.

[3] Prayers and Meditations, p. 44.

marginal line:
*with him . . . specimen
of* [H]

marginal line:
name to . . . to it [H]

marginal line:
*Feeling,' was . . .
young Irish* [H]

accordingly.' Rolt, who wrote a great deal for the book-sellers, was, as Johnson told me, a singular character. Though not in the least acquainted with him, he used to say, 'I am just come from Sam. Johnson.' This was a sufficient specimen of his vanity and impudence. But he gave a more eminent proof of it in our sister kingdom, as Dr. Johnson informed me. When Akenside's 'Pleasures of the Imagination' first came out, he did not put his name to the poem. Rolt went over to Dublin, published an edition of it, and put his own name to it. Upon the fame of this he lived for several months, being entertained at the best tables as 'the ingenious Mr. Rolt.'[1] His conversation indeed, did not discover much of the fire of a poet; but it was recollected, that both Addison and Thomson were equally dull till excited by wine. Akenside having been informed of this imposition, vindicated his right by pub-lishing the poem with its real authour's name. Several instances of such literary fraud have been detected. The Reverend Dr. Campbell, of St. Andrew's, wrote 'An Enquiry into the original of Moral Virtue,' the manuscript of which he sent to Mr. Innes, a clergyman in England, who was his countryman and acquaintance. Innes published it with his own name to it; and before the imposition was discovered, obtained considerable pro-motion, as a reward of his merit.[2] The celebrated Dr. Hugh Blair, and his cousin Mr. George Bannatine, when students in divinity, wrote a poem, entitled 'The Resurrection,' copies of which were handed about in manuscript. They were, at length, very much surprized to see a pompous edition of it in folio, dedicated to the Princess Dowager of Wales, by a Dr. Douglas, as his own. Some years ago a little novel, entitled 'The Man of Feeling,' was assumed by Mr. Eccles, a young Irish clergyman, who was afterwards

---

[1] I have had enquiry made in Ireland as to this story, but do not find it recollected there. I give it on the authority of Dr. Johnson, to which may be added, that of the 'Biographical Dictionary,' and 'Biographia Dramatica;' in both of which it has stood many years. Mr. Malone observes, that the truth probably is, not that an edition was published with Rolt's name in the title-page, but, that the poem being then anonymous, Rolt acquiesced in its being attributed to him in conversation.

[2] I have both the books. Innes was the clergyman who brought Psalma-nazar to England, and was an accomplice in his extraordinary fiction.

drowned near bath. He had been at the pains to transcribe
the whole book, with blottings, interlineations, and corrections, that it might be shewn to several people as an
original. It was, in truth, the production of Mr. Henry
Mackenzie, an attorney in the Exchequer at Edinburgh,[a]
who is the authour of several other ingenious pieces; but
the belief with regard to Mr. Eccles became so general,
that it was thought necessary for Messieurs Strahan and
Cadell to publish an advertisement in the newspapers,
contradicting the report, and mentioning that they
purchased the copy-right of Mr. Mackenzie. I can conceive
this kind of fraud to be very easily practised with successful
effrontery. The *Filiation* of a literary performance is
difficult of proof; seldom is there any witness present at its
birth. A man, either in confidence or by improper means,
obtains possession of a copy of it in manuscript, and boldly
publishes it as his own. The true authour, in many cases,
may not be able to make his title clear. Johnson, indeed,
from the peculiar features of his literary offspring, might
bid defiance to any attempt to appropriate them to others:

> 'But Shakspeare's magick could not copied be,
> Within that circle none durst walk but he.'

He this year lent his friendly assistance to correct and
improve a pamphlet written by Mr. Gwyn, the architect,
entitled 'Thoughts on the Coronation of George III.'*

Johnson had now for some years admitted Mr. Baretti
to his intimacy; nor did their friendship cease upon their
being separated by Baretti's revisiting his native country,
as appears from Johnson's letters to him.

'TO MR. JOSEPH BARETTI, AT MILAN[1]

'You reproach me very often with parsimony of writing;
but you may discover by the extent of my paper, that I
design to recompense rarity by length. A short letter to a
distant friend is, in my opinion, an insult like that of a
slight bow or cursory salutation;—a proof of unwillingness

[a] *& who is yet alive
1819.* [H]

marginal line:
to the . . . first appeared
[H]

---

[1] The originals of Dr. Johnson's three letters to Mr. Baretti, which are
among the very best he ever wrote, were communicated to the proprietors
of that instructive and elegant monthly miscellany, 'The European
Magazine,' in which they first appeared.

to do much, even where there is a necessity of doing something. Yet it must be remembered, that he who continues
the same course of life in the same place, will have little
to tell. One week and one year are very like one another.
The silent changes made by time are not always perceived;
and if they are not perceived, cannot be recounted. I have
risen and laid down, talked and mused, while you have
roved over a considerable part of Europe; yet I have not
envied my Baretti any of his pleasures, though, perhaps,
I have envied others his company: and I am glad to have
other nations made acquainted with the character of the
English, by a traveller who has so nicely inspected our
manners, and so successfully studied our literature. I
received your kind letter from Falmouth, in which you
gave me notice of your departure for Lisbon; and another
from Lisbon, in which you told me, that you were to leave
Portugal in a few days. To either of these how could any
answer be returned? I have had a third from Turin, complaining that I have not answered the former. Your English
style still continues in its purity and vigour. With vigour
your genius will supply it: but its purity must be continued
by close attention. To use two languages familiarly, and
without contaminating one by the other, is very difficult;
and to use more than two, is hardly to be hoped. The
praises which some have received for their multiplicity of
languages, may be sufficient to excite industry, but can
hardly generate confidence.

index sign:
To use etc. [H]

'I know not whether I can heartily rejoice at the kind
reception which you have found, or at the popularity to
which you are exalted. I am willing that your merit should
be distinguished; but cannot wish that your affections
may be gained. I would have you happy wherever you
are: yet I would have you wish to return to England. If
ever you visit us again you will find the kindness of your
friends undiminished. To tell you how many enquiries
are made after you, would be tedious, or if not tedious,
would be vain; because you may be told in a very few
words, that all who knew you wish you well; and that all
that you embraced at your departure, will caress you at
your return: therefore do not let Italian academicians nor
Italian ladies drive us from your thoughts. You may find

among us what you will leave behind, soft smiles and easy sonnets. Yet I shall not wonder if all our invitations should be rejected: for there is a pleasure in being considerable at home, which is not easily resisted.

'By conducting Mr. Southwell to Venice, you fulfilled, I know, the original contract: yet I would wish you not wholly to lose him from your notice, but to recommend him to such acquaintance as may best secure him from suffering by his own follies, and to take such general care both of his safety and his interest as may come within your power. His relations will thank you for any such gratuitous attention: at least they will not blame you for any evil that may happen, whether they thank you or not for any good.

'You know that we have a new King and a new Parliament. Of the new Parliament Fitzherbert is a member. We were so weary of our old King, that we are much pleased with his successor;[a] of whom we are so much inclined to hope great things, that most of us begin already to believe them. The young man is hitherto blameless; but it would be unreasonable to expect much from the immaturity of juvenile years, and the ignorance of princely education. He has been long in the hands of the Scots, and has already favoured them more than the English will contentedly endure. But, perhaps, he scarcely knows whom he has distinguished, or whom he has disgusted.

'The Artists have instituted a yearly Exhibition of pictures and statues, in imitation, as I am told, of foreign academies. This year was the second exhibition. They please themselves much with the multitude of spectators, and imagine that the English School will rise in reputation. Reynolds is without a rival, and continues to add thousands to thousands, which he deserves, among other excellencies, by retaining his kindness for Baretti. This Exhibition has filled the heads of the Artists and lovers of art. Surely life, if it be not long, is tedious, since we are forced to call in the assistance of so many trifles to rid us of our time, of that time which never can return.

'I know my Baretti will not be satisfied with a letter in which I give him no account of myself: yet what account shall I give him; I have not, since the day of our separation,

marginal line:
a member . . . old King [H]

underlined:
weary of our old King [I]

[a] *it was* not *so; The Mob huzzaed our* old King *whenever, & where ever he moved—I have seen him applauded at the Theatres with enthusiastic Fondness H: L: P. 1808.* [I]

marginal line:
School will . . . is without (H)

suffered or done any thing considerable. The only change in my way of life is, that I have frequented the theatre

marginal line:
former seasons . . . new farces [H]

more than in former seasons. But I have gone thither only to escape from myself. We have had many new farces, and the comedy called "The Jealous Wife," which, though not written with much genius, was yet so well adapted to the

marginal line:
the actors . . . the play-house [H]

underlined:
twenty [H]

stage, and so well exhibited by the actors, that it was crowded for near twenty nights. I am digressing from myself to the playhouse; but a barren plan must be filled with episodes. Of myself I have nothing to say, but that I have hitherto lived without the concurrence of my own judgement; yet I continue to flatter myself, that, when you return, you will find me mended. I do not wonder that, where the monastick life is permitted, every order finds votaries, and every monastery inhabitants. Men will submit to any rule, by which they may be exempted from the tyranny of caprice and of chance. They are glad to supply by external authority their own want of constancy and resolution, and court the government of others, when long experience has convinced them of their own inability to govern themselves. If I were to visit Italy, my curiosity would be more attracted by convents than by palaces; though I am afraid that I should find expectation in both

marginal line:
disappointed, and . . . must be [H]

places equally disappointed, and life in both places supported with impatience and quitted with reluctance. That it must be so soon quitted, is a powerful remedy against impatience; but what shall free us from reluctance? Those who have endeavoured to teach us to die well, have taught

underlined:
might [H]

few to die willingly: yet I cannot but hope that a good life might end at last in a contented death.[a]

[a] *I suppose it* might: *but who leads a good Life* [H]

'You see to what a train of thought I am drawn by the mention of myself. Let me now turn my attention upon you. I hope you take care to keep an exact journal, and to register all occurrences and observations; for your friends here expect such a book of travels as has not been often seen. You have given us good specimens in your letters from Lisbon. I wish you had staid longer in Spain, for no country is less known to the rest of Europe; but the quickness of your discernment must make amends for the celerity of your motions. He that knows which way to direct his view, sees much in a little time.

'Write to me very often, and I will not neglect to write
to you; and I may, perhaps, in time, get something to
write: at least, you will know by my letters, whatever else
they may have or want, that I continue to be

'Your most affectionate friend,

'[London] June 10, 1761.'   'SAM. JOHNSON'

In 1762 he wrote for the Reverend Dr. Kennedy, Rector
of Bradley in Derbyshire,[a] in a strain of very courtly
elegance, a Dedication to the King* of that gentleman's
work, entitled 'A complete System of Astronomical
Chronology, unfolding the Scriptures.' He had certainly
looked at this work before it was printed; for the concluding paragraph is undoubtedly of his composition, of which
let my readers judge:

[a] was that the poor old Man I saw wth. his Wife & Miss J. said they were like Baucis & Philemon? [1]

'Thus have I endeavoured to free Religion and History
from the darkness of a disputed and uncertain chronology;
from difficulties which have hitherto appeared insuperable,
and darkness which no luminary of learning has hitherto
been able to dissipate. I have established the truth of the
Mosaical account, by evidence which no transcription can
corrupt, no negligence can lose, and no interest can
pervert. I have shewn that the universe bears witness to
the inspiration of its historian, by the revolution of its
orbs and the succession of its seasons; *that the stars in their
courses fight against* incredulity, that the works of GOD give
hourly confirmation to the *law*, the *prophets*, and the *gospel*,
of which *one day telleth another, and one night certifieth another;*
and that the validity of the sacred writings never can be
denied, while the moon shall increase and wane, and the
sun shall know his going down.'

He this year wrote also the Dedication† to the Earl of
Middlesex of Mrs. Lennox's 'Female Quixote,' and the
Preface to the 'Catalogue of the Artists' Exhibition.'†

The following letter, which, on account of its intrinsick
merit, it would have been unjust both to Johnson and the
publick to have withheld, was obtained for me by the
solicitation of my friend Mr. Seward:

'TO DR. STAUNTON, (NOW SIR GEORGE STAUNTON, BARONET)

'DEAR SIR,

'I MAKE haste to answer your kind letter, in hope of hearing again from you before you leave us. I cannot but regret that a man of your qualifications should find it necessary to seek an establishment in Guadaloupe, which if a peace should restore to the French, I shall think it some alleviation of the loss, that it must restore likewise Dr. Staunton to the English.

'It is a melancholy consideration, that so much of our time is necessarily to be spent upon the care of living, and that we can seldom obtain ease in one respect but by resigning it in another: yet I suppose we are by this dispensation not less happy in the whole, than if the spontaneous bounty of Nature poured all that we want into our hands. A few, if they were left thus to themselves, would, perhaps, spend their time in laudable pursuits; but the greater part would prey upon the quiet of each other, or, in the want of other objects, would prey upon themselves.

'This, however, is our condition, which we must improve and solace as we can: and though we cannot choose always our place of residence, we may in every place find rational amusements, and possess in every place the comforts of piety and a pure conscience.[a]

a *Thank God for* that.
[1]

'In America there is little to be observed except natural curiosities. The new world must have many vegetables and animals with which philosophers are but little acquainted. I hope you will furnish yourself with some books of natural history, and some glasses and other instruments of observation. Trust as little as you can to report; examine all you can by your own senses. I do not doubt but you will be able to add much to knowledge, and, perhaps, to medicine. Wild nations trust to simples; and, perhaps, the Peruvian bark is not the only specifick which those extensive regions may afford us.

'Wherever you are, and whatever be your fortune, be certain, dear Sir, that you carry with you my kind wishes; and that whether you return hither, or stay in the other hemisphere, to hear that you are happy will give pleasure to, Sir,

'Your most affectionate humble servant,

'June 1, 1762.'   'SAM. JOHNSON'

A lady having at this time solicited him to obtain the Archbishop of Canterbury's patronage to have her son sent to the University, one of those solicitations which are too frequent, where people, anxious for a particular object, do not consider propriety, or the opportunity which the persons whom they solicit have to assist them, he wrote to her the following answer; with a copy of which I am favoured by the Reverend Dr. Farmer, Master of Emanuel College, Cambridge.

'MADAM,

'I HOPE you will believe that my delay in answering your letter could proceed only from my unwillingness to destroy any hope that you had formed.[a] Hope is itself a species of happiness, and, perhaps, the chief happiness which this world affords: but, like all other pleasures immoderately enjoyed, the excesses of hope must be expiated by pain: and expectations improperly indulged, must end in disappointment. If it be asked, what is the improper expectation which it is dangerous to indulge, experience will quickly answer, that it is such expectation as is dictated not by reason, but by desire; expectation raised, not by the common occurrences of life, but by the wants of the expectant; an expectation that requires the common course of things to be changed, and the general rules of action to be broken.

'When you made your request to me, you should have considered, Madam, what you were asking. You ask me to solicit a great man, to whom I never spoke, for a young person whom I had never seen, upon a supposition which I had no means of knowing to be true. There is no reason why, amongst all the great, I should chuse to supplicate the Archbishop, nor why, among all the possible objects of his bounty, the Archbishop should chuse your son. I know, Madam, how unwillingly conviction is admitted, when interest opposes it; but surely, Madam, you must

[a] *A Charming Letter.*
[1]

allow, that there is no reason why that should be done by me, which every other man may do with equal reason, and which, indeed, no man can do properly, without some very particular relation both to the Archbishop and to you. If I could help you in this exigence by any proper means, it would give me pleasure; but this proposal is so very remote from usual methods, that I cannot comply with it, but at the risk of such answer and suspicions as I believe you do not wish me to undergo.

'I have seen your son this morning; he seems a pretty youth, and will, perhaps, find some better friend than I can procure him; but though he should at last miss the University, he may still be wise, useful, and happy.

'I am, Madam,

'Your most humble servant,

'June 8, 1762.'   'SAM. JOHNSON'

'TO MR. JOSEPH BARETTI, AT MILAN

'SIR,   'London, July 20, 1762

'HOWEVER justly you may accuse me for want of punctuality in correspondence, I am not so far lost in negligence as to omit the opportunity of writing to you, which Mr. Beauclerk's passage through Milan affords me.

'I suppose you received the Idlers, and I intend that you shall soon receive Shakspeare, that you may explain his works to the ladies of Italy, and tell them the story of the editor, among the other strange narratives with which your long residence in this unknown region has supplied you.

'As you have now been long away, I suppose your curiosity may pant for some news of your old friends. Miss Williams and I live much as we did. Miss Cotterel still continues to cling to Mrs. Porter, and Charlotte is now big of the fourth child. Mr. Reynolds gets six thousands a year. Levet is lately married,[a] not without much suspicion that he has been wretchedly cheated in his match. Mr. Chambers is gone this day, for the first time, the circuit with the

ᵃ *I never knew he was a married Man before.*
[1]

Judges. Mr. Richardson[1] is dead of an apoplexy, and his second daughter has married a merchant.

'My vanity, or my kindness, makes me flatter myself, that you would rather hear of me than of those whom I have mentioned; but of myself I have very little which I care to tell. Last winter I went down to my native town, where I found the streets much narrower and shorter than I thought I had left them, inhabited by a new race of people, to whom I was very little known. My play-fellows were grown old, and forced me to suspect that I was no longer young. My only remaining friend has changed his principles, and was become the tool of the predominant faction. My daughter-in-law, from whom I expected most, and whom I met with sincere benevolence, has lost the beauty and gaiety of youth, without having gained much of the wisdom of age.[a] I wandered about for five days, and took the first convenient opportunity of returning to a place, where, if there is not much happiness, there is, at least, such a diversity of good and evil, that slight vexations do not fix upon the heart.

a Comical enough [H]

marginal line: *where, if . . . that slight* [H]

'I think in a few weeks to try another excursion; though to what end? Let me know, my Baretti, what has been the result of your return to your own country: whether time has made any alteration for the better, and whether, when the first raptures of salutation were over, you did not find your thoughts confessed their disappointment.

'Moral sentences appear ostentatious and tumid, when they have no greater occasions than the journey of a wit to his own town: yet such pleasures and such pains make up the general mass of life; and as nothing is little to him that feels it with great sensibility, a mind able to see common incidents in their real state, is disposed by very common incidents to very serious contemplations. Let us trust that a time will come, when the present moment shall be no longer irksome; when we shall not borrow all our happiness from hope, which at last is to end in disappointment.

'I beg that you will shew Mr. Beauclerk all the civilities which you have in your power; for he has always been kind to me.

---

[1] [Samuel Richardson, the authour of Clarissa, Sir Charles Grandison, &c. He died July 4, 1761, aged 72. MALONE.]

'I have lately seen Mr. Stratico, Professor of Padua, who has told me of your quarrel with an Abbot of the Celestine order; but had not the particulars very ready in his memory. When you write to Mr. Marsili, let him know that I remember him with kindness.

'May you, my Baretti, be very happy at Milan, or some other place nearer to, Sir,

'Your most affectionate humble servant,

'SAM. JOHNSON'

The accession of George the Third to the throne of these kingdoms, opened a new and brighter prospect to men of literary merit, who had been honoured with no mark of royal favour in the preceding reign. His present Majesty's education in this country, as well as his taste and beneficence, prompted him to be the patron of science and the arts; and early this year Johnson having been represented to him as a very learned and good man, without any certain provision, his Majesty was pleased to grant him a pension of three hundred pounds a year. The Earl of Bute, who was then Prime Minister, had the honour to announce this instance of his Sovereign's bounty, concerning which, many and various stories, all equally erroneous, have been propagated; maliciously representing it as a political bribe to Johnson, to desert his avowed principles, and become the tool of a government which he held to be founded in usurpation. I have taken care to have it in my power to refute them from the most authentick information. Lord Bute told me, that Mr. Wedderburne, now Lord Loughborough, was the person who first mentioned this subject to him. Lord Loughborough told me, that the pension was granted to Johnson solely as the reward of his literary merit, without any stipulation whatever, or even tacit understanding that he should write for administration. His Lordship added, that he was confident the political tracts which Johnson afterwards did write, as they were entirely consonant with his own opinions, would have been written by him, though no pension had been granted to him.

Mr. Thomas Sheridan and Mr. Murphy, who then lived a good deal both with him and Mr. Wedderburne, told me, that they previously talked with Johnson upon this matter, and that it was perfectly understood by all parties that the pension was merely honorary. Sir Joshua Reynolds told me, that Johnson called on him after his Majesty's intention had been notified to him, and said he wished to consult his friends as to the propriety of his accepting this mark of the royal favour, after the definitions which he had given in his Dictionary of *pension* and *pensioners*. He said he should not have Sir Joshua's answer till next day, when he would call again, and desired he might think of it. Sir Joshua answered that he was clear to give his opinion then, that there could be no objection to his receiving from the King a reward for literary merit; and that certainly the definitions in his Dictionary were not applicable to him. Johnson, it should seem, was satisfied, for he did not call again till he had accepted the pension, and had waited on Lord Bute to thank him. He then told Sir Joshua that Lord Bute said to him expressly, 'It is not given you for any thing you are to do, but for what you have done.'[1] His Lordship, he said, behaved in the handsomest manner. He repeated the words twice, that he might be sure Johnson heard them, and thus set his mind perfectly at ease. This nobleman, who has been so virulently abused, acted with great honour in this instance, and displayed a mind truly liberal. A minister of a more narrow and selfish disposition would have availed himself of such an opportunity to fix an implied obligation on a man of Johnson's powerful talents to give him his support.

Mr. Murphy and the late Mr. Sheridan severally contended for the distinction of having been the first who mentioned to Mr. Wedderburne that Johnson ought to have a pension. When I spoke of this to Lord Loughborough, wishing to know if he recollected the prime mover in the business, he said, 'All his friends assisted:' and when I told him that Mr. Sheridan strenuously asserted his claim to it, his Lordship said, 'He rang the bell.' And it is but just to add, that Mr. Sheridan told me, that when he

---

[1] [This was said by Lord Bute, as Dr. Burney was informed by Johnson himself, in answer to a question which he put, previously to his acceptance of the intended bounty: 'Pray, my lord, what am I expected to do for this pension?' MALONE.]

communicated to Dr. Johnson that a pension was to be granted him, he replied in a fervour of gratitude, 'The English language does not afford me terms adequate to my feelings on this occasion. I must have recourse to the French. I am *penetré* with his Majesty's goodness.' When I repeated this to Dr. Johnson, he did not contradict it.

His definitions of *pension* and *pensioner*, partly founded on the satirical verses of Pope, which he quotes, may be generally true; and yet every body must allow, that there may be, and have been, instances of pensions given and received upon liberal and honourable terms. Thus, then, it is clear, that there was nothing inconsistent or humiliating in Johnson's accepting of a pension so unconditionally and so honourably offered to him.

But I shall not detain my readers longer by any words of my own, on a subject on which I am happily enabled, by the favour of the Earl of Bute, to present them with what Johnson himself wrote; his lordship having been pleased to communicate to me a copy of the following letter to his late father, which does great honour both to the writer, and to the noble person to whom it is addressed:

'TO THE RIGHT HONOURABLE THE EARL OF BUTE

'MY LORD,

'WHEN the bills were yesterday delivered to me by Mr. Wedderburne, I was informed by him of the future favours which his Majesty has, by your Lordship's recommendation, been induced to intend for me.

'Bounty always receives part of its value from the manner in which it is bestowed; your Lordship's kindness includes every circumstance that can gratify delicacy, or enforce obligation. You have conferred your favours on a man who has neither alliance nor interest, who has not merited them by services, nor courted them by officiousness; you have spared him the shame of solicitation, and the anxiety of suspense.

'What has been thus elegantly given, will, I hope, not be reproachfully enjoyed; I shall endeavour to give your Lordship the only recompense which generosity desires,—

the gratification of finding that your benefits are not improperly bestowed. I am, my Lord,

'Your Lordship's most obliged,
'Most obedient, and most humble servant,

'July 20 1762.'   'SAM. JOHNSON'

This year his friend, Sir Joshua Reynolds, paid a visit of some weeks to his native country, Devonshire, in which he was accompanied by Johnson, who was much pleased with this jaunt, and declared he had derived from it a great accession of new ideas. He was entertained at the seats of several noblemen and gentlemen in the west of England;[1] but the greatest part of this time was passed at Plymouth, where the magnificence of the navy, the ship-building and all its circumstances, afforded him a grand subject of contemplation. The Commissioner of the Dock-yard paid him the compliment of ordering the yacht to convey him and his friend to the Eddystone, to which they accordingly sailed. But the weather was so tempestuous that they could not land.

Reynolds and he were at this time the guests of Dr. Mudge, the celebrated surgeon, and now physician of that place, not more distinguished for quickness of parts and variety of knowledge, than loved and esteemed for his amiable manners; and here Johnson formed an acquaintance with Dr. Mudge's father, that very eminent divine, the Reverend Zachariah Mudge, Prebendary of Exeter, who was idolised in the west, both for his excellence as a preacher and the uniform perfect propriety of his private conduct. He preached a sermon purposely that Johnson might hear him; and we shall see afterwards that Johnson honoured his memory by drawing his character.[a] While Johnson was at Plymouth, he saw a great many of its inhabitants, and was not sparing of his very entertaining

underlined:
his character [H]

[a] *& so it is—very finely drawn* [H]

---

[1] At one of these seats Dr. Amyat, Physician in London, told me he happened to meet him. In order to amuse him till dinner should be ready, he was taken out to walk in the garden. The master of the house thinking it proper to introduce something scientifick into the conversation, addressed him thus: 'Are you a botanist, Dr. Johnson?' 'No, Sir, (answered Johnson,) I am not a botanist; and, (alluding, no doubt, to his near sightedness) should I wish to become a botanist, I must first turn myself into a reptile.'[b]

[b] *very comical* [I]

marginal line:
truly original ... ignorance, pure [H]

conversation. It was here that he made that frank and truly original confession, that 'ignorance, pure ignorance,' was the cause of a wrong definition in his Dictionary of the word *pastern*,[1] to the no small surprise of the Lady who put the question to him; who having the most profound reverence for his character, so as almost to suppose him endowed with infallibility, expected to hear an explanation (of what, to be sure, seemed strange to a common reader,) drawn from some deep-learned source with which she was unacquainted.

Sir Joshua Reynolds, to whom I was obliged for my information concerning this excursion, mentions a very characteristical anecdote of Johnson while at Plymouth. Having observed, that in consequence of the Dock-yard

index sign:
knowing from his sagacity etc. [H]

a new town had arisen about two miles off as a rival to the old; and knowing from his sagacity, and just observation of human nature that it is certain if a man hates at all, he will hate his next neighbour; he concluded that this new and rising town could not but excite the envy and jealousy of the old, in which conjecture he was very soon confirmed; he therefore set himself resolutely on the side of the old town, the *established* town, in which his lot was cast, considering it as a kind of duty to *stand by* it. He accordingly entered warmly into its interests, and upon every occasion talked of the *dockers*, as the inhabitants of the new town were called, as upstarts and aliens. Plymouth is very plentifully supplied with water by a river brought into it from a great distance, which is so abundant that it runs to waste in the town. The Dock, or New-town, being totally destitute of water, petitioned Plymouth that a small portion of the conduit might be permitted to go to them, and this was now under consideration. Johnson, affecting to entertain the passions of the place, was violent in opposition; and half-laughing at himself for his pretended zeal, where he had no concern, exclaimed, 'No, no! I am against the *dockers;* I am a Plymouth-man. Rogues! let them die

[a] *how droll!* [J]

of thirst. They shall not have a drop!'[2][a]

Lord Macartney obligingly favoured me with a copy

[1] See p. 205.

[2] [A friend of mine once heard him, during this visit, exclaim with the utmost vehemence, 'I HATE a Docker.' BLAKEWAY.]

of the following letter, in his own hand-writing, from the original, which was found, by the present Earl of Bute, among his father's papers.

'TO THE RIGHT HONOURABLE THE EARL OF BUTE

'MY LORD,

'THAT generosity by which I was recommended to the favour of his Majesty, will not be offended at a solicitation necessary to make that favour permanent and effectual.

'The pension appointed to be paid me at Michaelmas I have not received, and know not where or from whom I am to ask it. I beg, therefore, that your lordship will be pleased to supply Mr. Wedderburne with such directions as may be necessary, which, I believe, his friendship will make him think it no trouble to convey to me.

'To interrupt your Lordship, at a time like this, with such petty difficulties, is improper and unseasonable; but your knowledge of the world has long since taught you, that every man's affairs, however little, are important to himself. Every man hopes that he shall escape neglect; and, with reason, may every man, whose vices do not preclude his claim, expect favour from that beneficence which has been extended to,

'My Lord,
'Your Lordship's
'Most obliged,
'And
'Most humble servant,

'Temple Lane,
Nov. 3, 1762.'   'SAM JOHNSON'

'TO MR. JOSEPH BARETTI, AT MILAN

'SIR,   'London, Dec. 21, 1762

'YOU are not to suppose, with all your conviction of my idleness, that I have passed all this time without writing to my Baretti. I gave a letter to Mr. Beauclerk, who in my opinion, and in his own, was hastening to Naples for the recovery of his health; but he has stopped at Paris, and I know not when he will proceed. Langton is with him.

'I will not trouble you with speculations about peace and war. The good or ill success of battles and embassies extends itself to a very small part of domestick life: we all have good and evil, which we feel more sensibly than our petty part of publick miscarriage or prosperity. I am sorry for your disappointment, with which you seem more touched than I should expect a man of your resolution and experience to have been, did I not know that general truths are seldom applied to particular occasions; and that the fallacy of our self-love extends itself as wide as our interest or affections. Every man believes that mistresses are unfaithful, and patrons capricious; but he excepts his own mistress, and his own patron. We have all learned that greatness is negligent and contemptuous, and that in Courts life is often languished away in ungratified expectation; but he that approaches greatness, or glitters in a Court, imagines that destiny has at last exempted him from the common lot.

'Do not let such evils overwhelm you as thousands have suffered, and thousands have surmounted; but turn your thoughts with vigour to some other plan of life, and keep always in your mind, that, with due submission to Providence, a man of genius has been seldom ruined but by himself. Your Patron's weakness or insensibility will finally do you little hurt, if he is not assisted by your own passions. Of your love I know not the propriety, nor can estimate the power; but in love, as in every other passion of which hope is the essence, we ought always to remember the uncertainty of events. There is, indeed, nothing that so much seduces reason from vigilance, as the thought of passing life with an amiable woman; and if all would happen that a lover fancies, I know not what other terrestrial happiness would deserve pursuit. But love and marriage are different states. Those who are to suffer the evils together,[1] and to suffer often for the sake of one another, soon lose that tenderness of look, and that benevolence of mind, which arose from the participation

two marginal lines:
would deserve . . .
marriage are [H]

---

[1] [Johnson probably wrote 'the evils *of life* together.' The words in Italicks, however, are not found in Baretti's original edition of this letter, but they may have been omitted inadvertently either in his transcript or at the press. MALONE.]

of unmingled pleasure and successive amusement. A woman, we are sure, will not be always fair; we are not sure she will always be virtuous: and man cannot retain through life that respect and assiduity by which he pleases for a day or for a month. I do not, however, pretend to have discovered that life has any thing more to be desired than a prudent and virtuous marriage; therefore know not what counsel to give you.

'If you can quit your imagination of love and greatness, and leave your hopes of preferment and bridal raptures to try once more the fortune of literature and industry, the way through France is now open. We flatter ourselves that we shall cultivate, with great diligence, the arts of peace; and every man will be welcome among us who can teach us any thing we do not know. For your part, you will find all your old friends willing to receive you.

'Reynolds still continues to increase in reputation and in riches. Miss Williams, who very much loves you, goes on in the old way. Miss Cotterel is still with Mrs. Porter. Miss Charlotte is married to Dean Lewis, and has three children. Mr. Levet has married a street-walker. But the gazette of my narration must now arrive to tell you, that Bathurst went physician to the army, and died at the Havannah.

marginal line: *married a . . . of my* [H]

'I know not whether I have not sent you word that Huggins and Richardson are both dead. When we see our enemies and friends gliding away before us, let us not forget that we are subject to the general law of mortality, and shall soon be where our doom will be fixed for ever.

queried and under- lined: *soon* [H]

'I pray GOD to bless you, and am, Sir,

'Your most affectionate humble servant,

'SAM. JOHNSON'

'Write soon.'

In 1763 he furnished to 'The Poetical Calendar,' pub- lished by Fawkes and Woty, a character of Collins,* which he afterwards ingrafted into his entire life of that admirable poet, in the collection of lives which he wrote for the body of English poetry, formed and published by the booksellers of London. His account of the melancholy depression with

which Collins was severely afflicted, and which brought
him to his grave, is, I think, one of the most tender and
interesting passages in the whole series of his writings. He
also favoured Mr. Hoole with the Dedication of his translations of Tasso to the Queen,* which is so happily conceived and elegantly expressed, that I cannot but point it
out to the peculiar notice of my readers.[1]

This is to me a memorable year; for in it I had the
happiness to obtain the acquaintance of that extraordinary
man whose memoirs I am now writing; an acquaintance
which I shall ever esteem as one of the most fortunate
circumstances in my life. Though then but two-and-
twenty, I had for several years read his works with delight
and instruction, and had the highest reverence for their
authour, which had grown up in my fancy into a kind of
mysterious veneration, by figuring to myself a state of
solemn elevated abstraction, in which I supposed him to
live in the immense metropolis of London. Mr. Gentleman,
a native of Ireland, who passed some years in Scotland as
a player, and as an instructor in the English language, a
man whose talents and worth were depressed by misfortunes, had given me a representation of the figure and

[1] 'MADAM,

'To approach the high and illustrious has been in all ages the privilege
of Poets; and though translators cannot justly claim the same honour, yet
they naturally follow their authours as attendants; and I hope that in return
for having enabled TASSO to diffuse his fame through the British dominions,
I may be introduced by him to the presence of YOUR MAJESTY.

'TASSO has a peculiar claim to YOUR MAJESTY's favour, as follower
and panegyrist of the House of *Este*, which has one common ancestor with
the House of HANOVER; and in reviewing his life it is not easy to forbear
a wish that he had lived in a happier time, when he might among the
descendants of that illustrious family have found a more liberal and potent
patronage.

'I cannot but observe, MADAM, how unequally reward is proportioned
to merit, when I reflect that the happiness which was withheld from
TASSO is reserved for me; and that the poem which once hardly procured
to its authour the countenance of the Princes of Ferrara, has attracted to its
translator the favourable notice of a BRITISH QUEEN.

'Had this been the fate of TASSO, he would have been able to have
celebrated the condescension of YOUR MAJESTY in nobler language, but
could not have felt it with more ardent gratitude than,

'MADAM,
'YOUR MAJESTY's
'Most faithful and devoted servant.'

manner of DICTIONARY JOHNSON! as he was then generally called;[1] and during my first visit to London, which was for three months in 1760, Mr. Derrick the poet, who was Gentleman's friend and countryman, flattered me with hopes that he could introduce me to Johnson, an honour of which I was very ambitious. But he never found an opportunity; which made me doubt that he had promised to do what was not in his power; till Johnson some years afterwards told me, 'Derrick, Sir, might very well have introduced you. I had a kindness for Derrick, and am sorry he is dead.'

In the summer of 1761, Mr. Thomas Sheridan was at Edinburgh, and delivered lectures upon the English Language and Publick Speaking to large and respectable audiences. I was often in his company, and heard him frequently expatiate upon Johnson's extraordinary knowledge, talents, and virtues, repeat his pointed sayings, describe his particularities, and boast of his being his guest sometimes till two or three in the morning. At his house I hoped to have many opportunities of seeing the sage, as Mr. Sheridan obligingly assured me I should not be disappointed.

When I returned to London in the end of 1762, to my surprise and regret I found an irreconcileable difference had taken place between Johnson and Sheridan. A pension of two hundred pounds a year had been given to Sheridan. Johnson, who, as has been already mentioned, thought slightingly of Sheridan's art, upon hearing that he was also pensioned, exclaimed, 'What! have they given *him* a pension? Then it is time for me to give up mine.' Whether this proceeded from a momentary indignation, as if it were an affront to his exalted merit that a player should be rewarded in the same manner with him, or was the sudden effect of a fit of peevishness, it was unluckily said, and, indeed, cannot be justified. Mr. Sheridan's pension was granted to him not as a player, but as a sufferer in the

marginal line: *was the ... it was* [H]

---

[1] As great men of antiquity such as Scipio *Africanus* had an epithet added to their names, in consequence of some celebrated action, so my illustrious friend was often called DICTIONARY JOHNSON, from that wonderful atchievement of genius and labour, his 'Dictionary of the English Language;' the merit of which I contemplate with more and more admiration.

cause of government, when he was manager of the Theatre
Royal in Ireland, when parties ran high in 1753. And it
must also be allowed that he was a man of literature,
and had considerably improved the arts of reading and
speaking with distinctness and propriety.

Besides, Johnson should have recollected that Mr.
Sheridan taught pronunciation to Mr. Alexander Wedderburne, whose sister was married to Sir Harry Erskine, an
intimate friend of Lord Bute, who was the favourite of the
King; and surely the most outrageous Whig will not
maintain, that whatever ought to be the principle in the
disposal of *offices*, a *pension* ought never to be granted from
any bias of court connection. Mr. Macklin, indeed, shared
with Mr. Sheridan the honour of instructing Mr. Wedderburne; and though it was too late in life for a Caledonian
to acquire the genuine English cadence, yet so successful
were Mr. Wedderburne's instructors, and his own un-
abating endeavours, that he got rid of the coarse part of
his Scotch accent, retaining only as much of the 'native
wood-note wild,' as to mark his country; which, if any
Scotchman should affect to forget, I should heartily
despise him. Notwithstanding the difficulties which are
to be encountered by those who have not had the advantage of an English education, he by degrees formed a mode
of speaking, to which Englishmen do not deny the praise
of elegance. Hence his distinguished oratory, which he
exerted in his own country as an advocate in the Court of
Session, and a ruling elder of the *Kirk*, has had its fame
and ample reward, in much higher spheres. When I look
back on this noble person at Edinburgh, in situations so
unworthy of his brilliant powers, and behold LORD
LOUGHBOROUGH at London, the change seems almost
like one of the metamorphoses in Ovid; and as his two
preceptors, by refining his utterance, gave currency to his
talents, we may say in the words of that poet, '*Nam vos
mutastis.*'

I have dwelt the longer upon this remarkable instance
of successful parts and assiduity; because it affords animating encouragement to other gentlemen of North-
Britain to try their fortunes in the southern part of the
island, where they may hope to gratify their utmost

marginal line:
mark his . . . him.
Notwithstanding [H]

ambition; and now that we are one people by the Union, it would surely be illiberal to maintain, that they have not an equal title with the natives of any other part of his Majesty's dominions.

Johnson complained that a man who disliked him repeated his sarcasm to Mr. Sheridan, without telling him what followed, which was, that after a pause he added, 'However, I am glad that Mr. Sheridan has a pension, for he is a very good man.' Sheridan could never forgive this hasty contemptuous expression. It rankled in his mind; and though I informed him of all that Johnson said, and that he would be very glad to meet him amicably, he positively declined repeated offers which I made, and once went off abruptly from a house where he and I were engaged to dine, because he was told that Dr. Johnson was to be there. I have no sympathetick feeling with such persevering resentment. It is painful when there is a breach between those who have lived together socially and cordially; and I wonder that there is not, in all such cases, a mutual wish that it should be healed. I could perceive that Mr. Sheridan was by no means satisfied with Johnson's acknowledging him to be a good man. That could not sooth his injured vanity. I could not but smile, at the same time that I was offended, to observe Sheridan in the Life of Swift, which he afterwards published, attempting, in the writhings of his resentment, to depreciate Johnson, by characterising him as 'A writer of gigantick fame, in these days of little men;' that very Johnson whom he once so highly admired and venerated.

This rupture with Sheridan deprived Johnson of one of his most agreeable resources for amusement in his lonely evenings; for Sheridan's well-informed, animated, and bustling mind never suffered conversation to stagnate; and Mrs. Sheridan was a most agreeable companion to an intellectual man. She was sensible, ingenious, unassuming, yet communicative. I recollect, with satisfaction, many pleasing hours which I passed with her under the hospitable roof of her husband, who was to me a very kind friend. Her novel, entitled 'Memoirs of Miss Sydney Biddulph,' contains an excellent moral, while it inculcates a future state of retribution;[1] and what it teaches is impressed upon the mind by a series of as deep distress as can affect humanity, in the amiable and pious heroine, who goes to her grave unrelieved, but resigned, and full of hope of 'heaven's mercy.' Johnson paid her this high compliment upon it: 'I know not, Madam, that you have a right, upon moral principles, to make your readers suffer so much.'[a]

[a] *It is exquisitely managed* [1]

Mr. Thomas Davies the actor, who then kept a bookseller's shop in Russell-street, Covent-garden,[2] told me that Johnson was very much his friend, and came frequently to his house, where he more than once invited me to meet him: but by some unlucky accident or other he was prevented from coming to us.

[1] My position has been very well illustrated by Mr. Belsham of Bedford, in his Essay on Dramatick Poetry. 'The fashionable doctrine (says he) both of moralists and criticks in these times is, that virtue and happiness are constant concomitants; and it is regarded as a kind of dramatick impiety to maintain that virtue should not be rewarded, nor vice punished in the last scene of the last act of every tragedy. This conduct in our modern poets is, however, in my opinion, extremely injudicious; for, it labours in vain to inculcate a doctrine in theory, which every one knows to be false in fact, *viz.* that virtue in real life is always productive of happiness; and vice of misery. Thus Congreve concludes the Tragedy of "The Mourning Bride" with the following foolish couplet:

> "For blessings ever wait on virtuous deeds,
> And, though a late, a sure reward succeeds."

'When a man eminently virtuous, a Brutus, a Cato, or a Socrates, finally sinks under the pressure of accumulated misfortune, we are not only led to entertain a more indignant hatred of vice, than if he rose from his distress, but we are inevitably induced to cherish the sublime idea that a day of future retribution will arrive when he shall receive not merely poetical, but real and substantial justice.' Essays Philosophical, Historical, and Literary, London, 1791, Vol II. 8vo. p. 317.

This is well reasoned and well expressed. I wish, indeed, that the ingenious authour had not thought it necessary to introduce any *instance* of 'a man eminently virtuous;' as he would then have avoided mentioning such a ruffian as Brutus under that description. Mr. Belsham discovers in his 'Essays' so much reading and thinking, and good composition, that I regret his not having been fortunate enough to be educated a member of our excellent national establishment. Had he not been nursed in nonconformity, he probably would not have been tainted with those heresies (as I sincerely, and on no slight investigation, think them) both in religion and politicks, which, while I read, I am sure, with candour, I cannot read without offence.

[2] No. 8.—The very place where I was fortunate enough to be introduced to the illustrious subject of this work, deserves to be particularly marked. I never pass by it without feeling reverence and regret.

Mr. Thomas Davies was a man of good understanding and talents, with the advantage of a liberal education. Though somewhat pompous, he was an entertaining companion; and his literary performances have no inconsiderable share of merit. He was a friendly and very hospitable man. Both he and his wife, (who had been celebrated for her beauty,)[a] though upon the stage for many years, maintained an uniform decency of character; and Johnson esteemed them, and lived in as easy an intimacy with them as with any family which he used to visit. Mr. Davies recollected several of Johnson's remarkable sayings, and was one of the best of the many imitators of his voice and manner, while relating them. He increased my impatience more and more to see the extraordinary man whose works I highly valued, and whose conversation was reported to be so peculiarly excellent.

[a] *with Justice* [1]

At last, on Monday the 16th of May, when I was sitting in Mr. Davies's back-parlour, after having drunk tea with him and Mrs. Davies, Johnson unexpectedly came into the shop;[1] and Mr. Davies having perceived him through the glass-door in the room in which we were sitting, advancing towards us,—he announced his awful approach to me, somewhat in the manner of an actor in the part of Horatio, when he addresses Hamlet on the appearance of his father's ghost, 'Look, my Lord, it comes.' I found that I had a very perfect idea of Johnson's figure, from the portrait of him painted by Sir Joshua Reynolds soon after he had published his Dictionary, in the attitude of sitting in his easy chair in deep meditation, which was the first picture his friend did for him, which Sir Joshua very kindly

---

[1] Mr. Murphy, in his 'Essay on the Life and Genius of Dr. Johnson,' has given an account of this meeting considerably different from mine, I am persuaded without any consciousness of errour. His memory, at the end of near thirty years, has undoubtedly deceived him,[b] and he supposes himself to have been present at a scene, which he has probably heard inaccurately described by others. In my note *taken on the very day*, in which I am confident I marked every thing material that passed, no mention is made of this gentleman; and I am sure, that I should not have omitted one so well known in the literary world. It may easily be imagined that this my first interview with Dr. Johnson. with all its circumstances, made a strong impression on my mind, and would be registered with peculiar attention. [It is remarkable, that in the editions of Murphy's Life of Johnson, published subsequently to the appearance of this note, in 1791, he never corrected the mis-statement here mentioned.[c] MALONE.]

underlined:
His memory, deceived [H]

[b] *not at all* [H]

[c] *why should he?* [H

presented to me, and from which an engraving has been made for this work. Mr. Davies mentioned my name, and respectfully introduced me to him. I was much agitated; and recollecting his prejudice against the Scotch, of which I had heard much, I said to Davies, 'Don't tell where I come from.'—'From Scotland,' cried Davies, roguishly. 'Mr. Johnson, (said I) I do indeed come from Scotland, but I cannot help it.' I am willing to flatter myself that I meant this as light pleasantry to sooth and conciliate him, and not as an humiliating abasement at the expence of my country. But however that might be, this speech was somewhat unlucky; for with that quickness of wit for which he was so remarkable, he seized the expression 'come from Scotland,' which I used in the sense of being of that country; and, as if I had said that I had come away from it, or left it, retorted, 'That, Sir, I find, is what a very great many of your countrymen cannot help.' This stroke stunned me a good deal; and when we had sat down, I felt myself not a little embarrassed, and apprehensive of what might come next. He then addressed himself to Davies: 'What do you think of Garrick? He has refused me an order for the play for Miss Williams, because he knows the house will be full, and that an order will be worth three shillings.' Eager to take any opening to get into conversation with him, I ventured to say, 'O, Sir, I cannot think Mr. Garrick would grudge such a trifle to you.' 'Sir, (said he, with a stern look,) I have known David Garrick longer than you have done: and I know no right you have to talk to me on the subject.' Perhaps I deserved this check; for it was rather presumptuous in me, an entire stranger, to express any doubt of the justice of his animadversion upon his old acquaintance and pupil.[1] I now felt myself much mortified, and began to think that the hope which I had long indulged of obtaining his acquaintance was blasted. And, in truth, had not my ardour been uncommonly strong,

[1] That this was a momentary sally against Garrick there can be no doubt; for at Johnson's desire he had, some years before, given a benefit-night at his theatre to this very person, by which she had got two hundred pounds. Johnson, indeed, upon all other occasions, when I was in his company, praised the very liberal charity of Garrick. I once mentioned to him, 'It is observed, Sir, that you attack Garrick yourself, but will suffer nobody else to do it' JOHNSON, (smiling) 'Why, Sir, that is true.'

and my resolution uncommonly persevering, so rough a reception might have deterred me for ever from making any further attempts. Fortunately, however, I remained upon the field not wholly discomfited; and was soon rewarded by hearing some of his conversation, of which I preserved the following short minute, without marking the questions and observations by which it was produced.

'People (he remarked) may be taken in once, who imagine that an authour is greater in private life than other men. Uncommon parts require uncommon opportunities for their exertion.

marginal line: *than other . . . their exertion* [H]

'In barbarous society, superiority of parts is of real consequence. Great strength or great wisdom is of much value to an individual. But in more polished times there are people to do every thing for money; and then there are a number of other superiorities, such as those of birth and fortune, and rank that dissipate men's attention, and leave no extraordinary share of respect for personal and intellectual superiority. This is wisely ordered by Providence, to preserve some equality among mankind.'

'Sir, this book ("The Elements of Criticism," which he had taken up,) is a pretty essay, and deserves to be held in some estimation, though much of it is chimerical.'

Speaking of one who with more than ordinary boldness attacked publick measures and the royal family, he said, 'I think he is safe from the law, but he is an abusive scoundrel; and instead of applying to my Lord Chief Justice to punish him, I would send half a dozen footmen and have him well ducked.'

marginal line: *applying to . . . him well* [H]

'The notion of liberty amuses the people of England, and helps to keep off the *tædium vitæ*. When a butcher tells you that *his heart bleeds for his country*, he has, in fact, no uneasy feeling.'

'Sheridan will not succeed at Bath with his oratory. Ridicule has gone down before him, and, I doubt, Derrick is his enemy.'[1]

'Derrick may do very well, as long as he can outrun his character; but the moment his character gets up with him, it is all over.'

---

[1] Mr. Sheridan was then reading lectures upon Oratory at Bath, where Derrick was Master of the Ceremonies; or, as the phrase is, KING.

It is however, but just to record, that some years afterwards, when I reminded him of this sarcasm, he said, 'Well, but Derrick has now got a character that he need not run away from.'

I was highly pleased with the extraordinary vigour of his conversation, and regretted that I was drawn away from it by an engagement at another place. I had, for a part of the evening, been left alone with him, and had ventured to make an observation now and then, which he received very civilly; so that I was satisfied that though there was a roughness in his manner, there was no ill-nature in his disposition. Davies followed me to the door, and when I complained to him a little of the hard blows which the great man had given me, he kindly took upon him to console me by saying, 'Don't be uneasy. I can see he likes you very well.'

A few days afterwards I called on Davies, and asked him if he thought I might take the liberty of waiting on Mr. Johnson at his chambers in the Temple. He said I certainly might, and that Mr. Johnson would take it as a compliment. So on Tuesday the 24th of May, after having been enlivened by the witty sallies of Messieurs Thornton, Wilkes, Churchill, and Lloyd, with whom I had passed the morning, I boldly repaired to Johnson. His Chambers were on the first floor of No. 1, Inner-Temple-lane, and I entered them with an impression given me by the Reverend Dr. Blair, of Edinburgh, who had been introduced to him not long before, and described his having 'found the Giant in his den;' an expression, which, when I came to be pretty well acquainted with Johnson, I repeated to him, and he was diverted at this picturesque account of himself. Dr. Blair had been presented to him by Dr. James Fordyce. At this time the controversy concerning the pieces published by Mr. James Macpherson, as translations of Ossian, was at its height. Johnson had all along denied their authenticity; and, what was still more provoking to their admirers, maintained that they had no merit. The subject having been introduced by Dr. Fordyce, Dr. Blair, relying on the internal evidence of their antiquity, asked Dr. Johnson whether he thought any man of a modern age could have written such poems? Johnson replied, 'Yes, Sir, many

marginal line:
His Chambers . . . an impression [H]

men, many women, and many children.' Johnson at this
time, did not know that Dr. Blair had just published a
Dissertation, not only defending their authenticity, but
seriously ranking them with the poems of Homer and
Virgil; and when he was afterwards informed of this
circumstance, he expressed some displeasure at Dr. Fordyce's having suggested the topick, and said, 'I am not
sorry that they got thus much for their pains. Sir, it was
like leading one to talk of a book, when the authour is
concealed behind the door.'

marginal line:
*their pains . . . behind
the* [H]

He received me very courteously; but, it must be confessed, that his apartment, and furniture, and morning
dress, were sufficiently uncouth. His brown suit of cloaths
looked very rusty; he had on a little old shrivelled un-
powdered wig, which was too small for his head; his shirt-
neck and knees of his breeches were loose; his black worsted
stockings ill drawn up; and he had a pair of unbuckled
shoes by way of slippers. But all these slovenly particularities were forgotten the moment that he began to talk.
Some gentlemen, whom I do not recollect, were sitting
with him; and when they went away, I also rose; but he
said to me, 'Nay, don't go.'—'Sir, (said I,) I am afraid
that I intrude upon you. It is benevolent to allow me to sit
and hear you.' He seemed pleased with this compliment,
which I sincerely paid him, and answered, 'Sir, I am
obliged to any man who visits me.'—I have preserved the
following short minute of what passed this day.

'Madness frequently discovers itself merely by unnecessary deviation from the usual modes of the world. My poor
friend Smart shewed the disturbance of his mind, by falling
upon his knees, and saying his prayers in the street, or in
any other unusual place. Now although, rationally speaking, it is greater madness not to pray at all, than to pray
as Smart did, I am afraid there are so many who do not
pray, that their understanding is not called in question.'

Concerning this unfortunate poet, Christopher Smart,
who was confined in a mad-house, he had, at another
time, the following conversation with Dr. Burney.—
BURNEY. 'How does poor Smart do, Sir; is he likely to
recover?' JOHNSON. 'It seems as if his mind had ceased to
struggle with the disease; for he grows fat upon it.'

BURNEY. 'Perhaps, Sir, that may be from want of exercise.' JOHNSON. 'No, Sir; he has partly as much exercise as he used to have, for he digs in the garden. Indeed, before his confinement, he used for exercise to walk to the ale-house; but he was *carried* back again. I did not think he ought to be shut up. His infirmities were not noxious to society. He insisted on people praying with him; and I'd as lief pray with Kit Smart as any one else. Another charge was, that he did not love clean linen; and I have no passion for it.'

Johnson continued. 'Mankind have a great aversion to intellectual labour; but even supposing knowledge to be easily attainable, more people would be content to be ignorant than would take even a little trouble to acquire it.'

'The morality of an action depends on the motive from which we act. If I fling half a crown to a beggar with intention to break his head, and he picks it up and buys victuals with it, the physical effect is good; but, with respect to me, the action is very wrong. So, religious exercises, if not performed with an intention to please GOD, avail us nothing. As our Saviour says of those who perform them from other motives, "Verily they have their reward."'

'The Christian religion has very strong evidences. It indeed, appears in some degree strange to reason; but in History we have undoubted facts, against which, in reasoning *à priori*, we have more arguments than we have for them; but then, testimony has great weight, and casts the balance. I would recommend to every man whose faith is yet unsettled, Grotius,—Dr. Pearson,—and Dr. Clarke.'

Talking of Garrick, he said, 'He is the first man in the world for sprightly conversation.'

When I rose a second time, he again pressed me to stay, which I did.

He told me, that he generally went abroad at four in the afternoon, and seldom came home till two in the morning. I took the liberty to ask if he did not think it wrong to live thus, and not make more use of his great talents. He owned it was a bad habit. On reviewing, at the distance of many years, my journal of this period, I wonder how, at my first visit, I ventured to talk to him so freely, and that he bore it with so much indulgence.

Before we parted, he was so good as to promise to favour me with his company one evening at my lodgings; and, as I took my leave, shook me cordially by the hand. It is almost needless to add, that I felt no little elation at having now so happily established an acquaintance of which I had been so long ambitious.

My readers will, I trust, excuse me for being thus minutely circumstantial, when it is considered that the acquaintance of Dr. Johnson was to me a most valuable acquisition, and laid the foundation of whatever instruction and entertainment they may receive from my collections concerning the great subject of the work which they are now perusing.

I did not visit him again till Monday, June 13, at which time I recollect no part of his conversation, except that when I told him I had been to see Johnson ride upon three horses, he said, 'Such a man, Sir, should be encouraged; for his performances shew the extent of the human powers in one instance, and thus tend to raise our opinion of the faculties of man. He shews what may be attained by persevering application; so that every man may hope, that by giving as much application, although perhaps he may never ride three horses at a time, or dance upon a wire, yet he may be equally expert in whatever profession he has chosen to pursue.'

He again shook me by the hand at parting, and asked me why I did not come oftener to him. Trusting that I was now in his good graces, I answered, that he had not given me much encouragement, and reminded him of the check I had received from him at our first interview. 'Poh, poh! (said he, with a complacent smile,) never mind these things. Come to me as often as you can. I shall be glad to see you.'

I had learnt that his place of frequent resort was the Mitre tavern in Fleet-street, where he loved to sit up late, and I begged I might be allowed to pass an evening with him there soon, which he promised I should. A few days afterwards I met him near Temple-bar, about one o'clock in the morning, and asked if he would then go to the Mitre. 'Sir, (said he) it is too late; they won't let us in. But I'll go with you another night with all my heart.'

marginal line:
*commission in . . . my
own* [H]

A revolution of some importance in my plan of life had just taken place; for instead of procuring a commission in the foot-guards, which was my own inclination, I had, in compliance with my father's wishes, agreed to study the law, and was soon to set out for Utrecht, to hear the lectures of an excellent Civilian in that University, and then to proceed on my travels. Though very desirous of obtaining Dr. Johnson's advice and instructions on the mode of pursuing my studies, I was at this time so occupied, shall I call it? or so dissipated by the amusements of London, that our next meeting was not till Saturday, June 25, when happening to dine at Clifton's eating-house, in Butcher-row, I was surprised to perceive Johnson come in and take his seat at another table. The mode of dining, or rather being fed, at such houses in London, is well known to many to be particularly unsocial, as there is no Ordinary, or united company, but each person has his own mess, and is under no obligation to hold any intercourse with any one. A liberal and full-minded man, however, who loves to talk, will break through this churlish and unsocial restraint. Johnson and an Irish gentleman got into a dispute concerning the cause of some part of mankind being black. 'Why, Sir, (said Johnson,) it has been accounted for in three ways: either by supposing that they are the posterity of Ham, who was cursed; or that GOD at first created two kinds of men, one black and another white; or that by the heat of the sun the skin is scorched, and so acquires a sooty hue. This matter has been much canvassed among naturalists, but has never been brought to any certain issue.' What the Irishman said is totally obliterated from my mind; but I remember that he became very warm and intemperate in his expressions: upon which Johnson rose, and quietly walked away. When he had retired, his antagonist took his revenge, as he thought, by saying, 'He has a most ungainly figure, and an affectation of pomposity, unworthy of a man of genius.'

Johnson had not observed that I was in the room. I followed him, however, and he agreed to meet me in the evening at the Mitre. I called on him, and we went thither at nine. We had a good supper, and port wine, of which he then sometimes drank a bottle. The orthodox high-church sound of the MITRE,—the figure and manner of the celebrated SAMUEL JOHNSON,—the extraordinary power and precision of his conversation, and the pride arising from finding myself admitted as his companion, produced a variety of sensations, and a pleasing elevation of mind beyond what I had ever before experienced. I find in my Journal the following minute of our conversation, which, though it will give but a very faint notion of what passed, is, in some degree, a valuable record; and it will be curious in this view, as shewing how habitual to his mind were some opinions which appear in his works.

marginal line:
SAMUEL JOHNSON
· · · *power and* [H]

'Colley Cibber, Sir, was by no means a blockhead: but by arrogating to himself too much, he was in danger of losing that degree of estimation to which he was entitled. His friends gave out that he *intended* his birth-day Odes should be bad: but that was not the case, Sir; for he kept them many months by him, and a few years before he died he shewed me one of them, with great solicitude to render it as perfect as might be, and I made some corrections, to which he was not very willing to submit. I remember the following couplet in allusion to the King and himself:

> "Perch'd on the eagle's soaring wing,
>   The lowly linnet loves to sing."

Sir, he had heard something of the fabulous tale of the wren sitting upon the eagle's wing, and he had applied it to a linnet.[a] Cibber's familiar style, however, was better than that which Whitehead has assumed. *Grand* nonsense is insupportable. Whitehead is but a little man to inscribe verses to players.'

[a] *& the Linnet rid as well as the Wren, for ought I see.* [H]

I did not presume to controvert this censure, which was tinctured with his prejudice against players, but I could not help thinking that a dramatick poet might with propriety pay a compliment to an eminent performer, as Whitehead has very happily done in his verses to Mr. Garrick.

'Sir, I do not think Gray a first-rate poet. He has not a bold imagination, nor much command of words. The obscurity in which he has involved himself will not persuade us that he is sublime. His Elegy in a Church-yard

queried twice:
He has not etc. [H]

has a happy selection of images, but I don't like what are called his great things. His Ode which begins

"Ruin seize thee, ruthless King,
Confusion on thy banners wait!"

has been celebrated for its abruptness, and plunging into the subject all at once. But such arts as these have no merit, unless when they are original. We admire them only once; and this abruptness has nothing new in it. We have had it often before. Nay, we have it in the old song of Johnny Armstrong:

"Is there ever a man in all Scotland,
From the highest estate to the lowest degree, &c."

And then, Sir,

"Yes, there is a man in Westmoreland
And Johnny Armstrong they do him call."

There, now, you plunge at once into the subject. You have no previous narration to lead you to it.—The two next lines in that Ode are, I think, very good:

"Though fann'd by conquest's crimson wing,
They mock the air with idle state." '[1]

marginal line:
I believe . . . by whom
[H]

Here let it be observed, that although his opinion of Gray's poetry was widely different from mine, and I believe from that of most men of taste, by whom it is with justice highly admired, there is certainly much absurdity in the clamour which has been raised, as if he had been culpably injurious to the merit of that bard, and had been actuated by envy. Alas! ye little short-sighted criticks, could Johnson be envious of the talents of any of his contemporaries? That his opinion on this subject was what in private and in publick he uniformly expressed, regardless of what others might think, we may wonder, and perhaps regret; but it is shallow and unjust to charge him with expressing what he did not think.

Finding him in a placid humour, and wishing to avail myself of the opportunity which I fortunately had of

[1] My friend Mr. Malone, in his valuable comments on Shakspeare, has traced in that great poet the *disjecta membra* of these lines.

consulting a sage, to hear whose wisdom, I conceived, in
the ardour of youthful imagination, that men filled with
a noble enthusiasm for intellectual improvement would
gladly have resorted from distant lands;—I opened my
mind to him ingenuously, and gave him a little sketch of
my life, to which he was pleased to listen with great
attention.

I acknowledged, that though educated very strictly in the
principles of religion, I had for some time been misled
into a certain degree of infidelity; but that I was come
now to a better way of thinking, and was fully satisfied
of the truth of the Christian revelation, though I was not
clear as to every point considered to be orthodox. Being
at all times a curious examiner of the human mind, and
pleased with an undisguised display of what had passed
in it, he called to me with warmth, 'Give me your hand;
I have taken a liking to you.' He then began to descant
upon the force of testimony, and the little we could know
of final causes; so that the objections of, why was it so? or
why was it not so? ought not to disturb us: adding, that he
himself had at one period been guilty of a temporary
neglect of religion, but that it was not the result of
argument, but mere absence of thought.

After having given credit to reports of his bigotry, I
was agreeably surprized when he expressed the following
very liberal sentiment, which has the additional value of
obviating an objection to our holy religion, founded upon
the discordant tenets of Christians themselves: 'For my
part, Sir, I think all Christians, whether Papists or
Protestants, agree in the essential articles, and that their
differences are trivial, and rather political than religious.'[a]

We talked of belief in ghosts. He said, 'Sir, I make a
distinction between what a man may experience by the
mere strength of his imagination, and what imagination
cannot possibly produce.[b] Thus, suppose I should think
that I saw a form, and heard a voice cry, "Johnson, you
are a very wicked fellow, and unless you repent you will
certainly be punished;" my own unworthiness is so deeply
impressed upon my mind, that I might *imagine* I thus saw
and heard, and therefore I should not believe that an
external communication had been made to me. But if a

index sign:
*their differences are
trivial* etc. [1]

[a] *he was a great Reader
of Leslie* [1]

[b] *wisely distinguished
—because Ghost-seers,
like other Men of dis-
order'd Minds, are all
Egotists: a Lunatic
never tells you that a
Chimney Sweeper is
crowned King of France,
or that the whole House
of Bourbon are turn'd*

Chimney Sweepers: He says how He—John Wilson, or Tom Jackson, is appointed King of the French; or condemn'd for his Sins to sweep Chimneys in London or Paris,—he would laugh at a similar Tale when not relating to himself. [H]

form should appear, and a voice should tell me that a particular man had died at a particular place, and a particular hour, a fact which I had no apprehension of, nor any means of knowing, and this fact, with all its circumstances, should afterwards be unquestionably proved, I should, in that case be persuaded that I had supernatural intelligence imparted to me.'

Here it is proper, once for all, to give a true and fair statement of Johnson's way of thinking upon the question, whether departed spirits are ever permitted to appear in this world, or in any way to operate upon human life. He has been ignorantly misrepresented as weakly credulous upon that subject; and, therefore, though I feel an inclination to disdain and treat with silent contempt so foolish a notion concerning my illustrious friend, yet as I find it has gained ground, it is necessary to refute it. The real fact then is, that Johnson had a very philosophical mind, and such a rational respect for testimony, as to make him submit his understanding to what was authentically proved, though he could not comprehend why it was so. Being thus disposed, he was willing to enquire into the truth of any relation of supernatural agency, a general belief of which has prevailed in all nations and ages. But so far was he from being the dupe of implicit faith, that he examined the matter with a jealous attention, and no man was more ready to refute its falsehood when he had discovered it. Churchill, in his poem entitled 'The Ghost,' availed himself of the absurd credulity imputed to Johnson, and drew a caricature of him under the name of 'POM-

marginal line: *Cock-lane . . . gained very* [H]

POSO,' representing him as one of the believers of the story of a Ghost in Cock-lane, which, in the year 1762, had gained very general credit in London. Many of my readers, I am convinced, are to this hour under an impression that Johnson was thus foolishly deceived. It will therefore surprize them a good deal when they are informed upon undoubted authority, that Johnson was one of those by whom the imposture was detected. The story had become so popular, that he thought it should be investigated; and in this research he was assisted by the Reverend Dr. Douglas, now Bishop of Salisbury, the great detector of impostures; who informs me, that after the gentlemen

who went and examined into the evidence were satisfied of its falsity, Johnson wrote in their presence an
account of it, which was published in the newspapers and
Gentleman's Magazine, and undeceived the world.[1]

Our conversation proceeded. 'Sir, (said he,) I am a
friend to subordination, as most conducive to the happiness of society. There is a reciprocal pleasure in governing
and being governed.'

marginal line:
the happiness . . . being
governed [H]

'Dr. Goldsmith is one of the first men we now have as
an authour, and he is a very worthy man too. He has
been loose in his principles, but he is coming right.'

I mentioned Mallet's tragedy of 'ELVIRA,' which had
been acted the preceding winter at Drury-lane, and that

[1] The account was as follows: 'On the night of the 1st of February, many
gentlemen eminent for their rank and character, were, by the invitation
of the Reverend Mr. Aldrich, of Clerkenwell, assembled at his house, for
the examination of the noises supposed to be made by a departed spirit, for
the detection of some enormous crime.

'About ten at night the gentlemen met in the chamber in which the girl,
supposed to be disturbed by a spirit, had, with proper caution, been put to
bed by several ladies. They sat rather more than an hour, and hearing
nothing, went down stairs, when they interrogated the father of the girl,
who denied, in the strongest terms, any knowledge or belief of fraud.

'The supposed spirit had before publickly promised, by an affirmative
knock, that it would attend one of the gentlemen into the vault under the
church of St. John, Clerkenwell, where the body is deposited, and give a
token of her presence there, by a knock upon her coffin; it was therefore
determined to make this trial of the existence or veracity of the supposed spirit.

'While they were enquiring and deliberating, they were summoned into
the girl's chamber by some ladies who were near her bed, and who had
heard knocks and scratches. When the gentlemen entered, the girl declared
that she felt the spirit like a mouse upon her back, and was required to hold
her hands out of bed. From that time, though the spirit was very solemnly
required to manifest its existence by appearance, by impression on the hand
or body of any present, by scratches, knocks, or any other agency, no evidence
of any preternatural power was exhibited.

'The spirit was then very seriously advertised that the person to whom
the promise was made of striking the coffin, was then about to visit the
vault, and that the performance of the promise was then claimed. The
company at one o'clock went into the church, and the gentleman to whom
the promise was made, went with another into the vault. The spirit was
solemnly required to perform its promise, but nothing more than silence
ensued: the person supposed to be accused by the spirit, then went down
with several others, but no effect was perceived. Upon their return they
examined the girl, but could draw no confession from her. Between two
and three she desired and was permitted to go home with her father.

'It is, therefore, the opinion of the whole assembly, that the child has some
art of making or counterfeiting a particular noise, and that there is no
agency of any higher cause.'

the Honourable Andrew Erskine, Mr. Dempster, and myself, had joined in writing a pamphlet, entitled, 'Critical Strictures' against it.[1] That the mildness of Dempster's disposition had, however, relented; and he had candidly said, 'We have hardly a right to abuse this tragedy; for bad as it is, how vain should either of us be to write one not near so good.' JOHNSON. 'Why no, Sir; this is not just reasoning. You *may* abuse a tragedy, though you cannot write one. You may scold a carpenter who has made you a bad table, though you cannot make a table. It is not your trade to make tables.'

When I talked to him of the paternal estate to which I was heir, he said, 'Sir, let me tell you, that to be a Scotch landlord, where you have a number of families dependent upon you, and attached to you, is, perhaps, as high a situation as humanity can arrive at. A merchant upon the 'Change of London, with a hundred thousand pounds, is nothing; an English Duke, with an immense fortune, is nothing: he has no tenants who consider themselves as under his patriarchal care, and who will follow him to the field upon an emergency.'

His notion of the dignity of a Scotch landlord had been formed upon what he had heard of the Highland Chiefs; for it is long since a lowland landlord has been so curtailed in his feudal authority, that he has little more influence over his tenants than an English landlord; and of late years most of the Highland Chiefs have destroyed, by means too well known, the princely power which they once enjoyed.

He proceeded: 'Your going abroad, Sir, and breaking off idle habits, may be of great importance to you. I would go where there are courts and learned men. There is a good deal of Spain that has not been perambulated. I would have you go thither. A man of inferiour talents to yours may furnish us with useful observations upon that country.' His supposing me, at that period of life, capable of writing an account of my travels that would deserve to be read, elated me not a little.

marginal line:
has been . . . of the
[H]

---

[1] The Critical Review, in which Mallet himself sometimes wrote, characterised this pamphlet as 'the crude efforts of envy, petulance, and self-conceit.' There being thus three epithets, we the three authours had a humourous contention how each should be appropriated.

I appeal to every impartial reader whether this faithful detail of his frankness, complacency, and kindness to a young man, a stranger and a Scotchman, does not refute the unjust opinion of the harshness of his general demeanour. His occasional reproofs of folly, impudence, or impiety, and even the sudden sallies of his constitutional irritability of temper, which have been preserved for the poignancy of their wit, have produced that opinion among those who have not considered that such instances, though collected by Mrs. Piozzi into a small volume, and read over in a few hours, were, in fact, scattered through a long series of years: years, in which his time was chiefly spent in instructing and delighting mankind by his writings and conversation, in acts of piety to GOD, and good-will to men.

I complained to him that I had not yet acquired much knowledge; and asked his advice as to my studies. He said, 'Don't talk of study now. I will give you a plan; but it will require some time to consider of it.' 'It is very good in you (I replied,) to allow me to be with you thus. Had it been foretold to me some years ago that I should pass an evening with the authour of the RAMBLER, how should I have exulted!' What I then expressed was sincerely from the heart. He was satisfied that it was, and cordially answered, 'Sir, I am glad we have met. I hope we shall pass many evenings and mornings too, together.' We finished a couple of bottles of port, and sat till between one and two in the morning.

He wrote this year in the Critical Review the account of 'Telemachus, a Mask,' by the Reverend George Graham, of Eton College. The subject of this beautiful poem was particularly interesting to Johnson, who had much experience of 'the conflict of opposite principles,' which he describes as 'The contention between pleasure and virtue, a struggle which will always be continued while the present system of nature shall subsist; nor can history or poetry exhibit more than pleasure triumphing over virtue, and virtue subjugating pleasure.'

As Dr. Oliver Goldsmith will frequently appear in this narrative, I shall endeavour to make my readers in some degree acquainted with his singular character. He was a native of Ireland, and a contemporary with Mr. Burke, at Trinity College, Dublin, but did not then give much promise of future celebrity.[1] He, however, observed to Mr. Malone, that 'though he made no great figure in mathematicks, which was a study in much repute there, he could turn an Ode of Horace into English better than any of them.' He afterwards studied physick at Edinburgh, and upon the Continent: and I have been informed, was enabled to pursue his travels on foot, partly by demanding at Universities to enter the lists as a disputant, by which, according to the custom of many of them, he was entitled to the premium of a crown, when luckily for him his challenge was not accepted; so that, as I once observed to Dr. Johnson, he *disputed* his passage through Europe. He then came to England, and was employed successively in the capacities of an usher to an academy, a corrector of the press, a reviewer, and a writer for a newspaper. He had sagacity enough to cultivate assiduously the acquaintance of Johnson, and his faculties were gradually enlarged by the contemplation of such a model. To me and many others it appeared that he studiously copied the manner of Johnson, though, indeed, upon a smaller scale.

At this time I think he had published nothing with his name, though it was pretty generally known that *one Dr. Goldsmith* was the authour of 'An Enquiry into the present State of polite Learning in Europe,' and of 'The Citizen of the World,' a series of letters supposed to be written from London by a Chinese.[2] No man had the art of displaying with more advantage as a writer, whatever literary acquisitions he made. '*Nihil quod tetigit non ornavit.*'[3] His mind resembled a fertile, but thin soil.[a] There was a

underlined:
mind resembled, fertile, thin soil [H]

[a] *So it did.* [H]

[1] [Goldsmith got a premium at a Christmas examination in Trinity College, Dublin, which I have seen. KEARNEY.]

[A premium obtained at the Christmas examination is generally more honourable than any other, because it ascertains the person who receives it to be the first in literary merit. At the other examinations, the person thus distinguished may be only the second in merit; he who has previously obtained the same honorary reward, sometimes receiving a written certificate that *he* was the best answerer, it being a rule that not more than one premium should be adjudged to the same person in one year. See p. 220. MALONE.]

[2] [He had also published in 1759, 'THE BEE, being Essays on the most interesting subjects.' MALONE.]

[3] See his Epitaph in Westminster Abbey, written by Dr. Johnson.

quick, but not a strong vegetation, of whatever chanced
to be thrown upon it. No deep root could be struck. The
oak of the forest did not grow there; but the elegant
shrubbery and the fragrant parterre appeared in gay
succession. It has been generally circulated and believed
that he was a mere fool in conversation;[1] but, in truth,
this has been greatly exaggerated. He had, no doubt, a
more than common share of that hurry of ideas which we
often find in his countrymen, and which sometimes
produces a laughable confusion in expressing them. He
was very much what the French call *un etourdi*, and from
vanity and an eager desire of being conspicuous wherever
he was, he frequently talked carelessly without knowledge
of the subject, or even without thought. His person was
short, his countenance coarse[a] and vulgar, his deportment
that of a scholar awkwardly affecting the easy gentleman.
Those who were in any way distinguished, excited envy in
him to so ridiculous an excess, that the instances of it are
hardly credible. When accompanying two beautiful young
ladies[2] with their mother on a tour in France, he was
seriously angry that more attention was paid to them than
to him; and once at the exhibition of the *Fantoccini* in
London, when those who sat next him observed with
what dexterity a puppet was made to toss a pike, he could
not bear that it should have such praise, and exclaimed
with some warmth, 'Pshaw! I can do it better myself!'[3]

underlined:
coarse [H]

[a] *more mean than
coarse.* [H]

[1] In allusion to this, Mr. Horace Walpole, who admired his writings, said
he was 'an inspired idiot;' and Garrick described him as one

   '————— for shortness call'd Noll,
    Who wrote like an angel, and talk'd like poor Poll.'

Sir Joshua Reynolds mentioned to me that he frequently heard Goldsmith
talk warmly of the pleasure of being liked, and observe how hard it would
be if literary excellence should preclude a man from that satisfaction, which
he perceived it often did, from the envy which attended it; and therefore
Sir Joshua was convinced that he was intentionally more absurd, in order
to lessen himself in social intercourse, trusting that his character would be
sufficiently supported by his work. If it indeed was his intention to appear
absurd in company, he was often very successful. But with due deference
to Sir Joshua's ingenuity, I think the conjecture too refined.

marginal line:
*man from . . . was con-
vinced* [H]

[2] Miss Hornecks, one of whom is now married to Henry Bunbury, Esq.
and the other to Colonel Gwyn.

[3] He went home with Mr. Burke to supper; and broke his shin by attempting
to exhibit to the company how much better he could jump over a stick than
the puppets.

He, I am afraid, had no settled system of any sort, so that his conduct must not be strictly scrutinized; but his affections were social and generous, and when he had money he gave it away very liberally. His desire of imaginary consequence predominated over his attention to truth. When he began to rise into notice, he said he had a brother who was Dean of Durham,[1] a fiction so easily detected, that it is wonderful how he should have been so inconsiderate as to hazard it. He boasted to me at this time of the power of his pen in commanding money, which I believe was true in a certain degree, though in the instance he gave he was by no means correct. He told me that he had sold a novel for four hundred pounds. This was his 'Vicar of Wakefield.' But Johnson informed me, that he had made the bargain for Goldsmith, and the price was sixty pounds. 'And, Sir, (said he,) a sufficient price too, when it was sold; for then the fame of Goldsmith had not been elevated, as it afterwards was, by his "Traveller;" and the bookseller had such faint hopes of profit by his bargain, that he kept the manuscript by him a long time, and did not publish it till after the "Traveller" had appeared. Then, to be sure, it was accidentally worth more money.'

queried and underlined:
accidentally [H]

Mrs. Piozzi[2] and Sir John Hawkins[3] have strangely misstated the history of Goldsmith's situation and Johnson's friendly interference, when this novel was sold. I shall give it authentically from Johnson's own exact narration:

'I received one morning a message from poor Goldsmith that he was in great distress, and as it was not in his power to come to me, begging that I would come to him as soon as possible. I sent him a guinea, and promised to come to him directly. I accordingly went as soon as I was dressed, and found that his landlady had arrested him for his rent, at which he was in a violent passion. I perceived that he had already changed my guinea, and had got a bottle of Madeira and a glass before him. I put the cork into the bottle, desired he would be calm, and began to talk to him

---

[1] I am willing to hope that there may have been some mistake as to this anecdote, though I had it from a Dignitary of the Church. Dr. Isaac Goldsmith, his near relation, was Dean of Cloyne, in 1747.

[2] Anecdotes of Johnson, p. 119.   [3] Life of Johnson, 420.

of the means by which he might be extricated. He then
told me that he had a novel ready for the press, which he
produced to me. I looked into it, and saw its merit; told
the landlady I should soon return, and having gone to a
bookseller, sold it for sixty pounds. I brought Goldsmith
the money, and he discharged his rent, not without rating
his landlady in a high tone for having used him so ill.'[1]

marginal line:
return, and . . . money,
and [H]

My next meeting with Johnson was on Friday the 1st
of July, when he and I and Dr. Goldsmith supped at the
Mitre. I was before this time pretty well acquainted with
Goldsmith, who was one of the brightest ornaments of the
Johnsonian school. Goldsmith's respectful attachment to
Johnson was then at its height; for his own literary reputation had not yet distinguished him so much as to excite
a vain desire of competition with his great Master. He had
increased my admiration of the goodness of Johnson's
heart, by incidental remarks in the course of conversation,
such as, when I mentioned Mr. Levet, whom he entertained under his roof, 'He is poor and honest, which is
recommendation enough to Johnson;' and when I wondered that he was very kind to a man of whom I had heard
a very bad character, 'He is now become miserable, and
that insures the protection of Johnson.'

Goldsmith attempting this evening to maintain, I
suppose from an affectation of paradox, 'that knowledge
was not desirable on its own account, for it often was a
source of unhappiness.' JOHNSON. 'Why, Sir, that knowledge may in some cases produce unhappiness, I allow.
But, upon the whole, knowledge, *per se*, is certainly an

---

[1] It may not be improper to annex here Mrs. Piozzi's account of this
transaction, in her own words, as a specimen of the extreme inaccuracy
with which all her anecdotes of Dr. Johnson are related, or rather discoloured
and distorted. 'I have forgotten the year, but it could scarcely, I think, be
later than 1765 or 1766, that he was *called abruptly from our house after dinner,*
and returning *in about three hours,* said he had been with an enraged authour,
whose landlady pressed him for payment within doors, while the bailiffs
beset him without; that he was *drinking himself drunk* with Madeira, to drown
care, and fretting over a novel, which, when *finished,* was to be his *whole
fortune,* but *he could not get it done for distraction,* nor could he step out of doors
to offer it for sale. Mr. Johnson, therefore, sent away the bottle, and went
to the bookseller, recommending the performance, and *desiring some immediate
relief;* which when he brought back to the writer, *he called the woman of the
house directly to partake of punch, and pass their time in merriment.'* Anecdotes of
Dr. Johnson, p. 119.

object which every man would wish to attain, although, perhaps, he may not take the trouble necessary for attaining it.'

Dr. John Campbell, the celebrated political and biographical writer, being mentioned, Johnson said, 'Campbell is a man of much knowledge, and has a good share of imagination. His "Hermippus Redivivus" is very entertaining, as an account of Hermetick philosophy, and as furnishing a curious history of the extravagancies of the human mind. If it were merely imaginary, it would be nothing at all. Campbell is not always rigidly careful of truth in his conversation; but I do not believe there is any thing of this carelessness in his books. Campbell is a good man, a pious man. I am afraid he has not been in the inside of a church for many years;[1] but he never passes a church without pulling off his hat. This shews that he has good principles. I used to go pretty often to Campbell's on a Sunday evening, till I began to consider that the shoals of Scotchmen who flocked about him might probably say, when any thing of mine was well done, "Ay, ay, he has learnt this of CAWMELL!"'

He talked very contemptuously of Churchill's poetry, observing, that 'it had a temporary currency, only from its audacity of abuse, and being filled with living names, and that it would sink into oblivion.' I ventured to hint that he was not quite a fair judge, as Churchill had attacked him violently. JOHNSON. 'Nay, Sir, I am a very fair judge. He did not attack me violently till he found I did not like his poetry; and his attack on me shall not prevent me from continuing to say what I think of him, from an

marginal line:
Campbell is . . . I used
[H]

---

[1] I am inclined to think that he was misinformed as to this circumstance. I own I am jealous for my worthy friend Dr. John Campbell. For though Milton could without remorse absent himself from public worship, I cannot. On the contrary, I have the same habitual impressions upon my mind, with those of a truly venerable Judge, who said to Mr. Langton, 'Friend Langton, if I have not been at church on Sunday, I do not feel myself easy.' Dr. Campbell was a sincerely religious man. Lord Macartney, who is eminent for his variety of knowledge, and attention to men of talents, and knew him well, told me, that when he called on him in a morning, he found him reading a chapter in the Greek New Testament, which he informed his Lordship was his constant practice. The quantity of Dr. Campbell's composition is almost incredible, and his labours brought him large profits. Dr. Joseph Warton told me that Johnson said of him, 'He is the richest authour that ever grazed the common of literature.'

apprehension that it may be ascribed to resentment. No, Sir, I called the fellow a blockhead at first, and I will call him a blockhead still. However, I will acknowledge that I have a better opinion of him now, than I once had; for he has shewn more fertility than I expected. To be sure, he is a tree that cannot produce good fruit: he only bears crabs.[a] But Sir, a tree that produces a great many crabs is better than a tree which produces only a few.'

In this depreciation of Churchill's poetry I could not agree with him. It is very true that the greatest part of it is upon the topicks of the day, on which account, as it brought him great fame and profit at the time, it must proportionably slide out of the public attention as other occasional objects succeed. But Churchill had extra-ordinary vigour both of thought and expression. His portraits of the players will ever be valuable to the true lovers of the drama; and his strong caricatures of several eminent men of his age, will not be forgotten by the curious. Let me add, that there are in his works many passages which are of a general nature; and his 'Prophecy of Famine' is a poem of no ordinary merit. It is, indeed, falsely injurious to Scotland; but therefore may be allowed a greater share of invention.

marginal line: *of Famine . . . of invention* [H]

Bonnell Thornton had just published a burlesque 'Ode on St. Cecilia's day,' adapted to the ancient British musick, viz. the salt-box, the jews-harp, the marrow-bones and cleaver, the hum-strum or hurdy-gurdy, &c. Johnson praised its humour, and seemed much diverted with it. He repeated the following passage:

'In strains more exalted the salt-box shall join,
And clattering and battering and clapping combine;
With a rap and a tap while the hollow side sounds,
Up and down leaps the flap, and with rattling rebounds.'[1]

index sign: footnote 1 [H]

[1] [In 1769 I set for Smart and Newberry, Thornton's burlesque Ode, on St. Cecilia's day. It was performed at Ranelagh in masks, to a very crowded audience, as I was told; for I then resided in Norfolk. Beard sung the salt-box song, which was admirably accompanied on that instrument by Brent, the Fencing-master, and father of Miss Brent, the celebrated singer; Skeggs on the broomstick, as bassoon; and a remarkable performer on the Jews-harp,—'Buzzing twangs the iron lyre.' Cleavers were cast in bell-metal for this entertainment. All the performers of the old woman's Oratory, employed by Foote, were, I believe, employed at Ranelagh, on this occasion. BURNEY.]

I mentioned the periodical paper called 'THE CON-NOISSEUR.' He said it wanted matter.—No doubt it had not the deep thinking of Johnson's writings. But surely it has just views of the surface of life, and a very sprightly manner. His opinion of THE WORLD was not much higher than of the Connoisseur.

Let me here apologize for the imperfect manner in which I am obliged to exhibit Johnson's conversation at this period. In the early part of my acquaintance with him, I was so wrapt in admiration of his extraordinary colloquial talents, and so little accustomed to his peculiar mode of expression, that I found it extremely difficult to recollect and record his conversation with its genuine vigour and vivacity. In progress of time, when my mind was, as it were, *strongly impregnated with the Johnsonian æther*, I could with much more facility and exactness, carry in my memory and commit to paper the exuberant variety of his wisdom and wit.

At this time *Miss* Williams,[1] as she was then called, though she did not reside with him in the Temple under his roof, but had lodgings in Bolt-court, Fleet-street, had so much of his attention, that he every night drank tea with her before he went home, however late it might be, and she always sat up for him. This, it may be fairly conjectured, was not alone a proof of his regard for *her*, but of his own unwillingness to go into solitude, before that unseasonable hour at which he had habituated himself to expect the oblivion of repose. Dr. Goldsmith, being a privileged man, went with him this night, strutting away, and calling to me with an air of superiority, like that of an esoterick over an exoterick disciple of a sage of antiquity, 'I go to Miss Williams.' I confess, I then envied him this mighty privilege, of which he seemed so proud; but it was not long before I obtained the same mark of distinction.

On Tuesday the 5th of July, I again visited Johnson. He told me he had looked into the poems of a pretty voluminous writer, Mr. (now Dr.) John Ogilvie, one of

---

[1] [See p. 157. This lady resided in Dr. Johnson's house in Gough-square from about 1753 to 1758; and in that year, on his removing to Gray's Inn, she went into lodgings. At a subsequent period, she again became an inmate with Johnson, in Johnson's-court. MALONE.]

the Presbyterian ministers of Scotland, which had lately
come out, but could find no thinking in them. BOSWELL.
'Is there not imagination in them, Sir?' JOHNSON.'Why,
Sir, there is in them what *was* imagination, but it is no
more imagination in *him*, than sound is sound in the echo.
And his diction too is not his own. We have long ago seen
white-robed innocence, and *flower-bespangled meads*.'

Talking of London, he observed, 'Sir, if you wish to
have a just notion of the magnitude of this city, you must
not be satisfied with seeing its great streets and squares,
but must survey the innumerable little lanes and courts.[a]   [a] *very true that* is [I]
It is not in the showy evolutions of buildings, but in the
multiplicity of human habitations which are crowded
together, that the wonderful immensity of London consists.'
—I have often amused myself with thinking how different
a place London is to different people. They, whose narrow
minds are contracted to the consideration of some one
particular pursuit, view it only through that medium.
A politician thinks of it merely as the seat of government
in its different departments; a grazier, as a vast market for
cattle; a mercantile man, as a place where a prodigious
deal of business is done upon 'Change; a dramatick
enthusiast, as the grand scene of theatrical entertainments;
a man of pleasure, as an assemblage of taverns, and the
great emporium for ladies of easy virtue. But the intellectual man is struck with it, as comprehending the whole
of human life in all its variety, the contemplation of which
is inexhaustible.

On Wednesday, July 6, he was engaged to sup with me
at my lodgings in Downing-street, Westminster. But on
the preceding night my landlord having behaved very
rudely to me and some company who were with me, I had
resolved not to remain another night in his house. I was
exceedingly uneasy at the awkward appearance I supposed
I should make to Johnson and the other gentlemen whom
I had invited, not being able to receive them at home, and
being obliged to order supper at the Mitre. I went to   marginal line:
Johnson in the morning, and talked of it as of a serious   *of a . . . a twelvemonth*
distress. He laughed, and said, 'Consider, Sir, how insig-   [H]
nificant this will appear a twelvemonth hence.'—Were this
consideration to be applied to most of the little vexatious

incidents of life, by which our quiet is too often disturbed, it would prevent many painful sensations. I have tried it frequently with good effect. 'There is nothing (continued he) in this mighty misfortune; nay, we shall be better at the Mitre.' I told him that I had been at Sir John Fielding's office, complaining of my landlord, and had been informed, that though I had taken my lodgings for a year, I might, upon proof of his bad behaviour, quit them when I pleased, without being under an obligation to pay rent for any longer time than while I possessed them. The fertility of Johnson's mind could shew itself even upon so small a matter as this. 'Why, Sir, (said he,) I suppose this must be the law, since you have been told so in Bow-street. But, if your landlord could hold you to your bargain, and the lodgings should be yours for a year, you may certainly use them as you think fit. So, Sir, you may quarter two life-guardmen upon him; or you may send the greatest scoundrel you can find into your apartments; or you may say that you want to make some experiments in natural philosophy, and may burn a large quantity of assafœtida in his house.'

I had as my guests this evening at the Mitre tavern, Dr. Johnson, Dr. Goldsmith, Mr. Thomas Davies, Mr. Eccles, an Irish gentleman, for whose agreeable company I was obliged to Mr. Davies, and the Reverend Mr. John Ogilvie,[1] who was desirous of being in company with my illustrious friend, while I, in my turn, was proud to have the honour of shewing one of my countrymen upon what easy terms Johnson permitted me to live with him.

Goldsmith, as usual, endeavoured, with too much eagerness, to *shine*, and disputed very warmly with Johnson against the well known maxim of the British constitution, 'the King can do no wrong;' affirming, that 'what was morally false could not be politically true; and as the King might, in the exercise of his regal power, command

[1] The Northern bard mentioned page 298. When I asked Dr. Johnson's permission to introduce him, he obligingly agreed; adding, however, with a sly pleasantry, 'but he must give us none of his poetry.' It is remarkable that Johnson and Churchill, however much they differed in other points, agreed on this subject. See Churchill's 'Journey.' It is, however, but justice to Dr. Ogilvie to observe that his 'Day of Judgment' has no inconsiderable share of merit.

and cause the doing of what was wrong, it certainly might be said, in sense and in reason, that he could do wrong.' JOHNSON. 'Sir, you are to consider, that in our constitution, according to its true principles, the King is the head, he is supreme; he is above every thing, and there is no power by which he can be tried. Therefore, it is, Sir, that we hold the King can do no wrong; that whatever may happen to be wrong in government may not be above our reach, by being ascribed to Majesty. Redress is always to be had against oppression, by punishing the immediate agents. The King, though he should command, cannot force a Judge to condemn a man unjustly; therefore it is the Judge whom we prosecute and punish. Political institutions are formed upon the consideration of what will most frequently tend to the good of the whole, although now and then exceptions may occur. Thus it is better in general that a nation should have a supreme legislative power, although it may at times be abused. And then, Sir, there is this consideration, that *if the abuse be enormous, Nature will rise up, and claiming her original rights, overturn a corrupt political system.*' I mark this animated sentence with peculiar pleasure, as a noble instance of that truly dignified spirit of freedom which ever glowed in his heart, though he was charged with slavish tenets by superficial observers; because he was at all times indignant against that false patriotism, that pretended love of freedom, that unruly restlessness which is inconsistent with the stable authority of any good government.

This generous sentiment, which he uttered with great fervour, struck me exceedingly, and stirred my blood to that pitch of fancied resistance, the possibility of which I am glad to keep in mind, but to which I trust I never shall be forced.

'Great abilities (said he) are not requisite for an Historian; for in historical composition, all the greatest powers of the human mind are quiescent. He has facts ready to his hand; so there is no exercise of invention. Imagination is not required in any high degree; only about as much as is used in the lower kinds of poetry. Some penetration, accuracy, and colouring, will fit a man for the task, if he can give the application which is necessary.'

'Bayle's Dictionary is a very useful work for those to consult who love the biographical part of literature, which is what I love most.'

Talking of the eminent writers in Queen Anne's reign, he observed, 'I think Dr. Arbuthnot the first man among them. He was the most universal genius, being an excellent physician, a man of deep learning, and a man of much humour. Mr. Addison was, to be sure, a great man; his learning was not profound; but his morality, his humour, and his elegance of writing, set him very high.'

Mr. Ogilvie was unlucky enough to choose for the topick of his conversation the praises of his native country. He began with saying, that there was very rich land around Edinburgh. Goldsmith, who had studied physick there, contradicted this, very untruly, with a sneering laugh. Disconcerted a little by this, Mr. Ogilvie then took a new ground, where, I suppose, he thought himself perfectly safe; for he observed, that Scotland had a great many noble wild prospects. JOHNSON. 'I believe, Sir, you have a great many. Norway, too, has noble wild prospects; and Lapland is remarkable for prodigious noble wild prospects. But, Sir, let me tell you, the noblest prospect which a Scotchman ever sees, is the high road that leads him to England!' This unexpected and pointed sally produced a roar of applause. After all, however, those who admire the rude grandeur of Nature cannot deny it to Caledonia.

On Saturday, July 9, I found Johnson surrounded with a numerous levee, but have not preserved any part of his conversation. On the 14th we had another evening by ourselves at the Mitre. It happening to be a very rainy night, I made some common place observations on the relaxation of nerves and depression of spirits which such weather occasioned;[1] adding, however, that it was good for the vegetable creation. Johnson, who, as we have already seen, denied that the temperature of the air had any influence on the human frame, answered, with a smile of ridicule, 'Why, yes, Sir, it is good for vegetables, and for the animals who eat those vegetables, and for the animals who eat those animals.' This observation of his aptly

two marginal lines: *prospects. But . . . and pointed* [H]

[1] [Johnson would suffer none of his friends to fill up chasms in conversation with remarks on the weather: 'Let us not talk of the weather.' BURNEY.]

enough introduced a good supper; and I soon forgot, in
Johnson's company, the influence of a moist atmosphere.

Feeling myself now quite at ease as his companion,
though I had all possible reverence for him, I expressed a
regret that I could not be so easy with my father, though
he was not much older than Johnson, and certainly however respectable had not more learning and greater abilities
to depress me. I asked him the reason of this. JOHNSON.
'Why, Sir, I am a man of the world. I live in the world,
and I take, in some degree, the colour of the world as it
moves along. Your father is a Judge in a remote part
of the island, and all his notions are taken from the old
world. Besides, Sir, there must always be a struggle between a father and a son, while one aims at power and the
other at independence.' I said, I was afraid my father
would force me to be a lawyer. JOHNSON. 'Sir, you need
not be afraid of his forcing you to be a laborious practising
lawyer; that is not in his power. For as the proverb says,
"One man may lead a horse to the water, but twenty
cannot make him drink." He may be displeased that you
are not what he wishes you to be; but that displeasure will
not go far. If he insists only on your having as much law
as is necessary for a man of property, and then endeavours
to get you into Parliament, he is quite in the right.'

two marginal lines:
*property, and . . . the
right* [H]

He enlarged very convincingly upon the excellence of
rhyme over blank verse in English poetry. I mentioned to
him that Dr. Adam Smith, in his lectures upon composition, when I studied under him in the College of Glasgow,
had maintained the same opinion strenuously, and I
repeated some of his arguments. JOHNSON. 'Sir, I was
once in company with Smith, and we did not take to each
other; but had I known that he loved rhyme as much as
you tell me he does, I should have HUGGED him.'

underlined:
*to get you into Parlia-
ment* [H]

marginal line:
*he does . . . of Christi-
anity* [H]

Talking of those who denied the truth of Christianity,
he said, 'It is always easy to be on the negative side. If a
man were now to deny that there is salt upon the table,
you could not reduce him to an absurdity. Come, let us
try this a little further. I deny that Canada is taken, and
I can support my denial by pretty good arguments. The
French are a much more numerous people than we; and
it is not likely that they would allow us to take it. "But the

ministry have assured us, in all the formality of the
Gazette, that it is taken,"—Very true. But the ministry
have put us to an enormous expence by the war in
America, and it is their interest to persuade us that we
have got something for our money.—"But the fact is
confirmed by thousands of men who were at the taking
of it."—Ay, but these men have still more interest in
deceiving us. They don't want that you should think the
French have beat them, but that they have beat the French.
Now suppose you should go over and find that it really is
taken, that would only satisfy yourself; for when you come
home we will not believe you. We will say, you have been
bribed.—Yet, Sir, notwithstanding all these plausible
objections, we have no doubt that Canada is really ours.
Such is the weight of common testimony. How much
stronger are the evidences of the Christian religion?'

'Idleness is a disease which must be combated; but I
would not advise a rigid adherence to a particular plan
of study. I myself have never persisted in any plan for two
days together. A man ought to read just as inclination
leads him; for what he reads as a task will do him little
good. A young man should read five hours in a day, and
so may acquire a great deal of knowledge.'

To a man of vigorous intellect and ardent curiosity like
his own, reading without a regular plan may be beneficial;
though even such a man must submit to it, if he would
attain a full understanding of any of the sciences.

To such a degree of unrestrained frankness had he now
accustomed me, that in the course of this evening I talked
of the numerous reflections which had been thrown out
against him on account of his having accepted a pension
from his present Majesty. 'Why, Sir, (said he, with a
hearty laugh,) it is a mighty foolish noise that they make.[1]
I have accepted of a pension as a reward which has been
thought due to my literary merit; and now that I have this
pension, I am the same man in every respect that I have
ever been; I retain the same principles. It is true, that I
cannot now curse (smiling) the House of Hanover; nor

[1] When I mentioned the same idle clamour to him several years afterwards
he said, with a smile, 'I wish my pension were twice as large, that they
might make twice as much noise.'

would it be decent for me to drink King James's health
in the wine that King George gives me money to pay for.
But, Sir, I think that the pleasure of cursing the House
of Hanover, and drinking King James's health, are amply
overbalanced by three hundred pounds a year.'

There was here, most certainly, an affectation of more
Jacobitism than he really had; and indeed an intention
of admitting, for the moment, in a much greater extent
than it really existed, the charge of disaffection imputed
to him by the world, merely for the purpose of shewing
how dexterously he could repel an attack, even though he
were placed in the most disadvantageous position; for I
have heard him declare, that if holding up his right hand
would have secured victory at Culloden to Prince Charles's
army, he was not sure he would have held it up; so little
confidence had he in the right claimed by the house of
Stuart, and so fearful was he of the consequences of
another revolution on the throne of Great-Britain; and
Mr. Topham Beauclerk assured me, he had heard him say
this before he had his pension. At another time he said to
Mr. Langton, 'Nothing has ever offered, that has made it
worth my while to consider the question fully.' He, however, also said to the same gentleman, talking of King
James the Second, 'It was become impossible for him to
reign any longer in this country.' He no doubt had an
early attachment to the House of Stuart; but his zeal had
cooled as his reason strengthened. Indeed I heard him
once say, 'that after the death of a violent Whig, with
whom he used to contend with great eagerness, he felt his
Toryism much abated.'[1] I suppose he meant Mr. Walmsley.

Yet there is no doubt that at earlier periods he was wont
often to exercise both his pleasantry and ingenuity in
talking Jacobitism. My much respected friend, Dr.
Douglas, now Bishop of Salisbury, has favoured me with
the following admirable instance from his Lordship's own
recollection. One day when dining at old Mr. Langton's,
where Miss Roberts, his niece, was one of the company,
Johnson, with his usual complacent attention to the fair
sex, took her by the hand, and said, 'My dear, I hope you
are a Jacobite.' Old Mr. Langton, who, though a high and

[1] Journal of a Tour to the Hebrides, 3d edit. p. 420.

steady Tory, was attached to the present Royal Family, seemed offended, and asked Johnson, with great warmth, what he could mean by putting such a question to his niece? 'Why, Sir, (said Johnson) I meant no offence to your niece, I meant her a great compliment. A Jacobite, Sir, believes in the divine right of Kings. He that believes in the divine right of Kings believes in a Divinity. A Jacobite believes in the divine right of Bishops. He that believes in the divine right of Bishops believes in the divine authority of the Christian religion. Therefore, Sir, a Jacobite is neither an Atheist nor a Deist. That cannot be said of a Whig; for *Whiggism is a negation of all principle*.'[1]

He advised me, when abroad, to be as much as I could with the Professors in the Universities, and with the Clergy; for from their conversation I might expect the best accounts of every thing in whatever country I should be, with the additional advantage of keeping my learning alive.

It will be observed, that when giving me advice as to my travels, Dr. Johnson did not dwell upon cities, and palaces, and pictures, and shows, and Arcadian scenes. He was of Lord Essex's opinion, who advises his kinsman Roger Earl of Rutland, 'rather to go a hundred miles to speak with one wise man, than five miles to see a fair town.'[2]

I described to him an impudent fellow from Scotland, who affected to be a savage, and railed at all established systems. JOHNSON. 'There is nothing surprizing in this, Sir. He wants to make himself conspicuous. He would tumble in a hogstye, as long as you looked at him and called to him to come out. But let him alone, never mind him, and he'll soon give it over.'

I added that the same person maintained that there was no distinction between virtue and vice. JOHNSON. 'Why, Sir, if the fellow does not think as he speaks, he is lying; and I see not what honour he can propose to himself from

---

[1] He used to tell, with great humour, from my relation to him, the following little story of my early years, which was literally true: 'Boswell, in the year 1745, was a fine boy, wore a white cockade, and prayed for King James, till one of his uncles (General Cochran) gave him a shilling on condition that he would pray for King George, which he accordingly did. So you see (says Boswell) that *Whigs of all ages are made the same way*.'

[2] Letter to Rutland on Travel, 16mo. 1596.

having the character of a lyar. But if he does really think that there is no distinction between virtue and vice, why, Sir, when he leaves our houses let us count our spoons.'

Sir David Dalrymple, now one of the Judges of Scotland by the title of Lord Hailes, had contributed much to increase my high opinion of Johnson, on account of his writings, long before I attained to a personal acquaintance with him; I, in return, had informed Johnson of Sir David's eminent character for learning and religion; and Johnson was so much pleased, that at one of our evening meetings he gave him for his toast. I at this time kept up a very frequent correspondence with Sir David; and I read to Dr. Johnson to-night the following passage from the letter which I had last received from him:

'It gives me pleasure to think that you have obtained the friendship of Mr. Samuel Johnson. He is one of the best moral writers which England has produced. At the same time, I envy you the free and undisguised converse with such a man. May I beg you to present my best respects to him, and to assure him of the veneration which I entertain for the authour of the Rambler and of Rasselas? Let me recommend this last work to you; with the Rambler you certainly are acquainted. In Rasselas you will see a tender-hearted operator, who probes the wound only to heal it. Swift, on the contrary, mangles human nature. He cuts and slashes, as if he took pleasure in the operation, like the tyrant who said, *Ita feri ut se sentiat emori.*' Johnson seemed to be much gratified by this just and well-turned compliment.

He recommended to me to keep a journal of my life, full and unreserved. He said it would be a very good exercise, and would yield me great satisfaction when the particulars were faded from my remembrance.[a] I was uncommonly fortunate in having had a previous coincidence of opinion with him upon this subject, for I had kept such a journal for some time; and it was no small pleasure to me to have this to tell him, and to receive his approbation. He counselled me to keep it private, and said I might surely have a friend who would burn it in case of my death. From this habit I have been enabled to give the world so many anecdotes, which would otherwise have been lost

to posterity. I mentioned that I was afraid I put into my
journal too many little incidents. JOHNSON. 'There is
nothing, Sir, too little for so little a creature as man. It
is by studying little things that we attain the great art of
having as little misery and as much happiness as possible.'

Next morning Mr. Dempster happened to call on me,
and was so much struck even with the imperfect account
which I gave him of Dr. Johnson's conversation, that to
his honour be it recorded, when I complained that drinking port and sitting up late with him, affected my nerves
for some time after, he said, 'One had better be palsied
at eighteen than not keep company with such a man.'

On Tuesday, July 18, I found tall Sir Thomas Robinson
sitting with Johnson. Sir Thomas said, that the King of
Prussia valued himself upon three things;—upon being a
hero, a musician, and an authour. JOHNSON. 'Pretty
well, Sir, for one man. As to his being an authour, I have
not looked at his poetry; but his prose is poor stuff. He
writes just as you may suppose Voltaire's footboy to do,
who has been his amanuensis. He has such parts as the
valet might have, and about as much of the colouring of
the style as might be got by transcribing his works.' When
I was at Ferney, I repeated this to Voltaire, in order to
reconcile him somewhat to Johnson, whom he, in affecting
the English mode of expression, had previously characterised as 'a superstitious dog;' but after hearing such a
criticism on Frederick the Great, with whom he was then
on bad terms, he exclaimed, 'An honest fellow!'

marginal line:
Frederick the
on bad [H]

But I think the criticism much too severe; for the
'Memoirs of the House of Brandenburgh' are written as
well as many works of that kind. His poetry, for the style
of which he himself makes a frank apology, '*Jargonnant un
François barbare*,' though fraught with pernicious ravings
of infidelity, has, in many places, great animation, and in
some a pathetick tenderness.

Upon this contemptuous animadversion on the King of
Prussia, I observed to Johnson, 'It would seem then, Sir,
that much less parts are necessary to make a King, than
to make an Authour: for the King of Prussia is confessedly
the greatest King now in Europe, yet you think he makes
a very poor figure as an Authour.'

Mr. Levet this day shewed me Dr. Johnson's library, which was contained in two garrets over his Chambers, where Lintot, son of the celebrated bookseller of that name, had formerly his warehouse. I found a number of good books, but very dusty and in great confusion. The floor was strewed with manuscript leaves, in Johnson's own hand-writing, which I beheld with a degree of veneration, supposing they perhaps might contain portions of the Rambler, or of Rasselas. I observed an apparatus for chymical experiments, of which Johnson was all his life very fond. The place seemed to be very favourable for retirement and meditation. Johnson told me, that he went up thither without mentioning it to his servant when he wanted to study, secure from interruption; for he would not allow his servant to say he was not at home when he really was. 'A servant's strict regard for truth, (said he) must be weakened by such a practice. A philosopher may know that it is merely a form of denial; but few servants are such nice distinguishers. If I accustom a servant to tell a lie for *me*, have I not reason to apprehend that he will tell many lies for *himself?*' I am, however, satisfied that every servant, of any degree of intelligence, understands saying his master is not at home, not at all as the affirmation of a fact, but as customary words, intimating that his master wishes not to be seen; so that there can be no bad effect from it.

Mr. Temple now vicar of St. Gluvias, Cornwall, who had been my intimate friend for many years, had at this time chambers in Farrar's-buildings, at the bottom of Inner Temple-lane, which he kindly lent me upon my quitting my lodgings, he being to return to Trinity Hall, Cambridge. I found them particularly convenient for me, as they were so near Dr. Johnson's.

On Wednesday, July 20, Dr. Johnson, Mr. Dempster, and my uncle Dr. Boswell, who happened to be now in London, supped with me at these Chambers. JOHNSON. 'Pity is not natural to man. Children are always cruel. Savages are always cruel. Pity is acquired and improved by the cultivation of reason. We may have uneasy sensations from seeing a creature in distress, without pity; for we have not pity unless we wish to relieve them. When

I am on my way to dine with a friend, and finding it late, have bid the coachman make haste, if I happen to attend when he whips his horses, I may feel unpleasantly that the animals are put to pain, but I do not wish him to desist. No, Sir, I wish him to drive on.'

Mr. Alexander Donaldson, bookseller, of Edinburgh, had for some time opened a shop in London, and sold his cheap editions of the most popular English books, in defiance of the supposed common-law right of *Literary Property*. Johnson, though he concurred in the opinion which was afterwards sanctioned by a judgement of the House of Lords, that there was no such right, was at this time very angry that the Booksellers of London, for whom he uniformly professed much regard, should suffer from an invasion of what they had ever considered to be secure; and he was loud and violent against Mr. Donaldson. 'He is a fellow who takes advantage of the law to injure his brethren; for notwithstanding that the statute secures only fourteen years of exclusive right, it has always been understood by the *trade*, that he, who buys the copy-right of a book from the authour, obtains a perpetual property; and upon that belief, numberless bargains are made to transfer that property after the expiration of the statutory term. Now Donaldson, I say, takes advantage here, of people who have really an equitable title from usage; and if we consider how few of the books, of which they buy the property, succeed so well as to bring profit, we should be of opinion that the term of fourteen years is too short; it should be sixty years.' DEMPSTER. 'Donaldson, Sir, is anxious for the encouragement of literature. He reduces the price of books, so that poor students may buy them.' JOHNSON, (laughing) 'Well, Sir, allowing that to be his motive, he is no better than Robin Hood, who robbed the rich in order to give to the poor.'

It is remarkable, that when the great question concerning Literary Property came to be ultimately tried before the supreme tribunal of this country, in consequence of the very spirited exertions of Mr. Donaldson, Dr. Johnson was zealous against a perpetuity; but he thought that the term of the exclusive right of authours should be considerably enlarged. He was then for granting a hundred years.

marginal line:
enlarged. He . . .
hundred years [H]

The conversation now turned upon Mr. David Hume's style. JOHNSON. 'Why, Sir, his style is not English; the structure of his sentences is French. Now the French structure and the English structure may, in the nature of things, be equally good. But if you allow that the English language is established, he is wrong. My name might originally have been Nicholson, as well as Johnson; but were you to call me Nicholson now, you would call me very absurdly.'

Rousseau's treatise on the inequality of mankind was at this time a fashionable topick. It gave rise to an observation by Mr. Dempster, that the advantages of fortune and rank were nothing to a wise man, who ought to value only merit. JOHNSON. 'If man were a savage, living in the woods by himself, this might be true; but in civilized society we all depend upon each other, and our happiness is very much owing to the good opinion of mankind. Now, Sir, in civilized society, external advantages make us more respected. A man with a good coat upon his back meets with a better reception than he who has a bad one. Sir, you may analyse this, and say what is there in it? But that will avail you nothing, for it is a part of a general system. Pound St. Paul's church into atoms, and consider any single atom; it is, to be sure, good for nothing: but, put all these atoms together, and you have St. Paul's church. So it is with human felicity, which is made up of many ingredients, each of which may be shewn to be very insignificant. In civilized society, personal merit will not serve you so much as money will. Sir, you may make the experiment. Go into the street, and give one man a lecture on morality, and another a shilling, and see which will respect you most. If you wish only to support nature, Sir William Petty fixes your allowance at three pounds a year; but as times are much altered, let us call it six pounds. This sum will fill your belly, shelter you from the weather, and even get you a strong lasting coat, supposing it to be made of good bull's hide. Now, Sir, all beyond this is artificial, and is desired in order to obtain a greater degree of respect from our fellow-creatures. And, Sir, if six hundred pounds a year procure a man more consequence, and, of course, more happiness than six pounds a year, the same proportion

queried:
Now, Sir etc. [H]

queried:
the same proportion etc.
[H]

will hold as to six thousand, and so on, as far as opu-
lence can be carried. Perhaps he who has a large
fortune may not be so happy as he who has a small one;
but that must proceed from other causes than from his
having the large fortune: for, *cæteris paribus*, he who is rich
in a civilized society, must be happier than he who is
poor; as riches, if properly used, (and it is a man's own
fault if they are not,) must be productive of the highest
advantages. Money, to be sure, of itself is of no use; for
its only use is to part with it. Rousseau, and all those who
deal in paradoxes, are led away by a childish desire of
novelty.[1] When I was a boy, I used always to choose the
wrong side of a debate, because most ingenious things,
that is to say, most new things, could be said upon it. Sir,
there is nothing for which you may not muster up more
plausible arguments, than those which are urged against
wealth and other external advantages. Why, now, there is
stealing; why should it be thought a crime? When we
consider by what unjust methods property has been often
acquired, and that what was unjustly got it must be unjust
to keep, where is the harm in one man's taking the
property of another from him?[a] Besides, Sir, when we
consider the bad use that many people make of their
property, and how much better use the thief may make of
it, it may be defended as a very allowable practice. Yet,
Sir, the experience of mankind has discovered stealing to
be so very bad a thing, that they make no scruple to hang
a man for it. When I was running about this town a very
poor fellow, I was a great arguer for the advantages of
poverty; but I was, at the same time, very sorry to be poor.
Sir, all the arguments which are brought to represent
poverty as no evil, shew it to be evidently a great evil.
You never find people labouring to convince you that
you may live very happily upon a plentiful fortune.—So
you hear people talking how miserable a King must be;
and yet they all wish to be in his place.'

It was suggested that Kings must be unhappy, because

[a] *The Democrats talk this very Talk now.* [I]

---

[1] [Johnson told Dr. Burney that Goldsmith said, when he first began to
write, he determined to commit to paper nothing but what was *new*; but
he afterwards found that what was *new* was generally false, and from that
time was no longer solicitous about novelty. BURNEY.]

they are deprived of the greatest of all satisfactions, easy and unreserved society. JOHNSON. 'That is an ill-founded notion. Being a King does not exclude a man from such society. Great Kings have always been social. The King of Prussia, the only great King at present, is very social. Charles the Second, the last King of England who was a man of parts, was social; and our Henrys and Edwards were all social.'

Mr. Dempster having endeavoured to maintain that intrinsick merit *ought* to make the only distinction amongst mankind. JOHNSON. 'Why, Sir, mankind have found that this cannot be. How shall we determine the proportion of intrinsick merit? Were that to be the only distinction amongst mankind, we should soon quarrel about the degrees of it. Were all distinctions abolished, the strongest would not long acquiesce, but would endeavour to obtain a superiority by their bodily strength. But, Sir, as subordination is very necessary for society, and contentions for superiority very dangerous, mankind, that is to say, all civilized nations, have settled it upon a plain invariable principle. A man is born to hereditary rank; or his being appointed to certain offices, gives him a certain rank. Subordination tends greatly to human happiness. Were we all upon an equality, we should have no other enjoyment than mere animal pleasure.'

I said, I considered distinction of rank to be of so much importance in civilized society, that if I were asked on the same day to dine with the first Duke in England, and with the first man in Britain for genius, I should hesitate which to prefer. JOHNSON. 'To be sure, Sir, if you were to dine only once, and it were never to be known where you dined, you would choose rather to dine with the first man for genius; but to gain most respect, you should dine with the first Duke in England. For nine people in ten that you meet with, would have a higher opinion of you for having dined with a Duke; and the great genius himself would receive you better, because you had been with the great Duke.'

He took care to guard himself against any possible suspicion that his settled principles of reverence for rank and respect for wealth were at all owing to mean or interested motives; for he asserted his own independence as a literary man. 'No man (said he) who ever lived by literature, has lived more independently than I have done.' He said he had taken longer time than he needed to have done in composing his Dictionary. He received our compliments upon that great work with complacency, and told us that the Academy *della Crusca* could scarcely believe that it was done by one man.

Next morning I found him alone, and have preserved the following fragments of his conversation. Of a gentleman who was mentioned, he said, 'I have not met with any man for a long time who has given me such general displeasure. He is totally unfixed in his principles, and wants to puzzle other people.' I said his principles had been poisoned by a noted infidel writer, but that he was, nevertheless, a benevolent good man. JOHNSON. 'We can have no dependance upon that instinctive, that constitutional goodness which is not founded upon principle. I grant you that such a man may be a very amiable member of society. I can conceive him placed in such a situation that he is not much tempted to deviate from what is right; and as every man prefers virtue, when there is not some strong incitement to transgress its precepts, I can conceive him doing nothing wrong. But if such a man[a] stood in need of money, I should not like to trust him; and I should certainly not trust him with young ladies, for *there* there is always temptation. Hume, and other sceptical innovators, are vain men, and will gratify themselves at any expence. Truth will not afford sufficient food to their vanity; so they have betaken themselves to errour. Truth, Sir, is a cow which will yield such people no more milk, and so they are gone to milk the bull. If I could have allowed myself to gratify my vanity at the expence of truth, what fame might I have acquired. Every thing which Hume has advanced against Christianity had passed through my mind long before he wrote. Always remember this, that after a system is well settled upon positive evidence, a few partial objections ought not to shake it. The human mind is so limited, that it cannot take in all the parts of a subject, so that there may be objections raised against any thing. There are objections against a

[a] *I fancy this was Seward who wrote the Anecdotes.* [H]

plenum, and objections against a *vacuum;* yet one of them must certainly be true.'

I mentioned Hume's argument against the belief of miracles, that it is more probable that the witnesses to the truth of them are mistaken, or speak falsely, than that the miracles should be true. JOHNSON. 'Why, Sir, the great difficulty of proving miracles should make us very cautious in believing them. But let us consider; although GOD has made Nature to operate by certain fixed laws, yet it is not unreasonable to think that he may suspend those laws, in order to establish a system highly advantageous to mankind. Now the Christian Religion is a most beneficial system, as it gives us light and certainty where we were before in darkness and doubt. The miracles which prove it are attested by men who had no interest in deceiving us; but who, on the contrary, were told that they should suffer persecution, and did actually lay down their lives in confirmation of the truth of the facts which they asserted. Indeed, for some centuries the heathens did not pretend to deny the miracles; but said they were performed by the aid of evil spirits. This is a circumstance of great weight. Then, Sir, when we take the proofs derived from prophecies which have been so exactly fulfilled, we have most satisfactory evidence. Supposing a miracle possible, as to which, in my opinion, there can be no doubt, we have as strong evidence for the miracles in support of Christianity, as the nature of the thing admits.'

At night, Mr. Johnson and I supped in a private room at the Turk's Head coffee-house, in the Strand. 'I encourage this house (said he,) for the mistress of it is a good civil woman, and has not much business.'

'Sir, I love the acquaintance of young people; because, in the first place, I don't like to think myself growing old. In the next place, young acquaintances must last longest, if they do last; and then, Sir, young men have more virtue than old men; they have more generous sentiments in every respect. I love the young dogs of this age, they have more wit and humour and knowledge of life than we had; but then the dogs are not so good scholars. Sir, in my early years I read very hard. It is a sad reflection, but a true one, that I knew almost as much at eighteen as

I do now.[1] My judgement, to be sure, was not so good; but I had all the facts. I remember very well, when I was at Oxford, an old gentleman said to me, "Young man, ply your book diligently now, and acquire a stock of knowledge; for when years come upon you, you will find that poring upon books will be but an irksome task."'

This account of his reading, given by himself in plain words, sufficiently confirms what I have already advanced upon the disputed question as to his application. It reconciles any seeming inconsistency in his way of talking upon it at different times; and shews that idleness and reading hard were with him relative terms, the import of which, as used by him, must be gathered from a comparison with what scholars of different degrees of ardour and assiduity have been known to do. And let it be remembered, that he was now talking spontaneously, and expressing his genuine sentiments; whereas at other times he might be induced, from his spirit of contradiction, or more properly from his love of argumentative contest, to speak lightly of his own application to study. It is pleasing to consider that the old gentleman's gloomy prophecy as to the irksomeness of books to men of an advanced age, which is too often fulfilled,[a] was so far from being verified in Johnson, that his ardour for literature never failed, and his last writings had more ease and vivacity than any of his earlier productions.

[a] not in me at 80 years old . . . being griev'd that Year particularly, I was forced upon Study to relieve my Mind, and it had the due Effect in 1819 . . . I write this Note in 1820. [H]

He mentioned to me now, for the first time, that he had been distressed by melancholy, and for that reason had been obliged to fly from study and meditation to the dissipating variety of life. Against melancholy he recommended constant occupation of mind, a great deal of exercise, moderation in eating and drinking, and especially to shun drinking at night. He said melancholy people were apt to fly to intemperance for relief, but that it sunk them much deeper in misery. He observed, that labouring men[b] who work hard, and live sparingly, are seldom or never troubled with low spirits.

underlined:
labouring men [I]
[b] we never ask such Men whether They are low spirited or not. [I]

He again insisted on the duty of maintaining subordination of rank. 'Sir, I would no more deprive a nobleman

[1] [His great period of study was from the age of twelve to that of eighteen as he told Mr. Langton, who gave me this information. MALONE.]

of his respect, than of his money. I consider myself as acting a part in the great system of society, and I do to others as I would have them to do to me. I would behave to a nobleman as I should expect he would behave to me, were I a nobleman and he Sam. Johnson. Sir, there is one Mrs. Macaulay[1] in this town, a great republican. One day when I was at her house, I put on a very grave countenance, and said to her, "Madam, I am now become a convert to your way of thinking. I am convinced that all mankind are upon an equal footing; and to give you an unquestionable proof, Madam, that I am in earnest, here is a very sensible, civil, well-behaved fellow-citizen, your footman; I desire that he may be allowed to sit down and dine with us." I thus, Sir, shewed her the absurdity of the levelling doctrine. She has never liked me since. Sir, your levellers wish to level *down* as far as themselves; but they cannot bear levelling *up* to themselves. They would all have some people under them; why not then have some people above them?' I mentioned a certain authour who disgusted me by his forwardness, and by shewing no deference to noblemen into whose company he was admitted. JOHNSON. 'Suppose a shoemaker should claim an equality with him, as he does with a Lord: how he would stare. "Why, Sir, do you stare? (says the shoemaker,) I do great service to society. 'Tis true, I am paid for doing it; but so are you, Sir: and I am sorry to say it, better paid than I am, for doing something not so necessary. For mankind could do better without your books, than without my shoes." Thus, Sir, there would be a perpetual struggle for precedence, were there no fixed invariable rules for the distinction of rank, which creates no jealousy, as it is allowed to be accidental.'

He said, Dr. Joseph Warton was a very agreeable man, and his 'Essay on the Genius and Writings of Pope,' a very pleasing book. I wondered that he delayed so long to give us the continuation of it. JOHNSON. 'Why, Sir, I suppose he finds himself a little disappointed, in not having been able to persuade the world to be of his opinion as to Pope.'[a]

We have now been favoured with the concluding volume,

marginal line: *desire that . . . of the* [H]

marginal line: *distinction of . . . is allowed* [H]

[a] *Just so.* [H]

---

[1] This *one* Mrs. Macaulay was the same personage who afterwards made herself so much known as 'the celebrated female historian.'

in which, to use a parliamentary expression, he has *explained*, so as not to appear quite so adverse to the opinion of the world, concerning Pope, as was at first thought; and we must all agree, that his work is a most valuable accession to English literature.

A writer of deserved eminence being mentioned, Johnson said; 'Why, Sir, he is a man of good parts, but being originally poor, he has got a love of mean company and low jocularity; a very bad thing, Sir. To laugh is good, and to talk is good. But you ought no more to think it enough if you laugh, than you are to think it enough if you talk. You may laugh in as many ways as you talk; and surely *every* way of talking that is practised cannot be esteemed.'

I spoke of Sir James Macdonald as a young man of most distinguished merit, who united the highest reputation at Eton and Oxford, with the patriarchal spirit of a great Highland Chieftain. I mentioned that Sir James had said to me, that he had never seen Mr. Johnson, but he had a great respect for him, though at the same time it was mixed with some degree of terrour. JOHNSON. 'Sir, if he were to be acquainted with me, it might lessen both.'

The mention of this gentleman led us to talk of the Western Islands of Scotland, to visit which he expressed a wish that then appeared to me a very romantick fancy, which I little thought would be afterwards realised. He told me, that his father had put Martin's account of those islands into his hands when he was very young, and that he was highly pleased with it; that he was particularly struck with the St. Kilda man's notion that the high church of Glasgow had been hollowed out of a rock; a circumstance to which old Mr. Johnson had directed his attention. He said, he would go to the Hebrides with me, when I returned from my travels, unless some very good companion should offer when I was absent, which he did not think probable; adding, 'There are few people whom I take so much to, as you.' And when I talked of my leaving England, he said with a very affectionate air, 'My dear Boswell, I should be very unhappy at parting, did I think we were not to meet again.'—I cannot too often remind my readers, that although such instances of his kindness are doubtless very flattering to me, yet I hope my recording them will be ascribed to a better motive than to vanity; for they afford unquestionable evidence of his tenderness and complacency, which some, while they were forced to acknowledge his great powers, have been so strenuous to deny.

He maintained that a boy at school was the happiest of human beings. I supported a different opinion, from which I have never yet varied, that a man is happier: and I enlarged upon the anxiety and sufferings which are endured at school.[a] JOHNSON. 'Ah! Sir, a boy's being flogged is not so severe as a man's having the hiss of the world against him. Men have a solicitude about fame; and the greater share they have of it, the more afraid they are of losing it.' I silently asked myself, 'Is it possible that the great SAMUEL JOHNSON really entertains any such apprehension, and is not confident that his exalted fame is established upon a foundation never to be shaken?'

He this evening drank a bumper to Sir David Dalrymple, 'as a man of worth, a scholar, and a wit.' 'I have (said he) never heard of him, except from you; but let him know my opinion of him: for as he does not shew himself much in the world, he should have the praise of the few who hear of him.'

On Tuesday, July 26, I found Mr. Johnson alone. It was a very wet day, and I again complained of the disagreeable effects of such weather. JOHNSON. 'Sir, this is all imagination, which physicians encourage; for man lives in air, as a fish lives in water; so that if the atmosphere press heavy from above, there is an equal resistance from below. To be sure, bad weather is hard upon people who are obliged to be abroad; and men cannot labour so well in the open air in bad weather, as in good; but, Sir, a smith or a taylor, whose work is within doors, will surely do as much in rainy weather, as in fair. Some very delicate frames, indeed, may be affected by wet weather; but not common constitutions.'

We talked of the education of children; and I asked him what he thought was best to teach them first. JOHNSON. 'Sir, it is no matter what you teach them first, any more than what leg you shall put into your breeches first. Sir,

queried:
He maintained etc. [H]

[a] *They are neither of 'em happy but as their Minds are torpid to Sensations of Misery. I had a 1st. Cousin Sir R. S. Cotton, he went thro' Westmr. School without ever receiving a Blow or a rough Word from Master or fellow Student—I know he did; How he went thro' Life I do not know . . . but I fancy very easily. He was a dull Fellow, & a severe Husband: Father to the 1st. Lord Combermere. That he was happy I have no great Notion.* [H]

queried:
Sir, this etc. [H]

queried: *Sir, it is* etc. [H]

you may stand disputing which is best to put in first, but in the mean time your breech is bare. Sir, while you are considering which of two things you should teach your child first, another boy has learnt them both.'

On Thursday, July 28, we again supped in private at the Turk's Head coffee-house. JOHNSON. 'Swift has a higher reputation than he deserves. His excellence is strong sense; for his humour, though very well, is not remarkably good. I doubt whether the "Tale of a Tub" be his; for he never owned it, and it is much above his usual manner.'[1]

'Thomson, I think, had as much of the poet about him as most writers. Every thing appeared to him through the medium of his favourite pursuit. He could not have viewed those two candles burning but with a poetical eye.'

a Burke perhaps [H]

'Has not ——ᵃ a great deal of wit, Sir?' JOHNSON. 'I do not think so, Sir. He is, indeed, continually attempting wit, but he fails. And I have no more pleasure in hearing a man attempting wit and failing, than in seeing a man trying to leap over a ditch and tumbling into it.'ᵇ

b Murphy used to say Johnson hates an Endeavouring Man. [I]

marginal line:
Why, Sir . . . of stupidity [H]

He laughed heartily when I mentioned to him a saying of his concerning Mr. Thomas Sheridan, which Foote took a wicked pleasure to circulate. 'Why, Sir, Sherry is dull, naturally dull; but it must have taken him a great deal of pains to become what we now see him. Such an excess of stupidity, Sir, is not in Nature.'—'So (said he,) I allowed him all his own merit.'

He now added, 'Sheridan cannot bear me. I bring his declamation to a point. I ask him a plain question, "What do you mean to teach?" Besides, Sir, what influence can Mr. Sheridan have upon the language of this great country, by his narrow exertions? Sir, it is burning a farthing candle at Dover, to shew light at Calais.'

Talking of a young man who was uneasy from thinking that he was very deficient in learning and knowledge, he said, 'A man has no reason to complain who holds a middle place, and has many below him: and perhaps he has not six of his years above him;—perhaps not one. Though he may not know any thing perfectly, the general mass of

---

[1] This opinion was given by him more at large at a subsequent period. See 'Journal of a Tour to the Hebrides,' 3d edit. p. 32.

knowledge that he has acquired is considerable. Time will do for him all that is wanting.'

The conversation then took a philosophical turn. JOHNSON. 'Human experience, which is constantly contradicting theory, is the great test of truth. A system, built upon the discoveries of a great many minds, is always of more strength, than what is produced by the mere workings of any one mind, which, of itself, can do little. There is not so poor a book in the world that would not be a prodigious effort were it wrought out entirely by a single mind, without the aid of prior investigators. The French writers are superficial, because they are not scholars, and so proceed upon the mere power of their own minds; and we see how very little power they have.'

'As to the Christian Religion, Sir, besides the strong evidence which we have for it, there is a balance in its favour from the number of great men who have been convinced of its truth, after a serious consideration of the question. Grotius was an acute man, a lawyer, a man accustomed to examine evidence, and he was convinced. Grotius was not a recluse, but a man of the world, who certainly had no bias to the side of religion. Sir Isaac Newton set out an infidel, and came to be a very firm believer.'

He this evening again recommended to me to perambulate Spain.[1] I said it would amuse him to get a letter from me dated at Salamancha. JOHNSON. 'I love the University of Salamancha; for when the Spaniards were in doubt as to the lawfulness of their conquering America, the University of Salamancha gave it as their opinion that it was not lawful.' He spoke this with great emotion, and with that generous warmth which dictated the lines in his 'London,' against Spanish encroachment.

marginal line: *their conquering . . . not lawful* [H]

I expressed my opinion of my friend Derrick as but a poor writer. JOHNSON. 'To be sure, Sir, he is: but you are to consider that his being a literary man has got for him all that he has. It has made him King of Bath. Sir,

---

[1] I fully intended to have followed advice of such weight; but having staid much longer both in Germany and Italy than I proposed to do, and having also visited Corsica, I found that I had exceeded the time allowed me by my father, and hastened to France in my way homewards.

he has nothing to say for himself but that he is a writer. Had he not been a writer, he must have been sweeping the crossings in the streets, and asking halfpence from
^a *Comical enough.* [H] every body that past.'^a

In justice, however, to the memory of Mr. Derrick, who was my first tutor in the ways of London, and shewed me the town in all its variety of departments both literary and sportive, the particulars of which Dr. Johnson advised me to put in writing, it is proper to mention what Johnson, at a subsequent period, said of him both as a writer and an editor: 'Sir, I have often said, that if Derrick's letters had been written by one of a more established name, they would have been thought very pretty letters.'[1] And, 'I sent Derrick to Dryden's relations to gather materials for his life; and I believe he got all that I myself should have got.'[2]

Poor Derrick! I remember him with kindness. Yet I cannot withhold from my readers a pleasant humourous sally which could not have hurt him had he been alive, and now is perfectly harmless. In his collection of poems, there is one upon entering the harbour of Dublin, his native city, after a long absence. It begins thus:

> 'Eblana! much lov'd city, hail!
>   Where first I saw the light of day.'

And after a solemn reflection on his being 'numbered with forgotten dead,' there is the following stanza:

> 'Unless my lines protract my fame,
>   And those, who chance to read them, cry,
> I knew him! Derrick was his name,
>   In yonder tomb his ashes lie.'

which was thus happily parodied by Mr. John Home, to whom we owe the beautiful and pathetick tragedy of 'Douglas:'

> 'Unless my *deeds* protract my fame,
>   *And he who passes sadly sings,*
> I knew him! Derrick was his name,
>   *On yonder tree his carcase swings!*'

[1] Journal of a Tour to the Hebrides, 2d edit. p. 104.   [2] Ibid. p. 142.

I doubt much whether the amiable and ingenious authour of these burlesque lines will recollect them; for they were produced extempore one evening while he and I were walking together in the dining room at Eglingtoune Castle, in 1760, and I have never mentioned them to him since.

Johnson said once to me, 'Sir, I honour Derrick for his presence of mind. One night, when Floyd,[1] another poor authour, was wandering about the streets in the night, he found Derrick fast asleep upon a bulk; upon being suddenly waked, Derrick started up, "My dear Floyd, I am sorry to see you in this destitute state: will you go home with me to *my lodgings?*"'

I again begged his advice as to my method of study at Utrecht. 'Come, (said he) let us make a day of it. Let us go down to Greenwich and dine, and talk of it there.' The following Saturday was fixed for this excursion.

As we walked along the Strand to-night, arm in arm, a woman of the town accosted us, in the usual enticing manner. 'No, no, my girl, (said Johnson) it won't do.' He, however, did not treat her with harshness; and we talked of the wretched life of such women, and agreed, that much more misery than happiness, upon the whole, is produced by illicit commerce between the sexes.

On Saturday, July 30, Dr. Johnson and I took a sculler at the Temple-stairs, and set out for Greenwich. I asked him if he really thought a knowledge of the Greek and Latin languages an essential requisite to a good education. JOHNSON. 'Most certainly, Sir; for those who know them have a very great advantage over those who do not. Nay, Sir, it is wonderful what a difference learning makes upon people even in the common intercourse of life, which does not appear to be much connected with it.' 'And yet, (said I) people go through the world very well, and carry on the business of life to good advantage, without learning.' JOHNSON. 'Why, Sir, that may be true in cases where learning cannot possibly be of any use; for instance, this boy rows us as well without learning, as if he could sing the song of Orpheus to the Argonauts, who were the first

---

[1] He published a biographical work, containing an account of eminent writers, in 3 vols. 8vo.

sailors.' He then called to the boy, 'What would you give, my lad, to know about the Argonauts?' 'Sir (said the boy), I would give what I have.' Johnson was much pleased with his answer, and we gave him a double fare. Dr. Johnson then turning to me, 'Sir, (said he) a desire of knowledge is the natural feeling of mankind; and every human being whose mind is not debauched, will be willing to give all that he has, to get knowledge.'

We landed at the Old Swan, and walked to Billingsgate, where we took oars and moved smoothly along the silver Thames. It was a very fine day. We were entertained with the immense number and variety of ships that were lying at anchor, and with the beautiful country on each side of the river.

I talked of preaching, and of the great success which those called methodists[1] have. JOHNSON. 'Sir, it is owing to their expressing themselves in a plain and familiar

marginal line:
the University . . . devout exercises [H]

[1] All who are acquainted with the history of religion, (the most important, surely, that concerns the human mind,) know that the appellation of *Methodists* was first given to a society of students in the University of Oxford, who about the year 1730, were distinguished by an earnest and *methodical* attention to devout exercises. This disposition of mind is not a novelty, or peculiar to any sect, but has been and still may be found, in many Christians of every denomination. Johnson himself was in a dignified manner, a Methodist. In his Rambler, No. 110, he mentions with respect 'the whole discipline of regulated piety;' and in his 'Prayers and Meditations,' many instances occur of his anxious examination into his spiritual state. That this religious earnestness, and in particular an observation of the influence of the Holy Spirit, has sometimes degenerated into folly, and sometimes been counterfeited for base purposes, cannot be denied. But it is not, therefore, fair to decry it when genuine. The principal argument in reason and good sense against methodism is, that it tends to debase human nature, and prevent the generous exertions of goodness, by an unworthy supposition that GOD will pay no regard to them; although it is positively said in the scriptures, that he 'will reward every man according to his works.' But I am happy to have it in my power to do justice to those whom it is the fashion to ridicule, without any knowledge of their tenets; and this I can do by quoting a passage from one of their best apologists, Mr. Milner, who thus expresses their doctrine upon this subject: 'Justified by faith, renewed in his faculties, and constrained by the love of Christ, their believer moves in the sphere of love and gratitude, and all his *duties* flow more or less from this principle. And though *they are accumulating for him in heaven a treasure of bliss proportioned to his faithfulness and activity, and it is by no means inconsistent with his principles to feel the force of this consideration,* yet love itself sweetens every duty to his mind; and he thinks there is no absurdity in his feeling the love of GOD as the grand commanding principle of his life.' *Essays on several religious Subjects, &c., by Joseph Milner, A. M. Master of the Grammar School of Kingston-upon-Hull,* 1789, *p.* 11.

manner, which is the only way to do good to the common people, and which clergymen of genius and learning ought to do from a principle of duty, when it is suited to their congregations; a practice, for which they will be praised by men of sense. To insist against drunkenness as a crime, because it debases reason, the noblest faculty of man, would be of no service to the common people; but to tell them that they may die in a fit of drunkenness, and shew them how dreadful that would be, cannot fail to make a deep impression. Sir, when your Scotch clergy give up their homely manner, religion will soon decay in that country.' Let this observation, as Johnson meant it, be ever remembered.

I was much pleased to find myself with Johnson at Greenwich, which he celebrates in his 'London' as a favourite scene. I had the poem in my pocket, and read the lines aloud with enthusiasm:

'On Thames's banks in silent thought we stood,
Where Greenwich smiles upon the silver flood:
Pleas'd with the seat which gave ELIZA birth,
We kneel, and kiss the consecrated earth.'

He remarked that the structure of Greenwich hospital was too magnificent for a place of charity, and that its parts were too much detached, to make one great whole.

Buchanan, he said, was a very fine poet; and observed, that he was the first who complimented a lady, by ascribing to her the different perfections of the heathen goddesses;[1] but that Johnston improved upon this, by making his lady, at the same time, free from their defects.

He dwelt upon Buchanan's elegant verses to Mary, Queen of Scots, *Nympha Caledoniæ*, &c. and spoke with enthusiasm of the beauty of Latin verse. 'All the modern languages (said he) cannot furnish so melodious a line as

'*Formosam resonare doces Amarillida silvas.*'

[1] [Epigram. Lib. II. 'In Elizabeth. Angliæ Reg.'—I suspect that the authour's memory here deceived him, and that Johnson said, 'the first *modern* poet;' for there is a well known Epigram in the ANTHOLOGIA, containing this kind of eulogy. MALONE.]

Afterwards he entered upon the business of the day, which was to give me his advice as to a course of study. And here I am to mention with much regret, that my record of what he said is miserably scanty. I recollect with admiration an animating blaze of eloquence, which roused every intellectual power in me to the highest pitch, but must have dazzled me so much, that my memory could not preserve the substance of his discourse; for the note which I find of it is no more than this:—'He ran over the grand scale of human knowledge; advised me to select some particular branch to excel in, but to acquire a little of every kind.' The defect of my minutes will be fully supplied by a long letter upon the subject, which he favoured me with, after I had been some time at Utrecht, and which my readers will have the pleasure to peruse in its proper place.

We walked in the evening in Greenwich Park. He asked me, I suppose, by way of trying my disposition, 'Is not this very fine?' Having no exquisite relish of the beauties of Nature, and being more delighted with 'the busy hum of men,' I answered 'Yes, Sir; but not equal to Fleet-street.' JOHNSON. 'You are right, Sir.'

I am aware that many of my readers may censure my want of taste. Let me, however, shelter myself under the authority of a very fashionable Baronet[1] in the brilliant world, who, on his attention being called to the fragrance of a May evening in the country, observed, 'This may be very well; but for my part, I prefer the smell of a flambeau at the play-house.'

We staid so long at Greenwich, that our sail up the river, in our return to London, was by no means so pleasant as in the morning; for the night air was so cold that it made me shiver. I was the more sensible of it from having sat up

---

[1] My friend Sir Michael Le Fleming. This gentleman, with all his experience of sprightly and elegant life, inherits, with the beautiful family domain, no inconsiderable share of that love of literature, which distinguished his venerable grandfather, the Bishop of Carlisle. He one day observed to me, of Dr. Johnson, in a felicity of phrase, 'There is a blunt dignity about him on every occasion.'

[Sir Michael Le Fleming died of an apoplectick fit, while conversing at the Admiralty with Lord Howick, (now the Earl Grey,) May 19, 1806. MALONE.]

all the night before recollecting and writing in my Journal what I thought worthy of preservation; an exertion, which, during the first part of my acquaintance with Johnson, I frequently made. I remember having sat up four nights in one week, without being much incommoded in the day time.

Johnson, whose robust frame was not in the least affected by the cold, scolded me, as if my shivering had been a paltry effeminacy, saying, 'Why do you shiver?' Sir William Scott, of the Commons, told me, that when he complained of a head-ach in the post-chaise, as they were travelling together to Scotland, Johnson treated him in the same manner: 'At your age, Sir, I had no head-ach.' It is not easy to make allowance for sensations in others, which we ourselves have not at the time. We must all have experienced how very differently we are affected by the complaints of our neighbours, when we are well and when we are ill. In full health, we can scarcely believe that they suffer much; so faint is the image of pain upon our imagination: when softened by sickness, we readily sympathize with the sufferings of others.

We concluded the day at the Turk's Head coffee-house very socially. He was pleased to listen to a particular account which I gave him of my family, and of its heredi-tary estate, as to the extent and population of which he asked questions, and made calculations; recommending, at the same time, a liberal kindness to the tenantry, as people over whom the proprietor was placed by Provi-dence. He took delight in hearing my description of the romantick seat of my ancestors. 'I must be there, Sir, (said he) and we will live in the old castle; and if there is not a room in it remaining, we will build one.' I was highly flattered, but could scarcely indulge a hope that Auchinleck would indeed be honoured by his presence, and celebrated by a description, as it afterwards was, in his 'Journey to the Western Islands.'

After we had again talked of my setting out for Holland, he said, 'I must see thee out of England; I will accompany you to Harwich.' I could not find words to express what I felt upon this unexpected and very great mark of his affectionate regard.

Next day, Sunday, July 31, I told him I had been that

morning at a meeting of the people called Quakers, where
I had heard a woman preach. JOHNSON. 'Sir, a woman's
preaching is like a dog's walking on his hind legs. It is not
done well; but you are surprised to find it done at all.'

On Tuesday, August 2, (the day of my departure from
London having been fixed for the 5th,) Dr. Johnson did

me the honour to pass a part of the morning with me at
my Chambers. He said, that 'he always felt an inclination
to do nothing.' I observed, that it was strange to think that
the most indolent man in Britain had written the most
laborious work, THE ENGLISH DICTIONARY.

I mentioned an imprudent publication, by a certain
friend of his, at an early period of life, and asked him if he

thought it would hurt him. JOHNSON. 'No, Sir; not much.
It may, perhaps, be mentioned at an election.'

I had now made good my title to be a privileged man,
and was carried by him in the evening to drink tea with
Miss Williams,[1] whom, though under the misfortune of

[1] [In a paper already referred to, (see p. 52,) a lady[a] who appears to have
been well acquainted with Mrs. Williams, thus speaks of her:

'Mrs. Williams was a person extremely interesting. She had an uncommon
firmness of mind, a boundless curiosity, retentive memory, and strong
judgement. She had various powers of pleasing. Her personal afflictions and
slender fortune she seemed to forget, when she had the power of doing an
act of kindness: she was social, cheerful, and active, in a state of body that
was truly deplorable. Her regard to Dr. Johnson was formed with such
strength of judgement and firm esteem, that her voice never hesitated when
she repeated his maxims, or recited his good deeds; though upon many
other occasions her want of sight had led her to make so much use of her

ear, as to affect her speech.[b]

'Mrs. Williams was blind before she was acquainted with Dr. Johnson.—
She had many resources, though none very great. With the Miss Wilkinsons
she generally passed a part of the year, and received from them presents,
and from the first who died, a legacy of cloaths and money. The last of them,
Mrs. Jane, left her an annual rent; but from the blundering manner of the
Will, I fear she never reaped the benefit of it. The lady left money to erect
an hospital for ancient maids: but the number she had allotted being too
great for the donation, the Doctor [Johnson] said, it would be better to
expunge the word *maintain*, and put in to *starve* such a number of old maids.
They asked him, What name should be given it? he replied, "Let it be called
JENNY'S WHIM." [The name of a well-known tavern near Chelsea, in
former days.]

'Lady Phillips made her a small annual allowance, and some other Welsh
ladies, to all of whom she was related. Mrs. Montague, on the death of Mr.
Montague, settled upon her [by deed] ten pounds per annum.—As near as
I can calculate, Mrs. Williams had about thirty-five or forty pounds a year.

having lost her sight, I found to be agreeable in conversation; for she had a variety of literature, and expressed herself well; but her peculiar value was the intimacy in which she had long lived with Johnson, by which she was well acquainted with his habits, and knew how to lead him on to talk.

After tea he carried me to what he called his walk, which was a long narrow paved court in the neighbourhood, overshadowed by some trees. There we sauntered a considerable time; and I complained to him that my love of London and of his company was such, that I shrunk almost from the thought of going away even to travel, which is generally so much desired by young men. He roused me by manly and spirited conversation. He advised me, when settled in any place abroad, to study with an eagerness after knowledge, and to apply to Greek an hour every day; and when I was moving about, to read diligently the great book of mankind.

On Wednesday, August 3, we had our last social evening at the Turk's Head coffee-house, before my setting out for foreign parts. I had the misfortune, before we parted, to irritate him unintentionally. I mentioned to him how common it was in the world to tell absurd satires of him, and to ascribe to him very strange sayings. JOHNSON. 'What do they make me say, Sir?' BOSWELL. 'Why, Sir, as an instance very strange indeed, (laughing heartily as I spoke,) David Hume told me, you said that you would stand before a battery of cannon to restore the Convocation to its full powers.'—Little did I apprehend that he had actually said this: but I was soon convinced of my errour; for, with a determined look, he thundered out 'And would I not, Sir? Shall the Presbyterian *Kirk* of Scotland have its

The furniture she used [in her apartment in Dr. Johnson's house] was her own; her expences were small, tea and bread and butter being at least half of her nourishment. Sometimes she had a servant or charewoman to do the ruder offices of the house: but she was herself active and industrious. I have frequently seen her at work. Upon remarking one day her facility in moving about the house, searching into drawers, and finding books, without the help of sight, "Believe me, (said she,) persons who cannot do those common offices without sight, did but little while they enjoyed that blessing."—Scanty circumstances, bad health, and blindness are surely a sufficient apology for her being sometimes impatient: her natural disposition was good, friendly, and humane.' MALONE.]

General Assembly, and the Church of England be denied its Convocation?' He was walking up and down the room, while I told him the anecdote; but when he uttered this explosion of high-church zeal, he had come close to my chair, and his eyes flashed with indignation. I bowed to the storm, and diverted the force of it, by leading him to expatiate on the influence which religion derived from maintaining the church with great external respectability.

I must not omit to mention that he this year wrote 'The Life of Ascham,'† and the Dedication to the Earl of Shaftesbury,† prefixed to the edition of that writer's English works, published by Mr. Bennet.

On Friday, August 5, we set out early in the morning in the Harwich stage-coach. A fat elderly gentlewoman, and a young Dutchman, seemed the most inclined among us to conversation. At the inn where we dined, the gentle-woman said that she had done her best to educate her children; and particularly, that she had never suffered them to be a moment idle. JOHNSON. 'I wish, Madam, you would educate me too; for I have been an idle fellow all my life.' 'I am sure, Sir, (said she) you have not been idle.' JOHNSON. 'Nay, Madam, it is very true; and that gentleman there, (pointing to me,) has been idle. He was idle at Edinburgh. His father sent him to Glasgow, where he continued to be idle. He then came to London, where he has been very idle; and now he is going to Utrecht, where he will be as idle as ever.' I asked him privately how he could expose me so. JOHNSON. 'Poh, poh! (said he) they knew nothing about you, and will think of it no more.' In the afternoon the gentlewoman talked violently against the Roman Catholicks, and of the horrours of the Inquisition. To the utter astonishment of all the passengers but myself, who knew that he could talk upon any side of a question, he defended the Inquisition, and maintained, that 'false doctrine should be checked on its first appearance; that the civil power should unite with the church in punishing those who dare to attack the established religion, and that such only were punished by the Inquisition.' He had in his pocket 'Pomponius Mela de Situ Orbis,' in which he read occasionally, and seemed very intent upon ancient geography. Though by no means niggardly, his attention to what was generally right was so minute, that having observed at one of the stages that I ostentatiously gave a shilling to the coachman, when the custom was for each passenger to give only six-pence, he took me aside and scolded me, saying that what I had done would make the coachman dissatisfied with all the rest of the passengers, who gave him no more than his due. This was a just reprimand; for in whatever way a man may indulge his generosity or his vanity in spending his money, for the sake of others he ought not to raise the price of any article for which there is a constant demand.

He talked of Mr. Blacklock's poetry, so far as it was descriptive of visible objects; and observed that 'as its authour had the misfortune to be blind, we may be absolutely sure that such passages are combinations of what he has remembered of the works of other writers who could see. That foolish fellow, Spence, has laboured to explain philosophically how Blacklock may have done, by means of his own faculties, what it is impossible he should do. The solution, as I have given it, is plain. Suppose, I know a man to be so lame that he is absolutely incapable to move himself, and I find him in a different room from that in which I left him; shall I puzzle myself with idle conjectures, that, perhaps, his nerves have by some unknown change all at once become effective? No, Sir, it is clear how he got into a different room: he was *carried*.'

Having stopped a night at Colchester, Johnson talked of that town with veneration, for having stood a siege for Charles the First. The Dutchman alone now remained with us. He spoke English tolerably well; and thinking to recommend himself to us by expatiating on the superiority of the criminal jurisprudence of this country over that of Holland, he inveighed against the barbarity of putting an accused person to the torture, in order to force a confession. But Johnson was as ready for this, as for the Inquisition. 'Why Sir, you do not, I find, understand the law of your own country. To torture in Holland is considered as a favour to an accused person; for no man is put to the torture there, unless there is as much evidence against him as would amount to conviction in England.

An accused person among you, therefore, has one chance more to escape punishment, than those who are tried among us.'

At supper this night he talked of good eating with uncommon satisfaction. 'Some people (said he,) have a foolish way of not minding, or pretending not to mind what they eat. For my part, I mind my belly very studiously, and very carefully; for I look upon it, that he who does not mind his belly, will hardly mind any thing else.' He now appeared to me *Jean Bull philosophe*, and he was for the moment, not only serious, but vehement. Yet I have heard him, upon other occasions, talk with great contempt of people who were anxious to gratify their palates; and the 206th number of his Rambler is a masterly essay against gulosity. His practice, indeed, I must acknowledge, may be considered as casting the balance of his different opinions upon this subject: for I never knew any man who relished good eating more than he did. When at table, he was totally absorbed in the business of the moment; his looks seemed rivetted to his plate; nor would he, unless when in very high company, say one word, or even pay the least attention to what was said by others, till he had satisfied his appetite: which was so fierce, and indulged with such intenseness, that while in the act of eating, the veins of his forehead swelled, and generally a strong perspiration was visible. To those whose sensations were delicate, this could not but be disgusting; and it was doubtless not very suitable to the character of a philosopher, who should be distinguished by self-command. But it must be owned, that Johnson, though he could be rigidly *abstemious*, was not a *temperate* man either in eating or drinking. He could refrain, but he could not use moderately. He told me that he had fasted two days without inconvenience, and that he had never been hungry but once. They who beheld with wonder how much he eat upon all occasions, when his dinner was to his taste, could not easily conceive what he must have meant by hunger; and not only was he remarkable for the extraordinary quantity which he eat, but he was, or affected to be, a man of very nice discernment, in the science of cookery. He used to descant critically on the

index sign:
For my part etc. [H]

index sign:
he who does no t etc. [I]

·

index sign:
while in the act etc. [H]

dishes which had been at table where he had dined or
supped, and to recollect very minutely what he had liked.
I remember when he was in Scotland, his praising
'*Gordon's palates*,' (a dish of palates at the Honourable
Alexander Gordon's) with a warmth of expression which
might have done honour to more important subjects. 'As
for Maclaurin's imitation of a *made dish*, it was a wretched
attempt.' He about the same time was so much displeased
with the performances of a nobleman's French cook, that
he exclaimed with vehemence, 'I'd throw such a rascal
into the river:' and he then proceeded to alarm a lady at
whose house he was to sup, by the following manifesto of
his skill: 'I, Madam, who live at a variety of good tables,
am a much better judge of cookery, than any person who
has a very tolerable cook, but lives much at home; for his
palate is gradually adapted to the taste of his cook:
whereas, Madam, in trying by a wider range, I can more
exquisitely judge.' When invited to dine, even with an
intimate friend, he was not pleased if something better
than a plain dinner was not prepared for him. I have
heard him say on such an occasion, 'This was a good
dinner enough, to be sure: but it was not a dinner to *ask*
a man to.' On the other hand, he was wont to express,
with great glee, his satisfaction when he had been entertained quite to his mind. One day when he had dined with
his neighbour and landlord, in Bolt-court, Mr. Allen, the
printer, whose old housekeeper had studied his taste in
every thing, he pronounced this eulogy: 'Sir, we could
not have had a better dinner, had there been a *Synod
of Cooks*.'

While we were left by ourselves, after the Dutchman
had gone to bed, Dr. Johnson talked of that studied
behaviour which many have recommended and practised.
He disapproved of it: and said, 'I never considered whether I should be a grave man, or a merry man, but just
let inclination, for the time, have its course.'

two marginal lines:
*and practised . . . for
the* [H]

He flattered me with some hopes that he would, in the
course of the following summer, come over to Holland,
and accompany me in a tour through the Netherlands.

I teased him with fanciful apprehensions of unhappiness.
A moth having fluttered round the candle, and burnt

itself, he laid hold of this little incident to admonish me; saying, with a sly look, and in a solemn but a quiet tone, 'That creature was its own tormentor, and I believe its name was BOSWELL.'

underlined:
Harwich [H]

Next day we got to Harwich, to dinner; and my passage in the packet-boat to Helvoetsluys being secured, and my baggage put on board, we dined at our inn by ourselves. I happened to say, it would be terrible if he should not find a speedy opportunity of returning to London, and be confined in so dull a place. JOHNSON. 'Don't, Sir, accustom yourself to use big words for little matters. It would *not* be *terrible*, though I *were* to be detained some time here.' The practice of using words of disproportionate magnitude, is, no doubt, too frequent every where; but, I think, most remarkable among the French, of which, all who have travelled in France must have been struck with innumerable instances.

two marginal lines:
of returning . . . dull a
[H]

We went and looked at the church, and having gone into it, and walked up to the altar, Johnson, whose piety was constant and fervent, sent me to my knees, saying, 'Now that you are going to leave your native country, recommend yourself to the protection of your CREATOR and REDEEMER.'

After we came out of the church, we stood talking for some time together of Bishop Berkeley's ingenious sophistry to prove the non-existence of matter, and that every thing in the universe is merely ideal. I observed, that though we are satisfied his doctrine is not true, it is impossible to refute it. I never shall forget the alacrity with which Johnson answered, striking his foot with mighty force against a large stone, till he rebounded from it, —'I refute it *thus*.'[1] This was a stout exemplification of the *first truths* of *Pere Bouffier*, or the *original principles* of Reid and of Beattie; without admitting which, we can no more argue in metaphysicks, than we can argue in mathematicks

---

[1] [Dr. Johnson seems to have been imperfectly acquainted with Berkeley's doctrine: as his experiment only proves that we have the sensation of solidity, which Berkeley did not deny.—He admitted that we had sensations or ideas that are usually called sensible qualities, one of which is solidity: he only denied the existence of *matter*, i.e. an inert senseless substance, in which they are supposed to subsist.—Johnson's exemplification concurs with the vulgar notion, that solidity is matter. KEARNEY.]

without axioms. To me it is not conceivable how Berkeley can be answered by pure reasoning; but I know that the nice and difficult task was to have been undertaken by one of the most luminous minds of the present age, had not politicks 'turned him from calm philosophy aside.' What an admirable display of subtilty, united with brilliance, might his contending with Berkeley have afforded us! How must we, when we reflect on the loss of such an intellectual feast, regret that he should be characterised as the man,

'Who born for the universe narrow'd his mind,
And to party gave up what was meant for mankind?'ᵃ   ᵃ *Burke.* [H]

My revered friend walked down with me to the beach, where we embraced and parted with tenderness, and engaged to correspond by letters. I said, 'I hope, Sir, you will not forget me in my absence.' JOHNSON. 'Nay, Sir, it is more likely you should forget me, than that I should forget you.' As the vessel put out to sea, I kept my eyes upon him for a considerable time, while he remained rolling his majestic frame in his usual manner; and at last I perceived him walk back into the town, and he disappeared.

Utrecht seeming at first very dull to me, after the animated scenes of London, my spirits were grievously affected; and I wrote to Johnson a plaintive and desponding letter, to which he paid no regard. Afterwards, when I had acquired a firmer tone of mind, I wrote him a second letter, expressing much anxiety to hear from him. At length I received the following epistle, which was of important service to me, and, I trust, will be so to many others.

'*A Mr. Mr.* BOSWELL, *à la Cour de l'Empereur,*
UTRECHT

'DEAR SIR,
'YOU are not to think yourself forgotten, or criminally neglected, that you have had yet no letter from me. I love to see my friends, to hear from them, to talk to them, and to talk of them; but it is not without a considerable effort

of resolution that I prevail upon myself to write. I would not, however, gratify my own indolence by the omission of any important duty, or any office of real kindness.

'To tell you that I am or am not well, that I have or have not been in the country, that I drank your health in the room in which we last sat together, and that your acquaintance continue to speak of you with their former kindness, topicks with which those letters are commonly filled which are written only for the sake of writing, I seldom shall think worth communicating; but if I can have it in my power to calm any harassing disquiet, to excite any virtuous desire, to rectify any important opinion, or fortify any generous resolution, you need not doubt but I shall at least wish to prefer the pleasure of gratifying a friend much less esteemed than yourself, before the gloomy calm of idle vacancy. Whether I shall easily arrive at an exact punctuality of correspondence, I cannot tell. I shall, at present, expect that you will receive this in return for two which I have had from you. The first, indeed, gave me an account so hopeless of the state of your mind, that it hardly admitted or deserved an answer; by the second I was much better pleased; and the pleasure will still be increased by such a narrative of the progress of your studies, as may evince the continuance of an equal and rational application of your mind to some useful enquiry.

'You will, perhaps, wish to ask, what study I would recommend. I shall not speak of theology, because it ought not to be considered as a question whether you shall endeavour to know the will of GOD.

'I shall, therefore, consider only such studies as we are at liberty to pursue or to neglect; and of these I know not how you will make a better choice, than by studying the civil law as your father advises, and the ancient languages, as you had determined for yourself; at least resolve, while you remain in any settled residence, to spend a certain number of hours every day amongst your books. The dissipation of thought of which you complain, is nothing more than the vacillation of a mind suspended between different motives, and changing its direction as any motive gains or loses strength. If you can but kindle in your mind any strong desire, if you can but keep predominant any wish for some particular excellence or attainment, the gusts of imagination will break away, without any effect upon your conduct, and commonly without any traces left upon the memory.

'There lurks, perhaps, in every human heart a desire of distinction, which inclines every man first to hope, and then to believe, that nature has given him something peculiar to himself. This vanity makes one mind nurse aversion, and another actuate desires, till they rise by art much above their original state of power: and as affectation in time improves to habit, they at last tyrannise over him who at first encouraged them only for show. Every desire is a viper in the bosom, who, while he was chill, was harmless; but when warmth gave him strength, exerted it in poison. You know a gentleman, who, when first he set his foot in the gay world, as he prepared himself to whirl in the vortex of pleasure, imagined a total indifference and universal negligence to be the most agreeable concomitants of youth, and the strongest indication of an airy temper and a quick apprehension. Vacant to every object, and sensible of every impulse, he thought that all appearance of diligence would deduct something from the reputation of genius; and hoped that he should appear to attain, amidst all the ease of carelessness, and all the tumults of diversion, that knowledge and those accomplishments which mortals of the common fabrick obtain only by mute abstraction and solitary drudgery. He tried this scheme of life awhile, was made weary of it by his sense and his virtue; he then wished to return to his studies; and finding long habits of idleness and pleasure harder to be cured than he expected, still willing to retain his claim to some extraordinary prerogatives, resolved the common consequences of irregularity into an unalterable degree of destiny, and concluded that Nature had originally formed him incapable of rational employment.[a]

[a] *I wonder who this was.* [H]

'Let all such fancies, illusive and destructive, be banished henceforward from your thoughts for ever. Resolve, and keep your resolution; choose, and pursue your choice. If you spend this day in study, you will find yourself still more able to study to-morrow; not that you are to expect that you shall at once obtain a complete victory. Depravity is not very easily overcome. Resolution will sometimes relax, and diligence will sometimes be interrupted; but let no accidental surprise or deviation, whether short or long, dispose you to despondency. Consider these failings as incident to all mankind. Begin again where you left off, and endeavour to avoid the seducements that prevailed over you before.

'This, my dear Boswell, is advice which, perhaps, has been often given you, and given you without effect. But this advice, if you will not take from others, you must take from your own reflections, if you purpose to do the duties of the station to which the bounty of Providence has called you.

'Let me have a long letter from you as soon as you can. I hope you continue your Journal, and enrich it with many observations upon the country in which you reside. It will be a favour if you can get me any books in the Frisick language, and can enquire how the poor are maintained in the Seven Provinces. I am, dear Sir,

'Your most affectionate servant,

'London, Dec. 8, 1763.'   'SAM. JOHNSON'

I am sorry to observe, that neither in my own minutes, nor in my letters to Johnson which have been preserved by him, can I find any information how the poor are maintained in the Seven Provinces. But I shall extract from one of my letters what I learnt concerning the other subject of his curiosity.

'I have made all possible enquiry with respect to the Frisick language, and find that it has been less cultivated than any other of the northern dialects; a certain proof of which is their deficiency of books. Of the old Frisick there are no remains, except some ancient laws preserved by Schotanus in his "*Beschryvinge van die Heerlykheid van Friesland;*" and his "*Historia Frisica.*" I have not yet been able to find these books. Professor Trotz, who formerly was of the University of Vranyken in Friesland, and is at present preparing an edition of all the Frisick laws, gave me this information. Of the modern Frisick, or what is

spoken by the boors of this day, I have procured a specimen. It is Gisbert Japix's "*Rymelerie*," which is the only
book that they have. It is amazing that they have no
translation of the bible, no treatises of devotion, nor even
any of the ballads and story-books which are so agreeable
to country people. You shall have Japix by the first convenient opportunity. I doubt not to pick up Schotanus.
Mynheer Trotz has promised me his assistance.'

Early in 1764 Johnson paid a visit to the Langton
family, at their seat of Langton in Lincolnshire, where he
passed some time, much to his satisfaction. His friend
Bennet Langton, it will not be doubted, did every thing
in his power to make the place agreeable to so illustrious
a guest; and the elder Mr. Langton and his lady, being
fully capable of understanding his value, were not wanting
in attention. He, however, told me, that old Mr. Langton,
though a man of considerable learning, had so little
allowance to make for his occasional 'laxity of talk,' that
because in the course of discussion he sometimes mentioned
what might be said in favour of the peculiar tenets of the
Romish church, he went to his grave believing him to be
of that communion.

Johnson, during his stay at Langton, had the advantage
of a good library, and saw several gentlemen of the
neighbourhood. I have obtained from Mr. Langton the
following particulars of this period.

He was now fully convinced that he could not have
been satisfied with a country living; for talking of a
respectable clergyman in Lincolnshire, he observed, 'This
man, Sir, fills up the duties of his life well. I approve of
him, but could not imitate him.'

To a lady who endeavoured to vindicate herself from
blame for neglecting social attention to worthy neighbours,
by saying, 'I would go to them if it would do them any
good;' he said, 'What good, Madam, do you expect to
have in your power to do them? It is shewing them respect,
and that is doing them good.'

So socially accommodating was he, that once when Mr.
Langton and he were driving together in a coach, and
Mr. Langton complained of being sick, he insisted that
they should go out, and sit on the back of it in the open

air, which they did. And being sensible how strange the appearance must be, observed, that a countryman whom they saw in a field would probably be thinking, 'If these two madmen should come down, what would become of me?'

Soon after his return to London, which was in February, was founded that CLUB which existed long without a name, but at Mr. Garrick's funeral became distinguished by the title of THE LITERARY CLUB. Sir Joshua Reynolds had the merit of being the first proposer of it, to which Johnson acceded; and the original members were, Sir Joshua Reynolds, Dr. Johnson, Mr. Edmund Burke, Dr. Nugent, Mr. Beauclerk, Mr. Langton, Dr. Goldsmith, Mr. Chamier, and Sir John Hawkins. They met at the Turk's Head, in Gerrard-street, Soho, one evening in every week, at seven, and generally continued their conversation till a pretty late hour. This club has been gradually increased to its present number, thirty-five. After about ten years, instead of supping weekly, it was resolved to dine together once a fortnight during the meeting of Parliament. Their original tavern having been converted into a private house, they moved first to Prince's in Sackville-street, then to Le Telier's in Dover-street, and now meet at Parsloe's, St. James's-street. Between the time of its formation, and the time at which this work is passing through the press, (June 1792,)[1] the following persons, now dead, were members of it: Mr. Dunning, (afterwards Lord Ashburton,) Mr. Samuel Dyer, Mr. Garrick, Dr. Shipley Bishop of St. Asaph, Mr. Vesey, Mr. Thomas Warton, and Dr. Adam Smith. The present members are, Mr. Burke, Mr. Langton, Lord Charlemont, Sir Robert Chambers, Dr. Percy Bishop of Dromore, Dr. Barnard Bishop of Killaloe, Dr. Marlay Bishop of Clonfert, Mr. Fox, Dr. George Fordyce, Sir William Scott, Sir Joseph Banks, Sir Charles Bunbury, Mr. Windham of Norfolk, Mr. Sheridan, Mr. Gibbon, Sir William Jones, Mr. Colman, Mr. Steevens, Dr. Burney, Dr. Joseph Warton, Mr. Malone, Lord Ossory, Lord Spencer, Lord Lucan, Lord Palmerston, Lord Eliot, Lord Macartney, Mr. Richard Burke, junior, Sir William Hamilton,

---

[1] [The second edition is here spoken of. MALONE.]

Dr. Warren, Mr. Courtenay, Dr. Hinchcliffe Bishop of Peterborough, the Duke of Leeds, Dr. Douglas Bishop of Salisbury, and the writer of this account.[1]

Sir John Hawkins[2] represents himself as a '*seceder*' from this society, and assigns as the reason of his '*withdrawing*' himself from it, that its late hours were inconsistent with his domestick arrangements. In this he is not accurate; for the fact was, that he one evening attacked Mr. Burke, in so rude a manner, that all the company testified their displeasure; and at their next meeting his reception was such, that he never came again.[3]

He is equally inaccurate with respect to Mr. Garrick, of whom he says, 'he trusted that the least intimation of a desire to come among us, would procure him a ready admission; but in this he was mistaken. Johnson consulted

[1] [The LITERARY CLUB has since been deprived by death of Dr. Hinchcliffe Bishop of Peterborough, Mr. Gibbon, Sir William Jones, Mr. Richard Burke, Mr. Colman, Mr. Boswell, (the author of this work,) the Marquis of Bath, Dr. Warren, Mr. Burke, the Rev. Dr. Farmer, the Duke of Leeds, the Earl of Lucan, James Earl of Charlemont, Mr. Steevens, Dr. Warton, Mr. Langton, Lord Palmerston, Dr. Fordyce, Dr. Marley Bishop of Waterford, Sir William Hamilton, Sir Robert Chambers, Lord Eliot, Lord Macartney, Dr. Barnard Bishop of Limerick, Mr. Fox, Dr. Horsley Bishop of St. Asaph, Dr. Douglas Bishop of Salisbury, and Dr. French Lawrence. Its latest and its irreparable loss was that of the Right Hon. William Windham, the delight and admiration of this society, and of every other with whom he ever associated.—Of the persons above-mentioned some were chosen members of it, after the preceding account was written. It has since that time acquired Sir Charles Blagden, Major Rennell, the Hon. Frederick North, the Right Hon. George Canning, Mr. Marsden, the Right Hon. J. H. Frere, the Right Hon. Thomas Grenville, the Reverend Dr. Vincent Dean of Westminster, Mr. William Lock, jun., Mr. George Ellis, Lord Minto, the Right Hon. Sir William Grant Master of the Rolls, Sir George Staunton, Bart., Mr. Charles Wilkins, the Right Hon. Sir William Drummond, Sir Henry Halford, M.D., Sir Henry Englefield, Bart., Henry Lord Holland, John Earl of Aberdeen, Mr. Charles Hatchett, Mr. Charles Vaughan, Mr. Humphrey Davy, and the Rev. Dr. Burney.—The Club, some years after Mr. Boswell's death, removed (in 1799,) from Parsloe's to the Thatched House in St. James's-street, where they still continue to meet.

The total number of those who have been members of this Club, from its foundation to the present time, (October 1810,) is SEVENTY-SIX; of whom FIFTY-FIVE have been authours. Of the seventy-six members above mentioned, forty-three are dead; thirty-three living. MALONE.]

[2] Life of Johnson, p. 425.

[3] From Sir Joshua Reynolds.

[The Knight having refused to pay his portion of the reckoning for supper, because he usually eat no supper at home, Johnson observed, 'Sir John, Sir, is a very *unclubable* man.' BURNEY.]

me upon it; and when I could find no objection to receiving him, exclaimed,—"He will disturb us by his buffoonery;"—and afterwards so managed matters, that he was never formally proposed, and, by consequence, never admitted.'[1]

In justice both to Mr. Garrick and Dr. Johnson, I think it necessary to rectify this mis-statement. The truth is, that not very long after the institution of our club, Sir Joshua Reynolds was speaking of it to Garrick. 'I like it much, (said he,) I think I shall be of you.' When Sir Joshua mentioned this to Dr. Johnson, he was much displeased with the actor's conceit. '*He'll be of us*, (said Johnson) how does he know we will *permit* him? the first Duke in England has no right to hold such language.' However, when Garrick was regularly proposed some time afterwards, Johnson, though he had taken a momentary offence at his arrogance, warmly and kindly supported him, and he was accordingly elected,[2] was a most agreeable member, and continued to attend our meetings to the time of his death.

Mrs. Piozzi[3] has also given a similar misrepresentation of Johnson's treatment of Garrick in this particular, as if he had used these contemptuous expressions: if Garrick *does* apply, I'll black-ball him.[a]—Surely, one ought to sit in a society like ours,

a he did *say so, & Mr. Thrale stood astonished.* [H]

They were his very words. [I]

'Unelbow'd by a gamester, pimp, or player.'

I am happy to be enabled by such unquestionable authority as that of Sir Joshua Reynolds, as well as from my own knowledge, to vindicate at once the heart of Johnson and the social merit of Garrick.

In this year, except what he may have done in revising Shakspeare, we do not find that he laboured much in literature. He wrote a review of Granger's 'Sugar Cane,' a poem, in the London Chronicle. He told me, that Dr. Percy wrote the greatest part of this review; but, I imagine, he did not recollect it distinctly, for it appears to be mostly, if not altogether, his own. He also wrote in the Critical

[1] Life of Johnson, p. 425.
[2] [Mr. Garrick was elected in March, 1773. MALONE.]
[3] Letters to and from Dr. Johnson. Vol. II. p. 278.

Review, an account† of Goldsmith's excellent poem, 'The Traveller.'

The ease and independence to which he had at last attained by royal munificence, increased his natural indolence. In his 'Meditations,' he thus accuses himself: 'GOOD FRIDAY, April 20, 1764. I have made no reformation; I have lived totally useless, more sensual in thought, and more addicted to wine and meat.'[1] And next morning he thus feelingly complains: 'My indolence, since my last reception of the sacrament, has sunk into grosser sluggishness, and my dissipation spread into wilder negligence. My thoughts have been clouded with sensuality; and, except that from the beginning of this year I have, in some measure, forborne excess of strong drink, my appetites have predominated over my reason. A kind of strange oblivion has overspread me, so that I know not what has become of the last year; and perceive that incidents and intelligence pass over me without leaving any impression.' He then solemnly says, 'This is not the life to which heaven is promised;'[2] and he earnestly resolves an amendment.

It was his custom to observe certain days with a pious abstraction: viz. New-year's day, the day of his wife's death, Good Friday, Easter-day, and his own birth-day. He this year says, 'I have now spent fifty-five years in resolving: having, from the earliest time almost that I can remember, been forming schemes of a better life. I have done nothing. The need of doing, therefore, is pressing, since the time of doing is short. O GOD, grant me to resolve aright, and to keep my resolutions, for JESUS CHRIST's sake. Amen.'[3] Such a tenderness of conscience, such a fervent desire of improvement, will rarely be found. It is surely, not decent in those who are hardened in indifference to spiritual improvement, to treat this pious anxiety of Johnson with contempt.

About this time he was afflicted with a very severe return of the hypochondriack disorder, which was ever lurking about him. He was so ill, as, notwithstanding his remarkable love of company, to be entirely averse to society, the most fatal symptom of that malady. Dr. Adams told me,

[1] Prayers and Meditations, p. 53.   [2] Ibid. p. 51.   [3] Ibid. p. 58.

that, as an old friend he was admitted to visit him, and that he found him in a deplorable state, sighing, groaning, talking to himself, and restlessly walking from room to room. He then used this emphatical expression of the misery which he felt: 'I would consent to have a limb amputated to recover my spirits.'

Talking to himself was, indeed, one of his singularities ever since I knew him. I was certain that he was frequently uttering pious ejaculations; for fragments of the Lord's Prayer have been distinctly overheard.[1] His friend Mr. Thomas Davies, of whom Churchill says,

'That Davies has a very pretty wife,——'

when Dr. Johnson muttered—'lead us not into temptation,' used with waggish and gallant humour to whisper Mrs. Davies, 'You, my dear, are the cause of this.'

He had another particularity, of which none of his friends ever ventured to ask an explanation. It appeared to me some superstitious habit, which he had contracted early, and from which he had never called upon his reason to disentangle him. This was his anxious care to go out or in at a door or passage, by a certain number of steps from a certain point, or at least so as that either his right or his left foot, (I am not certain which,) should constantly make the first actual movement when he came close to the door or passage. Thus I conjecture: for I have, upon innumerable occasions, observed him suddenly stop, and then seem to count his steps with a deep earnestness; and when he had neglected or gone wrong in this sort of magical movement, I have seen him go back again, put himself in a proper posture to begin the ceremony, and,

---

[1] [It used to be imagined at Mr. Thrale's, when Johnson retired to a window or corner of the room, by perceiving his lips in motion, and hearing a murmur without audible articulation, that he was praying; but this was not *always* the case, for I was once, perhaps unperceived by him, writing at a table, so near the place of his retreat, that I heard him repeating some lines in an ode of Horace, over and over again, as if by iteration to exercise the organs of speech, and fix the ode in his memory:

> *Audiet cives accuisse ferrum,*
> *Quo graves* Persæ *melius perirent,*
> *Audiet pugnas . . .*

It was during the American war. BURNEY.]

having gone through it, break from his abstraction, walk briskly on, and join his companion. A strange instance of something of this nature, even when on horseback, happened when he was in the Isle of Sky.[1] Sir Joshua Reynolds has observed him to go a good way about, rather than cross a particular alley in Leicester-fields; but this Sir Joshua imputed to his having had some disagreeable recollection associated with it.

That the most minute singularities which belonged to him, and made very observable parts of his appearance and manner, may not be omitted, it is requisite to mention, that while talking or even musing as he sat in his chair, he commonly held his head to one side towards his right shoulder, and shook it in a tremulous manner, moving his body backwards and forwards, and rubbing his left knee in the same direction, with the palm of his hand. In the intervals of articulating he made various sounds with his mouth; sometimes as if ruminating, or what is called chewing the cud, sometimes giving a half whistle, sometimes making his tongue play backwards from the roof of his mouth, as if clucking like a hen, and sometimes protruding it against his upper gums in front, as if pronouncing quickly under his breath, *too, too, too:* all this accompanied sometimes with a thoughtful look, but more frequently with a smile. Generally when he had concluded a period, in the course of a dispute, by which time he was a good deal exhausted by violence and vociferation, he used to blow out his breath like a whale. This I suppose was a relief to his lungs; and seemed in him to be a contemptuous mode of expression, as if he had made the arguments of his opponent fly like chaff before the wind.

I am fully aware how very obvious an occasion I here give for the sneering jocularity of such as have no relish of an exact likeness; which to render complete, he who draws it must not disdain the slightest strokes. But if witlings should be inclined to attack this account, let them have the candour to quote what I have offered in my defence.

He was for some time in the summer at Easton Maudit, Northamptonshire, on a visit to the Reverend Dr. Percy,

[1] Journal of a Tour to the Hebrides, 3d. edit. p. 316.

now Bishop of Dromore. Whatever dissatisfaction he felt
at what he considered as a slow progress in intellectual
improvement, we find that his heart was tender, and his
affections warm, as appears from the following very
kind letter:

'TO JOSHUA REYNOLDS, ESQ. IN LEICESTER-FIELDS,
LONDON
    'DEAR SIR,

    'I DID not hear of your sickness till I heard likewise
of your recovery, and therefore escaped that part of your
pain, which every man must feel, to whom you are known
as you are known to me.

    'Having had no particular account of your disorder,
I know not in what state it has left you. If the amusement
of my company can exhilarate the languor of a slow
recovery, I will not delay a day to come to you; for I know
not how I can so effectually promote my own pleasure as
by pleasing you, or my own interest as by preserving you,
in whom, if I should lose you, I should lose almost the
only man whom I call a friend.

    'Pray, let me hear of you from yourself, or from dear
Miss Reynolds.[1] Make my compliments to Mr. Mudge.

            I am, dear Sir,
                    'Your most affectionate
                        'And most humble servant,
'At the Rev. Mr. Percy's, at Easton   'SAM. JOHNSON'
Maudit, Northamptonshire, (by
Castle Ashby,) Aug. 19, 1764.'

Early in the year 1765 he paid a short visit to the
University of Cambridge, with his friend Mr. Beauclerk.
There is a lively picturesque account of his behaviour on
this visit, in the Gentleman's Magazine for March, 1785,
being an extract of a letter from the late Dr. John Sharp.
The two following sentences are very characteristical: 'He
drank his large potations of tea with me, interrupted by
many an indignant contradiction, and many a noble

    [1] Sir Joshua's sister, for whom Johnson had a particular affection, and
to whom he wrote many letters which I have seen, and which I am sorry
her too nice delicacy will not permit to be published.

sentiment.'—'Several persons got into his company the last evening at Trinity, where, about twelve, he began to be very great; stripped poor Mrs. Macaulay to the very skin, then gave her for his toast, and drank her in two bumpers.'

The strictness of his self-examination, and scrupulous Christian humility, appear in his pious meditation on Easter-day this year.—'I purpose again to partake of the blessed sacrament; yet when I consider how vainly I have hitherto resolved at this annual commemoration of my Saviour's death, to regulate my life by his laws, I am almost afraid to renew my resolutions.'

The concluding words are very remarkable, and shew that he laboured under a severe depression of spirits. 'Since the last Easter I have reformed no evil habit; my time has been unprofitably spent, and seems as a dream that has left nothing behind. *My memory grows confused, and I know not how the days pass over me.* Good Lord, deliver me!'[1]

No man was more gratefully sensible of any kindness done to him than Johnson. There is a little circumstance in his diary this year, which shews him in a very amiable light.

'July 2. I paid Mr. Simpson ten guineas, which he had formerly lent me in my necessity, and for which Tetty expressed her gratitude.'

'July 8. I lent Mr. Simpson ten guineas more.'

Here he had a pleasing opportunity of doing the same kindness to an old friend, which he had formerly received from him. Indeed his liberality as to money was very remarkable. The next article in his diary is, 'July 16th, I received seventy-five pounds. Lent Mr. Davies twenty-five.'

Trinity College, Dublin, at this time surprised Johnson with a spontaneous compliment of the highest academical honours, by creating him Doctor of Laws. The diploma, which is in my possession, is as follows:

'*OMNIBUS ad quos præsentes literæ pervenerint, salutem. Nos Præpositus et Socii seniores Collegii sacrosanctæ et individuæ Trinitatis Reginæ Elizabethæ juxta Dublin, testamur,* Samueli Johnson, *Armigero, ob egregiam scriptorum elegantiam et*

[1] Prayers and Meditations, p. 61.

utilitatem, gratiam concessam fuisse pro gradu Doctoratûs in utroque Jure, octavo die Julii, Anno Domini millesimo septingentesimo sexagesimo-quinto. In cujus rei testimonium singulorum manus et sigillum quo in hisce utimur apposuimus; vicesimo tertio die Julii, Anno Domini millesimo septingentesimo sexagesimoquinto.

GUL. CLEMENT	FRAN. ANDREWS	R. MURRAY
THO. WILSON	*Præp*.	ROB^tus LAW
THO. LELAND		MICH. KEARNEY'

This unsolicited mark of distinction, conferred on so great a literary character, did much honour to the judgement and liberal spirit of that learned body. Johnson acknowledged the favour in a letter to Dr. Leland, one of their number; but I have not been able to obtain a copy of it.[1]

He appears this year to have been seized with a temporary fit of ambition, for he had thoughts both of studying law, and of engaging in politicks. His 'Prayer before the Study of Law' is truly admirable:

'Sept. 26, 1765

'Almighty GOD, the giver of wisdom, without whose help resolutions are vain, without whose blessing study is ineffectual; enable me, if it be thy will, to attain such

---

[1] [Since the publication of the edition in 1804, a copy of this letter has been obligingly communicated to me by John Leland, Esq. son to the learned Historian, to whom it is addressed:

'TO THE REV. DR. LELAND
'SIR,
'Among the names subscribed to the degree which I have had the honour of receiving from the University of Dublin, I find none of which I have any personal knowledge but those of Dr. Andrews and yourself.

'Men can be estimated by those who know them not, only as they are represented by those who know them; and therefore I flatter myself that I owe much of the pleasure which this distinction gives me, to your concurrence with Dr. Andrews in recommending me to the learned society.

'Having desired the Provost to return my general thanks to the University, I beg that you, Sir, will accept my particular and immediate acknowledgments.   'I am, Sir,
'Your most obedient and most humble servant,

'Johnson's-court, Fleet-street,   'SAM. JOHNSON'
London, Oct. 17, 1765.'

I have not been able to recover the letter which Johnson wrote to Dr. Andrews on this occasion. MALONE.]

knowledge as may qualify me to direct the doubtful, and instruct the ignorant; to prevent wrongs and terminate contentions; and grant that I may use that knowledge which I shall attain, to thy glory and my own salvation, for JESUS CHRIST's sake. Amen.'[1]

His prayer in the view of becoming a politician is entitled, 'Engaging in POLITICKS with H——n,' no doubt, his friend, the Right Honourable William Gerard Hamilton, for whom, during a long acquaintance, he had a great esteem, and to whose conversation he once paid this high compliment: 'I am very unwilling to be left alone, Sir, and therefore I go with my company down the first pair of stairs, in some hopes that they may, perhaps, return again; I go with you, Sir, as far as the street-door.' In what particular department he intended to engage,[2] does not appear, nor can Mr. Hamilton explain. His prayer is in general terms: 'Enlighten my understanding with knowledge of right, and govern my will by thy laws, that no deceit may mislead me, nor temptation corrupt me; that I may always endeavour to do good, and hinder evil.'[3] There is nothing upon the subject in his diary.

This year was distinguished by his being introduced into the family of Mr. Thrale, one of the most eminent brewers in England, and member of Parliament for the borough of Southwark. Foreigners are not a little amazed, when they hear of brewers, distillers, and men in similar departments of trade, held forth as persons of considerable consequence. In this great commercial country it is natural that a situation which produces much wealth should be considered as very respectable; and, no doubt, honest

[1] Prayers and Meditations, p. 66.

[2] [In the Preface to a late Collection of Mr. Hamilton's Pieces, it has been observed, that our authour was, by the generality of Johnson's words, 'led to suppose that he was seized with a temporary fit of amibition, and that hence he was induced to apply his thoughts to law and politicks. But Mr. Boswell was certainly mistaken in this respect; and these words merely allude to Johnson's having at that time entered into some engagement with Mr. Hamilton occasionally to furnish him with his sentiments on the great political topicks which should be considered in parliament.' In consequence of this engagement, Johnson, in November, 1766, wrote a very valuable tract, entitled, 'Considerations on Corn,' which is printed as an Appendix to the works of Mr. Hamilton, published by T. Payne in 1808. MALONE.]

[3] Prayers and Meditations, p. 67.

industry is entitled to esteem. But, perhaps, the too rapid
advances of men of low extraction tends to lessen the value
of that distinction by birth and gentility, which has ever
been found beneficial to the grand scheme of subordination. Johnson used to give this account of the rise of
Mr. Thrale's father: 'He worked at six shillings a week
for twenty years[a] in the great brewery, which afterwards
was his own. The proprietor of it[1] had an only daughter,
who was married to a nobleman. It was not fit that a peer
should continue the business. On the old man's death,
therefore, the brewery was to be sold. To find a purchaser
for so large a property was a difficult matter; and, after
some time, it was suggested, that it would be adviseable
to treat with Thrale, a sensible, active, honest man, who
had been employed in the house, and to transfer the whole
to him for thirty thousand pounds, security being taken
upon the property. This was accordingly settled. In eleven
years Thrale paid the purchase-money. He acquired a
large fortune, and lived to be a member of Parliament for
Southwark.[2] But what was most remarkable was the
liberality with which he used his riches. He gave his son
and daughters the best education. The esteem which his
good conduct procured him from the nobleman who had
married his master's daughter, made him be treated with
much attention; and his son, both at school and at the
University of Oxford, associated with young men of the
first rank. His allowance from his father, after he left
college, was splendid; not less than a thousand a year.
This, in a man who had risen as old Thrale did, was a very

index sign:
this account etc. [I]
underlined:
twenty years [H]
[a] *no no, he wd. never
have got rich* that way
[H]

[b] *Edmund Halsey was
Son to a Miller at St.
Albans wth. whom he
quarrel'd—like Ralph
in the Maid of the
Mill,—and ran away
to London with a very
few Shillings in his
Pocket. He was emi-
nently handsome . . .
& Old Child of
the Anchor Brewhouse
Southwark took him
in . . . as what we
call a Broomstick Clerk
to sweep the Yard
&c. Edmund Halsey*

1 [The predecessor of old Thrale was Edmund Halsey, Esq.;[b] the nobleman
who married his daughter, was Lord Cobham, great uncle of the Marquis
of Buckingham. But I believe, Dr. Johnson was mistaken in assigning so
very low an origin to Mr. Thrale. The Clerk of St. Alban's, a very aged man,
told me, that he, (the elder Thrale,) married a sister of Mr. Halsey. It is at
least certain that the family of Thrale was of some consideration in that
town: in the abbey church is a handsome monument to the memory of Mr.
John Thrale, late of London, Merchant, who died in 1704, aged 54;
Margaret, his wife, and three of their children who died young, between
the years 1676 and 1690. The arms upon this monument are, paly of eight,
gules and or, impaling, ermine, on a chief indented vert, three wolves (or
gryphons') heads, or, couped at the neck:—Crest on a ducal coronet, a tree,
vert. BLAKEWAY.]

2 [In 1733 he served the office of High Sheriff for Surrey; and died April
9, 1758. A. CHALMERS.]

extraordinary instance of generosity. He used to say, "If this young dog does not find so much after I am gone as he expects, let him remember that he has had a great deal in my own time." '

The son, though in affluent circumstances, had good sense enough to carry on his father's trade, which was of such extent, that I remember he once told me, he would not quit it for an annuity of ten thousand a year; 'Not (said he,) that I get ten thousand a year by it, but it is an estate to a family.' Having left daughters only, the property was sold for the immense sum of one hundred and thirty-five thousand pounds; a magnificent proof of what may be done by fair trade in a long period of time.

There may be some who think that a new system of gentility[1] might be established, upon principles totally different from what have hitherto prevailed. Our present heraldry, it may be said, is suited to the barbarous times in which it had its origin. It is chiefly founded upon ferocious merit, upon military excellence. Why, in civilized times, we may be asked, should there not be rank and honours, upon principles, which, independent of long custom, are certainly not less worthy, and which, when once allowed to be connected with elevation and precedency, would obtain the same dignity in our imagination? Why should not the knowledge, the skill, the expertness, the assiduity, and the spirited hazards of trade and commerce, when crowned with success, be entitled to give those flattering distinctions by which mankind are so universally captivated?

Such are the specious, but false arguments for a proposition which always will find numerous advocates in a nation where men are every day starting up from obscurity to wealth. To refute them is needless. The general sense

[1] Mrs. Burney informs me that she heard Dr. Johnson say, 'An English Merchant is a new species of Gentleman.' He, perhaps, had in his mind the following ingenious passage in 'The Conscious Lovers,' Act. iv. Scene ii. where Mr. Sealand thus addresses Sir John Bevil: 'Give me leave to say, that we merchants are a species of gentry that have grown into the world this last century, and are as honourable, and almost as useful as you landed-folks, that have always thought yourselves so much above us; for your trading forsooth is extended no farther than a load of hay, or a fat ox.—You are pleasant people indeed! because you are generally bred up to be lazy, therefore, I warrant you, industry is dishonourable.'

behav'd so well he was soon prefer'd to be a House Clerk . . . & then having free Access to his Master's Table — married his only Daughter, & succeeded to the Business upon Child's Demise. being now rich & prosperous, he turnd his Eyes homewards, where he learn'd that Sister Sukey had married a hard-working Man at Offley in Hertfordshire & had many Children by her. He sent for one of them to London,—my Mr. Thrale's Father, said he would make a Man of him, & did so; but made him work very hard, & treated him very roughly. Halsey being more proud than tender, . . . and his only Child—a Daughter —married to Ld Cobham — Old Thrale however, as these fine Writers call him—then a Young Fellow, & like his Uncle Eminent for personal Beauty;— made himself so useful to Mr. Halsey, that the Weight of Business fell entirely on him; & while Edmund was canvassing the Borough, & Visiting the Vicountess, Ralph Thrale was getting Money both for himself & his Principal . . . who envious of his Success with a Wench they both liked . . . but who prefer'd the Young Man to the Old one; died: — leaving him ne'er a Guinea, & He bought the Brewhouse of Lord & Lady Cobham—making an excellent Bargain . . . with the money he got & saved. [H]

Edmund Halsey was Son to a Miller at St.

Albans, who quarrel'd
wth. his Father &
walk'd up to London in
a Passion: when arriv'd
he had but 1s 6d in his
Pocket, and wander-
ing about ye. Door
of Child's Brewhouse
gain'd Employment as
a Broomstick Clerk 6s
a Week, but he rose
gradually to be the 1st
Clerk, married his
Master's Daughter &
got Possession of the
Brewhouse—When he
found himself rich &
with one Daughter only
—he looked out for a
Nephew, & found his
sister Sukey's Son by a
poor old Man at Offley
in Herts; whence he
drove an Ass loaded
with apples to Hitchin
Market—This Son was
Father to Henry Thrale
who married the Niece
of Sir Thos. Salusbury
in whose Dogkennel his
Father was born. [I]
underlined:
English 'Squire [I]
[a] no no; Mr. Thrale's
manners presented the
Character of a Gay
Man of the Town: like
Millamant in Con-
greve's Comedy, he ab-
horred the Country &
Every thing in it. [H]
not at All like an
English Squire [I]

marginal line:
learning: he . . . lower
forms [H]

of mankind cries out, with irresistible force, ' Un gentilhomme
est toujours gentilhomme.'

Mr. Thrale had married Miss Hesther Lynch Salusbury,
of good Welch extraction, a lady of lively talents, improved by education. That Johnson's introduction into
Mr. Thrale's family, which contributed so much to the
happiness of his life, was owing to her desire for his conversation, is a very probable and the general supposition: but
it is not the truth. Mr. Murphy, who was intimate with
Mr. Thrale, having spoken very highly of Dr. Johnson,
he was requested to make them acquainted. This being
mentioned to Johnson, he accepted of an invitation to
dinner at Thrale's, and was so much pleased with his
reception, both by Mr. and Mrs. Thrale, and they so much
pleased with him, that his invitations to their house were
more and more frequent, till at last he became one of the
family, and an apartment was appropriated to him, both
in their house at Southwark and in their villa at Streatham.

Johnson had a very sincere esteem for Mr. Thrale, as a
man of excellent principles, a good scholar, well skilled in
trade, of a sound understanding, and of manners such as
presented the character of a plain independent English
'Squire.[a] As this family will frequently be mentioned in the
course of the following pages, and as a false notion has
prevailed that Mr. Thrale was inferiour, and in some
degree insignificant, compared with Mrs. Thrale, it may
be proper to give a true state of the case from the authority
of Johnson himself in his own words.

'I know no man, (said he,) who is more master of his
wife and family than Thrale. If he but holds up a finger, he
is obeyed. It is a great mistake to suppose that she is above
him in literary attainments. She is more flippant; but he
has ten times her learning: he is a regular scholar; but her
learning is that of a school-boy in one of the lower forms.'
My readers may naturally wish for some representation of
the figures of this couple. Mr. Thrale was tall, well proportioned, and stately. As for Madam, or my Mistress, by
which epithets Johnson used to mention Mrs. Thrale, she
was short, plump, and brisk. She has herself given us a
lively view of the idea which Johnson had of her person,
on her appearing before him in a dark-coloured gown:

'You little creatures should never wear those sort of clothes, however; they are unsuitable in every way. What! have not all insects gay colours?'[1] Mr. Thrale gave his wife a liberal indulgence, both in the choice of their company, and in the mode of entertaining them. He understood and valued Johnson, without remission, from their first acquaintance to the day of his death. Mrs. Thrale was enchanted with Johnson's conversation for its own sake, and had also a very allowable vanity in appearing to be honoured with the attention of so celebrated a man.

marginal line: *had also ... a man* [H]

Nothing could be more fortunate for Johnson than this connection. He had at Mr. Thrale's all the comforts and even luxuries of life: his melancholy was diverted, and his irregular habits lessened by association with an agreeable and well-ordered family. He was treated with the utmost respect, and even affection. The vivacity of Mrs. Thrale's literary talk roused him to cheerfulness and exertion, even when they were alone. But this was not often the case; for he found here a constant succession of what gave him the highest enjoyment, the society of the learned, the witty, and the eminent in every way; who were assembled in numerous companies; called forth his wonderful powers, and gratified him with admiration, to which no man could be insensible.

marginal line: *In the ... it had* [H]

In the October of this year[2] he at length gave to the world his edition of Shakspeare, which, if it had no other merit but that of producing his Preface, in which the excellencies and defects of that immortal bard are displayed with a masterly hand, the nation would have had no reason to complain. A blind indiscriminate admiration

---

[1] Mrs. Piozzi's Anecdotes, p. 279.

[2] [From a letter written by Dr. Johnson to Dr. Joseph Warton, the day after the publication of his Shakspeare, Oct. 9, 1765, (See Wooll's Memoirs of Dr. Warton, 4to. 1806) it appears that Johnson spent some time with that gentleman at Winchester in this year. In a letter written by Dr. Warton to Mr. Thomas Warton, not long afterwards (January 28, 1766) is a paragraph, which may throw some light on various passages in Dr. Warton's edition of Pope, relative to Johnson:—'I only dined with Johnson, who seemed cold and indifferent, and scarce said any thing to me: perhaps he has heard what I said of his Shakspeare, or rather was offended at what I wrote to him:—as he pleases.' The letter here alluded to, it is believed, has not been preserved: at least, it does not appear in the collection above referred to. MALONE.]

of Shakspeare had exposed the British nation to the ridicule of foreigners. Johnson, by candidly admitting the faults of his poet, had the more credit in bestowing on him deserved and indisputable praise; and doubtless none of all his panegyrists have done him half so much honour. Their praise was like that of a counsel, upon his own side of the cause; Johnson's was like the grave, well considered, and impartial opinion of the judge, which falls from his lips with weight, and is received with reverence. What he did as a commentator has no small share of merit, though his researches were not so ample, and his investigations so acute as they might have been; which we now certainly know from the labours of other able and ingenious criticks who have followed him. He has enriched his edition with a concise account of each play, and of its characteristick excellence. Many of his notes have illustrated obscurities in the text, and placed passages eminent for beauty in a more conspicuous light; and he has, in general, exhibited such a mode of annotation, as may be beneficial to all subsequent editors.

His Shakspeare was virulently attacked by Mr. William Kenrick, who obtained the degree of LL.D. from a Scotch University, and wrote for the booksellers in a great variety of branches. Though he certainly was not without considerable merit, he wrote with so little regard to decency, and principles, and decorum, and in so hasty a manner, that his reputation was neither extensive nor lasting. I remember one evening, when some of his works were mentioned, Dr. Goldsmith said he had never heard of them; upon which Dr. Johnson observed, 'Sir, he is one of the many who have made themselves *publick*, without making themselves *known*.'

A young student of Oxford, of the name of Barclay, wrote an answer to Kenrick's review of Johnson's Shakspeare. Johnson was at first angry that Kenrick's attack should have the credit of an answer. But afterwards, considering the young man's good intention, he kindly noticed him, and probably would have done more, had not the young man died.

In his Preface to Shakspeare, Johnson treated Voltaire very contemptuously, observing, upon some of his remarks,

'These are the petty cavils of petty minds.' Voltaire, in revenge, made an attack upon Johnson, in one of his numerous literary sallies which I remember to have read; but there being no general index to his voluminous works, have searched in vain, and therefore cannot quote it.

Voltaire was an antagonist with whom I thought Johnson should not disdain to contend. I pressed him to answer. He said, he perhaps might; but he never did.

Mr. Burney having occasion to write to Johnson for some receipts for subscriptions to his Shakspeare, which Johnson had omitted to deliver when the money was paid, he availed himself of that opportunity of thanking Johnson for the great pleasure which he had received from the perusal of his Preface to Shakspeare; which, although it excited much clamour against him at first, is now justly ranked among the most excellent of his writings. To this letter Johnson returned the following answer:

'TO CHARLES BURNEY, ESQ. IN POLAND-STREET

'SIR,

'I AM sorry that your kindness to me has brought upon you so much trouble, though you have taken care to abate that sorrow, by the pleasure which I receive from your approbation. I defend my criticism in the same manner with you. We must confess the faults of our favourite, to gain credit to our praise of his excellencies. He that claims, either in himself or for another, the honours of perfection, will surely injure the reputation which he designs to assist.[a]

'Be pleased to make my compliments to your family. I am, Sir,

> 'Your most obliged
> 'And most humble servant,

'Oct. 16, 1765.'   'SAM. JOHNSON'

[a] *Boswell should have remember'd that Sentence when he blamed H. L. P.* [H & I]

From one of his Journals I transcribe what follows:

'At church, Oct.—65.

'To avoid all singularity; *Bonaventura*.[1]

[1] He was probably proposing to himself the model of this excellent person, who for his piety was named *the Seraphick Doctor*.

To come in before service, and compose my mind by meditation, or by reading some portions of scripture. *Tetty.*

'If I can hear the sermon, to attend it, unless attention be more troublesome than useful.

'To consider the act of prayer as a reposal of myself upon God, and a resignation of all into his holy hand.'

In 1764 and 1765 it should seem that Dr. Johnson was so busily employed with his edition of Shakspeare, as to have had little leisure for any other literary exertion, or, indeed, even for private correspondence. He did not favour me with a single letter for more than two years, for which it will appear that he afterwards apologised.

He was, however, at all times ready to give assistance to his friends, and others, in revising their works, and in writing for them, or greatly improving, their Dedications. In that courtly species of composition no man excelled Dr. Johnson. Though the loftiness of his mind prevented him from ever dedicating in his own person, he wrote a very great number of Dedications for others. Some of these, the persons who were favoured with them, are unwilling should be mentioned, from a too anxious apprehension, as I think, that they might be suspected of having received larger assistance; and some, after all the diligence I have bestowed, have escaped my enquiries. He told me, a great many years ago, 'he believed he had dedicated to all the Royal Family round;' and it was indifferent to him what was the subject of the work dedicated, provided it were innocent. He once dedicated some Musick for the German Flute to Edward, Duke of York. In writing Dedications for others, he considered himself as by no means speaking his own sentiments.

Notwithstanding his long silence, I never omitted to write to him, when I had any thing worthy of communicating. I generally kept copies of my letters to him, that I might have a full view of our correspondence, and never be at a loss to understand any reference in his letters. He kept the greater part of mine very carefully; and a short time before his death was attentive enough to seal them up in bundles, and order them to be delivered to me, which was accordingly done. Amongst them I found one, of

index sign:
and order them etc. [H]

which I had not made a copy, and which I own I read with pleasure at the distance of almost twenty years. It is dated November, 1765, at the palace of Pascal Paoli, in Corte, the capital of Corsica, and is full of generous enthusiasm. After giving a sketch of what I had seen and heard in that island, it proceeded thus: 'I dare to call this a spirited tour. I dare to challenge your approbation.'

This letter produced the following answer, which I found on my arrival at Paris.

'*A Mr. Mr.* BOSWELL, *chez Mr.* WATERS, *Banquier, à Paris*

'DEAR SIR,

'APOLOGIES are seldom of any use. We will delay till your arrival the reasons, good or bad, which have made me such a sparing and ungrateful correspondent. Be assured, for the present, that nothing has lessened either the esteem or love with which I dismissed you at Harwich. Both have been increased by all that I have been told of you by yourself or others; and when you return, you will return to an unaltered, and, I hope, unalterable friend.

'All that you have to fear from me is the vexation of disappointing me. No man loves to frustrate expectations which have been formed in his favour; and the pleasure which I promise myself from your journals and remarks is so great, that perhaps no degree of attention or discernment will be sufficient to afford it.

'Come home, however, and take your chance. I long to see you, and to hear you; and hope that we shall not be so long separated again. Come home, and expect such welcome as is due to him, whom a wise and noble curiosity has led, where perhaps no native of this country ever was before.

'I have no news to tell you that can deserve your notice; nor would I willingly lessen the pleasure that any novelty may give you at your return. I am afraid we shall find it difficult to keep among us a mind which has been so long feasted with variety. But let us try what esteem and kindness can effect.

'As your father's liberality has indulged you with so long a ramble, I doubt not but you will think his sickness, or even his desire to see you, a sufficient reason for hastening your return. The longer we live, and the more we think, the higher value we learn to put on the friendship and tenderness of parents and of friends. Parents we can have but once; and he promises himself too much, who enters life with the expectation of finding many friends. Upon some motive, I hope, that you will be here soon; and am willing to think that it will be an inducement to your return, that it is sincerely desired by, dear Sir,

'Your affectionate humble servant,

'Johnson's Court, Fleet-street,   'SAM. JOHNSON'
    January 14, 1766.'

I returned to London in February, and found Dr. Johnson in a good house in Johnson's-court, Fleet-street, in which he had accommodated Miss Williams with an apartment on the ground floor, while Mr. Levett occupied his post in the garret: his faithful Francis was still attending upon him. He received me with much kindness. The fragments of our first conversation, which I have preserved, are these: I told him that Voltaire, in a conversation with me, had distinguished Pope and Dryden thus:—'Pope drives a handsome chariot, with a couple of neat trim nags; Dryden a coach, and six stately horses.' JOHNSON. 'Why, Sir, the truth is, they both drive coaches and six; but Dryden's horses are either galloping or stumbling: Pope's go at a steady even trot.'[1] He said of Goldsmith's 'Traveller,' which had been published in my absence, 'There has not been so fine a poem since Pope's time.'

And here it is proper to settle, with authentick precision, what has long floated in publick report, as to Johnson's being himself the authour of a considerable part of that

---

[1] It is remarkable that Mr. Gray has employed somewhat the same image to characterise Dryden. He, indeed, furnishes his car with but two horses; but they are of 'ethereal race:'

> 'Behold where Dryden's less presumptuous car,
> Wide o'er the fields of glory bear
> Two coursers of ethereal race,
> With necks in thunder cloath'd, and long resounding pace.'
>
> *Ode on the Progress of Poesy.*

poem. Much, no doubt, both of the sentiments and expression were derived from conversation with him; and it was certainly submitted to his friendly revision: but in the year 1783, he at my request marked with a pencil the lines which he had furnished, which are only line 420th,

two marginal lines: to his . . . which he [H]

'To stop too fearful, and too faint to go;'

and the concluding ten lines, except the last couplet but one, which I distinguish by the Italick character:

'How small of all that human hearts endure,
That part which kings or laws can cause or cure.
Still to ourselves in every place consign'd,
Our own felicity we make or find;
With secret course, which no loud storms annoy,
Glides the smooth current of domestick joy:
The lifted axe, the agonizing wheel,
Luke's iron crown, and Damien's bed of steel,
To men remote from power, but rarely known,
Leave reason, faith, and conscience, all our own.'

queried: With secret course etc. [H]

He added, 'These are all of which I can be sure.' They bear a small proportion to the whole, which consists of four hundred and thirty-eight verses. Goldsmith, in the couplet which he inserted, mentions *Luke* as a person well known, and superficial readers have passed it over quite smoothly; while those of more attention have been as much perplexed by *Luke* as by *Lydiat,* in 'The Vanity of Human Wishes.' The truth is, that Goldsmith himself was in a mistake. 'In the *Respublica Hungarica,*' there is an account of a desperate rebellion in the year 1514, headed by two brothers, of the name of *Zeck,* George and Luke. When it was quelled, *George,* not *Luke,* was punished by his head being encircled with a red hot iron crown: '*coronâ candescente ferreâ coronatur.*' The same severity of torture was exercised on the Earl of Athol, one of the murderers of King James I. of Scotland.[1]

[1] [On the iron crown, see Mr. Steevens's note 7, on Act iv. sc. i. of RICHARD III. It seems to be alluded to in MACBETH, Act iv. sc. i. 'Thy crown does sear,' &c. See also Gough's Camden, vol. iii. p. 396. BLAKEWAY.]

marginal line:
*marking the . . . last
four* [H]

Dr. Johnson at the same time favoured me by marking the lines which he furnished to Goldsmith's 'Deserted Village,' which are only the last four:

'That trade's proud empire hastes to swift decay,
As ocean sweeps the labour'd mole away:
While self-dependent power can time defy,
As rocks resist the billows and the sky.'

Talking of education, 'People have now-a-days, (said he,) got a strange opinion that every thing should be taught by lectures. Now, I cannot see that lectures can do so much good as reading the books from which the lectures are taken. I know nothing that can be best taught by lectures, except where experiments are to be shewn. You may teach chymistry by lectures:—You might teach making of shoes by lectures!'

At night I supped with him at the Mitre Tavern, that we might renew our social intimacy at the original place of meeting. But there was now a considerable difference in his way of living. Having had an illness, in which he was advised to leave off wine, he had, from that period, continued to abstain from it, and drank only water, or lemonade.

a who was this? [J]

I told him that a foreign friend of his,ª whom I had met with abroad, was so wretchedly perverted to infidelity, that he treated the hopes of immortality with brutal levity; and said, 'As man dies like a dog, let him lie like a dog.' JOHNSON. '*If* he dies like a dog, *let* him lie like a dog.' I added, that this man said to me, 'I hate mankind, for I think myself one of the best of them, and I know how bad I am.' JOHNSON. 'Sir, he must be very singular in his opinion, if he thinks himself one of the best of men; for none of his friends think him so.'—He said, 'No honest man could be a Deist; for no man could be so after a fair examination of the proofs of Christianity.' I named Hume. JOHNSON. 'No, Sir; Hume owned to a clergyman in the bishoprick of Durham, that he had never read the New Testament with attention.'—I mentioned Hume's notion, that all who are happy are equally happy; a little Miss with a new gown at a dancing-school ball, a General at the head of a victorious army, and an orator, after having made an eloquent speech in a great assembly. JOHNSON. 'Sir, that all who are happy, are equally happy, is not true. A peasant and a philosopher may be equally *satisfied*, but not equally *happy*. Happiness consists in the multiplicity of agreeable consciousness. A peasant has not capacity for having equal happiness with a philosopher.' I remember this very question very happily illustrated in opposition to Hume, by the Reverend Mr. Robert Brown, at Utrecht. 'A small drinking-glass and a large one, (said he,) may be equally full; but the large one holds more than the small.'[1]

Dr. Johnson was very kind this evening, and said to me, 'You have now lived five-and-twenty years, and you have employed them well.' 'Alas, Sir, (said I,) I fear not. Do I know history? Do I know mathematicks? Do I know law?' JOHNSON. 'Why, Sir, though you may know no science so well as to be able to teach it, and no profession so well as to be able to follow it, your general mass of knowledge of books and men renders you very capable to make yourself master of any science, or fit yourself for any profession.' I mentioned that a gay friend had advised me against being a lawyer, because I should be excelled by plodding blockheads. JOHNSON. 'Why, Sir, in the formulary and statutory part of law, a plodding blockhead may excel; but in the ingenious and rational part of it a plodding blockhead can never excel.'

marginal line: *in the . . . never excel* [H]

I talked of the mode adopted by some to rise in the world, by courting great men, and asked him whether he

---

[1] [Bishop Hall, in discussing this subject, has the same image: 'Yet so conceive of these heavenly degrees, that the least is glorious. *So do these vessels differ, that all are full.*' EPISTLES, Dec. iii. cp. 6. 'Of the different degrees of heavenly glory.' This most learned and ingenious writer, however, was not the first who suggested this image; for it is found also in an old book entitled 'A Work worth the reading,' by Charles Gibbon, 4to, 1591. In the fifth dialogue of this work, in which the question debated is, 'whether there be degrees of glorie in heaven, or difference of paines in hell,' one of the speakers observes, that 'no doubt in the world to come, (where the least pleasure is unspeakable,) it cannot be but that he which hath bin most afflicted here, shall conceive and receive more exceeding joy, than he which hath bin touched with lesse tribulation; and yet the joyes of heaven are fitlie compared to *vessels filled with licour, of all quantities;* for everie man shall have his full measure there.' By '*all* quantities' this writer (who seems to refer to a still more ancient authour than himself) I suppose, means *different* quantities. MALONE.]

had ever submitted to it. JOHNSON. 'Why, Sir, I never
was near enough to great men, to court them. You may be
prudently attached to great men, and yet independent.
You are not to do what you think wrong; and, Sir, you
are to calculate, and not pay too dear for what you get.

You must not give a shilling's worth of court for sixpence
worth of good. But if you can get a shilling's worth of good
for sixpence worth of court, you are a fool if you do not
pay court.'

He said, 'If convents should be allowed at all, they
should only be retreats for persons unable to serve the
publick, or who have served it. It is our first duty to serve
society; and, after we have done that, we may attend wholly
to the salvation of our own souls. A youthful passion for
abstracted devotion should not be encouraged.'

I introduced the subject of second sight, and other
mysterious manifestations; the fulfilment of which, I suggested, might happen by chance. JOHNSON. 'Yes, Sir,
but they have happened so often, that mankind have
agreed to think them not fortuitous.'

I talked to him a great deal of what I had seen in Corsica,
and of my intention to publish an account of it. He encouraged me by saying, 'You cannot go to the bottom of
the subject; but all that you tell us will be new to us. Give
us as many anecdotes as you can.'

Our next meeting at the Mitre was on Saturday the
15th of February, when I presented to him my old and
most intimate friend, the Reverend Mr. Temple, then of
Cambridge. I having mentioned that I had passed some
time with Rousseau in his wild retreat, and having quoted
some remark made by Mr. Wilkes, with whom I had spent
many pleasant hours in Italy, Johnson said, (sarcastically,)
'It seems, Sir, you have kept very good company abroad,
Rousseau and Wilkes!' Thinking it enough to defend one
at a time, I said nothing as to my gay friend, but answered
with a smile, 'My dear Sir, you don't call Rousseau bad
company. Do you really think *him* a bad man?' JOHNSON.
'Sir, if you are talking jestingly of this, I don't talk with
you. If you mean to be serious, I think him one of the
worst of men; a rascal, who ought to be hunted out of
society, as he has been. Three or four nations have

1766. Ætat. 57]   DR. JOHNSON   363

expelled him: and it is a shame that he is protected in this country.' BOSWELL. 'I don't deny, Sir, but that his novel may, perhaps, do harm; but I cannot think his intention was bad.' JOHNSON. 'Sir, that will not do. We cannot prove any man's intention to be bad. You may shoot a man through the head, and say you intended to miss him; but the Judge will order you to be hanged. An alleged want of intention, when evil is committed, will not be allowed in a court of justice. Rousseau, Sir, is a very bad man. I would sooner sign a sentence for his transportation, than that of any felon who has gone from the Old Bailey these many years. Yes, I should like to have him work in the plantations.'ᵃ BOSWELL. 'Sir, do you think him as bad a man as Voltaire?' JOHNSON. 'Why, Sir, it is difficult to settle the proportion of iniquity between them.'

ᵃ *It would have cur'd Rousseau & have made him a very good Man* [I]

This violence seemed very strange to me, who had read many of Rousseau's animated writings with great pleasure, and even edification; had been much pleased with his society, and was just come from the Continent, where he was very generally admired. Nor can I yet allow that he deserves the very severe censure which Johnson pronounced upon him. His absurd preference of savage to civilised life, and other singularities, are proofs rather of a defect in his understanding, than of any depravity in his heart. And notwithstanding the unfavourable opinion which many worthy men have expressed of his '*Profession de Foi du Vicaire Savoyard,*' I cannot help admiring it as the performance of a man full of sincere reverential submission to Divine Mystery, though beset with perplexing doubts: a state of mind to be viewed with pity rather than with anger.

On his favourite subject of subordination, Johnson said, 'So far is it from being true that men are naturally equal, that no two people can be half an hour together, but one shall acquire an evident superiority over the other.'

marginal line: *said, 'So . . . half an* [H]

I mentioned the advice given us by philosophers, to console ourselves, when distressed or embarrassed, by thinking of those who are in a worse situation than ourselves. This, I observed, could not apply to all, for there must be some who have nobody worse than they are. JOHNSON. 'Why, to be sure, Sir, there are; but they don't know it. There is no being so poor and so contemptible, who does not think there is somebody still poorer, and still more contemptible.'ᵃ

As my stay in London at this time was very short, I had not many opportunities of being with Dr. Johnson; but I felt my veneration for him in no degree lessened, by my having seen *multorum hominum mores et urbes*. On the contrary, by having it in my power to compare him with many of the most celebrated persons of other countries, my admiration of his extraordinary mind was increased and confirmed.

The roughness, indeed, which sometimes appeared in his manners, was more striking to me now, from my having been accustomed to the studied smooth complying habits of the Continent; and I clearly recognised in him, not without respect for his honest conscientious zeal, the same indignant and sarcastical mode of treating every attempt to unhinge or weaken good principles.

One evening, when a young gentleman teased him with an account of the infidelity of his servant, who, he said, would not believe the scriptures, because he could not read them in the original tongues, and be sure that they were not invented;—'Why, foolish fellow, (said Johnson,) has he any better authority for almost every thing that he believes?'—BOSWELL. 'Then the vulgar, Sir, never can know they are right, but must submit themselves to the learned.'—JOHNSON. 'To be sure, Sir. The vulgar are the children of the State, and must be taught like children.'—BOSWELL. 'Then, Sir, a poor Turk must be a Mahometan, just as a poor Englishman must be a Christian?'—JOHNSON. 'Why, yes, Sir; and what then? This now is such stuff as I used to talk to my mother, when I first began to think myself a clever fellow; and she ought to have whipt me for it.'

Another evening Dr. Goldsmith and I called on him, with the hope of prevailing on him to sup with us at the Mitre. We found him indisposed, and resolved not to go abroad. 'Come then, (said Goldsmith,) we will not go to the Mitre to-night, since we cannot have the big man with us.' Johnson then called for a bottle of port, of which Goldsmith and I partook, while our friend, now a water-drinker, sat by us. GOLDSMITH. 'I think, Mr. Johnson, you don't

underlined: *big* [H]

go near the theatres now. You give yourself no more concern about a new play, than if you had never had any
thing to do with the stage.' JOHNSON. 'Why, Sir, our tastes
greatly alter. The lad does not care for the child's rattle,
and the old man does not care for the young man's whore.'
GOLDSMITH. 'Nay, Sir; but your Muse was not a whore.'
JOHNSON. 'Sir, I do not think she was. But as we advance
in the journey of life we drop some of the things which have
pleased us; whether it be that we are fatigued and don't
choose to carry so many things any farther, or that we
find other things which we like better.' BOSWELL. 'But,
Sir, why don't you give us something in some other way?'
GOLDSMITH. 'Ay, Sir, we have a claim upon you.'
JOHNSON. 'No, Sir, I am not obliged to do any more.
No man is obliged to do as much as he can do. A man is to
have part of his life to himself. If a soldier has fought a
good many campaigns, he is not to be blamed, if he retires
to ease and tranquillity. A physician, who has practised
long in a great city, may be excused, if he retires to a small
town, and takes less practice. Now, Sir, the good I can do
by my conversation bears the same proportion to the good
I can do by my writings, that the practice of a physician,
retired to a small town, does to his practice in a great city.'
BOSWELL. 'But I wonder, Sir, you have not more pleasure
in writing than in not writing.' JOHNSON. 'Sir, you *may*
wonder.'

He talked of making verses, and observed, 'The great
difficulty is, to know when you have made good ones.
When composing, I have generally had them in my mind,
perhaps fifty at a time, walking up and down in my room;
and then I have written them down, and often, from laziness, have written only half lines. I have written a hundred
lines in a day. I remember, I wrote a hundred lines of
"The Vanity of Human Wishes" in a day. Doctor,
(turning to Goldsmith,) I am not quite idle; I made one
line t'other day; but I made no more.' GOLDSMITH.
'Let us hear it; we'll put a bad one to it.' JOHNSON. 'No,
Sir; I have forgot it.'

Such specimens of the easy and playful conversation
of the great Dr. Samuel Johnson are, I think, to be prized;
as exhibiting the little varieties of a mind so enlarged and

so powerful when objects of consequence required its exertions, and as giving us a minute knowledge of his character and modes of thinking.

'TO BENNET LANGTON, ESQ. AT LANGTON, NEAR
SPILSBY, LINCOLNSHIRE

'DEAR SIR,

'WHAT your friends have done, that from your departure till now nothing has been heard of you, none of us are able to inform the rest; but as we are all neglected alike, no one thinks himself entitled to the privilege of complaint.

'I should have known nothing of you or of Langton, from the time that dear Miss Langton left us, had not I met Mr. Simpson, of Lincoln, one day in the street, by whom I was informed that Mr. Langton, your Mamma, and yourself, had been all ill, that that you were all recovered.

'That sickness should suspend your correspondence, I did not wonder; but hoped that it would be renewed at your recovery.

'Since you will not inform us where you are, or how you live, I know not whether you desire to know any thing of us. However, I will tell you that THE CLUB subsists; but we have the loss of Burke's company since he has been engaged in publick business, in which he has gained more reputation than perhaps any man at his [first] appearance ever gained before. He made two speeches in the House for repealing the Stamp-act, which were publickly commended by Mr. Pitt, and have filled the town with wonder.

'Burke is a great man by nature, and is expected soon to attain civil greatness. I am grown greater too, for I have maintained the newspapers these many weeks; and what is greater still, I have risen every morning since New-year's day, at about eight: when I was up, I have indeed done but little; yet it is no slight advancement to obtain for so many hours more, the consciousness of being.

'I wish you were in my new study; I am now writing the first letter in it. I think it looks very pretty about me.

'Dyer[1] is constant at THE CLUB; Hawkins is remiss; I am not over diligent. Dr. Nugent, Dr. Goldsmith, and Mr. Reynolds, are very constant. M. Lye is printing his Saxon and Gothick Dictionary: all THE CLUB subscribes.

'You will pay my respects to all my Lincolnshire friends. I am, dear Sir,
                                   'Most affectionately your's,

'March 9, 1766,   'SAM. JOHNSON'
Johnson's-court, Fleet-street.'

'TO BENNET LANGTON, ESQ. AT LANGTON, NEAR
               SPILSBY, LINCOLNSHIRE

'DEAR SIR,

' IN supposing that I should be more than commonly affected by the death of Peregrine Langton,[2] you were not mistaken; he was one of those whom I loved at once by instinct and by reason. I have seldom indulged more hope of any thing than of being able to improve our acquaintance to friendship. Many a time have I placed myself again at Langton, and imagined the pleasure with which I should walk to Partney[3] in a summer morning; but this is no longer possible. We must now endeavour to preserve what is left us,—his example of piety and œconomy. I hope you make what enquiries you can, and write down what is told you. The little things which distinguish domestick characters are soon forgotten: if you delay to enquire, you will have no information; if you neglect to write, information will be vain.[4]

[1] [Samuel Dyer, Esq., a most learned and ingenious Member of the LITERARY CLUB, for whose understanding and attainments Dr. Johnson had great respect. He died Sept. 14, 1772. A more particular account of this gentleman may be found in a Note on the Life of Dryden, p. 186, prefixed to the edition of that great writer's PROSE WORKS, in four volumes, 8vo. 1800: in which his character is vindicated, and the very unfavourable and unjust representation of it, given by Sir John Hawkins in his Life of Johnson, pp. 222–232, is minutely examined. MALONE.]

[2] Mr. Langton's uncle.

[3] The place of residence of Mr. Peregrine Langton.

[4] Mr. Langton did not disregard this counsel, but wrote the following account which he has been pleased to communicate to me:
'The circumstances of Mr. Peregrine Langton were these. He had an annuity for life of two hundred pounds *per annum*. He resided in a village in Lincolnshire: the rent of his house, with two or three small fields, was twenty-eight pounds; the county he lived in was not more than moderately cheap; his family consisted of a sister, who paid him eighteen pounds

'His art of life certainly deserves to be known and studied. He lived in plenty and elegance upon an income which to many would appear indigent, and to most, scanty. How he lived, therefore, every man has an interest in knowing. His death, I hope, was peaceful; it was surely happy.

'I wish I had written sooner, lest, writing now, I should renew your grief; but I would not forbear saying what I have now said.

annually for her board, and a niece. The servants were two maids, and two men in livery. His common way of living, at his table, was three or four dishes; the appurtenances to his table were neat and handsome; he frequently entertained company at dinner, and then his table was well served with as many dishes as were usual at the tables of the other gentlemen in the neighbourhood. His own appearance, as to clothes, was genteelly neat and plain. He had always a post-chaise, and kept three horses.

'Such, with the resources I have mentioned, was his way of living, which he did not suffer to employ his whole income: for he had always a sum of money lying by him for any extraordinary expences that might arise. Some money he put into the stocks; at his death, the sum he had there amounted to one hundred and fifty pounds. He purchased out of his income his household-furniture and linen, of which latter he had a very ample store; and, as I am assured by those that had very good means of knowing, not less than the tenth part of his income was set apart for charity: at the time of his death, the sum of twenty-five pounds was found, with a direction to be employed in such uses.

'He had laid down a plan of living proportioned to his income, and did not practise any extraordinary degree of parsimony, but endeavoured that in his family there should be plenty without waste. As an instance that this was his endeavour, it may be worth while to mention a method he took in regulating a proper allowance of malt liquor to be drunk in his family, that there might not be a deficiency, or any intemperate profusion: On a complaint made that his allowance of a hogshead in a month, was not enough for his own family, he ordered the quantity of a hogshead to be put into bottles, had it locked up from the servants, and distributed out, every day, eight quarts, which is the quantity each day at one hogshead in a month; and told his servants, that if that did not suffice, he would allow them more; but, by this method, it appeared at once that the allowance was much more than sufficient for his small family; and this proved a clear conviction, that could not be answered, and saved all future dispute. He was, in general, very diligently and punctually attended and obeyed by his servants; he was very considerate as to the injunctions he gave, and explained them distinctly; and, at their first coming to his service, steadily exacted a close compliance with them, without any remission: and the servants finding this to be the case, soon grew habitually accustomed to the practice of their business, and then very little further attention was necessary. On extraordinary instances of good behaviour, or diligent service, he was not wanting in particular encouragements and presents above their wages; it is remarkable that he would permit their relations to visit them, and stay at his house two or three days at a time.

'The wonder, with most that hear an account of his œconomy, will be, how he was able, with such an income, to do so much, especially when it is

'This loss is, I hope, the only misfortune of a family to whom no misfortune at all should happen, if my wishes could avert it. Let me know how you all go on. Has Mr. Langton got him the little horse that I recommended? It would do him good to ride about his estate in fine weather.

'Be pleased to make my compliments to Mrs. Langton, and to dear Miss Langton, and Miss Di, and Miss Juliet, and to every body else.

'THE CLUB holds very well together. Monday is my night.[1] I continue to rise tolerably well, and read more than I did. I hope something will yet come on it. I am, Sir,

'Your most affectionate servant,

'May 10, 1766,   'SAM. JOHNSON'
Johnson's-court, Fleet-street.'

considered that he paid for every thing he had. He had no land, except the two or three small fields which I have said he rented; and, instead of gaining any thing by their produce, I have reason to think he lost by them; however, they furnished him with no further assistance towards his housekeeping, than grass for his horses, (not hay, for that I know he bought,) and for two cows. Every Monday morning he settled his family accounts and so kept up a constant attention to the confining his expences within his income; and to do it more exactly, compared those expences with a computation he had made, how much that income would afford him every week and day of the year. One of his œconomical practices was, as soon as any repair was wanting in or about his house, to have it immediately performed. When he had money to spare, he chose to lay in a provision of linen or clothes, or any other necessaries; as then, he said, he could afford it, which he might not be so well able to do when the actual want came; in consequence of which method, he had a considerable supply of necessary articles lying by him, beside what was in use.

'But the main particular that seems to have enabled him to do so much with his income, was, that he paid for every thing as soon as he had it, except, alone, what were current accounts, such as rent for his house, and servants' wages; and these he paid at the stated times with the utmost exactness. He gave notice to the tradesmen of the neighbouring market-towns that they should no longer have his custom, if they let any of his servants have any thing without their paying for it. Thus he put it out of his power to commit those imprudences to which those are liable that defer their payments by using their money some other way than where it ought to go. And whatever money he had by him, he knew that it was not demanded elsewhere, but that he might safely employ it as he pleased.

'His example was confined, by the sequestered place of his abode, to the observation of few, though his prudence and virtue would have made it valuable to all who could have known it.—These few particulars, which I knew myself, or have obtained from those who lived with him, may afford instruction, and be an incentive to that wise art of living, which he so successfully practised.'

[1] Of his being in the chair of THE LITERARY CLUB, which at this time met once a week in the evening.

After I had been some time in Scotland, I mentioned to him in a letter that 'On my first return to my native country, after some years of absence, I was told of a vast number of my acquaintance who were all gone to the land of forgetfulness, and I found myself like a man stalking over a field of battle, who every moment perceives some one lying dead.' I complained of irresolution, and mentioned my having made a vow as a security for good conduct. I wrote to him again without being able to move his indolence: nor did I hear from him till he had received a copy of my inaugural Exercise, or Thesis in Civil Law, which I published at my admission as an Advocate, as is the custom in Scotland. He then wrote to me as follows:

'TO JAMES BOSWELL, ESQ.

'DEAR SIR,

'The reception of your Thesis put me in mind of my debt to you. Why did you * * * * * * * * * * * *.[1] I will punish you for it, by telling you that your Latin wants correction.[2] In the beginning, *Spei alteræ*, not to urge that it should be *primæ*, is not grammatical: *alteræ* should be *alteri*. In the next line you seem to use *genus* absolutely, for what we call *family*, that is, for *illustrious extraction*, I doubt without authority. *Homines nullius originis*, for *Nullis orti majoribus*, or, *Nullo loco nati*, is, as I am afraid, barbarous. — Ruddiman is dead.

[1] The passage omitted alluded to a private transaction.

[2] This censure of my Latin relates to the Dedication, which was as follows:

VIRO NOBILISSIMO, ORNATISSIMO,
JOANNI,
VICECOMITI MOUNTSTUART,
ATAVIS EDITO REGIBUS
EXCELSÆ FAMILIÆ DE BUTE SPEI ALTERÆ;
LABENTE SECULO,
QUUM HOMINES NULLIUS ORIGINIS
GENUS ÆQUARE OPIBUS AGGREDIUNTUR,
SANGUINIS ANTIQUI ET ILLUSTRIS
SEMPER MEMORI,
NATALIUM SPLENDOREM VIRTUTIBUS AUGENTI:
AD PUBLICA POPULI COMITIA
JAM LEGATO;
IN OPTIMATIUM VERO MAGNÆ BRITANNIÆ SENATU,
JURE HÆREDITARIO,

'I have now vexed you enough, and will try to please you. Your resolution to obey your father I sincerely approve; but do not accustom yourself to enchain your volatility by vows; they will sometime leave a thorn in your mind, which you will, perhaps, never be able to extract or eject. Take this warning; it is of great importance.[a]

marginal line: *sincerely approve . . . will, perhaps* [H]

[a] *So it is.* [H]

'The study of the law is what you very justly term it, copious and generous;[1] and in adding your name to its professors, you have done exactly what I always wished, when I wished you best. I hope that you will continue to pursue it vigorously and constantly. You gain, at least, what is no small advantage, security from those troublesome and wearisome discontents, which are always obtruding themselves upon a mind vacant, unemployed, and undetermined.

'You ought to think it no small inducement to diligence and perseverance, that they will please your father. We all live upon the hope of pleasing somebody; and the pleasure of pleasing ought to be greatest, and at last always will be greatest, when our endeavours are exerted in consequence of our duty.

underlined: *We all live, hope of pleasing somebody* [H]

'Life is not long, and too much of it must not pass in idle deliberation how it shall be spent: deliberation, which those who begin it by prudence, and continue it with subtilty, must, after long expence of thought, conclude by chance. To prefer one future mode of life to another, upon

OLIM CONSESSURO:

VIM INSITAM VARIA DOCTRINA PROMOVENTE,

NEC TAMEN SE VENDITANTE,

PRÆDITO:

PRISCA FIDE ANIMO LIBERRIMO,

ET MORUM ELEGANTIA

INSIGNI:

IN ITALIÆ VISITANDÆ ITINERE,

SOCIO SUO HONORATISSIMO,

HASCE JURISPRUDENTIÆ PRIMITIAS

DEVINCTISSIMÆ AMICITIÆ ET OBSERVANTIÆ,

MONUMENTUM,

D. D. C. Q.

JACOBUS BOSWELL

[1] This alludes to the first sentence of the *Prœmium* of my Thesis. 'JURISPRUDENTIÆ *studio nullum uberius, nullum generosius: in legibus enim agitandis, populorum mores, variasque fortunæ vices ex quibus leges oriuntur, contemplari simul solemus.*'

just reasons, requires faculties which it has not pleased our Creator to give us.

'If therefore the profession you have chosen has some unexpected inconveniences, console yourself by reflecting that no profession is without them; and that all the importunities and perplexities of business are softness and luxury, compared with the incessant cravings of vacancy, and the unsatisfactory expedients of idleness.

"*Hæc sunt quæ nostrâ potui te voce monere;*
Vade, age."

'As to your History of Corsica, you have no materials which others have not, or may not have. You have, somehow, or other, warmed your imagination. I wish there were some cure, like the lover's leap, for all heads of which some single idea has obtained an unreasonable and irregular possession. Mind your own affairs, and leave the Corsicans to theirs. I am, dear Sir,

'Your most humble servant,
'London, Aug. 21, 1766.'   'SAM. JOHNSON'

'TO DR. SAMUEL JOHNSON

'Auchinleck, Nov. 6, 1766

"MUCH ESTEEMED AND DEAR SIR,

'I PLEAD not guilty to[1] * * * * * * * * * * * * * *
* * * * * * * * * * *.

'Having thus, I hope, cleared myself of the charge brought against me, I presume you will not be displeased if I escape the punishment which you have decreed for me unheard. If you have discharged the arrows of criticism against an innocent man, you must rejoice to find they have missed him, or have not been pointed so as to wound him.

'To talk no longer in allegory, I am, with all deference, going to offer a few observations in defence of my Latin, which you have found fault with.

'You think I should have used *spei primæ*, instead of

[1] The passage omitted explained the transaction to which the preceding letter had alluded.

spei alteræ. Spes is, indeed, often used to express something
on which we have a future dependence, as in Virg. Eclog.
i. l. 14.

> "———— *modo namque gemellos*
> Spem *gregis ah silice in nudâ connixa reliquit.*"

and in Georg. iii. l. 473.

> "Spemque *gregemque simul,*"

for the lambs and the sheep. Yet it is also used to express
any thing on which we have a present dependence, and is
well applied to a man of distinguished influence,—our
support, our refuge, our *præsidium,* as Horace calls Mæcenas.
So Æneid xii. l. 57, Queen Amata addresses her son-in-
law, Turnus:—"Spes *tu nunc una:*" and he was then no
future hope, for she adds,

> "——— *decus imperiumque Latini*
> *Te penes;*"

which might have been said of my Lord Bute some years
ago. Now I consider the present Earl of Bute to be
"*Excelsæ familiæ de Bute* spes prima;" and my Lord Mountstuart, as his eldest son, to be "*spes altera.*" So in Æneid
xii. l. 168, after having mentioned Pater Æneas, who was
the *present* spes, the *reigning* spes, as my German friends
would say, the *spes prima,* the poet adds,

> "*Et juxta Ascanius, magnæ* spes altera *Romæ.*"

'You think *alteræ* ungrammatical, and you tell me it
should have been *alteri.* You must recollect, that in old
times *alter* was declined regularly; and when the ancient
fragments preserved in the *Juris Civilis Fontes* were written,
it was certainly declined in the way that I use it. This, I
should think, may protect a lawyer who writes *alteræ* in a
dissertation upon part of his own science. But as I could
hardly venture to quote fragments of old law to so classical
a man as Mr. Johnson, I have not made an accurate search
into these remains, to find examples of what I am able to
produce in poetical composition. We find in Plaut. Rudens,
act iii, scene 4,

> "*Nam huic* alteræ *patria quæ sit profecto nescio.*"

Plautus is, to be sure, an old comick writer; but in the days of Scipio and Lelius, we find Terent. Heautontim. act. ii. scene 3,

> "———— *hoc ipsa in itinere* alteræ
> *Dum narrat, forte audivi.*"

'You doubt my having authority for using *genus* absolutely, for what we call *family*, that is, for *illustrious extraction*. Now I take *genus* in Latin, to have much the same signification with *birth* in English; both in their primary meaning expressing simply descent, but both made to stand κατ' ἐξοχήν, for noble descent. *Genus* is thus used in Hor. lib. ii. Sat. v. l. 8.

> "*Et* genus *et virtus, nisi cum re, vilior alga est.*"

And in lib. i. Epist. vi. l. 37,

> "*Et* genus *et formam Regina pecunia donat.*"

marginal line:
And in . . . l. 140 [H] And in the celebrated contest between Ajax and Ulysses, Ovid's Metamorph. lib. xiii. l. 140,

> "*Nam* genus *et proavos, et quæ non fecimus ipsi,*
> *Vix ea nostra voco.*"

'*Homines nullius originis,* for *nullis orti majoribus,* or *nullo loco nati,* is "you are afraid, barbarous."
'*Origo* is used to signify extraction, as in Virg. Æneid i. l. 286,

> "*Nascetur pulchrâ Trojanus* origine *Cæsar.*"

And in Æneid x. l. 618,

> "*Ille tamen nostrâ deducit* origine *nomen.*"

And as *nullus* is used for obscure, is it not in the genius of the Latin language to write *nullius originis,* for obscure extraction?
'I have defended myself as well as I could.
'Might I venture to differ from you with regard to the utility of vows? I am sensible that it would be very dangerous to make vows rashly, and without a due consideration. But I cannot help thinking that they may often

be of great advantage to one of a variable judgement and irregular inclinations. I always remember a passage in one of your letters to our Italian friend Baretti: where talking of the monastick life, you say you do not wonder that serious men should put themselves under the protection of a religious order, when they have found how unable they are to take care of themselves. For my own part, without affecting to be a Socrates, I am sure I have a more than ordinary struggle to maintain with *the Evil Principle;* and all the methods I can devise are little enough to keep me tolerably steady in the paths of rectitude.

* * * * * * *

'I am ever, with the highest veneration,

'Your affectionate humble servant,

'JAMES BOSWELL'

It appears from Johnson's diary, that he was this year at Mr. Thrale's, from before Midsummer till after Michaelmas, and that he afterwards passed a month at Oxford. He had then contracted a great intimacy with Mr. Chambers of that University, afterwards Sir Robert Chambers, one of the Judges in India.

He published nothing this year in his own name; but the noble dedication* to the King, of Gwyn's 'London and Westminster Improved,' was written by him; and he furnished the Preface,† and several of the pieces, which compose a volume of Miscellanies by Mrs. Anna Williams, the blind lady who had an asylum in his house.[1] Of these,

---

[1] [In a paper already mentioned, (see pp. 52 and 328) the following account of this publication is given by a lady well acquainted with Mrs. Williams:

'As to her poems, she many years attempted to publish them: the half-crowns she had got towards the publication, she confessed to me, went for necessaries, and that the greatest pain she ever felt was from the appearance of defrauding her subscribers: 'but what can I do? the Doctor [Johnson] always puts me off with "Well, we'll think about it," and Goldsmith says, "Leave it to me." However, two of her friends, under her directions, made a new subscription at a crown, the whole price of the work, and in a very little time raised sixty pounds. Mrs. Carter was applied to by Mrs. Williams's desire, and she, with the utmost activity and kindness, procured a long list of names. At length the work was published, in which is a fine written but gloomy tale of Dr. Johnson.[a] The money Mrs. Williams had various uses for, and a part of it was funded.'

By this publication Mrs. Williams got 150*l*. Ibid. MALONE.]

underlined:
fine written but gloomy tale [1]
[a] *is Floretta a gloomy Tale?* [H]
Does he mean The Fountains? is that a gloomy Tale? [1]

there are his 'Epitaph on Phillips;'* 'Translation of a Latin Epitaph on Sir Thomas Hanmer;'✝ 'Friendship, an Ode;'* and 'The Ant,'* a paraphrase from the Proverbs, of which I have a copy in his own hand-writing; and, from internal evidence, I ascribe to him, 'To Miss —— on her giving the Authour a gold and silver net-work Purse of her own weaving;'✝ and 'The happy Life.'✝ — Most of the pieces in this volume have evidently received additions from his superiour pen, particularly 'Verses to Mr. Richardson, on his Sir Charles Grandison;' 'The Excursion;' 'Reflections on a Grave digging in Westminster Abbey.' There is in this collection a poem, 'On the death of Stephen Grey, the Electrician;'* which, on reading it, appeared to me to be undoubtedly Johnson's. I asked Mrs. Williams whether it was not his. 'Sir, (said she, with some warmth,) I wrote that poem before I had the honour of Dr. Johnson's acquaintance.' I, however, was so much impressed with my first notion, that I mentioned it to Johnson, repeating, at the same time, what Mrs. Williams had said. His answer was, 'It is true, Sir, that she wrote it before she was acquainted with me; but she has not told you that I wrote it all over again, except two lines.' 'The Fountains,'✝ᵃ a beautiful little Fairy tale in prose, written with exquisite simplicity, is one of Johnson's productions; and I cannot withhold from Mrs. Thrale the praise of being the authour of that admirable poem, 'The Three Warnings.'ᵇ

He wrote this year a letter, not intended for publication, which has, perhaps, as strong marks of his sentiment and style, as any of his compositions. The original is in my possession. It is addressed to the late Mr. William Drummond, bookseller in Edinburgh, a gentleman of good family, but small estate, who took arms for the house of Stuart in 1745; and during his concealment in London till the act of general pardon came out, obtained the acquaintance of Dr. Johnson, who justly esteemed him as a very worthy man. It seems, some of the members of the society in Scotland for propagating Christian knowledge had opposed the scheme of translating the holy scriptures into the Erse or Gaelic language, from political considerations of the disadvantage of keeping up the

ᵃ *Where's the Reference to this Mark?* [I] underlined: *cannot withhold* [H]

ᵇ *how sorry he is!* [H]

distinction between the Highlanders and the other inhabitants of North-Britain. Dr. Johnson being informed of this, I suppose by Mr. Drummond, wrote with a generous indignation as follows:

'TO MR. WILLIAM DRUMMOND

'SIR,

'I DID not expect to hear that it could be, in an assembly convened for the propagation of Christian knowledge, a question whether any nation uninstructed in religion should receive instruction; or whether that instruction should be imparted to them by a translation of the holy books into their own language. If obedience to the will of GOD be necessary to happiness, and knowledge of his will be necessary to obedience, I know not how he that withholds this knowledge, or delays it, can be said to love his neighbour as himself. He, that voluntarily continues ignorance, is guilty of all the crimes which ignorance produces; as to him that should extinguish the tapers of a light-house, might justly be imputed the calamities of shipwrecks. Christianity is the highest perfection of humanity; and as no man is good but as he wishes the good of others, no man can be good in the highest degree, who wishes not to others the largest measures of the greatest good. To omit for a year, or for a day, the most efficacious method of advancing Christianity, in compliance with any purposes that terminate on this side of the grave, is a crime of which I know not that the world has yet had an example, except in the practice of the planters of America, a race of mortals whom, I suppose, no other man wishes to resemble.

'The Papists have, indeed, denied to the laity the use of the bible; but this prohibition, in few places now very rigorously enforced, is defended by arguments, which have for their foundation the care of souls. To obscure, upon motives merely political, the light of revelation, is a practice reserved for the reformed; and, surely, the blackest midnight of popery is meridian sunshine to such a reformation. I am not very willing that any language should be totally extinguished. The similitude and derivation of languages afford the most indubitable proof of the traduction of nations, and the genealogy of mankind. They add often physical certainty to historical evidence; and often supply the only evidence of ancient migrations, and of the revolutions of ages which left no written monuments behind them.

'Every man's opinions, at least his desires, are a little influenced by his favourite studies. My zeal for languages may seem, perhaps, rather over-heated, even to those by whom I desire to be well esteemed. To those who have nothing in their thoughts but trade or policy, present power, or present money, I should not think it necessary to defend my opinions; but with men of letters I would not unwillingly compound, by wishing the continuance of every language, however narrow in its extent, or however incommodious for common purposes, till it is reposited in some version of a known book, that it may be always hereafter examined and compared with other languages, and then permitting its disuse. For this purpose the translation of the bible is most to be desired. It is not certain that the same method will not preserve the High-land language, for the purposes of learning, and abolish it from daily use. When the Highlanders read the Bible, they will naturally wish to have its obscurities cleared, and to know the history, collateral or appendant. Knowledge always desires increase; it is like fire, which must first be kindled by some external agent, but which will afterwards propagate itself. When they once desire to learn, they will naturally have recourse to the nearest language by which that desire can be gratified; and one will tell another that if he would attain knowledge, he must learn English.

'This speculation may, perhaps, be thought more subtle than the grossness of real life will easily admit. Let it, however, be remembered, that the efficacy of ignorance has long been tried, and has not produced the consequence expected. Let knowledge, therefore, take its turn; and let the patrons of privation stand awhile aside, and admit the operation of positive principles.

'You will be pleased, Sir, to assure the worthy man who is employed in the new translation,[1] that he has my

---

[1] The Rev. Mr. John Campbell, Minister of the parish of Kippen, near Stirling, who has lately favoured me with a long, intelligent, and very

wishes for his success; and if here or at Oxford I can be of any use, that I shall think it more than honour to promote his undertaking.

'I am sorry that I delayed so long to write.

'I am, Sir,

'Your most humble servant,

'Johnson's-court, Fleet-street,   'SAM. JOHNSON'
    Aug. 16, 1766.'

The opponents of this pious scheme being made ashamed of their conduct, the benevolent undertaking was allowed to go on.

The following letters, though not written till the year after, being chiefly upon the same subject, are here inserted.

'TO MR. WILLIAM DRUMMOND

'DEAR SIR,

'THAT my letter should have had such effects as you mention, gives me great pleasure. I hope you do not flatter me by imputing to me more good than I have really done. Those whom my arguments have persuaded to change their opinion, shew such modesty and candour as deserve great praise.

'I hope the worthy translator goes diligently forward. He has a higher reward in prospect than any honours which this world can bestow. I wish I could be useful to him.

'The publication of my letter, if it could be of use in a cause to which all other causes are nothing, I should not prohibit. But first, I would have you to consider whether the publication will really do any good; next, whether by

obliging letter upon this work, makes the following remark. 'Dr. Johnson has alluded to the worthy man employed in the translation of the New Testament. Might not this have afforded you an opportunity of paying a proper tribute of respect to the memory of the Rev. Mr. James Stuart, late Minister of Killin, distinguished by his eminent Piety, Learning, and Taste. The amiable simplicity of his life, his warm benevolence, his indefatigable and successful exertions for civilizing and improving the Parish of which he was Minister for upwards of fifty years, entitle him to the gratitude of his country, and the veneration of all good men. It certainly would be a pity, if such a character should be permitted to sink into oblivion.'

printing and distributing a very small number, you may not attain all that you propose; and, what perhaps I should have said first, whether the letter, which I do not now perfectly remember, be fit to be printed.

'If you can consult Dr. Robertson, to whom I am a little known, I shall be satisfied about the propriety of whatever he shall direct. If he thinks that it should be printed, I entreat him to revise it; there may, perhaps, be some negligent lines written, and whatever is amiss, he knows very well how to rectify.[1]

'Be pleased to let me know, from time to time, how this excellent design goes forward.

'Make my compliments to young Mr. Drummond, whom I hope you will live to see such as you desire him.

'I have not lately seen Mr. Elphinston, but believe him to be prosperous, I shall be glad to hear the same of you, for I am, Sir,

'Your affectionate humble servant,

'Johnson's-court, Fleet-street,   'SAM. JOHNSON'
     April 21, 1767.'

TO THE SAME

'SIR,

'I RETURNED this week from the country, after an absence of near six months, and found your letter with many others, which I should have answered sooner, if I had sooner seen them.

'Dr. Robertson's opinion was surely right. Men should not be told of the faults which they have mended. I am glad the old language is taught, and honour the translator as a man whom GOD has distinguished by the high office of propagating his word.

'I must take the liberty of engaging you in an office of charity. Mrs. Heely, the wife of Mr. Heely, who had lately some office in your theatre, is my near relation, and now in great distress. They wrote me word of their situation some time ago, to which I returned them an answer which raised hopes of more than it is proper for me to

---

[1] This paragraph shews Johnson's real estimation of the character and abilities of the celebrated Scottish Historian, however lightly, in a moment of caprice, he may have spoken of his works.

give them. Their representation of their affairs I have
discovered to be such as cannot be trusted: and at this
distance, though their case requires haste, I know not how
to act. She, or her daughters, may be heard of at Canongate
Head. I must beg, Sir, that you will enquire after them,
and let me know what is to be done. I am willing to go to
ten pounds, and will transmit you such a sum, if upon
examination you find it likely to be of use. If they are in
immediate want, advance them what you think proper.
What I could do, I would do for the woman, having no
great reason to pay much regard to Heely himself.[1]

'I believe you may receive some intelligence from Mrs.
Baker, of the theatre, whose letter I received at the same
time with yours; and to whom, if you see her, you will
make my excuse for the seeming neglect of answering her.

'Whatever you advance within ten pounds shall be
immediately returned to you, or paid as you shall order.
I trust wholly to your judgment.

'I am, Sir, &c.

'London, Johnson's-court, Fleet-   'SAM. JOHNSON'
    street, Oct. 24, 1767.'

Mr. Cuthbert Shaw,[2] alike distinguished by his genius,
misfortunes, and misconduct, published this year a poem,
called 'The Race, by Mercurius Spur, Esq.' in which he
whimsically made the living poets of England contend
for pre-eminence of fame by running:

'Prove by their heels the prowess of the head.'

In this poem there was the following portrait of Johnson:

'Here Johnson comes,—unblest with outward grace,
His rigid morals stamp'd upon his face.
While strong conceptions struggle in his brain;
(For even wit is brought to bed with pain:)
To view him, porters with their loads would rest,
And babes cling frighted to the nurses' breast.

[1] This is the person concerning whom Sir John Hawkins has thrown out
very unwarrantable reflections both against Dr. Johnson and Mr. Francis
Barber.

[2] See an account of him in the European Magazine, Jan. 1786.

With looks convuls'd he roars in pompous strain,
And, like an angry lion, shakes his mane.
The nine, with terrour struck, who ne'er had seen,
Aught human with so terrible a mien,
Debating whether they should stay or run,
Virtue steps forth and claims him for her son.
With gentle speech she warns him now to yield,
Nor stain his glories in the doubtful field;
But wrapt in conscious worth, content sit down,
Since Fame, resolv'd his various pleas to crown,
Though forc'd his present claim to disavow,
Had long reserv'd a chaplet for his brow.
He bows, obeys; for time shall first expire,
Ere Johnson stay, when Virtue bids retire.'

The Honourable Thomas Hervey[1] and his lady, having unhappily disagreed, and being about to separate, Johnson interfered as their friend, and wrote him a letter of expostulation, which I have not been able to find; but the substance of it is ascertained by a letter to Johnson in answer to it, which Mr. Hervey printed. The occasion of this correspondence between Dr. Johnson and Mr. Hervey, was thus related to me by Mr. Beauclerk. 'Tom Hervey had a great liking for Johnson, and in his will had left him a legacy of fifty pounds. One day he said to me, "Johnson may want this money now, more than afterwards. I have a mind to give it him directly. Will you be so good as to carry a fifty pound note from me to him?" This I positively refused to do, as he might, perhaps, have knocked me down for insulting him, and have afterwards put the note in his pocket. But I said, if Hervey would write him a letter, and enclose a fifty pound note, I should take care to deliver it. He accordingly did write him a letter, mentioning that he was only paying a legacy a little sooner. To his letter he added, "*P. S. I am going to part with my wife.*" Johnson then wrote to him, saying nothing of the note, but remonstrating with him against parting with his wife.'

---

a & divorced her or denied her for his Wife rather—& said in Excuse that She eat Duck & Onions. [1]

[1] [The Honourable Thomas Hervey, whose letter to Sir Thomas Hanmer in 1742, was much read at that time. He was the second son of John, the first Earl of Bristol, and one of the brothers of Johnson's early friend, Henry Hervey. He married[a] in 1744, Anne, daughter of Francis Coughlan, Esq. and died Jan. 20, 1775. MALONE.]

When I mentioned to Johnson this story, in as delicate terms as I could, he told me that the fifty pound note was given to him by Mr. Hervey in consideration of his having written for him a pamphlet against Sir Charles Hanbury Williams, who, Mr. Hervey imagined, was the authour of an attack upon him; but that it was afterwards discovered to be the work of a garreteer, who wrote 'The Fool:' the pamphlet, therefore, against Sir Charles was not printed.

In February, 1767, there happened one of the most remarkable incidents of Johnson's life, which gratified his monarchical enthusiasm, and which he loved to relate with all its circumstances, when requested by his friends. This was his being honoured by a private conversation with his Majesty, in the library at the Queen's house. He had frequently visited those splendid rooms, and noble collection of books,[1] which he used to say was more numerous and curious than he supposed any person could have made in the time which the King had employed. Mr. Barnard, the librarian, took care that he should have every accommodation that could contribute to his ease and convenience, while indulging his literary taste in that place: so that he had here a very agreeable resource at leisure hours.

His Majesty having been informed of his occasional visits, was pleased to signify a desire that he should be told when Dr. Johnson came next to the library. Accordingly, the next time that Johnson did come, as soon as he was fairly engaged with a book, on which, while he sat by the fire, he seemed quite intent, Mr. Barnard stole round to the apartment where the King was, and, in obedience to his Majesty's commands, mentioned that Dr. Johnson was then in the library. His Majesty said he was at leisure, and would go to him: upon which Mr. Barnard took one of the candles that stood on the King's table, and lighted his Majesty through a suite of rooms, till they came to a

[1] Dr. Johnson had the honour of contributing his assistance towards the formation of this library; for I have read[a] a long letter from him to Mr. Barnard, giving the most masterly instructions on the subject. I wished much to have gratified my readers with the persual of this letter, and have reason to think that his Majesty would have been graciously pleased to permit its publication; but Mr. Barnard, to whom I applied, declined it 'on his own account.'

[a] *so have I.* [1]

private door into the library, of which his Majesty had the
key. Being entered, Mr. Barnard stepped forward hastily
to Dr. Johnson, who was still in a profound study, and
whispered him, 'Sir, here is the King.' Johnson started up,
and stood still. His Majesty approached him, and at once
was courteously easy.[1]

His Majesty began by observing, that he understood he
came sometimes to the library; and then mentioned his
having heard that the Doctor had been lately at Oxford,
asked him if he was not fond of going thither. To which
Johnson answered, that he was indeed fond of going to
Oxford sometimes, but was likewise glad to come back
again. The King then asked him what they were doing at
Oxford. Johnson answered, he could not much commend
their diligence, but that in some respects they were mended,
for they had put their press under better regulations and
were at that time printing Polybius. He was then asked
whether there were better libraries at Oxford or Cambridge.
He answered, he believed the Bodleian was larger than
any they had at Cambridge; at the same time adding, 'I
hope, whether we have more books or not than they have
at Cambridge, we shall make as good use of them as they
do.' Being asked whether All-Souls or Christ-Church
library was the largest, he answered, 'All-Souls library is
the largest we have, except the Bodleian.' 'Ay, (said the
King,) that is the publick library.'

[1] The particulars of this conversation I have been at great pains to collect
with the utmost authenticity, from Dr. Johnson's own detail to myself; from
Mr. Langton who was present when he gave an account of it to Dr. Joseph
Warton, and several other friends at Sir Joshua Reynolds's; from Mr.
Barnard; from the copy of a letter written by the late Mr. Strahan, the
printer, to Bishop Warburton; and from a minute, the original of which is
among the papers of the late Sir James Caldwell, and a copy of which was
most obligingly obtained for me from his son Sir John Caldwell, by Sir
Francis Lumm. To all these gentlemen I beg leave to make my grateful
acknowledgements, and particularly to Sir Francis Lumm, who was pleased
to take a great deal of trouble, and even had the minute laid before the
King by Lord Caermarthen, now Duke of Leeds, then one of his Majesty's
Principal Secretaries of State, who announced to Sir Francis the Royal
pleasure concerning it by a letter, in these words: 'I have the King's commands to assure you, Sir, how sensible his Majesty is of your attention in
communicating the minute of the conversation previous to its publication.
As there appears no objection to your complying with Mr. Boswell's wishes
on the subject, you are at full liberty to deliver it to that gentleman, to make
such use of in his Life of Dr. Johnson, as he may think proper.'

His Majesty enquired if he was then writing any thing. He answered, he was not, for he had pretty well told the world what he knew, and must now read to acquire more knowledge. The King, as it should seem with a view to urge him to rely on his own stores as an original writer, and to continue his labours, then said 'I do not think you borrow much from any body.' Johnson said, he thought he had already done his part as a writer. 'I should have thought so too, (said the King,) if you had not written so well.'—Johnson observed to me, upon this, that 'No man could have paid a handsomer compliment; and it was fit for a King to pay. It was decisive.' When asked by another friend, at Sir Joshua Reynolds's, whether he made any reply to this high compliment, he answered, 'No, Sir. When the King had said it, it was to be so. It was not for me to bandy civilities with my Sovereign.' Perhaps no man who had spent his whole life in courts could have shewn a more nice and dignified sense of true politeness than Johnson did in this instance.

His Majesty having observed to him that he supposed he must have read a great deal; Johnson answered, that he thought more than he read; that he had read a great deal in the early part of his life, but having fallen into ill health, he had not been able to read much, compared with others: for instance, he said he had not read much, compared with Dr. Warburton. Upon which the King said, that he heard Dr. Warburton was a man of such general knowledge, that you could scarce talk with him on any subject on which he was not qualified to speak; and that his learning resembled Garrick's acting, in its universality.[1] His Majesty then talked of the controversy between Warburton and Lowth, which he seemed to have read, and asked Johnson what he thought of it. Johnson answered, 'Warburton has most general, most scholastic learning; Lowth is the more correct scholar. I do not know which of them calls names best.' The King was pleased to say he was of the same opinion; adding, 'You do not think

index sign:
he said etc. [1]

---

[1] The Reverend Mr. Strahan clearly recollects having been told by Johnson, that the King observed that Pope made Warburton a Bishop. 'True, Sir, (said Johnson,) but Warburton did more for Pope; he made him a Christian:' alluding no doubt, to his ingenious comments on the 'Essay on Man.'

then, Dr. Johnson, that there was much argument in the case.' Johnson said, he did not think there was. 'Why truly, (said the King,) when once it comes to calling names, argument is pretty well at an end.'

His Majesty then asked him what he thought of Lord Lyttelton's history, which was then just published. Johnson said, he thought his style pretty good, but that he had blamed Henry the Second rather too much. 'Why, (said the King,) they seldom do these things by halves.' 'No, Sir, (answered Johnson,) not to Kings.' But fearing to be misunderstood, he proceeded to explain himself; and immediately subjoined, 'That for those who spoke worse of Kings than they deserved, he could find no excuse; but that he could more easily conceive how some might speak better of them than they deserved, without any ill intention; for, as Kings had much in their power to give, those who were favoured by them would frequently, from gratitude, exaggerate their praises: and as this proceeded from a good motive, it was certainly excusable, as far as errour could be excusable.'

The King then asked him what he thought of Dr. Hill. Johnson answered, that he was an ingenious man, but had no veracity; and immediately mentioned, as an instance of it, an assertion of that writer, that he had seen objects magnified to a much greater degree by using three or four microscopes at a time than by using one. 'Now, (added Johnson,) every one acquainted with microscopes knows, that the more of them he looks through, the less the object will appear.' 'Why, (replied the King,) this is not only telling an untruth, but telling it clumsily; for, if that be the case, every one who can look through a microscope will be able to detect him.'

'I now, (said Johnson to his friends, when relating what had passed,) began to consider that I was depreciating this man in the estimation of his Sovereign, and thought it was time for me to say something that might be more favourable.' He added, therefore, that Dr. Hill was, notwithstanding, a very curious observer; and if he would have been contented to tell the world no more than he knew, he might have been a very considerable man, and needed not to have recourse to such mean expedients to raise his reputation.

The King then talked of literary journals, mentioned particularly the *Journal des Savans*, and asked Johnson if it was well done. Johnson said, it was formerly very well done, and gave some account of the persons who began it, and carried it on for some years: enlarging at the same time, on the nature and use of such works. The King asked him if it was well done now. Johnson answered, he had no reason to think that it was. The King then asked him if there were any other literary journals published in this kingdom, except the Monthly and Critical Reviews; and on being answered there was no other, his Majesty asked which of them was the best: Johnson answered, that the Monthly Review was done with most care, the Critical upon the best principles; adding that the authours of the Monthly Review were enemies to the Church. This the King said he was sorry to hear.

The conversation next turned on the Philosophical Transactions, when Johnson observed that they had now a better method of arranging their materials than formerly. 'Ay, (said the King,) they are obliged to Dr. Johnson for that;' for his Majesty had heard and remembered the circumstance, which Johnson himself had forgot.

His Majesty expressed a desire to have the literary biography of this country ably executed, and proposed to Dr. Johnson to undertake it. Johnson signified his readiness to comply with his Majesty's wishes.

During the whole of this interview, Johnson talked to his Majesty with profound respect, but still in his firm manly manner, with a sonorous voice, and never in that subdued tone which is commonly used at the levee and in the drawing-room. After the King withdrew, Johnson shewed himself highly pleased with his Majesty's conversation, and gracious behaviour. He said to Mr. Barnard, 'Sir, they may talk of the King as they will; but he is the finest gentleman I have ever seen.' And he afterwards observed to Mr. Langton, 'Sir, his manners are those of as fine a gentleman as we may suppose Lewis the Fourteenth or Charles the Second.'

marginal line:
talk of . . . he afterwards [H]

marginal line:
those of . . . may suppose [H]

At Sir Joshua Reynolds's, where a circle of Johnson's friends was collected round him to hear his account of this memorable conversation, Dr. Joseph Warton, in his frank and lively manner, was very active in pressing him to mention the particulars. 'Come now, Sir, this is an interesting matter; do favour us with it.' Johnson, with great good humour, complied.

He told them, 'I found his Majesty wished I should talk, and I made it my business to talk. I find it does a man good to be talked to by his Sovereign. In the first place, a man cannot be in a passion—.' Here some question interrupted him, which is to be regretted, as he certainly would have pointed out and illustrated many circumstances of advantage, from being in a situation, where the powers of the mind are at once excited to vigorous exertion, and tempered by reverential awe.

During all the time in which Dr. Johnson was employed in relating to the circle at Sir Joshua Reynolds's the particulars of what passed between the King and him, Dr. Goldsmith remained unmoved upon a sopha at some distance, affecting not to join in the least in the eager curiosity of the company. He assigned as a reason for his gloom and seeming inattention, that he apprehended Johnson had relinquished his purpose of furnishing him with a Prologue to his play, with the hopes of which he had been flattered; but it was strongly suspected that he was fretting with chagrin and envy at the singular honour Dr. Johnson had lately enjoyed. At length, the frankness, and simplicity of his natural character prevailed. He sprung from the sopha, advanced to Johnson, and in a kind of flutter, from imagining himself in the situation which he had just been hearing described, exclaimed, 'Well, you acquitted yourself in this conversation better than I should have done; for I should have bowed and stammered through the whole of it.'

I received no letter from Johnson this year: nor have I discovered any of the correspondence[1] he had, except the

---

[1] It is proper here to mention, that when I speak of his correspondence, I consider it independent of the voluminous collection of letters which, in the course of many years, he wrote to Mrs. Thrale, which forms a separate part of his works: and as a proof of the high estimation set on any thing which came from his pen, was sold by that lady for the sum of five hundred pounds.[a]

two letters to Mr. Drummond, which have been inserted, for the sake of connection, with that to the same gentleman in 1766. His diary affords no light as to his employment at this time. He passed three months at Lichfield:[1] and I cannot omit an affecting and solemn scene there, as related by himself:

'Sunday, Oct. 18, 1767. Yesterday, Oct. 17, at about ten in the morning, I took my leave for ever of my dear old friend, Catharine Chambers, who came to live with my mother about 1724, and has been but little parted from us since. She buried my father, my brother, and my mother. She is now fifty-eight years old.

'I desired all to withdraw, then told her that we were to part for ever; that as Christians, we should part with prayer; and that I would, if she was willing, say a short prayer beside her. She expressed great desire to hear me: and held up her poor hands, as she lay in bed, with great fervour, while I prayed, kneeling by her, nearly in the following words:

index sign: Almighty etc. [H]

'Almighty and most merciful Father, whose loving kindness is over all thy works, behold, visit, and relieve this thy servant, who is grieved with sickness. Grant that the sense of her weakness may add strength to her faith, and seriousness to her repentance. And grant that by the help of thy Holy Spirit, after the pains and labours of this short life, we may all obtain everlasting happiness, through JESUS CHRIST our Lord, for whose sake hear our prayers. Amen. Our father, &c.

'I then kissed her. She told me, that to part was the greatest pain that she had ever felt, and that she hoped we should meet again in a better place. I expressed, with swelled eyes, and great emotion of tenderness, the same hopes. We kissed, and parted, I humbly hope to meet again, and to part no more.'[2a]

By those who have been taught to look upon Johnson as a man of a harsh and stern character, let this tender and affectionate scene be candidly read; and let them

a *Johnson told me this tender Story with many Tears; & cried Poor Kitty! Poor dear Kitty! so often in the Course of the Evene—I rejoyced to see new Faces come in, & turn the Course of his Ideas.* [H]

[1] [In his letter to Mr. Drummond, dated Oct. 24, 1767, he mentions that he had arrived in London, after an absence, of nearly *six months*, in the country. Probably part of that time was spent at Oxford. MALONE.]

[2] Prayers and Meditations, pp. 77 and 78.

then judge whether more warmth of heart, and grateful kindness, is often found in human nature.

We have the following notice in his devotional record:

'August 2, 1767. I have been disturbed and unsettled for a long time, and have been without resolution to apply to study or to business, being hindered by sudden snatches.'[1]

He, however, furnished Mr. Adams with a Dedication* to the King of that ingenious gentleman's 'Treatise on the Globes,' conceived and expressed in such a manner as could not fail to be very grateful to a Monarch, distinguished for his love of the sciences.

This year was published a ridicule of his style, under the title of 'Lexiphanes.' Sir John Hawkins ascribes it to Dr. Kenrick; but its authour was one Campbell, a Scotch purser in the navy. The ridicule consisted in applying Johnson's 'words of large meaning,' to insignificant matters, as if one should put the armour of Goliath upon a dwarf. The contrast might be laughable; but the dignity of the armour must remain the same in all considerate minds. This malicious drollery, therefore, it may easily be supposed, could do no harm to its illustrious object.[a]

a *It vex'd him how-*
ever I well remember.
[H]

'TO BENNET LANGTON, ESQ. AT MR. ROTHWELL'S, PERFUMER, IN NEW BOND-STREET, LONDON

'DEAR SIR,

'THAT you have been all summer in London is one more reason for which I regret my long stay in the country. I hope that you will not leave the town before my return. We have here only the chance of vacancies, in the passing carriages, and I have bespoken one that may, if it happens, bring me to town on the fourteenth of this month: but this is not certain.

'It will be a favour if you communicate this to Mrs. Williams: I long to see all my friends.

'I am, dear Sir,

'Your most humble servant,

'Lichfield, Oct. 10, 1767.'   'SAM. JOHNSON'

1 Prayers and Meditations, p. 73.

It appears from his notes of the state of his mind,[1] that
he suffered great perturbation and distraction in 1768.
Nothing of his writings was given to the public this year,
except the Prologue* to his friend Goldsmith's comedy of
'The Good-natured Man.' The first lines of this Prologue
are strongly characteristical of the dismal gloom of his
mind; which in his case, as in the case of all who are
distressed with the same malady of imagination, transfers
to others its own feelings. Who could suppose it was to
introduce a comedy, when Mr. Bensley solemnly began,[a]

> 'Press'd with the load of life, the weary mind
> Surveys the general toil of human kind.'

marginal line:
*public this . . . Good-
natured Man [H]*

underlined:
Mr. Bensley [H]

[a] *& with his gloomy
Look too. I hear he is
still alive 1820. [H]*

But this dark ground might make Goldsmith's humour
shine the more.[2]

In the spring of this year, having published my 'Account
of Corsica, with the Journal of a Tour to that Island,' I
returned to London, very desirous to see Dr. Johnson, and
hear him upon the subject. I found he was at Oxford, with
his friend Mr. Chambers, who was now Vinerian Professor,
and lived in New Inn Hall. Having had no letter from him
since that in which he criticised the Latinity of my Thesis,
and having been told by somebody that he was offended
at my having put into my book an extract of his letter to
me at Paris, I was impatient to be with him, and therefore
followed him to Oxford, where I was entertained by Mr.
Chambers, with a civility which I shall ever gratefully
remember. I found that Dr. Johnson had sent a letter to
me to Scotland, and that I had nothing to complain of
but his being more indifferent to my anxiety than I wished

[1] Prayers and Meditations, p. 81.

[2] [In this prologue, as Mr. John Taylor informs me, after the fourth line—
'And social sorrow loses half its pain,' the following couplet was inserted:

> 'Amidst the toils of this returning year
> When senators and nobles learn to fear;
> Our little bard without complaint may share
> The bustling season's epidemick care:'

So the Prologue appeared in 'the Publick Advertiser,' (the theatrical gazette
of that day) soon after the first representation of this comedy in 1768.—
Goldsmith probably thought that the lines printed in Italick characters,
which, however, seem necessary, or at least improve the sense, might give
offence, and therefore prevailed on Johnson to omit them. The epithet
little, which perhaps the authour thought might diminish his dignity, was
also changed to anxious. MALONE.]

him to be. Instead of giving, with the circumstances of time and place, such fragments of his conversation as I preserved during this visit to Oxford, I shall throw them together in continuation.

I asked him whether, as a moralist, he did not think that the practice of the law, in some degree, hurt the nice feeling of honesty. JOHNSON. 'Why no, Sir, if you act properly. You are not to deceive your clients with false representations of your opinion: you are not to tell lies to a judge.' BOSWELL. 'But what do you think of supporting a cause which you know to be bad?' JOHNSON. 'Sir, you do not know it to be good or bad till the judge determines it. I have said that you are to state facts fairly; so that your thinking, or what you call knowing, a cause to be bad, must be from reasoning, must be from your supposing your arguments to be weak and inconclusive. But, Sir, that is not enough. An argument which does not convince yourself, may convince the Judge to whom you urge it; and if it does convince him, why, then, Sir, you are wrong, and he is right. It is his business to judge; and you are not to be confident in your own opinion that a cause is bad, but to say all you can for your client, and then hear the Judge's opinion.' BOSWELL. 'But, Sir, does not affecting a warmth when you have no warmth, and appearing to be clearly of one opinion when you are in reality of another opinion, does not such dissimulation impair one's honesty? Is there not some danger that a lawyer may put on the same mask in common life, in the intercourse with his friends?' JOHNSON. 'Why no, Sir. Every body knows you are paid for affecting warmth for your client; and it is, therefore, properly no dissimulation: the moment you come from the bar you resume your usual behaviour. Sir, a man will no more carry the artifice of the bar into the common intercourse of society, than a man who is paid for tumbling upon his hands will continue to tumble upon his hands when he should walk on his feet.'[1]

Talking of some of the modern plays, he said, 'False Delicacy' was totally void of character. He praised Goldsmith's 'Good-natured Man;' said, it was the best comedy

[1] [See 'The Journal of a Tour to the Hebrides,' 4th edit. p. 14, where Johnson has supported the same argument. J. BOSWELL.]

that had appeared since 'The Provoked Husband,' and that there had not been of late any such character exhibited on the stage as that of Croaker. I observed it was the Suspirius of his Rambler. He said, Goldsmith had owned he had borrowed it from thence. 'Sir, (continued he) there is all the difference in the world between characters of nature and characters of manners; and *there* is the difference between the characters of Fielding and those of Richardson. Characters of manners are very entertaining; but they are to be understood, by a more superficial observer, than characters of nature, where a man must dive into the recesses of the human heart.'

It always appeared to me that he estimated the compositions of Richardson too highly, and that he had an unreasonable prejudice against Fielding. In comparing those two writers, he used this expression: 'that there was as great a difference between them, as between a man who knew how a watch was made, and a man who could tell the hour by looking on the dial-plate.' This was a short and figurative state of his distinction between drawing characters of nature and characters only of manners. But I cannot help being of opinion, that the neat watches of Fielding are as well constructed as the large clocks of Richardson, and that his dial-plates are brighter. Fielding's characters, though they do not expand themselves so widely in dissertation, are as just pictures of human nature, and I will venture to say, have more striking features, and nicer touches of the pencil; and though Johnson used to quote with approbation a saying of Richardson's, 'that the virtues of Fielding's heroes were the vices of a truly good man,' I will venture to add, that the moral tendency of Fielding's writings, though it does not encourage a strained and rarely possible virtue, is ever favourable to honour and honesty, and cherishes the benevolent and generous affections. He who is as good as Fielding would make him, is an amiable member of society, and may be led on by more regulated instructors, to a higher state of ethical perfection.

Johnson proceeded: 'Even Sir Francis Wronghead is a character of manners, though drawn with great humour.' He then repeated, very happily, all Sir Francis's credulous account to Manly of his being with 'the great man,' and securing a place. I asked him, if 'The Suspicious Husband' did not furnish a well-drawn character, that of Ranger. JOHNSON. 'No, Sir; Ranger is just a rake, a mere rake, and a lively young fellow, but no *character*.'

The great Douglas Cause was at this time a very general subject of discussion. I found he had not studied it with much attention, but had only heard parts of it occasionally. He, however, talked of it, and said, 'I am of opinion that positive proof of fraud should not be required of the plaintiff, but that the Judges should decide according as probability shall appear to preponderate, granting to the defendant the presumption of filiation to be strong in his favour. And I think too, that a good deal of weight should be allowed to the dying declarations, because they were spontaneous. There is a great difference between what is said without our being urged to it, and what is said from a kind of compulsion. If I praise a man's book without being asked my opinion of it, that is honest praise, to which one may trust. But if an authour asks me if I like his book, and I give him something like praise, it must not be taken as my real opinion.'

'I have not been troubled for a long time with authours desiring my opinion of their works. I used once to be sadly plagued with a man who wrote verses, but who literally had no other notion of a verse, but that it consisted of ten syllables. *Lay your knife and your fork, across your plate*, was to him a verse:

Lay yōur knife ānd your fŏrk, acrŏss your plāte.

As he wrote a great number of verses, he sometimes by chance made good ones, though he did not know it.'

He renewed his promise of coming to Scotland, and going with me to the Hebrides, but said he would now content himself with seeing one or two of the most curious of them. He said 'Macaulay, who writes the account of St. Kilda, set out with a prejudice against prejudices, and wanted to be a smart modern thinker; and yet affirms for a truth, that when a ship arrives there all the inhabitants are seized with a cold.'[a]

[a] *why?* [1]

Dr. John Campbell, the celebrated writer, took a great

deal of pains to ascertain this fact, and attempted to account for it on physical principles, from the effect of
effluvia from human bodies. Johnson, at another time
praised Macaulay for his '*magnanimity*,' in asserting this
wonderful story, because it was well attested. A lady of
Norfolk, by a letter to my friend Dr. Burney, has favoured
me with the following solution: 'Now for the explication
of this seeming mystery, which is so very obvious as, for
that reason, to have escaped the penetration of Dr. Johnson
and his friend, as well as that of the authour. Reading the
book with my ingenious friend, the late Reverend Mr.
Christian of Docking—after ruminating a little, "The
cause, (says he,) is a natural one. The situation of St. Kilda
renders a North-East Wind indispensably necessary[a] before
a stranger can land. The wind, not the stranger, occasions
an epidemick cold." If I am not mistaken, Mr. Macaulay is
dead; if living, this solution might please him, as I hope
it will Mr. Boswell, in return for the many agreeable hours
his works have afforded us.'

marginal line:
is a . . . before a [H]
[a] *Oh!* [I]

Johnson expatiated on the advantages of Oxford for
learning. 'There is here, Sir, (said he,) such a progressive
emulation. The students are anxious to appear well to
their tutors; the tutors are anxious to have their pupils
appear well in the college; the colleges are anxious to have
their students appear well in the University; and there are
excellent rules of discipline in every college. That the rules
are sometimes ill observed, may be true; but is nothing
against the system. The members of an University may,
for a season, be unmindful of their duty. I am arguing for
the excellency of the institution.'

Of Guthrie, he said, 'Sir, he is a man of parts. He has
no great regular fund of knowledge; but by reading so
long, and writing so long, he no doubt has picked up a
good deal.'

He said he had lately been a long while at Lichfield, but
had grown very weary before he left it. BOSWELL. 'I
wonder at that, Sir; it is your native place.' JOHNSON.
'Why, so is Scotland *your* native place.'

marginal line:
place.' JOHNSON . . .
native place [H]

His prejudice against Scotland appeared remarkably
strong at this time. When I talked of our advancement in
literature, 'Sir, (said he,) you have learnt a little from us,

and you think yourselves very great men. Hume would never have written History, had not Voltaire written it before him. He is an echo of Voltaire.' BOSWELL. 'But, Sir, we have Lord Kames.' JOHNSON. 'You *have* Lord Kames. Keep him; ha, ha, ha! We don't envy you him. Do you ever see Dr. Robertson?' BOSWELL. 'Yes, Sir.' JOHNSON. 'Does the dog talk of me?' BOSWELL. 'Indeed, Sir, he does, and loves you.' Thinking that I now had him in a corner, and being solicitous for the literary fame of my country, I pressed him for his opinion on the merit of Dr. Robertson's History of Scotland. But, to my surprize, he escaped.—'Sir, I love Robertson, and I won't talk of his book.'

It is but justice both to him and Dr. Robertson to add, that though he indulged himself in this sally of wit, he had too good taste not to be fully sensible of the merits of that admirable work.

An essay, written by Mr. Deane, a Divine of the Church of England, maintaining the future life of brutes, by an explication of certain parts of the scriptures, was mentioned, and the doctrine insisted on by a gentleman who seemed fond of curious speculation. Johnson, who did not like to hear of any thing concerning a future state which was not authorized by the regular canons of orthodoxy, discouraged this talk; and being offended at its continuation, he watched an opportunity to give the gentleman a blow of reprehension. So, when the poor speculatist, with a serious metaphysical pensive face, addressed him, 'But really, Sir, when we see a very sensible dog, we don't know what to think of him.' Johnson, rolling with joy at the thought which beamed in his eye, turned quickly round, and replied, 'True, Sir: and when we see a very foolish *fellow*, we don't know what to think of *him*.' He then rose up, strided to the fire, and stood for some time laughing and exulting.

I told him that I had several times when in Italy, seen the experiment of placing a scorpion within a circle of burning coals; that it ran round and round in extreme pain; and finding no way to escape, retired to the centre, and like a true Stoick philosopher, darted its sting into its head, and thus at once, freed itself from its woes. ' *This*

marginal line:
have Lord . . . don't envy [H]

marginal line:
True, Sir . . . and exulting [H]

must end 'em.' I said, this was a curious fact,[a] as it shewed deliberate suicide in a reptile. Johnson would not admit the fact. He said, Maupertuis[1] was of opinion that it does not kill itself, but dies of the heat; that it gets to the centre of the circle, as the coolest place; that its turning its tail in upon its head is merely a convulsion, and that it does not sting itself. He said he would be satisfied if the great anatomist Morgagni, after dissecting a scorpion on which the experiment had been tried, should certify that its sting had penetrated into its head.

He seemed pleased to talk of natural philosophy. 'That woodcocks, (said he,) fly over the northern countries, is proved, because they have been observed at sea. Swallows certainly sleep all the winter. A number of them conglobulate together, by flying round and round, and then all in a heap throw themselves under water, and lye in the bed of a river.' He told us, one of his first essays was a Latin poem upon the glow-worm. I am sorry I did not ask where it was to be found.

Talking of the Russians and the Chinese, he advised me to read Bell's Travels. I asked him whether I should read Du Halde's Account of China. 'Why yes, (said he) as one reads such a book; that is to say, consult it.'

He talked of the heinousness of the crime of adultery, by which the peace of families was destroyed. He said, 'Confusion of progeny constitutes the essence of the crime; and therefore a woman who breaks her marriage vows is much more criminal than a man who does it. A man, to

[a] *It is true tho!* [1]

marginal line:
had been . . . its head
[H]

queried:
A number of them etc.
[H]

---

[1] I should think it impossible not to wonder at the variety of Johnson's reading, however desultory it might have been. Who could have imagined that the High Church of England-man would be so prompt in quoting *Maupertuis*, who, I am sorry to think, stands in the list of those unfortunate mistaken men, who call themselves *esprits forts*. I have, however, a high respect for that Philosopher whom the Great Frederick of Prussia loved and honoured, and addressed pathetically in one of his Poems,

'*Maupertuis cher Maupertuis*
Que notre vie est peu de chose.'

There was in Maupertuis a vigour and yet a tenderness of sentiment, united with strong intellectual powers, and uncommon ardour of soul. Would he had been a Christian! I cannot help earnestly venturing to hope that he is one now.

[Maupertuis died in 1759 at the age of 62, in the arms of the Bernoullis, *très Chrétiennement*. BURNEY.]

be sure, is criminal in the sight of GOD; but he does not do his wife a very material injury, if he does not insult her; if, for instance, from mere wantonness of appetite, he steals privately to her chambermaid. Sir, a wife ought not greatly to resent this. I would not receive home a daughter who had run away from her husband on that account. A wife should study to reclaim her husband by more atten-

tion to please him. Sir, a man will not, once in a hundred instances, leave his wife and go to a harlot, if his wife has not been negligent of pleasing.'

Here he discovered that acute discrimination, that solid judgement, and that knowledge of human nature, for which he was upon all occasions remarkable. Taking care to keep in view the moral and religious duty, as understood in our nation, he shewed clearly from reason and good sense, the greater degree of culpability in the one sex deviating from it than the other; and, at the same time, inculcated a very useful lesson as to *the way to keep him.*

I asked him if it was not hard that one deviation from

chastity should so absolutely ruin a young woman. JOHNSON. 'Why no, Sir; it is the great principle which she is taught. When she has given up that principle, she has given up every notion of female honour and virtue, which are all included in chastity.'

A gentleman talked to him of a ladyª whom he greatly admired and wished to marry, but was afraid of her

superiority of talents. 'Sir, (said he,) you need not be afraid; marry her. Before a year goes about, you'll find that reason much weaker, and that wit not so bright.' Yet the gentleman may be justified in his apprehension by one of Dr. Johnson's admirable sentences in his life of Waller: 'He doubtless praised many whom he would have been afraid to marry; and, perhaps, married one whom he would have been ashamed to praise. Many qualities contribute to domestick happiness, upon which poetry has no colours to bestow: and many airs and sallies may delight imagination, which he who flatters them never can approve.'

He praised Signor Baretti. 'His account of Italy is a very entertaining book; and, Sir, I know no man who carries his head higher in conversation than Baretti. There are strong powers in his mind. He has not, indeed, many hooks; but with what hooks he has, he grapples very forcibly.'

At this time I observed upon the dial-plate of his watch a short greek inscription, taken from the New Testament, Νὺξ γὰρ ἔρχεται, being the first words of our SAVIOUR's solemn admonition to the improvement of that time which is allowed us to prepare for eternity; 'the night cometh when no man can work.' He sometime afterwards laid aside this dial-plate; and when I asked him the reason, he said, 'It might do very well upon a clock which a man keeps in his closet; but to have it upon his watch which he carries about with him, and which is often looked at by others, might be censured as ostentatious.' Mr. Steevens is now possessed of the dial-plate inscribed as above.

marginal line:
ostentatious.' Mr. . . .
as above [H]

He remained at Oxford a considerable time; I was obliged to go to London, where I received this letter, which had been returned from Scotland.

'TO JAMES BOSWELL, ESQ.

'MY DEAR BOSWELL,

'I have omitted a long time to write to you, without knowing very well why. I could now tell why I should not write; for who would write to men who publish the letters of their friends, without their leave? Yet I write to you in spite of my caution, to tell you that I shall be glad to see you, and that I wish you would empty your head of Corsica, which I think has filled it rather too long. But, at all events, I shall be glad, very glad to see you.

'I am, Sir,
'Yours affectionately,
'Oxford, March 23, 1768.'   'SAM. JOHNSON'

I answered thus:

'TO MR. SAMUEL JOHNSON

'MY DEAR SIR,   'London, 26th April, 1768

'I HAVE received your last letter, which, though very short, and by no means complimentary, yet gave me real pleasure, because it contains these words, "I shall be glad, very glad to see you."—Surely you have no reason to complain of my publishing a single paragraph of one of your letters; the temptation to it was so strong. An irrevocable grant of your friendship, and your dignifying my desire of visiting Corsica with the epithet of "a wise and noble curiosity," are to me more valuable than many of the grants of kings.

'But how can you bid me "empty my head of Corsica?" My noble-minded friend, do you not feel for an oppressed nation bravely struggling to be free? Consider fairly what is the case. The Corsicans never received any kindness from the Genoese. They never agreed to be subject to them. They owe them nothing, and when reduced to an abject state of slavery, by force, shall they not rise in the great cause of liberty, and break the galling yoke? And shall not every liberal soul be warm for them? Empty my head of Corsica?[a] Empty it of honour, empty it of humanity, empty it of friendship, empty it of piety. No! while I live, Corsica and the cause of the brave islanders, shall ever employ much of my attention, shall ever interest me in the sincerest manner.

[a] 'Banish plump Jack & banish all the World.' [1]

*   *   *   *   *   *   *

'I am, &c.

'JAMES BOSWELL'

['TO MRS. LUCY PORTER, IN LICHFIELD

'MY DEAR DEAR LOVE,   'Oxford, Apr. 18, 1768

'You have had a very great loss. To lose an old friend, is to be cut off from a great part of the little pleasure that this life allows. But such is the condition of our nature, that as we live on we must see those whom we love drop successively, and find our circle of relation grow less and less, till we are almost unconnected with the world; and then it must soon be our turn to drop into the grave. There is always this consolation, that we have one Protector who can never be lost but by our own fault, and every new experience of the uncertainty of all other comforts should determine us to fix our hearts where true joys are to be found. All union with the inhabitants of earth must in time be broken; and all the hopes that terminate here, must on [one] part or other end in disappointment.

'I am glad that Mrs. Adey and Mrs. Cobb do not leave you alone. Pay my respects to them, and the Sewards, and all my friends. When Mr. Porter comes, he will direct you. Let me know of his arrival, and I will write to him. index sign: *the Sewards* etc. [1]

'When I go back to London, I will take care of your reading glass. Whenever I can do any thing for you, remember, my dear darling, that one of my greatest pleasures is to please you.

'The punctuality of your correspondence I consider as a proof of great regard. When we shall see each other, I know not, but let us often think on each other, and think with tenderness. Do not forget me in your prayers. I have for a long time back been very poorly; but of what use is it to complain?

'Write often, for your letters always give great pleasure to,
'My dear,
'Your most affectionate,
'And most humble servant,
'SAM. JOHNSON']

Upon his arrival in London in May, he surprized me one morning with a visit at my lodging in Half-Moon-street, was quite satisfied with my explanation, and was in the kindest and most agreeable frame of mind. As he had objected to a part of one of his letters being published, I thought it right to take this opportunity of asking him explicitly whether it would be improper to publish his letters after his death. His answer was, 'Nay, Sir, when I am dead, you may do as you will.'

He talked in his usual style with a rough contempt of popular liberty. 'They make a rout about *universal* liberty, without considering that all that is to be valued, or indeed can be enjoyed by individuals, is *private* liberty. Political liberty is good only so far as it produces private liberty. Now, Sir, there is the liberty of the press, which you know is a constant topick. Suppose you and I and two hundred more were restrained from printing our thoughts: what then? What proportion would that restraint upon us bear to the private happiness of the nation.'

This mode of representing the inconveniences of restraint as light and insignificant, was a kind of sophistry in which he delighted to indulge himself, in opposition to the extreme laxity for which it has been fashionable for too many to argue, when it is evident upon reflection, that the very essence of government is restraint; and certain it is, that as government produces rational happiness, too much restraint is better than too little. But when restraint is unnecessary, and so close as to gall those who are subject to it, the people may and ought to remonstrate; and, if relief is not granted, to resist. Of this manly and spirited principle, no man was more convinced than Johnson himself.

About this time Dr. Kenrick attacked him, through my sides, in a pamphlet, entitled 'An Epistle to James Boswell, Esq. occasioned by his having transmitted the moral Writings of Dr. Samuel Johnson to Pascal Paoli, General of the Corsicans.' I was at first inclined to answer this pamphlet; but Johnson, who knew that my doing so would only gratify Kenrick, by keeping alive what would soon die away of itself, would not suffer me to take any notice of it.

His sincere regard for Francis Barber, his faithful negro servant, made him so desirous of his further improvement, that he now placed him at a school at Bishop Stortford, in Hertfordshire. This humane attention does Johnson's heart much honour. Out of many letters which Mr. Barber received from his master, he has preserved three, which he kindly gave me, and which I shall insert according to their dates.

'TO MR. FRANCIS BARBER

'DEAR FRANCIS,

'I HAVE been very much out of order. I am glad to hear that you are well, and design to come soon to you. I would have you stay at Mrs. Clapp's for the present, till I can determine what we shall do. Be a good boy.[a]

'My compliments to Mrs. Clapp and to Mr. Fowler. I am,

'Your's affectionately,

'May 28, 1768.'   'SAM. JOHNSON'

[a] *a good Boy!!* [1]

Soon afterwards, he supped at the Crown and Anchor tavern, in the Strand, with a company whom I collected to meet him. They[a] were Dr. Percy, now Bishop of Dromore, Dr. Douglas, now Bishop of Salisbury, Mr. Langton, Dr. Robertson the Historian, Dr. Hugh Blair, and Mr. Thomas Davies, who wished much to be introduced to these eminent Scotch literati; but on the present occasion he had very little opportunity of hearing them talk, for with an excess of prudence, for which Johnson afterwards found fault with them, they hardly opened their lips, and that only to say something which they were certain would not expose them to the sword of Goliath; such was their anxiety for their fame when in the presence of Johnson. He was this evening in remarkable vigour of mind, and eager to exert himself in conversation, which he did with great readiness and fluency; but I am sorry to find that I have preserved but a small part of what passed.

[a] *all dead—but Percy.*
[1]

He allowed high praise to Thomson as a poet; but when one of the company said he was also a very good man, our moralist contested this with great warmth, accusing him of gross sensuality and licentiousness of manners. I was very much afraid that in writing Thomson's life, Dr. Johnson would have treated his private character with a stern severity, but I was agreeably disappointed; and I may claim a little merit in it, from my having been at pains to send him authentick accounts of the affectionate and generous conduct of that poet to his sisters, one of whom, the wife of Mr. Thomson, schoolmaster at Lanark, I knew, and was presented by her with three of his letters, one of which Dr. Johnson has inserted in his life.

He was vehement against old Dr. Mounsey,[1] of Chelsea College, as 'a fellow who swore and talked bawdy.' 'I have often been in his company, (said Dr. Percy,) and never heard him swear or talk bawdy.' Mr. Davies, who sat next to Dr. Percy, having after this had some conversation aside with him, made a discovery which, in his zeal to pay court to Dr. Johnson, he eagerly proclaimed aloud

[1] [Messenger Mounsey, M.D. died at his apartments in Chelsea College, Dec. 26, 1788, at the great age of ninety-five. An extraordinary direction in his will may be found in the GENTLEMAN'S MAGAZINE, vol. 50, p. ii. p. 1183. MALONE.]

from the foot of the table: 'O, Sir, I have found out a very good reason why Dr. Percy never heard Mounsey swear or talk bawdy, for he tells me he never saw him but at the Duke of Northumberland's table.' 'And so, Sir, (said Dr. Johnson loudly to Dr. Percy) you would shield this man from the charge of swearing and talking bawdy, because he did not do so at the Duke of Northumberland's table. Sir, you might as well tell us that you had seen him hold up his hand at the Old Bailey, and he neither swore nor talked bawdy; or that you had seen him in the cart at Tyburn, and he neither swore nor talked bawdy. And is it thus, Sir, that you presume[a] to controvert what I have related?'[b] Dr. Johnson's animadversion was uttered in such a manner, that Dr. Percy seemed to be displeased, and soon afterwards left the company, of which Johnson did not at that time take any notice.

Swift having been mentioned, Johnson, as usual, treated him with little respect as an authour. Some of us endeavoured to support the Dean of St. Patrick's, by various arguments. One in particular praised his 'Conduct of the Allies.' JOHNSON. 'Sir, his "Conduct of the Allies" is a performance of very little ability.' 'Surely, Sir, (said Dr. Douglas,) you must allow it has strong facts.'[1] JOHNSON. 'Why yes, Sir; but what is that to the merit of the composition? In the Sessions-paper of the Old Bailey there are strong facts. Housebreaking is a strong fact; robbery is a strong fact; and murder is a *mighty* strong fact: but is great praise due to the historian of those strong facts? No, Sir, Swift has told what he had to tell distinctly enough, but that is all. He had to count ten, and he has counted it right.'—Then recollecting that Mr. Davies, by acting as an *informer*, had been the occasion of his talking somewhat too harshly to his friend Dr. Percy, for which, probably,

exclamation point:
And is it etc. [H]

underlined:
presume [I]

[a] *too bad.* [I]

[b] *He did spurn poor Cantilanus always.* [H]

[c] *'Tis all right, Johnson repeated the Anecdote to me himself giving Acct. of the Conversation* [I]

[1] My respectable friend, upon reading this passage, observed that he probably must have said not simply 'strong facts,' but 'strong facts well arranged.' His lordship, however, knows too well the value of written documents to insist on setting his recollection against my notes taken at the time.[c] He does not attempt to *traverse the record*. The fact, perhaps, may have been, either that the additional words escaped me in the noise of a numerous company, or that Dr. Johnson, from his impetuosity, and eagerness to seize an opportunity to make a lively retort, did not allow Dr. Douglas to finish his sentence.

when the first ebullition was over, he felt some compunction, he took an opportunity to give him a hit: so added,
with a preparatory laugh, 'Why, Sir, Tom Davies might
have written "the Conduct of the Allies." ' Poor Tom
being thus suddenly dragged into ludicrous notice in
presence of the Scottish Doctors, to whom he was ambitious
of appearing to advantage, was grievously mortified. Nor
did his punishment rest here; for upon subsequent occasions, whenever he, 'statesman all o'er,'[1] assumed a
strutting importance, I used to hail him—'*the Authour of
the Conduct of the Allies.*'

When I called upon Dr. Johnson next morning, I found
him highly satisfied with his colloquial prowess the
preceding evening. 'Well, (said he,) we had good talk.'
BOSWELL. 'Yes, Sir, you tossed and gored several
persons.'

The late Alexander Earl of Eglintoune, who loved wit
more than wine, and men of genius more than sycophants,
had a great admiration of Johnson; but from the remarkable elegance of his own manners, was, perhaps, too
delicately sensible of the roughness which sometimes
appeared in Johnson's behaviour. One evening about this
time, when his Lordship did me the honour to sup at my
lodgings with Dr. Robertson, and several other men of
literary distinction, he regretted that Johnson had not
been educated with more refinement, and lived more in
polished society. 'No, no, my Lord, (said Signor Baretti,)
do with him what you would, he would always have been
a bear.' 'True, (answered the Earl, with a smile,) but he
would have been a *dancing* bear.'

To obviate all the reflections which have gone round
the world to Johnson's prejudice, by applying to him the
epithet of a *bear*, let me impress upon my readers a just
and happy saying of my friend Goldsmith, who knew him
well: 'Johnson, to be sure, has a roughness in his manner:
but no man alive has a more tender heart. *He has nothing
of the bear but his skin.*'

In 1769, so far as I can discover, the publick was
favoured with nothing of Johnson's composition, either
for himself or any of his friends. His 'Meditations' too

---

[1] See the hard drawing of him in Churchill's ROSCIAD.

underlined:
evil [H]
ª *Ay & against the
King's Evil.* [H]

strongly prove that he suffered much both in body and mind; yet was he perpetually striving against *evil*,ª and nobly endeavouring to advance his intellectual and devotional improvement. Every generous and grateful heart must feel for the distresses of so eminent a benefactor to mankind; and now that his unhappiness is certainly known, must respect that dignity of character which prevented him from complaining.

His Majesty having the preceding year instituted the Royal Academy of Arts in London, Johnson had now the honour of being appointed Professor in Ancient Literature.[1] In the course of the year he wrote some letters to Mrs. Thrale, passed some part of the summer at Oxford and at Lichfield, and when at Oxford he wrote the following letter:

'TO THE REVEREND MR. THOMAS WARTON

'DEAR SIR,

'MANY years ago, when I used to read in the library of your College, I promised to recompence the college for that permission, by adding to their books a Baskerville's Virgil. I have now sent it, and desire you to reposit it on the shelves in my name.[2]

'If you will be pleased to let me know when you have an hour of leisure, I will drink tea with you. I am engaged for the afternoon, to-morrow and on Friday: all my mornings are my own.[3]

          'I am, &c.

'May 31, 1769.'   'SAM. JOHNSON'

[1] In which place he has been succeeded by Bennet Langton, Esq. When that truly religious gentleman was elected to this honorary Professorship, at the same time that Edward Gibbon, Esq. noted for introducing a kind of sneering infidelity into his Historical Writings, was elected Professor in Ancient History, in the room of Dr. Goldsmith, I observed that it brought to my mind, 'Wicked Will Whiston and good Mr. Ditton.'—I am now also of that admirable institution as Secretary for Foreign Correspondence, by the favour of the Academicians, and the approbation of the Sovereign.

[2] It has this inscription in a blank-leaf: '*Hunc librum D.D. Samuel Johnson, eo quod hic loci studiis interdum vacaret.*' Of this library, which is an old Gothic room, he was very fond. On my observing to him that some of the *modern* libraries of the University were more commodious and pleasant for study, as being more spacious and airy, he replied, 'Sir, if a man has a mind to *prance*, he must study at Christ-Church and All-Souls.'

[3] During this visit he seldom or never dined out. He appeared to be deeply engaged in some literary work. Miss Williams was now with him at Oxford.

I came to London in the autumn, and having informed him that I was going to be married in a few months, I wished to have as much of his conversation as I could before engaging in a state of life which would probably keep me more in Scotland, and prevent me seeing him so often as when I was a single man; but I found he was at Brighthelmstone with Mr. and Mrs. Thrale. I was very sorry that I had not his company with me at the Jubilee, in honour of Shakspeare, at Stratford-upon-Avon, the great poet's native town. Johnson's connection both with Shakspeare and Garrick founded a double claim to his presence; and it would have been highly gratifying to Mr. Garrick. Upon this occasion I particularly lamented that he had not that warmth of friendship for his brilliant pupil, which we may suppose would have had a benignant effect on both. When almost every man of eminence in the literary world was happy to partake in this festival of genius, the absence of Johnson could not but be wondered at and regretted. The only trace of him there, was in the whimsical advertisement of a haberdasher, who sold *Shaksperian ribbands* of various dyes; and, by way of illustrating their appropriation to the bard, introduced a line from the celebrated Prologue at the opening of Drury-lane theatre:

'Each change of *many-colour'd* life he drew.'

From Brighthelmstone Dr. Johnson wrote me the following letter, which they who may think that I ought to have suppressed, must have less ardent feelings than I have always avowed.[1]

'TO JAMES BOSWELL, ESQ.

'DEAR SIR,

'WHY do you charge me with unkindness? I have omitted nothing that could do you good, or give you pleasure, unless it be that I have forborne to tell you my

[1] In the Preface to my Account of Corsica, published in 1768, I thus express myself:

'He who publishes a book affecting not to be an authour, and professing an indifference for literary fame, may possibly impose upon many people such an idea of his consequence as he wishes may be received. For my part, I should be proud to be known as an authour, and I have an ardent ambition for literary fame; for, of all possessions I should imagine literary fame to be

opinion of your 'Account of Corsica.' I believe my opinion, if you think well of my judgement, might have given you pleasure; but when it is considered how much vanity is excited by praise, I am not sure that it would have done you good. Your History is like other histories, but your Journal is in a very high degree curious and delightful. There is between the history and the journal that difference which there will always be found between notions borrowed from without, and notions generated within. Your history was copied from books; your journal rose out of your own experience and observation. You express images which operated strongly upon yourself, and you have impressed them with great force upon your readers. I know not whether I could name any narrative by which curiosity is better excited, or better gratified.

'I am glad that you are going to be married; and as I wish you well in things of less importance, wish you well with proportionate ardour in this crisis of your life. What I can contribute to your happiness, I should be very unwilling to withhold; for I have always loved and valued you, and shall love you and value you still more, as you become more regular and useful: effects which a happy marriage will hardly fail to produce.

'I do not find that I am likely to come back very soon from this place. I shall, perhaps, stay a fortnight longer; and a fortnight is a long time to a lover absent from his mistress. Would a fortnight ever have an end?

'I am, dear Sir,
'Your most affectionate humble servant,

'Brighthelmstone,   'SAM. JOHNSON'
  Sept. 9, 1769.'

the most valuable. A man who has been able to furnish a book, which has been approved by the world, has established himself as a respectable character in distant society, without any danger of having that character lessened by the observation of his weaknesses. To preserve an uniform dignity among those who see us every day, is hardly possible; and to aim at it, must put us under the fetters of perpetual restraint. The authour of an approved book may allow his natural disposition an easy play, and yet indulge the pride of superiour genius, when he considers that by those who know him only as an authour, he never ceases to be respected. Such an authour, when in his hours of gloom and discontent, may have the consolation to think, that his writings are, at that very time, giving pleasure to numbers; and such an authour may cherish the hope of being remembered after death, which has been a great object to the noblest minds in all ages.'

After his return to town, we met frequently, and I continued the practice of making notes of his conversation, though not with so much assiduity as I wish I had done. At this time, indeed, I had a sufficient excuse for not being able to appropriate so much time to my journal; for General Paoli, after Corsica had been overpowered by the monarchy of France, was now no longer at the head of his brave countrymen, but having with difficulty escaped from his native island, had sought an asylum in Great-Britain; and it was my duty, as well as my pleasure, to attend much upon him. Such particulars of Johnson's conversation at this period as I have committed to writing, I shall here introduce, without any strict attention to methodical arrangement. Sometimes short notes of different days shall be blended together, and sometimes a day may seem important enough to be separately distinguished.

He said, he would not have Sunday kept with rigid severity and gloom, but with a gravity and simplicity of behaviour.

I told him that David Hume had made a short collection of Scotticisms. 'I wonder, (said Johnson,) that *he* should find them.'[1]

He would not admit the importance of the question concerning the legality of general warrants. 'Such a power (he observed) must be vested in every government, to answer particular cases of necessity; and there can be no just complaint but when it is abused, for which those who administer government must be answerable. It is a matter of such indifference, a matter about which the people care so very little, that were a man to be sent over Britain to offer them an exemption from it at a half-penny a piece, very few would purchase it.' This was a specimen of that laxity of talking, which I had heard him fairly acknowledge; for, surely, while the power of granting general warrants was supposed to be legal, and the apprehension of them hung over our heads, we did not possess that security of freedom, congenial to our happy constitution, and which, by the intrepid exertions of Mr. Wilkes, has been happily established.

two marginal lines: laxity of . . . of granting [H]

---

[1] [The first edition of Hume's History of England was full of Scotticisms, many of which he corrected in subsequent editions. MALONE.]

He said, 'The duration of Parliament, whether for seven years or the life of the King, appears to me so immaterial, that I would not give half a crown to turn the scale one way or the other. The *habeas corpus* is the single advantage which our government has over that of other countries.'ᵃ

On the 30th of September we dined together at the Mitre. I attempted to argue for the superiour happiness of the savage life, upon the usual fanciful topicks. JOHN-SON. 'Sir, there can be nothing more false. The savages have no bodily advantages beyond those of civilized men. They have not better health; and as to care or mental uneasiness, they are not above it, but below it, like bears. No, Sir; you are not to talk such paradox: let me have no more on't. It cannot entertain, far less can it instruct. Lord Monboddo, one of your Scotch Judges, talked a great deal of such nonsense. I suffered *him;* but I will not suffer *you.*' BOSWELL. 'But, Sir, does not Rousseau talk such non-sense?' JOHNSON. 'True, Sir, but Rousseau *knows* he is talking nonsense, and laughs at the world for staring at him.' BOSWELL. 'How so, Sir?' JOHNSON. 'Why Sir, a man who talks nonsense so well, must know that he is talking nonsense. But I am *afraid*, (chuckling and laugh-ing,) Monboddo does *not* know that he is talking nonsense.'[1] BOSWELL. 'Is it wrong then, Sir, to affect singularity, in order to make people stare?' JOHNSON. 'Yes, if you do it by propagating errour; and, indeed, it is wrong in any way. There is in human nature a general inclination to make people stare, and every wise man has himself to cure of it, and does cure himself. If you wish to make people stare by doing better than others, why make them stare till they stare their eyes out. But consider how easy it is' to make people stare, by being absurd. I may do it by going into a drawing-room without my shoes. You remember the gentleman in "The Spectator," who had a commission of lunacy taken out against him for his extreme singularity,

[1] His Lordship having frequently spoken in an abusive manner of Dr. Johnson, in my company, I on one occasion during the life-time of my illustrious friend could not refrain from retaliation, and repeated to him this saying. He has since published I don't know how many pages in one of his curious books, attempting in much anger, but with pitiful effect, to persuade mankind that my illustrious friend was not the great and good man which they esteemed and ever will esteem him to be.

such as never wearing a wig, but a night-cap. Now, Sir, abstractedly, the night-cap was best: but, relatively, the advantage was overbalanced by his making the boys run after him.'

Talking of a London life, he said, 'The happiness of London is not to be conceived but by those who have been in it. I will venture to say, there is more learning and science within the circumference of ten miles from where we now sit, than in all the rest of the kingdom.' BOSWELL. 'The only disadvantage is the great distance at which people live from one another.' JOHNSON. 'Yes, Sir; but that is occasioned by the largeness of it, which is the cause of all the other advantages.' BOSWELL. 'Sometimes I have been in the humour of wishing to retire to a desart.' JOHNSON. 'Sir, you have desart enough in Scotland.'

Although I had promised myself a great deal of instructive conversation with him on the conduct of the married state, of which I had then a near prospect, he did not say much upon that topick. Mr. Seward heard him once say, that 'a man has a very bad chance for happiness in that state, unless he marries a woman of very strong and fixed principles of religion.' He maintained to me contrary to the common notion, that a woman would not be the worse wife for being learned; in which, from all that I have observed of *Artemisias*, I humbly differed from him. That a woman should be sensible and well informed, I allow to be a great advantage; and think that Sir Thomas Overbury,[1] in his rude versification, has very judiciously pointed out that degree of intelligence which is to be desired in a female companion:

marginal line: *that Sir . . . rude versification* [H]

> 'Give me, next *good*, an *understanding wife*,
>   By Nature *wise*, not *learned* by much art:
> Some *knowledge* on her side will all my life
>   More scope of conversation impart;
> Besides, her inborne virtue fortifie;
> They are most firmly good, who best know why.'

When I censured a gentleman of my acquaintance for marrying a second time, as it shewed a disregard of his first wife, he said, 'Not at all, Sir. On the contrary, were he

---

[1] 'A Wife,' a poem, 1614.

not to marry again, it might be concluded that his first
wife had given him a disgust to marriage; but by taking a
second wife he pays the highest compliment to the first, by
shewing that she made him so happy as a married man,
that he wishes to be so a second time.' So ingenious a turn
did he give to this delicate question. And yet, on another
occasion, he owned that he once had almost asked a
promise of Mrs. Johnson that she would not marry again,
but had checked himself. Indeed I cannot help thinking,
that in his case the request would have been unreasonable;
for if Mrs. Johnson forgot, or thought it no injury to the
memory of her first love,—the husband of her youth and
the father of her children,—to make a second marriage,
why should she be precluded from a third, should she be
so inclined? In Johnson's persevering fond appropriation
of his *Tetty*, even after her decease, he seems totally to have
overlooked the prior claim of the honest Birmingham
trader. I presume that her having been married before
had, at times, given him some uneasiness; for I remember
his observing upon the marriage of one of our common
friends, 'He has done a very foolish thing, Sir; he has
married a widow, when he might have had a maid.'

We drank tea with Mrs. Williams. I had last year the
pleasure of seeing Mrs. Thrale at Dr. Johnson's one
morning, and had conversation enough with her to admire
her talents; and to shew her that I was as Johnsonian as
herself. Dr. Johnson had probably been kind enough to
speak well of me, for this evening he delivered me a very
polite card from Mr. Thrale and her, inviting me to
Streatham.

On the 6th of October I complied with this obliging
invitation, and found, at an elegant villa, six miles from
town, every circumstance that can make society pleasing.
Johnson, though quite at home, was yet looked up to with
an awe, tempered by affection, and seemed to be equally
the care of his host and hostess. I rejoiced at seeing him
so happy.

He played off his wit against Scotland with a good
humoured pleasantry, which gave me, though no bigot to
national prejudices, an opportunity for a little contest
with him. I having said that England was obliged to us

for gardeners, almost all their good gardeners being Scotchmen;—JOHNSON. 'Why, Sir, that is because gardening is much more necessary amongst you than with us, which makes so many of your people learn it. It is *all* gardening with you. Things which grow wild here, must be cultivated with great care in Scotland. Pray now (throwing himself back in his chair, and laughing,) are you ever able to bring the *sloe* to perfection?'

I boasted that we had the honour of being the first to abolish the inhospitable, troublesome, and ungracious custom of giving vails to servants. JOHNSON. 'Sir, you abolished vails, because you were too poor to be able to give them.'

Mrs. Thrale disputed with him on the merit of Prior. He attacked him powerfully; said he wrote of love like a man who had never felt it: his love verses were college verses; and he repeated the song 'Alexis shunn'd his fellow swains,' &c. in so ludicrous a manner, as to make us all wonder how any one could have been pleased with such fantastical stuff. Mrs. Thrale stood to her gun with great courage, in defence of amorous ditties, which Johnson despised, till he at last silenced her by saying, 'My dear Lady, talk no more of this. Nonsense can be defended but by nonsense.'

Mrs. Thrale then praised Garrick's talents for light gay poetry; and, as a specimen, repeated his song in 'Florizel and Perdita,' and dwelt with peculiar pleasure on this line:

'I'd smile with the simple, and feed with the poor.'

JOHNSON. 'Nay, my dear Lady, this will never do. Poor David! Smile with the simple;—What folly is that? And who would feed with the poor that can help it? No, no; let me smile with the wise, and feed with the rich.' I repeated this sally to Garrick,[a] and wondered to find his sensibility as a writer not a little irritated by it. To sooth him I observed, that Johnson spared none of us; and I quoted the passage in Horace, in which he compares one who attacks his friends for the sake of a laugh, to a pushing ox, that is marked by a bunch of hay put upon his horns: *'fœnum habet in cornu.'* 'Ay, (said Garrick vehemently,) he has a whole *mow* of it.'

[a] *how odd to go and tell the Man!!* [H]

Talking of history, Johnson said, 'We may know historical facts to be true, as we may know facts in common life to be true. Motives are generally unknown. We cannot trust to the characters we find in history, unless when they are drawn by those who knew the persons, as those, for instance, by Sallust and by Lord Clarendon.'

He would not allow much merit to Whitfield's oratory. 'His popularity, Sir, (said he,) is chiefly owing to the peculiarity of his manner. He would be followed by crowds were he to wear a night-cap in the pulpit, or were he to preach from a tree.'

I know not from what spirit of contradiction he burst out into a violent declamation against the Corsicans, of whose heroism I talked in high terms. 'Sir, (said he,) what is all this rout about the Corsicans? They have been at war with the Genoese for upwards of twenty years, and have never yet taken their fortified towns. They might have battered down their walls, and reduced them to powder in twenty years. They might have pulled the walls in pieces, and cracked the stones with their teeth in twenty years.' It was in vain to argue with him upon the want of artillery: he was not to be resisted for the moment.

On the evening of October 10, I presented Dr. Johnson to General Paoli. I had greatly wished that two men, for whom I had the highest esteem, should meet. They met with a manly ease, mutually conscious of their own abilities, and of the abilities of each other. The General spoke Italian, and Dr. Johnson English, and understood one another very well, with a little aid of interpretation from me, in which I compared myself to an isthmus which joins two great continents. Upon Johnson's approach, the General said, 'From what I have read of your works, Sir, and from what Mr. Boswell has told me of you, I have long held you in great veneration.' The General talked of languages being formed on the particular notions and manners of a people, without knowing which, we cannot know the language. We may know the direct signification of single words; but by these no beauty of expression, no sally of genius, no wit is conveyed to the mind. All this must be by allusion to other ideas. 'Sir, (said Johnson,) you talk of language, as if you had never done any thing else but study it, instead of governing a nation.' The General said, '*Questo e un troppo gran complimento;*' this is too great a compliment. Johnson answered, 'I should have thought so, Sir, if I had not heard you talk.' The General asked him what he thought of the spirit of infidelity which was so prevalent. JOHNSON. 'Sir, this gloom of infidelity, I hope, is only a transient cloud passing through the hemisphere, which will soon be dissipated, and the sun break forth with his usual splendour.' 'You think then, (said the General,) that they will change their principles like their clothes.' JOHNSON. 'Why, Sir, if they bestow no more thought on principles than on dress, it must be so.' The General said, that 'a great part of the fashionable infidelity was owing to a desire of shewing courage. Men who have no opportunities of shewing it as to things in this life, take death and futurity as objects on which to display it.' JOHNSON. 'That is mighty foolish affectation. Fear is one of the passions of human nature, of which it is impossible to divest it. You remember that the Emperour Charles V. when he read upon the tomb-stone of a Spanish nobleman, "Here lies one who never knew fear," wittily said, "Then he never snuffed a candle with his fingers." '

He talked a few words of French to the General; but finding he did not do it with facility, he asked for pen, ink, and paper, and wrote the following note:

'*J'ai lu dans la geographie de Lucas de Linda un Pater-noster écrit dans une langue tout à-fait differente de l'Italienne, et de toutes autres lesquelles se derivent du Latin. L'auteur l'appelle* linguam Corsicæ rusticam: *elle a peut-être passé, peu à peu; mais elle a certainement prevalue autrefois dans les montagnes et dans la campagne. Le même auteur dit la même chose en parlant de Sardaigne; qu'il y a deux langues dans l'Isle, une des villes, l'autre de la campagne.*'

The General immediately informed him that the *lingua rustica* was only in Sardinia.

Dr. Johnson went home with me, and drank tea till late in the night. He said, 'General Paoli had the loftiest port of any man he had ever seen.' He denied that military men were always the best bred men. 'Perfect good breeding (he observed) consists in having no particular mark of any profession, but a general elegance of manners; whereas, in a military man, you can commonly distinguish the *brand* of a soldier, *l'homme d'epée.*'

Dr. Johnson shunned to-night any discussion of the perplexed question of fate and free will, which I attempted to agitate: 'Sir, (said he,) we *know* our will is free, and *there's* an end on't.'

He honoured me with his company at dinner on the 16th of October, at my lodgings in Old Bond-street, with Sir Joshua Reynolds, Mr. Garrick, Dr. Goldsmith, Mr. Murphy, Mr. Bickerstaff, and Mr. Thomas Davies. Garrick played round him with a fond vivacity, taking hold of the breasts of his coat, and, looking up in his face with a lively archness, complimented him on the good health which he seemed then to enjoy; while the sage, shaking his head, beheld him with a gentle complacency. One of the company not being come at the appointed hour, I proposed, as usual upon such occasions, to order dinner to be served; adding, 'Ought six people to be kept waiting for one?' 'Why, yes, (answered Johnson, with a delicate humanity,) if the one will suffer more by your sitting down, than the six will do by waiting.' Goldsmith, to divert the tedious minutes, strutted about, bragging of his dress, and I believe was seriously vain of it, for his mind was wonderfully prone to such impressions. 'Come, come, (said Garrick,) talk no more of that. You are perhaps, the worst—eh, eh!'—Goldsmith was eagerly attempting to interrupt him, when Garrick went on, laughing ironically, 'Nay, you will always *look* like a gentleman; but I am talking of being well or ill *drest.*' 'Well, let me tell you, (said Goldsmith,) when my taylor brought home my bloom-coloured coat, he said, "Sir, I have a favour to beg of you. When any body asks you who made your clothes, be pleased to mention John Filby, at the Harrow, in Water-lane."' JOHNSON. 'Why, Sir, that was because he knew the strange colour would attract crowds to gaze at it, and thus they might hear of him, and see how well he could make a coat even of so absurd a colour.'

After dinner our conversation first turned upon Pope. Johnson said, his characters of men were admirably drawn, those of women not so well. He repeated to us, in his forcible melodious manner, the concluding lines of the Dunciad.[1] While he was talking loudly in praise of those lines, one of the company ventured to say, 'Too fine for such a poem:—a poem on what?' JOHNSON, (with a disdainful look,) 'Why, on *dunces*. It was worth while being a dunce then. Ah, Sir, hadst *thou* lived in those days! It is not worth while being a dunce now, when there are no wits.' Bickerstaff observed, as a peculiar circumstance, that Pope's fame was higher when he was alive than it was then. Johnson said, his Pastorals were poor things, though the versification was fine. He told us, with high satisfaction, the anecdote of Pope's enquiring who was the authour of his 'London,' and saying, he will be soon *deterré*. He observed, that in Dryden's poetry there were passages drawn from a profundity which Pope could never reach.[a] He repeated some fine lines on love, by the former, (which I have now forgotten,) and gave great applause to the character of Zimri. Goldsmith said, that Pope's character of Addison shewed a deep knowledge of the human heart. Johnson said, that the description of the temple, in 'The Mourning Bride,'[2] was the finest poetical passage he had ever read; he recollected none in Shakspeare equal to it.—'But, (said Garrick, all alarmed for "the God of his idolatry,") we know not the extent and variety of his powers. We are to suppose there are such passages in his works. Shakspeare must not suffer from the badness of our memories.' Johnson, diverted by this enthusiastick jealousy, went on with great ardour: 'No, Sir; Congreve has *nature*;'[b] (smiling on the tragick eagerness of Garrick;) but composing himself, he added, 'Sir, this is not comparing Congreve on the whole with Shakspeare on the whole; but only maintaining that Congreve has one finer passage than any that can be found in Shakspeare. Sir, a man may have no more than ten guineas in the world, but he may have those ten guineas in one piece; and so may have a finer piece than a man

exclamation point: *It is not* etc. [H]

underlined: *profundity, reach* [H]
[a] *ill express'd* [H]

queried: *finest poetical passage* etc. [H]

[b] *In the First Place it is not* Nature, *it is the* Art *of* Man, *a Piece of Architecture which is the Subject of Congreve's Description. in the second Place It is not Original; it is a ten Pound Bank Note only, & that Note forged.* [I]
queried: *on the whole* etc. [H]

[c] *& whatever else it may be, Mr. Malone knows it is not original* [H]

---

[1] [Mr. Langton informed me that he once related to Johnson (on the authority of Spence) that Pope himself admired those lines so much, that when he repeated them, his voice faltered: 'and well it might, Sir, (said Johnson) for they are noble lines.' J. BOSWELL.]

[2] [Act ii. sc. 3. MALONE.][c]

who has ten thousand pound: but then he has only one
ten-guinea piece.—What I mean is, that you can shew me
no passage where there is simply a description of material
objects, without any intermixture of moral notions,[1]
which produces such an effect.' Mr. Murphy mentioned
Shakspeare's description of the night before the battle of
Agincourt; but it was observed it had *men* in it. Mr. Davies
suggested the speech of Juliet, in which she figures herself
awaking in the tomb of her ancestors. Some one mentioned
the description of Dover Cliff. JOHNSON. 'No, Sir; it
should be all precipice,—all vacuum. The crows impede
your fall. The diminished appearance of the boats, and
other circumstances, are all very good description; but do
not impress the mind at once with the horrible idea of
immense height. The impression is divided; you pass on
by computation, from one stage of the tremendous space
to another. Had the girl in "The Mourning Bride" said,
she could not cast her shoe to the top of one of the pillars
in the temple, it would not have aided the idea, but
weakened it.'

Talking of a Barrister who had a bad utterance, some
one, (to rouse Johnson,) wickedly said, that he was unfortunate in not having been taught oratory by Sheridan.
JOHNSON. 'Nay, Sir, if he had been taught by Sheridan,
he would have cleared the room.' GARRICK. 'Sheridan
has too much vanity to be a good man.'—We shall now see
Johnson's mode of *defending* a man; taking him into his own
hands, and discriminating. JOHNSON. 'No, Sir. There is,
to be sure, in Sheridan, something to reprehend and every
thing to laugh at; but, Sir, he is not a bad man. No, Sir;
were mankind to be divided into good and bad, he would
stand considerably within the ranks of good. And, Sir, it
must be allowed that Sheridan excels in plain declamation,
though he can exhibit no character.'

I should, perhaps, have suppressed this disquisition
concerning a person of whose merit and worth I think with
respect, had he not attacked Johnson so outrageously in

[1] [In Congreve's description there seems to be *an intermixture of moral
notions;* as the affecting power of the passage arises from the vivid impression
of the described objects on the mind of the speaker: 'And shoots a chillness,'
&c. KEARNEY.]

his Life of Swift, and, at the same time, treated us his admirers as a set of pigmies. He who has provoked the lash of wit, cannot complain that he smarts from it.

Mrs. Montague, a lady distinguished for having written an Essay on Shakspeare, being mentioned;—REYNOLDS. 'I think that essay does her honour.' JOHNSON. 'Yes, Sir; it does *her* honour, but it would do nobody else honour. I have, indeed, not read it all. But when I take up the end of a web, and find it packthread, I do not expect, by looking further to find embroidery. Sir, I will venture to say, there is not one sentence of true criticism in her book.' GARRICK. 'But, Sir, surely it shews how much Voltaire has mistaken Shakspeare, which nobody else has done.' JOHNSON. 'Sir, nobody else has thought it worth while. And what merit is there in that? You may as well praise a schoolmaster for whipping a boy who has construed ill. No, Sir, there is no real criticism in it: none shewing the beauty of thought, as formed on the workings of the human heart.'

The admirers of this Essay[1] may be offended at the slighting manner in which Johnson spoke of it: but let it be remembered, that he gave his honest opinion unbiassed by any prejudice, or any proud jealousy of a woman intruding herself into the chair of criticism; for Sir Joshua Reynolds has told me, that when the Essay first came out, and it was not known who had written it, Johnson wondered how Sir Joshua could like it. At this time Sir Joshua himself had received no information concerning the authour, except being assured by one of our most eminent literati, that it was clear its authour did not know the Greek tragedies in the original. One day at Sir Joshua's table, when it was related that Mrs. Montague, in an excess of compliment to the authour of a modern tragedy,[a] had

marginal line:
JOHNSON. '*Yes* . . .
but it [H]

[a] *Braganza* [I]

---

[1] Of whom I acknowledge myself to be one, considering it as a piece of the secondary or comparative species of criticism; and not of that profound species which alone Dr. Johnson would allow to be 'real criticism.' It is, besides, clearly and elegantly expressed, and has done effectually what it professed to do, namely, vindicated Shakspeare from the misrepresentations of Voltaire; and considering how many young people were misled by his witty, though false observations, Mrs. Montague's Essay was of service to Shakspeare with a certain class of readers, and is, therefore, entitled to praise. Johnson, I am assured, allowed the merit which I have stated, saying, (with reference to Voltaire,) 'it is conclusive *ad hominem*.'

exclaimed, 'I tremble for Shakspeare;' Johnson said,
'When Shakspeare has got ——ᵃ for his rival, and Mrs.
Montague for his defender, he is in a poor state indeed.'

ᵃ *Jephson* [H & I]

Johnson proceeded: 'The Scotchman has taken the right
method in his "Elements of Criticism." I do not mean
that he has taught us any thing; but he has told us old
things in a new way.' MURPHY. 'He seems to have read
a great deal of French criticism, and wants to make it his
own; as if he had been for years anatomising the heart of
man, and peeping into every cranny of it.' GOLDSMITH.
'It is easier to write that book, than to read it.' JOHNSON.
'We have an example of true criticism in Burke's "Essay
on the Sublime and Beautiful;" and, if I recollect, there
is also Du Bos; and Bouhours, who shews all beauty to
depend on truth. There is no great merit in telling how
many plays have ghosts in them, and how this Ghost is
better than that. You must shew how terrour is impressed
on the human heart.—In the description of night in Macbeth, the beetle and the bat detract from the general idea
of darkness,—inspissated gloom.'

Politicks being mentioned, he said, 'This petitioning is
a new mode of distressing government, and a mighty easy
one. I will undertake to get petitions either against quarter
guineas or half guineas, with the help of a little hot wine.
There must be no yielding to encourage this. The object
is not important enough. We are not to blow up half a
dozen palaces, because one cottage is burning.'

The conversation then took another turn. JOHNSON.
'It is amazing what ignorance of certain points one sometimes finds in men of eminence. A wit about town,ᵇ who
wrote Latin bawdy verses, asked me, how it happened that
England and Scotland, which were once two kingdoms,
were now one:—and Sir Fletcher Norton did not seem to
know that there were such publications as the Reviews.'

ᵇ *I wonder who that was!* [I]

'The ballad of Hardyknute has no great merit, if
it be really ancient.¹ People talk of nature. But mere
obvious nature may be exhibited with very little power
of mind.'

¹ [It is unquestionably a modern fiction. It was written by Sir John Bruce
of Kinross, and first published at Edinburgh in folio, 1719. See 'Percy's
Reliques of ancient English Poetry,' vol. ii. pp. 96, 111, 4th edit. MALONE.]

On Thursday, October 19, I passed the evening with him at his house. He advised me to complete a Dictionary of words peculiar to Scotland, of which I shewed him a specimen. 'Sir, (said he,) Ray has made a collection of north-country words. By collecting those of your country, you will do a useful thing towards the history of the language.' He bade me also go on with collections which I was making upon the antiquities of Scotland. 'Make a large book; a folio.' BOSWELL. 'But of what use will it be, Sir?' JOHNSON. 'Never mind the use; do it.'

I complained that he had not mentioned Garrick in his Preface to Shakspeare; and asked him if he did not admire him. JOHNSON. 'Yes, as "a poor player, who frets and struts his hour upon the stage;"—as a shadow.' BOSWELL. 'But has he not brought Shakspeare into notice?' JOHNSON. 'Sir, to allow that, would be to lampoon the age. Many of Shakspeare's plays are the worse for being acted: Macbeth, for instance.' BOSWELL. 'What, Sir, is nothing gained by decoration and action? Indeed, I do wish that you had mentioned Garrick.' JOHNSON. 'My dear Sir, had I mentioned him, I must have mentioned many more; Mrs. Pritchard, Mrs. Cibber,—nay, and Mr. Cibber too; he too altered Shakspeare.' BOSWELL. 'You have read his apology, Sir?' JOHNSON. 'Yes, it is very entertaining. But as for Cibber himself, taking from his conversation all that he ought not to have said, he was a poor creature. I remember when he brought me one of his Odes to have my opinion of it, I could not bear such nonsense, and would not let him read it to the end; so little respect had I for *that great man!* (laughing.) Yet I remember Richardson wondering that I could treat him with familiarity.'

I mentioned to him that I had seen the execution of several convicts at Tyburn, two days before, and that none of them seemed to be under any concern. JOHNSON. 'Most of them, Sir, have never thought at all.' BOSWELL. 'But is not the fear of death natural to man?' JOHNSON. 'So much so, Sir, that the whole of life is but keeping away the thoughts of it.' He then, in a low and earnest tone, talked of his meditating upon the awful hour of his own dissolution, and in what manner he should conduct himself upon that occasion: 'I know not (said he,) whether I

marginal line:
JOHNSON. '*Most...
of death* [H]

should wish to have a friend by me, or have it all between GOD and myself.'

Talking of our feeling for the distresses of others;— JOHNSON. 'Why, Sir, there is much noise made about it, but it is greatly exaggerated. No, Sir, we have a certain degree of feeling to prompt us to do good; more than that, Providence does not intend. It would be misery to no purpose.' BOSWELL. 'But suppose now, Sir, that one of your intimate friends were apprehended for an offence for which he might be hanged.' JOHNSON. 'I should do what I could to bail him, and give him any other assistance; but if he were once fairly hanged, I should not suffer.' BOSWELL. 'Would you eat your dinner that day, Sir?' JOHNSON. 'Yes, Sir; and eat it as if he were eating with me. Why, there's Baretti, who is to be tried for his life to-morrow, friends have risen up for him on every side; yet if he should be hanged, none of them will eat a slice of plumb-pudding the less. Sir, that sympathetick feeling goes a very little way in depressing the mind.'

marginal line:
up for . . . plumb-
pudding the [H]

I told him that I had dined lately at Foote's, who shewed me a letter which he had received from Tom Davies, telling him that he had not been able to sleep from the concern he felt on account of '*This sad affair of Baretti,*' begging of him to try if he could suggest any thing that might be of service; and, at the same time, recommending to him an industrious young man who kept a pickle-shop.' JOHNSON. 'Ay, Sir, here you have a specimen of human sympathy; a friend hanged, and a cucumber pickled. We know not whether Baretti or the pickle-man has kept Davies from sleep: nor does he know himself. And as to his not sleeping, Sir; Tom Davies is a very great man; Tom has been upon the stage, and knows how to do those things: I have not been upon the stage, and cannot do those things.' BOSWELL. 'I have often blamed myself, Sir, for not feeling for others, as sensibly as many say they do.' JOHNSON. 'Sir, don't be duped by them any more. You will find these very feeling people are not very ready to do you good. They *pay* you by *feeling*.'

BOSWELL. 'Foote has a great deal of humour.' JOHNSON. 'Yes, Sir.' BOSWELL. 'He has a singular talent of exhibiting character.' JOHNSON. 'Sir, it is not a talent; it is a vice; it is what others abstain from. It is not comedy, which exhibits the character of a species, as that of a miser gathered from many misers: it is farce which exhibits individuals.' BOSWELL. 'Did not he think of exhibiting you, Sir?' JOHNSON. 'Sir, fear restrained him; he knew I would have broken his bones. I would have saved him the trouble of cutting off a leg; I would not have left him a leg to cut off.' BOSWELL. 'Pray, Sir, is not Foote an infidel?' JOHNSON. 'I do not know, Sir, that the fellow is an infidel; but if he be an infidel, he is an infidel as a dog is an infidel; that is to say, he has never thought upon the subject.'[1] BOSWELL. 'I suppose, Sir, he has thought superficially, and seized the first notions which occurred to his mind.' JOHNSON. 'Why then, Sir, still he is like a dog, that snatches the piece next him. Did you never observe that dogs have not the power of comparing? A dog will take a small bit of meat as readily as a large, when both are before him.'[a]

[a] *Which Johnson would never have done* [H]

'Buchanan (he observed,) has fewer *centos* than any modern Latin poet. He has not only had great knowledge of the Latin language, but was a great poetical genius. Both the Scaligers praise him.'

He again talked of the passage in Congreve with high commendation, and said, 'Shakespeare never has six lines together without a fault. Perhaps you may find seven: but this does not refute my general assertion. If I come to an orchard, and say there's no fruit here, and then comes a poring man, who finds two apples and three pears, and tells me, "Sir, you are mistaken, I have found both apples and pears," I should laugh at him: what would that be to the purpose?'

[1] When Mr. Foote was at Edinburgh, he thought fit to entertain a numerous Scotch company, with a great deal of coarse jocularity, at the expence of Dr. Johnson, imagining it would be acceptable. I felt this as not civil to me; but sat very patiently till he had exhausted his merriment on that subject; and then observed, that surely Johnson must be allowed to have some sterling wit, and that I had heard him say a very good thing of Mr. Foote himself. 'Ah, my old friend Sam, (cried Foote,) no man says better things: do let us have it.' Upon which I told the above story, which produced a very loud laugh from the company. But I never saw Foote so disconcerted. He looked grave and angry and entered into a serious refutation of the justice of the remark, 'What, Sir, (said he,) talk thus of a man of liberal education:—a man who for years was at the University of Oxford:—a man who has added sixteen new characters to the English drama of his country!'

BOSWELL. 'What do you think of Dr. Young's "Night Thoughts," Sir?' JOHNSON. 'Why, Sir, there are very fine things in them.' BOSWELL. 'Is there not less religion in the nation now, Sir, than there was formerly?' JOHNSON. 'I don't know, Sir, that there is.' BOSWELL. 'For instance, there used to be a chaplain in every great family, which we do not find now.' JOHNSON. 'Neither do you find any of the state servants which great families used formerly to have. There is a change of modes in the whole department of life.'

Next day, October 20, he appeared, for the only time I suppose in his life, as a witness in a Court of Justice, being called to give evidence to the character of Mr. Baretti, who having stabbed a man in the street, was arraigned at the Old Bailey for murder. Never did such a constellation of genius enlighten the awful Sessions House, emphatically called JUSTICE HALL; Mr. Burke, Mr. Garrick, Mr. Beauclerk, and Dr. Johnson: and undoubtedly their favourable testimony had due weight with the Court and Jury. Johnson gave his evidence in a slow, deliberate, and distinct manner, which was uncommonly impressive. It is well known that Mr. Baretti was acquitted.

On the 26th of October, we dined together at the Mitre tavern. I found fault with Foote for indulging his talent of ridicule at the expence of his visitors, which I colloquially termed making fools of his company. JOHNSON. 'Why, Sir, when you go to see Foote, you do not go to see a saint: you go to see a man who will be entertained at your house, and then bring you on a publick stage; who will entertain you at his house, for the very purpose of bringing you on a publick stage. Sir, he does not make fools of his company; they whom he exposes are fools already: he only brings them into action.'

Talking of trade, he observed, 'It is a mistaken notion that a vast deal of money is brought into a nation by trade. It is not so. Commodities come from commodities; but trade produces no capital accession of wealth. However, though there should be little profit in money, there is a considerable profit in pleasure, as it gives to one nation the productions of another; as we have wines and fruits, and many other foreign articles brought to us.' BOSWELL.

'Yes, Sir, and there is a profit in pleasure, by its furnishing occupation to such numbers of mankind.' JOHNSON. 'Why, Sir, you cannot call that pleasure to which all are averse, and which none begin but with the hope of leaving off; a thing which men dislike before they have tried it, and when they have tried it.' BOSWELL. 'But, Sir, the mind must be employed, and we grow weary when idle.' JOHNSON. 'That is, Sir, because others being busy, we want company; but if we were all idle, there would be no growing weary; we should all entertain one another. There is, indeed, this in trade:—it gives men an opportunity of improving their situation. If there were no trade, many who are poor would always remain poor. But no man loves labour for itself.' BOSWELL. 'Yes, Sir, I know a person who does. He is a very laborious Judge, and he loves the labour.' JOHNSON. 'Sir, that is because he loves respect and distinction. Could he have them without labour, he would like it less.' BOSWELL. 'He tells me he likes it for itself.'—'Why, Sir, he fancies so, because he is not accustomed to abstract.'

queried: *no man* etc. [H]

We went home to his house to tea. Mrs. Williams made it with sufficient dexterity, notwithstanding her blindness, though her manner of satisfying herself that the cups were full enough, appeared to me a little aukward; for I fancied she put her finger down a certain way, till she felt the tea touch it.[1] In my first elation at being allowed the privilege of attending Dr. Johnson at his late visits to this lady, which was like being *è secretioribus consiliis*, I willingly drank cup after cup, as if it had been the Heliconian spring. But as the charm of novelty went off, I grew more fastidious; and besides, I discovered that she was of a peevish temper.

There was a pretty large circle this evening. Dr. Johnson was in very good humour, lively, and ready to talk upon all subjects. Mr. Fergusson, the self-taught philosopher, told him of a new-invented machine which went without

[1] I have since had reason to think that I was mistaken; for I have been informed by a lady, who was long intimate with her, and likely to be a more accurate observer of such matters, that she had acquired such a niceness of touch, as to know, by the feeling on the outside of the cup, how near it was to being full.[a]

[a] *not She poor Soul. The 1st. Story is the truest.* [H]

horses: a man who sat in it turned a handle, which worked a spring that drove it forward. 'Then, Sir, (said Johnson,) what is gained is, the man has his choice whether he will move himself alone, or himself and the machine too.' Dominicetti being mentioned, he would not allow him any merit. 'There is nothing in all this boasted system. No, Sir; medicated baths can be no better than warm water: their only effect can be that of tepid moisture.' One of the company took the other side, maintaining that medicines of various sorts, and some too of most powerful effect, are introduced into the human frame by the medium of the pores; and, therefore, when warm water is impregnated with salutiferous substances, it may produce great effects as a bath. This appeared to me very satisfactory. Johnson did not answer it; but talking for victory, and determined to be master of the field, he had recourse to the device which Goldsmith imputed to him in the witty words of one of Cibber's comedies: 'There is no arguing with Johnson; for when his pistol misses fire, he knocks you down with the butt end of it.' He turned to the gentleman,ᵃ 'Well, Sir, go to Dominicetti, and get thyself fumigated; but be sure that the steam be directed to thy *head*, for *that* is the *peccant part*.' This produced a triumphant roar of laughter from the motley assembly of philosophers, printers, and dependents, male and female.

I know not how so whimsical a thought came into my mind, but I asked, 'If, Sir, you were shut up in a castle, and a new-born child with you, what would you do?' JOHNSON. 'Why, Sir, I should not much like my company.' BOSWELL. 'But would you take the trouble of rearing it?' He seemed, as may well be supposed, unwilling to pursue the subject: but upon my persevering in my question, replied, 'Why yes, Sir, I would; but I must have all conveniences. If I had no garden, I would make a shed on the roof, and take it there for fresh air. I should feed it, and wash it much, and with warm water to please it, not with cold water to give it pain.' BOSWELL. 'But, Sir, does not heat relax?' JOHNSON. 'Sir, you are not to imagine the water is to be very hot. I would not *coddle* the child. No, Sir, the hardy method of treating children does no good. I'll take you five children from London, who shall

Marginal notes:
queried:
no better etc. [H]

underlined:
gentleman [H]
ᵃ *Bozzy himself.* [H]

cuff five Highland children. Sir, a man bred in London will carry a burthen, or run, or wrestle, as well as a man brought up in the hardest manner in the country.' BOSWELL. 'Good living, I suppose, makes the Londoners strong.' JOHNSON. 'Why, Sir, I don't know that it does. Our chairmen from Ireland, who are as strong men as any, have been brought up upon potatoes. Quantity makes up for quality.' BOSWELL. 'Would you teach this child that I have furnished you with, any thing?' JOHNSON. 'No, I should not be apt to teach it.' BOSWELL. 'Would not you have a pleasure in teaching it?' JOHNSON. 'No, Sir, I should *not* have a pleasure in teaching it.' BOSWELL. 'Have you not a pleasure in teaching men!— *There* I have you. You have the same pleasure in teaching men, that I should have in teaching children.' JOHNSON. 'Why, something about that.'

BOSWELL. 'Do you think, Sir, that what is called natural affection is born with us? It seems to me to be the effect of habit, or of gratitude for kindness. No child has it for a parent whom it has not seen.'[a] JOHNSON. 'Why, Sir, I think there is an instinctive natural affection in parents towards their children.'

a *No—nor whom it has seen I believe— unless by Chance.* [H]

Russia being mentioned as likely to become a great empire, by the rapid increase of population:—JOHNSON. 'Why, Sir, I see no prospect of their propagating more, They can have no more children than they can get. I know of no way to make them breed more than they do. It is not from reason and prudence that people marry, but from inclination. A man is poor; he thinks, "I cannot be worse, and so I'll e'en take Peggy."' BOSWELL. 'But have not nations been more populous at one period than another?' JOHNSON. 'Yes, Sir; but that has been owing to the people being less thinned at one period than another, whether by emigrations, war, or pestilence, not by their being more or less prolifick. Births at all times bear the same proportion to the same number of people.' BOSWELL. 'But, to consider the state of our own country;—does not throwing a number of farms into one hand hurt population?' JOHNSON. 'Why no, Sir; the same quantity of food being produced, will be consumed by the same number of mouths, though the people may be disposed of in different ways. We see, if corn be dear, and butchers' meat cheap, the farmers all apply themselves to the raising of corn, till it becomes plentiful and cheap, and then butchers' meat becomes dear; so that an equality is always preserved. No, Sir, let fanciful men do as they will, depend upon it, it is difficult to disturb the system of life.' BOSWELL. 'But, Sir, is it not a very bad thing for land-lords to oppress their tenants, by raising their rents?' JOHNSON. 'Very bad. But, Sir, it never can have any general influence: it may distress some individuals. For, consider this: landlords cannot do without tenants. Now tenants will not give more for land, than land is worth. If they can make more of their money by keeping a shop, or any other way, they'll do it, and so oblige landlords to let land come back to a reasonable rent, in order that they may get tenants. Land, in England, is an article of com-merce. A tenant who pays his landlord his rent, thinks himself no more obliged to him than you think yourself obliged to a man in whose shop you buy a piece of goods. He knows the landlord does not let him have his land for less than he can get from others, in the same manner as the shopkeeper sells his goods. No shopkeeper sells a yard of ribband for six-pence when seven-pence is the current price.' BOSWELL. 'But, Sir, is it not better that tenants should be dependent on landlords?' JOHNSON. 'Why, Sir, as there are many more tenants than landlords, perhaps strictly speaking, we should wish not. But if you please you may let your lands cheap, and so get the value, part in money and part in homage. I should agree with you in that.' BOSWELL. 'So, Sir, you laugh at schemes of political improvement.' JOHNSON. 'Why, Sir, most schemes of political improvement are very laughable things.'

He observed, 'Providence has wisely ordered that the more numerous men are, the more difficult it is for them to agree in any thing, and so they are governed. There is no doubt, that if the poor should reason, "We'll be the poor no longer, we'll make the rich take their turn," they could easily do it, were it not that they can't agree. So the common soldiers, though so much more numerous than their officers, are governed by them for the same reason.'

index sign:
We'll be etc. [H]

He said, 'Mankind have a strong attachment to the habitations to which they have been accustomed. You see the inhabitants of Norway do not with one consent quit it, and go to some part of America, where there is a mild climate, and where they may have the same produce from land, with the tenth part of the labour. No, Sir; their affection for their old dwellings, and the terrour of a general change, keep them at home. Thus, we see many of the finest spots in the world thinly inhabited, and many rugged spots well inhabited.'

'The London Chronicle,' which was the only newspaper he constantly took in, being brought, the office of reading it aloud was assigned to me. I was diverted by his impatience. He made me pass over so many parts of it, that my task was very easy. He would not suffer one of the petitions to the King about the Middlesex election to be read.

I had hired a Bohemian as my servant while I remained in London, and being much pleased with him I asked Dr. Johnson whether his being a Roman Catholick should prevent my taking him with me to Scotland. JOHNSON. 'Why no, Sir. If *he* has no objection, you can have none.' BOSWELL. 'So, Sir, you are no great enemy to the Roman Catholick Religion.' JOHNSON. 'No more, Sir, than to the Presbyterian religion.' BOSWELL. 'You are joking.' JOHNSON. 'No, Sir, I really think so. Nay, Sir, of the two, I prefer the Popish.' BOSWELL. 'How so, Sir?' JOHNSON. 'Why, Sir, the Presbyterians have no church, no apostolical ordination.' BOSWELL. 'And do you think that absolutely essential, Sir?' JOHNSON. 'Why, Sir, as it was an apostolical institution, I think it is dangerous to be without it. And, Sir, the Presbyterians have no publick worship: they have no form of prayer in which they know they are to join. They go to hear a man pray, and are to judge whether they will join with him.' BOSWELL. 'But Sir, their doctrine is the same with that of the Church of England. Their confession of faith, and the thirty-nine articles, contain the same points, even the doctrine of predestination.' JOHNSON. 'Why, yes, Sir; predestination was a part of the clamour of the times, so it is mentioned in our articles, but with as little positiveness as could be.'

Boswell. 'Is it necessary, Sir, to believe all the thirty-nine articles?' Johnson. 'Why, Sir, that is a question which has been much agitated. Some have thought it necessary that they should all be believed; others have considered them to be only articles of peace,[1] that is to say, you are not to preach against them.' Boswell. 'It appears to me, Sir, that predestination, or what is equivalent to it, cannot be avoided, if we hold an universal prescience in the Deity.' Johnson. 'Why, Sir, does not God every day see things going on without preventing them?' Boswell. 'True, Sir, but if a thing be *certainly* foreseen, it must be fixed, and cannot happen otherwise; and if we apply this consideration to the human mind, there is no free will, nor do I see how prayer can be of any avail.' He mentioned Dr. Clarke, and Bishop Bramhall on Liberty and Necessity, and bid me read South's Sermons on Prayer; but avoided the question which has excruciated philosophers and divines, beyond any other. I did not press it further, when I perceived that he was displeased, and shrunk from any abridgement of an attribute usually ascribed to the Divinity, however irreconcileable in its full extent with the grand system of moral government. His supposed orthodoxy here cramped the vigorous powers of his understanding. He was confined by a chain which early imagination and long habit made him think massy and strong, but which, had he ventured to try, he could at once have snapt asunder.

I proceeded: 'What do you think, Sir, of Purgatory, as believed by the Roman Catholicks?' Johnson. 'Why, Sir, it is a very harmless doctrine. They are of opinion that

[1] [Dr. Simon Patrick, (afterwards Bishop of Ely) thus expresses himself on this subject, in a letter to the learned Dr. John Mapletoft, dated Feb. 8, 1682–3:

'I always took the Articles to be only articles of communion; and so Bishop Bramhall expressly maintains against the Bishop of Chalcedon; and I remember well, that Bishop Sanderson, when the King was first restored, received the subscription of an acquaintance of mine, which he declared was not to them as articles of *faith*, but *peace*. I think you need make no scruple of the matter, because all that I know so understand the meaning of subscription, and upon other terms would not subscribe.'—The above was printed some years ago in the European Magazine, from the original, now in the hands of Mr. Mapletoft, surgeon at Chertsey, grandson to Dr. John Mapletoft. Malone.]

the generality of mankind are neither so obstinately wicked as to deserve everlasting punishment, nor so good as to merit being admitted into the society of blessed spirits; and therefore that GOD is graciously pleased to allow of a middle state, where they may be purified by certain degrees of suffering. You see, Sir, there is nothing unreasonable in this.' BOSWELL. 'But then, Sir, their masses for the dead?' JOHNSON. 'Why, Sir, if it be once established that there are souls in purgatory, it is as proper to pray for *them*, as for our brethren of mankind who are yet in this life.' BOSWELL. 'The idolatry of the Mass?' — JOHNSON, 'Sir, there is no idolatry in the Mass. They believe GOD to be there, and they adore him.' BOSWELL. 'The worship of Saints?'—JOHNSON. 'Sir, they do not worship saints; they invoke them; they only ask their prayers. I am talking all this time of the *doctrines* of the Church of Rome. I grant you that in *practice*, Purgatory is made a lucrative imposition, and that the people do become idolatrous as they recommend themselves to the tutelary protection of particular saints. I think their giving the sacrament only in one kind is criminal, because it is contrary to the express institution of CHRIST, and I wonder how the Council of Trent admitted it.' BOSWELL. 'Confession?'— JOHNSON. 'Why, I don't know but that is a good thing. The scripture says "Confess your faults one to another," and the priests confess as well as the laity. Then it must be considered that their absolution is only upon repentance, and often upon penance also.[a] You think your sins may be forgiven without penance, upon repentance alone.'

[a] *Their Absolution is the same as ours—Word for Word.* [H & I]

I thus ventured to mention all the common objections against the Roman Catholick Church, that I might hear so great a man upon them. What he said is here accurately recorded. But it is not improbable that if one had taken the other side, he might have reasoned differently.

two marginal lines: *improbable that . . . respect for* [H]

I must however mention, that he had a respect for '*the old religion*,' as the mild Melancthon called that of the Roman Catholick Church, even while he was exerting himself for its reformation in some particulars. Sir William Scott informs me, that he heard Johnson say, 'A man who is converted from Protestantism to Popery, may be sincere: he parts with nothing: he is only superadding to what he already had. But a convert from Popery to Protestantism, gives up so much of what he has held as sacred as any thing that he retains: there is so much *laceration of mind* in such a conversion, that it can hardly be sincere and lasting.' The truth of this reflection may be confirmed by many and eminent instances, some of which will occur to most of my readers.

When we were alone, I introduced the subject of death, and endeavoured to maintain that the fear of it might be got over. I told him that David Hume said to me, he was no more uneasy to think he should *not be* after his life, than that he *had not been* before he began to exist. JOHNSON. 'Sir, if he really thinks so, his perceptions are disturbed; he is mad; if he does not think so, he lies. He may tell you, he holds his finger in the flame of a candle, without feeling pain; would you believe him? When he dies, he at least gives up all he has.' BOSWELL. 'Foote, Sir, told me, that when he was very ill he was not afraid to die.' JOHNSON. 'It is not true, Sir. Hold a pistol to Foote's breast, or to Hume's breast, and threaten to kill them, and you'll see how they behave.' BOSWELL. 'But may we not fortify our minds for the approach of death?'—Here I am sensible I was in the wrong, to bring before his view what he ever looked upon with horrour; for although when in a celestial frame of mind in his 'Vanity of Human Wishes,' he has supposed death to be 'kind Nature's signal for retreat,' from this state of being to 'a happier seat,' his thoughts upon this awful change were in general full of dismal apprehensions. His mind resembled the vast amphi-theatre, the Colisæum at Rome. In the centre stood his judgement, which like a mighty gladiator, combated those apprehensions that, like the wild beasts of the *Arena*, were all around in cells, ready to be let out upon him. After a conflict, he drives them back into their dens; but not killing them, they were still assailing him. To my question, whether we might not fortify our minds for the approach of death, he answered, in a passion, 'No, Sir, let it alone. It matters not how a man dies, but how he lives. The act of dying is not of importance, it lasts so short a time.' He added, (with an earnest look,) 'A man knows it must be so, and submits. It will do him no good to whine.'

I attempted to continue the conversation. He was so provoked, that he said: 'Give us no more of this;' and was thrown into such a state of agitation, that he expressed himself in a way that alarmed and distressed me; shewed an impatience that I should leave him, and when I was going away, called to me sternly, 'Don't let us meet to-morrow.'

I went home exceedingly uneasy. All the harsh observations which I had ever heard made upon his character, crowded into my mind; and I seemed to myself like the man who had put his head into the lion's mouth a great many times with perfect safety, but at last had it bit off.

exclamation point: *into the lion's mouth* etc. [H]

Next morning I sent him a note, stating that I might have been in the wrong, but it was not intentionally; he was therefore, I could not help thinking, too severe upon me. That notwithstanding our agreement not to meet that day, I would call on him in my way to the city, and stay five minutes by my watch. 'You are, (said I) in my mind, since last night, surrounded with cloud and storm. Let me have a glimpse of sunshine, and go about my affairs in serenity and cheerfulness.'

Upon entering his study, I was glad that he was not alone, which would have made our meeting more awkward. There were with him Mr. Steevens and Mr. Tyers, both of whom I now saw for the first time. My note had, on his own reflection, softened him, for he received me very complacently; so that I unexpectedly found myself at ease; and joined in the conversation.

He said, the criticks had done too much honour to Sir Richard Blackmore, by writing so much against him. That in his 'Creation' he had been helped by various wits, a line by Phillips, and a line by Tickell; so that by their aid, and that of others, the poem had been made out.[1]

I defended Blackmore's supposed lines, which have been ridiculed as absolute nonsense:

'A painted vest Prince Vortiger had on,
Which from a naked Pict his grandsire won.'[2]

[1] [Johnson himself has vindicated Blackmore upon this very point. See the Lives of the Poets, vol. iii. p. 75. 8vo. 1791. J. BOSWELL.]

[2] An acute correspondent of the European Magazine, April 1792, has completely exposed a mistake which has been unaccountably frequent in

I maintained it to be a poetical conceit. A Pict being painted, if he is slain in battle, and a vest is made of his skin, it is a painted vest won from him, though he was naked.

Johnson spoke unfavourably of a certain pretty voluminous authour, saying, 'He used to write anonymous books, and then other books commending those books, in which there was something of rascality.'

I whispered him, 'Well, Sir, you are now in good humour.' JOHNSON. 'Yes, Sir.' I was going to leave him, and had got as far as the staircase. He stopped me, and smiling, said, 'Get you gone in;'ᵃ a curious mode of inviting me to stay, which I accordingly did for some time longer.

ᵃ Such a strange Fellow could scarce have been otherwise dealt with. [H & I; I omits otherwise]

This little incidental quarrel and reconciliation, which, perhaps, I may be thought to have detailed too minutely, must be esteemed as one of many proofs which his friends had, that though he might be charged with *bad humour* at times, he was always a *good-natured* man; and I have heard Sir Joshua Reynolds, a nice and delicate observer of manners, particularly remark, that when upon any occasion Johnson had been rough to any person in company, he took the first opportunity of reconciliation, by drinking to him, or addressing his discourse to him; but if he found his dignified indirect overtures sullenly neglected, he was quite indifferent, and considered himself as

ascribing these lines to Blackmore, notwithstanding that Sir Richard Steele, in that very popular work 'The Spectator,' mentions them as written by the authour of 'The British Princes,' the Hon. Edward Howard. The correspondent above mentioned, shews this mistake to be so inveterate, that not only *I* defended the lines as Blackmore's, in the presence of Dr. Johnson, without any contradiction or doubt of their authenticity, but that the Reverend Mr. Whitaker has asserted in print, that he understands they were *suppressed* in the late edition or editions of Blackmore. 'After all (says this intelligent writer) it is not unworthy of particular observation, that these lines so often quoted do not exist either in Blackmore or Howard.' In 'The British Princes,' 8vo. 1669, now before me, p. 96, they stand thus:

'A vest as admir'd Vortiger had on,
Which from this Island's foes, his grandsire won,
Whose artful colour pass'd the Tyrian dye,
Oblig'd to triumph in this legacy.'

marginal line:
It is . . . now circulates
[H]

It is probable, I think, that some wag, in order to make Howard still more ridiculous than he really was, has formed the couplet as it now circulates.

having done all that he ought to do, and the other as now in the wrong.

Being to set out for Scotland on the 10th of November, I wrote to him at Streatham, begging that he would meet me in town on the 9th; but if this should be very inconvenient to him, I would go thither. His answer was as follows:

'TO JAMES BOSWELL, ESQ.

'DEAR SIR,

'UPON balancing the inconveniences of both parties, I find it will less incommode you to spend your night here, than me to come to town. I wish to see you, and am ordered by the lady of this house to invite you hither. Whether you can come or not, I shall not have any occasion of writing to you again before your marriage, and therefore tell you now, that with great sincerity I wish you happiness. I am, dear Sir,

'Your most affectionate humble servant,
'Nov. 9, 1769.'   'SAM. JOHNSON'

I was detained in town till it was too late on the ninth, so went to him early in the morning of the tenth of November. 'Now (said he,) that you are going to marry, do not expect more from life, than life will afford. You may often find yourself out of humour, and you may often think your wife not studious enough to please you; and yet you may have reason to consider yourself as upon the whole very happily married.'

Talking of marriage in general, he observed, 'Our marriage service is too refined. It is calculated only for the best kind of marriages; whereas, we should have a form for matches of convenience, of which there are many.' He agreed with me that there was no absolute necessity for having the marriage ceremony performed by a regular clergyman, for this was not commanded in scripture.

marginal line: *Our marriage . . . is calculated* [H]
two marginal lines: *we should . . . of convenience* [H]

I was volatile enough to repeat to him a little epigrammatick song of mine, on matrimony, which Mr. Garrick had a few days before procured to be set to music by the very ingenious Mr. Dibden.

A MATRIMONIAL THOUGHT

'In the blithe days of honey-moon,
    With Kate's allurements smitten,
I lov'd her late, I lov'd her soon,
    And call'd her dearest kitten.

But now my kitten's grown a cat,
    And cross like other wives,
O! by my soul, my honest Mat,
    I fear she has nine lives.'

My illustrious friend said, 'It is very well, Sir; but you should not swear.' Upon which I altered 'O! by my soul,' to 'alas, alas!'

He was so good as to accompany me to London, and see me into the post-chaise which was to carry me on my road to Scotland. And sure I am, that however inconsiderable many of the particulars recorded at this time may appear to some, they will be esteemed by the best part of my readers as genuine traits of his character, contributing together to give a full, fair, and distinct view of it.

In 1770, he published a political pamphlet, entitled 'The False Alarm,' intended to justify the conduct of ministry and their majority in the House of Commons for having virtually assumed it as an axiom, that the expulsion of a Member of Parliament was equivalent to exclusion, and thus having declared Colonel Lutterel to be duly elected for the county of Middlesex, notwithstanding Mr. Wilkes had a great majority of votes. This being justly considered as a gross violation of the right of election, an alarm for the constitution extended itself all over the kingdom. To prove this alarm to be false, was the purpose of Johnson's pamphlet; but even his vast powers are inadequate to cope with constitutional truth and reason, and his argument failed of effect; and the House of Commons have since expunged the offensive resolution from their Journals. That the House of Commons might have expelled Mr. Wilkes repeatedly, and as often as he should be re-chosen, was not denied; but incapacitation cannot be but by an act of the whole legislature. It was wonderful to see how a prejudice in favour of government in general,

marginal line:
of effect . . . their
Journals [H]

and an aversion to popular clamour, could blind and contract such an understanding as Johnson's, in this particular case; yet the wit, the sarcasm, the eloquent vivacity which this pamphlet displayed, made it be read with great avidity at the time, and it will ever be read with pleasure, for the sake of its composition. That it endeavoured to infuse a narcotick indifference, as to publick concerns, into the minds of the people, and that it broke out sometimes into an extreme coarseness of contemptuous abuse, is but too evident.

It must not, however, be omitted, that when the storm of his violence subsides, he takes a fair opportunity to pay a grateful compliment to the King, who had rewarded his merit: 'These low-born railers have endeavoured, surely without effect, to alienate the affections of the people from the only King who for almost a century has much appeared to desire, or much endeavoured to deserve them.' And, 'Every honest man must lament, that the faction has been regarded with frigid neutrality by the Tories, who being long accustomed to signalise their principles by opposition to the Court, do not yet consider, that they have at last a King who knows not the name of party, and who wishes to be the common father of all his people.'

To this pamphlet, which was at once discovered to be Johnson's, several answers came out, in which care was taken to remind the public of his former attacks upon government, and of his now being a pensioner, without allowing for the honourable terms upon which Johnson's pension was granted and accepted, or the change of system which the British court had undergone upon the accession of his present Majesty. He was, however, soothed in the highest strain of panegyrick, in a poem called 'The Remonstrance,' by the Reverend Mr. Stockdale, to whom he was, upon many occasions, a kind protector.

The following admirable minute made by him, describes so well his own state, and that of numbers to whom self-examination is habitual, that I cannot omit it:

'June 1, 1770. Every man naturally persuades himself that he can keep his resolutions, nor is he convinced of his imbecility but by length of time and frequency of experiment. This opinion of our own constancy is so prevalent, that we always despise him who suffers his general and settled purpose to be overpowered by an occasional desire. They, therefore, whom frequent failures have made desperate, cease to form resolutions; and they who are become cunning, do not tell them. Those who do not make them are very few, but of their effect little is perceived: for scarcely any man persists in a course of life planned by choice, but as he is restrained from deviation by some external power. He who may live as he will, seldom lives long in the observation of his own rules.'[1]

Of this year I have obtained the following letters:

'TO THE REVEREND DR. FARMER, CAMBRIDGE

'SIR,

'As no man ought to keep wholly to himself any possession that may be useful to the publick, I hope you will not think me unreasonably intrusive, if I have recourse to you for such information as you are more able to give me than any other man.

'In support of an opinion which you have already placed above the need of any more support, Mr. Steevens, a very ingenious gentleman, lately of King's College, has collected an account of all the translations which Shakspeare might have seen and used. He wishes his catalogue to be perfect, and therefore intreats that you will favour him by the insertion of such additions as the accuracy of your enquiries has enabled you to make. To this request, I take the liberty of adding my own solicitation.

'We have no immediate use for this catalogue, and therefore do not desire that it should interrupt or hinder your more important employments. But it will be kind to let us know that you receive it.

'I am, Sir, &c.

'Johnson's-court, Fleet-street,
   March 21, 1770.'   'SAM. JOHNSON'

'TO THE REVEREND MR. THOMAS WARTON

'DEAR SIR,

'THE readiness with which you were pleased to promise me some notes on Shakspeare, was a new instance

[1] Prayers and Meditations, p. 95.

of your friendship. I shall not hurry you; but am desired
by Mr. Steevens, who helps me in this edition, to let you
know, that we shall print the tragedies first, and shall
therefore want first the notes which belong to them. We
think not to incommode the readers with a supplement;
and therefore, what we cannot put into its proper place,
will do us no good. We shall not begin to print before the
end of six weeks, perhaps not so soon.

'I am, &c.

'London, June 23, 1770.'   'SAM. JOHNSON'

'TO THE REV. DR. JOSEPH WARTON

'DEAR SIR,

'I AM revising my edition of Shakspeare, and remember that I formerly misrepresented your opinion of Lear.
Be pleased to write the paragraph as you would have it,
and send it. If you have any remarks of your own upon that
or any other play, I shall gladly receive them.

'Make my compliments to Mrs. Warton. I sometimes
think of wandering for a few days to Winchester, but am
apt to delay. I am, Sir,

'Your most humble servant,

'Sept. 21, 1770.'   'SAM. JOHNSON'

'TO MR. FRANCIS BARBER, AT MRS. CLAPP'S,
BISHOP-STORTFORD, HERTFORDSHIRE

'DEAR FRANCIS,

'I AM at last sat down to write to you, and should very
much blame myself for having neglected you so long, if I
did not impute that and many other failings to want of
health. I hope not to be so long silent again. I am very well
satisfied with your progress, if you can really perform the
exercises which you are set; and I hope Mr. Ellis does not
suffer you to impose on him, or on yourself.

'Make my compliments to Mr. Ellis, and to Mrs. Clapp,
and Mr. Smith.

'Let me know what English books you read for your
entertainment. You can never be wise unless you love
reading.

'Do not imagine that I shall forget or forsake you; for if, when I examine you, I find that you have not lost your time, you shall want no encouragement from

'Yours affectionately,

'London, Sept. 25, 1770.'   'SAM. JOHNSON'

TO THE SAME

'DEAR FRANCIS,

'I HOPE you mind your business. I design you shall stay with Mrs. Clapp these holidays. If you are invited out you may go, if Mr. Ellis gives leave. I have ordered you some clothes, which you will receive, I believe, next week. My compliments to Mrs. Clapp and to Mr. Ellis, and Mr. Smith, &c.

'I am

'Your affectionate,

'December 7, 1770.'   'SAM. JOHNSON'

During this year there was a total cessation of all correspondence between Dr. Johnson and me, without any coldness on either side, but merely from procrastination, continued from day to day; and as I was not in London, I had no opportunity of enjoying his company and record-ing his conversation. To supply this blank, I shall present my readers with some *Collectanea*, obligingly furnished to me by the Rev. Dr. Maxwell, of Falkland, in Ireland, some time assistant preacher at the Temple, and for many years the social friend of Johnson, who spoke of him with a very kind regard.

marginal line:
Dr. Maxwell . . . time assistant [H]

'MY acquaintance with that great and venerable character commenced in the year 1754. I was introduced to him by Mr. Grierson,[1] his Majesty's printer at Dublin, a gentleman of uncommon learning, and great wit and vivacity. Mr. Grierson died in Germany, at the age of

[1] Son of the learned Mrs. Grierson, who was patronized by the late Lord Granville, and was the editor of several of the classicks.

[Her edition of Tacitus, with the notes of Ryckius, in three volumes, 8vo. 1730, was dedicated in very elegant Latin to John, Lord Carteret, (afterwards Earl Granville,) by whom she was patronized during his residence in Ireland as Lord Lieutenant between 1724 and 1730. MALONE.]

twenty-seven. Dr. Johnson highly respected his abilities, and often observed, that he possessed more extensive knowledge than any man of his years he had ever known. His industry was equal to his talents; and he particularly excelled in every species of philological learning, and was, perhaps, the best critick of the age he lived in.

'I must always remember with gratitude my obligation to Mr. Grierson, for the honour and happiness of Dr. Johnson's acquaintance and friendship, which continued uninterrupted and undiminished to his death: a connection, that was at once the pride and happiness of my life.

'What pity it is, that so much wit and good sense as he continually exhibited in conversation, should perish unrecorded! Few persons quitted his company without perceiving themselves wiser and better than they were before. On serious subjects he flashed the most interesting conviction upon his auditors; and upon lighter topicks, you might have supposed—*Albano musas de monte locutas*.

'Though I can hope to add but little to the celebrity of so exalted a character, by any communications I can furnish, yet out of pure respect to his memory, I will venture to transmit to you some anecdotes concerning him, which fell under my own observation. The very *minutiæ* of such a character must be interesting, and may be compared to the filings of diamonds.

'In politicks he was deemed a Tory, but certainly was not so in the obnoxious or party sense of the term; for while he asserted the legal and salutary prerogatives of the crown, he no less respected the constitutional liberties of the people. Whiggism, at the time of the Revolution, he said, was accompanied with certain principles; but latterly, as a mere party distinction under Walpole and the Pelhams, was no better than the politicks of stock jobbers, and the religion of infidels.

'He detested the idea of governing by parliamentary corruption, and asserted most strenuously, that a prince steadily and conspicuously pursuing the interests of his people, could not fail of parliamentary concurrence. A prince of ability, he contended, might and should be the directing soul and spirit of his own administration; in short, his own minister, and not the mere head of a party:

and then, and not till then, would the royal dignity be sincerely respected.

'Johnson seemed to think that a certain degree of crown influence over the Houses of Parliament, (not meaning a corrupt and shameful dependence,) was very salutary, nay, even necessary, in our mixed government. "For, (said he,) if the members were under no crown influence, and disqualified from receiving any gratification from Court, and resembled, as they possibly might, Pym and Haslerig, and other stubborn and sturdy members of the long Parliament, the wheels of government would be totally obstructed. Such men would oppose, merely to shew their power, from envy, jealousy, and perversity of disposition; and not gaining themselves, would hate and oppose all who did: not loving the person of the prince, and conceiving they owed him little gratitude, from the mere spirit of insolence and contradiction, they would oppose and thwart him upon all occasions."

marginal line:
Such men . . . of disposition [H]

'The inseparable imperfection annexed to all human governments, consisted, he said, in not being able to create a sufficient fund of virtue and principle to carry the laws into due and effectual execution. Wisdom might plan, but virtue alone could execute. And where could sufficient virtue be found? A variety of delegated, and often discretionary, powers must be entrusted somewhere: which, if not governed by integrity and conscience, would necessarily be abused, till at last the constable would sell his for a shilling.

'This excellent person was sometimes charged with abetting slavish and arbitrary principles of government. Nothing in my opinion could be a grosser calumny and misrepresentation; for how can it be rationally supposed, that he should adopt such pernicious and absurd opinions, who supported his philosophical character with so much dignity, was extremely jealous of his personal liberty and independence,[1] and could not brook the smallest appearance of neglect or insult, even from the highest personages?

[1] [On the necessity of crown influence, see Boucher's Sermons on the American Revolution, p. 218; and Paley's Moral Philosophy, B. VI. c. vii. p. 491, 4to. there quoted. BLAKEWAY.]

'But let us view him in some instances of more familiar life.

'His general mode of life, during my acquaintance, seemed to be pretty uniform. About twelve o'clock I commonly visited him, and frequently found him in bed, or declaiming over his tea, which he drank very plentifully. He generally had a levee of morning visitors, chiefly men of letters; Hawkesworth, Goldsmith, Murphy, Langton, Steevens, Beauclerk, &c. &c. and sometimes learned ladies; particularly I remember a French lady of wit and fashion[a] doing him the honour of a visit. He seemed to me to be considered as a kind of publick oracle, whom every body thought they had a right to visit and consult; and doubtless they were well rewarded. I never could discover how he found time for his compositions. He declaimed all the morning, then went to dinner at a tavern, where he commonly staid late, and then drank his tea at some friend's house, over which he loitered a great while, but seldom took supper. I fancy he must have read and wrote chiefly in the night, for I can scarcely recollect that he ever refused going with me to a tavern, and he often went to Ranelagh, which he deemed a place of innocent recreation.

'He frequently gave all the silver in his pocket to the poor, who watched him, between his house and the tavern where he dined. He walked the streets at all hours, and said he was never robbed, for the rogues knew he had little money, nor had the appearance of having much.

'Though the most accessible and communicative man alive, yet when he suspected he was invited to be exhibited, he constantly spurned the invitation.

'Two young women from Staffordshire visited him when I was present, to consult him on the subject of Methodism, to which they were inclined. "Come, (said he,) you pretty fools, dine with Maxwell and me at the Mitre, and we will talk over that subject;" which they did, and after dinner he took one of them upon his knee, and fondled her for half an hour together.

'Upon a visit to me at a country lodging near Twickenham, he asked what sort of society I had there. I told him, but indifferent; as they chiefly consisted of opulent traders, retired from business. He said, he never much liked that

[a] *Comtesse Boufflers* [H]
  Comptesse de la Boufflers [I]

marginal line:
one of . . . hour together
[H]

marginal line:
For, Sir . . . of gentle-
men [H]

class of people; "For, Sir, (said he) they have lost the civility of tradesmen, without acquiring the manners of gentlemen."

'Johnson was much attached to London:[1] he observed, that a man stored his mind better there, than any where else; and that in remote situations a man's body might be feasted, but his mind was starved, and his faculties apt to degenerate, from want of exercise and competition. No place, (he said) cured a man's vanity or arrogance, so well as London; for as no man was either great or good *per se*, but as compared with others not so good or great,

marginal line:
London was . . . of a
[H]

he was sure to find in the metropolis many his equals, and some his superiours. He observed, that a man in London was in less danger of falling in love indiscreetly, than any where else; for there the difficulty of deciding between the conflicting pretensions of a vast variety of objects, kept him safe. He told me, that he had frequently been offered country preferment, if he would consent to take orders; but he could not leave the improved society of the capital, or consent to exchange the exhilarating joys and splendid decorations of publick life, for the obscurity, insipidity, and uniformity of remote situations.

'Speaking of Mr. Harte, Canon of Windsor, and writer of "The History of Gustavus Adolphus," he much commended him as a scholar, and a man of the most companionable talents he had ever known. He said, the defects in his history proceeded not from imbecility, but from foppery.

'He loved, he said, the old black letter books; they were rich in matter, though their style was inelegant; wonderfully so, considering how conversant the writers were with the best models of antiquity.

'Burton's "Anatomy of Melancholy," he said, was the only book that ever took him out of bed two hours sooner than he wished to rise.

[1] [Montaigne had the same affection for Paris, which Johnson had for London.—'Je l'aime tendrement, (says he in his Essay on Vanity,) jusque à ses verrues et à ses taches. Je ne suis François, que par cette grande cité, grande en peuples, grande en felicité de son assiette, mais sur tout grande et incomparable en varieté et diversité des commoditez: la gloire de la France, et l'un des plus nobles ornamens du monde.' Vol. iii. p. 321, edit. Amsterdam, 1781. BLAKEWAY.]

'He frequently exhorted me to set about writing a History of Ireland, and archly remarked, there had been some good Irish writers, and that one Irishman might at least aspire to be equal to another. He had great compassion for the miseries and distresses of the Irish nation, particularly the Papists; and severely reprobated the barbarous debilitating policy of the British government, which, he said, was the most detestable mode of persecution. To a gentleman, who hinted such policy might be necessary to support the authority of the English government, he replied by saying, "Let the authority of the English government perish, rather than be maintained by iniquity. Better would it be to restrain the turbulence of the natives by the authority of the sword, and to make them amenable to law and justice by an effectual and vigorous police, than to grind them to powder by all manner of disabilities and incapacities. Better (said he) to hang or drown people at once, than by an unrelenting persecution to beggar and starve them." The moderation and humanity of the present times have, in some measure, justified the wisdom of his observations.

'Dr. Johnson was often accused of prejudices, nay, antipathy, with regard to the natives of Scotland. Surely, so illiberal a prejudice never entered his mind: and it is well known, many natives of that respectable country possessed a large share in his esteem: nor were any of them ever excluded from his good offices as far as opportunity permitted. True it is, he considered the Scotch, nationally, as a crafty, designing people, eagerly attentive to their own interest, and too apt to overlook the claims and pretensions of other people. "While they confine their benevolence, in a manner, exclusively to those of their own country, they expect to share in the good offices of other people. Now (said Johnson) this principle is either right or wrong; if right, we should do well to imitate such conduct; if wrong, we cannot too much detest it."

'Being solicited to compose a funeral sermon for the daughter of a tradesman, he naturally inquired into the character of the deceased; and being told she was remarkable for her humility and condescension to inferiours, he observed, that those were very laudable qualities,

marginal line: *laudable qualities . . . inferiours were* [H]

index sign:
easy to discover etc. [1]

but it might not be so easy to discover who the lady's inferiours were.

'Of a certain player he remarked, that his conversation usually threatened and announced more than it performed; that he fed you with a continual renovation of hope, to end in a constant succession of disappointment.

'When exasperated by contradiction, he was apt to treat his opponents with too much acrimony: as, "Sir, you don't see your way through that question:"—"Sir, you talk the language of ignorance." On my observing to him that a certain gentleman had remained silent the whole evening, in the midst of a very brilliant and learned society, "Sir, (said he,) the conversation overflowed, and drowned him."

index sign:
the conversation etc. [H]

'His philosophy, though austere and solemn, was by no means morose and cynical, and never blunted the laudable sensibilities of his character, or exempted him from the influence of the tender passions. Want of tenderness, he always alledged, was want of parts, and was no less a proof of stupidity than depravity.

'Speaking of Mr. Hanway, who published "An Eight Days' Journey from London to Portsmouth," "Jonas, (said he,) acquired some reputation by travelling abroad, but lost it all by travelling at home."

'Of the passion of love he remarked, that its violence and ill effects were much exaggerated; for who knows any real sufferings on that head, more than from the exorbitancy of any other passion?

'He much commended "Law's Serious Call," which he said was the finest piece of hortatory theology in any language. "Law, (said he,) fell latterly into the reveries of Jacob Behmen, whom Law alledged to have been somewhat in the same state with St. Paul, and to have seen *unutterable things*. Were it even so, (said Johnson,) Jacob would have resembled St. Paul still more, by not attempting to utter them."

'He observed, that the established clergy in general did not preach plain enough; and that polished periods and glittering sentences flew over the heads of the common people, without any impression upon their hearts. Something might be necessary, he observed, to excite the affections of the common people, who were sunk in languor and lethargy, and therefore he supposed that the new concomitants of methodism might probably produce so desirable an effect. The mind, like the body, he observed, delighted in change and novelty, and even in religion itself, courted new appearances and modifications. Whatever might be thought of some methodist teachers, he said, he could scarcely doubt the sincerity of that man, who travelled nine hundred miles in a month, and preached twelve times a week; for no adequate reward, merely temporal, could be given for such indefatigable labour.

'Of Dr. Priestly's theological works, he remarked, that they tended to unsettle every thing, and yet settled nothing.

'He was much affected by the death of his mother, and wrote to me to come and assist him to compose his mind, which indeed I found extremely agitated. He lamented that all serious and religious conversation was banished from the society of men, and yet great advantages might be derived from it. All acknowledged, he said, what hardly any body practised, the obligations we were under of making the concerns of eternity the governing principles of our lives. Every man, he observed, at last wishes for retreat: he sees his expectations frustrated in the world, and begins to wean himself from it, and to prepare for everlasting separation.

'He observed, that the influence of London now extended every where, and that from all manner of communication being opened, there shortly would be no remains of the ancient simplicity, or places of cheap retreat to be found.

'He was no admirer of blank verse, and said it always marginal line: *always failed . . . language suffered* [H] failed, unless sustained by the dignity of the subject. In blank verse, he said, the language suffered more distortion, marginal line: to keep it out of prose, than any inconvenience or limitation *any inconvenience . . . of rhyme* [H] to be apprehended from the shackles and circumspection of rhyme.

'He reproved me once for saying grace without mention of the name of our LORD JESUS CHRIST, and hoped in future I would be more mindful of the apostolical injunction.

'He refused to go out of a room before me at Mr. Langton's house, saying, he hoped he knew his rank better

—

than to presume to take place of a Doctor in Divinity.
I mention such little anecdotes, merely to shew the
peculiar turn and habit of his mind.

'He used frequently to observe, that there was more to
be endured than enjoyed, in the general condition of
human life; and frequently quoted those lines of Dryden:

> "Strange cozenage! none would live past years again,
> Yet all hope pleasure from what still remain."

exclamation point
and marginal line:
For his . . . to him [H]

For his part, he said, he never passed that week in his life
which he would wish to repeat, were an angel to make the
proposal to him.

'He was of opinion, that the English nation cultivated
both their soil and their reason better than any other
people; but admitted that the French, though not the
highest, perhaps, in any department of literature, yet
in every department were very high. Intellectual pre-
eminence, he observed, was the highest superiority; and
that every nation derived their highest reputation from
the splendour and dignity of their writers. Voltaire, he
said, was a good narrator, and that his principal merit
consisted in a happy selection and arrangement of
circumstances.

'Speaking of the French novels, compared with Richardson's, he said, they might be pretty baubles, but a wren
was not an eagle.

'In a Latin conversation with the Pere Boscovitch, at
the house of Mrs. Cholmondely, I heard him maintain the
superiority of Sir Isaac Newton over all foreign philosophers,[1] with a dignity and eloquence that surprised that
learned foreigner. It being observed to him, that a rage
for every thing English prevailed much in France after

three marginal lines:
*proper reverence . . .
periodical chastisement*
[H]

Lord Chatham's glorious war, he said, he did not wonder
at it, for that we had drubbed those fellows into a proper
reverence for us, and that their national petulance required
periodical chastisement.

[1] [In a Discourse by Sir William Jones, addressed to the Asiatick Society,
Feb. 24, 1785, is the following passage:
'One of the most sagacious men in this age who continues, I hope, to
improve and adorn it, Samuel Johnson, remarked in my hearing, that if
Newton had flourished in ancient Greece, he would have been worshipped
as a Divinity.' MALONE.]

'Lord Lyttelton's Dialogues, he deemed a nugatory performance. "That man, (said he,) sat down to write a book, to tell the world what the world had all his life been telling him."

'Somebody observing that the Scotch Highlanders, in the year 1745, had made surprising efforts, considering their numerous wants and disadvantages: "Yes, Sir, (said he,) their wants were numerous: but you have not mentioned the greatest of them all,—the want of law."

'Speaking of the *inward light*, to which some methodists pretended, he said, it was a principle utterly incompatible with social or civil security. "If a man (said he,) pretends to a principle of action of which I can know nothing, nay, not so much as that he has it, but only that he pretends to it; how can I tell what that person may be prompted to do? When a person professes to be governed by a written ascertained law, I can then know where to find him."

'The poem of Fingal, he said, was a mere unconnected rhapsody, a tiresome repetition of the same images. "In vain shall we look for the *lucidus ordo*, where there is neither end or object, design or moral, *nec certa recurrit imago*."

'Being asked by a young nobleman, what was become of the gallantry and military spirit of the old English nobility, he replied, "Why, my Lord, I'll tell you what is become of it: it is gone into the city to look for a fortune."

marginal line: *I'll tell . . . a fortune* [H]

'Speaking of a dull tiresome fellow, whom he chanced to meet, he said, "That fellow seems to me to possess but one idea, and that is a wrong one."

'Much enquiry having been made concerning a gentleman, who had quitted a company where Johnson was, and no information being obtained; at last Johnson observed, that "he did not care to speak ill of any man behind his back, but he believed the gentleman was an *attorney*."

marginal line: *of any . . . an* attorney [H]

'He spoke with much contempt of the notice taken of Woodhouse, the poetical shoemaker. He said, it was all vanity and childishness: and that such objects were, to those who patronized them, mere mirrors of their own superiority. "They had better (said he,) furnish the man with good implements for his trade, than raise subscriptions for his poems. He may make an excellent shoemaker, but can never make a good poet. A school-boy's exercise may be a pretty thing for a school-boy; but it is no treat for a man."

'Speaking of Boetius, who was the favourite writer of the middle ages, he said it was very surprising, that upon such a subject, and in such a situation, he should be *magis philosophus quàm Christianus*.

'Speaking of Arthur Murphy, whom he very much loved, "I don't know (said he,) that Arthur can be classed with the very first dramatick writers; yet at present I doubt much whether we have any thing superiour to Arthur."

'Speaking of the national debt, he said, it was an idle dream to suppose that the country could sink under it. Let the publick creditors be ever so clamorous, the interest of millions must ever prevail over that of thousands.

'Of Dr. Kennicott's Collations, he observed, that though the text should not be much mended thereby, yet it was no small advantage to know that we had as good a text as the most consummate industry and diligence could procure.

'Johnson observed, that so many objections might be made to every thing, that nothing could overcome them but the necessity of doing something. No man would be of any profession, as simply opposed to not being of it: but every one must do something.

'He remarked, that a London parish was a very comfortless thing: for the clergyman seldom knew the face of one out of ten of his parishioners.

'Of the late Mr. Mallet he spoke with no great respect: said, he was ready for any dirty job: that he had wrote against Byng at the instigation of the ministry, and was equally ready to write for him, provided he found his account in it.

a not immediately at all—Tho' I forget who it was. [H]

two marginal lines: *Johnson said . . . over experience* [H]

'A gentleman who had been very unhappy in marriage, married immediately after his wife died:ª Johnson said, it was the triumph of hope over experience.

two marginal lines: *be such . . . about that* [H]

'He observed, that a man of sense and education should meet a suitable companion in a wife. It was a miserable thing when the conversation could only be such as, whether the mutton should be boiled or roasted, and probably a dispute about that.

'He did not approve of late marriages, observing that more was lost in point of time, than compensated for by any possible advantages. Even ill assorted marriages were preferable to cheerless celibacy.

'Of old Sheridan he remarked, that he neither wanted parts nor literature; but that his vanity and Quixotism obscured his merits.

'He said, foppery was never cured; it was the bad stamina of the mind, which, like those of the body, were never rectified: once a coxcomb, and always a coxcomb.

'Being told that Gilbert Cowper called him the Caliban of literature; "Well, (said he,) I must dub him the Punchinello."[a]

'Speaking of the old Earl of Cork and Orrery, he said, "that man spent his life in catching at an object, [literary eminence,] which he had not power to grasp."

'To find a substitution for violated morality, he said, was the leading feature in all perversions of religion.

'He often used to quote, with great pathos, those fine lines of Virgil:

> "*Optima quæque dies miseris mortalibus ævi,*
> *Prima fugit; subeunt morbi, tristisque senectus,*
> *Et labor, et duræ rapit inclementia mortis.*"

'Speaking of Homer, whom he venerated as the prince of poets, Johnson remarked that the advice given to Diomed[1] by his father, when he sent him to the Trojan war, was the noblest exhortation that could be instanced in any heathen writer, and comprised in a single line:

Αἰὲν ἀριϛεύειν, καὶ ὑπείροχον ἔμμεναι ἄλλων:

which, if I recollect well, is translated by Dr. Clarke thus: *semper appetere præstantissima, et omnibus aliis antecellere.*

'He observed, "it was a most mortifying reflection for any man to consider, *what he had done*, compared with what *he might have done.*"

---

[a] *That would have been better said of Foote than of Gilbert Cowper* [1]

[1] [Dr. Maxwell's memory has deceived him. Glaucus is the person who received this counsel; and Clarke's translation of the passage (Il. vi. l. 208,) is as follows:

'Ut semper fortissime rem gererem, et superior virtute essem aliis.'
J. BOSWELL.]

'He said few people had intellectual resources sufficient to forego the pleasures of wine. They could not otherwise contrive how to fill the interval between dinner and supper.

'He went with me, one Sunday, to hear my old Master, Gregory Sharpe, preach at the Temple.—In the prefatory prayer, Sharpe ranted about *Liberty*, as a blessing most fervently to be implored, and its continuance prayed for. Johnson observed that our *liberty* was in no sort of danger:— he would have done much better, to pray against our *licentiousness*.

'One evening at Mrs. Montagu's, where a splendid company was assembled, consisting of the most eminent literary characters, I thought he seemed highly pleased with the respect and attention that were shewn him, and asked him, on our return home, if he was not highly *gratified* by his visit: "No, Sir, (said he) not highly *gratified;* yet I do not recollect to have passed many evenings *with fewer objections*."

'Though of no high extraction himself, he had much respect for birth and family, especially among ladies. He said, "adventitious accomplishments may be possessed by all ranks; but one may easily distinguish the *born gentlewoman*."

'He said, "the poor in England were better provided for, than in any other country of the same extent: he did not mean little Cantons, or petty Republicks. Where a great proportion of the people (said he,) are suffered to languish in helpless misery, that country must be ill policed, and wretchedly governed: a decent provision for the poor is the true test of civilization.—Gentlemen of education, he observed, were pretty much the same in all countries; the condition of the lower orders, the poor especially, was the true mark of national discrimination."

'When the corn laws were in agitation in Ireland, by which that country has been enabled not only to feed itself, but to export corn to a large amount; Sir Thomas Robinson observed, that those laws might be prejudicial to the corn-trade of England. "Sir Thomas, (said he,) you talk the language of a savage: what, Sir, would you prevent any people from feeding themselves, if by any honest means they can do it."

'It being mentioned, that Garrick assisted Dr. Browne, the authour of the "Estimate," in some dramatick composition, "No, Sir; (said Johnson,) he would no more suffer Garrick to write a line in his play, than he would suffer him to mount his pulpit."

'Speaking of Burke, he said, "It was commonly observed he spoke too often in Parliament; but nobody could say he did not speak well, though too frequently and too familiarly."

'Speaking of economy, he remarked, it was hardly worth while to save anxiously twenty pounds a year. If a man could save to that degree, so as to enable him to assume a different rank in society, then, indeed, it might answer some purpose.

'He observed, a principal source of erroneous judgement was, viewing things partially and only on *one side;* as for instance, *fortune-hunters*, when they contemplated the fortunes *singly* and *separately*, it was a dazzling and tempting object; but when they came to possess the wives and their fortunes *together*, they began to suspect they had not made quite so good a bargain.

'Speaking of the late Duke of Northumberland living very magnificently when Lord Lieutenant of Ireland, somebody remarked, it would be difficult to find a suitable successor to him: then, exclaimed Johnson, *he is only fit to succeed himself*.

'He advised me, if possible, to have a good orchard. He knew, he said, a clergyman of small income, who brought up a family very reputably, which he chiefly fed with apple dumplins.

'He said, he had known several good scholars among the Irish gentlemen; but scarcely any of them correct in *quantity*. He extended the same observation to Scotland.

'Speaking of a certain Prelate, who exerted himself very laudably in building churches and parsonage-houses; "however, said he, I do not find that he is esteemed a man of much professional learning, or a liberal patron of it;— yet, it is well, where a man possesses any strong positive excellence.—Few have all kinds of merit belonging to their character. We must not examine matters too deeply—No, Sir, a *fallible being will fail somewhere*."

'Talking of the Irish clergy, he said, Swift was a man of
great parts, and the instrument of much good to his
country.—Berkeley was a profound scholar, as well as a
man of fine imagination; but Usher, he said, was the great
luminary of the Irish church; and a greater, he added, no
church could boast of; at least in modern times.

'We dined *tête-à-tete* at the Mitre, as I was preparing to
return to Ireland, after an absence of many years. I
regretted much leaving London, where I had formed
many agreeable connexions: "Sir, (said he,) I don't
wonder at it: no man, fond of letters, leaves London without regret. But remember, Sir, you have seen and enjoyed
a great deal:—you have seen life in its highest decorations,
and the world has nothing new to exhibit.—No man is so
well qualified to leave publick life as he who has long tried
it and known it well. We are always hankering after untried
situations, and imagining greater felicity from them than
they can afford. No, Sir, knowledge and virtue may be
acquired in all countries, and your local consequence will
make you some amends for the intellectual gratifications
you relinquish." Then he quoted the following lines with
great pathos:

> "He who has early known the pomps of state,
>   (For things unknown, 'tis ignorance to condemn;)
> And after having view'd the gaudy bait,
>   Can boldly say, the trifle I contemn;
> With such a one contented could I live,
>   Contented could I die."[1]—

---

[1] [Being desirous to trace these verses to the fountain-head, after having in
vain turned over several of our elder poets with the hope of lighting on them,
I applied to Dr. Maxwell, now resident at Bath, for the purpose of ascertaining their authour: but that gentleman could furnish no aid on this occasion.
At length the lines have been discovered by the authour's second son, Mr.
James Boswell, in the London Magazine for July, 1732, where they form
part of a poem on RETIREMENT, there published anonymously, but in
fact (as he afterwards found) copied with some slight variations from one
of Walsh's smaller poems, entitled 'The Retirement;' and they exhibit
another proof of what has been elsewhere observed by the authour of the
work before us, that Johnson retained in his memory fragments of obscure
or neglected poetry. In quoting verses of that description, he appears by a
slight variation to have sometimes given them a moral turn, and to have
dexterously adapted them to his own sentiments, where the original had a
very different tendency. Thus, in the present instance, (as Mr. J. Boswell
observes to me) 'the authour of the poem above-mentioned exhibits himself

'He then took a most affecting leave of me; said he knew it was a point of *duty* that called me away.—"We shall all be sorry to lose you, said he: *laudo tamen*." '

In 1771 he published another political pamphlet entitled 'Thoughts on the late Transactions respecting Falkland's Islands,' in which, upon materials furnished to him by ministry, and upon general topicks expanded in his rich style, he successfully endeavoured to persuade the nation that it was wise and laudable to suffer the question of right to remain undecided, rather than involve our country in another war. It has been suggested by some, with what truth I shall not take upon me to decide, that he rated the consequence of those islands to Great Britain too low. But

as having retired to the country, to avoid the vain follies of a town life,— ambition, avarice, and the pursuit of pleasure, contrasted with the enjoy-ments of the country, and the delightful conversation that the brooks, &c. furnish; which he holds to be infinitely more pleasing and instructive than any which towns afford. He is then led to consider the weakness of the human mind, and after lamenting that he (the writer) who is neither en-slaved by avarice, ambition, or pleasure, has yet made himself a slave to *love*, he thus proceeds:

> 'If this dire passion never will be done,
>   If beauty always must my heart enthral,
> O, rather let me be enslaved by *one*,
>   Than madly thus become a slave to all:
>
> One *who has early known the pomp of state,*
>   *For things unknown 'tis ignorance to condemn,*
> *And, after having view'd the gawdy bait,*
>   *Can coldly say, the trifle I contemn;*
>
> In her blest arms *contented could I live,*
>   *Contented could I die.* But, O my mind
> Imaginary scenes of bliss deceive
>   With hopes of joys impossible to find.'

Another instance of Johnson's retaining in his memory verses by obscure authours is given in Mr. Boswell's 'Journal of a Tour to the Hebrides;' where, in consequence of hearing a girl spinning in a chamber over that in which he was sitting, he repeated these lines, which he said were written by one Giffard, a clergyman; but the poem in which they are introduced, has hitherto been undiscovered:

> 'Verse sweetens toil, however rude the sound:
>   All at her work the village maiden sings;
> Nor while she turns the giddy wheel around,
>   Revolves the sad vicissitude of things.'

In the autumn of 1782, when he was at Brighthelmstone, he frequently accompanied Mr. Philip Metcalfe in his chaise, to take the air; and the con-versation in one of their excursions happening to turn on a celebrated

underlined:
celebrated historian [H]

however this may be, every humane mind must surely applaud the earnestness with which he averted the calamity of war; a calamity so dreadful, that it is astonishing how civilised, nay, Christian nations, can deliberately continue to renew it. His description of its miseries in this pamphlet, is one of the finest pieces of eloquence in the English language. Upon this occasion, too, we find Johnson lashing the party in opposition with unbounded severity, and making the fullest use of what he ever reckoned a most effectual argumentative instrument,—contempt. His character of their very able mysterious champion, JUNIUS, is executed with all the force of his genius, and finished with the highest care. He seems to have exulted in sallying forth to single combat against the boasted and formidable hero, who bade defiance to 'principalities and powers, and the rulers of this world.'

This pamphlet, it is observable, was softened in one particular, after the first edition; for the conclusion of Mr. George Grenville's character stood thus: 'Let him not, however, be depreciated in his grave. He had powers not universally possessed: could he have enforced payment of the Manilla ransom, *he could have counted it.*' Which, instead of retaining its sly sharp point, was reduced to a

^a *It was no greater a Person than poor HLP who adapted the Lines to Gibbon: I wrote them in his first 4to Volume. They are translated from some old Latin Verses at the End of Cluverius's Geography.* [H & I]

^b *fruitful* [I]

^c *& sometimes both— or either,* [I]

^d *So have I seen some Youth set out* [I]

^e *Some new Religion to find out* [I]

^f *The Verses are in Cluverius's Geography —Latin Verses; I know not who translated them.* [I]

historian, since deceased, he repeated, with great precision, some verses,^a as very characteristick of that gentleman. These furnish another proof of what has been above observed; for they are found in a very obscure quarter, among some anonymous poems appended to the second volume of a collection frequently printed by Lintot, under the title of Pope's MISCELLANIES:

'See how the wand'ring^b Danube flows,
    Realms and religions parting;
A friend to all true christian foes,
    To Peter, Jack, and Martin.

Now Protestant, and Papist now,
    Not constant long to either,^c
At length an infidel does grow,
    And ends his journey neither.

Thus many a youth I've known set out,^d
    Half Protestant, half Papist,
And rambling long the world about,^e
    Turn infidel or atheist.'^f

In reciting these verses I have no doubt that Johnson substituted some word for *infidel* in the second stanza, to avoid the disagreeable repetition of the same expression. MALONE.]

mere flat unmeaning expression, or, if I may use the word, —*truism:* 'He had powers not universally possessed: and if he sometimes erred, he was likewise sometimes right.'

'TO BENNET LANGTON, ESQ.

'DEAR SIR,

'AFTER much lingering of my own, and much of the ministry, I have, at length, got out my paper.[1] But delay is not yet at an end: Not many had been dispersed, before Lord North ordered the sale to stop. His reasons I do not distinctly know. You may try to find them in the perusal.[2] Before his order, a sufficient number were dispersed to do all the mischief, though, perhaps, not to make all the sport that might be expected from it.

'Soon after your departure, I had the pleasure of finding all the danger pass with which your navigation was threatened. I hope nothing happens at home to abate your satisfaction; but that Lady Rothes, and Mrs. Langton, and the young ladies, are all well.

'I was last night at THE CLUB. Dr. Percy has written a long ballad in many *fits:* it is pretty enough. He has printed, and will soon publish it. Goldsmith is at Bath, with Lord Clare. At Mr. Thrale's, where I am now writing, all are well. I am, dear Sir,

'Your most humble servant,

'March 20, 1771.'   'SAM. JOHNSON'

Mr. Strahan, the printer, who had been long in intimacy with Johnson, in the course of his literary labours, who was at once his friendly agent in receiving his pension for him, and his banker in supplying him with money when he wanted it; who was himself now a Member of Parliament, and who loved much to be employed in political negociation; thought he should do eminent service, both to government and Johnson, if he could be the means of his getting a seat in the House of Commons. With this view,

[1] 'Thoughts on the late Transactions respecting Falkland's Islands.'

[2] By comparing the first with the subsequent editions, this curious circumstance of ministerial authourship may be discovered.

[It can only be discovered (as Mr. Bindley observes to me) by him who possesses a copy of the first edition issued out before the sale was stopped. MALONE.]

he wrote a letter to one of the Secretaries of the Treasury, of which he gave me a copy, in his own hand-writing, which is as follows:

'SIR,

'You will easily recollect, when I had the honour of waiting upon you some time ago, I took the liberty to observe to you, that Dr. Johnson would make an excellent figure in the House of Commons, and heartily wished he had a seat there. My reasons are briefly these:

'I know his perfect good affection to his Majesty, and his government, which I am certain he wishes to support by every means in his power.

'He possesses a great share of manly, nervous, and ready eloquence; is quick in discerning the strength and weakness of an argument; can express himself with clearness and precision, and fears the face of no man alive.

'His known character, as a man of extraordinary sense and unimpeached virtue, would secure him the attention of the House, and could not fail to give him a proper weight there.

'He is capable of the greatest application, and can undergo any degree of labour, where he sees it necessary, and where his heart and affections are strongly engaged. His Majesty's ministers might therefore securely depend on his doing, upon every proper occasion, the utmost that could be expected from him. They would find him ready to vindicate such measures as tended to promote the stability of government, and resolute and steady in carrying them into execution. Nor is any thing to be apprehended from the supposed impetuosity of his temper. To the friends of the King you will find him a lamb, to his enemies a lion.

'For these reasons, I humbly apprehend that he would be a very able and useful member. And I will venture to say, the employment would not be disagreeable to him; and knowing, as I do, his strong affection to the King, his ability to serve him in that capacity, and the extreme ardour with which I am convinced he would engage in that service, I must repeat, that I wish most heartily to see him in the House.

'If you think this worthy of attention, you will be pleased to take a convenient opportunity of mentioning it to Lord North. If his Lordship should happily approve of it, I shall have the satisfaction of having been, in some degree, the humble instrument of doing my country, in my opinion, a very essential service. I know your good-nature, and your zeal for the publick welfare, will plead my excuse for giving you this trouble. I am, with the greatest respect, Sir,

'Your most obedient and humble servant,

'New-street,   'WILLIAM STRAHAN'
March 30, 1771.'

This recommendation, we know, was not effectual; but how, or for what reason, can only be conjectured. It is not to be believed that Mr. Strahan would have applied, unless Johnson had approved of it.[a] I never heard him mention the subject; but at a later period of his life, when Sir Joshua Reynolds told him that Mr. Edmund Burke had said, that if he had come early into Parliament, he certainly would have been the greatest speaker that ever was there, Johnson exclaimed, 'I should like to try my hand now.'

It has been much agitated among his friends and others, whether he would have been a powerful speaker in Parliament, had he been brought in when advanced in life. I am inclined to think, that his extensive knowledge, his quickness and force of mind, his vivacity and richness of expression, his wit and humour, and above all his poignancy of sarcasm, would have had great effect in a popular assembly; and that the magnitude of his figure, and striking peculiarity of his manner, would have aided the effect. But I remember it was observed by Mr. Flood, that Johnson, having been long used to sententious brevity, and the short flights of conversation, might have failed in that continued and expanded kind of argument, which is requisite in stating complicated matters in publick speaking; and as a proof of this he mentioned the supposed speeches in Parliament written by him for the magazine, none of which, in his opinion, were at all like real debates. The opinion of one who was himself so eminent an orator, must

[margin: a *Yes, Yes: he would have* approved *it* [H]]

[margin: marginal line: *Parliament written ... real debates* [H]] be allowed to have great weight. It was confirmed by Sir William Scott, who mentioned that Johnson had told him, that he had several times tried to speak in the Society of Arts and Manufactures, but 'had found he could not get on.'[1] From Mr. William Gerard Hamilton I have heard, that Johnson, when observing to him that it was prudent for a man who had not been accustomed to speak in publick, to begin his speech in as simple a manner as possible, acknowledged that he rose in that society to deliver a speech which he had prepared; 'but (said he,) all my flowers of oratory forsook me.' I however cannot help wishing, that he *had* 'tried his hand' in Parliament; and I wonder that ministry did not make the experiment.[a]

I at length renewed a correspondence which had been too long discontinued:

[a] *Boswell had Leisure for Curiosity; Ministers had not: Boswell would have been equally amused by his Failure as by his Success; but to Lord North, there would have been no Joke at all in the Experiment ending untowardly.* [H & I]

'TO DR. JOHNSON

'MY DEAR SIR,   'Edinburgh, April 18, 1771

'I CAN now fully understand those intervals of silence in your correspondence with me, which have often given me anxiety and uneasiness; for although I am conscious that my veneration and love for Mr. Johnson have never in the least abated, yet I have deferred for almost a year and a half to write to him.'

In the subsequent part of this letter, I gave him an account of my comfortable life as a married man, and a lawyer in practice at the Scotch bar; invited him to Scotland, and promised to attend him to the Highlands, and Hebrides.

'TO JAMES BOSWELL, ESQ.

'DEAR SIR,

'IF you are now able to comprehend that I might neglect to write without diminution of affection, you have

[1] [Dr. Kippis, however, (BIOGRAPH. BRITAN. article 'J. Gilbert Cooper,' p. 266, n. new edit.) says, that he 'once heard Dr. Johnson speak in the Society of Arts and Manufactures, upon a subject relative to mechanicks, with a propriety, perspicuity, and energy, which excited general admiration.' MALONE.]

taught me, likewise, how that neglect may be uneasily felt without resentment. I wished for your letter a long time, and when it came it amply recompensed the delay. I never was so much pleased as now with your account of yourself; and sincerely hope, that between publick business, improving studies, and domestick pleasures, neither melancholy nor caprice will find any place for entrance. Whatever philosophy may determine of material nature, it is certainly true of intellectual nature, that it *abhors a vacuum:* our minds cannot be empty; and evil will break in upon them, if they are not pre-occupied by good. My dear Sir, mind your studies, mind your business, make your lady happy, and be a good Christian. After this,

> "————*tristitiam et metus*
> *Trades protervis in mare Creticum*
> *Portare ventis.*"

'If we perform our duty, we shall be safe and steady, "*Sive per,*" &c. whether we climb the Highlands, or are tossed among the Hebrides; and I hope the time will come when we may try our powers both with cliffs and water. I see but little of Lord Elibank, I know not why; perhaps by my own fault. I am this day going into Staffordshire and Derbyshire for six weeks.

'I am, dear Sir,
'Your most affectionate,
'And most humble servant,
'London, June 20, 1771.'   'SAM. JOHNSON'

'TO SIR JOSHUA REYNOLDS, IN LEICESTER-FIELDS

'DEAR SIR,
'WHEN I came to Lichfield, I found that my portrait[1] had been much visited, and much admired. Every man has a lurking wish to appear considerable in his native place; and I was pleased with the dignity conferred by such a testimony of your regard.

---

[1] [The second portrait of Johnson, painted by Sir Joshua Reynolds; with his arms raised, and his hands bent. It was at this time, it is believed, in the possession of Miss Lucy Porter, and is still probably at Lichfield. MALONE.]

'Be pleased, therefore, to accept the thanks of, Sir, your most obliged,
                                   'And most humble servant,

'Ashbourne in Derbyshire,   'SAM. JOHNSON'
    July 17, 1771.'

'Compliments to Miss Reynolds.'

'TO DR. JOHNSON

'MY DEAR SIR,   'Edinburgh, July 27, 1771

'The bearer of this, Mr. Beattie, Professor of Moral Philosophy at Aberdeen, is desirous of being introduced to your acquaintance. His genius and learning, and labours in the service of virtue and religion, render him very worthy of it; and as he has a high esteem of your character, I hope you will give him a favourable reception. I ever am, &c.
                                   'JAMES BOSWELL'

'TO BENNET LANGTON, ESQ. AT LANGTON, NEAR
              SPILSBY, LINCOLNSHIRE

'DEAR SIR,

'I AM lately returned from Staffordshire and Derbyshire. The last letter mentions two others which you have written to me since you received my pamphlet. Of these two I never had but one, in which you mentioned a design of visiting Scotland, and, by consequence, put my journey to Langton out of my thoughts. My summer wanderings are now over, and I am engaging in a very great work, the revision of my Dictionary; from which I know not, at present, how to get loose.

'If you have observed, or been told, any errours or omissions, you will do me a great favour by letting me know them.

'Lady Rothes, I find, has disappointed you and herself. Ladies will have these tricks. The Queen and Mrs. Thrale, both ladies of experience, yet both missed their reckoning this summer. I hope, a few months will recompense your uneasiness.

'Please to tell Lady Rothes how highly I value the honour of her invitation, which it is my purpose to obey as soon as I have disengaged myself. In the mean time I shall hope to hear often of her Ladyship, and every day better news and better, till I hear that you have both the happiness, which to both is very sincerely wished, by, Sir,

'Your most affectionate, and

'Most humble servant,

'August 29, 1771.'   'SAM. JOHNSON'

In October I again wrote to him, thanking him for his last letter, and his obliging reception of Mr. Beattie; informing him that I had been at Alnwick lately, and had good accounts of him from Dr. Percy.

In his religious record of this year we observe that he was better than usual, both in body and mind, and better satisfied with the regularity of his conduct. But he is still 'trying his ways' too rigourously. He charges himself with not rising early enough; yet he mentions what was surely a sufficient excuse for this, supposing it to be a duty seriously required, as he all his life appears to have thought it. 'One great hindrance is want of rest; my nocturnal complaints grow less troublesome towards morning; and I am tempted to repair the deficiencies of the night.'[1] Alas! how hard would it be, if this indulgence were to be imputed to a sick man as a crime. In his retrospect on the following Easter-eve, he says, 'When I review the last year, I am able to recollect so little done, that shame and sorrow, though perhaps too weakly, come upon me.' Had he been judging of any one else in the same circumstances, how clear would he have been on the favourable side. How very difficult, and in my opinion almost constitutionally impossible it was for him to be raised early, even by the strongest resolutions, appears from a note in one of his little paper-books, (containing words arranged for his Dictionary,) written, I suppose, about 1753: 'I do not remember that since I left Oxford, I ever rose early by mere choice, but once or twice at Edial, and two or three times for the Rambler.' I think he had fair ground enough to have quieted his mind on the subject, by concluding that he was physically incapable of what is at best but a commodious regulation.

marginal line:
my nocturnal . . . hard would [H]

---

[1] Prayers and Meditations, p. 101.

In 1772 he was altogether quiescent as an authour; but it will be found, from the various evidences which I shall bring together, that his mind was acute, lively, and vigorous.

'TO SIR JOSHUA REYNOLDS

'DEAR SIR,

'BE pleased to send to Mr. Banks, whose place of residence I do not know, this note, which I have sent open, that, if you please, you may read it.

'When you send it, do not use your own seal.

'I am, Sir,
'Your most humble servant,

'Feb. 27, 1772.'   'SAM. JOHNSON'

'TO JOSEPH BANKS, ESQ.

'*Perpetua ambitâ bis terrâ præmia lactis*
Hæc habet altrici Capra secunda Jovis.'[1]

'SIR,

'I RETURN thanks to you and to Dr. Solander for the pleasure which I received in yesterday's conversation. I could not recollect a motto for your Goat, but have given her one. You, Sir, may perhaps have an epick poem from some happier pen than, Sir,

'Your most humble servant,

'Johnson's-court, Fleet-street,   'SAM. JOHNSON'
   February 27, 1772.'

'TO DR. JOHNSON

'MY DEAR SIR,

'IT is hard that I cannot prevail on you to write to me oftener. But I am convinced that it is in vain to expect from you a private correspondence with any regularity. I must, therefore, look upon you as a fountain of wisdom,

---

[1] Thus translated by a friend:

'In fame scarce second to the nurse of Jove,
   This Goat, who twice the world had traversed round,
Deserving both her master's care and love,
   Ease and perpetual pasture now has found.'

from whence few rills are communicated to a distance, and which must be approached at its source, to partake fully of its virtues.

* * * * * *

'I am coming to London soon, and am to appear in an appeal from the Court of Session in the House of Lords. A schoolmaster in Scotland was, by a court of inferior jurisdiction, deprived of his office, for being somewhat severe in the chastisement of his scholars. The Court of Session considering it to be dangerous to the interest of learning and education, to lessen the dignity of teachers, and make them afraid of too indulgent parents, instigated by the complaints of their children, restored him. His enemies have appealed to the House of Lords, though the salary is only twenty pounds a year. I was Counsel for him here. I hope there will be little fear of a reversal; but I must beg to have your aid in my plan of supporting the decree. It is a general question, and not a point of particular law.

* * * * * *

'I am, &c.
'JAMES BOSWELL'

'TO JAMES BOSWELL, ESQ.

'DEAR SIR,

'THAT you are coming so soon to town I am very glad; and still more glad that you are coming as an advocate. I think nothing more likely to make your life pass happily away, than that consciousness of your own value, which eminence in your profession will certainly confer. If I can give you any collateral help, I hope you do not suspect that it will be wanting. My kindness for you has neither the merit of singular virtue, nor the reproach of singular prejudice. Whether to love you be right or wrong, I have many on my side: Mrs. Thrale loves you,[a] and Mrs. Williams loves you, and what would have inclined me to love you, if I had been neutral before, you are a great favourite of Dr. Beattie.

'Of Dr. Beattie I should have thought much, but that his lady puts him out of my head; she is a very lovely woman.

underlined: *Thrale* [H]

[a] *not I, I never lov'd him.* [H]

'The ejection which you come hither to oppose, appears very cruel, unreasonable, and oppressive. I should think there could not be much doubt of your success.

'My health grows better, yet I am not fully recovered. I believe it is held, that men do not recover very fast after threescore. I hope yet to see Beattie's College: and have not given up the western voyage. But however all this may be or not, let us try to make each other happy when we meet, and not refer our pleasure to distant times or distant places.

'How comes it that you tell me nothing of your lady? I hope to see her some time, and till then shall be glad to hear of her.

'I am, dear Sir, &c.

'March 15, 1772.'   'SAM. JOHNSON'

'TO BENNET LANGTON, ESQ. NEAR SPILSBY,
        LINCOLNSHIRE

'DEAR SIR,

'I CONGRATULATE you and Lady Rothes[1] on your little man, and hope you will all be many years happy together.

'Poor Miss Langton can have little part in the joy of her family. She this day called her aunt Langton to receive the sacrament with her; and made me talk yesterday on such subjects as suit her condition. It will probably be her *viaticum*. I surely need not mention again that she wishes to see her mother. I am, Sir,

'Your most humble servant,

'March 14, 1772.'   'SAM. JOHNSON'

[1] [Mr. Langton married, May 24, 1770, Jane, the daughter of —— Lloyd, Esq. and widow of John Earl of Rothes, many years Commander in Chief of the Forces in Ireland, who died in 1767. MALONE.]

END OF VOLUME I